THE EVOLVING ROLE OF ASIA IN GLOBAL FINANCE

FRONTIERS OF ECONOMICS AND GLOBALIZATION

9

FRONTIERS OF ECONOMICS AND GLOBALIZATION VOLUME 9

THE EVOLVING ROLE OF ASIA IN GLOBAL FINANCE

Edited by

Yin-Wong Cheung

Economics Department, University of California, Santa Cruz, CA, USA

Vikas Kakkar

Department of Economics and Finance, City University of Hong Kong, Hong Kong

Guonan Ma

Representative Office for Asia and the Pacific, Bank for International Settlements, Hong Kong

Emerald

Emerald Group Publishing Limited
Howard House, Wagon Lane, Bingley BD16 1WA, UK

First edition 2011

British Library Cataloguing in Publication Data
A catalogue record for this book is available from the British Library

ISBN: 978-0-85724-745-2
ISSN: 1574-8715 (Series)

ABOUT THE SERIES: FRONTIERS OF ECONOMICS AND GLOBALIZATION

This series is aimed at economists and financial economists worldwide and will provide an in-depth look at current global topics. Each volume in the series will focus on specialized topics for greater understanding of the chosen subject and provide a detailed discussion of emerging issues. The target audiences are professional researchers, graduate students, and policy makers. It will offer cutting-edge views on new horizons and deepen the understanding in these emerging topics.

With contributions from leading researchers, each volume presents a fresh look at today's current topics. This series will present primarily original works, and employ references appropriate to the topic being explored.

Each volume will bring a set of highly concentrated chapters that will provide in-depth knowledge to a target audience, while the entire series will appeal to a wide audience by providing them with deeper knowledge on a broad set of emerging topics in the global economy.

The *Frontiers of Economics and Globalization* series will publish on topics such as:

- Frontiers of Trade Negotiations
- Frontiers of Derivative Pricing
- Frontiers of International Lending and Debt Problems
- Frontiers of Economics Integration
- Frontiers of Trade and Environment
- Frontiers of Foreign Exchange
- Frontiers of International Finance
- Frontiers of Growth of Open Economies
- Frontiers of Futures Pricing
- Frontiers of International Financial Markets
- Frontiers of Investment Banking
- Frontiers of Mergers and Acquisitions
- Frontiers of Government Policy and Regulations
- Frontiers of Multi-Sector Growth Models
- Frontiers of Intellectual Property Rights
- Frontiers of Fragmentations and Outsourcing

Hamid Beladi
E. Kwan Choi
Series Editors

ABOUT THE EDITORS

Yin-Wong Cheung obtained his bachelor's and master's degrees, respectively, from the University of Hong Kong and the University of Essex. After graduating from the University of Pennsylvania in 1990, Cheung joined the University of California in Santa Cruz. Currently, Cheung is a professor in the economics department at the University of California, Santa Cruz.

Concurrently, Cheung is a member of the Council of Advisers, HKIMR/HKMA, a research fellow of the CESifo in Germany, a founding and board member of the Methods in International Finance Network in Europe, an adjunct professor of the City University of Hong Kong, and a chair professor of the Shandong University.

Vikas Kakkar is an associate professor at the City University of Hong Kong. He specializes in international finance and applied econometrics, and his research interests also include behavioral economics and finance. His publications have appeared in the *Review of Economics and Statistics*, *Journal of International Economics*, and the *Journal of Money, Credit and Banking*. He obtained his Ph.D. in economics from the University of Rochester and is a CFA charter holder.

Guonan Ma is a senior economist at the Representative Office for Asia and the Pacific of the Bank for International Settlements (BIS). Before joining the BIS in 2001, he worked as a chief North Asia economist for 10 years at various investment banks, including Merrill Lynch, Salomon Smith Barney, and Bankers Trust. Prior to his investment bank career, he was a lecturer of economics and research fellow at the Australian National University for four years following the completion of his Ph.D. in economics at the University of Pittsburgh (1990). Dr Ma was born in China where he obtained his undergraduate degree at Beijing University (1982). He has many publications on the Asian and Chinese economies and financial markets over the years.

About the volume

The process of Asia's rise to a position of eminence in global finance has accelerated in the wake of the international financial crisis, posing new opportunities and challenges to both the Asian economies and the global financial and trade systems. This volume represents a significant new endeavor to explore and understand the dynamics created by this process of transition. Specifically, it addresses the following four contemporary themes of the evolving role of Asia in global finance: (a) real and financial interactions among economies and across markets, both within Asia and beyond; (b) regional monetary cooperation in Asia; (c) the decoupling debate over Asia's evolving economic and financial ties with major industrial economies; and (d) the changing roles of domestic finance and capital flows in the developing Asian economies. It sheds light on various dimensions of Asia's economy and finance, ranging from business cycles, exchange rate movements, regional policy coordination, domestic financial development, capital flows, and financial market behavior. These analyses are pooled in a book that is a must read for market participants, policymakers, and academics alike.

LIST OF CONTRIBUTORS

Bertrand Candelon	Department of Economics, Maastricht University, Maastricht, The Netherlands
Chunlai Chen	Policy and Governance Program, Crawford School of Economics and Government, The Australian National University, Canberra, ACT, Australia
Yin-Wong Cheung	Department of Economics, University of California, Santa Cruz, CA, USA; Department of Economics and Finance, City University of Hong Kong, and School of Economics, Shandong University, China
Tsz-Kin Chung	Research Department, Hong Kong Monetary Authority, Central, Hong Kong, China
Chadwick C. Curtis	Department of Economics, University of Notre Dame, Notre Dame, IN, USA
Hans Genberg	Independent Evaluation Office, International Monetary Fund, N.W., Washington DC, USA
Galina Hale	Research Department, Federal Reserve Bank of San Francisco, San Francisco, CA, USA
Cho-Hoi Hui	Research Department, Hong Kong Monetary Authority, Central, Hong Kong, China
Shawn Chen-Yu Leu	School of Economics and Finance, La Trobe University, Melbourne, VIC, Australia
Priscilla Liang	Claremont Institute for Economic Policy Studies, Claremont, CA , USA; Martin V. Smith School of Business & Economics, California State University, Channel Islands, Camarillo, CA, USA
Cheryl Long	Department of Economics, Colgate University, Hamilton, NY, USA
Antonia López-Villavicencio	CEPN-CNRS, University of Paris 13, Villetaneuse, France

Guonan Ma	Bank for International Settlements, Representative Office for Asia and the Pacific, Bank for International Settlements, Central, Hong Kong
Nelson C. Mark	Department of Economics, University of Notre Dame and NBER, Notre Dame, IN USA
Robert N. McCauley	Monetary and Economic Department, Bank for International Settlements, Basel, Switzerland
Norbert Metiu	Department of Economics, University of Maastricht, Maastricht, The Netherlands
Valérie Mignon	EconomiX-CNRS, University of Paris Ouest, Nanterre Cedex, France; CEPII, Paris, France
Eiji Ogawa	Graduate School of Commerce and Management, Hitotsubashi University, Tokyo, Japan
Tuomas A. Peltonen	European Central Bank, Frankfurt am Main, Germany
Gabor Pula	European Central Bank, Frankfurt am Main, Germany
XingWang Qian	Department of Economics and Finance, SUNY, Buffalo State, Buffalo, NY 14222, USA
Jeffrey Sheen	Department of Economics, Macquarie University, Sydney, NSW, Australia
Junko Shimizu	School of Commerce, Senshu University, Tama-ku, Kawasaki, Japan
Peter T. Treadway	Department of Economics and Finance, City University of Hong Kong, Kowloon Tong, Hong Kong
Ulrich Volz	German Development Institute, Bonn, Germany
Thomas D. Willett	Claremont Institute for Economic Policy Studies; Department of Economics, Claremont McKenna College; Department of Economics, School of Politics and Economics, Claremont Graduate University, Claremont, CA, USA
Alfred Wong	Research Department, Hong Kong Monetary Authority, Central, Hong Kong, China
James Yetman	Representative Office for Asia and the Pacific, Bank for International Settlements, Central, Hong Kong

Yushi Yoshida	Faculty of Economics, Kyushu Sangyo University, Fukuoka, Japan
Nan Zhang	Claremont Institute for Economic Policy Studies; Department of Economics, School of Politics and Economics, Claremont Graduate University, Claremont, CA, USA

CONTENTS

PART III: DECOUPLING

INTRODUCTION: THE EVOLVING ROLE OF ASIA IN GLOBAL FINANCE

The rise of Asia in general and China in particular has markedly changed the landscape of the global economy and marketplace, especially after the global financial crisis of 2007–2009. The region has evolved from a sweatshop to a trading powerhouse and become a major growth engine globally today. Its economic rise will profoundly affect its relationship with the rest of the world, change the interactions among economies in the region, impact on an individual economy's domestic development pattern, and alter the linkages across various financial markets. Academics, policymakers, and market participants alike would like to have an enhanced understanding of this unfolding new world order. At the same time, the rapid rise of Asia has also prompted researchers to reexamine the conventional wisdom about the changing role of Asia in the global economy and different dimensions of its dynamic growth process.

This volume offers a timely collection of the latest research works that shed light on the evolving roles of a rising Asia in the global economic system. The contributors are experts on Asian economic issues. They are from the United States, Europe, and Asia, with diverse backgrounds ranging from academia, think tanks, monetary authorities, and international organizations, and of very different perspectives and styles. The volume consists of four main sections, with a total of 16 chapters. The four sections each address one of the following four broad themes: (a) real and financial interactions among economies and across markets, both within Asia and beyond; (b) regional monetary cooperation in Asia; (c) the decoupling debate over Asia's evolving economic and financial ties with major industrial economies; and (d) the changing roles of domestic finance and capital flows in the developing Asian economies.

1. Real and financial interactions

Asia's economic integration into the global system has many dimensions. It is part of the broader globalization process that has taken place over the past two decades and involves dynamics of convergence, integration, and interactions of both real and financial activities. Section 1 examines some of the recent trends in the real and financial interactions between Asia and the rest of the world and among different markets within Asia. It contains four chapters on this theme, addressing the issues of macroeconomic similarities and differences, interactions among Asian stock markets and between them and the US equity market, as well as spillovers across various types of financial markets in the region in response to shocks.

In Chapter 1 Curtis and Mark identify how the Chinese macroeconomy differs from large developed economies, such as the United States or Canada, by applying a standard real business cycle model to China. Their main finding is that while the standard model fits China well along several dimensions, it predicts a consumption share in GDP that is significantly larger than that observed in the data. They then proceed to examine whether the relatively low consumption in China could be due to the lack of adequate risk-sharing across the provinces. They document that the degree of risk-sharing across Chinese provinces is strikingly low and constitutes one of the major differences between China and the industrialized countries, suggesting that low risk-sharing across provinces in China could be a key to its much lower observed consumption share in GDP. Their analysis raises questions about the possible causes behind the low interregional risk-sharing and has important implications for macroeconomic policy as the Chinese government moves away the export-led model and increases reliance on domestic demand as a more important engine of economic growth.

Candelon and Metiu focus on the linkages between stock market fluctuations and business cycles in several Asian economies in Chapter 2. The economies covered in their sample include China, Indonesia, Japan, South Korea, Malaysia, the Philippines, Taiwan, and Thailand. They use a recently developed band-pass filter to extract cycles from the data. Similar to what has been documented for developed economies, they find that stock markets lead business cycles by about 6 months on average for most Asian countries in their sample. The key exceptions to this stylized fact are China, Taiwan, and South Korea, for which the real business cycles are contemporaneously synchronized with the stock market cycles. They conjecture that this could be due these markets being less mature in terms of asset market capitalization and turnover. This interesting conjecture stands in sharp contrast to the prevailing market view that Taiwan and South Korea have deeper and more liquid stock markets than most other emerging Asian markets.

In the third Chapter Yoshida investigates and compares the linkages between the United States and 13 Asian stock markets during the Asian financial crisis of 1997–1998 and the more recent subprime crisis of 2007–2008 using a smooth-transition correlation VAR-GARCH model. He discovers significant differences in the dynamics of the two crises. During the Asian financial crisis, the volatility in Asian equity markets Granger-caused volatility in the U.S. stock market, whereas in the subprime crisis the volatility causality ran from the United States to Asia. This result makes sense, as the Asian crisis started in Asia while the subprime crisis originated in the United States. Also, during the Asian financial crisis, the correlation between Asian and U.S. stock markets decreased for several Asian economies, but a similar decline was not apparent during the subprime crisis. This finding suggests that relative market size matters, as spillover from smaller markets tends to be less pronounced than vice versa. Both crises also shared something in common – a transition in correlation took place well in advance of the largest drop in equity prices, suggesting that the market participants were, at least to some extent, anticipating the upcoming crash.

One of the interesting features of the subprime crisis was that, as market participants re-evaluated counterparty risk, the turbulence in money markets spilled over to the foreign exchange swap markets. In Chapter 4, Genberg, Hui, Wong, and Chung examine the links between foreign exchange swaps and currency strength during the subprime crisis of 2007–2008. Their main findings are that the currency risk premiums are positively correlated with the spreads of money market rates over their corresponding overnight index swap rates and negatively correlated with the strength of the spot rates of their respective currencies. These facts are consistent with the notion that the flow of funds during the credit crunch was guided by perceptions about the relative safety and soundness of different countries' banking systems, and had associated consequences for their currencies.

2. *Regional monetary cooperation in Asia*

The future of exchange rate cooperation among Asian economies has been a topic of intense research for several reasons. For one, relative stability among regional currencies may matter a lot, given a large trade sector and a high degree of openness for most Asian economies. Both concerns over competitiveness and risks associated with excessive exchange rate volatility favor some degree of intraregional currency stability. Yet, so far Asian policymakers find few feasible options of coordination in enhancing stable and yet flexible Asian currencies against each other. Section 2 is a collection of four papers from experts on this subject. Chapters 5 through 7 investigate exchange rate regimes in East Asian economies, and a unifying thread across them is the view that even in the absence of formal monetary or exchange rate agreements, currency stability may be achieved if each country manages its own currency against an appropriately defined currency basket. Chapter 8 discusses the possibility that competitive devaluation may be one of the factors behind the undervaluation of most Asian currencies since the Asian financial crisis.

In Chapter 5 Ma and McCauley investigate the recent evolution of the renminbi (RMB) since its unpegging from the US dollar in 2005. The authors discuss the implications of the basket management of the RMB for currency stability in Asia. The paper points to an important, but often overlooked, feature of the RMB's evolution – from mid-2006 through mid-2008 the RMB's *effective* exchange rate was confined to a narrow band of and trended along a gradual upward crawl against its trade-weighted basket of partner currencies. The conventional wisdom, by contrast, is that the RMB was no more than a dollar peg since 2005. This policy experiment was apparently interrupted by the intensification of the global financial crisis in 2008. Yet an important implication is that even without explicit and formal monetary cooperation, a policy of managing currencies against their own respective baskets by regional monetary authorities could lead to greater currency stability within Asia.

In Chapter 6, Volz considers the problem of the choice of an optimal exchange rate regime in the context of East Asian economies. He extends the literature on the optimal peg by taking into account considerations of international financial relations, and proposes a blend of real and financial exchange rate baskets. The key recommendation of the author is a gradual reduction of the East Asian economies' close linkage with the U.S. dollar, and a corresponding increase in the weights on the euro and the Japanese yen in their currency baskets. This would naturally lead to a relatively homogenous exchange rate policy for the region and could evolve into a more formal exchange rate arrangement at an appropriate stage.

In Chapter 7, Shimizu and Ogawa study during the recent subprime crisis the fluctuations in the nominal bilateral exchange rates and nominal effective exchange rates (NEERs) for East Asian economies and the Asian monetary unit (AMU), which is a weighted average of the East Asian currencies with weights based on purchasing-power-parity-measured GDP and trade volumes. Their key finding is that while the nominal exchange rates of East Asian economies become more volatile vis-à-vis the US dollar, the euro, and the Japanese yen in 2008, currencies that were pegged to a basket experienced relatively minor fluctuations. The AMU, in particular, was significantly more stable compared with the individual East Asian currencies in bilateral terms. They also reach similar conclusions as Chapters 5 and 6 and argue that stabilizing a currency against its NEER would result in a *de facto* coordinated exchange rate policy. In addition, they also emphasize the possibility of coordinated monetary policies in East Asia in the future.

One topic that has led to heated and intense debate in recent years is whether observed exchange rates in Asian economies, especially China, reflect their underlying equilibrium values. In Chapter 8 López-Villavicencio and Mignon provide estimates of the real exchange rate misalignment for a large set of countries based on a version of the behavioral equilibrium exchange rate model. They also study the dynamics of how real exchange rates converge to these long-run equilibrium values, allowing for the possibility of a nonlinear adjustment mechanism. A key finding is that while Asian real exchange rates were overvalued during most of the 1980s, they have since been significantly undervalued. They interpret these undervalued real exchange rates as being driven by competitive devaluations of Asian currencies given their reliance on export-led growth. This in turn highlights the potentials for some informal exchange rate coordination within Asia.

3. The decoupling debate

In the past decade or so, academics, analysts, and policy makers have vigorously debated whether emerging Asian economies have become decoupled from the developed western world. This debate has become all the more relevant with the outburst of the global financial crisis during 2007–2009 and the gradual but remarkable ascent of Asia. Section 3 explores the various dimensions of this ongoing debate and casts new light on it using novel techniques and data.

Chapter 9 by Willett, Liang, and Zhang provide an overview of the concept of decoupling and distinguishes the various notions and definitions associated with it. Decoupling could, for instance, be viewed as economic growth in one area occurring independently of another area. Alternatively, it could be defined in terms of a reduction in business cycle synchronization or lower stock return correlations. The authors demonstrate that the structure of correlations between advanced and emerging economies is susceptible to significant time variation, and caution against reading too much into these changes given their dependence on the patterns of underlying shocks. In particular, the authors argue that even for the more insulated economies like China and India, their slowdowns from trend growth have been similar to that of the United States. Thus, their decoupling has not been as great as many popular analyses have suggested.

In Chapter 10 Yetman focuses on the "business cycle synchronization" version of the decoupling concept and asks whether emerging Asia-Pacific economies have decoupled from the US economy. He shows that the variation in the business cycle correlations is related to the phase of the business cycle, with correlations being relatively high during recessions and low during other phases. He also constructs a measure of decoupling that adjusts for countries' long-run average growth rates and, based on this measure, shows that the evidence does not support decoupling of the Asia-Pacific economies with the US economy. On the contrary, the author contends that Asia has become less decoupled from the United States over time.

In Chapter 11 Pula and Peltonen analyze the sensitivity of emerging Asia's business cycle dynamics to intraregional demand and demands from the United States, the EU15, and Japan by using an Asian input–output table. They find that about one-third of the value added in the emerging Asian economies depends on external demand and that trade and production linkages between Asia and the rest of the world have strengthened in recent years, casting doubt on the decoupling hypothesis. At the same time, Asia itself has become more integrated in trade. Moreover, they caution that inference based on raw trade data alone can be misleading as it significantly overstates the Asian economies' actual dependence on exports when measured in value-added terms.

Leu and Sheen investigate the evolution of the association of the Australian business cycle vis-à-vis its trading partners in Europe, North America, and Asia using a dynamic latent factor model in Chapter 12. Their variance decomposition exercise for the Australian output growth variations shows that the most significant factors explaining the variation, in descending order of importance, were the global factor, the European factor, the Asian factor, and the North American factor. A striking finding is that the correlation between the Australian output growth rate and the Asian business cycle factor has, over the past eight years, become large and positive from an initially negative and small value. Other than during the global financial crisis period of 2007–2008, which was arguably an exceptional time period, the correlations of Australian output growth with the North American and European business cycle factors have been negative. This prompts the authors to conclude that Australia has indeed become more closely "coupled" with Asia in recent years.

4. Domestic finance and capital flows

Both internal and external financing have been an important factor influencing economic development and financial stability and will remain key to future high economic growth for the Asian economies. Nevertheless, the global financial crisis in 2008 reminds us that their relationships are far from straightforward. In the absence of appropriate regulation, the financial sector can become more self-serving, giving rise to unpleasant externalities. Cross-border capital flows can strengthen or destabilize an economy. Section 4 comprises four papers discussing the Asian experiences related to issues such as firm financing, capital flows, foreign direct investment (FDI), and international financial hubs.

The positive relationship between economic growth and the financial sector development is well established for many economies. Yet China has witnessed remarkable growth over the past couple of decades, far outpacing its relatively underdeveloped financial sector. Hale and Long investigate the various sources of financing for Chinese firms in Chapter 13. Utilizing a large database of firms, they find that state-owned enterprises (SOEs) in China enjoy significant advantages relative to other types of firms in obtaining external financing. In addition to SOE status, the size of a firm also plays an important role, with small private firms facing greater financial constraints relative to their larger counterparts. Most local Chinese private firms rely more on internal financing and more expensive external financing, though they seem to have gained improved access to formal external financing in recent years. The authors identify private firms' inability to obtain adequate long-term financing as the most severe financial constraint facing Chinese firms and argue that alleviating this constraint should be the focus of financial reforms in China.

One of the key ingredients in China's economic success has been the persistent and large inward flow of FDI into China ever since the opening up of the economy in 1979. In Chapter 14, Chen provides an overview of FDI in China and analyzes its sources and the regional and sectoral distribution of inflows. An important conclusion of the chapter is that FDI inflows have made a significant positive impact on China's economic prospects and have contributed to capital formation, export promotion, and integration of China in the world economy. Despite the recent slowdown in FDI inflows, attributable to the subprime crisis, China is expected to retain its position as one of the most attractive FDI destinations globally. The author also casts doubt over the view that the large inward FDI into China has taken place at the expense of its emerging market peers.

Cheung and Qian in Chapter 15 conduct an empirical assessment of the primary determinants of the Chinese renminbi's covered interest rate differential, which can be interpreted as a proxy for the effectiveness of capital controls. In addition to the usual macroeconomic variables, such as capital flight and various components of country risk, they also examine the impact of three China-specific regulatory and institutional factors. They find that the effects of the canonical macroeconomic variables on the RMB covered interest differential are largely consistent with *a priori* expectations and robust to the choice of onshore and offshore RMB forward rates. They also show that China-specific factors, such as the exchange rate reform program and capital control policy, affect the RMB covered differential, but political risk does not.

In Chapter 16 Treadway explores the future of Hong Kong as a major public securities market and argues persuasively that Hong Kong has the potential to become the world's pre-eminent equity market venue, if certain important conditions are met. These conditions include granting Chinese firms the freedom to list in Hong Kong and Chinese retail and institutional investors the option to invest in Hong Kong – events which would be facilitated by lifting capital controls on the renminbi. He also underscores the importance of remaining open to new technologies that reduce the cost of trading and enhance Hong Kong's competitiveness, maintaining Hong Kong's stable exchange rate regime with full capital mobility, and preserving Hong Kong's legal and economic structure as specified in the Basic Law.

In the coming decades, Asia is set to become an even more important leading force contributing to the global economic growth and driving global financial markets. This prospect is more than amply demonstrated by the rapid rise of both China and India, the two dynamic and most important emerging market giants on the world stage. During this process, there will be many new challenges to both Asia and the world and to business, market participants and policymakers alike. We all need to climb the learning curve quickly, in order to grasp the many new issues arising from a fast-changing Asia, as the storm of the global financial crisis gradually subsides. This edited volume represents an attempt to shed light on only a small set of such questions. Much more remains to be explored going forward.

This edited volume is a collective and collaborative effort by many. The authors of the 16 chapters undoubtedly deserve most of the credit, as it is their contributions, cooperation, and willingness to share their insights that have made the volume possible. The editors also wish to express their appreciation to the referees for their timely and quality services. Last, but certainly not least, we would also like to thank Kwan Choi of the Iowa State University, Hamid Beladi of the University of Texas, and Chris Hart, Emma Whitfield, and Sarah Baxter of the Emerald Group Publishing for their encouragement and professional support.

Yin-Wong Cheung
Vikas Kakkar
Guonan Ma
Editors

PART I

Real and Financial Interactions

CHAPTER 1

Business Cycles, Consumption, and Risk Sharing: How Different Is China?☆

Chadwick C. Curtis[a] and Nelson C. Mark[b]

[a]*Department of Economics, University of Notre Dame, Notre Dame, IN, USA*
E-mail address: ccurtis1@nd.edu
[b]*Department of Economics, University of Notre Dame and NBER, Notre Dame, IN, USA*
E-mail address: nmark@nd.edu

Abstract

Can standard business cycle methodology be applied to China? In this chapter, we address this question by examining the macroeconomic time series and identifying dimensions in which China differs from economies (such as Canada and the United States) that are typically the subject of business cycle research. We show that naively applying the standard business cycle tools to China is no more ridiculous than applying it to Canada, although the dimensions along which the model struggles is different. For China, the model cannot account for the low level of consumption (or high saving) as a proportion of income observed in the data. An examination of provincial level consumption data suggests that the absence of channels for intranational consumption risk sharing may be an important reason why the business cycle model has trouble accounting for Chinese consumption and saving behavior.

Keywords: China, business cycles, consumption, risk sharing

JEL classifications: E32, O11, E13

1. Introduction

The economic importance of China in the world economy is difficult to overstate. Simply by virtue of China's 1.3 billion people, its economy is large in an absolute terms and is poised to overtake Japan as the world's second largest. Its sustained growth in real per capita GDP, at an average

☆Prepared for *The Evolving Role of Asia in Global Finance*, Yin-Wong Cheung, Vikas Kakkar, and Guonan Ma (Eds).

[1] Source: China National Bureau of Statistics.

Frontiers of Economics and Globalization
Volume 9 ISSN: 1574-8715
DOI: 10.1108/S1574-8715(2011)0000009006

of 8.6% from 1978 to 2007, is high by any standard.[1] While there has been a good deal of economic research done on China, most of it has been on microeconomic issues. Given the pace of globalization and China's role in international economics, surprisingly little research on China has been done on the macroeconomic side by academic economists.

There may be several reasons for this, but two possibilities jump to mind. The first concerns doubts about data quality. In one example of potential measurement error, in revising PPP exchange rates used to deflate nominal GDP, the World Bank revised the real GDP data for China downwards by about 40%. On the other hand, following the 2004 Chinese Economic Census, the National Bureau of Statistics (NBS) revised GDP from 1993 to 2004 upward so that by 2004, nominal and real GDP were modified to be 16% and 6% higher, respectively. Whether one believes in the accuracy of these revisions or not, the magnitude of the revisions serves to underscore some of the uncertainty surrounding the data. A second possibility stems from China's ongoing transition from a centrally planned to a market-based economy but with continued heavy involvement of the government. Researchers may be skeptical as to whether a transitional economy such as China's is appropriate for analysis by the current generation of business cycle models. These models are typically solved as approximations around the steady state, but one can question whether China has converged to the steady-state growth path. In this sense, China may be "too different" from the typical country that macroeconomists study with the standard toolkit of business cycle models.

In this chapter, we examine the extent to which China's macroeconomy is suitable for business cycle modeling. Using the available data, we address whether China is sufficiently similar or different, say in comparison with Canada and the United States. Of course, if we find that China is too different for business cycle modeling, it is possible that the underlying cause is data quality. In any event, it is beyond our manpower resources and our expertise to do anything about data quality issues and understanding the macroeconomics of China is too important to wait until the "high-quality data" are available.

We focus on two issues. First, we investigate the extent to which the cyclical properties of the post-reform Chinese economy (1978–2007) can be understood with a very basic real business cycle model. The model we use is nearly identical to Mendoza (1991), who studied the Canadian economy from 1946 to 1985. The only part of the model that is specific to China are the parameters of the exogenous processes (government spending and productivity) that we estimate from the Chinese data. Otherwise, we employ the same parameter values as Mendoza to facilitate the comparison between Chinese and Canadian macroeconomic behavior.

The main finding from this analysis is that China is not so very different. The business cycle model works about as well for China as it does for Canada in terms of matching the volatility and persistence of the macroeconomic data. For China, the model's primary shortcoming is in explaining consumption and saving behavior, whereas for Canada it is in explaining the persistence of investment and the trade balance. The model predicts consumption to be too smooth and to be too large a fraction of GDP as compared to the data.

The second issue we address is motivated by the "failure" of the business cycle model to explain household consumption behavior. Here, we examine the extent to which either markets or institutions in China carry out intranational risk sharing as a potential cause of the anomalous consumption/saving behavior. Since the representative agent setup in the business cycle model that we employ rests on an assumption of perfect within country risk sharing, severe violations of the risk-sharing assumption may explain the inability of the model to account for this aspect of the data. If opportunities for consumption risk-sharing are absent, people will have a strong precautionary saving motive that normally does not arise in the model.

Using provincial level data on real per capita consumption and income, we conduct a formal test of the risk-sharing assumption. We follow Crucini's (1999) study of risk sharing across the US states and among G-7 countries. By employing the same methodology as Crucini, we can directly compare our results for China with his results for the United States and across the industrialized economies.

The primary finding from this analysis is the degree of within China risk sharing is strikingly low. During the post market reform period (1979–2004), the data tell us that there was about as much risk sharing across Chinese provinces (i.e., very little) as there was internationally among G-7 countries from 1970 to 1987. Since many capital controls were still in place during the 1970s and 1980s, it is perhaps not surprising that international risk sharing was imperfect.[2] We find the degree of risk sharing across Chinese Provinces is much lower than that across the US states.[3] The differences in risk-sharing opportunities (and by implication of consumption and saving ratios) constitute one of the major differences between China and the industrialized countries.

The remainder of the chapter proceeds as follows. The next section covers the application of the business cycle model to China. Section 3 presents an informal examination of the provincial level data. The formal

---

[2] See Pierfederico *et al.* (1996) and Ostegaard *et al.* (2002) who test the risk-sharing hypothesis across the United States, and Lewis (1996) and Canova and Ravn (1996) who test the risk-sharing hypothesis internationally.

[3] While our primary focus is on risk sharing during the post-reform years, we also conduct our analyses on pre-reform data from 1954 to 1977. This analysis finds that consumption risk was shared even less under central planning than that has been observed in the post-reform period. The central planning committee evidently did not direct allocations in the same way as the social planner of our macro models.

test of the risk-sharing hypothesis and comparison of our results to Crucini's for the United States and G-7 countries is undertaken in Section 4, and Section 5 concludes.

2. *Does the business cycle framework work for China?*

In this section, we investigate the extent the cyclical properties of the post-reform Chinese economy be understood with a very basic real business cycle model.

The model we employ is a variant of Mendoza (1991) and Schmitt-Grohe and Uribe (2003). It is a one-good small open economy model with a representative consumer/producer who seeks to maximize expected lifetime utility,

$$E_t \sum_{j=0}^{\infty} \beta^j \frac{(c_{t+j} - (h_{t+j}^{\omega}/\omega))^{1-\gamma} - 1}{1-\gamma}$$

where $\beta \in [0,1)$ is the subjective discount factor, c_t is consumption, h_t is hours worked, and $\gamma \in [0,\infty)$ is the coefficient of relative risk aversion. This is same the period utility function used by Mendoza. The difference is that he assumes an endogenous subjective discount factor. Agents can issue or hold an internationally traded one-period non-state contingent bond that pays off one unit of the consumption good next period. The current resources available to the agent are the value of the bond holdings b_t and income y_t. These are consumed c_t, saved, and paid as lump sum taxes τ_t. Taxes fund wasteful government purchases g_t, and the government runs a balanced budget so that $g_t = \tau_t$. Saving is achieved by investment i_t in real capital or bond purchases b_{t+1}. The period budget constraint facing the agent is

$$c_t + \tau_t + i_t + \frac{b_{t+1}}{1+R_{t+1}} = y_t + b_t$$

where R_{t+1} is the rate of return on the bond between time t and $t+1$.

Output is produced by the Cobb–Douglas technology

$$y_t = a_t k_t^{\alpha} h_t^{1-\alpha}$$

where a_t is an exogenous technology shock and the capital stock k_t accumulates according to

$$k_{t+1} = (1-\delta)k_t + i_t - \frac{\varphi}{2}\left(\frac{k_{t+1}-k_t}{k_t}\right)^2.$$

The last term in the accumulation equation is an adjustment cost that imposes a penalty for rapid changes in the capital stock. In open economy models, including the adjustment cost is standard and necessary to prevent international investment flows from being overly responsive.

The exogenous state variables are government purchases, technology, and the world interest rate, r_t, which are assumed to evolve according to the first-order autoregressive processes,

$$\ln(g_t) = (1 - \rho_g)\ln(\bar{g}) + \rho_g \ln(g_{t+1}) + \varepsilon_t^g,$$
$$\ln(a_t) = \rho_a \ln(a_{t-1}) + \varepsilon_t^a,$$
$$r_t = (1 - \rho_r)\bar{r} + \rho_r r_{t-1} + \varepsilon_t^r,$$

where $\varepsilon_t^g(\overset{\text{iid}}{\sim} N(0, \sigma_g^2)$, $\varepsilon_t^a(\overset{\text{iid}}{\sim} N(0, \sigma_a^2)$, and $\varepsilon_t^r(\overset{\text{iid}}{\sim} N(0, \sigma_r^2)$. The subjective rate of time preference is set to the long-run (steady-state) interest rate such that it equals $(1 + \bar{r})^{-1}$. As in Schmitt-Grohe and Uribe (2003), we achieve a stationary steady-state level of bonds $\bar{b}$ by introducing a country premium $R_t - r_t$ that is increasing in deviations from a fixed debt level,[4]

$$R_{t+1} = r_{t+1} + \psi[\exp(\bar{b} - b_{t+1}) - 1].$$

The model is completed by imposing the national income accounting identity

$$y_t = c_t + i_t + g_t + tb_t,$$

where tb_t is the trade balance. Given the solution of the model, construction of auxiliary variables such as the current account,

$$ca_t = tb_t + \frac{R_t}{1 + R_t} b_t,$$

and national saving,

$$s_t = i_t + ca_t$$

follow directly.

2.1. Calibration and simulation

The data that we employ in our quantitative analysis are annual observations from the China Statistical Yearbook (various issues, see statistical appendix) spanning 1978–2007. In calibrating the model, the parameters that govern the exogenous state variables (g_t, r_t, a_t) are estimated from the data by least-squares of the AR(1) models. The capital adjustment parameter ϕ is chosen to match the volatility of investment. In setting the remaining parameter values, we draw from the literature and make no special adjustments specific to China. Table 1 reports the parameter values that we use. We take ω from Mendoza (1991) and ψ from

[4] Mendoza achieves a stationary steady state by assuming that the subjective discount factor is endogenous.

Table 1. Parameter values

	Parameter	Value		Parameter	Value
Preferences	β	0.978	Exogenous processes	ρ_a	0.600
	ω	1.45		ρ_g	0.809
	λ	2		ρ_r	0.434
	α	0.33			
	δ	0.1		σ_a	0.017
	ψ	0.00074		σ_g	0.010
	ϕ	2		σ_r	0.010
				$\bar{r}$	0.023
Bonds (SS)	$\bar{b}$	−0.05		$\bar{g}$	0.140

Schmitt-Grohe and Uribe (2003). We set the discount factor $\beta = (1 + \bar{r})^{-1}$ where $\bar{r}$ is the mean world real interest rate. The values for γ, α, and δ are all standard in the business cycle literature (recall that this is an annual model).

We examine four versions of the model that differ by the shocks that are allowed to hit the economy. They are:

1. The *All Shocks* model, which has all three shocks (g_t, r_t, a_t) running.
2. The *No Government* model, which allows productivity and interest rate shocks only.
3. The *Domestic Shocks* model, which shuts down world interest rate shocks but leaves productivity and government shocks running.
4. The *Productivity Shocks* model, which shuts down interest rate and government spending shocks.

Table 2 shows implied volatility of the key variables from the model and in the data since 1978.[5] Let us begin with the "All Shocks" model. In the data, consumption is somewhat more volatile than output, a feature that the model has trouble explaining. The high consumption volatility is not a feature specific to China, as this is a feature of many emerging market economies and also of some industrialized countries such as Great Britain. While also understating the volatility of net exports and the current account, the model overstates the relative volatility of investment, employment, and savings.

World interest rate shocks have a mall contribution to the volatility of the endogenous variables. Eliminating government spending shocks, however, results in consumption being even quieter (and saving being much too volatile). The ability of either the "All Shocks" or the "Domestic Shocks" model to generate the correct amount of volatility is mixed.

[5] We are working with a stationary model so the data have all been passed through the Hodrick-Prescott filter.

Table 2. Volatilities: Open economy (1978–2007)

Series	Data	All shocks	No government	Domestic shocks	Productivity only
$\sigma(y)$	0.048	0.050	0.049	0.050	0.049
$\frac{\sigma(c)}{\sigma(y)}$	1.167	0.877	0.660	0.883	0.721
$\frac{\sigma(i)}{\sigma(y)}$	1.792	1.687	1.703	1.677	1.682
$\frac{\sigma(h)}{\sigma(y)}$	0.458	0.664	0.662	0.664	0.663
$\frac{\sigma(s)}{\sigma(y)}$	1.500	1.237	2.003	1.273	1.882
$\frac{\sigma(g)}{\sigma(y)}$	0.958	0.904		0.910	
$\sigma\left(\frac{nx}{y}\right)$	0.027	0.016	0.014	0.017	0.015
$\sigma\left(\frac{ca}{y}\right)$	0.033	0.013	0.015	0.012	0.013

Table 3. Autocorrelations: Open economy (1978–2007)

	Data	All shocks	No government	Domestic shocks	Productivity only
GDP	0.730	0.722	0.724	0.720	0.719
Consumption	0.685	0.787	0.763	0.793	0.790
Employment	0.454	0.747	0.739	0.745	0.744
Investment	0.685	0.424	0.409	0.425	0.417
Saving	0.764	0.701	0.691	0.695	0.681
Current account/GDP	0.664	0.612	0.884	0.606	0.868
Net exports/GDP	0.667	0.755	0.870	0.750	0.893

Table 3 reports (model) implied and data values of the first-order autocorrelation of the macro time series. Keeping government spending shocks in the model are important, otherwise the implied trade balance (and current account) to GDP ratio becomes too persistent. The persistence of the other variables is little affected by the inclusion of government spending. The primary shortcomings of all four versions of the model are that implied persistence of employment is overstated and that of investment is understated.

Table 4 examines the co-movements of the macro variables. Consumption, investment, and saving all co-move with output in the appropriate direction. The last two rows highlight the importance of the government shocks, for the external balances become much too procyclical when they are omitted. Although slightly positive, the low cyclicality of the external balances comes from the fact that government spending is procyclical. The

Table 4. Correlations: Open economy (1978–2007)

Series	Data	All shocks	No government	Domestic shocks	Productivity only
$\rho(y,c)$	0.834	0.933	0.985	0.916	0.942
$\rho(y,i)$	0.800	0.812	0.817	0.826	0.824
$\rho(y,s)$	0.829	0.994	0.993	0.992	0.993
$\rho(c,i)$	0.437	0.705	0.759	0.703	0.719
$\rho(c,s)$	0.384	0.910	0.987	0.879	0.907
$\rho(s,i)$	0.890	0.827	0.832	0.849	0.857
$\rho(y,g)$	0.391	0.399		0.398	
$\rho\left(\frac{nx}{y},y\right)$	−0.098	0.058	0.529	0.025	0.439
$\rho\left(\frac{ca}{y},y\right)$	−0.167	0.020	0.534	0.021	0.510

Table 5. Results for Canada, 1946–1985

Variable	Data volatility	Model volatility	Data autocorrelation	Model autocorrelation
GDP	2.81	2.81	0.615	0.615
Consumption	2.46	2.25	0.701	0.689
Saving	7.31	5.58	0.543	0.629
Investment	9.82	9.89	0.314	−0.017
Hours	2.02	1.94	0.541	0.615
Productivity	1.71	0.87	0.372	0.615
TB/Y	1.87	1.97	0.663	0.032

Source: Mendoza (1991).

other difficulty in the model is that the predicted co-movements between saving and consumption are much higher than in the data.

To compare how China's business cycle differs from developed economies, Table 5 shows the main results from Mendoza's (1991) simulations from the model calibrated to Canadian data from 1946 to 1985. He calibrates his model to exactly match the volatility of GDP. In doing so, the model is able to match the volatility of consumption, investment, hours, and the trade balance to GDP ratio. Saving and productivity implied by the model are not volatile enough but the most obvious shortcoming of the model is the lack of persistence that it generates in investment and in the trade balance.

How different is China? Overall, the model actually works about as well for China as it does for Canada, although the dimensions along which it fares poorly is different in each case. A pretty consistent theme that emerges from the analysis of China is that the standard specification and calibration has trouble explaining household consumption, which in the data is too volatile and too low relative to GDP. The other side of this problem is that both the investment and saving ratios implied by the model are too low. To give one more illustration of this difficulty, we note that the mean values of consumption, investment, and saving in the data (as a fraction of GDP) are 0.465, 0.375, and 0.393, respectively. China's current account surplus did not accelerate until around 2004, so the national saving ratio is only around 2 percentage points higher than the investment ratio. These values contrast with the steady-state ratios implied by the model, which are 0.600 for consumption, 0.268 for investment, and 0.268 for saving.

One potential explanation for these deviations between the moments in the data and those implied by the model is a severe violation of the perfect within country risk-sharing assumption. We now turn to an investigation of this idea.

3. *Informal examination of China's provincial data*

The business cycle model assumes that markets are complete and/or a social planner directs allocations to achieve a Pareto Optimum. In either case, consumption growth across households are predicted to be highly (possibly perfectly) correlated. This section focuses on that prediction.

We employ provincial level data, which we obtain from the China Statistical Yearbook (various issues) and the China Statistical Data Compilation 1949–2003. We refer to "provinces" as regions classified as provinces, autonomous regions, and municipalities. These exclude Hong Kong and Macau. These are annual observations spanning from 1954 to 2004 and have not been subjected to the NBS revisions.[6,7] Nominal values are deflated with the aggregate price deflator. We also deflated provincial nominal figures using provincial price deflators. The main results are unchanged by doing this. We are primarily interested in consumption behavior during the post-reform (1978–2004) period. However, since they are available, we also examine the data from the pre-reform (1954–1977) period that allows us to assess consumption allocations determined under central planning.

We begin with an examination of provincial real per capita consumption growth. Average growth rates over the subsamples are displayed in Figure 1, where a large jump in growth can be observed for every region in the post-reform period. At the aggregate level, consumption growth nearly triples from 2.5% to 7.2% per year. In provinces such as Shanghai, the

[6] Provincial data is reported by each Provincial Statistical Bureau, not the NBS. So, the dates of revisions to provincial accounts data are staggered.

[7] The provincial data only spans up to 2004 where the aggregate data used in business cycle calibration extends to 2007. We used the revised aggregate data but the business cycle moments are similar to the unrevised series.

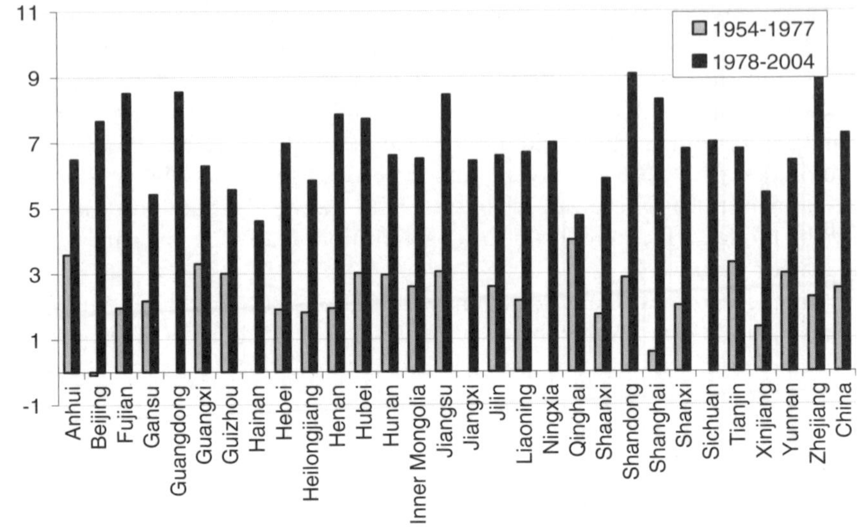

Fig. 1. Per capita consumption growth rates.

growth rate went from 0.6% during the pre-reform era to 8.3% in the post-reform period. However, Shanghai is an example of a province that suffered a great deal from the Great Leap Forward (1958–1961) that resulted in widespread famine. Omitting these years, the growth rate is slightly under 3%. In fact, eight provinces experienced an annual consumption growth rate of less than −20% in at least one year during this period. This contrasts with the much more modest change in Qinghai province. Qinghai, which seemed to be doing relatively well in the pre-reform period, had an average growth rate of 4.0%. In the post-reform era, its growth increased only to 4.7%.

In addition to raising consumption growth, the economic reforms after 1978 also seemed to have reduced the overall riskiness of life. Figure 2 shows provincial volatility (standard deviation) of consumption growth in the two periods. Volatility declines in every province except for the southern province of Yunnan and Zhejiang bordering Shanghai to the south on the eastern coast. Gansu, an economy based heavily on mining in the interior western region, shows a huge decline in consumption growth volatility. A curious (perhaps troubling) feature of the data is that consumption growth volatility reported in the aggregate China figures lies below most of the provincial volatility levels.

Turning to output, Figure 3 shows the well-known and corresponding acceleration of average annual growth rate of real per capita provincial GDP in the post-reform era. An interesting feature of this figure is the unevenness of output growth across the provinces. During the pre-reform period, the interior provinces such as Xinjiang (1.2%) and Inner Mongolia (0.5%) experienced very low growth. Even when omitting years of the

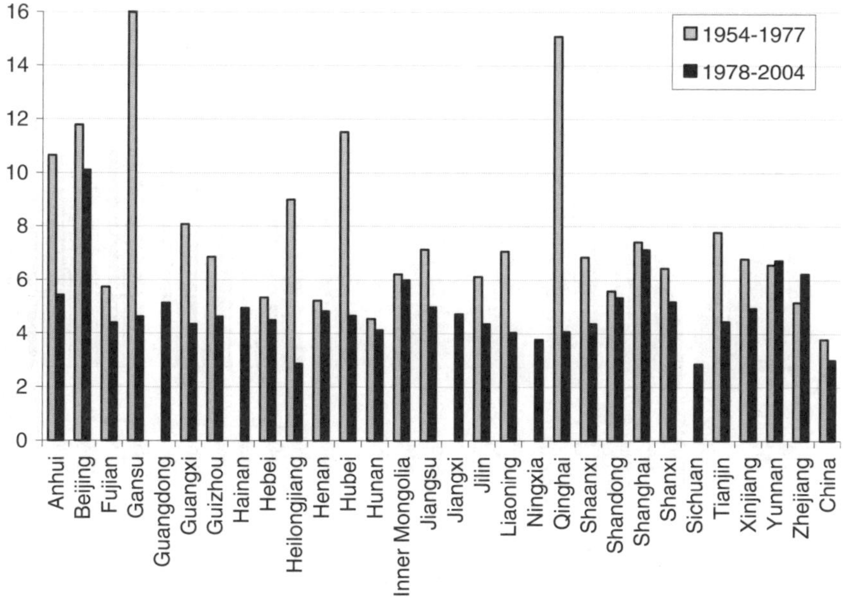

Fig. 2. Volatility of per capita consumption growth.

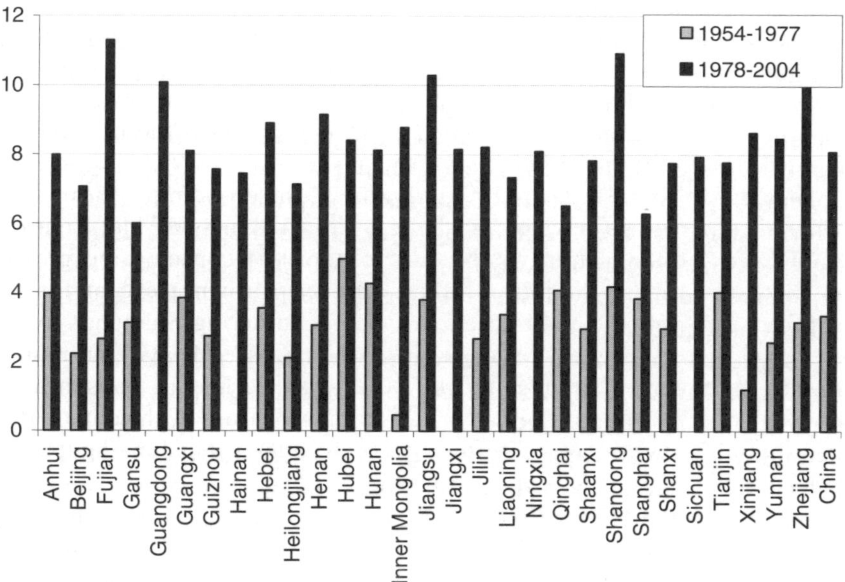

Fig. 3. Growth rate of output.

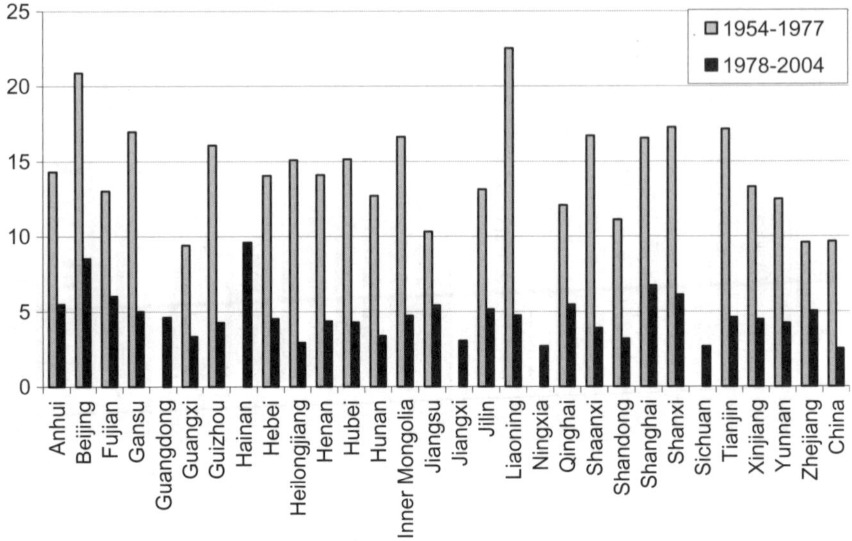

Fig. 4. Volatility of output growth.

Great Leap Forward, growth rates are a low 1.8% for Xinjiang and 1.7% for Inner Mongolia whereas areas such as Hubei grew at nearly 5%. Similarly, post-reform output growth is unbalanced and ranges from 6% in Gansu to 11.7% in Zhejiang.

The volatility of provincial output growth is displayed in Figure 4 shows the huge reduction in volatility following the market reforms. Pre-reform output volatility during our sample was largely self-inflicted by central planning disasters such as the Great Leap forward (1958–1961) and the Cultural Revolution (1966–1976), which resulted in serious economic upheaval. While pre-reform China seems unimaginably unstable, post-reform China has been quite the opposite. The aggregate volatility of per capita output growth of 2.5% from 1979–2004 is roughly the same level experienced in the United States during the years (1969–1983) before the "Great Moderation."

To get an idea of the degree of integration or coordination across provinces, Figure 5 shows the correlation between provincial output growth and aggregate output growth. Correlations during the Mao Zedong years are relatively high with an average value of 0.84. This is higher than output growth correlations among US states shown in Figure 6. For the United States, the correlation average is 0.7 from 1969 to 1983 and 0.56 from 1984 to 2008. In post-central planning China, the average correlation falls to 0.4, which suggests a low level of integration across provinces on the production side and an increase in the relative importance of idiosyncratic (provincial level) risk.

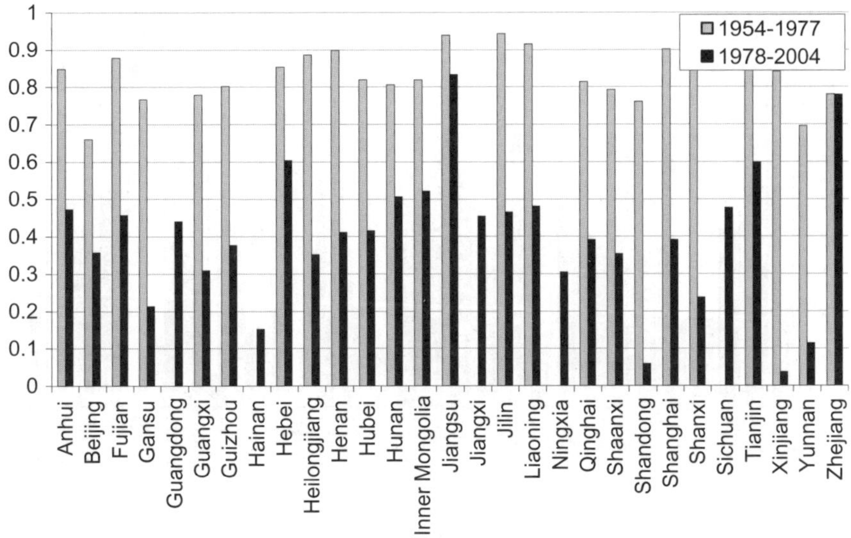

Fig. 5. Correlation between provincial aggregate output growth.

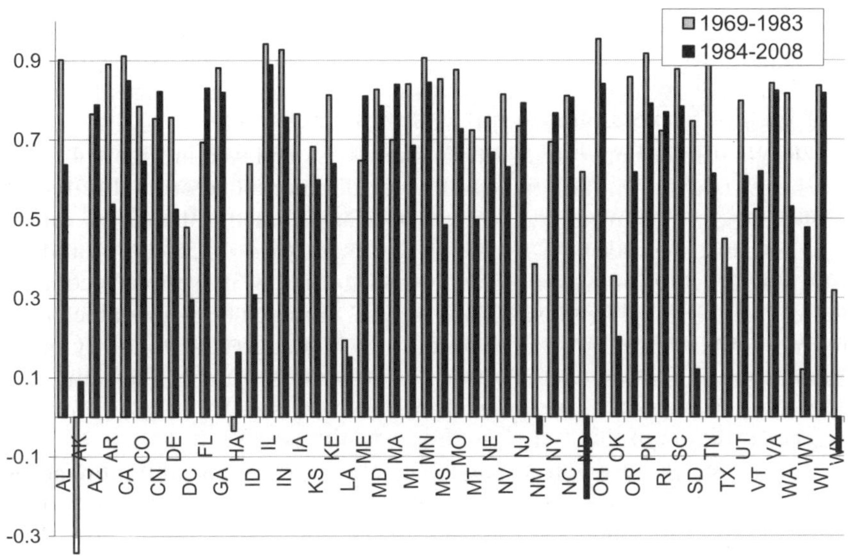

Fig. 6. Output growth correlations in the United States.

We next proceed to get a sense of the ability to insure against idiosyncratic income risk. The typical approach to risk sharing is an environment of complete financial markets where a full menu of state-contingent assets is traded. China's pre-reform environment was

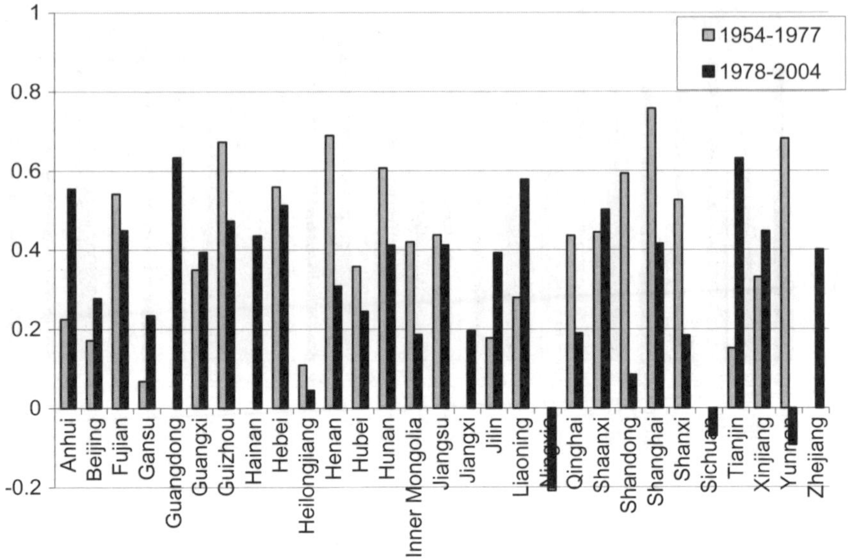

Fig. 7. Correlation between provincial and aggregate consumption growth.

perhaps the farthest thing possible from complete markets. But, by the second theorem of welfare economics, if the leadership acts to maximize social welfare, any Pareto Optimal allocation achieved can also be achieved by a competitive equilibrium. China potentially had at its disposal an institutional setup that could actually achieve perfect consumption insurance. A benevolent social planner would have ordered that consumption be directed across provinces such that consumption growth between any two provinces is perfectly correlated. Such is the basic tenet of communism: "From each according to his ability, to each according to his need," as the Marxist slogan goes.

The key figure of this section and the one that speaks directly to the risk-sharing issue is Figure 7. It displays the correlation between provincial and aggregate per capita consumption growth, which should be close to 1 under perfect insurance.[8] In 15 of the 24 provinces for which we have data over the two subsamples, the correlation declines. So for slightly more than half of the provinces, the pre-reform regime was better able to provide consumption insurance. The average correlation declines from 0.42 to 0.32 in the post-reform period, a statistically significant difference

[8] The existence of non-traded goods and differences in consumption weights across provinces would cause the correlation to drop below, but not far from 1 even with complete risk sharing.

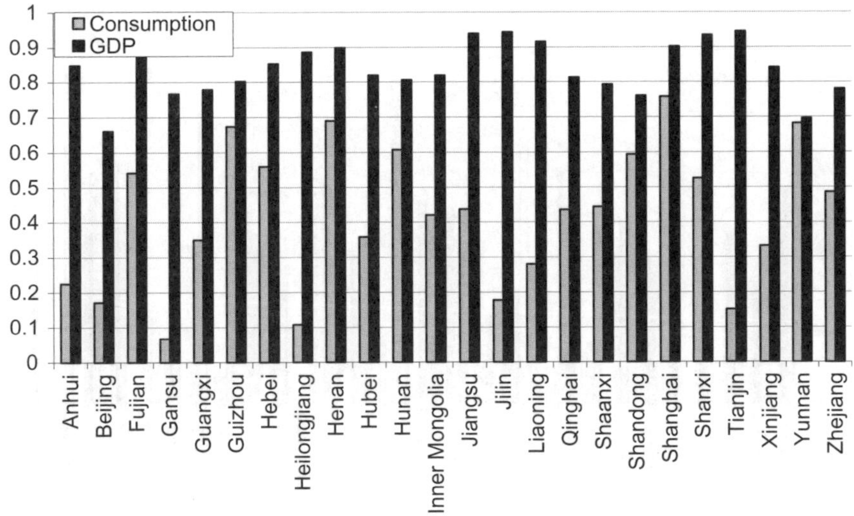

Fig. 8. Correlation between provincial and aggregate growth 1954–1977.

at the 10% level, and the correlation for three of the provinces in the latter period are negative.

The degree of risk sharing across countries is a topic also studied by international economists.[9] In the international economics literature, a widely documented fact, known as the "consumption correlation puzzle," is that the correlation of consumption growth between two countries is typically smaller than the correlation between output growth between the same two countries. For example, Choi and Mark (2010) report an average consumption correlation across G-7 countries and the aggregate of 0.4 and an output correlation of 0.5. This is a puzzle, because even if financial markets are incomplete (say there is only a single non-state contingent bond traded across countries), we expect the correlation between the two countries' consumption to be much higher than the correlation between their outputs. It is against this backdrop that we present in Figures 8 and 9, which plots the correlation between provincial and aggregate consumption and output. During the pre-reform years, there is a substantial consumption correlation puzzle as provincial consumption correlations (average value 0.42) lie far below the output correlations

[9] The puzzle was noted by Backus *et al.* (1992) who find that a two-country business cycle model fails to explain most of co-movements of major macroeconomic variables across countries. Subsequent studies that attempt to explain the puzzle include Baxter and Crucini (1995), Kehoe and Perri (2002), Kollmann (1996), and Iacoviello and Minetti (2006) who study the role of the asset market incompleteness in the international business cycles, whereas Stockman and Tesar (1995), Wen (2007), Xiao (2004) introduce taste or demand shocks in their models.

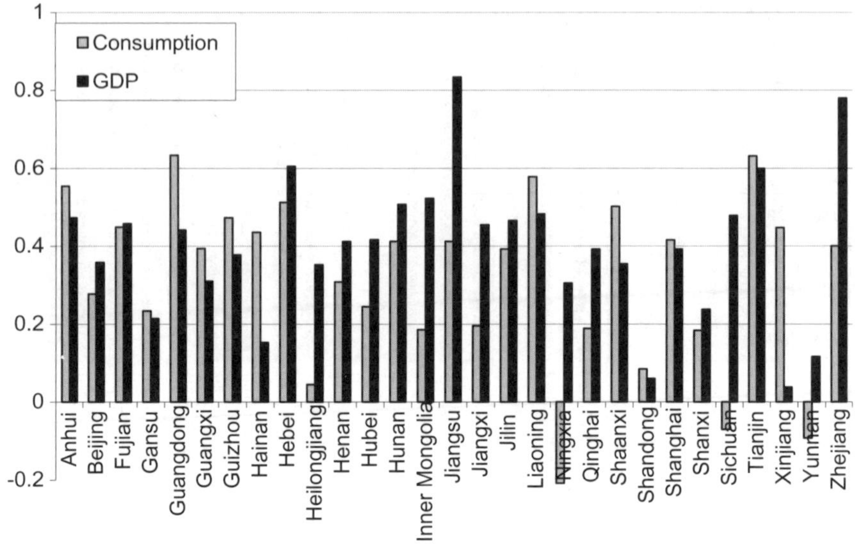

Fig. 9. Correlation between provincial and aggregate growth 1978–2004.

(average value 0.84). During the post-reform period, the puzzle is attenuated to the extent that provinces look like the industrialized countries in this dimension with an average consumption correlation of 0.32 against an average output correlation of 0.40.

4. A test of the perfect risk-sharing hypothesis

In this section, we employ a methodology used by Crucini (1999) to formally test the risk-sharing hypothesis across Chinese provinces. Since Crucini applied the same test to US states and G-7 countries, we can use our results to assess the degree of within country risk-sharing in China to that in the United States and to international risk sharing across industrialized countries.

Let c_{jt} be log real per capita consumption of province *j* in year *t*, and C_t be log aggregate real per capita consumption. If there is perfect risk sharing, provincial consumption growth should be perfectly correlated with aggregate consumption growth. A testable implication of the hypothesis of perfect risk sharing is that a regression of the change in provincial consumption, Δc_{jt}, on the change of aggregate consumption, ΔC_t, will yield a unit-valued slope coefficient and that coefficients on any additional regressors will be zero. Let Δy^p_{jt} be the innovation (unexpected change) to province *j*'s permanent income. Crucini (1999) suggest running the regression

$$\Delta c_{jt} = \alpha_j + \lambda_j \Delta C_t + (1 - \lambda_j)\Delta y^p_{jt} + \varepsilon_{jt} \tag{1}$$

and testing the null hypothesis (perfect risk sharing) that $\lambda_j = 1$

Table 6. Tests of perfect risk sharing on 24 Chinese provinces

Income model	$\bar{\lambda}$	Average S.E. ($\bar{\lambda}$)	Values R^2	No. of provinces for which a 95% confidence interval contains the value of λ such that			
				$\lambda = 1$	$0 < \lambda < 1$	$\lambda = 0$	$\lambda = 0$ or 1
1954–1977							
I	0.45	0.43	0.38	6	2	8	8
II	0.39	0.40	0.42	6	1	9	8
III	0.33	0.38	0.43	5	2	11	6
1978–2004							
I	0.50	0.32	0.26	9	2	5	7
II	0.49	0.32	0.27	8	1	7	8
III	0.43	0.31	0.27	6	1	10	7

against the alternative hypothesis (imperfect risk sharing) that $0 \leq \lambda_j < 1$. The innovation to permanent income is unobserved and must be estimated. As in his paper, we consider three alternative estimates of this variable. Income model I assumes that provincial and aggregate income growth, Δy_{jt} and ΔY_t, are generated by a first-order vector autoregression. Income model II assumes that provincial income growth follows a first-order autoregression. Income model III assumes that log provincial income is a driftless random walk. The residual from estimating the income model serves as the estimated innovation to permanent income, Δy^p_{jt}.

For each income model specification, we estimate 24 regressions of Equation (1). Although there are 31 provinces, we have continuous observations from 1954 to 2004 for only 24 of these provinces. To summarize the results, we report average figures in Table 6.

We do not get exceedingly precise estimates of λ as the standard errors are about the same size as the estimates. In the pre-reform era, under income model I [provincial and aggregate income growth generated by a VAR(1)], perfect risk sharing is not be rejected at the 5 percent level for 6 provinces. In 8 provinces, the hypothesis of zero risk sharing could not be rejected, and in 8 others, the data are uninformative as neither the hypothesis that $\lambda = 1$ or $\lambda = 0$ can be rejected. The evidence for effective consumption risk sharing is not much different when innovations to permanent income are modeled by income models II [AR(1)] and III (random walk).

In post-reform China, there is some evidence of a slightly increased degree of risk sharing. The magnitude of our estimated λ coefficients is bigger, and perfect risk sharing is not rejected for nine provinces under income model I.

To compare China to within United States and international G-7 risk sharing, Table 7 reproduces Crucini's results. Since state level consumption data is unavailable for the United States, he uses retail sales as the proxy. It can be seen on the basis of retail sales, there appears to be a great

Table 7. Tests of perfect risk sharing on US states and G-7 countries

Income model	$\bar{\lambda}$	Average S.E. ($\bar{\lambda}$)	Values R^2	No. of provinces for which a 95% confidence interval contains the value of λ such that			
				$\lambda = 1$	$0<\lambda<1$	$\lambda = 0$	$\lambda = 0$ or 1
US states, 1972–1990							
I	0.94	0.31	0.51	31	3	2	9
II	0.84	0.34	0.50	29	2	3	13
III	0.88	0.32	0.50	33	3	2	10
G-7 countries, 1972–1990							
I	0.60	0.26	0.45	2	2	2	1
II	0.44	0.44	0.57	1	2	4	0
III	0.37	0.37	0.57	1	2	4	0

deal of risk-sharing within the United States. Perfect insurance cannot be rejected for 33 states (66% of the sample) using income model III. The international story, at least among the G-7 during the 1970s and 1980s, is one of substantially less risk sharing. Perfect risk sharing cannot be rejected for at most 28% of the sample.

Thus for post-reform China, the degree of risk sharing is substantially below that in the United States and about at the same level across industrialized countries in the 1970s and 1980s. It makes sense that international risk sharing may have been low at that time since there were still many capital controls in place (1970–1987). Overall, the conclusion has to be that there is very little consumption risk sharing across Chinese provinces.[10]

To summarize the findings on risk sharing; first, as measured by income volatility, the pre-reform era was a riskier environment than post reform. Although riskier, the state run model appears not to have done substantially worse at implementing a program of consumption risk sharing than post-reform China. Nevertheless, the ability to hedge against idiosyncratic provincial level income risk appears modest. The absence of effective risk-sharing channels tells us that the precautionary saving motive must be very strong for Chinese households. Presumably, this is an important factor driving high household saving rates and the current account. We caution the reader not to infer normative implications of this analysis. Even though risk sharing is still quite modest, the growths enabled by the post-1978 reforms have undoubtedly improved welfare.

[10] Xu (2008) employs the Crucini test but employs household survey data spanning 1980–2004 and reaches conclusions similar to ours.

5. Conclusion

To answer the questions posed in the introduction, we do find that China's macroeconomics are different from developed countries that are usually studied in business cycle research, but not so different that it is an unsuitable target for this research. One of the most prominent differences in the Chinese data that sets it apart lies in the consumption/saving decisions by households. The business cycle model cannot explain why Chinese households consume such a small fraction of income, why consumption moves around so much relative to income, and why the co movement between consumption and saving is so low.

We get a clue as to why the model falls short in this dimension from the analysis on intranational consumption risk sharing. As in Xu (2008), we detect a low degree of cross-province risk sharing. In this dimension, each province is about as segmented from one another as between the G-7 countries during the 1970s and 1980s. Given the difficulty of hedging income risk and natural household concerns about income security, the environment would seem to create a significant motive for precautionary saving, which is not present say within the United States.[11]

Statistical Appendix

The sources of the Chinese provincial and aggregate data are:

- All China Marketing Research Co., Ltd (2004).
- NBS of China. The China Statistical Yearbook (2005, 2006, 2007, 2008). China Statistics Press, Beijing.

The data set contains 31 provinces for which only 24 cover the entire sample 1954–2004.

List of 24 provinces (1954–2004): Beijing, Tianjin, Hebei, Shanxi, Inner Mongolia, Liaoning, Jilin, Heilongjiang, Shanghai, Jiangsu, Zhejiang, Anhui, Fujian, Henan, Hubei, Hunan, Guangxi, Guizhou, Yunnan, Shaanxi, Gansu, Qinhai, Ningxia, and Xinjiang.

Gross State Product data in the United States comes from US Bureau of Economic Analysis at http://www.bea.gov/regional/gsp/.

References

Backus, D.K., Kehoe, P.J., Kydland, F.E. (1992), International real business cycles. *Journal of Political Economy* 100 (4), 745–775.

[11] Wei and Zhang (2009) investigate the interesting idea that competition for marriage partners combined with a surplus of Chinese males drive the high saving rates.

Baxter, M., Crucini, M.J. (1995), Business cycles and the asset structure of foreign trade. *International Economic Review* 6 (4), 821–854.

Canova, F., Ravn, M,O. (1996), International consumption risk sharing. *International Economic Review* 37 (3), 573–601.

Choi, H., Mark, N. (2010), trending current accounts, mimeo, University of Notre Dame.

Crucini, M. (1999), On international and national dimensions of risk sharing. *Review of Economics and Statistics* 81 (1), 73–84.

Iacoviello, M., Minetti, R. (2006), International business cycles with domestic and foreign lenders. *Journal of Monetary Economics* 53 (8), 2267–2282.

Kehoe, P.J., Perri, F. (2002), International business cycles with endogenous incomplete markets. *Econometrica* 70 (3), 907–928.

Kollmann, R. (1996), Incomplete asset markets and the cross-country consumption correlation puzzle. *Journal of Economic Dynamics and Control* 20 (5), 945–961.

Lewis, K.K. (1996), What can explain the apparent lack of international consumption risk sharing? *Journal of Political Economy* 104 (2), 267–297.

Mendoza, E.G. (1991), Real business cycles in a small open economy. *American Economic Review* 81 (4), 797–818.

Ostegaard, C., Sørenson, B.E., Yosha, O. (2002), Consumption and aggregate constraints: evidence from U.S. States and Canadian provinces. *Journal of Political Economy* 110 (3), 634–645.

Schmitt-Grohe, S., Uribe, M. (2003), Closing small open economy models. *Journal of International Economics* 61, 163–185.

Stockman, A.C., Tesar, L.L. (1995), Tastes and technology in a two-country model of the business cycle: Explaining international comovements. *American Economic Review* 85 (1), 168–185.

Wei, S-J., Zhang, X. (2009). Sex ratios and saving rates: Evidence from "Excess Men" in China, mimeo, Columbia University.

Wen, Y. (2007), By force of demand: Explaining international comovements. *Journal of Economic Dynamics and Control* 31 (1), 1–23.

Xiao, W. (2004), Can Indeterminacy resolve the cross-country correlation puzzle? *Journal of Economic Dynamics and Control* 28 (12), 2341–2366.

Xu, X. (2008), Consumption risk sharing in china. *Economica* 75, 326–341.

CHAPTER 2

Linkages between Stock Market Fluctuations and Business Cycles in Asia

Bertrand Candelon[a] and Norbert Metiu[a]

[a]*Department of Economics, Maastricht University, P.O. Box 616, Maastricht, MD6200, Netherlands*
E-mail address: b.candelon@maastrichtuniversity.nl; n.metiu@maastrichtuniversity.nl

Abstract
This chapter sheds new light on the linkages between stock market fluctuations and business cycles in Asia. It shows that at cyclical frequencies stock markets lead business cycles by six months on average. China, Korea, and Taiwan constitute exceptions, as their real and stock market cycles are contemporaneously synchronized. The low level of maturity of these markets offers a potential explanation of this outcome. Furthermore, we find that the linkage also holds during phases of cyclical upswing and downturn, with the exception of China, where the financial market lags behind industrial production during expansions. Finally, for most of the countries (except Thailand and Malaysia), the linkage is also robust to the presence of financial crises.

Keywords: Business cycles, economic integration, financial cycles, synchronization

JEL classifications: C19, E32, F36

1. Introduction

A large number of studies have shown that if stock markets are efficient, prices in these markets reflect underlying economic forces. Consequently, financial markets should react to news concerning the present or future evolution of real economic activity, or in other words, macroeconomic fundamentals should constitute explanatory variables for stock market indices. However, the pronounced boom-bust cycles in emerging stock markets experienced during the recent decades together with rather moderate macroeconomic fluctuations point to a possible disruption of

Frontiers of Economics and Globalization
Volume 9 ISSN: 1574-8715
DOI: 10.1108/S1574-8715(2011)0000009007

the financial sector from the real economy, fueled by global financial liberalization. The "decoupling" of financial markets from real fundamentals during periods of financial boom suggests that the impact of macroeconomic news on financial price movements is related to the state of the business cycle. Moreover, stock market fluctuations may have repercussions on economic activity. Through their impact on corporate balance sheets, financial cycles can create inflationary or deflationary pressures, which is of concern to monetary policymakers.

Empirical support for the interactions between financial and real markets has been provided by, among others, Fama (1990), Schwert (1989, 1990), Chen (1991), Ferson and Harvey (1993), and Binswanger (2000) for the United States, as well as by Cheung *et al.* (1997), Cheung and Ng (1998) and Maysami and Sim (2001) for a group of countries. These studies include short- and long-run analyses, employing various econometric tools. Nevertheless, the cyclical links between the two sectors have been investigated by only few papers. In a seminal work, Hamilton and Lin (1996) established the most robust stylized fact on cyclical interaction. They found that stock market downturns precede economic recessions, while stock market upswings anticipate business cycle expansions. Hence, stock market indices constitute potential leading indicators of economic activity, which can be exploited for economic prediction (see, e.g., Estrella and Mishkin, 1998; Chauvet, 1998; Beaudry and Portier, 2006).

The aim of this chapter is to unravel the relation between stock market fluctuations and business cycles in Asia. The literature proposes several methods to analyze cyclical interactions between time series. The first method, which is the most popular, consists of testing for a short-run co-movement (also called common feature) between series, using raw data.[1] For example, Breitung and Candelon (2001) proposed a frequency domain test for co-movements at specified frequencies in particular at business cycle ones. An alternative route consists of directly working on the cyclical components obtained by filtering the raw series in a preliminary stage. It is then possible to perform a correlation and concordance analysis on the extracted cycles. Both approaches are interesting *per se*, and offer complementary results. Nevertheless, we implement the second approach, as it permits to investigate the potential asymmetries in the link between the two sectors during expansions and recessions, and is less subject to identification problems. Finally, its implementation is scarce in the literature.

The cyclical relationship is investigated for several Asian countries (China, Indonesia, Japan, Korea, Malaysia, the Philippines, Taiwan, and Thailand). We also integrate the possible distorting effect on the links

[1] See Engle and Kozicki (1993) for the seminal paper and Cheung and Westermann (2000, 2003) for empirical applications.

between financial and real markets that is potentially introduced by successive crises (the 1997 "Asian flu" and the 2007 subprime crisis). In principle, removing cyclical phases associated with financial crises should increase the strength of the relationship; during bull market phases, stock market prices disconnect from their fundamentals and reconnect only after the bubble bursts. Thus, it would not be surprising if, without controlling for these periods, the linkages between the stock market and the real sector appeared less strong than they are in reality, as indicated by Hamao *et al.* (2003) in the case of Japan.

Anticipating our results, we confirm that the relationship between stock markets and industrial production prevails and financial cycles lead real cycles by six months on average. China, Korea, and Taiwan constitute exceptions; their cycles appear to be synchronized contemporaneously. This result finds its justification in the low level of maturity of these markets (in terms of asset market capitalization). Looking specifically at the expansion phase of the cycle, we find that cyclical asymmetry is rejected for all countries except China, for which financial markets lag behind industrial production during expansions. Finally, the results prove to be robust to the presence of financial crises. In countries where extreme financial cyclical phases are detected (Thailand and Malaysia), the degree of synchronization is higher after controlling for the crisis periods, which supports the idea of a disconnection of the stock market from fundamental values during crises.

The rest of this chapter is organized as follows: Section 2 presents the data as well as the filters used to extract the cyclical fluctuations. Sections 3–5 cover the analysis using cyclical series. Specifically, Section 3 considers the linkage between the cycles extracted from stock market and industrial production indices. Section 4 considers the relationship between phases of expansion and contraction in the cycles. Finally, the potential asymmetries within the cycle and the robustness of the relationship to financial crises are investigated in Section 5. Section 6 offers conclusions.

2. *Preliminary analysis*

2.1. The data

Our sample consists of stock market indices and indicators of real economic activity for China, Indonesia, Japan, Korea, Malaysia, the Philippines, Taiwan, and Thailand. Several proxies are available for real economic activity, the most popular being gross domestic product, gross national product, and industrial production. We use the industrial production index because unlike the data issued from quarterly national accounts, it is available monthly and is less subject to revisions. Stock market series are represented by indices of the largest national stock

Table 1. Glossary and definitions of data

China	Shanghai index, Shenzhen index; industrial production index; 1992m2–2009m7
Indonesia	Jakarta SE composite index; manufacturing production index; 1986m1–2009m7
Japan	TOPIX index; industrial production index; 1959m10–2009m7
Korea	KOSPI index; industrial production index; 1975m1–2009m6
Malaysia	FTSE Bursa Malaysia KLCI index; industrial production index; 1980m1–2009m7
Philippines	Philippine SE; manufacturing production index; 1986m1–2009m7
Taiwan	Taiwan SE weighted index; industrial production index; 1971m1–2009m7
Thailand	SET index; manufacturing production index; 1987m1–2009m7
USA	S&P 500 index; industrial production index; 1964m1–2009m7
Regional stock index	IBES MSCI EM FAR EAST index (comprised of China, Indonesia, Korea, Malaysia, Philippines, Taiwan, Thailand); 1988m2–2009m7

Note: All variables are taken in logs.

market. The only uncertainty comes from China, where two stock markets coexist (the Shanghai and Shenzhen stock exchanges), as do two types of shares (the A-shares are domestic shares that can be traded only by Chinese citizens, while the B-shares can be traded only by foreign investors). Both shares are traded on both markets, but the A-shares are more actively traded on the Shanghai Stock Exchange, while the B-shares are more actively traded on the Shenzhen Stock Exchange. The latter market is thus comparatively less liquid; one would expect the B-share market to be less efficient than the A-share market. We therefore report results only for the Shanghai stock market.[2]

All series have been extracted from Datastream. The data are monthly and are expressed in local currency to exclude movements that are due specifically to the exchange rate. The industrial production series were seasonally adjusted before the analysis. A glossary and definitions of the data are reported in Table 1.

The choice of countries is motivated by the fact that the countries considered have emerging economies – that is, they are experiencing swiftly growing financial markets. Garcia and Liu (1999) analyzed average market capitalization for the period 1980–1995 and found that it skyrocketed for the countries in our sample after 1990. To indicate an order of magnitude of the increase after 1990, asset market capitalization was multiplied by a number between 3 (in Korea, from 8% to 24% of the GDP) and 17 (in Indonesia, from 1% to 17% of the GDP); this is much

[2] The analysis has also been performed using the Shenzhen stock market index, and the outcomes appear to be similar even if they are quoted in different currencies. We thank an anonymous referee for pointing out this issue. Outcomes are available at http://www.personeel.unimaas.nl/b.candelon or upon request from the authors.

Table 2. Stock market capitalization (in % of GDP)

Country	1980–1991	1992–1995	1996–2001
China	–	–	37.60
Indonesia	1.05	17.99	44.45
Japan	74.73	71.76	63.85
Korea	8.78	24.05	40.00
Malaysia	66.76	231.60	179.23
Philippines	9.24	56.05	72.05
Taiwan	6.05	42.81	–
Thailand	6.07	40.95	43.89
USA	53.39	75.73	172.95

Notes: The first two columns are extracted from Garcia and Liu (1999, p. 47), while the third column comes from an IMF series and the authors' calculations.

more pronounced than for other emerging economies – e.g., in Latin America (see Garcia and Liu, 1999, p. 47, Table 2). The increase in asset market capitalization signals that Asian stock markets are becoming more mature, thus enhancing economic efficiency and leading to a stronger connection with economic activity. Well-developed financial markets can aid the efficient functioning of real markets by enforcing the survival of firms with healthy balance sheets, competitive products, and innovative technologies. However, if the liquidity originates to a large extent from speculative foreign capital inflow that is not matched by comprehensive financial market regulation, this can potentially lead to an excessive credit boom, where all stock markets co-move independently of the underlying macroeconomic fundamentals. The 1997 Asian financial crisis is commonly attributed to the adverse consequences of this so-called decoupling hypothesis.[3] Recent values for stock market capitalization are reported in Table 2.

Despite this common evolution, the countries are still heterogeneous in terms of levels of stock market capitalization: Korea and China exhibit the lowest ratios on average and Malaysia the highest. This evidence highlights the fact that the level of stock market maturity is not identical in all countries, and thus a country-level analysis of the relationship between stock markets and the real economy is needed.

The analysis can be performed at the level of individual countries considered in isolation, or at the level of a specific group (clustered by region or with the degree of development). However, considering the system as a whole faces econometric difficulties. In our case, considering a set of 8 countries would result in a system of 16 variables to be analyzed

[3] Calvo *et al.* (1996) give an account of excessive liquidity inflow to emerging markets, while Chang and Velasco (1998) illustrate its role in the 1997 Asian financial crisis.

with approximately 200 observations. This would lead to huge test distortions. Second, the identification of the relationships appears difficult in the multivariate case because of the restrictions to be imposed to ascertain the drivers of multivariate co-movement. In particular, the presence of common cycles does not necessarily mean an effective interaction between the financial and the real sector; the co-movement can be driven by the links between stock market cycles because of international financial integration. Hence, we assess the links between the stock market and the business cycle considering countries in isolation. Moreover, we introduce the international dimension via an Asian regional stock market index. We also present results from the United States as a global benchmark.

2.2. The cyclical filter

The cyclical components of the data are defined as the transitory fluctuations around their trends – that is, growth cycles. Several methods are available for extracting growth cycles from time series, the most popular being the filters proposed by Hodrick and Prescott (1997), Baxter and King (1999), and Christiano and Fitzgerald (2003).[4]

Hodrick and Prescott (1997) proposed a heuristic method of trend-cycle decomposition.[5] Although the method produces reasonably robust results and is widely used, it has several disadvantages. In particular, Cogley and Nason (1995) showed that the Hodrick–Prescott (HP) filter is optimal if the time series is integrated of order two. Therefore, when applied to first-order integrated processes, the HP filter can produce spurious cycles. Second, the choice of the trend-smoothing parameter is debatable, and common choices for this parameter result in a large amount of variability in the trend being attributed to the cycle, as pointed out by Canova (1998). Moreover, Mise *et al.* (2005) showed that the filter is suboptimal at the endpoints of the series, which can be a matter for concern if the most recent pattern of the cycle is of particular interest.

To circumvent the deficiencies of the HP filter, we employ the band-pass frequency filter developed by Christiano and Fitzgerald (2003), hereafter called the CF filter. The ideal band-pass filter extracts cycles from the data as components within a specified frequency band, while the components

---

[4] For a comparative statistical analysis of these methods, see Estrella (2007).

[5] Cycles are obtained with the Hodrick–Prescott filter as a result of minimizing a weighted average of the rate of change of the trend and the gap between the actual series and trend. It is postulated that trend growth follows a smooth path while the cyclical component is transitory. In the frequency domain, the filter approximates a particular high-pass filter (see King and Rebelo, 1993), and the frequency components passed through are determined by the trend-smoothing parameter (Christiano and Fitzgerald (2003) show that their method provides a better approximation of this high-pass filter).

at all other frequencies are filtered out. The CF filter provides an optimal finite sample linear approximation to this ideal filter. In practice, it is a two-sided asymmetric weighted moving average of the original series. The analytical details are presented in Appendix A.

The CF filter differs from the band-pass filters proposed by Baxter and King (1999) and Pedersen (2001), in that it takes into account the observations available at all leads and lags when constructing the filter weights at each data point. Therefore, it is an asymmetric filter. The main advantage of the CF filter is that it can be computed at the ends of the original sample; it therefore integrates the most recent information about the evolution of the growth cycle. In light of the latest sub-prime crisis, this advantage constitutes a strong motivation for the use of the CF filter, even if it is used at the cost of sample size dependence.[6]

Burns and Mitchell (1946) describe business cycle fluctuations as follows: "Business cycles are a type of fluctuation found in the aggregate economic activity of nations that organize their work mainly in business enterprises: a cycle consists of expansions occurring at about the same time in many economic activities, followed by similarly general recessions, contractions, and revivals which merge in the expansion phase of the next cycle" (p. 3.). This characterization has two defining features. First, business cycle fluctuations generate co-movement among financial and real variables with possible leads and lags in timing. Second, business cycles separate into different phases (expansion and recession). Henceforth, we analyze the linkages between the growth cycles extracted from the stock market and industrial production indices with the CF filter, addressing specifically the two aspects of cycles stressed by Burns and Mitchell (1946).

3. Short-run cyclical linkages

The cyclical components of the industrial production and stock market indices of each country are represented in Figure 1.

From Figure 1, it is possible to ascertain some stylized facts regarding short-run fluctuations as summarized in Table 3. It is apparent that the descriptive statistics reported are qualitatively matched with the respective statistics for the United States.

Table 3 shows that cyclical variability is higher in stock markets than in the case of industrial production. This result is theoretically and empirically well documented by several papers, and it finds its foundations in the differences between the degree of nominal and real rigidities in the

---

[6] For this reason, it is advisable to apply the CF filter once the seasonal pattern is removed from the data. It is nevertheless noticeable that if the sample is large enough, the coefficients of the CF filter are stable.

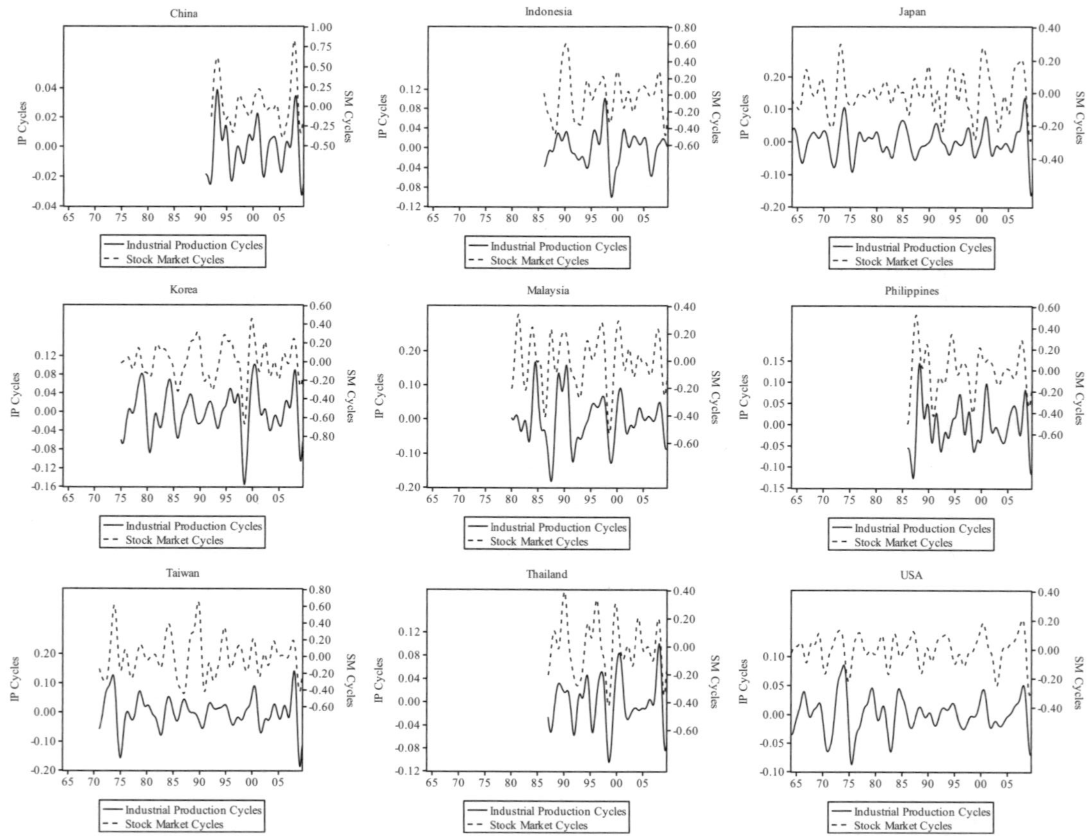

***Fig. 1.* Band-pass cycles extracted with the CF filter. Notes: Dashed lines indicate stock market cycles and solid lines indicate industrial production cycles.**

Table 3. Cyclical features

	China	Indonesia	Japan	Korea	Malaysia	Philippines	Taiwan	Thailand	USA
$\hat{\sigma}(sm_t)$	0.27	0.24	0.12	0.19	0.18	0.20	0.22	0.18	0.10
$\hat{\sigma}(ip_t)$	0.02	0.03	0.04	0.05	0.06	0.05	0.05	0.04	0.03
$\hat{\sigma}(sm_t)/\hat{\sigma}(ip_t)$	17.38	7.30	2.78	4.07	2.91	4.00	4.25	4.32	3.18
$\hat{\rho}(sm_t, ip_t)$	0.74	0.22	0.40	0.61	0.47	0.26	0.36	0.52	0.39
	[0.67; 0.80]	[0.11; 0.33]	[0.33; 0.47]	[0.55; 0.67]	[0.38; 0.55]	[0.15; 0.37]	[0.28; 0.44]	[0.43; 0.60]	[0.32; 0.46]

Notes: $\hat{\sigma}(sm_t)$ and $\hat{\sigma}(ip_t)$ indicate the standard deviation of the cyclical component in the stock market index and the industrial production index, respectively. $\hat{\rho}(sm_t, ip_t)$ refers to the sample correlation between these variables. 95% confidence intervals for the correlation coefficients are reported between brackets.

two sectors. In particular, real markets exhibit a more sluggish adjustment to shocks than financial markets.

The pro-/counter-cyclicality and time lead and lag relationships between cycles are typically analyzed using contemporaneous and lagged cross-correlations. This approach is used by, for example, Backus and Kehoe (1992). The correlation between stock market and industrial production cycles [$\rho(sm_t, ip_t)$] is significantly positive (ranging from 0.22 in Indonesia to 0.74 in China). Thus, financial cycles are pro-cyclical with respect to real cycles – that is, movements are positively synchronized over the course of the cycle. Schwert (1989) showed that stock market volatility is counter-cyclical, as it is greater in real recessions than in expansions. His finding intuitively complements the concept of pro-cyclicality of stock market cycles: periods of low financial volatility usually prevail during stock market and real economic upswings, while high volatility is typically induced by financial downturns which are accompanied by a real recession. It is also interesting to note that the correlation is the highest for Korea (0.61) and China (0.74) the two countries for which market capitalization is on average the lowest in our sample. Indeed, because the Chinese and Korean stock markets have been the least mature over the past 30 years, foreign investors are less present, leading to higher sensitivity of these markets to news from their respective domestic real sectors. For the other countries, the correlation is either in line with the U.S. benchmark (0.39) or much lower (falling to 0.22 for Indonesia and 0.26 for the Philippines), indicating a weaker linkage over the cycle because these markets are more sensitive to real and financial news from foreign markets than to local activity.

Having established that financial and real markets are positively synchronized over the course of the cycle, we expect that stock markets anticipate upswings or downturns in the real sector, as was shown originally for the United States by Fama (1990), Schwert (1990) and Hamilton and Lin (1996). Therefore, the greatest linkage should prevail at the lagged cross-correlation $\rho(sm_{t-h}, ip_t)$ with $h>0$. Cross-correlations for leads and lags up to 24 months are illustrated in Figure 2. The highest lagged cross-correlation between cycles obtained with the CF filter ($\hat{\rho}^{CF}_{max}$) for each country and the associated lead or lag ($\hat{h}^{CF}$) are reported in the upper panel of Table 4.

As expected, cross-correlation is highest at lags of the stock market index, indicating that the stock market integrates new information on the future evolution of real activity and therefore that the financial cycle leads the real cycle. This implicitly suggests a causal relationship (in the sense of Granger) between the financial and real sectors, which would imply that the stock market is a good leading indicator of the business cycle, as suggested by, for example, Hamilton and Lin (1996). For Japan, Indonesia, Malaysia, Thailand, and the Philippines, the stock market leads the real sector by around six months, which is similar to the benchmark

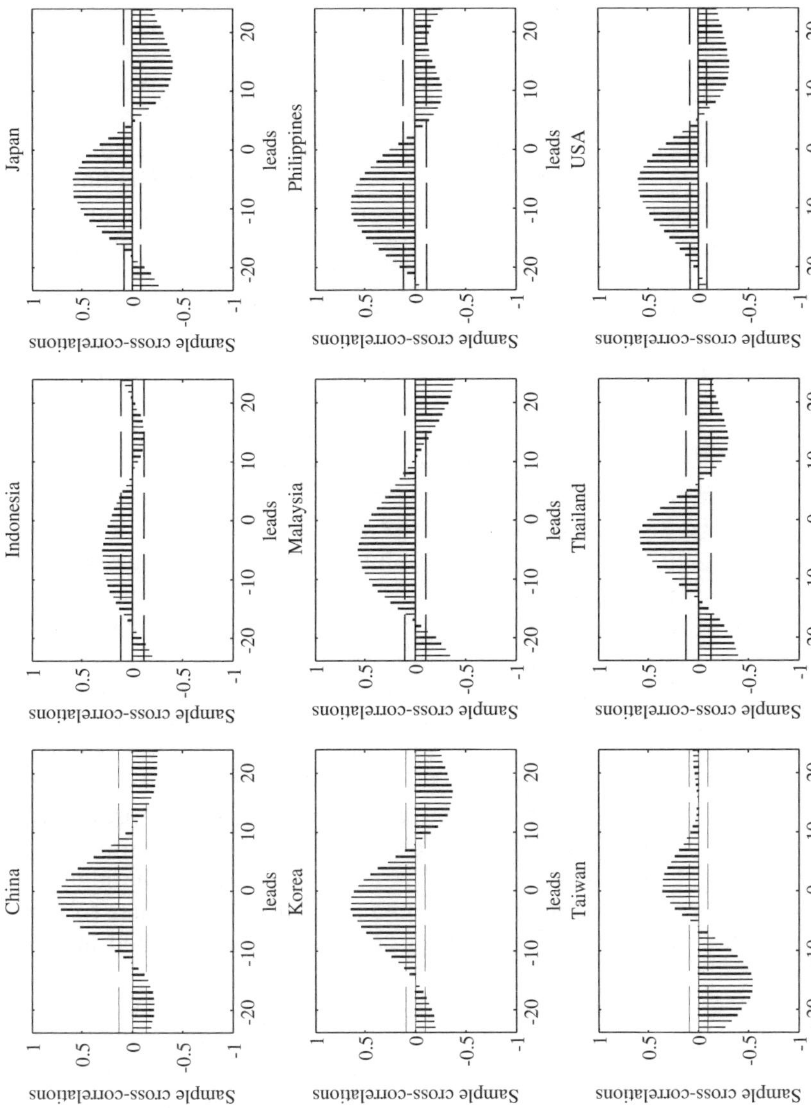

Fig. 2. ***Lagged cross-correlation ($\hat{\rho}(sm_{t-h}, ip_t)$). Note: 95% confidence bounds for $\hat{\rho}_0(sm_{t-h}, ip_t)$ are indicated by horizontal dashed lines.***

Table 4. Highest lagged correlations

	China	Indonesia	Japan	Korea	Malaysia	Phil.	Taiwan	Thailand	USA
$\hat{h}^{CF}$	1	6	6	2	5	9	−1	3	6
$\hat{\rho}^{CF}_{max}$	0.74	0.29	0.59	0.64	0.56	0.64	0.36	0.59	0.60
	[0.67;0.80]	[0.18;0.39]	[0.54;0.64]	[0.58;0.69]	[0.48;0.63]	[0.56;0.70]	[0.28;0.44]	[0.51;0.66]	[0.54;0.65]
$\hat{h}^{HP}$	13	3	−1	1	22	11	0	2	5
$\hat{\rho}^{HP}_{max}$	0.45	0.23	0.13	0.57	0.23	0.35	0.43	0.45	0.52
	[0.34;0.55]	[0.12;0.34]	[0.05;0.21]	[0.50;0.63]	[0.13;0.33]	[0.24;0.45]	[0.35;0.50]	[0.35;0.54]	[0.46;0.58]
$\hat{h}^{reg}$	4	−24	−16	−9	−24	−23	−13	−13	−5
$\hat{\rho}^{reg}_{max}$	0.23	0.74	0.30	0.33	0.34	0.60	0.32	0.84	0.23
	[0.10;0.35]	[0.68;0.79]	[0.23;0.37]	[0.24;0.41]	[0.25;0.42]	[0.52;0.67]	[0.24;0.40]	[0.80;0.87]	[0.15;0.31]

Notes: $\hat{\rho}^{CF}_{max}$ and $\hat{\rho}^{HP}_{max}$ are the highest lagged cross-correlations between the domestic stock market and industrial production index with the CF and HP filters, respectively, while $\hat{h}^{CF}$ $\hat{h}^{HP}$ are their associated lags. A positive (negative) value indicates a lag (lead). $\hat{\rho}^{reg}_{max}$ and $\hat{h}^{reg}$ are the associated figures between the domestic and the regional stock market index. 95% confidence intervals are reported between brackets.

obtained for the United States. Again, in China and Korea, the delay in the reaction is shorter than in other countries (around two months), indicating a strong orientation toward local investors with greater reaction to news on domestic activity. Taiwan is an interesting exception because its lag order at the highest lagged cross correlation ($\hat{h}^{CF}$) suggests that the Taiwanese stock market reacts with one month lag to news concerning domestic macroeconomic fundamentals. A possible explanation may lie in the fact the Taiwan has a large (albeit quite inactive) market; for example, Garcia and Liu (1999) found a turnover ratio of 24% compared to a ratio of 219% for Indonesia. Thus, news coming from the real sector will have a sluggish effect on the stock market because of the low level of transactions on this market.

The robustness of the results to the filter is checked by calculating the cross-correlation on variables filtered by the HP filter (see the middle panel of Table 4). It turns out that even if the general picture remains similar (the correlation being generally lower than the one obtained with CF filtered data), major differences are observed in particular for Japan and Taiwan. This outcome highlights the importance of the filter used and the potential biases resulting from using the HP filter (see Section 2). To assess the underlying determinants of the decoupling of the stock markets from the real sector, we also calculated the cross-correlations between the local stock market indices and an Asian regional stock market index (bottom panel of Table 4). The outcomes suggest that there is substantial cross-country heterogeneity in the decoupling of the financial sector from the real sector, which can be attributed to the degree of financial market openness.

4. Short-run linkages between cyclical phases

The cross-correlation between cyclical components is a simple and straightforward indicator of co-movement along the full cycle. Nevertheless, the traditional business cycle definition of Burns and Mitchell (1946) points out that business cycles separate into different phases (expansion and recession), and it has been acknowledged (since Neftci, 1984, and Hamilton, 1989) that cyclical behavior is asymmetric; in particular, the downturn is typically shorter and deeper than the upturn. Therefore, we investigate co-movement at the cyclical phase level to detect potential asymmetries.[7] We identify the phases of cyclical expansion and

[7] Several papers have analyzed business cycle features since Burns and Mitchell (1946), whereas only a few have identified and investigated univariate features of stock market cycles – see, for instance, Edwards *et al.* (2003), Gomez Biscarri and Perez de Gracia (2004), Pagan and Sossounov (2003) and Lunde and Timmermann (2004). An even smaller set of papers looked into whether stock market cycles co-move; see, for instance, Gomez Biscarri and Perez de Gracia (2004), Edwards et al. (2003), Harding and Pagan (2006), and Candelon et al. (2008).

contraction via dichotomous binary variables. This characterization presents the advantage of removing the presence of volatility clusters (ARCH) and rendering the econometric refinements associated with it redundant.

4.1. Dating cycle turning points

The cycles of the real and financial sectors alternate between periods of prolonged increase and decline; this alternation enables the classification of the business (financial) cycles into phases of expansion and recession (bulls and bears, respectively). To identify these phases, we date turning points as follows. First, the local minima (troughs) and maxima (peaks) are identified from the cyclical components. Second, we revise peaks that are located below and troughs that are located above the time series average of the cycle. Finally, we enforce the alternation of peaks and troughs. Consequently, expansions (bulls) correspond to trough-to-peak periods in the cycles of the respective series, while recessions (bears) correspond to peak-to-trough periods. The binary random variable S_t takes the value of 1 if the cycle is in an expansion (bull) period and 0 if it is in a recession (bear). Table 5 reports the dates corresponding to the turning points of the phases.[8]

At first sight, it is possible to detect similar turning points in the stock market and industrial production cycles. For example, almost all markets in Asia reached a peak around 1997 (± 6 months, except for Korean and Taiwanese industrial production), which can be associated with the 1997 Asian financial crisis. Similarly, the year 2000 (± 6 months) corresponds to a peak that preceded the collapse of the dot-com bubble. The recent recession triggered by the 2007 subprime crisis is also observed among all countries from early 2008 onwards.

4.2. Synchronization of cyclical phases

To assess the synchronization among expansions/bulls and recessions/bears, we refer to the concepts of perfect and multivariate synchronization proposed by Harding and Pagan (2006) and Candelon *et al.* (2009), which are described in Appendix B.

---

[8] The methodology to date turning points presented in this paper produces results that are reasonably in line with dates obtained in earlier studies that use similar methods. For instance, in case of the United States, the business cycle turning points approximately match the ones reported by the NBER, in case of Japan the dates are close to the ones found by Yamada et al. (2009). Regarding the stock market cycles, the turning points reported here are in correspondence with the dating in Pagan and Sossounov (2003) for the United States and Candelon et al. (2008) for the Asian economies.

Table 5. Dating of cyclical phases

China				Indonesia				Japan			
IP Cycles		SM Cycles		IP Cycles		SM Cycles		IP Cycles		SM Cycles	
P	T	P	T	P	T	P	T	P	T	P	T
93m2	94m2	93m2	94m9	90m4	92m8		88m2	61m1	63m1		59m12
94m10	95m11	97m5	99m3	97m8	98m11	90m4	92m1	64m5	65m12	61m4	62m5
97m1	98m2	01m1	03m8	01m4	06m6	94m3	95m3	70m1	71m12	63m5	65m4
00m1	01m12	04m4	05m7	08m9		97m3	98m7	73m11	75m5	66m9	68m10
03m11	05m4	07m9	08m12			00m1	01m3	79m12	82m1	69m7	71m6
07m12	09m3					02m1	03m1	84m12	87m5	73m3	77m12
						04m12	06m6	91m5	93m11	79m2	80m3
						07m11	09m2	97m6	98m8	81m8	82m11
								00m1	03m7	83m11	86m2
								08m2	09m5	87m4	88m8
										89m11	92m7
										94m4	95m7
										96m6	98m9
										00m4	05m1
										07m7	09m3

Korea				Malaysia				Philippines			
IP Cycles		SM Cycles		IP Cycles		SM Cycles		IP Cycles		SM Cycles	
P	T	P	T	P	T	P	T	P	T	P	T
	75m5	76m4	77m4		81m11	81m4	82m8	86m2	87m2	87m8	88m11
79m1	82m6	78m4	80m7	84m7	85m11	83m11	86m5	88m4	90m9	89m9	90m11
84m3	85m1	81m11	85m1	90m5	93m1	87m6	88m5	91m6	93m1	94m5	95m8
88m3	89m9	89m7	92m5	97m5	98m11	90m1	92m11	95m12	96m11	96m7	98m6
91m12	93m6	94m9	98m7	00m8	03m3	97m1	98m8	97m9	99m1	99m9	03m4
95m1	98m7	99m11	01m4	04m4	06m12	00m3	01m6	00m12	02m2	07m8	09m1
00m5	05m4	02m5	04m12	08m2	09m5	02m4	03m3	06m3	07m5		
08m1	09m2	07m1	09m2			04m3	06m5	08m5	09m6		
						07m1	09m2				

Taiwan				Thailand				USA			
IP Cycles		SM Cycles		IP Cycles		SM Cycles		IP Cycles		SM Cycles	
P	T	P	T	P	T	P	T	P	T	P	T
73m8	75m1		72m2		87m8	90m2	92m7		64m1	64m1	66m1
78m9	82m9	73m11	75m2	89m2	91m12	96m3	98m7	66m5	67m7	69m2	70m5
84m2	85m1	75m12	77m2	94m5	95m7	99m1	03m1	69m4	70m11	73m2	74m1
87m2	90m8	78m11	80m2	97m3	98m8	04m2	06m11	73m12	75m6	76m1	79m1
92m1	98m1	81m6	82m8	00m7	07m1	07m12	09m2	79m4	80m6	81m2	82m5
00m6	01m9	84m2	87m1	08m2	09m5			81m5	82m11	83m7	84m8
04m4	05m4	89m9	92m9					84m5	86m9	87m2	88m8
08m1	09m2	94m1	96m1					88m5	89m6	89m9	90m8
		97m8	99m1					90m3	91m5	93m4	95m1
		00m4	01m5					94m8	98m8	96m8	98m3

Table 5. *(Continued)*

Taiwan				Thailand				USA			
IP Cycles		SM Cycles		IP Cycles		SM Cycles		IP Cycles		SM Cycles	
P	T	P	T	P	T	P	T	P	T	P	T
		02m5	03m2					00m6	03m9	00m5	01m12
		04m2	06m7					08m1	09m5	07m1	09m3
		07m1	09m1								

Notes: IP and SM cycles refer to industrial production and stock market series. P and T indicate peak and trough. Extreme phases are highlighted in grey.

Table 6. Harding and Pagan (2006) synchronization tests

	China	Indonesia	Japan	Korea	Malaysia	Philippines	Taiwan	Thailand	USA
SPPS(i)	0.41	0.63	9.34*	0.58	0.26	0.40	0.01	1.23	0.12
SPPS(ii)	35.54*	39.44*	87.80*	46.65*	30.47*	93.31*	71.23*	26.88*	80.23*
$SPPS^{reg}$(ii)	0.40	0.02	1.73	0.83	3.75	1.44	0.00	3.82	0.16
$SPPS^{reg}$(ii)	58.45*	17.25*	23.60*	23.63*	8.84*	36.60*	20.65*	21.50*	50.94*

Notes: The test statistics SPPS(i) and SPPS(ii) indicate strong positive synchronization between the domestic stock market and industrial production index, while $SPPS^{reg}$(i) and $SPPS^{reg}$(ii) indicate strong positive synchronization between the domestic and the regional stock market index. The test statistics are calculated using eq. (31) and eq. (32) in Harding and Pagan (2006, p. 70). The 95% critical value is 3.842. Asterisks denote rejection of the null hypothesis at 5%.

In the first step, we test for perfect positive synchronization between cyclical phases of the stock market and industrial production. Series are perfectly synchronized if they satisfy both of the following moment conditions:

$$\text{SPPS(i)} : E(S_t^{\text{IP}}) - E(S_t^{\text{SM}}) = 0$$

and

$$\text{SPPS(ii)} : E(S_t^{\text{SM}}) - E(S_t^{\text{SM}} S_t^{\text{IP}}) = 0.$$

The results of these tests are reported in Table 6, and they clearly indicate that phases of the stock market are not perfectly synchronized with those of industrial production; the null of perfect synchronization is rejected in all cases for at least one of the above conditions.

In the second step, we estimate the degree of synchronization between the cyclical phases. To allow for a comparison with the cross-correlation statistics, Figure 3 illustrates an estimator of the contemporaneous

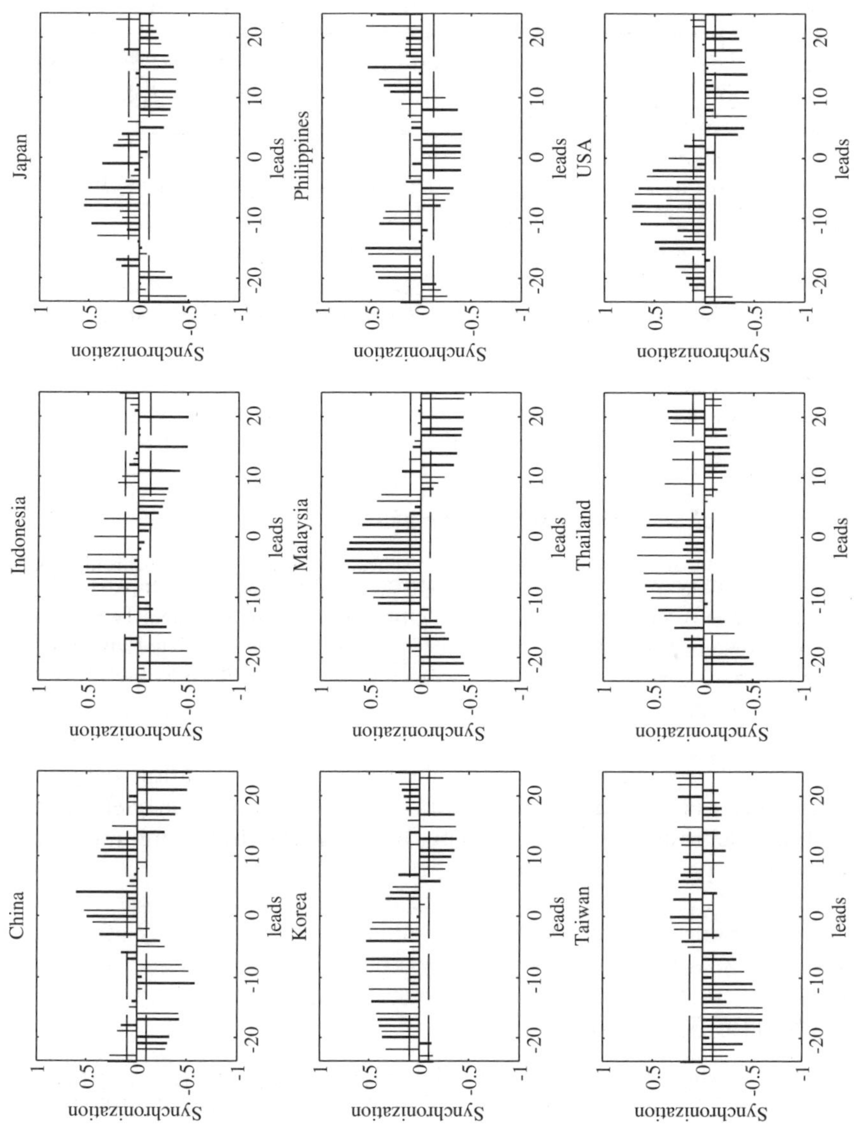

Fig. 3. Degree of synchronization ($\hat{\rho}_{0,max}(sm_{t-h}, ip_t)$). Note: 95% confidence bounds for $\hat{\rho}_0(sm_{t-h}, ip_t)$ are indicated by horizontal dashed lines.

$[\hat{\rho}_0(sm_t, ip_t)]$, and of the lagged degree of synchronization $[\hat{\rho}_0(sm_{t-h}, ip_t)]$. Table 7 reports the highest value for the degree of synchronization (and the associated lag order) between phases of financial and real expansion, as well as between bull phases of the domestic stock market index and the regional stock market index.

The picture obtained with $\hat{\rho}_0(sm_{t-h}, ip_t)$ resembles closely the results obtained with the lagged cross-correlation, and the highest degree of synchronization is of the same magnitude as the highest lagged cross-correlation. Moreover, the leads and lags in timing of full cycles also carry over to the cyclical phase level. In particular, a bull stock market leads an expansion in industrial production between 4 and 15 months for most countries (with the exception of China and Taiwan). Hence, the relationship between the two markets does not exhibit asymmetric behavior. Concerning Taiwan, upswings on the stock market and expansions of industrial production are synchronized contemporaneously. The case of China is rather special, as we observe a clear asymmetry between expansions and recessions: the bull stock market is lagging and not leading the upswing in the real economy.

5. *Cyclical synchronization and extreme phases*

Some cycles may exhibit extreme features – due, for instance, to an unusually deep recession or a major meltdown in the stock market. Such extreme events can induce an extreme phase length corresponding to an extended period of increase preceding a financial bubble. In this section, we intend to control for the potential distortionary effect of extreme lengths on the degrees of synchronization found in the previous section.

The two consecutive crises that hit the Asian economies, the 1997 Asian flu and the 2007 subprime crisis, may bias the synchronization tests toward decoupling. In principle, removing cyclical phases associated with financial crises should increase the strength of the relationship: during bulls, stock markets disconnect from their fundamentals and reconnect only after the explosion of the bubble. Thus, it would not be surprising if the linkages between the stock market and real activity appeared stronger, when controlling for extreme phases.

Let S_t be a dummy variable, taking the value of 1 when the cycle is in an expansion (recession) and 0 otherwise. The length of each phase is measured by the number of months spent in it – that is, the duration (D) statistic. Formally,

$$D = \sum_{t=t_1}^{t_2} S_t,$$

Table 7. Highest degree of (lagged) synchronization

	China	Indonesia	Japan	Korea	Malaysia	Philippines	Taiwan	Thailand	USA
$\hat{h}_0$	−4	5	7	4	4	15	0	3	8
$\hat{\rho}_{0,\max}$	0.60	0.53	0.54	0.52	0.75	0.55	0.32	0.66	0.72
	[0.51;0.68]	[0.44;0.61]	[0.48;0.59]	[0.45;0.59]	[0.70;0.79]	[0.46;0.63]	[0.24;0.39]	[0.59;0.72]	[0.68;0.76]
$\hat{h}_0^{reg}$	−9	1	0	0	0	−14	−1	−1	3
$\hat{\rho}_{0,\max}^{reg}$	0.55	0.81	0.74	0.75	0.69	0.55	0.73	0.78	0.48
	[0.45;0.64]	[0.77;0.85]	[0.70;0.77]	[0.70;0.79]	[0.63;0.74]	[0.46;0.63]	[0.68;0.77]	[0.73;0.82]	[0.41;0.54]

Notes: $\hat{\rho}_{0,\max}$ indicates the highest degree of synchronization and $\hat{h}_0$ is the associated lag between the domestic stock market and industrial production index. $\hat{\rho}_{0,\max}^{reg}$ is the highest degree of synchronization and $\hat{h}_0^{reg}$ is the associated lag between the domestic and the regional stock market index. A positive (negative) value of $\hat{h}_0$ and $\hat{h}_0^{reg}$ indicates a lag (lead). 95% confidence intervals are reported between brackets.

where t_1 and $t_2$correspond to two consecutive turning points, marking the beginning and the end of the phase, respectively.

In the context of financial cycles, Candelon and Metiu (2009) developed a method of testing for extreme phases conditional to predetermined characteristics. The major challenge of such a test is that the underlying distribution of the phase durations is unknown. Therefore, a distribution-free test was proposed, in which the extremes are defined as outliers in the empirical distribution of the duration measures. The non-parametric outlier test is presented in Appendix C.

Applying this procedure to the stock market indices, it appears that only a few extreme cyclical phases are detected: in Malaysia, Thailand, and the United States. For the two Asian countries, the extreme phases correspond to the bulls that preceded the 1997 Asian financial crisis, whereas in the United States, the extreme phase length can be associated with the subprime crisis.

To control for the effect of bubbles, the degree of synchronization, ρ_1, is estimated again for these three countries for up to 24 leads and lags of the stock market indices in a sample excluding the extreme cyclical phases – that is, 1996m4–2009m2 for Thailand, 1997m2–2009m2 for Malaysia and 1964m2–2001m12 for the U.S. The results are reported in Figure 4 and Table 8.

Comparing the results with those of the previous section, the shape of $\hat{\rho}_1$ is quite similar to the shapes obtained in Figure 3. Similarly, the lag order $\hat{h}_1$ maximizing the degree of synchronization differs only up to one month from those in Table 7. As expected, it is noticeable that $\hat{\rho}_{1,\max}$ is significantly higher when excluding financial crisis periods. The increase in synchronization in the aftermath of the crises supports the idea that stock market indices disconnect from their fundamental values during extreme bulls – that is, the decoupling increases during the bull phase before a crisis, and the stock market can be more closely associated with the macroeconomic fundamentals only after the explosion of the bubble, during the bear phase. A possible explanation of this synchronization pattern is offered by the imposition of capital controls in Malaysia in the midst of the Asian crisis, in September 1998. Capital controls might have strengthened the linkage between domestic financial and real markets by limiting the exposure to foreign shocks. However, we also observe an increase in synchronization in Thailand after the crisis, although it did not limit capital flows. Therefore, we suspect that decoupling is weaker in normal times irrespective of government policies.

6. *Conclusion*

This chapter investigates the linkages prevailing between the stock market and economic activity in Asian countries. Our findings show that the

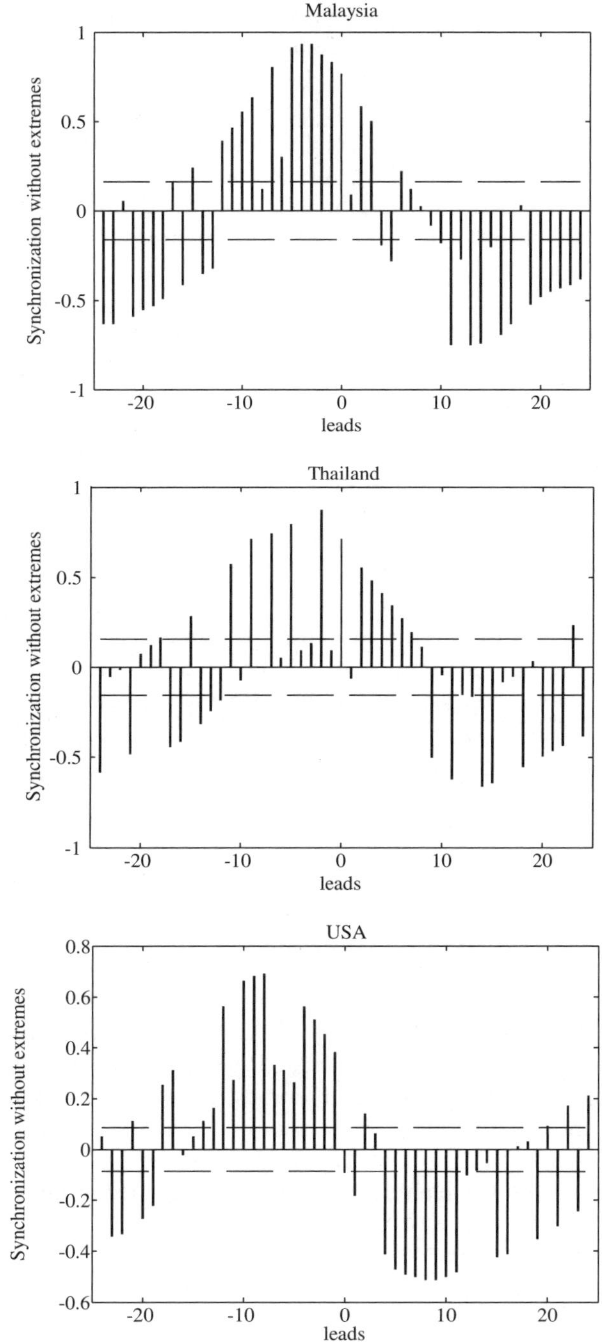

Fig. 4. Degree of synchronization ($\hat{\rho}_{1,max}(sm_{t-h}, ip_t)$) excluding crisis periods. Note: 95% confidence bounds for $\hat{\rho}_1(sm_{t-h}, ip_t)$ are indicated by horizontal dashed lines.

Table 8. Highest degree of (lagged) synchronization excluding crisis periods

	China	Indonesia	Japan	Korea	Malaysia	Philippines	Taiwan	Thailand	USA
$\hat{h}_1$	–	–	–	–	4	–	–	2	8
$\hat{\rho}_{1,\max}$	–	–	–	–	0.93 [0.91;0.94]	–	–	0.87 [0.84;0.90]	0.69 [0.64;0.73]

Notes: $\hat{\rho}_{1,\max}$ indicates the highest lagged degree of synchronization for the subsamples without crisis periods, and $\hat{h}_1$ is the associated lag. A positive (negative) value of $\hat{h}_1$ indicates a lag (lead). 95% confidence intervals are reported between brackets.

stock market leads the real sector by around six months for most of the countries, considering both the cycle and its phases. This is very much in line with the results obtained for the United States, our benchmark. For China, Korea, and Taiwan, linkages are stronger and more synchronous. Because these markets are the less mature in terms of asset market capitalization and turnover, this result leaves us with the feeling that a greater proportion of foreign investors respond to news other than that regarding domestic real activity, which increases the liquidity and thus the efficiency of the market, and at the same time it weakens the stock market/output relationship. This idea is supported by our finding that during the bubble phase, decoupling between real and financial spheres is observed, and that the most financially open countries show the highest correlation with the region. The precise role of foreign investors should be evaluated and estimated, but this would require *inter alii* a structural model, which is beyond the scope of this paper but could constitute an objective of future research.

Acknowledgments

The authors thank Yin-Wong Cheung as well as an anonymous referee for useful comments. The usual disclaimer applies.

Appendix A. The CF filter (Christiano and Fitzgerald, 2003)

To isolate the cyclical component of the original series x_t, with periodicities between p_l and p_u, where $2 \leq p_l < p_u < \infty$,[9] the CF filter, c_t,

[9] Following Baxter and King (1999) and Christiano and Fitzgerald (2003), typical business (and financial) cycles correspond to periodicities between 1.5–8 years (18–96 months). Thus, $p_l = 18$ and $p_u = 96$.

is computed as follows:

$$c_t = B_0 x_t + B_1 x_{t+1} + \ldots + B_{T-1-t} x_{T-1} + \tilde{B}_{T-t} x_T + B_1 x_{t-1} + \ldots + B_{t-2} x_2 + \tilde{B}_{t-1} x_1$$

for $t = 3, 4, \ldots, T-2$, and where

$$B_j = \frac{\sin(jb) - \sin(ja)}{\pi j}, \; j \geq 1,$$

$$B_0 = \frac{b-a}{\pi}, \; a = \frac{2\pi}{p_u}, \; b = \frac{2\pi}{p_l},$$

and

$$\tilde{B}_k = -\frac{1}{2} B_0 - \sum_{j=1}^{k-1} B_j.$$

The cyclical component, c_t, is covariance stationary. The filter weights are selected to minimize a mean squared error criterion corresponding to the deviation of the ideal band-pass filter from its linear approximation. Christiano and Fitzgerald (2003) showed that for a large set of macroeconomic series, including U.S. data on interest rates, unemployment, inflation, and output, the CF filter appropriately approximates the ideal filter without knowledge of the true time series representation of x_t. Instead, it can be assumed that the data follows a pure random walk (if the series is drifting, the drift is assumed to be removed before the analysis).

Appendix B. Perfect and multivariate synchronization (Harding and Pagan, 2006)

Harding and Pagan (2006) defined strong perfect positive synchronization (SPPS) between the phases of two cycles as follows. Two binary random variables, S_t^{IP} and S_t^{SM} are in SPPS if they satisfy the following necessary and sufficient conditions:

$$Pr(S_t^{\mathrm{IP}} = 1, S_t^{\mathrm{SM}} = 0) = 0$$

and

$$Pr(S_t^{\mathrm{IP}} = 0, S_t^{\mathrm{SM}} = 1) = 0.$$

Harding and Pagan (2006) propose Generalized Method of Moments (GMM)-based heteroscedasticity and serial correlation robust tests of the hypotheses indicating that cycles are perfectly synchronized. In the bivariate case, the following moment conditions need to hold under the null hypothesis of SPPS:

$$\mathrm{SPPS(i)} : E(S_t^{\mathrm{IP}}) - E(S_t^{\mathrm{SM}}) = 0$$

and

$$\mathrm{SPPS(ii)} : E(S_t^{\mathrm{SM}}) - E(S_t^{\mathrm{SM}} S_t^{\mathrm{IP}}) = 0.$$

Addressing the multivariate case, Harding and Pagan (2006) propose a test of strong multivariate non-synchronization (SMNS). Consider n countries with S_t^i phases of the cyclical component ($i = 1, \ldots, n$). We define sample means and pairwise correlations as follows:

$$E(S_t^i) = \mu_i$$

and

$$\rho^{ij} = \frac{E(S_t^i S_t^j) - \mu_i \mu_j}{\sqrt{\mu_i(1-\mu_i)\mu_j(1-\mu_j)}}, \quad \text{where } t = 1, \ldots, T, \ (i \times j) \in (1, \ldots, n)^2.$$

The following $n(n+1)/2$ stacked moment conditions need to hold for the hypothesis of SMNS to hold:

$$\mathrm{SMNS} : E(h_t(\theta, S_t)) = 0,$$

with

$$h_t(\theta, S_t) = \begin{bmatrix} S_{1t} - \mu_{S_1} \\ \vdots \\ S_{nt} - \mu_{S_n} \\ \dfrac{(S_{1t} - \mu_{S_1})(S_{2t} - \mu_{S_2})}{\sqrt{\mu_{S_1}(1-\mu_{S_1})\mu_{S_2}(1-\mu_{S_2})}} - \rho_S^{12} \\ \vdots \\ \dfrac{(S_{(n-1)t} - \mu_{S_{(n-1)}})(S_{nt} - \mu_{S_n})}{\sqrt{\mu_{S_{(n-1)}}(1-\mu_{S_{(n-1)}})\mu_{S_n}(1-\mu_{S_n})}} - \rho_S^{(n-1)n} \end{bmatrix}$$

and

$$g(\theta, \{S\}_{t=1}^T) = \frac{1}{T}\sum_{t=1}^{T} h_t(\theta, S_t).$$

Let $\hat{\theta}' = [\hat{\mu}_1, \ldots, \hat{\mu}_n, \hat{\rho}^{12}, \ldots, \hat{\rho}^{n(n-1)}]$ be the vector of unrestricted parameter estimates, and let $\theta_0' = [\mu_1, \ldots, \mu_n, 0, \ldots, 0]$ be the restricted vector under the null hypothesis of *SMNS*. The first test statistic proposed by Harding and Pagan (2006) is as follows:

$$W_{\text{SMNS and SPPS(i)}} = \sqrt{T}g\left(\theta_0, \{S\}_{t=1}^{T}\right)' \hat{V}^{-1} \sqrt{T}g\left(\theta_0, \{S\}_{t=1}^{T}\right) \xrightarrow{d} \chi^2_{(n-1)n/2}.$$

The estimated covariance matrix $\hat{V}$ is heteroskedasticity and autocorrelation consistent (HACC) (see Newey and West, 1987). The null hypothesis of SPPS(i) can be tested using the W-statistic, with $n-1$ degrees of freedom for the limiting distribution. The null hypothesis of SPPS(ii) can be tested using the second test statistic:

$$W_{\text{SPPS(ii)}} = T\left(\hat{\rho}_S - \rho_{S_0}\right)' V^{-1} \left(\hat{\rho}_S - \rho_{S_0}\right),$$

where ρ_S is the $n(n-1)/2$ vector of correlations and V is the asymptotic covariance matrix of $\sqrt{T}(\hat{\rho}_S - \rho_{S_0})$.

Candelon, Piplack and Straetmans (2009) suggested using tests of perfect synchronization before identifying imperfect synchronization. In the case where SPPS(i) or SPPS(ii) is rejected, they propose testing the weaker null hypothesis that the phases of the cycles are synchronized to a certain degree, $\rho^{12} = \ldots = \rho^{n(n-1)/2} = \rho_0$, with $-1 \leq \rho_0 < 1$. This is the null hypothesis of strong multivariate synchronization of order ρ_0 (SMS(ρ_0)). The order of synchronization ρ_0 corresponds to the GMM point estimate that does not lead to the rejection of the null hypothesis at a specified nominal size and that minimizes the test statistic; that is,

$$\hat{\rho}_0 = \arg\min \sqrt{T}g\left(\theta_0, \{S\}_{t=1}^{T}\right)' \hat{V}^{-1} \sqrt{T}g\left(\theta_0, \{S\}_{t=1}^{T}\right).$$

Appendix C. Detecting extreme cyclical phases (Candelon and Metiu, 2009)

In what follows, the analytical details of the Candelon and Metiu (2009) nonparametric outlier detection method are presented.

Consider a sample $D = [D_1, \ldots D_n]$ of phase durations issued from an unknown distribution. Singh and Xie (2003) developed a graphical tool for detecting outliers in D, the so-called Bootlier plot. Take the bootstrap sample $D^* = \left[D_1^*, \ldots D_n^*\right]$. It is possible to calculate the mean-trimmed mean (MTM) of D^*:

$$\text{MTM}(D^*) = \frac{1}{n}\sum_{i=1}^{n} D_i^* - \frac{1}{n-2k}\sum_{i=k+1}^{n-k} D_{(i)}^*.$$

The limiting bootstrap distribution of MTM(D^*) can be expressed as a mixture of normal distributions, where outliers cause the separation. Because only a certain fraction of all bootstrap samples contains the outliers, the mixture density (the Bootlier plot) will be multimodal. Thus, testing for the presence of outliers in D boils down to testing for the modality of the density of MTM(D^*).

Silverman (1981) proposed a seminal test of the modality of a density function $f(x)$ corresponding to an unknown distribution. It is based on the kernel density estimator:

$$\hat{f}_h = \frac{1}{nh}\sum_{i=1}^{n} K\left(\frac{x - \mathrm{MTM}(D^*)}{h}\right).$$

For a standard normal kernel function, $K(.)$, if the bandwidth h is sufficiently large, $\hat{f}_h$ will have a single mode in the interior of a given closed interval $\Im$. Thus, for the density $f(x)$ it is possible to find the narrowest bandwidth $\hat{h}_{\text{crit}}$ for which the kernel density $\hat{f}_h$ is unimodal, and $\hat{h}_{\text{crit}}$ will be larger for a multimodal density function than for a unimodal one. Silverman's modality test explores this property by drawing bootstrap samples from the kernel density with the critical bandwidth $\hat{f}_{h_{\text{crit}}}$ and by determining the empirical distribution of the bootstrap critical bandwidths $\hat{h}^*_{crit}$. The null hypothesis of unimodality (no outliers) is then rejected at α if $Pr(\hat{h}^*_{\text{crit}} \leq \lambda_\alpha \hat{h}_{\text{crit}}) \geq 1 - \alpha$. The method of Candelon and Metiu (2009) calibrates the scaling parameter λ_α to obtain an appropriate empirical size. Combining the Bootlier plot with Silverman's test yields a method to test for the presence of outliers in D.

To isolate the outliers in D, the test is performed sequentially on subsamples issued from the order statistics $\left[D_{(1)}, \ldots, D_{(n)}\right]$. In each sequence, a set of potential outliers is dropped from the sample, and the test is performed on the remainder until the largest subsample is found, for which the null of unimodality cannot be rejected. The complementary sample will contain the outliers.

References

Backus, D.K., Kehoe, P.J. (1992), International evidence on the historical properties of business cycles. *American Economic Review* 82, 864–888.

Baxter, M., King, R.G. (1999), Measuring business cycles: Approximate band-pass filters for economic time series. *The Review of Economics and Statistics* 81, 575–593.

Beaudry, P., Portier, F. (2006), Stock prices, news, and economic fluctuations. *The American Economic Review* 96 (4), 1293–1307.

Binswanger, M. (2000), Stock market booms and real economic activity: Is this time different. *International Review of Economics and Finance* 9, 387–415.

Breitung, J., Candelon, B. (2001), Is there a common European business cycle? New insights from a frequency domain analysis. *Vierteljahrshefte zur Wirschaftsforschung* 70 (3), 331–338.

Burns, A.F., Mitchell, W.C. (1946), *Measuring Business Cycles*. NBER, New York.

Calvo, G.A., Leiderman, L., Reinhart, C.M. (1996), Inflows of capital to developing countries in the 1990s. *Journal of Economic Perspectives* 10 (2), 123–139.

Candelon, B., Metiu, N. (2009), Testing for extreme bulls and bears: a non-parametric perspective. Working Paper, Maastricht University. Available at http://www.personeel.unimaas.nl/b.candelon/

Candelon, B., Piplack, J., Straetmans, S. (2008), On measuring synchronization of bulls and bears: The case of East Asia. *Journal of Banking and Finance* 32, 1022–1035.

Candelon, B., Piplack, J., Straetmans, S. (2009), Multivariate business cycle synchronization in small samples. *Oxford Bulletin of Economics and Statistics* 71 (5), 715–737.

Canova, F. (1998), Detrending and business cycle facts. *Journal of Monetary Economics* 41, 475–512.

Chang, R., Velasco, A. (1998), The Asian liquidity crisis. NBER Working Paper No. 6796.

Chauvet, M. (1998), Stock market fluctuations and the business cycle. *Journal of Economic and Social Measurement* 25, 235–257.

Chen, N. (1991), Financial investment opportunities and macroeconomy. *Journal of Finance* 46, 529–554.

Cheung, Y.W., He, J., Ng, L. (1997), Common predictable components in regional stock markets. *Journal of Business and Economic Statistics* 15, 35–42.

Cheung, Y.-W., Ng, L. (1998), International evidence on the stock market and aggregate economic activity. *Journal of Empirical Finance* 5 (3), 281–296.

Cheung, Y.-W., Westermann, F. (2000), Does Austria respond to the German or the US business cycle? *International Journal of Finance & Economics* 5 (1), 33–42.

Cheung, Y.-W., Westermann, F. (2003), Sectoral trends and cycles in Germany. *Empirical Economics* 28 (1), 141–156.

Christiano, L.J., Fitzgerald, T.J. (2003), The band pass filter. *International Economic Review* 44 (2), 435–465.

Cogley, T., Nason, J.M. (1995), Effects of the Hodrick-Prescott filter on trend and difference stationary time series – Implications for business cycle research. *Journal of Economic Dynamics and Control* 19, 253–278.

Edwards, S., Gomez Biscarri, J., Perez de Gracia, H.F. (2003), Stock market cycles, financial liberalization and volatility. *Journal of International Money and Finance* 22, 925–955.

Engle, R.F., Kozicki, S. (1993), Testing for common features. *Journal of Business & Economic Statistics* 11 (4), 369–380.

Estrella, A. (2007), Extracting business cycle fluctuations: what do time series filters really do? Staff Report No. 289, Federal Reserve Bank of New York.

Estrella, A., Mishkin, F.S. (1998), Predicting U.S. recessions: Financial variables as leading indicators. *The Review of Economics and Statistics* 80, 45–61.

Fama, E.F. (1990), Stock returns, expected returns, and real activity. *Journal of Finance* 45, 1089–1108.

Ferson, W.E., Harvey, C.R. (1993), The risk and predictability of international equity returns. *Review of Financial Studies* 6, 527–566.

Garcia, F.V., Liu, L. (1999), Macroeconomic determinants of stock market development. *Journal of Applied Economics* 2 (1), 29–59.

Gomez Biscarri, J., Perez de Gracia, H.F. (2004), Stock market cycles and stock market development in Spain. *Spanish Economic Review* 6, 127–151.

Hamao, Y., Mei J., Xu, Y. (2003). Idiosyncratic risk and the creative destruction in Japan. NBER Working Paper No. 9642.

Hamilton, J.D. (1989), A new approach to the economic analysis of nonstationary time series and the business cycle. *Econometrica* 57 (2), 357–384.

Hamilton, J.D., Lin, G. (1996), Stock market volatility and the business cycle. *Journal of Applied Econometrics* 11, 573–593.

Harding, D., Pagan, A. (2006), Synchronization of cycles. *Journal of Econometrics* 132, 59–79.

Hodrick, R., Prescott, E.C. (1997), Postwar U.S. business cycles: An empirical investigation. *Journal of Money, Credit, and Banking* 29, 1–16.

King, R.G., Rebelo, S.T. (1993), Low frequency filtering and real business cycles. *Journal of Economic Dynamics and Control* 17, 207–231.

Lunde, A., Timmermann, A. (2004), Duration dependence in stock prices: An analysis of bull and bear markets. *Journal of Business and Economic Statistics* 22 (3), 253–273.

Maysami, R.C., Sim, H.H. (2001), An empirical investigation of the dynamic relations between macroeconomics variable and the stock markets of Malaysia and Thailand. *The Management Journal* 20, 1–20.

Mise, E., Kim, T.-H., Newbold, P. (2005), On suboptimality of the hodrick-prescott filter at time series endpoints. *Journal of Macroeconomics* 27, 53–67.

Neftci, S.N. (1984), Are economic time series asymmetric over the business cycle. *Journal of Political Economy* 92, 307–328.

Newey, W.K., West, K.D. (1987), A simple positive semi-definite, heteroskedasticity and autocorrelation consistent covariance matrix. *Econometrica* 55 (3), 703–708.

Pagan, A., Sossounov, K.A. (2003), A simple framework for analysing bull and bear markets. *Journal of Applied Econometrics* 18, 233–246.

Pedersen, T.M. (2001), The hodrick-prescott filter, the slutzky effect and the distortionary effect of filters. *Journal of Economic Dynamics and Control* 25, 1081–1101.

Schwert, G.W. (1989), Why does stock market volatility change over time? *Journal of Finance* 44, 1115–1153.

Schwert, G.W. (1990), Stock returns and real activity: A century of evidence. *Journal of Finance* 45, 1237–1257.

Silverman, B.W. (1981), Using Kernel density estimates to investigate multimodality. *Journal of the Royal Statistical Society: Series B* 43 (1), 97–99.

Singh, K., Xie, M. (2003), Bootlier-plot – Bootstrap based outlier detection plot. *Sankhya: The Indian Journal of Statistics* 65 (3), 532–559.

Yamada, H., Nagata, S., Honda, Y. (2009), A comparison of two alternative composite leading indicators for detecting Japanese business cycle turning points. *Applied Economics Letters* 17 (9), 875–879.

CHAPTER 3

Stock Market Linkage between Asia and the United States in Two Crises: Smooth-Transition Correlation VAR-GARCH Approach

Yushi Yoshida

Faculty of Economics, Kyushu Sangyo University, 2-3-1 Matsukadai Higashi-ku, Fukuoka, 813-8503 Japan
E-mail address: yushi@ip.kyusan-u.ac.jp

Abstract
We investigate whether or not the effects of the subprime financial crisis on 12 Asian economies are similar to those of the Asian financial crisis by examining volatility spillovers and time-varying correlation between the US and Asian stock markets. After pretesting volatility causality and constancy of correlation, we estimate an appropriate smooth-transition correlation VAR-GARCH model for each Asian stock market. First, the empirical evidence indicates stark differences in stock market linkages between the two crises. The volatility causality comes from the crises-originating country. Volatility in Asian stock markets Granger-caused volatility in the US market during the Asian crisis, whereas volatility in the US stock market Granger-caused volatility in Asian stock markets during the subprime crisis. Second, decreased correlations during the period of financial turmoil were observed, especially during the Asian financial crisis. Third, the estimated points of transition in the correlation are indicative of market participants' awareness of the ensuing stock market crashes in July 1997 and in September 2008.

Keywords: Asia stock markets, financial crisis, smooth-transition correlation, VAR-GARCH, volatility spillover

JEL classifications: F31, F36, G15

1. Introduction

The financial turmoil that originated from the US housing market caused the market values of listed firms to plummet in stock markets all over the

Frontiers of Economics and Globalization
Volume 9 ISSN: 1574-8715
DOI: 10.1108/S1574-8715(2011)0000009008

world. The globalization of financial markets enabled risky lending practices in the United States, in the form of housing loans to subprime borrowers, to be shared worldwide via the securitization of loans as mortgage-backed securities, and their collapse consequently affected financial markets everywhere. While the most severely affected countries are in Europe, severe downturns were also experienced in many Asian countries. In fact, the initial impact on Asian economies was so severe that output in most of these countries contracted more than in the United States.

The negative impact on Asian financial markets was also spectacular. For example, in Singapore, the FTSTI index bottomed out from its most recent peak of 3,875 points in October 2007 to 1,456 points in March 2009. The Shanghai Stock Exchange Composite also plummeted from its peak of 6,036 point on October 17, 2007 to 1,706 points on November 4, 2008. However, since February 2009, Asia's economy began to revive (International Monetary Fund, 2009), and stock markets seemed to regain their confidence in the last half of 2009.

Twelve Asian countries experienced an average GDP growth of 1.2% in 2009, while the United States, EU15, and Japan experienced sharp declines in GDP growth in 2009 of −2.4%, −4.3%, and −5.2%, respectively.[1] The GDP growth rates in 2010 are forecasted to be 5.7% on average for the 12 Asian countries. Even after excluding China and India, the average GDP growth rate for the remaining 10 Asian countries is 5.0%, whereas the EU15 is expected to achieve less than 1% growth (International Monetary Fund World Economic Outlook, 2010).

Asia's quick rebound from the recession can be attributed to three factors (International Monetary Fund, 2009). First, one of the largest economies in the region demonstrated the fastest recovery. China's growth indicator was shown to surpass its own long-term trend rate. Second, external factors for Asia quickly returned to precrisis levels well before the overall economic activity stabilized in the West. Asia began to recover because trade and finance started to normalize in February 2009. Third, the region's aggressive countercyclical response helped its economy to move back onto its precrisis track.

Preliminary evidence seems to suggest that the recovery of Asian economies from this crisis may have proceeded faster than that of the rest of the world and than their own experience in the 1997 Asian financial crisis. The effects of the current subprime financial crisis on Asia may be different because Asia went through structural changes during the recovery from the Asian financial crisis. This process might have also changed the transmission structure between Asian economies and the United States. Simultaneously, regional linkages may have been

[1] The 12 Asian countries we study in this chapter are China, Hong Kong, Korea, Singapore, Taiwan, Indonesia, Malaysia, the Philippines, Thailand, India, Pakistan, and Sri Lanka.

strengthened in the past decade, thus limiting Asia's external dependence. In this chapter, we measure the degree of financial linkage of Asian markets with the United States, including the sample period after the subprime financial crisis, to provide a partial explanation for the observed resilience of the Asian economy during this crisis.

This chapter investigates the degree of financial linkage of Asian markets with the United States during two crisis episodes. We specifically define three channels of financial linkages by mean causality, volatility causality, and innovation correlation linkages. By *mean causality* we mean that a higher return in one market causes a higher return in the other market. Between two markets with different time zones, this linkage can also be considered an information flow between markets (King and Wadhwani, 1990). If mean causality is specified for only short lags, this linkage channel is effective only for the short term. On the other hand, *volatility causality* is observed if a higher volatility in one market causes a higher volatility in the other market. If volatility has a persistent effect, as observed in many financial data, this channel has a relatively longer effect, which we call the medium-term effect. However, by only observing the volatility–causality relationship, we cannot determine whether or not two markets move in the same direction. Having a close connection to mean causality, *correlation* captures long-term comovement of two stock markets. Because correlation measures long-term comovement, it is likely to undergo a structural change in the observed period. For estimating the correlation between two stock markets, we implement a method of smooth-transition in this possible structural change.

For analyzing the financial linkage between the United States and Asia, we adopt a multivariate VAR-GARCH model with a possible change in correlation. To determine the specification for the GARCH process, we test the direction of a volatility Granger-causality using tests proposed in Cheung and Ng (1996) and Hong (2001). We also test whether innovation correlation between the two markets is constant and estimate a smooth-transition correlation (STC) VAR-GARCH model if the tests reject the constancy of correlation. More importantly, we apply the same methodology to both the Asian crisis in 1997 and the subprime financial crisis in 2008.

The most interesting findings from empirical exercises are threefold. First, the empirical evidence indicates a stark difference between these two crises. The volatility causality comes from the crisis-originating country: the volatility causality runs from Asia to the United States in 1997 and vice versa in 2008. Second, the estimated points of transition in the correlation are indicative of market participants' awareness of the ensuing stock market crashes in September 2008 and in July 1997. Third, the decline in volatility spillovers during the period of financial turmoil was more pervasive for the Asian financial crisis.

The structure of this chapter is as follows. Section 2 reviews previous studies investigating financial linkages between the US and Asian stock markets. Section 3 describes three econometric approaches: a volatility causality test, tests for constancy of correlation, and the STC-VAR-GARCH model. Section 4 provides empirical evidence of financial linkages between the United States and Asia in the two crises. Section 5 provides the robustness of the results, and Section 6 concludes the chapter.

2. Review on the financial linkage of Asian stock markets with the United States

Two related literatures are relevant to this study: the financial linkage of Asian stock markets with external markets and financial market integration within Asia. We discuss the implications to our study of the integration within Asia in the concluding remarks. However, in this chapter, we focus on reviewing the existing empirical studies that investigate the financial linkage of Asian stock markets with the United States.

There exist many empirical studies that examine the spillover effect from the US market to other stock markets. It is natural to assume that any national market may be strongly associated with the United States, which is the world's largest stock market. In some studies, indeed, the US stock market is treated as the world factor. Many studies can be classified as relating to one of the following two models: the incomplete information model of King and Wadhwani (1990) and the world factor model of Bekeart and Harvey (1997).

King and Wadhwani (1990) specify an incomplete information model for two stock markets in which agents in one market learn about unobservable, common shocks through price changes in the other stock market. For stock markets with nonoverlapping trading hours, the reduced model includes, as an explanatory variable, the preceding returns in the other stock market, and this coefficient is called the contagion coefficient. Applying this model in the context of Asia-Pacific stock markets, Kim (2005) examines empirical evidence of information flows from the United States and Japan to Australia, Hong Kong, and Singapore. Kim finds that dynamic information spillover effects are significant from the United States but less so from Japan. Examining the change in information flows during the Asian currency crisis, Cheung *et al.* (2007) split the sample into precrisis, crisis, and postcrisis periods. They find that the US market is Granger-caused by the Asian markets only during the crisis period, while the US market leads the Asian markets in all three periods.

Extending the world-factor model of Bekeart and Harvey (1997) to a two-factor model, Ng (2000) examines the effect of the United States as a global shock and Japan as a regional shock on Asian markets. In contrast with Kim (2005), she finds significant spillovers from the region to many of the Pacific Basin countries. Yi and Tan (2009) find that the level of integration for Singapore and Malaysia with external markets is even higher when the MSCI global and regional indices are used instead of the US and Japanese national stock market indices. Applying a band spectrum approach, Chan *et al.* (2008) find that the US market effect on Hong Kong comes from the higher frequency of cycles during the postcrisis period.

The mere existence of high correlations of stock market returns between an emerging country and developed countries may only indicate that fluctuations in the Dow Jones ripple around the world. Nevertheless, by examining 14 emerging countries Cuadro-Sáez *et al.* (2009) demonstrate that shocks in emerging markets have significant impacts on global equity markets.

From our review of the existing studies, we summarize the three main findings most relevant to this study. First, the US stock market has a significant influence on Asian stock markets. We also investigate the financial linkages between the US and Asian markets, especially by identifying three channels of financial linkages. Second, the US effect may change during or after the crisis periods. Reflecting on this second point, we implement an estimation model that is capable of encompassing time-varying coefficients. Third, reverse causality may occur only during the crisis period. The third point requires our model to be a priori symmetric between the United States and Asian countries. For this reason, the single-variable structures of Bekeart and Harvey (1997), Ng (2000), Yi and Tan (2009), and Chan *et al.* (2008), which assume that the US stock market, being the largest in the world, influences the Asian markets unidirectionally, are not appropriate, and we propose a bivariate model in the following section.

3. Econometric approach

To investigate the linkages between Asian stock markets and the US market in the econometric framework, we first need to give precise definitions for financial linkages. To be specific about the term "linkages" for two financial markets in this study, we postulate the following three linkages to hold between returns in the Asian and US stock markets: (i) mean causality, (ii) volatility causality, and (iii) nonzero correlation. To capture these linkages, we apply a bivariate VAR-GARCH model.

In accordance with evidence in the literature, we implement a framework that allows the degree of correlation to change during financial crises. Instead of specifying correlation to be fully time-varying, we assume that there are two correlation regimes corresponding to before and after the crisis, and that the transition process between two regimes occurs gradually. Therefore, we apply a bilateral VAR-GARCH model with STC specification. Two of the advantages of using STC over fully time-varying correlation specification are that the timing of transitions in correlation can be investigated and that the computational burden can be decreased.

3.1. A baseline model

In the following, we let P_t^i be the log of the stock index in one of the Asian markets and P_t^U be the log of the US stock index. We define the returns on Asian markets and the US market as the log difference of the stock indices multiplied by 100 and denote them by R_t^i and R_t^U, respectively. Before we turn to our fully specified model, we begin by introducing a baseline model, described by the following Equations (1) through (5). Each return is assumed to possess a mean, an autoregressive term, a cross-market effect term, and a disturbance term, as in Equation (1). This framework is also adopted for the pair of Japan and the United States in Ng (2000). In addition to allowing *mean causality* from the United States to Asia, it is also important ex ante to allow for a possible mean causality from developing countries to the United States, as found in the study of Cuadro-Sáez *et al.* (2009).

$$\begin{bmatrix} R_t^i \\ R_t^U \end{bmatrix} = \begin{bmatrix} \alpha_1 \\ \alpha_2 \end{bmatrix} + \begin{bmatrix} \beta_{11} & \beta_{12} \\ \beta_{21} & \beta_{22} \end{bmatrix} \begin{bmatrix} R_{t-1}^i \\ R_{t-1}^U \end{bmatrix} + \begin{bmatrix} \varepsilon_{1t} \\ \varepsilon_{2t} \end{bmatrix}. \tag{1}$$

The variances of disturbance terms are modeled with a GARCH(1,1) structure in which the variances are conditionally dependent on past squared residuals and past variances (Bollerslev, 1988). Therefore, our model is a variant of the VAR-GARCH model investigated in Ling and McAleer (2003).

$$\begin{bmatrix} \varepsilon_{1,t} \\ \varepsilon_{2,t} \end{bmatrix} \sim \mathbf{N}(0, H_t), \text{ where } H_t = \begin{bmatrix} h_{11,t} & h_{12,t} \\ h_{21,t} & h_{22,t} \end{bmatrix}. \tag{2}$$

The symmetric covariance can be simplified in the vector representation (Vech) form, following Bollerslev *et al.* (1988).

$$\boldsymbol{h}_t = \boldsymbol{w} + \boldsymbol{A}\boldsymbol{\varepsilon}_{t-1}^2 + \boldsymbol{B}\boldsymbol{h}_{t-1}. \tag{3}$$

To impose the conditions for the positive definiteness of the covariance matrix with a simpler parameterization, Bollerslev (1990) introduces a constant correlation assumption in a GARCH(1,1) model. Each variance term follows a GARCH process in Equation (4). Equation (5) demonstrates that the covariance term is restricted with constant correlation parameters and variance terms in Equation (4):

$$\begin{bmatrix} h_{11,t} \\ h_{22,t} \end{bmatrix} = \begin{bmatrix} w_1 \\ w_2 \end{bmatrix} + \begin{bmatrix} a_{11} & a_{12} \\ a_{21} & a_{22} \end{bmatrix} \begin{bmatrix} \varepsilon_{1t-1}\varepsilon_{1t-1} \\ \varepsilon_{2t-1}\varepsilon_{2t-1} \end{bmatrix} + \begin{bmatrix} b_{11} & b_{12} \\ b_{21} & b_{22} \end{bmatrix} \begin{bmatrix} h_{11,t-1} \\ h_{22,t-1} \end{bmatrix}, \tag{4}$$

where volatility causality in off-diagonal components is restricted to zero, that is, $a_{12} = a_{21} = b_{12} = b_{21} = 0$ and

$$h_{21,t} = \rho(h_{11,t}h_{22,t})^{1/2}. \tag{5}$$

This baseline model imposes two restrictions: no volatility causality and constant correlation. In the following two subsections, we will discuss the tests to determine whether or not these two restrictions are valid. In the case that these restrictions are rejected, we will introduce a more flexible model that allows volatility causality and time-varying correlations. We describe this model as STC-VAR-GARCH in Section 3.4.

3.2. Causality in volatility

Cheung and Ng (1996) propose a test of causality in variance between two time-series variables by using the residual cross-correlation function. The test for causality in variance involves the sum of squared cross-correlations with equal weight up to the chosen lag size, M, and zero weight for cross-correlations with larger lags. Hong (2001) generalizes the test of Cheung and Ng (1996) by introducing kernel functions for the nonuniform weighting and provides simulation results that the Hong test performs better in the power. In this chapter, we implement the Daniel kernel for the causality-in-variance test (Hong, 2001).

After fitting each return variable to the univariate generalized ARCH specification, the squared standardized residuals are calculated as[2]

$$\hat{u}_t = \frac{\hat{\varepsilon}_{1t}^2}{\hat{h}_{1t}} - \bar{u}, \quad \hat{v}_t = \frac{\hat{\varepsilon}_{2t}^2}{\hat{h}_{2t}} - \bar{v}. \tag{6}$$

Then, the sample cross-correlations between $\hat{u}_t$ and $\hat{v}_t$ are defined as

$$\hat{\rho}_{uv}(j) = \left\{\hat{C}_{uu}(0)\hat{C}_{vv}(0)\right\}^{-1/2}\hat{C}_{uv}(j), \tag{7}$$

where the sample cross-covariance is

$$\hat{C}_{uu}(0) = T^{-1}\sum_{t=1}^{T}\hat{u}_t^2,\ \hat{C}_{vv}(0) = T^{-1}\sum_{t=1}^{T}\hat{v}_t^2,$$

$$\text{and } \hat{C}_{uv}(j) = \begin{cases} T^{-1}\sum\limits_{t=j+1}^{T}\hat{u}_t\hat{v}_{t-j}, \text{ if } j \geq 0 \\ T^{-1}\sum\limits_{t=-j+1}^{T}\hat{u}_{t+j}\hat{v}_t, \text{ if } j<0 \end{cases}. \tag{8}$$

---

[2] Hong (2001) suggests the use of the centered squared standardized residuals by subtracting 1, whereas Cheung and Ng (1996) use the sample means, $\bar{u}$ and $\bar{v}$. In a simulation study, virtually no difference was found (Hong, 2001). In this chapter, we use the sample mean to calculate cross-correlations.

The Cheung and Ng (1996) statistic is based on the sum of the first M squared cross-correlation

$$S = T\sum_{j=1}^{M}\hat{\rho}_{uv}^{2}(j), \tag{9}$$

which is asymptotically χ_M^2 under the null hypothesis of no volatility spillovers.

By introducing the kernel function, $k(z)$, as a weighting function, Hong (2001) generalized Cheung and Ng's (1996) statistic as

$$Q_1 = \frac{\left\{T\sum_{j=1}^{T-1}k^2(j/M)\hat{\rho}_{uv}^{2}(j) - C_{1T}(k)\right\}}{\left\{2D_{1T}(k)\right\}^{1/2}}, \tag{10}$$

where

$$\begin{aligned} C_{1T}(k) &= \sum_{j=1}^{T-1}(1-j/T)k^2(j/M),\ D_{1T}(k) \\ &= \sum(1-j/T)\{1-(j+1)/T\}k^4(j/M). \end{aligned} \tag{11}$$

Among alternative kernels, we use the Daniel kernel, as suggested by Hong (2001):

$$k(z) = \frac{\sin(\pi z)}{\pi z}. \tag{12}$$

For the above test, we set $M = 10$ in Equations (10) and (11). As a robustness check, we also used different values for $M = 5$ and $M = 20$. The Hong statistic asymptotically follows the standard normal distribution under the null hypothesis.

If the Hong test rejects the null hypothesis of no volatility causality, we allow corresponding off-diagonal components of the matrix in the GARCH process in Equation (4) to be nonzero. To allow for possible volatility spillovers between two stock markets, we choose the specification of nonzero, off-diagonal components in matrix $\boldsymbol{A}$, as in Equation (13). We assume that the effect of volatility spillover is rather short-lived. As a robustness check in Section 5, we also allow nonzero, off-diagonal components in matrix $\boldsymbol{B}$.

$$\begin{bmatrix} h_{11,t} \\ h_{22,t} \end{bmatrix} = \begin{bmatrix} w_1 \\ w_2 \end{bmatrix} + \begin{bmatrix} a_{11} & a_{12} \\ a_{21} & a_{22} \end{bmatrix}\begin{bmatrix} \varepsilon_{1t-1}\varepsilon_{1t-1} \\ \varepsilon_{2t-1}\varepsilon_{2t-1} \end{bmatrix} + \begin{bmatrix} b_{11} & 0 \\ 0 & b_{22} \end{bmatrix}\begin{bmatrix} h_{11,t-1} \\ h_{22,t-1} \end{bmatrix}. \tag{13}$$

3.3. Constant correlation model and tests for constancy of correlation

We implement the tests for constancy of correlation proposed by Bera and Kim (2002) and Berben and Jansen (2005). Both tests use estimates under the null of constant correlation specification in Equations (1) through (5). In the case that no volatility causality is rejected by Hong's test, we replace Equation (4) with (13). To simplify the presentation of the test statistics below, we denote the scaled residuals as $\hat{\varepsilon}^*_{i,t} = \hat{\varepsilon}_{i,t}/\sqrt{h_{i,t}}$ and the scaled residual premultiplied by the inverse of correlation matrix as

$$(\hat{v}^*_{1t}, \quad \hat{v}^*_{2t})' = \left(\frac{\hat{\varepsilon}^*_{1,t} - \hat{\rho}\hat{\varepsilon}^*_{2,t}}{\sqrt{1-\rho^2}}, \quad \frac{\hat{\varepsilon}^*_{2,t} - \hat{\rho}\hat{\varepsilon}^*_{1,t}}{\sqrt{1-\rho^2}} \right). \tag{14}$$

Bera and Kim (2002) propose two versions of information matrix (IM) tests. The efficient score test is

$$\mathrm{IM_e} = \frac{\left[\sum_{t=1}^{T}(\eta_t)\right]^2}{4T(1+4\hat{\rho}^2+\hat{\rho}^4)}, \quad \text{where } \eta_t = \hat{v}^{*2}_{1t}\hat{v}^{*2}_{2t} - 1 - 2\hat{\rho}^2, \tag{15}$$

and the studentized test for nonnormal distribution is

$$\mathrm{IM_s} = \frac{\left[\sum_{t=1}^{T}\eta_t\right]^2}{\sum_{t=1}^{T}(\eta_t - \bar{\eta})^2}. \tag{16}$$

Alternatively, Berben and Jansen (2005) apply Tse's (2000) Lagrange multiplier test for an STC-GARCH model (the STC-GARCH model will be described in the following section). Asymptotic distribution of the Wald, Lagrange multiplier, and likelihood ratio tests for the STC-GARCH model are nonstandard because nuisance parameters are not identified under the null hypothesis of constant correlation (Davies, 1977; Hansen, 1996). To circumvent the nuisance parameter problem, Berben and Jansen (2005) adopt an auxiliary STC-GARCH model by Taylor approximation and derive LMC test statistics:

$$\mathrm{LMC} = \frac{\left(\sum_{t=1}^{T}\partial l_t/\partial\hat{\gamma}\right)\left(\sum_{t=1}^{T}\partial l_t/\partial\hat{\gamma}\right)}{\sum_{t=1}^{T}\left((\partial l_t/\partial\hat{\gamma})(\partial l_t/\partial\hat{\gamma})\right)}, \tag{17}$$

where

$$\frac{\partial l_t}{\partial\hat{\gamma}} = \left[\left(\frac{\hat{v}^*_{1t}\hat{v}^*_{2t}}{1-\rho^2}\right) + \left(\frac{\rho}{1-\rho^2}\right)\right]. \tag{18}$$

The limiting distributions of all three test statistics are $\chi^2(1)$. Small sample properties determined by Monte Carlo simulation indicate that the IMs test performs better than the IMe test in terms of power when the disturbance term follows the t-distribution (Bera and Kim, 2002).

The power of the LMC test declines when the transition is linear and the location of the transition is closer to either end of the sample period (Berben and Jansen, 2005).

3.4. VAR-GARCH model with smooth-transition correlation

In estimating the financial linkages between the US and Asian stock markets, we propose to proceed by the following three steps. In the first step, we test whether or not a volatility–causality relationship exists between the two markets. Then, accordingly, we determine the specification of off-diagonal components of matrix $\boldsymbol{A}$ in the GARCH structure. In the second step, we apply tests for constancy of correlation to the VAR-GARCH model. If the constant correlation assumption is rejected, then, as the third step, we specify two correlation regimes and investigate how the correlation evolves between the two regimes.

Following Lin and Terasvirta (1994), we model the correlation between the US and Asian stock markets to follow a smooth transition over the sample period. We follow the specifications of Berben and Jansen (2005).[3] Variance terms follow a GARCH process in Equation (4) or (13), and the covariance term is defined as time-varying in Equation (19), with parameter restrictions given in Equations (20) and (21).

$$h_{21,t} = \rho_t (h_{11,t} h_{22,t})^{1/2}, \tag{19}$$

$$\rho_t = \rho_0 (1 - G(s_t; \gamma, c)) + \rho_1 G(s_t; \gamma, c), \tag{20}$$

$$G(s_t; \gamma, c) = \frac{1}{1 + \exp(-\gamma(s_t - c))}, \quad \gamma > 0. \tag{21}$$

The correlations in the first and second regimes are denoted by ρ_0 and ρ_1, respectively. The time-varying correlation is therefore a weighted average of these two correlations, as in Equation (20). The weighting function, $G(s_t; \gamma, c)$, follows the logistic specification, and γ and c denote the "speed" of transition and the (mid) "point" of transition, respectively. The transition variable s_t is defined as t divided by the number of observations; therefore, $s_t \in (0, 1]$. Then the weight becomes a monotonic function of the transition variable.

A few restrictions need to be imposed on the parameters of the estimation algorithm in Equations (19) through (21). The correlation parameters in both regimes, ρ_0 and ρ_1, have to be between -1 and 1. The parameter for the speed of transition, γ, needs to be strictly positive. The parameter for the midpoint of the transition, c, must be within the

---

[3] Yoshida (2009) also applies this approach to investigate the shift in correlations between the US and Japanese stock markets.

range of 0 and 1. For parameters associated with STC, we use the following transformations to abide by restrictions on these parameters:

$$\begin{aligned} \gamma &= (\gamma^0)^2, \\ c &= \Phi(c^0), \\ \rho_0 &= -1 + 2\Phi(\rho_0^0), \\ \rho_1 &= -1 + 2\Phi(\rho_1^0), \end{aligned} \tag{22}$$

where $\Phi(\ )$ is the cumulated standard normal distribution function. We denote parameters by a 0 superscript, that is, γ^0, c^0, ρ_0^0, and ρ_1^0, and regain model parameters from the above transformation equations. After we obtain the estimated coefficients for ρ_0, ρ_1, γ, and c, we can calculate the time-varying correlation between US and Asian stock market innovations.

For the estimation of the multivariate GARCH model, it is essential to set appropriate initial values to obtain the maximum of the quasi-likelihood function. First, we obtain consistent estimators for parameters in the VAR model, $\hat{\alpha}_i$ and $\hat{\beta}_{ij}$, in Equation (1) by using ordinary least squares. For the diagonal components in the matrices in GARCH components, we obtain initial values, $\hat{a}_{11}, \hat{b}_{11}, \hat{a}_{22}$, and $\hat{b}_{22}$, by estimating a single-variable GARCH(1,1) model for each Asian country and the United States. Then, using these estimators as initial values and setting $\rho_0^0 = -1$, $\rho_1^0 = 1$, $c^0 = 0$, and $\gamma^0 = 1$, we obtain maximum-likelihood estimators for the parameters in Equation (1) as well as the GARCH component of time-varying variances in Equations (19) through (21). In case Hong's test indicates volatility causality between two stock markets, we set cross-coefficients to be equal to 0.01. In addition, we estimate with varied initial conditions for $c^0 \in \{-3, -1, 0, 0.01, 0.1\}$and $\gamma^0 \in \{1, 2, 3, 5\}$ to correctly obtain the maximum of the quasi-likelihood function when convergence in estimation cannot be reached with our default setting. If convergence is obtained for more than one set of initial values, we compare the log likelihood of each estimate to find the maximum-likelihood estimates.

4. Empirical results for the Asian financial crisis and subprime loan crisis

Applying the methodologies described in the previous section to 12 Asian countries, this section presents the empirical results of (1) volatility Granger-causality tests, (2) testing of the constancy of correlation during crisis periods, and (3) estimates of STC-VAR-GARCH models for each of 12 Asian stock markets with the US stock market.

4.1. Data

Daily stock market returns are calculated as the log difference between the current and previous-day stock market index. For Asian stock market indices, we use SSEC for China, HIS for Hong Kong, JKSE for Indonesia, KS11 for Korea, BSESN for India, KLSE for Malaysia, KSE for Pakistan, PSI for the Philippines, FTSTI for Singapore, CSE for Sri Lanka, TWII for Taiwan, and SETI for Thailand. For US stock market indices, we use the Dow Jones Industrial Average. These data are retrieved in terms of the national currency from *Thomson Reuter 3000Xtra*. To maintain balanced panel data, we limited our sample to days for which all indices are available. For the following analysis, we use two subsample periods with equal lengths of 33 months: the Asian financial crisis period from April 1996 to October 1998 and the subprime financial crisis from June 2007 to December 2009.

4.2. Volatility causality during crises

To investigate the direction of the volatility spillover, we apply the volatility Granger-causality test developed by Cheung and Ng (1996) and Hong (2001) to the pairs of US and Asian economies. Table 1 provides the summary of test statistics for the Asian financial crisis sample. During the Asian financial crisis, Asian volatility spillovers to the US market are found for the markets in Malaysia, the Philippines, Thailand, and Taiwan, whereas there is no causality in the reverse direction, except for in Sri Lanka. It is noteworthy that the test statistics are the highest for the most crisis-affected countries, namely, the Philippines and Thailand.

Table 1. Granger-causality in volatility tests, April 1996 to Oct 1998 (Asian financial crisis)

	United States to Asia	Asia to United States
China	−0.056	−0.430
Hong Kong	−1.169	0.305
Korea	−1.029	−1.171
Singapore	0.799	−0.416
Taiwan	−0.313	2.031^{**}
Indonesia	0.363	−1.237
Malaysia	−0.909	1.307^{*}
Philippines	0.016	4.137^{***}
Thailand	−0.119	5.764^{***}
India	−1.158	0.097
Pakistan	0.270	−0.567
Sri Lanka	3.420^{***}	0.291

Note: The test statistic is the Q_1 test developed by Hong (2001). The test statistic asymptotically converges to the standard normal distribution. M is set to 10. Statistical significance at the 1%, 5% and 10% levels is indicated by ***, ** and *, respectively.

Table 2. Granger-causality in volatility tests, June 2007 to December 2009 (subprime loan crisis)

	United States to Asia	Asia to United States
China	−0.348	0.638
Hong Kong	2.471***	−1.454
Korea	1.071	−1.053
Singapore	−0.871	−1.352
Taiwan	−0.668	−1.253
Indonesia	1.785**	−1.335
Malaysia	0.232	−0.716
Philippines	1.868**	1.332*
Thailand	0.488	−1.130
India	2.907***	−1.177
Pakistan	−0.077	−0.864
Sri Lanka	0.066	−1.148

Note: See notes in Table 1.

Additionally, during the subprime loan crisis, we have very strong evidence that the US volatility Granger-caused Asian market volatility for Hong Kong, India, Indonesia, and the Philippines. From the Asian markets to the US market, we found weak evidence of volatility Granger-causality only for the Philippines (Table 2).[4]

The striking difference between the two crises found in volatility Granger-causality among the US and Asian markets suggests that the direction of volatility causality coincides with the location of the crisis-originating region. This finding is consistent with Cheung *et al.* (2007), in which reversed mean causality (from Asia to the United States) is only found during the Asian crisis period.

4.3. Testing the constancy of correlation during crises

Table 3 summarizes the test results when applying three tests for constancy of correlation to 12 Asian economies with the United States for the Asian financial crisis period. The sample extends 16 months both before and after July 1997, in which the Thai baht was pressured to depreciate after depletion of foreign currency reserves. The evidence for a change in correlation is strong in the Asian crisis. IMs rejects the null hypothesis

[4] We set the parameter in Equation (1) to $M = 10$ throughout the analysis in the chapter. To check the sensitivity of results with respect to the selection of lag length, we also obtained test statistics for $M = 5$ and $M = 20$. Most of the results remain qualitatively the same. In the small sample, however, Hong's test tends to reject the null less often with a shorter lag length. A notable difference is for the following two cases. For $M = 5$, US volatility causality in subprime loan crisis rejects only for Philippines. For $M = 20$, US volatility causality is additionally found for Indonesia in the 1997 crisis and Korea in the 2008 crisis.

Table 3. Test for the constancy of correlation

	(April 1996 to October 1998)			(June 2007 to December 2009)		
	LMC	IMe	IMs	LMC	IMe	IMs
China	0.01	122.88	2.42	0.29	0.63	0.26
Hong Kong	0.23	40.00	2.94	0.71	1.46	0.27
Korea	0.16	16.31	2.55	0.22	19.03	2.79
Singapore	0.05	50.91	1.98	0.23	3.00	0.40
Taiwan	0.03	25.75	2.86	0.03	6.24	1.04
Indonesia	0.12	12.26	1.11	0.57	11.27	1.63
Malaysia	0.51	10.09	0.87	0.55	49.14	1.45
Philippines	1.90	39.65	2.73	0.16	9.92	0.81
Thailand	1.42	55.27	0.96	0.06	31.09	2.61
India	0.53	52.34	2.65	0.54	15.48	1.12
Pakistan	0.40	28.55	2.14	0.70	31.45	0.97
Sri Lanka	0.36	117.02	3.25	0.00	9.23	1.43

Note: The LMC statistic is suggested by Berben and Jansen (2005) and the IMe and IMs are provided by Bera and Kim (2002). All test statistics follow $\chi^2(1)$. The critical values are 2.71, 3.84, and 6.63 for significance levels of 10%, 5%, and 1%, respectively. The specifications for volatility causality are determined by Hong's test.

for four countries with a significance level of 10%, while the IMe test rejects the null hypothesis of constant correlation for all countries, even at the 1% significance level. LMC, on the other hand, cannot reject the null hypothesis for any countries.

Table 3 also provides test statistics for the subprime crisis. The IMe tests overwhelmingly indicate rejection of the null hypothesis of constant correlations, while the LMC and IMs tests do not reject the null hypothesis for most of the cases. Specifically, IMe rejects the null hypothesis for 10 countries at the 10% significance level. The null hypothesis of constant correlation of China and Hong Kong with the United States cannot be rejected at any traditional significance level. On the other hand, the LMC test does not reject the null of constant correlation for any countries, while the IMs test only rejects the constant correlation for the case of Korea. Given the mixed results of these tests, we proceed to apply a STC framework to a country if one of the three test statistics rejects the null. Consequently, we investigate a possible change in volatility spillover by applying STC-VAR-GARCH(1,1) model to all 12 Asian countries in both crises, except for China and Hong Kong in the subprime loan crisis.

4.4. Smooth-transition correlation VAR-GARCH estimates

Tables 4 and 5 provide the estimates for the STC-VAR-GARCH model for the Asian and subprime financial crisis, respectively. In the following,

Table 4. STC-VAR-GARCH estimators (Asian financial crisis)

	China	Hong Kong	Korea	Singapore	Taiwan	Indonesia	Malaysia	Philippines	Thailand	India	Pakistan	Sri Lanka
α_1	0.128	0.093	−0.192	−0.121	0.103	0.031	−0.055	−0.019	−0.398	−0.025	−0.124	−0.009
	(0.112)	(0.088)	(0.123)	(0.068)*	(0.090)	(0.094)	(0.077)	(0.087)	(0.147)***	(0.106)	(0.137)	(0.043)
α_2	0.203	0.193	0.178	0.188	0.183	0.196	0.163	0.154	0.166	0.177	0.171	0.198
	(0.069)***	(0.070)***	(0.070)**	(0.070)***	(0.069)***	(0.069)***	(0.071)**	(0.069)**	(0.072)**	(0.068)***	(0.069)**	(0.066)***
β_{11}	0.107	0.137	0.078	0.192	0.102	0.159	0.118	0.199	0.156	0.077	0.072	0.279
	(0.065)	(0.058)**	(0.057)	(0.062)***	(0.060)*	(0.064)**	(0.063)*	(0.055)***	(0.065)**	(0.053)	(0.061)	(0.061)***
β_{12}	0.025	0.286	0.050	0.048	0.125	0.096	0.032	0.135	0.016	0.069	0.123	0.069
	(0.076)	(0.076)***	(0.088)	(0.049)	(0.066)*	(0.064)	(0.057)	(0.076)*	(0.105)	(0.072)	(0.088)	(0.041)*
β_{21}	−0.036	0.039	−0.020	0.005	0.000	0.010	0.005	−0.029	0.014	0.007	0.022	0.030
	(0.024)	(0.032)	(0.023)	(0.038)	(0.043)	(0.025)	(0.030)	(0.033)	(0.024)	(0.033)	(0.024)	(0.060)
β_{22}	−0.023	−0.040	−0.001	−0.022	−0.007	−0.029	−0.013	−0.032	−0.021	−0.007	−0.020	−0.038
	(0.057)	(0.060)	(0.058)	(0.058)	(0.056)	(0.057)	(0.058)	(0.059)	(0.057)	(0.057)	(0.057)	(0.057)
w_1	0.301	0.240	0.251	0.389	1.907	0.156	0.044	0.284	4.838	0.223	0.826	0.124
	(0.117)***	(0.089)***	(0.133)*	(0.150)***	(0.554)***	(0.072)**	(0.031)	(0.129)**	(0.911)***	(0.210)	(0.369)**	(0.042)***
w_2	0.209	0.403	0.233	0.292	0.249	0.224	0.436	1.116	0.339	0.247	0.228	0.207
	(0.105)**	(0.211)*	(0.120)*	(0.158)*	(0.110)**	(0.115)*	(0.242)*	(0.468)**	(0.246)	(0.128)*	(0.115)**	(0.109)*
a_{11}	0.178	0.234	0.167	0.427	0.200	0.240	0.248	0.311	0.392	0.030	0.093	0.556
	(0.051)***	(0.052)***	(0.053)***	(0.087)***	(0.089)**	(0.049)***	(0.047)***	(0.065)***	(0.158)**	(0.018)*	(0.034)***	(0.135)***
a_{12}												0.054
												(0.028)*
a_{22}	0.122	0.116	0.110	0.112	0.072	0.119	0.110	0.117	0.112	0.120	0.117	0.117
	(0.036)***	(0.039)***	(0.033)***	(0.036)***	(0.035)**	(0.036)***	(0.038)***	(0.048)**	(0.036)***	(0.036)***	(0.035)***	(0.035)***
a_{21}					0.039		0.011	0.030	0.001			
					(0.017)**		(0.008)	(0.026)	(0.003)			

Table 4. *(Continued)*

	China	Hong Kong	Korea	Singapore	Taiwan	Indonesia	Malaysia	Philippines	Thailand	India	Pakistan	Sri Lanka
b_{11}	0.805 (0.042)***	0.760 (0.044)***	0.824 (0.052)***	0.551 (0.081)***	0.249 (0.190)	0.786 (0.034)***	0.806 (0.028)***	0.703 (0.052)***	0.236 (0.111)**	0.921 (0.056)***	0.810 (0.067)***	0.493 (0.061)***
b_{22}	0.787 (0.060)***	0.706 (0.107)***	0.784 (0.067)***	0.760 (0.083)***	0.741 (0.070)***	0.786 (0.063)***	0.640 (0.141)***	0.257 (0.253)	0.724 (0.144)***	0.770 (0.071)***	0.782 (0.065)***	0.796 (0.060)***
gm_0	11.75 (13.97)	19.56 (24.71)	15.55 (42.81)	20.89 (17.87)	41.67 (71.50)	15.77 (19.85)	19.05 (17.96)	6.091 (2.420)**	7.050 (4.146)*	5.869 (1.929)***	13.27 (16.39)	21.19 (13.53)
cc_0	0.338 (0.110)***	−0.732 (0.033)***	−0.342 (0.101)***	−1.285 (0.046)***	−1.616 (0.025)***	−0.374 (0.041)***	−0.700 (0.035)***	0.287 (0.112)**	0.333 (0.133)**	−0.714 (0.201)***	−0.003 (0.064)	−0.856 (0.026)***
pp_0	−0.151 (0.079)*	1.050 (0.114)***	0.060 (0.122)	1.058 (0.170)***	−0.558 (0.277)**	0.533 (0.115)***	0.762 (0.132)***	0.003 (0.106)	−0.134 (0.105)	−0.379 (0.171)**	0.296 (0.100)***	0.836 (0.133)***
pp_1	0.102 (0.124)	0.366 (0.070)***	0.338 (0.075)***	0.239 (0.068)***	0.243 (0.066)***	0.139 (0.076)*	0.221 (0.071)***	0.587 (0.104)***	0.428 (0.110)***	0.189 (0.081)**	0.028 (0.083)	0.207 (0.069)***
LL	−1559.2	−1479.9	−1590.9	−1404.3	−1422.2	−1522	−1501.8	−1491.5	−1626.4	−1489.9	−1590.2	−1237.8

Note: The coefficients are estimated for Equations (1), (2), (5), (13), (19), (20), (21), and (22) by maximizing the quasi-likelihood. The figures in parentheses are standard deviations calculated from numeric second derivatives. LL is the log likelihood. Statistical significance at the 1%, 5% and 10% levels is indicated by ***, ** and *, respectively.

Table 5. STC-VAR-GARCH estimators (subprime crisis)

	China	Hong Kong	Korea	Singapore	Taiwan	Indonesia	Malaysia	Philippines	Thailand	India	Pakistan	Sri Lanka
α_1	0.102	0.072	0.102	0.040	0.141	0.108	0.032	0.047	0.089	0.087	0.103	0.055
	(0.137)	(0.104)	(0.090)	(0.080)	(0.097)	(0.097)	(0.060)	(0.095)	(0.100)	(0.111)	(0.087)	(0.054)
α_2	0.033	0.066	0.040	0.048	0.082	0.061	0.023	0.052	0.038	0.070	0.028	0.003
	(0.073)	(0.071)	(0.072)	(0.072)	(0.073)	(0.071)	(0.074)	(0.071)	(0.072)	(0.072)	(0.072)	(0.072)
β_{11}	0.029	−0.097	−0.119	−0.069	−0.018	0.061	0.024	−0.027	0.008	−0.048	0.153	0.220
	(0.052)	(0.057)*	(0.058)**	(0.060)	(0.059)	(0.058)	(0.059)	(0.059)	(0.059)	(0.059)	(0.060)**	(0.063)***
β_{12}	0.148	0.491	0.319	0.325	0.227	0.230	0.174	0.392	0.232	0.391	0.027	0.128
	(0.075)**	(0.085)***	(0.069)***	(0.064)***	(0.066)***	(0.077)***	(0.041)***	(0.064)***	(0.068)***	(0.093)***	(0.039)	(0.031)***
β_{21}	0.005	0.026	−0.030	0.008	0.012	0.037	−0.069	0.016	0.017	0.032	−0.034	0.060
	(0.026)	(0.034)	(0.042)	(0.044)	(0.039)	(0.039)	(0.062)	(0.040)	(0.039)	(0.032)	(0.036)	(0.056)
β_{22}	−0.115	−0.107	−0.096	−0.107	−0.123	−0.094	−0.090	−0.119	−0.108	−0.107	−0.098	−0.108
	(0.053)**	(0.057)*	(0.056)*	(0.057)*	(0.054)**	(0.055)*	(0.055)	(0.054)**	(0.055)**	(0.057)*	(0.052)*	(0.052)**
w_1	0.323	0.009	0.113	0.024	0.090	0.000	0.071	0.367	0.455	0.034	0.666	0.152
	(0.250)	(0.086)	(0.068)*	(0.031)	(0.072)	(0.001)	(0.044)	(0.148)**	(0.166)***	(0.114)	(0.216)***	(0.044)***
w_2	0.072	0.105	0.117	0.134	0.105	0.105	0.125	0.072	0.127	0.089	0.082	0.075
	(0.044)*	(0.051)**	(0.054)**	(0.063)**	(0.052)**	(0.054)**	(0.061)**	(0.047)	(0.061)**	(0.047)*	(0.047)*	(0.045)*
a_{11}	0.057	0.076	0.142	0.128	0.121	0.059	0.107	0.031	0.104	0.110	0.221	0.314
	(0.027)**	(0.032)**	(0.041)***	(0.026)***	(0.035)***	(0.030)**	(0.030)***	(0.025)	(0.037)***	(0.046)**	(0.068)***	(0.071)***
a_{12}		0.267				0.229		0.112		0.287		
		(0.071)***				(0.054)***		(0.039)***		(0.087)***		
a_{22}	0.116	0.122	0.114	0.123	0.112	0.127	0.125	0.111	0.112	0.120	0.127	0.114
	(0.030)***	(0.032)***	(0.030)***	(0.035)***	(0.030)***	(0.037)***	(0.036)***	(0.031)***	(0.033)***	(0.032)***	(0.033)***	(0.030)***

Table 5. (*Continued*)

	China	Hong Kong	Korea	Singapore	Taiwan	Indonesia	Malaysia	Philippines	Thailand	India	Pakistan	Sri Lanka
a_{21}								0.004 (0.012)				
b_{11}	0.906 (0.042)***	0.828 (0.030)***	0.852 (0.038)***	0.895 (0.017)***	0.880 (0.030)***	0.838 (0.025)***	0.872 (0.033)***	0.796 (0.056)***	0.817 (0.052)***	0.809 (0.033)***	0.647 (0.091)***	0.680 (0.046)***
b_{22}	0.866 (0.034)***	0.848 (0.038)***	0.850 (0.038)***	0.837 (0.045)***	0.857 (0.037)***	0.847 (0.043)***	0.842 (0.043)***	0.864 (0.035)***	0.849 (0.044)***	0.859 (0.037)***	0.854 (0.037)***	0.867 (0.034)***
gm_0			14.595 (48.394)	32.100 (24.658)	8.860 (3.284)***	7.545 (5.916)	11.237 (8.766)	17.479 (67.360)	32.172 (19.501)*	13.098 (8.570)	4.676 (2.141)**	6.878 (2.359)***
cc_0			−0.236 (0.105)**	−1.358 (0.024)***	−1.710 (0.237)***	0.025 (0.163)	0.521 (0.104)***	−0.558 (0.105)***	−1.359 (0.021)***	0.030 (0.037)	−0.476 (0.265)*	−1.990 (0.297)***
pp_0	0.147 (0.048)***	0.460 (0.039)***	0.732 (0.088)***	0.066 (0.345)	−1.246 (0.797)	0.344 (0.089)***	0.357 (0.072)***	0.593 (0.110)***	−0.240 (0.340)	0.432 (0.083)***	0.528 (0.141)***	−5.066 (106.260)
pp_1			0.504 (0.077)***	0.672 (0.060)***	0.542 (0.063)***	0.703 (0.106)***	0.864 (0.127)***	0.295 (0.077)***	0.556 (0.061)***	0.784 (0.081)***	−0.002 (0.089)	0.154 (0.065)**
LL	−1844.0	−1745.4	−1676.2	−1669.8	−1706.6	−1720.9	−1501.4	−1675.9	−1700.9	−1780	−1681.1	−1518.6

Note: The coefficients are estimated for Equations (1), (2), (5), (13), (19), (20), (21), and (22) by maximizing the quasi-likelihood. The figures in parentheses are standard deviations calculated from numeric second derivatives. LL is log likelihood. Statistical significance at the 1%, 5% and 10% levels is indicated by ***, ** and *, respectively.

we break down the coefficient estimates of the model into three components (VAR, volatility, and STC) and discuss each component in turn.

First, we compare the estimates of VAR components between two crises, especially focusing on the cross-lag coefficients, $\hat{\beta}_{ij}, i \neq j$. On the one hand, there is no mean causality from Asia to the United States in either crisis. On the other hand, the effects of the US market on the Asian markets are strong and pervasive. The lagged returns in the US market, the largest stock market of the world, influenced the four Asian markets (Hong Kong, the Philippines, Sri Lanka, and Taiwan) even during the Asian financial crisis, with statistical significance at the 10% level. During the subprime loan crisis, all the Asian markets are affected by the previous-day outcome of the US stock market, except for Pakistan.

Second, as in many other studies on financial returns, $\hat{a}_{ii}$ are relatively smaller than $\hat{b}_{ii}$ (see Jensen and Lange, 2010). For the Asian financial crisis period, the coefficient $\hat{a}_{21}$, which corresponds to the volatility causality from the Asian countries, is statistically significant for only one case (Taiwan) out of four candidate countries, for which Hong's test rejected the null of no volatility causality. However, we find supporting evidence for all four countries when we use an alternative specification for volatility spillovers. The details of the robustness check are provided in Section 5. For the subprime loan financial crisis period, the coefficient $\hat{a}_{12}$, which corresponds to the US volatility that Granger-causes Asian volatility, is statistically significant for all four candidate countries.

Third, regarding the dynamic behaviors of correlations, Table 6 summarizes the correlation at the beginning, end, and changes in correlation during the period. In addition, for a smooth transition, the midpoint of the transition is provided. Figures 1 and 2 provide the full dynamics of time-varying correlations for the subprime financial crisis and the Asian financial crisis, respectively.

Comparing smooth-transition specification for correlation dynamics for the Asian crisis and subprime financial crisis, we find the following three striking features. First, the correlation declined during financial turmoil for some countries in both crises. This decline in correlation is more pervasive during the Asian crisis period. This result adds new, interesting evidence to the contagion literature [see Edwards (2000) and Forbes and Rigobon (2001) for the survey]. Suggesting a bias-correction measure for contagion, Forbes and Rigobon (2002) argue that there is a high degree of interdependence but no contagion, that is, a shift in transmission parameters, during the Asian financial crisis.[5] The debate in the literature strictly focuses on the increase in transmission, but we find for some

---

[5] Rigobon (2003) and Corsetti et al. (2005) use a different approach to indicate that there is a contagion as well as interdependence.

Table 6. Change in correlation and transition date

	Asian crisis				Subprime financial crisis			
	Initial	End	Change	Trans. date	Initial	End	Change	Trans. date
China	−0.12	0.08	0.20	1997/12/09	0.08	0.42	0.34	2009/03/18
Hong Kong	0.71	0.29	−0.42	1996/12/17	0.35	0.57	0.22	2008/08/29
Korea	0.05	0.26	0.22	1997/05/13	0.54	0.39	−0.15	2008/06/23
Singapore	0.71	0.19	−0.52	1996/07/23	0.05	0.50	0.45	2007/08/06
Taiwan	−0.42	0.19	0.61	1996/06/11	−0.79	0.41	1.20	2007/07/06
Indonesia	0.41	0.11	−0.30	1997/04/25	0.27	0.52	0.25	2008/09/11
Malaysia	0.55	0.18	−0.38	1997/01/07	0.28	0.61	0.33	2009/03/27
Philippines	0.00	0.44	0.44	1997/11/25	0.45	0.23	−0.21	2008/03/13
Thailand	−0.11	0.33	0.44	1997/12/09	−0.19	0.42	0.61	2007/08/06
India	−0.30	0.15	0.45	1996/12/19	0.33	0.57	0.23	2008/09/12
Pakistan	0.23	0.02	−0.21	1997/08/22	0.40	0.00	−0.40	2008/04/03
Sri Lanka	0.60	0.16	−0.43	1996/11/14	−1.00	0.12	1.12	2007/06/21

Note: The estimated parameters in Tables 4 and 5 are converted back to figures in this table by Equation (22). The initial (end) correlation is under the first (second) regime. The estimated parameter for the transition point is converted back to the exact date under the heading "Trans. date."

economies that there are decreasing cases in the transmission channel during the Asian financial crisis.

Second, a transition in correlation took place well in advance of the crashes in both crises, that is, July 1997 in the Asian financial crisis and September 2008 in the subprime financial crisis. The estimated midpoint of transition, *c*, converted back to the date, is before the crash date for eight countries in both crises. Particularly, for the case of the subprime loan financial crisis, these results are indicative of market participants' awareness of the upcoming stock market crash well before the collapse of government-sponsored enterprises and investment banks. This is no

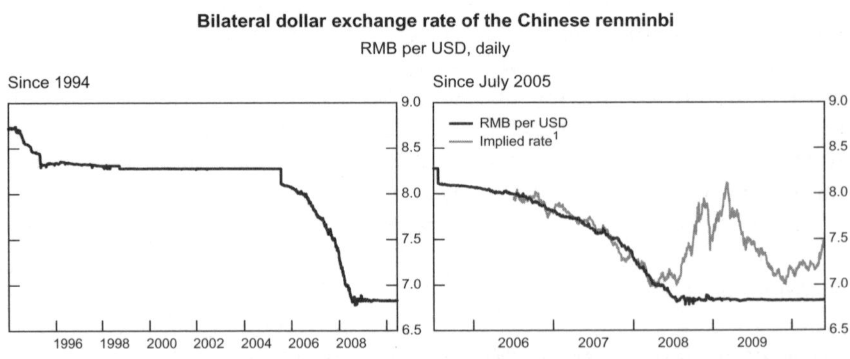

Fig. 1. Smooth-transition correlation, April 1996 to October 1998.

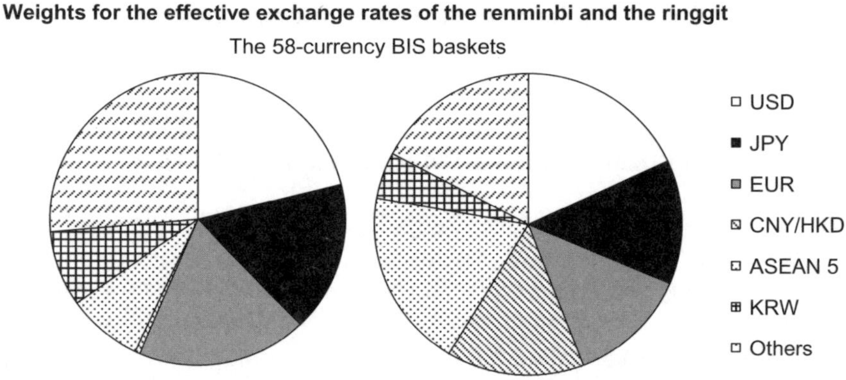

Fig. 2. Smooth-transition correlation, June 2007 to December 2009. Note: China and Hong Kong are excluded because their correlations are constant at 0.147 and 0.460, respectively.

surprise to anyone who closely followed the subprime loan problem because there were many early warnings, such as declining housing prices, well before September 2008.

Third, the range of correlations substantially narrowed in the wake of the Asian financial crisis, but correlations continued to have wide values even after the collapse of Lehman Brothers. We should note that the formal test could not reject the null hypothesis of constancy of correlation for China and Hong Kong during the subprime loan crisis.

Some caveats for interpretation of correlation shifts should be noted. First, results from both LMC and IMs tests are more in support of constant correlations. Our choice of STC-VAR-GARCH cannot be justified by depending solely on the result of IMe test statistics. Second, the coefficient γ^0 is statistically significant for only a few countries. From Equation (21), the weighting function becomes constant at 0.5 when $\gamma^0 = 0$, and, consequently, the correlation is also constant. γ^0 is statistically significant for India, the Philippines, and Thailand in the Asian financial crisis and for Pakistan, Sri Lanka, and Thailand in the subprime loan crisis. For these countries, except for Pakistan, the correlation actually increases during the subprime loan crisis. Given this weak evidence for shifts in correlation, we should interpret the results of correlation analysis more modestly. We further discuss this issue in the following section.

5. *Robustness check*

To examine the degree to which the empirical evidence from previous sections is robust, we consider the following three issues: alternative volatility causality specification in GARCH, volatility causality in tranquil periods, and tests of constancy of correlation.

5.1. Alternative volatility causality specification in GARCH

By applying Hong's (2001) test, we find evidence that volatility in Asian stock markets Granger-caused volatility in the US market for four Asian countries during the Asian financial crisis period. Similarly, we also find that volatility in the US stock market Granger-caused volatility in Asian stock markets during the subprime crisis period. To capture the volatility causality in a VAR-GARCH model, we chose the specification in which off-diagonal components of the **A** matrix in Equation (4) are nonzero. However, the cross-coefficients of lagged squared residuals are not statistically significant for three Asian stock markets in the Asian financial crisis. We suspect that this failure to capture the volatility spillover effect may be caused by a misspecification in GARCH components. Alternatively, we estimated the STC-VAR-GARCH model with a nonzero off-diagonal **B** matrix.

$$\begin{bmatrix} h_{11,t} \\ h_{22,t} \end{bmatrix} = \begin{bmatrix} w_1 \\ w_2 \end{bmatrix} + \begin{bmatrix} a_{11} & 0 \\ 0 & a_{22} \end{bmatrix} \begin{bmatrix} \varepsilon_{1t-1}\varepsilon_{1t-1} \\ \varepsilon_{2t-1}\varepsilon_{2t-1} \end{bmatrix} + \begin{bmatrix} b_{11} & 0 \\ b_{21} & b_{22} \end{bmatrix} \begin{bmatrix} h_{11,t-1} \\ h_{22,t-1} \end{bmatrix}. \tag{23}$$

Table 7 provides the estimated result of the STC-VAR-GARCH model with Equation (23) for Malaysia, the Philippines, and Thailand during the Asian financial crisis. Volatility spillover effects from Asia to the United States are supported by this alternative specification. The estimated coefficients for b_{21} are statistically significant at the 1% level for the Philippines and Thailand and at the 5% level for Malaysia. Interestingly, for the Philippines and Thailand, the sign of volatility spillover is negative, although the magnitude is very small.[6]

It is noteworthy that the estimates for other parameters are both qualitatively and quantitatively similar to previous estimates. The only exceptions are parameters regarding the variance of the US stock market, that is, w_2 and b_{22}. The results for mean causality and correlation shifts continue to hold for the alternative specification of volatility spillovers.

---

[6] For the Philippines and Thailand, we also obtained similar results for the volatility spillover effect, even when we used the specification that allowed both a_{21} and b_{21} to be nonzero simultaneously.

Table 7. STC-VAR-GARCH estimators (robustness check)

	Malaysia	Philippines	Thailand
α_1	−0.066	−0.030	−0.388
	(0.077)	(0.087)	(0.149)***
α_2	0.147	0.209	0.180
	(0.072)**	(0.066)***	(0.066)***
β_{11}	0.116	0.206	0.145
	(0.063)*	(0.054)***	(0.066)**
β_{12}	0.034	0.144	0.037
	(0.057)	(0.076)*	(0.106)
β_{21}	−0.005	−0.006	0.021
	(0.026)	(0.029)	(0.023)
β_{22}	0.003	−0.046	−0.042
	(0.060)	(0.056)	(0.055)
w_1	0.049	0.281	4.045
	(0.033)	(0.127)**	(1.308)***
w_2	1.624	0.166	0.134
	(0.303)***	(0.065)**	(0.040)***
a_{11}	0.262	0.309	0.292
	(0.049)***	(0.064)***	(0.163)*
a_{22}	0.161	0.090	0.071
	(0.056)***	(0.027)***	(0.026)***
b_{11}	0.797	0.703	0.371
	(0.028)***	(0.051)***	(0.203)*
b_{22}	−0.102	0.861	0.920
	(0.137)	(0.040)***	(0.026)***
b_{21}	0.028	−0.007	−0.009
	(0.012)**	(0.002)***	(0.003)***
gm_0	19.161	11.602	6.795
	(17.482)	(17.171)	(5.027)
cc_0	−0.707	0.375	0.337
	(0.033)***	(0.090)***	(0.181)*
pp_0	0.771	0.055	−0.117
	(0.133)***	(0.099)	(0.114)
pp_1	0.220	0.599	0.430
	(0.071)***	(0.101)***	(0.114)***
LL	−1501.4	−1490.2	−1621.1

Note: The coefficients are estimated for Equations (1), (2), (5), (19), (20), (21), (22), and (23) by maximizing the quasi-likelihood. The figures in parentheses are standard deviations calculated from numeric second derivatives. LL is log likelihood. Statistical significance at the 1%, 5% and 10% levels is indicated by ***,** and *, respectively.

5.2. Volatility causality in tranquil period

By applying Hong's test to stock market returns in the US and Asian countries during two crises, we found evidence that volatility causality runs from the crisis-originating country to the rest of world. However, we cannot claim that volatility causality across stock markets only arises or increases in crisis period unless we show that there is no volatility causality in a tranquil period.

Defining a tranquil period is as difficult as defining a crisis period. Therefore, we proceed by using several subsamples that do not overlap with two crisis periods, according to our definitions. We also maintained the length of the sample period to be the same 33 months, which is used for the length of each crisis period. We also intend to leave a sufficient time gap from either crisis period and avoid the period of turbulence that began in March 2000 when the dot-com bubble burst and proceeded to the terrorist attacks that occurred in September 2001. Then, we are left with three overlapping periods: June 2002 to December 2004, June 2003 to December 2005, and June 2004 to December 2006. It is noteworthy that this pervasiveness of US volatility Granger-causality is consistent with the findings in Cheung *et al.* (2007).

The Hong test on the first subsample (June 2002 to December 2004) indicated that there is only volatility causality from the United States to Asia in four countries. We suspect that this first subsample is still affected by the 9/11 attack and consequent turbulence in the US stock market. In the third subsample (June 2004 to December 2006), the Hong test also indicates that the US stock market volatility Granger-causes volatility in two Asian countries but not vice versa. This volatility causality may be associated with market participants' fear of upcoming collapse of subprime loans, especially after the peak of housing prices was reached in July of 2006.

Most interestingly, during the second subsample period (June 2003 to December 2005), we do not find volatility causality for any countries in either direction. This period is, in broad terms, furthest away from any turbulent incidents in financial markets. By finding no volatility causality in a tranquil period, our previous results on volatility causality directions during a crisis period are fortified.

5.3. Tests of constancy of correlation

We rejected the null hypothesis of constancy of correlation for most of the countries in both crises, according to the IMe statistics proposed by Bera and Kim (2002). However, LMC could not reject the constancy of correlation for any country in either crisis, and IMs could reject the null hypothesis for four countries in the Asian crisis and one country in the subprime crisis, but only at the 10% significance level. Regarding the different results obtained from these three test statistics, we need to consider the simulation results when the data are generated from the

t-distribution in Bera and Kim (2002). IMe rejects the hypothesis of constancy of correlation for 22.5% at the nominal significance level of 1% under t-distribution for the sample size of 400 with constant correlation of 0.5, whereas IMs rejects for only 0.32%. Given the voluminous evidence of the fat-tailedness of financial time series, the strong rejection of constancy of correlation by IMe test statistics in Table 3 is due to nonnormal distribution of innovations in stock markets. This concern leaves us to rely more on the results of the LMC and IMs. Still, consistently with our previous results, the evidence provided by IMs indicates that a correlation shift is more pervasive during the Asian crisis than during the subprime crisis; it includes rejection of the null for four countries and one country, respectively.

6. Conclusions

The recent subprime financial crisis initially affected the Asian economy to a degree comparable to that of the 1997 Asian crisis, although the epicenters of the two crises were different. Reinhart and Rogoff (2008, 2009a, 2009b) demonstrate that all past financial crises share striking similarities in the run-up of asset prices, debt accumulation, growth patterns, and current account deficits, although each crisis is distinctively different. While the current crisis may follow the same pattern for the United States, the contagion effect on Asia may not be the same as in past experience. We investigate whether or not the effects of the subprime financial crisis on 12 Asian economies are similar to those of the previous crisis by examining the mean causality, volatility causality, and correlation between the US and Asian stock markets. We find three interesting features regarding the relationship of Asian economies with the United States.

First, the empirical evidence indicates stark differences between these two crises. The volatility causality runs from the crisis-originating country. Evidence of volatility-causality from Asian economies to the United States is found during the Asian financial crisis, whereas volatility of the US market Granger-caused volatility in the Asian market during the recent subprime financial crisis.

Second, the correlation decreased during the financial turmoil for some countries in both crises. This decreased correlation was more pervasive for the Asian crisis period. An important implication can be drawn from this evidence. With respect to international investment diversification, the benefits of risk management are higher among financial products with low (or even negative) correlations. Our result indicates that the benefit of international investment diversification between the United States and Asia was higher after the Asian financial crisis. However, we need to remain conservative on this statement because the statistical significance of the shift in correlation is not overwhelming.

Third, a transition in correlation took place well in advance of the largest impact of September 2008 during the subprime financial crisis as well as in July 1997 during the Asian crisis. This result is indicative of market participants' awareness of the upcoming stock market crash well before the collapse of government-sponsored enterprises and investment banks.

According to the evidence in this chapter and subject to limitations due to the preliminary nature of the results, the spillover or contagion effect on Asian markets of the subprime financial crisis originating in the United States presents a striking difference from past experience during the Asian financial crisis in 1997. This difference may come from the fact that Asia learned the lesson from its past experience to adopt faster, larger, and more effective policy measures than other regions in the world.

Alternatively, we can also argue that the increased integration of anticrisis measures in the region, such as a multilateral currency swap arrangement under the Chiang Mai Initiatives, may have helped Asian markets to be better prepared for the second crisis. In fact, using stock market returns, there are numerous studies which find the degree of regional integration among Asian economies increased (Majid *et al.*, 2008; Awokuse *et al.*, 2009; Baur and Fry, 2009; Khan and Park, 2009).[7] These studies employ various econometric methodologies such as bilateral time-varying correlations and the cointegration approach. Despite the differences in econometric approaches, most of the studies indicate that the degree of market integration among Asian economies increased either during or after the Asian crisis period.

Acknowledgments

I would like to thank an anonymous referee, Seung C. Ahn, Yin-Wong Cheung, Taufiq Choudhry, Taro Esaka, Alexander Hoffmaister, Yoshitsugu Kitazawa, and Tatsuyoshi Miyakoshi for their helpful comments on the earlier version of this draft "Is this time different for Asia?: Evidence from stock markets." This research is financially supported by a Grant-in-Aid for Scientific Research (C)(22530253) from JSPS.

[7] There are also empirical studies that examine real components of the economy in the Asian region. By applying a dynamic factor model to macroeconomic variables for 10 Asian economies, Moneta and Rffer (2009) find that the degree of synchronization increased in Asia.

References

Awokuse, T.O., Chopra, A., Bessler, D.A. (2009), Structural change and international stock market interdependence: evidence from Asian emerging markets. *Economic Modeling* 26, 549–559.

Baur, D.G., Fry, R.A. (2009), Multivariate contagion and interdependence. *Journal of Asian Economics* 20, 353–366.

Bekeart, G., Harvey, C.R. (1997), Emerging equity market volatility. *Journal of Financial Economics* 43, 29–77.

Bera, A.K., Kim, S. (2002), Testing constancy of correlation and other specifications of the BGARCH model with an application to international equity returns. *Journal of Empirical Finance* 9, 171–195.

Berben, R.P., Jansen, W.J. (2005), Comovement in international equity markets: a sectoral view. *Journal of International Money and Finance* 24, 832–857.

Bollerslev, T. (1988), On the correlation structure for the generalized autoregressive conditional heteroskesastic process. *Journal of Time Series Analysis* 9, 121–131.

Bollerslev, T. (1990), Modeling the coherence in short-run nominal exchange rates: a multivariate generalized ARCH model. *Review of Economics and Statistics* 72, 498–505.

Bollerslev, T., Engle, R.F., Wooldridge, J.M. (1988), A capital asset pricing model with time-varying covariances. *Journal of Political Economy* 96 (1), 116–131.

Chan, L., Lien, D., Weng, W. (2008), Financial interdependence between Hong Kong and the US: a band spectrum approach. *International Review of Economics and Finance* 17, 507–516.

Cheung, Y.L., Cheung, Y.W., Ng, C.C. (2007), East Asian equity markets, financial crises, and the Japanese currency. *Journal of the Japanese and International Economics* 21, 138–152.

Cheung, Y.W., Ng, L.L. (1996), A causality-in-variance test and its application to financial market prices. *Journal of Econometrics* 72, 33–48.

Corsetti, G., Pericoli, M., Sbracia, M. (2005), 'Some contagion, some interdependence': more pitfalls in tests of financial contagion. *Journal of International Economics* 24, 1177–1199.

Cuadro-Sáez, L., Fratzscher, M., Thimann, C. (2009), The transmission of emerging market shocks to global equity markets. *Journal of Empirical Finance* 16, 2–17.

Davies, R.B. (1977), Hypothesis testing when a nuisance parameter is present only under the alternative. *Biometrika* 64 (2), 247–254.

Edwards, S. (2000), Contagion. *World Economy* 23, 873–900.

Forbes, K.J., Rigobon, R. (2001), Measuring Contagion: Conceptual and Empirical Issues. In: Claessens, S., Forbes, K. (Eds.), International Financial Contagion, World Bank, Washington, DC.

Forbes, K.J., Rigobon, R. (2002), No contagion, only interdependence: measuring stock market comovements. *Journal of Finance* 57 (5), 2223–2261.

Hansen, B.E. (1996), Inferences when a nuisance parameter is not identified under the null hypothesis. *Econometrica* 64 (2), 413–430.

Hong, Y. (2001), A test for volatility spillover with application to exchange rates. *Journal of Econometrics* 103, 183–224.

International Monetary Fund. (2009), *Regional Economic Outlook: Asia and Pacific*, October issue, IMF, Washington, DC.

International Monetary Fund. (2010), *World Economic Outlook*, IMF, Washington, DC.

Jensen, A.T., Lange, T. (2010), On convergence of the QMLE for misspecified GARCH models. *Journal of Time Series Econometrics* 2 (1), 1–29, Article 3.

Khan, S., Park, K.W. (2009), Contagion in the stock markets: the Asian Financial crisis revisited. *Journal of Asian Economics* 20, 561–569.

Kim, S.J. (2005), Information leadership in the advanced Asia-Pacific stock markets: return, volatility and volume information spillovers from the US and Japan. *Journal of the Japanese and International Economics* 19, 338–365.

King, M.A., Wadhwani, S. (1990), Transmission of volatility between stock markets. *The Review of Financial Studies* 3 (1), 5–33.

Lin, C.F.J., Terasvirta, T. (1994), Testing the constancy of regression parameters against continuous structural change. *Journal of Econometrics* 62, 211–228.

Ling, S., McAleer, M. (2003), Asymptotic theory for a vector ARMA-GARCH model. *Econometric Theory* 19, 280–310.

Majid, M.S.A., Meera, A.K.M., Omar, M.A. (2008), Interdependence of ASEAN-5 stock markets from the US and Japan. *Global Economic Review* 37 (2), 201–225.

Moneta, F., Rüffer, R. (2009), Business cycle synchronization in East Asia. *Journal of Asian Economics* 20, 1–12.

Ng, A. (2000), Volatility spillover effects from Japan and the US to the Pacific-Basin. *Journal of International Money and Finance* 19, 207–233.

Reinhart, C.M., Rogoff, K.S. (2008), Is the 2007 US sub-prime financial crisis so different? An international historical comparison. *American Economic Review* 98 (2), 339–344.

Reinhart, C.M., Rogoff, K.S. (2009a), The aftermath of financial crisis. *American Economic Review* 99 (2), 466–472.

Reinhart, C.M., Rogoff, K.S. (2009b), *This Time is Different: Eight Centuries of Financial Folly*. Princeton University Press, Princeton, PA.

Rigobon, R. (2003), Identification through heteroskedasticity. *Review of Economics and Statistics* 85 (4), 777–792.

Tse, Y.K. (2000), A test for constant correlations in a multivariate GARCH model. *Journal of Econometrics* 98 (1), 107–127.

Yi, Z., Tan, S.L. (2009), An empirical analysis of stock market integration: comparison study of Singapore and Malaysia. *The Singapore Economic Review* 54 (2), 217–232.

Yoshida, Y. (2009). Financial crisis, exchange rate and stock market integration. Kyushu Sangyo University, Discussion Paper No. 38.

CHAPTER 4

The Link between FX Swaps and Currency Strength during the Credit Crisis of 2007–2008

Hans Genberg[a], Cho-Hoi Hui[b], Alfred Wong[b] and Tsz-Kin Chung[b]

[a]*Independent Evaluation Office, International Monetary Fund, N.W., Washington DC, USA*
E-mail address: hgenberg@imf.org
[b]*Research Department, Hong Kong Monetary Authority, Hong Kong, China*
E-mail address: chhui@hkma.gov.hk; alfred_yt_wong@hkma.gov.hk; btkchung@hkma.gov.hk

Abstract
This chapter analyses the impact of the global credit crisis on the money market and discusses its potential implications. The turbulence in money markets has spilled over to foreign exchange (FX)-swap markets amid a reappraisal of counterparty risks during the recent financial turmoil. We examine the situations of six currencies: the euro, the British pound, the Australian dollar, the Japanese yen, the Hong Kong dollar, and the Singapore dollar. We find that (i) the risk premiums have indeed gone in tandem with the spreads of money market rates over their corresponding overnight index swaps across the economies, a popular measure of potential banking insolvency; and (ii) the risk premiums bear a negative relationship with the strength of the spot rates of the respective currencies, which is consistent with the increased pressure in the money and swap markets.

Keywords: FX swaps, covered interest parity, counterparty risk

JEL classifications: F31, G15

1. Introduction

The abrupt escalation of the recent global credit crisis last September marked an important turning point for many currencies. Those that had exhibited remarkable strength in early 2008 (e.g., the British pound, the euro, the Australia dollar) depreciated abruptly, while others (e.g., the Japanese yen, the Hong Kong dollar) rallied strongly. At the same time, unusual pricing behavior occurred in the money and foreign exchange (FX)-swap markets, revealing significant and persistent departure from covered interest parity, a well-established and well-tested theory in

Frontiers of Economics and Globalization
Volume 9 ISSN: 1574-8715
DOI: 10.1108/S1574-8715(2011)0000009009

international finance. What messages are these atypical phenomena sending us? This chapter attempts to shed light on these questions by looking at the FX-swap market more closely and finding that the two phenomena appear to be linked.

2. Covered interest parity in financial turmoil

The interest parity theory states that the equilibrium forward exchange rate F is:

$$F = \frac{S(1+r)}{(1+q)}, \tag{1}$$

where S is the spot exchange rate (the domestic currency value of a unit of the US dollar), r and q are, respectively, the domestic and the US dollar rates of interest on securities that are identical in all respects except for the currency of denomination. The market forward exchange rate F^* gives a swap-implied US dollar interest rate q^*. Therefore, the return of investing a sum of money in a domestic interest-bearing asset for a certain period of time is the same as the return of investing in a similar foreign interest-bearing asset by converting the sum into a foreign currency while simultaneously purchasing a futures contract to convert the investment back at the end of the period. If the returns are different, an arbitrage transaction could, in theory, produce a risk-free return.

It is important to note that covered interest parity assumes that assets denominated in domestic and foreign currency are freely traded internationally (i.e., no capital controls) and have negligible transaction costs and similar risks. Given today's technology, these assumptions normally hold in the international financial markets, and so the parity condition is observed almost all the time (except for those countries where capital controls are still in place). However, there are times and situations in which the condition breaks down. Taylor (1989) finds that during the floating of the sterling in 1972 and the inception of the European Monetary System in 1979, significant departure had occurred from covered interest parity for periods long enough to challenge the theory.[1]

One possibility is that in times of financial turmoil, true risks, or risks as perceived by market participants, might have changed, rendering the assumptions of covered interest parity inapplicable. Indeed, a recent BIS study by Baba and Packer (2009) finds that in the recent global financial crisis the turbulence in money markets has spilled over to FX-swap markets amid a reappraisal of counterparty risks.[2] The spillover occurred,

---

[1] Other studies have attempted to rationalize these departures in terms of transactions costs, for example, Frenkel and Levich (1977) and Clinton (1988).

[2] The chapter covers the study until September 12, 2008, that is, before the Lehman default.

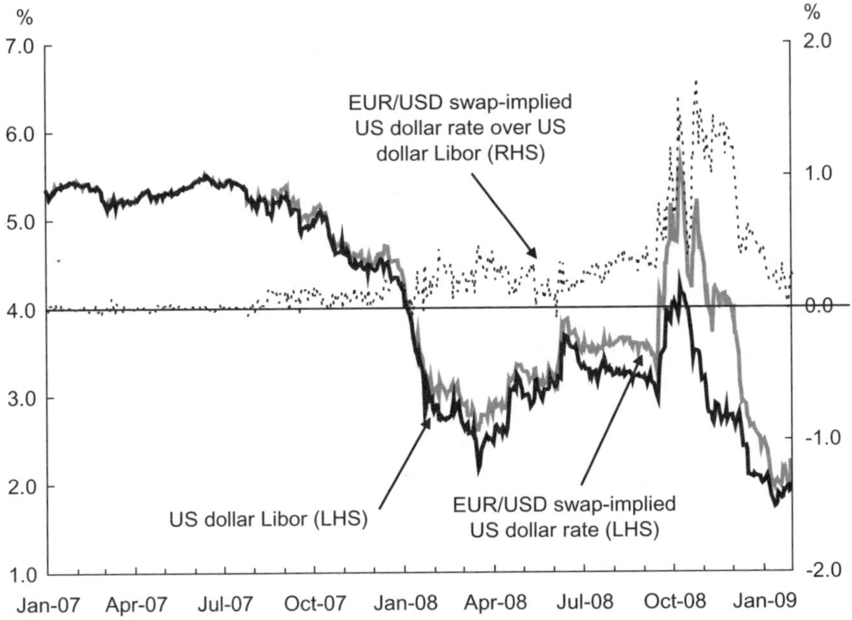

Fig. 1. ***12-month FX-swap-implied US dollar rate from euro.***

as European banks needed to secure US dollar funding to support their US conduits, while US banks – also facing increased financing difficulties and having to preserve funds on hand – became cautious in lending to their European counterparts, forcing the latter to resort to converting euros into dollars in the swap market. As soon as European banks (borrowers), perhaps with the exception of the well-known members on the London Interbank Offered Rate (LIBOR) panel, were perceived to be riskier by US banks (lenders), a risk premium quickly developed, adding to the dollar funding rates in the swap.

In Figure 1, the dotted line measures how much the implied 12-month US dollar funding rate deviates from the corresponding LIBOR – the risk premium demanded by dollar lenders in the swap market or the departure from covered interest parity.[3,4] As can be seen, before the summer 2007 it oscillated around 0% but after that it started to follow an upward trend. Around the beginning of September 2008, it shot up and fluctuated widely. Baba and Packer focus on the shorter end of the market in their study, and their findings yield similar results. Using credit default swap (CDS) spreads and LIBOR-overnight index swap (OIS) spreads as proxies, they find evidence that an increase in counterparty risks of European banks in general

[3] The three-month contracts show similar results.

[4] The data used in this chapter are from Bloomberg. While interbank interest rates are in general bank specific, this study uses LIBORs that are the aggregate rates of panels of banks.

was the main driving force behind the departure from the parity condition during the turmoil.[5] The LIBOR-OIS spread is commonly used as a measure of market perceptions of potential insolvency of counterparties, that is, a higher LIBOR-OIS spread implies higher counterparties' default risk.[6]

3. Effects of counterparty risks on deviations from covered interest parity

As compared to financial crises in the past, one of the distinct characteristics of this crisis is how the resulting increase in counterparty risks paralyses the money market. The significance of the Baba–Packer study lies in the uncovering of the mechanism in which the rise in counterparty risks among European banks as a result of the turmoil feeds through from the money to the swap market. Given that European banks are not alone in this global crisis, the same should also be observed in economies where financial institutions also suffered from a rise in counterparty risks. In Figure 2, we plot the deviations of the various currencies' swap-implied US dollar funding rates from the corresponding LIBOR (or Hong Kong Interbank Offered Rate, HIBOR).

If Baba and Packer are right in pointing out that what recently happened in the swap market reflects essentially a rise in counterparty risks spilling over from the money market, the amount of premium or discount as reflected in the swap-implied US dollar funding rates of different FX swaps can be taken a measure of relative risk of the banking sectors of the economies concerned. The results of such measure should be supported by the evidence in the LIBOR-OIS spread that reflects market perceptions of potential banking insolvency.[7] The LIBOR-OIS spread indirectly measure the availability of funds in the interbank market. The spreads reflect the aggregate counterparty risk of the financial institutions in the economy. The rise in spreads represents heightened perceived default risk or higher premium demanded by risk-averse investors against the risk

---

[5] An OIS is a currency-specific interest rate swap in which the floating leg is linked to an index of daily overnight rates. The two parties agree to exchange at maturity, on an agreed notional amount, the difference between interest accrued at the agreed fixed rate and interest accrued at the floating index rate over the life of the swap. The fixed rate is a proxy for expected future overnight interest rates. As overnight lending generally bears lower credit and liquidity risks, the credit risk and liquidity risk premiums contained in the overnight index swap rates should be small. By contrast, an interbank loan is an unsecured lending and is subjected to both credit and liquidity risks. Therefore, the spread of the 12-month LIBOR relative to 12-month OIS rate generally reflects the credit and liquidity risks of the interbank market.

[6] See an article written by Alan Greenspan in the last 2008 issue of *The Economist*, advocating the use of the LIBOR-OIS spread as a measure of market perceptions of extra capital needs for banks.

[7] The CDS market only covers a few banks in Hong Kong and Singapore. Therefore, their CDS spreads do not represent the risk of the banking sectors as a whole.

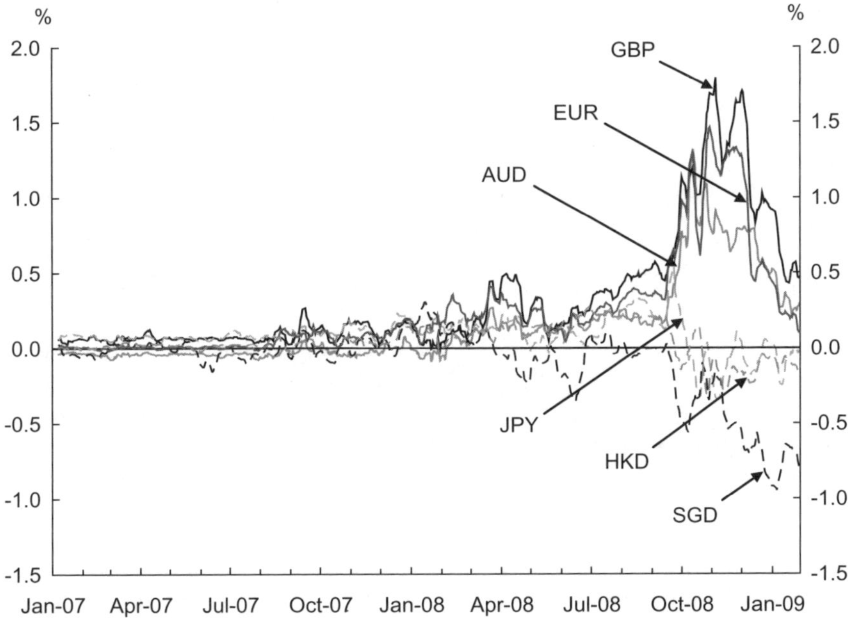

***Fig. 2.* Deviations of 12-month FX-swaps-implied US dollar rate from dollar LIBOR. Note: Five-day moving average of daily data. The currencies included are: the euro (EUR), British pound (GBP), Australian dollar (AUD), Japanese yen (JPY), Hong Kong dollar (HKD), and Singapore dollar (SGD).**

of default.[8] The 12-month LIBOR (or HIBOR)-OIS spreads of the respective economies in Figure 3 clearly show that the banking sectors in the United States, the Euro area, the United Kingdom, and Australia had a substantial higher default risk than that in Hong Kong, Japanese, and Singapore in the last quarter of 2008. These observations are consistent with the premium or discount as reflected in the swap-implied US dollar funding rates of different FX swaps.

To test statistically whether the changes of the differences between the LIBOR-OIS spreads of the currencies concerned and the US dollar had effects on the changes and volatility of their FX-swap deviations, we employ the EGARCH(1,1) model proposed by Nelson (1991) to test their data series from August 9, 2007 to March 31, 2009.[9] Table 1 shows that the series are not stationary in level but are stationary in the first difference

---

[8] Taylor and Williams (2009) find that counterparty risk is a key factor in the movements of the term-lending spreads including LIBOR-OIS spreads.

[9] This follows Taylor and Williams (2008, 2009) to choose August 9, 2007 to mark the inception of the turmoil, when BNP Paribas frozen redemptions for three of its investment funds.

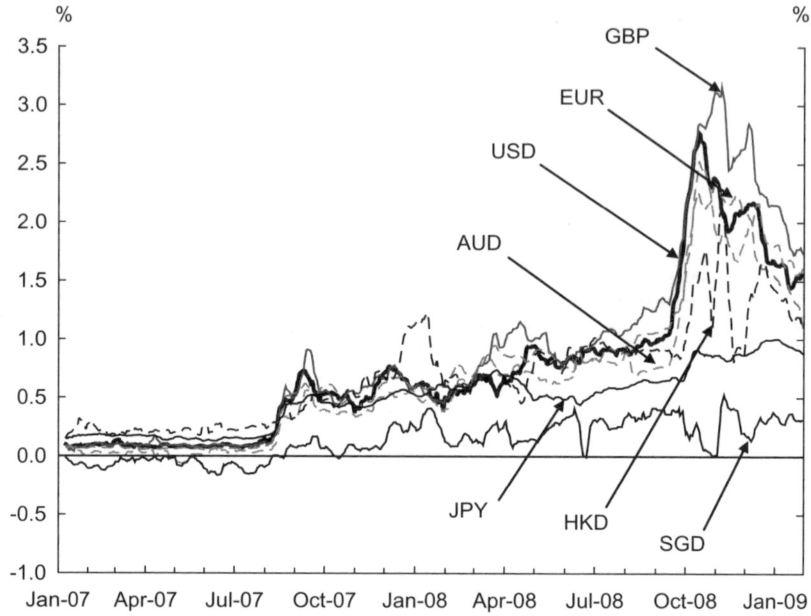

***Fig. 3.** 12-month LIBOR (HIBOR)-OIS spreads. Notes: (1) Five-day moving average of daily data. The currencies included are: the US dollar (USD), euro (EUR), British pound (GBP), Australian dollar (AUD), Japanese yen (JPY), Hong Kong dollar (HKD), and Singapore dollar (SGD). (2) For Hong Kong and Singapore, the interbank rates are Hong Kong Interbank Offered Rate (HIBOR) and Singapore Interbank Offered Rate (SIBOR), respectively.*

according to the augmented Dickey–Fuller test. The EGARCH(1,1) model in the first difference we use can be written as[10]

Mean equation:

$$\Delta \text{FXdev}_t = a + b\Delta \text{LSS}_t + \varepsilon_t, \tag{2}$$

where

$$\text{FXdev}_t = \frac{S_t}{F_t^*}(1 + r_t) - (1 + q_t) \equiv q_t^* - q_t$$

and

$$\text{LSS}_t = (\text{LIBOR-OIS})_t^{\text{FC}} - (\text{LIBOR-OIS})_t^{\text{USD}}.$$

[10] The specification assumes that the FX-swap spread has negligible feedback effect on the LIBOR-OIS spread.

Table 1. Augmented Dickey–Fuller test on the variables of Equation (2)

Currency	FX-swap deviation ($FXdev_t$)		LIBOR-OIS spread (LSS_t)	
	Level	Daily change	Level	Daily change
GBP	−2.600*	−5.161***	−2.647*	−5.520***
EUR	−2.173	−3.995***	−2.306	−4.796***
AUD	−2.237	−4.147***	−2.326	−6.702***
JPY	−2.273	−5.934***	−2.106	−4.465***
HKD	−0.445	−5.780***	−2.191	−5.681***
SGD	−0.789	−5.529***	−2.302	−5.237***

Notes:

1. The sample period is from August 9, 2007 to March 31, 2009.
2. ADF statistics are from the Augmented Dickey–Fuller unit root test. The critical ADF values at the 10%, 5%, and 1% significance level are −2.57, −2.87, and −3.44, respectively.
3. *, **, and *** indicate significant at 10%, 5%, and 1% levels, respectively.
4. The lag length of the ADF test is selected according to the Schwarz Information Criteria with maximum lags of 16.

Variance equation:

$$\varepsilon_t \sim N(0, \sigma_t^2)$$

$$\ln(\sigma_t^2) = \alpha + \beta \ln(\sigma_{t-1}^2) + \gamma \frac{\varepsilon_{t-1}}{\sigma_{t-1}} + \eta \left(\left| \frac{\varepsilon_{t-1}}{\sigma_{t-1}} \right| - \sqrt{\frac{2}{\pi}} \right) \quad (3)$$

If the relative risk of the banking systems of the economies concerned is a determinant of the premium or discount as reflected in the swap-implied US dollar funding rates of different FX swaps, the coefficient b in Equation (2) should be positive and statistically significant.

The results in Table 2 show the coefficients b for the six currencies are positive and significant at the 1% level.[11] This indicates that under the turmoil, FX-swap deviations in the euro, the pound, and the Australian dollar tended to widen upward when counterparty risk was heightened for the financial institution in these economies relative to US counterparts. On the other hand, the deviations in the Hong Kong dollar, the yen, and the Singapore dollar tended to go downward as counterparty risk of the financial institutions in these economies were perceived to low relative to US counterparts.

[11] The estimation results based on the two subsamples of data (i.e., before and after the Lehman failure, respectively) are qualitatively the same. Nevertheless, the adjusted R-squares for the post-Lehman failure period is lower, possibly due to the unprecedented policy measures taken by central banks during this period of time. The impact of these policy measures on the FX-swap market is beyond the scope of this chapter.

Table 2. ***Estimation results of EGARCH(1,1) model***

Currency	Mean equation		Variance equation				Ljung–Box test up to lag 24		
	a	*b*	*a*	*b*	*g*	*h*	Standardized residuals (*P*-value)	Squared standardized residuals (*P*-value)	Adj. R^2
GBP	0.0006	0.883**	−0.694**	0.953**	0.163	0.537**	18.324	16.548	0.721
	(0.002)	(0.023)	(0.224)	(0.024)	(0.086)	(0.134)	(0.787)	(0.867)	
EUR	0.002	0.853**	−0.363	0.984**	0.161	0.398*	16.055	12.908	0.516
	(0.002)	(0.024)	(0.202)	(0.018)	(0.112)	(0.192)	(0.886)	(0.968)	
AUD	0.002	0.716**	−0.377**	0.970**	0.109	0.284**	36.734	18.137	0.469
	(0.003)	(0.034)	(0.101)	(0.016)	(0.066)	(0.071)	(0.047)	(0.796)	
JPY	−0.002	0.869**	−0.737*	0.940**	0.008	0.524*	30.997	21.77	0.431
	(0.003)	(0.023)	(0.331)	(0.037)	(0.096)	(0.226)	(0.154)	(0.593)	
HKD	0.001	0.397**	−0.737	0.929**	0.015	0.405**	43.559	40.534	0.430
	(0.002)	(0.027)	(0.312)	(0.046)	(0.085)	(0.084)	(0.009)	(0.019)	
SGD	−0.002	0.311**	−0.590	0.931**	−0.079	0.315**	45.693	26.748	0.162
	(0.003)	(0.029)	(0.318)	(0.053)	(0.082)	(0.099)	(0.005)	(0.316)	

Notes:

1. The sample period is from August 9, 2007 to March 31, 2009.
2. Numbers in parentheses are Bollerslev–Wooldrige robust standard errors. * and ** indicate significant at 5% and 1% levels, respectively.
3. The Ljung–Box test (Q-statistics) identifies whether the autocorrelations among data are jointly zero up to a specified lag. Accepting the null hypothesis of the test means the data is not serial correlated. The standardized residual is the residual divided by the estimated volatility. The number of lag is selected to be 24.
4. If the model fits well, the standardized residual will be serial uncorrelated and homoskedastic. If the mean equation is correctly specified, the Q-statistic of the standardized residual should not be significant; if the variance equation is correctly specified, the Q-statistics of the standardized residuals should not be significant.

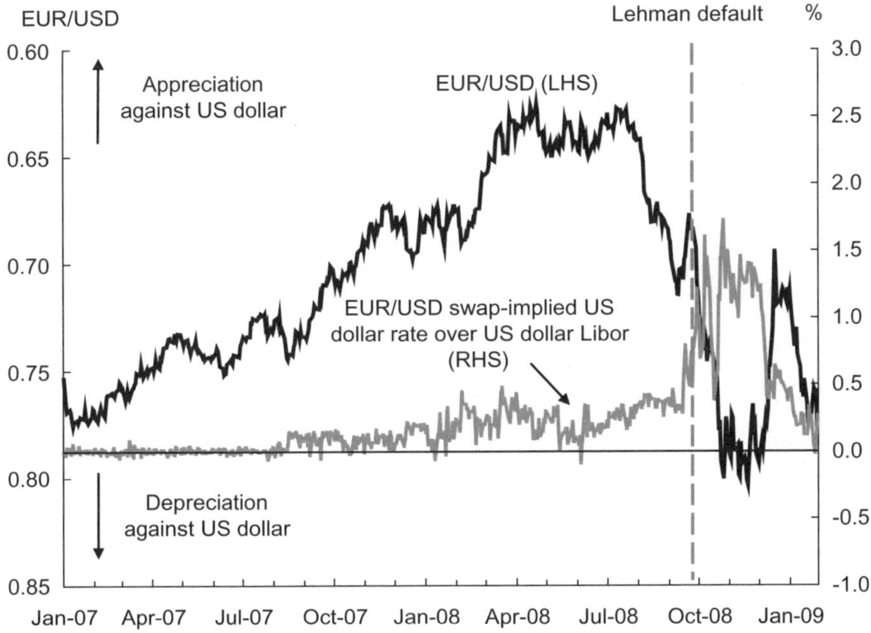

Fig. 4. Deviation of 12-month FX-swap-implied US dollar rate from dollar LIBOR and EUR/USD exchange rate.

Regarding the causality between the FX-swap deviations and the LIBOR-OIS spreads of the currencies, no evidence is found to support any causality between them based on the Granger causality test.

4. Deviations from covered interest parity and currency strength

The financial turmoil in turn has had a significant impact on the foreign exchange market – a feature of the crisis that so far has gone almost unnoticed by economists and policymakers. This section points out that the financial turmoil has led to a reappraisal of counterparty risks of different banking sectors, which has in turn led to fundamental changes in international currency markets.

As European banks resorted to converting their euros into dollars to meet their funding requirements, the euro began to depreciate rapidly. The euro had been on a long-term upward trend vis-à-vis the dollar before the news of the near-collapse of Bears Sterns in March 2008 (Figure 4). It had begun to stabilize since then. And when severe financial difficulties of Freddie and Fannie surfaced in around August 2008, it fell sharply.

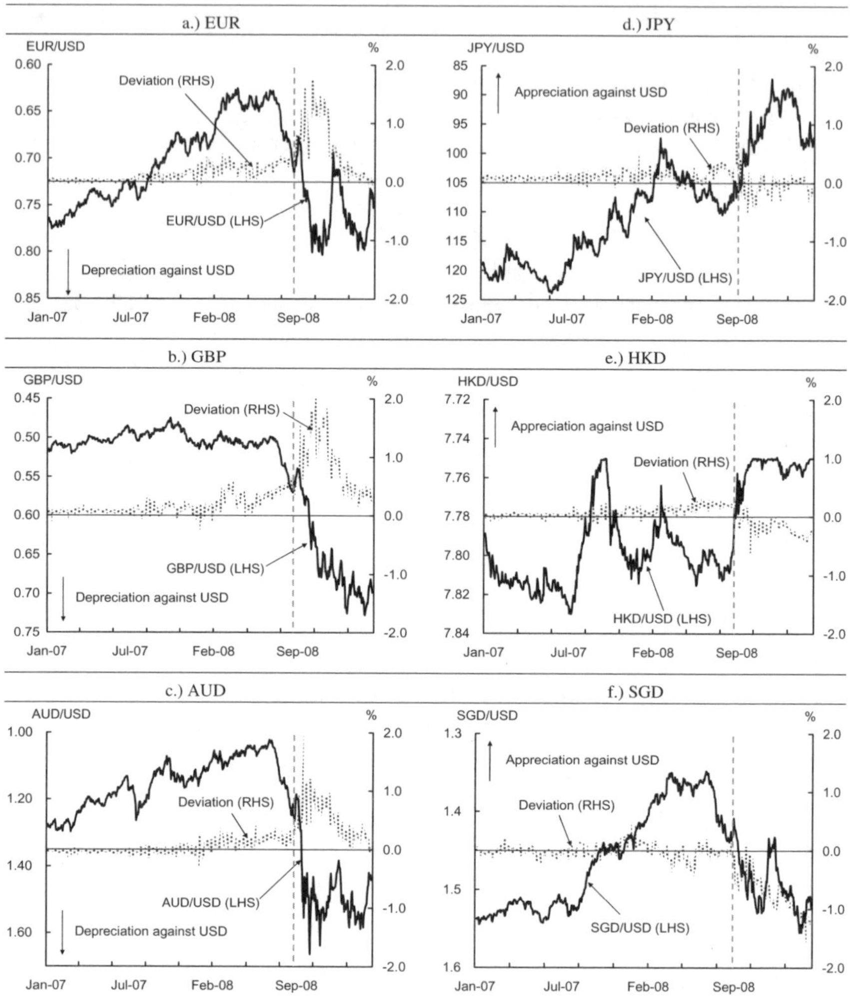

Fig. 5. Deviations of 12-month FX-swaps-implied US dollar rate from dollar LIBOR and their respective exchange rates.

In this global crisis, where economies' financial institutions also suffered from a rise in counterparty risks, their currencies should also experience sell-off to a similar extent. In Figure 5, we plot the deviations of the various currencies' swap-implied US dollar funding rates from the corresponding LIBOR and their exchange rates. As can be seen, some economies saw a significantly higher swap-implied funding rate over the US dollar LIBOR after mid-September 2008 and, at the same time, a sharply lower currency (i.e., the pound and the Australian dollar), while others enjoyed a swap-implied discount from the US dollar LIBOR and, at the same time, a much stronger currency (i.e., the yen and the Hong Kong dollar).[12]

Therefore, in contrast to European and Australian banks (which need to convert their currencies into US dollars to meet their funding requirements), Hong Kong, Japanese, and Singapore banks with swap-implied discounts from the US dollar LIBOR (i.e., with less default risk) attract financial institutions (probably US banks) with US dollars on hand to sell US dollars to these Asian banks at spot in the FX swaps.[13] In this connection, it becomes readily understandable why the yen and the Hong Kong dollar appreciated against the US dollar after the Lehman default. Having said that, Hui *et al.* (2009) find that the appreciation of the yen during the financial turmoil was partially attributed to the unwinding of carry trades.

5. Conclusion

This chapter analyses the impact of the global credit crisis on the money market and discusses its potential implications. A recent BIS study finds that the turbulence in money markets has spilled over to FX-swap markets amid a reappraisal of counterparty risks during the recent financial turmoil. The spillover occurred, as European banks needed to secure US dollar funding to support their US conduits while US banks were cautious in lending to them. This forced the European banks to resort to converting their euros into dollars in the swap market, giving rise to a risk premium in the dollar funding rates in the swap.

Our finding bears similarities with the Japan premium episode in the late 1990s when the creditworthiness of Japanese banks had substantially deteriorated. Given the extreme difficulty of raising US dollars in money markets, Japanese banks turned to FX-swap markets, which resulted in substantial deviations from covered interest parity (Covrig *et al.* 2004).

We extend the BIS analysis to examine the situations of five other currencies. We find that (i) the risk premiums have indeed gone in tandem with the spreads of money market rates over their corresponding OISs across the economies, a popular measure of potential banking insolvency and (ii) the risk premiums bear a negative relationship with the strength of the spot rates of the respective currencies, which is consistent with the increased pressure in the swap markets. The implication of the analysis is that the directions of fund flows among different economies may reflect the relative safety and soundness of their banking systems during the credit crisis period.

---

[12] The picture is less clear for the Singapore dollar. This may be due to the monetary policy for a stable Singapore dollar in effective terms (see Section 3 in Ma and McCauley (2009) for the discussion on the evolution of the Singapore dollar).

[13] The counterparty risk at the forward legs of the swaps is also relative low for these Asian banks.

Acknowledgments

The authors gratefully acknowledge Naohiko Baba, Charles Calomiris, Yin-Wong Cheung, Anella Munro, Giorgio Valente, Shang-Jin Wei, and the participants at the conferences on "The Global Financial Turmoil and the Evolving Financial Interdependence in Asia" organized by Columbia University, Lingnan University and the Hong Kong Institute for Monetary Research, and "Exchange Rate Systems and Currency Markets in Asia" organized by Keio University, Financial Services Agency, and the Asian Development Bank Institute for their helpful suggestions and comments on the chapter. The conclusions herein do not represent the views of the Hong Kong Monetary Authority.

References

Baba, N., Packer, F. (2009), Interpreting derivations from covered interest parity during the financial market turmoil of 2007–2008. *Journal of Banking and Finance* 33 (11), 1953–1962.

Clinton, K. (1988), Transaction costs and covered interest arbitrage: theory and evidence. *Journal of Political Economy* 96, 358–370.

Covrig, V., Low, B.S., Melvin, M. (2004), A yen is not a yen: TIBOR/LIBOR and the determinants of the Japan premium. *Journal of Financial and Quantitative Analysis* 39, 193–208.

Frenkel, J.A., Levich, R.M. (1977), Transaction costs and interest arbitrage: tranquil versus turbulent periods. *Journal of Political Economy* 85, 1209–1226.

Hui, C.H., Genberg, H., Chung, T.K. (2009), Liquidity, risk appetite and exchange rate movements during the financial crisis of 2007–2009. HKMA Working Paper 11/2009, Hong Kong Monetary Authority.

Ma, G., McCauley, R.N. (2009), The evolving renminbi regime and implications for Asian currency stability. BIS Working Paper No 321, Bank of International Settlement.

Nelson, B. (1991), Conditional heteroskedasticity in asset returns: a new approach. *Econometrica* 59, 347–370.

Taylor, M. (1989), Covered interest arbitrage and market turbulence. *Economic Journal* 99, 376–391.

Taylor, J.B., Williams, J.C. (2008), Further results on a black swan in the money market. SIEPR Discussion Paper No. 07-046, Stanford Institute for Economic Policy Research, Stanford University.

Taylor, J.B., Williams, J.C. (2009), A black swan in the money market. *American Economic Journal: Macroeconomics* 1 (1), 58–83.

PART II

Regional Monetary Cooperation

CHAPTER 5

The Implications of Renminbi Basket Management for Asian Currency Stability

Guonan Ma[a] and Robert N McCauley[b]

[a]*Bank for International Settlements, Representative Office for Asia and the Pacific, 78/F International Financial Centre Two, 8 Finance Street, Central, Hong Kong*
E-mail address: guonan.ma@bis.org
[b]*Bank for International Settlements, Monetary and Economics Department, Centralbahnpltz 2, CH-402, Basel, Switzerland*
E-mail address: robert.mccauley@bis.org

Abstract
The renminbi (RMB) has evolved in four phases since its mid-2005 unpegging from the US dollar. After a year's transition, the RMB's *effective* exchange rate traded for two years within narrow bands around an appreciating trend. That is, the RMB behaved as if it were managed to strengthen gradually against trading partners' currencies. This experiment was interrupted in mid-2008 and the RMB stabilized against a strong dollar amidst the global financial crisis. If Chinese policy were to return to effective currency stability and other East Asian countries were to pursue similar policies, regional currency stability would be enhanced. That would create more favorable conditions for an evolution towards monetary cooperation.

Keywords: Exchange rate regime, exchange rate policy, effective exchange rate, renminbi, Asian currencies, currency basket weights, regional currency stability, regional monetary cooperation

JEL classifications: F31, F33

1. Introduction

In July 2005, the People's Bank of China (PBC) announced that the renminbi (RMB) was unpegged from the US dollar and that the currency would be managed "with reference to a basket of currencies" (PBC, 2005). This statement has since been doubted, both in principle and in practice. Citing China's relatively closed economy, McCallum (2006) concludes: "In

Frontiers of Economics and Globalization
Volume 9 ISSN: 1574-8715
DOI: 10.1108/S1574-8715(2011)0000009010

sum, there is little or no reason to believe that a system like that of Singapore's will or has been adopted by China." Shah *et al.* (2006), Frankel and Wei (2007) and Ito (2008) find that the RMB has little but idiosyncratic variation against the US dollar, a finding inconsistent with the notion that the RMB is managed against a basket of currencies. Frankel (2009) finds a substantial weight on the euro by mid-2007 but still does not give credence to the idea that the RMB was being managed against a basket of trading partner currencies. These views contrast starkly to not only the PBC statement in 2005 but also the PBC policy statement in June 2010 that China would exit from the "special measure" of a tight dollar peg adopted during the global financial crisis and would return to a managed float in reference of a basket of currencies (PBC, 2010).

Research has been interpreting the RMB was doing little other than crawling upward against the US dollar. We contend that such interpretation was correct only for the first phase which lasted no more than a year after July 2005. We contend that the second phase differed. Consistent with the May 2008 Monetary Policy Report statement of the PBC (2008) and the 2007 Annual Balance of Payments Report of the State Administration of Foreign Exchange (SAFE, 2008), the RMB was managed against a basket of currencies within a narrow band during the second phase between mid-2006 and mid-2008.

However, in mid-2008, the management of the RMB reverted to "hugging the shore": stability against a generally strong US dollar in the midst of the worst storm in international finances since the founding of the People's Republic. This policy carried the RMB onto a path of uneven but substantial appreciation in effective terms and definitely interrupted the two-year policy experiment in basket management. The June 2010 PBC policy statement seems to signal an end to this third phase and the start of a new phase.

A return to managing the RMB against a currency basket would have important implications for East Asian exchange rate stability. To this end, it has been argued that East Asian currencies *should* be managed against a common basket.[1] We point to evidence that East Asian currencies *were* managed against their own respective trade-weighted baskets in 2006–2008 and as a result *already* traded with considerable stability against each other.[2] Cooperation, including a concerted choice of currency basket, is sufficient but not necessary for intra-Asian currency stability. Nevertheless, this informal approach to intra-regional currency stability cracked

---

[1] For discussion of motives for intra-regional exchange rate stability in Asia, see Williamson, 1999, 2001; Dornbusch and Park, 1999; Ogawa and Ito, 2002; Mori *et al.*, 2002; Kuroda and Kawai, 2003; Ogawa *et al.*, 2004; Kawai, 2004; Ogawa, 2006; Ogawa and Shimizu, 2006; Ito, 2008.

[2] This is foreseen as an "attractive solution" by Park and Wyplosz (2010).

under the weight of the global financial crisis that triggered a reversal of capital flows, and led to a sharp recovery of the dollar.

The plan of this chapter is as follows. In Section 2, we recall the conventional short history of the RMB against the US dollar since July 2005. Section 3 offers a four-phase interpretation of that short history. The first phase was a transitional one in which the RMB crawled upward against the US dollar peg. Policy in the second phase from mid-2006 to mid-2008 resembled a Singapore-style basket, band, and crawl (BBC) that confined the RMB's nominal effective rate to a narrow band around an appreciating centre. In the third phase from mid-2008, the RMB held firm against a generally stronger US dollar. It remains to be seen how the RMB behaves in the fourth phase that began in June 2010 when the PBC announced a return to a basket management of the RMB.

In Section 4, we draw the implications of the second phase of effective RMB management for Asian exchange rates. What happens when several neighboring economies manage their currencies against their trade-weighted baskets? Can substantial exchange rate stability arise within Asia? The answers to these questions point to the possibility of a domain of currency stability in East Asia wider than the ASEAN countries (Kenen and Meade, 2007). The final section concludes.

2. *The renminbi and the dollar since July 2005*

For more than 10 years after the unification of its multiple exchange rates in 1994, the RMB traded quite stably against the US dollar. During the Asian financial crisis, its flexibility against the dollar was reduced. At the time, this stability against the US dollar was appreciated by China's neighbors, whose currencies almost surely would have come under renewed downward pressure in the event of any substantial depreciation of the RMB against the dollar.

In July 2005, the Chinese authorities allowed a 2% appreciation (Ma *et al.*, 2005). From then until mid-2008, the RMB appreciated gradually against the US dollar, gaining a cumulative 20% (Graph 1). However, this trend appreciation vis-à-vis the dollar came to an abrupt halt in mid-2008, and the RMB approximated the dollar peg of the old days.

Naturally, market participants have focused on the daily movements of the RMB against the dollar, which have been quite limited. Analyses of daily and even intraday movements of the RMB in relation to various currencies have also concluded that the RMB's exchange rate is little more than an upward crawl against the dollar. Such analyses have used regression analysis to pose the question whether the movement of the RMB against the dollar shows any reflection of movement of the dollar against the euro or yen. They have found that it is generally very

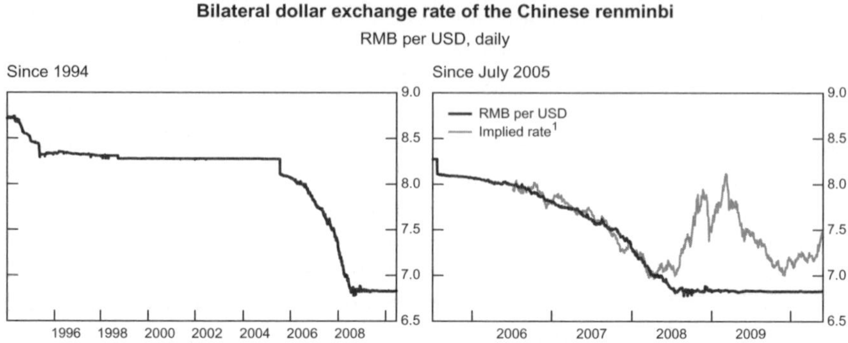

Graph 1. Bilateral dollar exchange rate of the Chinese renminbi. Notes: [1]Rate implied by the estimated linear trend of the RMB NEER. The trend line is estimated over a two-year period of mid-2006 and mid-2008, regressing the RMB NEER against a constant and a trading day trend. See note to Graph 6 for more details. Source: BIS, authors' estimations.

hard to detect a substantial reflection of these movements in other currencies in the rate at which the RMB has moved upward against the dollar. In particular, Frankel and Wei (2007) found that the weight on the US dollar was no less than 90% in the July 2005 to early 2007 sample.[3] Ito (2008) runs the Frankel and Wei (1994) analysis and concludes, "The renminbi hews very close to the dollar peg." Shah *et al.* (2006) concur. Taking this work as a whole, one would conclude that the reference in July 2005 to a basket was just talk. As Crockett (2008) observed: "if there is a basket, the weight of the US dollar must be pretty close to one in that basket, and therefore it is not nearly as effective as it should be."[4]

To summarize the short history since July 2005: There was a trend of appreciation vis-à-vis the US dollar that carried this bilateral rate up 20% by mid-2008, after which the RMB leveled off against the dollar. For the post-July 2005 period as a whole, the RMB has remained tightly managed against the US dollar on a daily basis, with little resonance at this frequency with movements in other currencies against the dollar. Management of the RMB against a basket of currencies is considered mostly a talk, even after Frankel (2009) inferred from monthly data that the management of the RMB put substantial weight on the euro by mid-2007. This is the conventional wisdom.

---

[3] They found in certain subsamples some evidence of the RMB's tracking the Korean won's, the Malaysian ringgit's and the Russian ruble's movement against the dollar.

[4] At the discussion of McKinnon and Schnabel (2009) at a BIS conference, there was no objection to the notion that the RMB is simply managed against the US dollar.

3. The evolving RMB management since July 2005

We propose an alternative interpretation. For one year after July 2005, the RMB regime behaved in a manner as described by the conventional wisdom: a peg against the dollar with a gradual upward trend. After this teething period, the Chinese authorities managed the RMB against its trade-weighted basket in a manner similar to the long-standing management of the Singapore dollar (SGD). This lasted from mid-2006 to mid-2008. As the global financial crisis approached its worst moments, the Chinese authorities abruptly interrupted this experiment, and held the RMB steady against a generally strong dollar from mid-2008 to mid-2010. We give most weight to documenting and analyzing this two-year policy experiment of a basket, band, crawl.

We take mid-2006 as the first break point of the post-July 2005 RMB regime for two reasons. First, in January 2006, the PBC announced a new rule of forming the daily central parity rate at the start of each trading day by pooling quotes from 13 RMB market makers. In contrast to the old rule of taking the closing of the previous trading day as today's opening, this move potentially allowed much greater flexibility of the bilateral RMB–USD exchange rate between two trading days. Second, there is evidence that this scope for greater flexibility was subsequently used as the ratio of bilateral dollar to effective volatility of the RMB rose noticeably around mid-2006.

3.1. Singapore-style basket management between mid-2006 and mid-2008

The Chinese monetary authorities (PBC, 2008; SAFE, 2008) interpreted the course of the RMB between mid-2006 and mid-2008 in terms of an effective exchange rate measure of the RMB.[5] The PBC argued against a widespread view that the appreciation of the RMB had accelerated in the first quarter of 2008. Not at all, the central bank replied: given the weakness of the US dollar against the euro and the yen at the time, the RMB had appreciated only 0.09% against the weighted average of its trading partner currencies. Taking these Chinese central bank reports seriously, we liken the management of the RMB to the long-standing management of the SGD and estimate the parameters in the policy experiment of managing the RMB's effective exchange within an appreciating band. Such a policy makes sense in terms of both competitiveness and price stability: effective RMB stability rather than bilateral dollar stability serves to keep China's exports competitive and traded goods prices stable (Fung *et al.*, 2009).

---

[5] Less specifically, Yi (2008, p 194) refers to the "appreciation of the nominal exchange rate." For a market analyst that takes the PBC's reference to the NEER of the RMB seriously, see Henderson (2008).

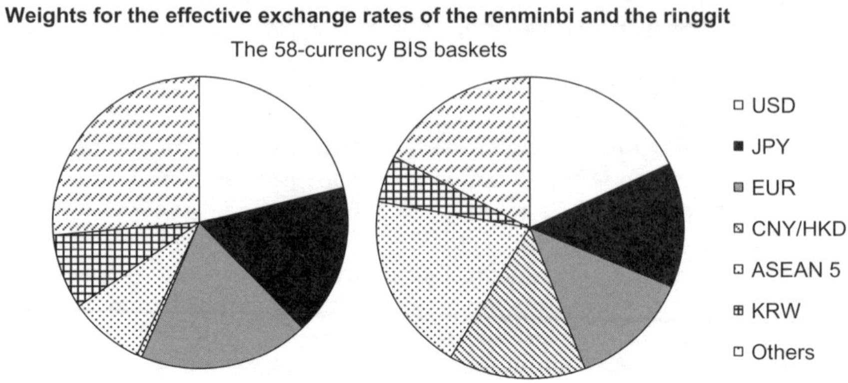

Graph 2. Weights for the effective exchange rates of the renminbi and the ringgit (the 58-currency BIS baskets). Source: BIS.

The PBC and SAFE both referred to the Bank for International Settlements (BIS) index of the nominal effective exchange rate (NEER) of the RMB, so it is worth examining (the left-hand panel of Graph 2), in part because our regression analysis below tests whether there is reversion to a path for the exchange rate defined in terms of the BIS index. The weights for this index are calculated from the merchandise trade among 58 economies (Klau and Fung, 2006). Importantly for China, allowance is made for entrepot trade through Hong Kong (Fung *et al.*, 2006). Without an adjustment for such trade, the weight on the HK dollar, and thus the US dollar, is too heavy while that on the yen, won and other neighboring currencies is too light. Adjusting for such trade, the weight on the G3 currencies amounts to about a half, the weight on Asian and Pacific currencies other than the yen amounts to about a third, and the weight on the rest of the world's currencies amounts to the remaining sixth.

The critical observation from the 14-year history of the NEER for the RMB is its steadiness over the episode between mid-2006 and mid-2008 (Graph 3). What first catches the eye, of course, is the effect of the dollar's cycle on the RMB NEER during its period of virtual peg against the dollar. The RMB strengthened in effective terms from its trough in early 1995, peaking in the first quarter of 2002, and declining into 2005. This is the dog that barks. The dog that does not bark is the marked steadiness in the RMB NEER in the two years up to July 2008, despite the further decline of the dollar in this period. Strikingly, the two indices moved in opposite directions during this two-year period, for the first time amply demonstrating an absence of the US dollar cycle on the effective RMB.

A comparison of the evolutions of the effective RMB and effective SGD helps to put the two-year Chinese policy experiment into perspective.

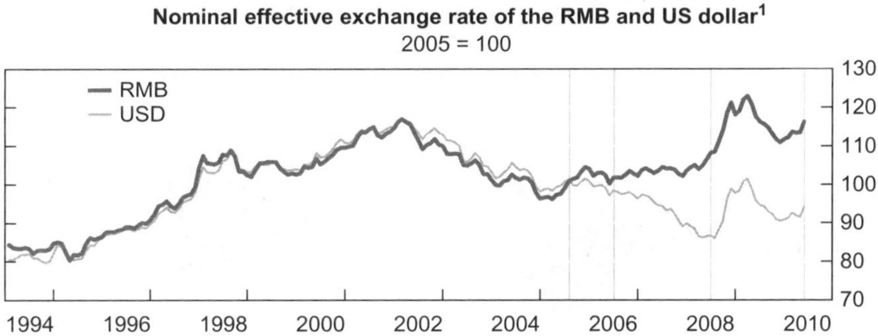

Graph 3. Nominal effective exchange rate of the RMB and US dollar[1] (2005 = 100). Note: [1]BIS broad indices, monthly data. Source: BIS.

The evolution of the RMB effective exchange rate calls to mind the graph for the SGD NEER that the Monetary Authority of Singapore (MAS) publishes twice a year with its monetary policy statement. Both show a steady upward movement from some time in 2006 into 2008.

The precise weights of the MAS effective SGD index have not been made public (MAS, 2001). Thus it is without much loss of generality that Graph 4 is drawn from a single such analyst (Baig, 2008a, 2008b).

The MAS has at various times called for a steady NEER, a gradually appreciating NEER or a slightly less gradual appreciation. These three settings of "crawl" are reflected in the three slopes of the imputed target in Graph 4. After the Asian financial crisis, after the bursting of the dot.com bubble and during the SARS scare, the target was taken to be a flat NEER. For a time in 2000–2001, and again from April 2004 to October 2007, the target was taken to be a 2% per annum rise. After October 2007, the target was taken as a 3% rise before the October 2008. In the face of a sharp contraction in exports and activity, the MAS re-centerd the target, in effect preventing appreciation of the NEER. Then, with a strong recovery in exports and activity, the MAS in April 2010 announced a return to an appreciating path. Around this target, market participants have inferred a band of tolerance of $\pm 2\%$ (Graph 4), as they see the MAS as prepared to intervene to buy or sell SGD to defend this band.

Having reviewed the manner in which market analysts interpret the MAS exchange rate policy, a parallel hypothesis can be sketched for the RMB. To start, the top panel of Graph 5 provides a close-up of the evolution of the NEER index for the RMB since July 2005. In the 12 months after July 2005, the effective RMB continued to move in line with the US dollar against major currencies. The effective RMB rose sharply as the RMB glided up against a recovering dollar, and then

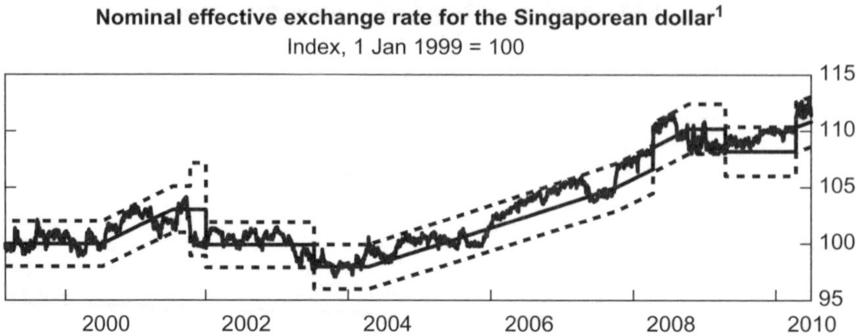

Graph 4. Nominal effective exchange rate for the Singaporean dollar[1] (index, January 1, 1999 = 100). Note: [1]Daily data. Source: Baig (2008a, 2008b) and update.

declined with a falling dollar. We judge that the Chinese authorities took a year to ease into the management of the RMB's effective rate.

On that hypothesis, the data can be allowed to speak on the question of the rate of crawl that the Chinese authorities were targeting between mid-2006 and mid-2008. If we take the two years' data to estimate the linear least squares line, we obtain a rise of 0.006 per day or an annual rate of crawl just shy of 2% (the middle panel of Graph 5).[6] On this showing, the least squares line is indicating something very close to the most frequent policy setting ascribed to the MAS.

To finish drawing the analogy, we hypothesize that a ±2% band is used, much like what the MAS is perceived to defend around its target for the effective SGD. A band of this width takes us some distance. Indeed, much of the variation takes place within ±1% sub-bands between mid-2006 and mid-2008 (the bottom panel of Graph 5).

The strangling of daily movements against the US dollar, which may be regarded as a side constraint on the management of the effective RMB, in part distinguishes the RMB's current management from that of Singapore. In particular, the announced intention is to keep daily RMB fluctuations against the dollar to ±0.3% (±0.5% from mid-2007). Thus, we have drawn a likeness to the Singaporean approach but the evolution is far from complete. This may be seen by comparing the volatility of the NEER to that of the US dollar bilateral rate at the weekly frequency (Graph 6). A characteristic of the SGD is observed from the rolling 13-week

[6] Since the NEER index is in the neighborhood of a hundred, this is about six-thousandths of a percent a day. Multiplying that by the number of the days in a year produces something just shy of 2%. Yin-Wong Cheung suggests a recursive, real-time estimation of the trend, rather than the retrospective estimation reported here. If the break-point is taken to be earlier, the estimated slope would be steeper.

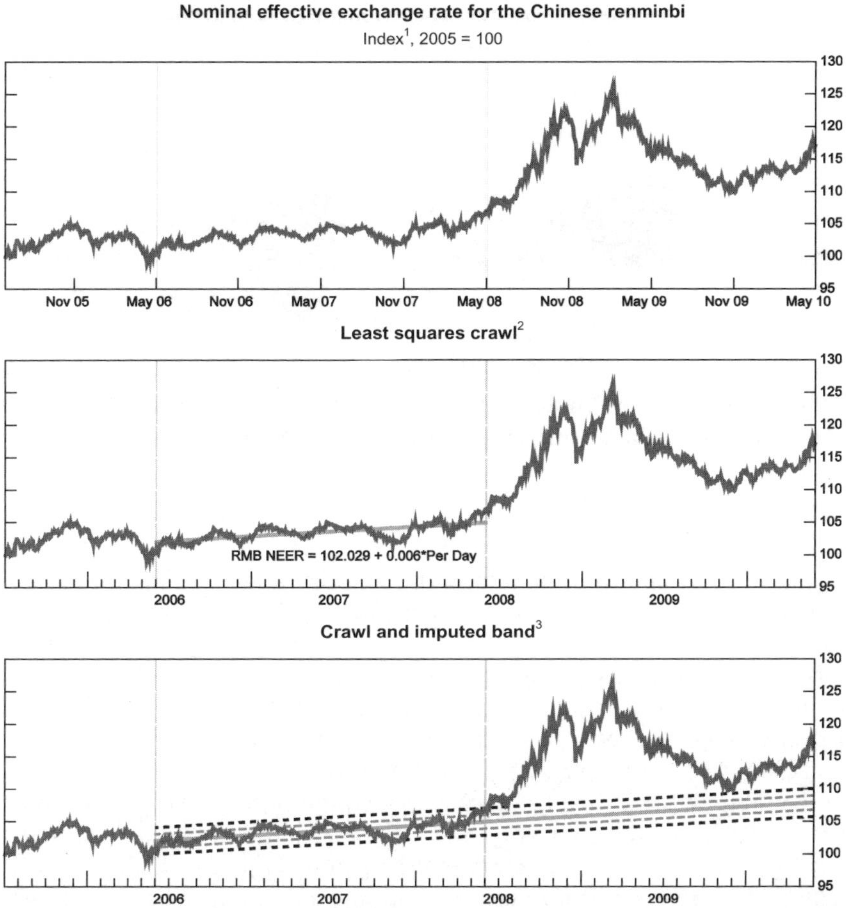

Graph 5. Nominal effective exchange rate for the Chinese renminbi Index[1] (2005 = 100). Notes: [1]BIS effective exchange rate index based on 58 economies. [2]The trend line is estimated over the two-year period of June 1, 2006, to May 30, 2008, regressing the RMB NEER against a trading day trend. The adjusted R-squared is 0.48, and both the constant term and trend coefficient are statistically significant at 1%. [3]The thick dotted lines represent ±2% of the trend line, while the thin dotted lines ±1% of the trend line. Sources: BIS; authors' estimations.

annualized volatility: the volatility of SGD against its basket of currencies (thin line) is uniformly below that against the US dollar (thick line).

The same measures for the RMB stand in the opposite relation (the right-hand panel of Graph 6). That is, even at the weekly frequency, the RMB's volatility against the US dollar has remained lower than that against the RMB's trade-weighted basket. It is worth noting, however, that the volatility of the RMB against its basket declined after July 2006

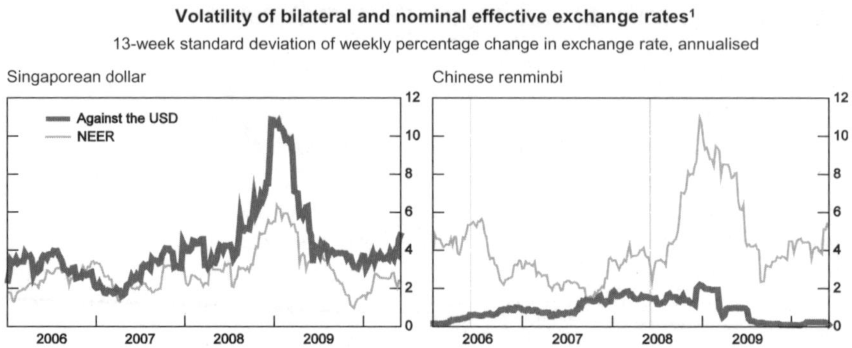

Graph 6. Volatility of bilateral and nominal effective exchange rates[1] (13-week standard deviation of weekly percentage change in exchange rate, annualized). Note: [1]Weekly data. Sources: BIS; authors' calculations.

only to pick up again in mid-2008.[7] This provides inductive evidence for our identifying mid-2006 as the break point between the first and second phase and using the data sample between mid-2006 and mid-2008 to estimate the rate of the basket crawl. In any case, the RMB's alignment to the US dollar is evident at both the daily and weekly frequency, which differs from the SGD management. Nevertheless, the RMB between mid-2006 and mid-2008 remained within the neighborhood of its imputed target of a gradual appreciation against its trade-weighted basket.

To sum up, the post-July 2005 RMB regime is not just a crawling dollar peg. We find evidence of a Singapore-style basket management of the RMB in the two years to mid-2008. The RMB traded as if it were managed to appreciate gradually against its trade weighted basket. Thus, the effective RMB and US dollar mostly moved in opposite directions during this two-year policy experiment. Much in the manner of Singaporean exchange rate policy, the effective RMB described a 2% annual crawl within a ±2% band.

Important differences remain, however. Unlike the SGD trading, the RMB's exchange rate movements against the dollar seemed to be constrained by certain de facto limits at daily frequency. Moreover, whereas the effective exchange rate is the principal policy lever in Singapore's monetary framework, the Chinese system features a hybrid of interest rate and exchange rate as means to respond to inflation and deviations of activity from trend. In any case, the two-year policy experiment was abruptly interrupted in mid-2008 against the backdrop of a sharp appreciation of the US dollar.

---

[7] Given that this measure looks back over 13 weeks of data, there is a suggestion that an important step away from the crawl against the dollar toward the crawl against the trade-weighted basket occurred in the second quarter of 2006.

3.2. Break-out from the crawling band after July 2008

In mid-2008, the effective RMB broke out above the upper limit of the estimated crawling basket band, ending a two-year policy experiment of a basket management. Indeed, all the key signs in this third phase of the evolution point to a return to the familiar pre-July 2005 dollar peg: (i) an abrupt ending of the trend appreciation of the RMB vis-à-vis the US dollar (Graph 1); (ii) a return of the close relationship between the US dollar's appreciating effective exchange rate and that of the RMB (Graph 3); (iii) a consequent steep appreciation of the NEER of the RMB during the second half of 2008 (Graph 5); and (iv) a sharp jump in the effective volatility of the RMB relative to its bilateral dollar volatility (Graph 6).

Why did the Chinese authorities revert to in effect a dollar peg in mid-2008? Basket management, in our view, was put on hold because of the unwillingness on the part of the Chinese policymakers to allow sustained depreciation of the RMB vis-à-vis the US dollar. This implicit constraint probably reflected two, not necessarily mutually exclusive, policy considerations. One possible objective may be to contain the structurally large bilateral trade surpluses. This implicit constraint may have been there since July 2005, but it did not bind during the policy experiment as long as the dollar was relatively steady or weakening against major currencies. But when the dollar strengthened sharply in late 2008, this implicit constraint bound.

Another important consideration behind this implicit constraint may have been the role of the bilateral dollar rate as a simple and long-held anchor of market expectations and confidence, especially in time of market turbulence. In the summer of 2008, to keep the basket management experiment going would have required the RMB to fall substantially against the US dollar (Graph 1, right-hand panel). After all, the dollar's move was among the sharpest upward moves since the inception of generalized floating a generation ago. As it was, the bellwether one-year non-deliverable forwards for the RMB swung from an implied appreciation of 5% to an implied depreciation of some 10% in a matter of weeks in mid-2008 as the Korean won depreciated sharply. To have let the RMB depreciate noticeably against the dollar would have given further impetus to such expectations and might have set in train a considerable outflow of the accumulated hot money in China. Such an outflow and any resulting decline in Chinese reserves could have contributed to market turbulence. The Chinese authorities may have chosen to hold fast to the US dollar, much like they did during the Asian financial crisis of 1997–1998 (Ma and McCauley, 2002).

3.3. Preliminary econometric evidence

Econometric analysis supports the graphical interpretation of the RMB having been managed to appreciate gradually against its trade-weighted basket in mid-2006 through mid-2008. The estimates below suggest both a slow tendency of the effective RMB to return to the centre of the crawling band *and* the short-term influence of the US dollar over the period July 2006-June 2008. These findings are consistent with basket management in the presence of a technical daily limit. The out-of-sample failure of our model for the effective RMB confirms that policy changed in mid-2008 either to respect an implicit constraint ruling out a sustained depreciation of the RMB against the dollar or to respond with a safe policy of dollar-pegging to the suddenly higher risks posed by the global financial crisis.

We analyze the ratio of the RMB's effective exchange rate to the centre of the band, as estimated by the least squares regression of the effective against time over the two-year period of July 2006 and June 2008. We consider the following two specifications.[8]

$$\Delta q_t = \alpha + \beta q_{t-1} + \sum \varphi_n \Delta q_{i,t-n} + \varepsilon_t \qquad (1)$$

$$\Delta q_t = \alpha + \beta q_{t-1} + \sum \varphi_n \Delta q_{i,t-n} + \theta \Delta p_{t-1} + \lambda_t \qquad (2)$$

where q is the log of the ratio of the RMB NEER over its linear least square line against time, p the log of the US Fed G7 USD NEER, and Δ the first difference operator. $\alpha = 0$ suggests an absence of drift from the basket target (which is true by construction), while $\beta < 0$ indicates that the effective RMB moves back to the centre of the band, with the speed of convergence given by the half-life of a shock to the ratio of the actual to trend effective exchange rate as $-\ln(2)/\ln(1+\beta)$. In the second specification, we add the lagged change in the NEER of the US dollar. This variable controls for the movement of the US dollar against the euro and the yen. A significantly positive coefficient on the effective dollar (θ) would confirm the influence on the effective RMB from the side constraint limiting daily bilateral movements against the US dollar. In particular, a stronger effective dollar yesterday would tend to produce a stronger effective RMB today.

In both specifications, the null hypothesis of $\alpha = 0$ cannot be rejected while the $\beta < 0$ is statistically favoured (Table 1). This seems to support the characteristics of a basket-oriented management, as Chinese policymakers aim to push the effective RMB towards the crawling target during the two-year basket policy experiment.

The first specification is just supported by the data. An estimated 2% of the gap between the effective RMB and its trend is closed every day, and this estimate is significant at the 90 percent level of significance. This makes for a very leisurely return to the centre, with a half-life of deviations of 33 trading days, or a half a quarter.

---

[8] For a more detailed technical discussion of the estimation equations, see Peng *et al.*, 2008.

Table 1. Reversion to trend of the renminbi NEER [July 2006 to June 2008, dependent variable: Δ Log(RMB NEER actual/RMB NEER estimated trend)$_t$]

	(1)	(2)
α	0.0042 (0.0087)	0.0074 (0.0088)
β	-0.0209^{*} (0.0107)	-0.0228^{**} (0.0107)
φ_1	−0.0620 (0.0460)	-0.1960^{***} (0.0511)
φ_2	0.0274 (0.0457)	0.0050 (0.0454)
θ	–	0.1613^{***} (0.0283)
Adjusted R^2	0.0078	0.0757
Number of observations	489	459
Half-life (number of days)	33	30

Notes: Sample period is between July 26, 2006, and June 9, 2008. ***1% significance; **5% significance; *10% significance.
Sources: Federal Reserve; BIS; authors' calculations.

The second specification is more strongly supported. The response to yesterday's change in the US dollar NEER is eight times stronger than the response to the gap between yesterday's effective RMB and the trend. The immediate effect of the US dollar on the RMB NEER is powerful. In contrast, the force of the reversion of the effective RMB to its trend appreciation remains subtle and slow-acting. When we add the effective dollar, the reversion to trend is estimated to occur marginally faster, with a half-life of 30 days.

The performance of this second specification out of sample provides strong evidence that the management of the RMB changed in the summer of 2008 rather than only the exchange rate environment. Given our characterization of the RMB policy, it is conceivable that a sustained and sharp upward movement of the US dollar would carry the effective RMB beyond the imputed policy band. And, indeed, there was a sustained and sharp movement of the dollar against major currencies in the second half of 2008. Had the RMB policy reacted to currency movements in the manner of the previous two years, the RMB would have been at the strong side of the inferred band, but would have remained within it. Instead, the RMB has traded as much as 15 percentage points stronger than the upper part of the estimated band at the height of global financial crisis in early 2009 (Graph 5). Thus the RMB policy has changed, in response either to the broad constraint limiting sustained bilateral RMB-USD depreciation or to the global financial crisis.

In sum, the RMB returned to a near-peg against the US dollar in mid-2008 and on balance the RMB appreciated substantially in effective terms as a result. The two-year experiment with an upward crawl against the RMB's trade-weighted basket was interrupted against the backdrop of a deepening global financial crisis. The shift to this third phase may have reflected broad concerns about a new balance of risks arising from global financial instability. If our explanations about the mid-2008 shift are accepted, one would not be surprised were the RMB's management to return a crawl against its basket in the fourth phase signalled by the PBC in June 2010 (PBC, 2010).

4. *Implications for intra-Asian exchange rate stability*

If China does pursue a policy of managing the RMB NEER over the medium term, then profound implications for intra-Asian exchange rate stability could follow. To assess these implications, it is useful to first review the proposals of McKinnon and Williamson, Kuroda and Ito for keeping Asian exchange rates relatively stable against each other.[9] Then we will argue that policies like that pursued by Singapore can be conducive to the stability of intro-Asian exchange rates even without either a common dollar orientation as proposed by McKinnon or coordination with a common basket as has been proposed by Williamson, Kuroda, Ito, and Kawai. We illustrate this point by examining the trading of the RMB against the Malaysian ringgit and against the SGD in mid-2006 to mid-2008. Nevertheless, the interruption of the RMB basket management in mid-2008 highlights the fragility of this informal route to intra-Asian currency stability.

McKinnon (2005) argues that the East Asian dollar standard has the benefit of providing for stability of exchange rates within Asia. This point can be illustrated by reference to the rate of exchange between the Malaysian ringgit and the RMB in the period from September 1998 to July 2005 (the left-hand panel of Graph 7). Clearly, the separate dollar pegs of the ringgit and RMB sufficed to achieve the stability of their bilateral exchange rate.

Ito *et al.* (1998) and Ogawa and Ito (2002) argued that the disadvantage of such a route to East Asian exchange rate stability is the destabilisation of the NEER.[10] These authors emphasized the loss of external competitiveness as the yen depreciated against the dollar in the lead-up to the Asian financial crisis. One can also lodge a monetary objection (Fung *et al.*, 2009). As the dollar rose from 1995–2002, the RMB appreciated

---

[9] We do not consider here the possibility of Asia's following the European approach step-by step, though the proposals for an Asian Monetary Unit or Asian Currency Unit do borrow from the ECU. See Wyplosz, 2001; Mundell, 2003; Padoa-Schioppa, 2004; Kenen and Meade, 2007; and Park and Wyplosz, 2010.

[10] See also Mundell, 2003, p. 2: "The low yen shut off Japanese foreign direct investment in South East Asia and closed down its engine of growth. At the same time the rising dollar appreciated pari passu the currencies of South East Asia to overvalued positions that made them sitting ducks for speculators. Thailand, Malaysia, Indonesia, and S. Korea were all caught up in the same boat. It was the instability of the dollar–yen exchange rates that brought about the crisis."

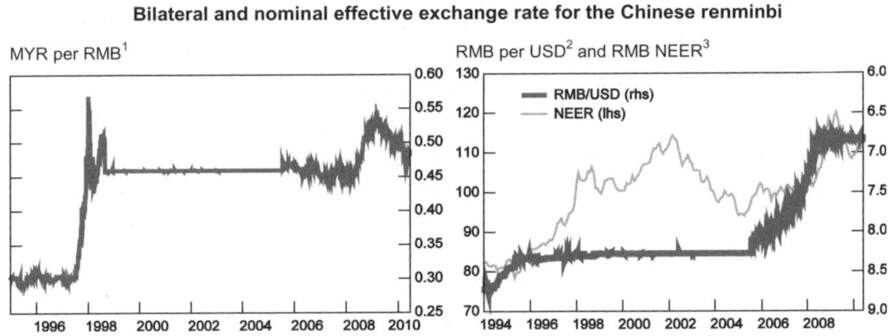

Graph 7. Bilateral and nominal effective exchange rate for the Chinese renminbi. Notes: [1]Daily data. [2]Inverted scale; a rise indicates an appreciation of the renminbi against the US dollar. [3]Sample average = 100; monthly data. Source: BIS.

by more than 40% in effective terms (the right-hand panel of Graph 7). In common with other dollar-linked economies like Hong Kong, China experienced deflating prices as the dollar peaked. Subsequent to the decline of the US dollar, inflation re-appeared in such economies with varying degrees of severity.

In view of these disadvantages inherent in the East Asian dollar standard, the proposal of Williamson (1999), Dornbusch and Park (1999), Ogawa and Ito (2002), Kuroda (2003), Kuroda and Kawai (2003), and Ito (2006, 2008) for a common basket peg promises to stabilize not only bilateral rates within Asia but also the overall effective exchange rates of the participating economies. Again, a common basket peg is a sufficient condition for intra-Asian exchange rate stability.

This proposal raises difficult questions, both in principle and in practice. Should the basket be composed of "outside" or "inside" currencies (Kenen and Meade, 2007)? In the original formulation, the common basket would be based on just the G3 currencies, the dollar, the euro and the yen. An alternative would be just inside currencies, possibly with the participating currencies combined into an Asian Currency Unit (ACU), analogous to the ECU used in Europe.[11] It should be noted that neither of these alternatives would build on the example of the SGD, the basket for which is widely taken to be a combination of outside and inside currencies – as are standard calculations of effective exchange rates like

[11] Padoa-Schioppa (2004, p 323) concludes: "the European experience with regional monetary arrangements may serve as a point of reference as it has allowed for the coexistence of a certain degree of *fixity inside* and, since the collapse of Bretton Woods, *flexibility outside* the region." The role of the ECU, especially in private use, in the lead up to the euro is often overstated in Asian discussions. See Dammers and McCauley (2006).

those produced by the BIS.[12] If the choice between outside, inside or both can be made, the common weights would have to be decided.

In view of the challenges to defining and agreeing on a common basket, it is interesting to discover to what extent intra-Asian exchange rate stability can arise out of similar, Singapore-style policies. We read the evidence from mid-2006 to mid-2008 to suggest that considerable intra-Asian exchange rate stability can arise from such similar policies. Nevertheless, such an informal approach did not prove robust to global financial instability, the associated reversal of capital flows and sharp rise of the dollar against major currencies.

Whether by policy or by market forces, a number of East Asian currencies trade with more volatility against the US dollar than against their trade-weighted indices (Ho *et al.*, 2005). It is no surprise that the SGD shows more volatility against the US dollar than against its basket (Graph 8; MAS, 2001). In addition, however, many currencies in the region show the same qualitative relationship between bilateral dollar volatility and effective exchange rate volatility (Ito, 2008). As depicted on Graph 8, the RMB's ratio moved before the mid-2008 reversion to a dollar peg.

On this measure, the Malaysian ringgit stands third after the SGD and the Thai baht in the relative stability of its NEER. Market participants interpret the Bank Negara Malaysia policy in much the same terms as the MAS (Graph 9). In particular, since July 2005, the ringgit is seen as appreciating at a rate of 2% per annum against the currencies of Malaysia's trading partners (Baig, 2008a, 2008b). Moreover, a ±2% band encompasses much of the movement of the ringgit against its basket.[13]

If the RMB, the ringgit, and the SGD were all managed against their trade-weighted baskets, does that imply that their exchange rates against each other are stabilized? The answer generally depends on the similarity of their trade-weighted baskets. In principle, there are differences, of course. Malaysia and Singapore are big trading partners so the ringgit and the SGD baskets put a heavier weight on each other's currency than the RMB basket puts on either one. In practice, however, the weights are not so different. The BIS weights for the ringgit give the G3 currencies a

[12] De Brouwer (2002, p 293) argued: "If a country has to target a basket of currencies, it may do better to target a basket peg based on its own rather than common, trade weights," emphasizing the differences across own weights in the region.

[13] Malaysia's capital account is more open than that of China and foreign investors invest freely in the local money and bond markets. The policy of guiding the effective exchange rate is thought to lean heavily on sterilized intervention. Even with such intervention, can the authorities sustain both policy targets? In the July 2005 to mid-2008 period, Malaysian interest rates were generally too high to be consistent with the appreciating path against the ringgit's trade-weighted basket as inferred by market participants. In this case, a lack of "credibility" in the technical sense of Svensson (1991) meant precisely that Malaysia retained two policy targets.

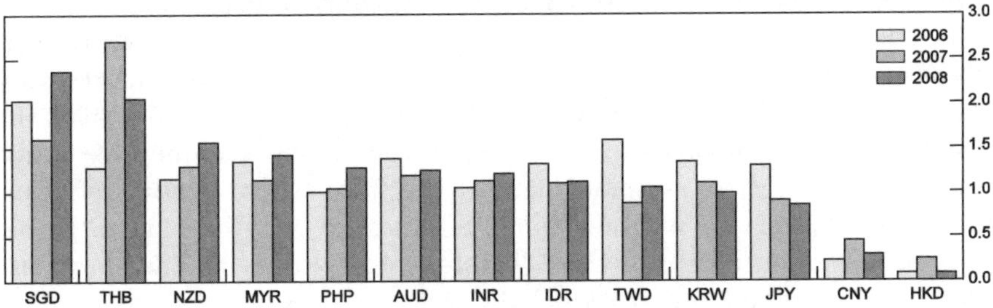

Graph 8. Ratio of dollar exchange rate volatility to effective rate volatility Ratio of standard deviation of weekly change in exchange rate. Sources: BIS; authors' calculations.

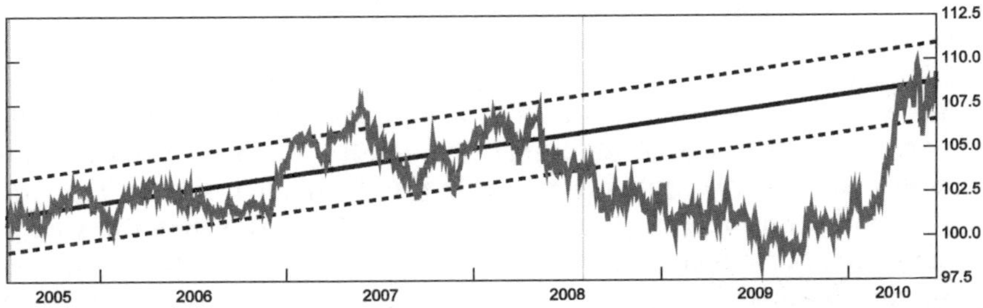

Graph 9. NEER of the Malaysian ringgit: imputed crawl and bands[1] (2005 = 100). Notes: [1]Daily data. The trend line is estimated over a three-year period of July 1, 2005, and July 31, 2008, and is given by MYR NEER = 101.1655 (0.0871)+0.0059 time (0.0001), where the adjusted $R^2 = 0.549$ and the numbers in the parentheses are standard errors. The dotted lines represent ±2% of the trend line. Sources: BIS; authors' estimations.

weight of about half, regional currencies about a third, much like the RMB (Graph 2). The RMB has a higher weight on the Korean won, while the ringgit has a higher weight on Malaysia's ASEAN trading partners.

It follows from the similarity of the composition of the baskets that, if the Chinese are managing the RMB's effective exchange rate and the Malaysians are managing the ringgit's effective exchange rate, then the ringgit/RMB is fairly stable. Again focusing on the observations from mid-2006 to mid-2008, this cross-rate traded in a fairly narrow band of two Malaysian cents around a rate near 50 Malaysian cents (the left-hand panel of Graph 10). Again plotting the least squares line and placing bands of ±2% around it, the overwhelming share of observations fall within such bands.

Let us be clear on our interpretation of this two-year episode. It is not that policy-makers in Beijing or Kuala Lumpur needed to manage this cross-rate in particular. Rather, if policy makers were managing their own currencies against their own (not dissimilar) respective baskets, they thereby produced the stability observed in this cross-rate. In June 2008, the Malaysian ringgit was trading at the weak edge of its band, and the RMB at the strong edge of its band, and already the bilateral rate had gone outside its band (Graph 5 and 9).

Similarly, the RMB-SGD exchange rate was quite stable during mid-2006 to mid-2008 (the right-hand panel of Graph 10). With a range of less than a Singapore cent, observations over this two-year period fell mostly within such $\pm 2\%$ bands. Again, this cross-rate stability ended in mid-2008.

In summary, a common basket adopted by East Asian authorities to manage their currencies would certainly be a *sufficient* condition for reducing intra-Asian currency volatility. But experience suggests that coordination is not a *necessary* condition to reduce such volatility substantially. Because the trade patterns are not all that different across the region, each authority's attending to its own effective exchange rate can produce quite stable cross-rates.[14] For both the Malaysian ringgit and the SGD, the volatility of the ringgit/SGD cross-rate was lower than the volatility of their other bilateral rates. The $\pm 2\%$ band, it should be noted, was narrower during the two-year period up to mid-2008 than those often recommended on the basis of the European experience (Latter, 2005; Park and Wyplosz, 2010).

Our empirical findings shed new light on the question of the likely geography of monetary cooperation in Asia. Kenen and Meade (2007) reviewed the prospects for exchange rate cooperation in East Asia and put most weight on the scenario in which the major ASEAN economies cooperate on exchange rates. They discounted the possibility of China's exchange rate management associating the RMB with such cooperation.

[14] Park and Wyplosz (2010) arrive at a similar conclusion by a different route. While we compare the weights in the BIS effective exchange rate indices for East Asian currencies, they compare the BIS indices with these currencies' exchange rates against the AMU (Asian Monetary Unit) as proposed by Ogawa (2006) and Ogawa and Shimizu (2006). In the terminology of Kenen and Meade (2007), the BIS baskets are a hybrid of inside and outside baskets, while the latter is an inside basket including only regional currencies. One might have thought that this difference in principle would make a big difference in practice. Instead, the authors find a remarkable similarity between the BIS effective exchange rate indices and the AMU exchange rates. Park and Wyplosz reason that, if stability against a common inside basket is sufficient for bilateral stability, and each currency's BIS indices tracks its exchange rates versus the AMU, then stability against the BIS indices is sufficient for bilateral stability. We reason simply that if stability against a common basket is sufficient for bilateral stability, and the composition of BIS baskets is similar, then stability against the BIS indices is sufficient for bilateral stability.

Graph 10. Bilateral exchange rate for the Chinese renminbi[1] (against the Malaysian ringgit and the Singaporean dollar). Notes: [1]Weekly data. The trend line is estimated over the two-year period of mid-2006 and mid-2008. The thick dotted lines represent $\pm 2\%$ of the trend line, while the thin dotted lines $\pm 1\%$ of the trend line. Source: Bloomberg; authors' estimations.

Our results point in the direction of a broader cooperation between China and ASEAN, as discussed by Mundell (2003). However, the idea of stable Asian cross rates arising out of a similarity of policies rather than leadership and followership leads us to resist viewing the RMB as a prospective "regional anchor currency" (Park, 2008) with that phrase's inevitable invocation of the asymmetric role of the Deutsche mark in Europe before the euro.

All that said, it must be recognized that this informal approach to currency stability in East Asia broke down in mid-2008. Even had the RMB remained stable in effective terms, the asymmetric response of capital flows to falling equity markets and global financial crisis would have challenged intra-Asian exchange rate stability. The equity market of China is effectively segmented as between the ("H" or "N") shares traded in Hong Kong or New York, on the one hand, and the ("S") shares traded in Shanghai and Shenzhen, on the other (Peng *et al.*, 2008). Non-resident holdings of the latter are strictly limited and therefore any disinvestment cannot generate a large capital outflow. Not so in economies like India, Korea or Malaysia, where non-resident holdings of equity are very large. In these economies, the global correction in equity prices in 2008 was associated with big capital outflows that put downward pressure on the domestic currencies. So, while the managers of the RMB could choose, for one reason or another, to allow an effective appreciation, the managers of other regional currencies faced strong market pressures for depreciation against the dollar and in effective terms.

Thus, it is not surprising that the Malaysian ringgit was allowed in early September 2008 to fall outside of the imputed lower band (Graph 9). Given the opposite sharp upward move of the effective RMB discussed above, the RMB/ringgit exchange rate lost the stability that was associated with both currencies' gradual appreciation between mid-2006 and mid-2008. Singapore, with a long track record and drawing down its huge reserves, continued to stabilize its effective exchange rate during the global financial crisis (Graph 4). Nevertheless, because of the RMB's reversion to a peg against a generally rising dollar, the SGD/RMB rate traded to nearly 23 cents, a rate not seen since the peak of the previous dollar cycle in 2002 (the right-hand panel of Graph 10). Nevertheless, Graphs 9 and 10 together suggest that, with the return of capital inflows to and rapid growth in Malaysia and Singapore, both the ringgit and SGD have returned to an appreciating NEER path, with the consequence of a recovery against the RMB.

5. *Conclusions*

To conclude, the RMB management has evolved in four phases since the July 2005 regime shift. Most observers think that the whole period has been characterized by an upward crawl or stall of the RMB versus the US dollar. The crawl against the dollar was a good characterization of the first phase lasting about a year to mid-2006 and the stall against the dollar was a good characterization of the period from mid-2008 through May 2010. It has generally escaped the notice of observers, however, that in mid-2006 to mid-2008, the RMB's effective exchange rate was confined to a fairly narrow band, resisting the ebb and flow of the effective dollar for the very first time. That is, despite the still narrow range of daily fluctuation of the RMB against the dollar, the RMB behaved over weeks and months in this second phase as if it were managed to appreciate gradually against its trade-weighted basket of partner currencies. However, this two-year basket policy experiment was interrupted in mid-2008 as the RMB reverted to a near-peg to the dollar as it strengthened sharply in the midst of a global financial crisis.

East Asia can be seen as taking an evolutionary path toward regional exchange rate stability and monetary cooperation. East Asian currencies managed against their respective trade-weighted currency baskets can show relative stability against each other, owing to the similarity of these baskets. Even without explicit cooperation, a similar policy of managing currencies against their own respective baskets can result in their trading relatively stably against each other. Nevertheless, the global financial crisis demonstrated that such convergent policy can break down when heavy outflows from the region's equity markets affect currencies differently owing to different degrees of capital controls or when dollar strength exposes asymmetric constraints to the trade-weighted basket policy.

The possibility of similar policies giving rise to currency stability is not an argument against furthering cooperation in the region. Rather, cooperative efforts might build on the achievements of the evolution witnessed to date.

This paper has not addressed the consequences of the use of currency baskets in Asia for the global financial system. For instance, Blanchard *et al.* (2005) discuss how a floating exchange rate of the RMB might affect the Asian portfolio allocation across currencies, and thus the euro-dollar exchange rate. It might be possible to say more about the effect of a basket policy, which will have predictable effects on the minimum-variance portfolio using the domestic currency numeraire (Genberg, *et al.*, 2005; and McCauley, 2008). More generally, the implication would seem to be that the dollar zone of the global economy, which had remained fairly stable (BIS, 2005), stands to shrink if much of East Asia comes to straddle the dollar, euro and yen zones. Finally, a basket management could facilitate the Chinese efforts to enhance the international use of the RMB (Cheung *et al.*, forthcoming).

Acknowledgment

Guonan Ma and Robert McCauley are staff members of the Bank for International Settlements (BIS). The authors thank Charles Adams, Yin-Wong Cheung, and Khor Hoe Ee and participants in seminars of the Hong Kong General Chamber of Commerce, the Hong Kong Institute for Monetary Research, the Hong Kong Treasury Markets Association, the Economic Society of Singapore/Singapore Training Institute, and Nanyang Technological University of Singapore, as well as two anonymous reviewers. We especially thank Mirza Baig for his market analysis and graphs of the SGD and Eric Chan and Lillie Lam for research assistance. All flaws remain those of the authors. The views expressed are those of the authors and not necessarily those of the BIS.

References

Baig, M. (2008a), SGD gets another leg up. Deutsche Bank Asia FX strategy notes, Global market research, 10 April.

Baig, M. (2008b), Foreign exchange strategy. Deutsche Bank Asia local markets market strategy, 5 September.

Bank for International Settlements. (2005), 75th annual report. Bank for International Settlements, Basel.

Blanchard, O., Giavazzi, F., Sa, F. (2005), The U.S. current account and the dollar. *Brookings Papers on Economic Activity* (1), 1–66.

de Brouwer, G. (2002), Does a formal common-basket peg in East Asia make economic sense? In: de Brouwer, G. (Ed.), *Financial Markets and Policies in East Asia*. Routledge, London, pp. 286–314.

Cheung, Y., Ma, G., McCauley, R. (forthcoming), Renminbising China's foreign assets. *Pacific Economic Review*.

Crockett, A. (2008), Comment. In: Goldstein, M., Lardy, N. (Eds.), *Debating China's Exchange Rate Policy*. Peterson Institute for International Economics, Washington, DC, pp. 341–344.

Dammers, R., McCauley, R. (2006), Basket weaving: the Euromarket experience with basket bonds. *BIS Quarterly Review* (March), 79–92.

Dornbusch, R., Park, Y. (1999), Flexibility or nominal anchors? In: Pisani-Ferry, C., Park, Y. (Eds.), *Exchange Rate Policies in Emerging Asian Countries*. Routledge, London.

Frankel, J. (2009), New estimates of China's exchange rate regime. NBER Working Paper No 14700, February.

Frankel, J., Wei, S. (1994), Yen bloc or dollar bloc? Exchange rate policies in East Asian economies. In: Ito, T., Krueger, A. (Eds.), *Macroeconomic Linkages: Savings. Exchange Rates, and Capital Flows*. University of Chicago Press, Chicago, pp. 295–329.

Frankel, J., Wei, S. (2007), Assessing China's exchange rate regime. *Economic Policy* 22 (51), 575–j627.

Fung, S., Klau, M., Ma, G., McCauley, R. (2006), Estimation of Asian effective exchange rates: a technical note. BIS Working Papers No 217.

Fung, S., Klau, M., Ma, G., McCauley, R. (2009), Implications of refined renminbi effective exchange rates with Asian entrepot and intraregional trade. In: Cheung, Y., Wong, K. (Eds.), *China and Asia: Economic and Financial Interactions*. Routledge, London, pp. 178–193.

Genberg, H., et al. (2005), Official reserves and currency management in Asia: Myth, reality and the future, Geneva reports on the world economy number 7, International Center for Monetary and Banking Studies and Centre for Economic Policy Research, Geneva and London.

Henderson, C. (2008), CNY may be being managed on a NEER basis. Standard Chartered FX Alert, 14 May.

Ho, C., Ma, G., McCauley, R. (2005), Trading Asian currencies. *BIS Quarterly Review* March, 49–58.

Ito, T. (2006), A case for a coordinated basket for Asian countries. In: Ito, T. (Ed.), *A Basket Currency for Asia*. Routledge, London.

Ito, T. (2007), The role of the exchange rate in inflation targeting. In: *Challenges to Inflation Targeting in Emerging Market Countries, Proceedings of an International Symposium Organized by the Bank of Thailand*. Bank of Thailand, Bangkok, pp. 243–275, 13–14 November 2006.

Ito, T. (2008), Influence of the renminbi on exchange rate policies of other Asian currencies. In: Goldstein, M., Lardy, N. (Eds.), *Debating China's Exchange Rate Policy*. Peterson Institute for International Economics, Washington, DC, pp. 239–258.

Ito, T., Ogawa, E., Sasaki, Y. (1998), How did the dollar peg fail in Asia? *Journal of the Japanese and International Economies* 12, 256–304.

Kawai, M. (2004), The case for a tri-polar currency basket for emerging East Asia. In: de Brouwer, G., Kawai, M. (Eds.), *Economic Linkages and Implications for Exchange Rate Regimes in East Asia*. Routledge, London, pp. 360–384.

Kenen, P., Meade, E. (2007), *Regional Monetary Integration*. Cambridge University Press, Oxford.

Klau, M., Fung, S. (2006), The new BIS effective exchange rate indices. *BIS Quarterly Review* March, 51–65.

Kuroda, H. (2003), Overview of financial and monetary cooperation in East Asia. In: Ahn, C., Ito, T., Kawai, M., Park, Y. (Eds.), *Financial Development and Integration in East Asia*. Korean Institute for International Economic Policy, Seoul, Tokyo: the Policy Research Institute, Ministry of Finance, Japan.

Kuroda, H., Kawai, M. (2003), Strengthening regional financial cooperation in East Asia. In: de Brouwer, G., Wang, Y. (Eds.), *Financial Governance in East Asia: Policy Dialogue, Surveillance and Cooperation*. Routledge, London, pp. 136–166.

Latter, T. (2005), Asian Monetary Union – Where do we go from here?" HKIMR Occasional Paper No 2. Hong Kong: Hong Kong Institute for Monetary Research.

Ma, G., Ho, C., McCauley, R., Remolona, E. (2005), Managing the renminbi regime shift. *BIS Quarterly Review* September, 7–8.

Ma, G., McCauley, R. (2002), Rising foreign currency liquidity of banks in China. *BIS Quarterly Review* September, 67–74.

McCallum, B. (2006), Singapore's exchange-rate based monetary policy and its relevance for China. *MAS Staff Paper No. 44*.

McCauley, R. (2008), Choosing the currency numeraire in managing official foreign exchange reserves. In: Pringle, R., Carver, N. (Eds.), *RBS Reserve Management Trends 2008*. Central Banking Publications, London, pp. 25–46.

McKinnon, R. (2005), *Exchange Rates Under the East Asian Dollar Standard: Living with Conflicted Virtue*. The MIT Press, Cambridge.

McKinnon, R., Schnabel, G. (2009). China's financial conundrum and global imbalances. BIS Working Papers No 277, first presented at the BIS conference in Lucerne in June 2008.

Monetary Authority of Singapore. (2001), Singapore's exchange rate policy, February.

Mori, J., Kinukawa, M., Nukaya, H., Hashimoto, M. (2002), Integration of East Asian economies and a step by step approach towards a currency basket regime. IIMA Research Report No. 2.

Mundell, R. (2003), Prospects for an Asian currency area. *Journal of Asian Economics* 14, 1–10.

Ogawa, E. (2006), AMU and AMU deviation indicators. Research Institute of Economy, Trade and Industry, Tokyo.

Ogawa, E., Ito, T. (2002), On the desirability of a regional basket currency arrangement. *Journal of the Japanese and International Economies* 16 (3), 317–334.

Ogawa, E., Ito, T., Sasaki, Y.N. (2004), Costs, benefits, and constraints of the currency basket regime for East Asia. In: *Asian Development Bank, Monetary and Financial Integration in East Asia: The Way Ahead*, vol. 2. Palgrave, Basingstoke, pp. 209–237.

Ogawa, E., Shimizu, J. (2006), AMU deviation indicator for coordinated exchange rate policies in East Asia and its relation with effective exchange rates. Research Institute of Economy, Trade and Industry, Discussion Paper Series 06-E-002.

Padoa-Schioppa, T. (2004), East Asian monetary arrangements: a European perspective. *International Finance* 7, 311–323.

Park, Y. (2008), The regional currency unit and exchange rate policy cooperation in East Asia. In: Goldstein, M., Lardy, M. (Eds.), *Debating China's Exchange Rate Policy*. Peterson Institute for International Economics, Washington, pp. 259–267.

Park, Y., Wyplosz, C. (2010). Monetary and financial integration in East Asia: the relevance of European experience. (May). Oxford University Press, Oxford.

Peng, W., Miao, H., Chow, N. (2008), Price convergence between dual-listed A and H shares. In: Genberg, H., He, D. (Eds.), *Macroeconomic Linkages between Hong Kong and Mainland China*. City University of Hong Kong, Hong Kong, pp. 295–315.

People's Bank of China. (2005), Public Announcement on Reforming the Renminbi Exchange Rate Regime, 21 July 2005. Available at http://www.pbc.gov.cn/english//detail.asp?col = 6400&ID = 542.

People's Bank of China. (2008), China's Monetary Policy Report, May.

People's Bank of China. (2010), Further reform the RMB exchange rate regime and enhance the RMB exchange rate flexibility. Announcement on 19 June 2010. Available at http://www.pbc.gov.cn/english/detail.asp?col = 6400&id = 1488.

Shah, A. Zeileis, A., Patnaik, I. (2006), What is the new Chinese currency regime? (4 April). Administration of Foreign Exchange, Beijing.

State Administration of Foreign Exchange. (2008), 2007 □□□□□□ (2007 Annual Balance of Payments Report of China).

Svensson, L. (1991), The simplest test of target zone credibility. *IMF Staff Papers* 38, 655–665.

Williamson, J. (1999), The case for a common basket peg for East Asian currencies. In: Collingnan, S., Pisani-Ferry, J., Park, Y. (Eds.), *Exchange Rate Policies in Emerging Asian Countries*. Routledge, London, pp. 327–343.

Williamson, J. (2001), The case for a basket, band and crawl (BBC) regime for East Asia. In: *Future Directions for Monetary Policies in East Asia*. Reserve Bank of Australia, Sydney, pp. 97–111.

Wyplosz, C. (2001), A monetary union in Asia? Some European lessons. In: *Future Directions for Monetary Policies in East Asia*. Reserve Bank of Australia, Sydney, pp. 124–155.

Yi, G. (2008), Renminbi exchange rates and relevant institutional factors. *Cato Journal* 28 (21, Spring/Summer), 187–196.

CHAPTER 6

On the Choice of Exchange Rate Regimes for East Asian Countries

Ulrich Volz

German Development Institute, Tulpenfeld 6, 53113 Bonn, Germany
E-mail address: ulrich.volz@die-gdi.de

Abstract
This chapter examines exchange rate options for East Asian countries, taking into account their real economic linkages as well as their international financial relations. Particular consideration is given to possible exchange rate cooperation within the region. For this purpose, the literature on the optimal peg is reconsidered and subsequently extended to include a country's international financial asset and liability situation. That is, instead of focusing solely on nominal or real effective exchange rates, the chapter proposes a blend of "real" and "financial" exchange rates for analyzing "optimal" exchange rate policy.

Keywords: Choice of exchange rate regime, optimal peg, monetary integration, East Asia

Jel Classification: F31, F33, F41, F42

1. Introduction

There is no consensus in the economics profession and thus little coherent guidance for policymakers on how countries should manage their exchange rates. Although fixed exchange rates have been discredited through the currency crises of the recent decades, there remain many reservations about free floating for any but the largest economies. This is reflected in the "fear of floating" that Calvo and Reinhart (2002) detect among many developing and emerging economies. In the second half of the 1990s, the "bipolar view" became fashionable, which suggests that countries should either irrevocably fix their exchange rate, that is, enter a currency union, or otherwise float their currency (e.g., Eichengreen, 1994; Fischer, 2001). Although the interest in monetary unification has increased

Frontiers of Economics and Globalization
Volume 9 ISSN: 1574-8715
DOI: 10.1108/S1574-8715(2011)0000009011

significantly since the creation of the European Monetary Union, and regional monetary unification is being discussed in various corners of the world, the fact that many countries today chose intermediate regimes over monetary union or a free float gives little support for the bipolar hypothesis.

Since the "East Asian dollar standard" (McKinnon, 2005) went into crisis in the late 1990s, many economists have advocated a free floating of East Asian currencies, including the Chinese yuan. Still, although most East Asian countries have allowed for a bit more flexibility in their exchange rates, the dollar standard resurrected after the crisis and today all East Asian countries with the exception of Japan essentially still peg to or manage their exchange rate vis-à-vis the dollar (McKinnon, 2001; McKinnon and Schnabl, 2004, 2009). While the dollar peg has served the region well in importing macroeconomic stability, promoting exports to the United States, and fostering real economic integration in East Asia, the adequacy of a continued dollar pegging or soft pegging has come under scrutiny. At the same time, free floating is not considered an option for the vast majority of policymakers in the region.

This chapter examines exchange rate options for East Asian countries, taking into account their real economic linkages as well as their international financial relations. Particular consideration is given to possible exchange rate cooperation within the region. For this purpose, the chapter first reconsiders the literature on the optimal peg, which it subsequently extends to include a country's international financial asset and liability situation. That is, instead of focusing solely on real effective exchange rates, the chapter proposes a blend of "real" and "financial" exchange rates for analyzing "optimal" exchange rate policy. It then analyzes these for the ASEAN+3[1] countries and Hong Kong. The simulations show that freely floating exchange rates would be potentially destabilizing for most East Asian economies, not only with respect to trade flows, but especially when taking into account their international investment positions. Moreover, the results suggest that no single currency would provide an optimal anchor for exchange rate stabilization of East Asian currencies.

Given the economic interdependencies that have developed within East Asia over the past decades, this chapter thus recommends a cooperative approach to exchange rate stabilization within the region based on currency baskets. As financial linkages with the United States are still very important today (much more than trade linkages, as commonly thought), a quick dissolution of the still close ties with the U.S. dollar would not only be destabilizing for the region, it would also entail the risk of a severe dollar crisis. Instead, this chapter proposes a gradual approach in which

[1] The 10 members of ASEAN are Brunei, Cambodia, Indonesia, Lao, Malaysia, Myanmar, Philippines, Singapore, Thailand, and Vietnam. The "+3" countries are China, Japan, and South Korea.

East Asian monetary authorities steadily reduce their linkages with the dollar and at the same time increase weights of other currencies – including the yen and the euro – in their currency baskets. Even if all countries chose the "optimal" basket composition tailored to their own economic circumstances, the result would be a relatively homogenous exchange rate policy across the region. In time, East Asian monetary authorities could harmonize their basket compositions and also introduce a virtual basket unit, which could be then used for more formal exchange rate coordination, if this is politically desired.

The next section discusses factors that need to be taken into consideration when choosing the appropriate exchange rate policy. This is followed in Section 3 by an analysis of the trade patterns of East Asian countries and calculations of "optimal" currency baskets that reflect these trade patterns. Section 4 extends the analysis to take account of East Asian countries' international asset and liability situation and how this affects exchange rate choices. Section 5 discusses currency baskets as a reasonable way forward for East Asian exchange rate policies. Section 6 concludes.

2. *Considerations regarding the choice of exchange rate regimes*

In theory, in the absence of capital controls, a country's monetary authority can target only either an internal target, such as a certain level of inflation or output growth, or an external target, such as the exchange rate vis-à-vis another country's currency.[2] Without any intention to dismiss the merits of a monetary policy solely directed at an internal target, the following analysis will concentrate on what factors should determine a country's exchange rate policy *if* the authorities have decided to run an active exchange rate policy.[3] That is, the question of what a central bank's monetary objective function should reasonably look like and whether a country should peg its currency or maintain a floating exchange rate will be blanked out; rather, the following analysis will take for granted that a fear of floating does exist among the developing and emerging economies

---

[2] The "impossibly trinity" hypothesis suggests that a country is unable to maintain open capital account, a fixed exchange rate and an independent monetary policy simultaneously. A "possible duality" is purported to exist, where only two of the three can be maintained at the same time. Recent empirical research, for example, by Fratzscher (2002), Frankel *et al.* (2004), and Reade and Volz (2011), however, has questioned this conventional view that exchange rate flexibility provides insulation for the conduct of monetary policy and come to the conclusion that in the face of globalized financial markets it has become ever more difficult to pursue independent monetary policy for all but the largest economies (the United States, the euro area, and Japan), even under flexible exchange rate arrangements.

[3] For a discussion of the problems that developing and emerging economies encounter when operating a monetary policy strategy that solely follows an internal target and disregards the exchange rate, see Chap. 9 of Volz (2010).

of East Asia, and hence focus on the question what kind of peg should be adopted by East Asian countries that have opted against floating rates.[4]

Before embarking on this exercise, it is important to reaffirm that there is no such thing as an "optimal" exchange rate policy; as Frankel (1999) pointed out, no single currency regime is right for all countries or at all times. Factors influencing the choice of the exchange rate regime are likely to change over time. Policy choices and economic structures are endogenous; a regime that has worked well over a certain period might hence become suboptimal over time, whereas choices that would have been inappropriate before might become superior.

There are two basic questions policymakers need to address when deciding on their country's exchange rate regime. First, should they fix their currency? Second, if they decide to fix, against what currency or currencies? Besides the openness of an economy, which for obvious reasons affects the importance of the exchange rate for a given economy and thus the attention policymakers will pay to exchange rate policy,[5] the literature on the optimal peg highlights the geographical distribution of trade as an important determinant in designing optimal exchange rate policy.[6] Trade is considered a crucial factor because it determines a country's (real) effective exchange rate, which in this literature is regarded as the most important influence on a country's macroeconomic development, including inflation and employment (Williamson, 2009). Hence, the analysis of an economy's trade patterns usually provides the basis for deciding upon the "optimal peg."

A factor that plays an important role in selecting the anchor currency to which to peg is the quality of this currency and the depth of financial markets of the economy issuing it. By pegging to a foreign currency, the pegging country links itself to the economy of that country and therefore should make sure that it does not import macroeconomic and financial instability from abroad. Historically, the quest for achieving macroeconomic stability has been an important incentive for weak currency countries or for countries that just lived through a currency crisis to peg to a strong currency. The idea is that governments "tie their hands" voluntarily by pegging to an external anchor, which would then impede discretionary monetary and exchange rate policy (Giavazzi and Pagano, 1988).

As mentioned above, the choice is not only between purely fixed and floating rates. Intermediate regimes, such as crawling pegs and managed

---

[4] Yoshino et al. (2004) discuss the desirability of various exchange rate regimes for East Asian countries using a three-country general equilibrium model.

[5] A closed economy obviously does not need to be concerned about its exchange rate. Note that "open" refers not only to trade, but also to financial openness of an economy, as will be lined out later.

[6] See Williamson (1982) for a survey of the analysis of the optimal peg.

floating offer an alternative to the corner solutions and are widely used in practice. Similarly, the choice of anchor country is not necessarily limited to a single currency. Currency baskets have particular appeal if the geographic distribution of trade points to no single currency area as an optimal anchor, or if the likely currency is not a good choice as an anchor, for instance, because of macroeconomic or financial instability of that currency area.

Exchange rate policy does not only have potential implications for trade, exchange rate swings can also have significant valuation effects on a country's international asset and liability position. Moreover, economies that exhibit a high degree of foreign currency substitution on domestic assets and liabilities, that is, dollarization or euroization, are susceptible to balance sheet effects of movements in the exchange rate of their national currency against the currency or currencies in which these assets and liabilities are denominated.[7] Although the impact of capital account transactions (which for most countries are much larger than the value of trade) on the foreign exchange market is acknowledged, the literature on optimal pegs so far has restricted itself to constructing trade-weighted exchange rate indices (e.g., Williamson, 2009). Against this backdrop, Lane and Shambaugh (2007) argue that trade-weighted exchange rate indices are insufficient to understand the financial impact of currency movements and suggest constructing "financial exchange rates."

In practice, an economy's foreign currency exposure can be expected to play an important role in how exchange rate policy is executed. In East Asia, many commentators highlight trade considerations as the main determinant of exchange rate policy. In particular, it is frequently argued that East Asian countries have linked their currencies (at undervalued rates) to the U.S. dollar to promote export growth, especially to the United States.[8] It can be taken for granted that the strategy to maintain an undervalued exchange rate has been part of the East Asian export-led growth model. And yet this is only one part of the story. McKinnon and Schnabl (2009) explain why continuing to peg to the dollar is entirely rational from the East Asian perspective and why the "East Asian dollar standard," as they call it, is likely to continue. Rather than undervaluing their currencies in order to promote exports, McKinnon and Schnabl argue that East Asian governments, in particular China, are trapped into maintaining (soft) dollar pegs. Because most East Asian economies have transformed themselves from dollar debtors into dollar creditors, they face what McKinnon and Schnabl call "conflicted virtue," pressure to appreciate their currencies that could lead to a deflationary spiral and zero interest liquidity trap. Prior to the Asian crisis, when many East Asian

---

[7] Bénassy-Quéré *et al.* (2001) highlight the effects of exchange rate policy for attracting foreign direct investment.

[8] See, for instance, the Bretton Woods II argument by Dooley *et al.* (2003, 2009a, 2009b).

countries ran current account deficits and were net debtors, stabilizing the exchange rate vis-à-vis the dollar was rational for central banks to facilitate financing from abroad.[9] The resulting currency mismatches caused big problems when the devaluation spiral started after the fall of the Thai baht. Having transformed themselves into net creditors, several East Asian countries nowadays face the problem that due to their inability to lend in domestic currency they have accumulated huge amounts of foreign currency holdings, both in the private and public sectors. An appreciation of the national currency would hence bring about distortive balance sheet effects.

A last point that needs to be highlighted is that the exchange rate regime is (or should be) in many cases not chosen in isolation from the decision of other countries. In the face of international interdependencies, the choice of monetary policy regime can be viewed as a strategic game (Hamada, 1985). As will be discussed in more detail later, the economic interdependencies between East Asian nations have become so close that for all but the largest countries in the region it becomes unrealistic to follow an exchange rate policy that ignores the choices of its neighbors.

3. *Trade considerations*

Table 1 shows the trade openness of East Asian countries and the euro area, that is, the ratio of total trade (imports plus exports) over GDP, for the period 1980–2007.[10] Except for Brunei and Singapore, the ratio increased over this period for all countries, in many cases quite dramatically. On average, total trade of ASEAN+4 countries equals almost 130 percent of GDP in 2007, nearly double that of the euro area, which itself has a relatively high degree of trade openness compared to other countries or regions, such as the United States and Mercosur. If, however, absolute values are used in place of unweighted averages (i.e., the sum of ASEAN/+3/+4 countries' imports and exports divided by the sum of these countries' GDPs), the situation looks different: in this

[9] The borrowing was almost entirely in foreign exchange, a problem that Eichengreen and Hausmann (2005) have termed "original sin."

[10] A caveat regarding the analysis of economic interdependencies based solely on trade data should be highlighted. Since the well-documented fragmentation and globalization of production processes, trade data cannot reliably capture the source of value-added. To more accurately capture the real linkages between economies, Pula and Peltonen (2011) propose the use of international input–output tables, which is not possible to do here due to data limitations. Based on international input–output data, Pula and Peltonen's analysis suggests that, due to the high import content of exports in these economies (which is a result of the increasing segmentation of production across the region), emerging Asia's dependence on exports is only about one-third of its GDP, well below the exposure suggested by trade data. This suggests that the results presented in this chapter might be a bit blurred, but the main message remains unaffected nonetheless.

Table 1. Total trade (imports plus exports) as percent of GDP, 1980–2007

	1980	1981	1982	1983	1984	1985	1986	1987	1988	1989	1990	1991	1992	1993	1994	1995	1996	1997	1998	1999	2000	2001	2002	2003	2004	2005	2006	2007
Brunei					88.7	87.7	100.6	90.9	92.0	91.8	91.3	96.6	151.2	162.9	148.0	134.1	140.5	137.1	106.5	84.3	76.5	83.0	86.8	87.9	78.1	76.6	75.2	78.0
Cambodia							6.9	16.2	11.7	21.0	10.9	5.9	37.6	51.4	50.5	56.5	55.3	51.4	66.4	65.1	69.7	69.1	73.9	75.2	79.9	88.5	90.1	109.0
China	12.2	14.8	14.6	14.5	16.4	22.9	25.3	25.7	25.7	25.0	30.1	33.5	34.7	31.9	42.3	38.6	33.9	34.1	31.8	33.3	39.6	38.5	42.7	51.9	59.8	63.4	66.6	67.2
Hong Kong	147.4	151.8	139.1	155.6	172.8	171.1	173.2	192.2	213.4	211.5	214.3	224.0	233.7	228.2	231.2	254.0	238.5	224.9	214.7	216.5	245.7	235.0	249.3	288.0	320.0	331.6	342.9	344.9
Indonesia	34.3	34.8	35.9	37.9	35.3	28.6	27.5	34.2	33.7	34.5	37.9	39.1	40.1	37.3	36.9	38.5	37.0	39.9	72.2	47.0	57.8	54.3	45.2	39.8	45.9	50.1	56.6	56.4
Japan	25.5	25.0	24.7	23.0	24.1	22.5	16.7	15.6	15.3	16.3	17.1	15.9	15.1	13.8	14.0	14.8	16.4	17.8	17.3	16.7	18.4	18.4	19.2	20.2	22.1	24.3	28.0	30.5
Korea	61.7	66.3	60.4	59.9	64.2	63.5	59.8	63.1	59.9	52.4	53.9	50.0	48.6	47.6	48.1	51.5	51.6	54.8	64.9	59.2	65.0	60.5	57.4	61.3	70.2	68.9	65.1	75.9
Lao	0.0	15.6	17.9	4.9	3.5	3.8	5.8	11.4	26.7	30.7	24.4	23.0	30.7	50.7	56.1	50.3	54.2	34.2	79.0	86.3	62.3	61.9	60.6	58.0	63.4	68.1	80.2	81.2
Malaysia	95.4	91.8	89.6	89.7	88.6	87.2	87.9	95.2	106.8	122.6	133.1	142.7	134.3	136.6	156.5	167.9	153.0	155.4	179.9	186.8	192.3	174.1	171.5	170.3	185.0	185.5	186.5	173.3
Myanmar	19.2	20.2	12.6	9.8	8.1	8.0	6.7	4.3	3.1	2.1	38.6	67.1	64.4	68.3	60.1	64.5	77.9	85.8	54.1	46.2	56.4	81.6	84.4	57.3	61.3	59.7	62.2	73.3
Philippines	43.4	39.8	35.8	38.5	36.9	32.4	33.5	38.1	41.5	44.4	48.0	48.1	46.1	53.2	56.2	60.5	62.1	76.9	88.6	87.0	95.8	91.6	92.0	92.6	96.3	89.8	83.8	95.7
Singapore	371.1	350.1	321.1	287.9	281.0	277.4	267.3	298.7	327.8	313.7	308.8	290.8	272.9	274.2	282.3	287.8	277.2	269.1	256.7	273.4	294.1	277.8	273.8	318.2	340.2	358.7	374.1	348.6
Thailand	48.6	48.7	42.3	41.6	42.7	42.1	41.9	48.6	58.7	63.1	66.0	69.5	66.9	68.6	70.1	80.8	72.2	80.8	88.6	88.8	106.6	110.1	105.3	109.5	118.1	129.4	126.3	119.6
Vietnam	0.0	5.1	3.3	2.2	1.6	16.9	8.7	7.9	16.3	87.5	82.9	61.1	60.3	52.4	60.7	67.4	76.0	79.6	76.0	81.2	96.5	96.1	103.7	114.6	128.3	130.5	138.5	154.6
ASEAN	58.7	62.0	58.8	58.7	53.3	55.9	51.3	58.9	71.5	78.0	87.7	89.4	87.7	89.3	94.6	101.6	96.1	102.8	126.5	116.9	132.1	125.7	118.1	120.1	132.1	137.0	137.2	133.1
ASEAN+3	29.0	29.9	29.6	28.3	29.1	28.7	22.8	22.6	22.9	24.4	26.9	26.0	25.5	24.3	26.2	28.0	30.3	32.6	32.0	31.1	35.2	35.2	37.3	40.9	46.4	50.8	56.1	60.3
ASEAN+4	31.0	32.0	31.7	30.3	31.5	31.1	25.0	25.2	25.8	27.6	30.4	29.8	29.7	28.4	30.5	32.4	35.1	37.7	37.1	35.6	40.2	40.2	42.4	46.2	51.9	56.5	62.1	66.1
ASEAN*	61.2	60.6	55.9	51.3	58.6	58.4	58.7	64.5	71.8	81.1	84.2	84.4	90.4	95.6	97.8	100.8	100.6	101.0	106.8	104.6	110.8	110.0	109.7	112.3	119.7	123.7	127.4	129.0
ASEAN+3*	54.7	54.8	50.6	46.9	53.2	53.3	53.0	57.7	63.0	69.6	72.5	72.6	77.1	80.7	83.2	85.6	85.2	85.9	90.9	88.9	94.7	93.6	93.6	96.7	103.8	107.2	110.3	112.6
ASEAN+4*	61.3	61.7	57.0	54.7	61.7	61.7	61.6	67.3	73.8	79.7	82.7	83.4	88.3	91.2	93.8	97.7	96.1	95.8	99.8	98.0	105.5	103.7	104.7	110.3	119.2	123.2	126.9	129.2
Euro area	46.4	48.0	47.8	47.1	49.9	50.7	44.1	43.3	43.9	46.4	44.8	42.7	40.5	39.0	42.2	44.4	44.6	48.8	49.7	52.1	59.7	59.4	57.1	56.1	58.9	61.5	65.4	66.6

Note: * denotes unweighted average.
Source: Calculations with data from DTS and WEO.

case trade openness of ASEAN is about 130 percent, while the trade openness of ASEAN+3 is just 60 percent.

The lower values for ASEAN+3 are a reflection of the relatively low degree of openness of Japan and China. While China and Japan are the regions' two largest traders, with total trade amounting to USD 2.2 trillion and USD 1.3 trillion, respectively, they also have the largest GDPs.[11] But while Japan has traditionally had low values of trade openness, openness has increased markedly in China over the past 25 years, a development that is likely to continue.[12] Among the ASEAN countries, only Indonesia (56 percent) was below the euro area openness value of 67 percent. In general, one can assert that East Asian countries, with the exception of Japan, are all open economies, making them sensitive to exchange rate fluctuations and reducing the ability of their central banks to influence the domestic price level.

Table 2 shows trade (i.e., exports plus imports) of the ASEAN+4 countries with their neighbors, as well as with the two most important extra-regional trading partners (the United States and the European Union), as the share of their total trade (world exports plus world imports) for 2007. The data show that intraregional trade (trade within ASEAN+4) on average accounts for almost 60 percent of total trade. When taking a weighted average for ASEAN+4 instead of an unweighted average, the ratio is still 47 percent, almost the same as the 49 percent for the euro area and higher than the 42 percent for NAFTA, and considerably higher than for other regional groupings such as Mercosur (16 percent), the Economic Community of West African States (ECOWAS, 9 percent), the Commonwealth of Independent States (CIS, 21 percent), the Central American Common Market (CACM, 14 percent), or the Andean Common Market (ANCOM, 9 percent) (Figure 1).

Looking at ASEAN alone, the share of trade within this group of countries is much lower than within ASEAN+4, amounting to a quarter of total trade on a weighted average as in Figure 1 (32 percent if taking an unweighted average as in Table 2). Trade with the "+4" countries is of great importance for all ASEAN countries except Lao (which has 68 percent of its trade with the other ASEAN countries), with an average of 30 percent of ASEAN countries' trade being conducted with China, Hong Kong, Japan, or Korea. On the other hand, trade with ASEAN is also important for China, Hong Kong, Japan, and Korea, but at a considerably lower level, 9, 10, 13, and 10 percent, respectively.

---

[11] In 2004, China for the first time exported (and imported) more than Japan; making it the world's third largest exporter behind the United States and Germany. In 2007, it overtook the United States to become the second largest exporter.

[12] In the case of Japan, trade openness had actually decreased in the 1980s and early 1990s, but has since increased again to 30 percent, a value a bit higher than the 26 percent in 1980.

Table 2. Trade of ... with ... (as percent of total trade), 2007

	USA	EU	China	HK	China+HK	Japan	Korea	ASEAN	ASEAN+3	ASEAN+4
Brunei	5.55	4.32	2.91	0.35	3.26	24.95	13.19	35.61	76.66	77.01
Cambodia	26.82	11.20	10.27	7.36	17.63	2.65	1.97	29.94	44.83	52.19
China	14.14	16.30		9.52	9.52	10.77	7.35	9.18	27.30	36.83
Hong Kong	9.15	10.23	47.46		47.46	7.33	3.10	9.91	67.80	67.80
Indonesia	7.57	9.84	10.28	1.59	11.87	13.87	6.22	29.32	59.68	61.27
Japan	16.30	12.78	17.74	3.02	20.76		6.10	13.01	36.86	39.88
Korea	11.43	11.95	21.20	2.95	24.15	11.63		10.36	43.19	46.14
Lao	1.03	6.38	7.69	0.45	8.14	1.61	1.34	67.84	78.48	78.93
Malaysia	13.45	12.42	10.63	3.84	14.47	10.88	4.32	25.14	50.97	54.82
Myanmar	0.10	5.73	21.85	1.28	23.13	4.67	2.52	47.14	76.17	77.45
Philippines	12.61	9.26	19.91	6.28	26.19	13.28	4.16	18.51	55.87	62.15
Singapore	10.58	11.52	10.81	6.26	17.07	6.39	4.16	28.60	49.97	56.22
Thailand	9.84	11.31	10.62	3.45	14.08	15.93	2.83	19.68	49.06	52.51
Vietnam	11.52	13.98	14.11	2.97	17.09	10.89	5.37	20.65	51.02	53.99
Mean ASEAN	9.91	9.59	11.91	3.38	15.29	10.51	4.61	32.24	59.27	62.65
Mean ASEAN+3	10.84	10.54	12.16	3.79	15.95	9.81	4.58	27.31	53.85	57.65
Mean ASEAN+4	10.72	10.51	14.68	3.52	18.20	9.63	4.47	26.06	54.85	58.37

Source: Calculations with data from DTS.
Mean ASEAN, ASEAN+3, ASEAN+4: unweighted average.

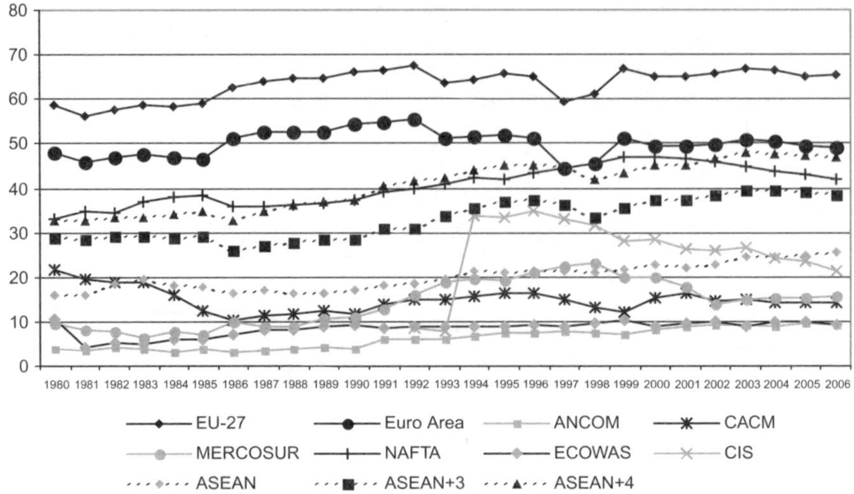

Fig. 1. ***Intraregional trade of group as percent of total trade, 1980–2006. Source: Calculations with data from UNCTAD and DTS.***

For most countries (Cambodia, Lao, Malaysia, Myanmar, the Philippines, Singapore, Vietnam, and Korea), trade with greater China (China and Hong Kong) has become more important now than trade with Japan. Moreover, greater China is a more important trading partner than the United States and the European Union for most East Asian countries, including Japan. Trade with the United States and the European Union makes up about 11 percent of the region's trade, respectively. This rather moderate share of trade with the United States is particularly interesting, as it is commonly claimed that East Asian countries maintain their (soft) pegs vis-à-vis the U.S. dollar because of strong trade ties with the U.S. (e.g., Dooley *et al.*, 2009a, 2009b). From this direction of trade analysis, it clearly follows that intraregional trade is much more important, and hence, from a trade-perspective, it is more crucial for East Asian countries to maintain intraregional exchange rate stability than to maintain stability toward the dollar. The solution is, of course, that the common dollar pegging also brings about intraregional exchange rate stability.[13] The question that follows is whether intraregional exchange rate stability could not better be achieved by direct exchange rate coordination between East Asian countries rather than by relying on an external anchor.

Going back to an individual country perspective, Table 3 lists the trading partners of East Asian countries, whose exports or imports account for at least 3 percent of total exports or imports. The disaggregated data

[13] As will be discussed later, the motivation for stabilizing the dollar exchange rates also stems from the problems associated with underdeveloped capital markets in East Asia.

Table 3. ***Exports, imports, and overall trade with … as percent of total exports, imports, and overall trade and individual basket weights***

Brunei	X to … as % of total X	I from … as % of total I	Trade with … as % of total trade	Individual country basket weight	Lao	X to … as % of total X	I from … as % of total I	Trade with … as % of total trade	Individual country basket weight
United States	7.72	2.65	6.57	6.76	China	4.07	11.33	8.4	10.48
Australia	11.46	1.14	9.1	9.36	Malaysia	4.03	0.38	1.85	2.31
Japan	30.54	5.56	24.84	25.56	Thailand	41.03	68.83	57.61	71.86
New Zealand	2.95	3.68	3.11	3.20	Vietnam	9.67	5.54	7.21	8.99
United Kingdom	1.88	8.07	3.29	3.39	Euro area	9.51	2.11	5.09	6.35
China	2.89	5.48	3.48	3.58					
Indonesia	19.86	2.72	15.95	16.41		68.31	88.19	80.17	99.99
Korea	14.86	1.09	11.72	12.06					
Malaysia	1.01	19	5.12	5.27					
Singapore	2.95	31.58	9.48	9.75					
Thailand	1.73	4.57	2.38	2.45					
Euro area	1.03	5.9	2.14	2.20					
	98.89	91.43	97.19	99.99					
Cambodia	X to … as % of total X	I from … as % of total I	Trade with … as % of total trade	Individual country basket weight	Malaysia	X to … as % of total X	I from … as % of total I	Trade with … as % of total trade	Individual country basket weight
United States	53.32	0.85	29.4	33.24	United States	15.62	10.84	13.45	16.80
Canada	3.23	0.09	1.8	2.04	Japan	9.13	12.98	10.88	13.59
Japan	0.96	4.34	2.5	2.83	Australia	3.37	2.02	2.76	3.45
United Kingdom	4.3	0.34	2.49	2.82	Hong Kong	4.62	2.91	3.84	4.80
China	0.44	17.55	8.24	9.32	India	3.34	1.4	2.46	3.07
Hong Kong	15.23	18.06	16.52	18.68	Indonesia	2.93	4.24	3.53	4.41

Table 3. *(Continued)*

Cambodia	X to … as % of total X	I from … as % of total I	Trade with … as % of total trade	Individual country basket weight	Malaysia	X to … as % of total X	I from … as % of total I	Trade with … as % of total trade	Individual country basket weight
Korea	0.09	4.89	2.28	2.58	Korea	3.8	4.93	4.32	5.39
Singapore	3.9	5.25	4.52	5.11	Singapore	14.63	11.48	13.19	16.47
Thailand	0.43	13.9	6.57	7.43	Thailand	4.95	5.35	5.13	6.41
Vietnam	2.11	9.04	5.27	5.96	China	8.77	12.86	10.63	13.27
Euro area	13.28	3.57	8.85	10.01	Euro area	10.07	9.66	9.88	12.34
	97.27	77.89	88.44	100.00		81.24	78.68	80.08	99.99
China	**X to … as % of total X**	**I from … as % of total I**	**Trade with … as % of total trade**	**Individual country basket weight**	**Myanmar**	**X to … as % of total X**	**I from … as % of total I**	**Trade with … as % of total trade**	**Individual country basket weight**
United States	19.14	7.32	13.94	24.88	Japan	5.16	3.01	4.16	4.77
Japan	8.38	14	10.85	19.36	China	5.25	35.07	19.08	21.88
Hong Kong	15.13	1.34	9.07	16.19	India	12.69	3.98	8.64	9.91
Korea	4.61	10.88	7.37	13.15	Korea	1.93	3.08	2.46	2.82
Malaysia	1.45	3.01	2.14	3.82	Malaysia	2.59	4.79	3.61	4.14
Euro area	14.98	9.71	12.66	22.60	Singapore	1.44	16.36	8.36	9.59
					Thailand	48.79	22.11	36.41	41.75
					Euro area	6.02	2.68	4.47	5.13
	63.69	46.26	56.03	100.00		83.86	91.08	87.21	99.98

Hong Kong	X to … as % of total X	I from … as % of total I	Trade with … as % of total trade	Individual country basket weight
United States	13.73	4.88	9.15	11.60
Japan	4.45	10.02	7.33	9.29
Korea. Republic of	1.97	4.17	3.10	3.93
Singapore	1.88	6.79	4.41	5.59
China	48.67	46.32	47.46	60.15
Euro area	9.37	5.65	7.45	9.44
	80.07	77.83	78.90	100.00

Philippines	X to … as % of total X	I from … as % of total I	Trade with … as % of total trade	Individual country basket weight
United States	18.32	16.31	17.27	20.52
Japan	16.48	13.59	14.97	17.79
China	9.83	7.13	8.41	9.99
Hong Kong	7.82	4.01	5.83	6.93
Korea	3	6.25	4.7	5.58
Malaysia	5.57	4.08	4.79	5.69
Singapore	7.34	8.45	7.92	9.41
Thailand	2.82	4.05	3.47	4.12
Iran	0.15	3.28	1.79	2.13
Saudi Arabia	0.11	5.78	3.08	3.66
Euro area	17.07	7.3	11.96	14.21
	88.51	80.22	84.17	100.02

Indonesia	X to … as % of total X	I from … as % of total I	Trade with … as % of total trade	Individual country basket weight
United States	11.48	3.66	7.97	9.86
Australia	2.85	3.95	3.34	4.13
Japan	19.38	8.76	14.61	18.08
China	7.7	11.24	9.29	11.49
India	3.19	1.4	2.39	2.96
Korea	6.44	5.29	5.93	7.34
Malaysia	3.96	4.84	4.36	5.39
Singapore	11.81	29.59	19.79	24.49
Thailand	2.77	3.97	3.31	4.10
Saudi Arabia	0.55	3.51	1.88	2.33
Euro area	9.76	5.76	7.96	9.85
	79.89	81.96	80.82	100.01

Singapore	X to … as % of total X	I from … as % of total I	Trade with … as % of total trade	Individual country basket weight
United States	8.91	12.48	10.58	13.51
Japan	4.81	8.18	6.39	8.16
Australia	3.74	1.2	2.55	3.26
Saudi Arabia	0.28	3.35	1.72	2.20
Hong Kong	10.47	1.46	6.26	7.99
India	3.34	2.23	2.82	3.60
Indonesia	9.85	5.57	7.84	10.01
Korea	3.55	4.87	4.16	5.31
Malaysia	12.91	13.07	12.99	16.59
Thailand	4.14	3.23	3.71	4.74
China	9.67	12.11	10.81	13.80
Euro area	7.5	9.62	8.49	10.84
	79.17	77.37	78.32	100.00

Table 3. (*Continued*)

Japan	X to … as % of total X	I from … as % of total I	Trade with … as % of total trade	Individual country basket weight	Thailand	X to … as % of total X	I from … as % of total I	Trade with … as % of total trade	Individual country basket weight
United States	20.38	11.62	16.3	23.09	United States	12.63	6.83	9.84	13.40
Australia	1.99	4.99	3.39	4.80	Japan	11.89	20.29	15.93	21.69
Saudi Arabia	0.94	5.72	3.17	4.49	Australia	3.76	2.72	3.26	4.44
United Arab Emirates	1.13	5.23	3.04	4.31	Saudi Arabia	0.9	3.27	2.04	2.78
Hong Kong	5.45	0.23	3.02	4.28	United Arab Emirates	1.45	4.88	3.1	4.22
Indonesia	1.27	4.22	2.64	3.74	Hong Kong	5.7	1.03	3.45	4.70
Korea	7.6	4.39	6.1	8.64	Indonesia	3.13	2.85	2.99	4.07
Singapore	3.06	1.13	2.16	3.06	Korea	1.95	3.78	2.83	3.85
Thailand	3.59	2.94	3.29	4.66	Malaysia	5.11	6.16	5.61	7.64
China	15.3	20.54	17.74	25.13	Singapore	6.25	4.49	5.4	7.35
Euro area	11.04	8.23	9.73	13.78	China	9.73	11.59	10.62	14.46
					Euro area	9.89	6.76	8.38	11.41
	71.74	69.27	70.59	99.99		72.37	74.63	73.45	100.00

Korea	X to … as % of total X	I from … as % of total I	Trade with … as % of total trade	Individual country basket weight	Vietnam	X to … as % of total X	I from … as % of total I	Trade with … as % of total trade	Individual country basket weight
United States	13.33	11.04	12.22	18.89	United States	21.23	2.6	11.17	14.50
Japan	8.13	16.76	12.33	19.06	Australia	9.4	2.7	5.78	7.50
Australia	1.47	3.6	2.5	3.86	Japan	12.28	9.78	10.93	14.19
Saudi Arabia	0.89	6.7	3.72	5.75	United Kingdom	3.42	0.42	1.8	2.34
United Arab Emirates	0.88	4.19	2.49	3.85	China	5.7	17.65	12.15	15.77
Hong Kong	5.86	0.69	3.34	5.16	Hong Kong	1.43	3.57	2.58	3.35
China	21.33	15.65	18.56	28.69	Korea	1.92	8.42	5.43	7.05
Euro area	11.04	7.93	9.52	14.72	Malaysia	3.24	4.16	3.74	4.85
					Singapore	3.78	12.9	8.7	11.29
					Thailand	2.07	7.32	4.91	6.37
					Euro area	14.68	5.73	9.85	12.79
	62.92	66.56	64.69	99.98		79.14	75.26	77.04	100.00

Note: Calculations are based on trade data for 2007. X, Exports; I, Imports.
Source: Calculations with data from DTS.

obviously show differences in the direction of trade between countries, but for almost all, trade with the United States, Japan, China, and the euro area is of great importance. The exceptions are Brunei, for which trade with China (3 percent) and the euro area (2 percent) is not important, whereas trade with Japan (25 percent), Indonesia (16 percent), and Korea (12 percent) are of utmost importance. Trade with Japan (2.5 percent) is not important for Cambodia. Lao trades predominantly with Thailand (58 percent), as well as with China (8 percent) and Vietnam (7 percent). Otherwise, trade with the United States, Japan, China and the euro area covers a great portion of trade, with each country usually having a few additional regional partners with whom they have particularly intense trade relations.

Table 3 also lists individual country currency basket weights that are based on these trade shares. Because the trade weights add up to less than 100 percent, since they exclude trade partners with whom either exports or imports account for less than 3 percent of total exports or imports, the weights are blown up to make the weights sum up to 100 percent.

To assess the effect of these individually tailored currency baskets, the behavior of the nominal effective exchange rates (NEERs) of ASEAN+4 countries under these baskets is compared with the NEERs under the actual policies that were followed.[14] To calculate both the NEERs of the actual historical experience as well as the hypothetical NEER under the basket scenario, the NEER weights for each of the ASEAN+4 countries are calculated on the basis of total trade shares.[15] For this purpose, the bilateral exchange rates are normalized to 1 for the starting period (January 1999). The NEER is then calculated as the sum of the bilateral exchange rates times the NEER weights.

To compare the volatility of the NEERs under the respective policies, the standard deviation of each country's NEER is computed for the period from January 1999 to April 2008. The results are presented in Table 4. The standard deviations of the NEERs under the baskets that are tailored to the trade patterns of each individual country are considerably lower than under the policies that were actually followed. That is, pegging to tailor-made currency baskets that reflect East Asian countries' patterns of trade would significantly reduce volatility of effective exchange rates.

[14] The nominal effective exchange rate (NEER) is the weighted average of a country's currency relative to an index or basket of other currencies. The weights are usually chosen to reflect the pattern of trade.

[15] It is most common to use total trade weights, but weights could be also based on import or export shares, or value added to exports. Alternatively, weighting could be based on trade elasticities, in order to also include important competitor countries and not only trading partners. Like for the calculation of the basket shares, all trading partners are included in the NEER calculation for which either exports or imports account for at least 3 percent of total exports or imports, respectively. Including trading partners with lower trade shares would only complicate calculations without changing the results.

Table 4. Standard deviation of NEERs, January 1999–April 2008

	NEER under actual policy	NEER if country had adopted individually tailored currency basket
Brunei	0.0340	0.0045
Cambodia	0.0584	0.0036
China	0.0399	0.0047
Hong Kong	0.0478	0.0022
Indonesia	0.1061	0.0026
Japan	0.0653	0.0037
Korea	0.0769	0.0038
Lao	0.3109	0.0019
Malaysia	0.0350	0.0030
Myanmar	0.0364	0.0020
Philippines	0.1433	0.0330
Singapore	0.0265	0.0032
Thailand	0.0544	0.0034
Vietnam	0.1183	0.0034

Source: Calculations with IFS and DTS data.

Because East Asian countries have roughly similar trade orientations, even basket policies that take account only of the national trade patterns would result in a relatively homogenous exchange rate policy across the region. And as the weights of the other East Asian countries make up important shares in the respective country baskets, intraregional exchange rate stability would in turn contribute to lower variability of effective exchange rates.

For East Asian countries, currency baskets have particular appeal because the geographic distribution of trade points to no single currency area as an optimal anchor. It was noted earlier that trade with the United States and the European Union each account for an average of about 11 percent for ASEAN+4 countries. This implies that, from a trade perspective, neither the dollar nor the euro is an optimal choice as an anchor currency for East Asian countries. Furthermore, trade with Japan on average accounts for 12 percent, which does not make the yen any more optimal a choice than the dollar or the euro. Finally, trade with China and Hong Kong makes up about 15 percent of trade for East Asian countries, only slightly more than trade with the United States, Europe, or Japan. Moreover, the Chinese currency is also inept in fulfilling the role of a regional currency anchor because of its inconvertibility and the weakness and shallowness of the Chinese financial markets. Thus, from the point of view of the literature on the optimum peg, no single currency would be a perfect anchor for East Asian countries. Currency baskets would thus be a superior alternative.

Moreover, currency baskets are an interesting option because they can also be used as a regional strategy for exchange rate cooperation.

As discussed, intraregional trade is of utmost importance for East Asia, with a weighted average of intra-ASEAN+4 trade of 48 percent, almost as high as the 51 percent of the euro area. The regional adoption of broadly similar currency baskets would contribute to intraregional exchange rate stability in the same way the common dollar peg does. Furthermore, as Williamson (2001) points out, a common basket peg would offer the important advantage of ensuring that the exchange rates of East Asian countries in relation to each other are not destabilized by shocks to the dollar/yen/euro rates.[16] This would prevent inadvertent competitive devaluation or the suspicion of instrumented competitive devaluation that could result from different pegging policies.

Because trade structures are broadly similar for most East Asian countries, individual country baskets to stabilize NEERs would in most cases include the same currencies with relatively similar weights. In other words, even if all countries in the region adopted baskets tailored to their individual trade structures, the result would be a relatively homogenous exchange rate policy throughout the region, which in effect would result in relative exchange rate stability between East Asian currencies (e.g., Williamson, 2001, 2009).[17] Williamson (2001, p. 104) hence concludes that a regional basket peg would offer "the advantages of the dollar peg without its disadvantages."

A currency basket could thus be a substitute for a peg to an international or regional anchor currency. In addition to supporting regional exchange rate stability, it could provide more flexibility than a full-fledged regional exchange rate system.[18] Another advantage of a currency basket over a regional currency system is that it would require less political commitment, as the former could be maintained by each country individually (although some coordination would be beneficial so as to avoid unintended beggar-thy-neighbor policies).

Given the high degree of economic interdependence within the region, a unilateral, noncooperative policy of East Asian countries would be problematic, as intraregional exchange rate volatility could have very disruptive effects on the regional economy. This would be aggravated because of poorly developed financial markets and missing hedging opportunities in most of the region. The fact that the East Asian dollar

[16] As Mundell (2003, p. 2) observes, "[a] major threat to the [current] system arises from gyrations of the major exchange rates. The instability of exchange rates between the large currencies has been enormous." The East Asian dollar standards arrangement, however, would become more sustainable, if also Japan were to peg its currency to the dollar, as suggested by McKinnon (2005). This would provide a uniform exchange rate policy for the *whole* region, as well as stability toward the dollar. It would also preclude instability of the dollar-yen rate, the results of which were painfully felt in the Asian crisis. A Japanese decision to link the yen to the dollar again, however, is very unlikely.

[17] Ma and McCauley (2009) argue in a similar direction.

[18] On the feasibility of a regional monetary system for East Asia see Volz (2006).

standard resurrected after the Asian crisis and still prevails is evidence of East Asian countries' (excluding Japan) fear of floating, and it is unlikely that this will change anytime soon. Floating exchange rates, or in general, unilateral exchange rate policies that might go into different directions, could have a highly destabilizing potential for the regional economy. Any monetary and exchange rate policy in East Asia should thus be directed at maintaining relative intraregional exchange rate stability.

4. International assets and liabilities

This section extends the previous analysis by taking account of East Asian countries' international asset and liability situation and how this affects exchange rate choices. As the data situation on the currency denomination of East Asian countries' international investment position is difficult, this section will focus mostly on conceptual issues, and do some simulations for Thailand based on the limited data available. It is hoped to conduct the suggested calculations with more comprehensive dataset at a later stage.

As highlighted by Lane and Milesi-Ferretti (2001), price and exchange rate changes have an impact on the value of external assets and liabilities that are not captured in the corresponding flows. For debt assets, debt liabilities, and foreign exchange reserves, valuation changes are primarily due to exchange rate fluctuations. Following Lane and Milesi-Ferretti (2005) and Lane and Shambaugh (2007), the change in the net foreign asset (NFA) position between periods $t-1$ and t can be formulated as

$$\mathrm{NFA}_t - \mathrm{NFA}_{t-1} = \mathrm{CA}_t + \mathrm{VAL}_t$$

where CA_t is the current account surplus and VAL_t describes the net capital gain on existing foreign assets and liabilities. Depending on the magnitude of NFA, the valuation impact of a shift in currency, $\partial \mathrm{VAL}_t / \partial E_t$, can have serious balance sheet effects for an economy, and might therefore become an important element in determining the exchange rate policy of that country.

First of all, to appraise the potential valuation effects it makes sense to look at the international financial exposure of an economy. A summary volume-based measure of international financial integration (Lane and Milesi-Ferretti, 2003) is

$$\mathrm{IFIGDP}_{it} = \frac{(\mathrm{FA}_{it} + \mathrm{FL}_{it})}{\mathrm{GDP}_{it}},$$

where IFIGDP_{it} stands for international financial integration for country i at time t and FA and FL refer to the stocks of aggregate foreign assets and liabilities, respectively. This data on countries' portfolios of external assets and liabilities – the so-called international investment position – summarize total holdings by domestic residents of financial claims on the

Table 5. International assets and liabilities as percent of GDP

	2000	2001	2002	2003	2004	2005	2006	2007
Cambodia	145.14	149.68	159.07	160.42	150.34	145.00	147.73	153.99
China					81.12	90.47	100.72	108.35
Hong Kong	1,218.77	1126.57	1,048.27	1,246.53	1,403.29	1,434.53	1,757.92	2,389.16
Indonesia		123.08	100.94	93.14	89.41	85.96	76.52	
Japan	102.41	107.44	118.26	131.90	142.13	154.58	173.08	194.35
Korea		90.02	88.34	97.60	108.41	113.62	124.22	145.15
Malaysia		167.50	167.65	174.87	197.02	183.70	204.67	243.53
Myanmar	96.70	136.31	141.39	102.87	106.44	90.06	93.42	
Philippines		132.29	129.66	131.75	122.24	119.43	112.40	112.13
Singapore		792.67	847.78	909.97	907.51	895.58	985.69	994.77
Thailand	136.92	138.91	128.62	129.05	123.73	122.82	132.64	142.79
Euro area	213.39	221.74	236.57	249.28	259.04	267.10	322.19	356.84

Note: No data available for Brunei, Lao, and Vietnam.
Source: Calculations with data from IFS and WEO.

rest of the world and nonresidents' claims on the domestic economy. External liabilities are divided into four main categories: foreign direct investment, portfolio investment (equity and debt securities), financial derivatives, and other investment (monetary authorities, general government, banks, and other sectors). Assets constitute the same four categories as liabilities, plus official reserves.

Table 5 gives an overview of the evolution of East Asian countries' and the euro area's international investment position relative to GDP since the year 2000. Compared with the euro area, most East Asian countries show a lower degree of international financial openness, with Hong Kong and Singapore being the two major exceptions, with international financial exposure equaling 2,389 percent of GDP in the case of Hong Kong and 995 percent in the case of Singapore. For all other, international assets and liabilities are on the magnitude of about 90–150 percent of GDP, with Japan's and Malaysia's exposure being greater at 194 and 244 percent, respectively.

The crucial question for our purpose is the currency denomination of these assets and liabilities. As discussed earlier, exchange rate swings will cause valuation effects if assets and liabilities are denominated in another currency than the domestic currency. Hence, a high ratio of international assets and liabilities relative to GDP does not automatically imply that this is a potential source of vulnerability for an economy; the composition of these assets and liabilities and the net value of these positions is what matters. For instance, Tille (2003) has highlighted that the foreign liabilities of the United States are mostly denominated in U.S. dollars, whereas there is a substantial foreign currency component in its foreign assets. On the other hand, most developing and emerging countries face

Table 6. ***Net value of international assets and liabilities (in million USD)***

	2000	2001	2002	2003	2004	2005	2006	2007
Cambodia	−635	−594	−616	−775	−899	−1,097	−1,112	−1,256
China					292,775	422,563	611,360	1,022,020
Hong Kong	221,850	265,221	343,337	394,159	424,752	439,360	518,330	483,700
Indonesia		−113,992	−98,621	−105,962	−116,758	−124,487	−139,996	
Japan	1,157,940	1,360,090	1,462,160	1,613,620	1,784,480	1,531,760	1,808,170	2,194,960
Korea		−63,783	−70,355	−81,759	−88,473	−179,476	−200,948	−232,459
Malaysia		−36,297	−36,871	−37,459	−33,513	−19,853	−6,553	−5,541
Myanmar	−8,031	−7,909	−8,462	−9,436	−9,896	−9,190	−9,478	
Philippines		−36,164	−37,601	−40,314	−38,611	−36,782	−31,312	−27,349
Singapore		60,990	81,748	98,205	112,577	143,227	160,797	154,683
Thailand	−60,444	−51,844	−45,741	−55,691	−53,481	−57,284	−59,369	−57,679
Euro area	−474,830	−349,160	−749,690	−994,000	−1,203,400	−981,400	−1,360,500	−1,881,200

Note: No data available for Brunei, Lao, and Vietnam.
Source: Calculations with data from IFS.

the problem of "original sin" (Eichengreen and Hausmann, 2005), a situation where countries cannot borrow internationally in domestic currency. Sometimes even domestic borrowing in domestic currency is difficult, if there is little trust in the stability of the domestic money. The problem of original sin was also a major problem during the Asian crisis, when East Asian currencies were forced to abandon their dollar pegs and devalue, which meant that their dollar debt increased dramatically in terms of domestic currency.

The situation in East Asia has changed in two ways. First, the problem of original sin has been recognized and as a consequence the region has started efforts to develop not only domestic bond markets but also a regional debt market in order to enable and facilitate borrowing in domestic currency.[19] Second, most East Asian countries have transformed their current account deficits into surpluses and some of them from net debtors into net creditors. Table 6 displays the net value of international assets and liabilities of East Asian countries. Among others, East Asian countries have accumulated vast amounts of foreign exchange reserves to fend off any future speculative attacks on their currencies. While this is a positive development, it has brought about the already mentioned problem of "conflicted virtue." Because most East Asian countries cannot lend in their home currency, the build-up of foreign assets makes them susceptible to large-scale appreciation of their home currencies. That is, because the majority of East Asian international assets is denominated on foreign currency, they face a currency mismatch again.

While it is known that international assets of East Asian countries are mostly denominated in foreign currency, especially the U.S. dollar,

[19] See, for instance, Ma and Remolona (2009) and Schou-Zibell (2008).

Table 7. Currency breakdown of portfolio investment assets (in million USD, end-2007)

Currency of denomination	Indonesia	Japan	Korea	Malaysia	Thailand
US dollar	2,081	1,047,293	82,595	4,983	12,030
Euro	13	493,872	8,772	1,138	866
British pound	....	107,941	1,675	189	473
Japanese yen	1	576,976	5,654	201	52
Swiss franc	....	16,571	524	24	32
Other	35	280,915	59,431	6,400	1,240
Total	2,129	2,523,566	158,651	12,935	14,692

Note: "..." indicates an unavailable term.
Source: IMF Coordinated Portfolio Investment Survey.

detailed information on the currency composition of these assets (as with liabilities) is in most cases hard to obtain or estimate. To fully assess the effects of exchange rate movements on a country's international investment position, it is necessary to know the magnitude and currency composition of assets and liabilities within the different classes, that is, foreign direct investment, portfolio investment (equity and debt securities), financial derivatives, other investment (monetary authorities, general government, banks, and other sectors), as well as official reserves in the case of assets. Lane and Shambaugh (2007) weigh these asset classes by their shares in the international balance sheet in order to construct an aggregate index to analyze valuation effects of exchange rate movements.[20]

We can get a rough idea of the overall currency composition by looking at different classes of investment. Tables 7 and 8 show the currency breakdown of portfolio investment assets for a couple of East Asian countries. The data show a strong dominance of the U.S. dollar for all countries with available data, reflecting the preeminent role that the USD still plays in the East Asia region. For all but Japan and Malaysia, the share of the USD in the international portfolio asset investments is above 50 percent.

Although most East Asian countries do not disclose the currency composition of their international reserves, one can safely assume that the dollar share of foreign reserves is even greater for most countries – given that the dollar has been the anchor country for most of them, which has implicated frequent intervention in the foreign exchange market and a subsequent accumulation of dollars to prevent appreciation of the domestic currency against the dollar.

[20] These authors collected data from various sources to compile a dataset and estimated the missing values for a panel of countries with the aim of analyzing valuation effects exchange rate changes. The Lane and Shambaugh data are not available for the time being, unfortunately.

Table 8. Currency breakdown of portfolio investment assets (as percent of total, end-2007)

Currency of denomination	Indonesia	Japan	Korea	Malaysia	Thailand
US dollar	97.72	41.50	52.06	38.52	81.88
Euro	0.62	19.57	5.53	8.80	5.89
British pound		4.28	1.06	1.46	3.22
Japanese yen	0.04	22.86	3.56	1.55	0.35
Swiss franc		0.66	0.33	0.18	0.22
Other	1.62	11.13	37.46	49.48	8.44
Total	100.00	100.00	100.00	100.00	100.00

Source: Calculations with data from IMF Coordinated Portfolio Investment Survey.

If one had complete data on currency denomination of debts and liabilities, one could construct what might be called "financial exchange rate baskets" (Lane and Shambaugh, 2007) for East Asian countries, analogue to the trade-weighted baskets of the last section. In a further step one could use both baskets to calculate a blend of "real" and "financial" exchange rate baskets for analyzing "optimal" exchange rate policy. While data limitations prevent us from effectively doing so, it is useful to illustrate this approach with a hypothetical example.

If we assume that the currency breakdown of Thailand's portfolio investment assets as presented as in Table 8 is representative of the currency denomination of all of Thailand's international assets and liabilities (a very simplifying yet not completely far-fetched assumption), then these figures could be used as weights for calculating a financial exchange rate basket for Thailand. From the data in Table 8 we would include five currencies into Thailand's "financial" currency basket, namely the U.S. dollar, the yen, the euro, the Swiss francs, and the British pound. Because the currency weights in Table 8 include the position "other currencies," the shares need to be adjusted as was the case with the trade-based weights. That is, the weights of the currencies that are included in the basket are blown up to make the weights sum up to 100 percent. This yields the financial basket weights presented in column three of Table 9. As is apparent, the weights for the trade baskets, which are presented in the second column of the same table, and those of the financial baskets differ markedly. Whereas the U.S. dollar gets only a share of 13.4 percent in the trade-based basket, it is dominating the finance-based basket with a share of 89.4 percent.[21] The yen, which on the basis of trade flows would get a share of 21.7 percent, is included in the financial basket with a

[21] As can be seen from Annex 1, which presents estimates of the actual currency weights for the Thai baht, the dollar share in the finance-based basket is not very far from the actual exchange rate policy conducted by the Bank of Thailand.

Table 9. Hypothetical currency baskets for Thailand

	Basket weights based on trade shares ("trade basket")	Basket weights based on currency shares ("financial basket")	Basket weights based on currency shares (blend of "trade" and "financial" baskets)
United States	13.40	89.43	54.77
Japan	21.69	0.38	10.09
Australia	4.44		2.02
Saudi Arabia	2.78		1.27
United Arab Emirates	4.22		1.92
Hong Kong	4.70		2.14
Indonesia	4.07		1.86
Korea	3.85		1.75
Malaysia	7.64		3.48
Singapore	7.35		3.35
China	14.46		6.59
Euro-area	11.41	6.43	8.70
Switzerland		0.24	0.13
United Kingdom		3.52	1.92
Total	100.01	100.00	100.00

miniscule 0.4 percent. The euro gets at least a 6.4 percent share, compared to the 11.4 percent for the trade-based basket. If we assume the denomination of Thai portfolio assets to be at least broadly similar to the denomination of other Thai asset and liability classes, the point to be made here is clear: an exchange rate policy for Thailand that aims at avoiding valuation changes of external assets and liabilities would be guided by a very different currency basket than an exchange rate policy targeted at stabilizing the NEER.

Which of these two factors should dominate in formulating exchange rate policy depends on the one hand on the importance of trade flows and the disruptive effects that exchange rate volatility or exchange rate appreciation might have on these, and on the other hand on the potentially disruptive effects on an economy's financial system caused by valuation changes due to exchange rate movements.

Both aspects can be included in the monetary authority's objective function. Assuming a simple objective function that takes into account both the stabilization of NEERs in order to minimize trade disruptions and valuation changes of external assets and liabilities, a basket for guiding optimal exchange rate policy can be constructed as a blend of "real" and "financial" exchange rate baskets. The optimal currency shares w_c^* of currency c in such a basket can be calculated as

$$w_c^* = \phi w_{tc} + (1 - \phi) w_{fc}$$

where w_{tc} and w_{fc} are the optimal weights of currency c in the purely trade-based and finance-based baskets, respectively, and where ϕ is the weight given to trade concerns and $(1 - \phi)$ the weight given to valuation effects.

If we base our calculations in the Thailand example on the basket shares from columns two (for w_{tc}) and three (for w_{fc}) of Table 9, and use figures for trade openness (from Table 1) and international financial integration (IFIGDP, from Table 5) to calculate ϕ and $(1 - \phi)$, respectively, we derive at the optimal currency shares w_c^* as listed in the fourth column of Table 9. The dollar now has a reduced share of 54.8 percent, compared with the finance-based weight of 89.4 percent. The yen gets at least a 10.1 percent share, the yuan 6.6 percent, and the euro 8.7.

It would be inept to suggest that such simple calculations should guide a country's "optimal" exchange rate policy. But an exchange rate rule taking into account effects of "real" and "financial" exchange rate swings that is based on comprehensive information on the denomination of financial stocks and assets can indeed be a helpful tool in guiding exchange rate policy, or at least for scrutinizing the appositeness of the policy that is currently operated.

5. *From the East Asia dollar standard to the East Asian basket standard*

While from a trade analysis one would conclude that the USD is currently overrepresented in the exchange rate policy of most East Asian countries, the financial analysis of the preceding section shows that there are good reasons indeed for a continued management of exchange rates against the dollar as it helps prevent major valuation effects for East Asian investors and debtors. (A further benefit of the East Asian dollar standard, as discussed, is that it provides relative exchange rate stability within the region, which has greatly helped in developing East Asia's trade and production network.)

However, there are three serious reservations against a continued reliance on the U.S. dollar. First, maintaining fixed parities with the dollar automatically brings about problems when there are swings in the dollar–euro and dollar–yen rates, as noted before.

Second, the risk of maintaining one-sided dollar pegs depends not only on domestic efforts to keep the dollar exchange rate stable, but also on the monetary policy in the anchor country and the international value of its currency (Schnabl, 2009). The problem is illustrated by the depreciation pressure on the dollar up to July 2008, which was in part a result of the historically low U.S. interest rate policy from 2001 up to 2004. To maintain the dollar parity in face of appreciation pressure on their own currencies, East Asian countries were forced to intervene heavily in the foreign exchange market and stockpile dollar reserves. As the scope for sterilization is limited, fast monetary expansion was a result in most

East Asian countries, which has led to a fast growth of monetary aggregates, contributed to surging stock and real estate prices (which in some parts of the region has led to financial bubbles that have burst in the meantime), and eventually, rising inflation. The zero interest rate policy and quantitative easing measures that the Federal Reserve has initiated as a response to the U.S. financial crisis carries the danger of high U.S. inflation and a devaluation pressure on the dollar in the medium run, which would erode the dollar's appeal as an anchor currency.

Last, the international creditor countries in the region face the already mentioned problem of conflicted virtue, that is, balance sheet losses on assets denominated in U.S. dollars as an appreciation of domestic currencies vis-à-vis the dollar reduces the value of these assets in terms of home currencies.

But even if the dollar maintains its strength, the question remains why a region as economically potent as East Asia should continuously bind itself to an external anchor. As noted earlier, the East Asian dollar standard also constitutes a form of implicit exchange rate coordination. While this system has served the majority of East Asian countries very well (with exception, of course, the period preceding the Asian crisis), a continued pegging to the dollar involves all the costs, but not all the gains of regional monetary integration. The current dollar pegging might well be feasible for a considerable amount of time as claimed by Dooley *et al.* (2009a, 2009b), but as a long-term strategy it is a dead end.

Still, the heavy dollar exposure of East Asian countries would make a quick dissolution of the linkages with the dollar a risky endeavor. The accumulation of huge amounts of private assets and dollar reserves to stem the appreciation of domestic currencies has led to a situation where a dollar-depreciation would cause significant balance sheet losses, which leads East Asian central banks to further intervene in the market, which increases reserves even more. To exit this "conflicted virtue circle" abruptly would risk a full-blown dollar crisis, something all parties wish to avoid.

Currency baskets would provide an elegant way out of the dollar dependency: dollar weights could be gradually reduced while the weights of other currencies could be increased.[22] The result would be a diversification of risk without unsettling currency markets. A first step of such a strategy could be a coordinated move of East Asian countries, including Japan, to adopt currency baskets that would take into account both their trade structures and international asset and liability position. This would create a situation where the East Asian dollar standard would be replaced by an "East Asian basket standard." While such a basket

---

[22] On the desirability of a regional basket arrangement for East Asia, see also Ogawa and Ito (2002) and Ito (2007).

standard would mark a departure from the current regime, the advantage is that it would not require a dramatic change of course. Indeed, dollar weights could be gradually reduced while the shares of other currencies in the baskets could be increased.[23] Each country could administer such a reorientation individually, although a coordinated move would facilitate adjustment. The only country for which the adoption of a basket regime would mean a substantial shift from its current exchange rate policy is Japan.[24] Still, Japan could converge to the other countries' policies gradually, without necessarily making radical policy moves.

In general, if countries wish to reap the benefits of relative intraregional and effective exchange rate stability but are reluctant to adhere strictly to a currency basket regime because they want to avoid the risk of pegging and maintain more flexibility than under a basket regime, they could adopt a managed float regime guided by the use of a common basket as numeraire as suggested by Williamson (2009). Compared with other options of maintaining relative regional exchange rate stability, namely a continuation of the East Asian dollar standard or the creation of an East Asian monetary system, this basket option compares favorably, as it would allow for a considerable degree of flexibility. This would not only reduce the risk of currency speculation, but also grant participating countries certain independence in conducting national economic policies.

A second step – which could be made parallel to the adoption of a region-wide currency basket regimes – could be the introduction of an Asian Currency Unit (ACU) as a virtual basket currency. The ACU could fulfill several functions (see Kawai, 2009). First, it could be useful as a statistical indicator that summarizes the collective movement of East Asian currencies against external key currencies such as the dollar and the euro. As a regional benchmark index, it could help to monitor regional foreign exchange market developments and help identify the degree of divergence of each component currency from the regional trend.[25] As such, the ACU would only serve as a monitoring device, without requiring any automatic policy reactions such as foreign exchange market interventions.

---

[23] China and Malaysia have made first moves into this direction since 2005. Once China allows for more flexibility in its exchange rate and effectively follows its announced basket regime, it is likely that Hong Kong (as well as the other dollar pegging countries in the region) will follow the mainland. Schnabl (2009) shows that several other East Asian countries have slightly reduced their dollar orientation recently. His estimations of the basket structures of East Asian countries suggest somewhat growing weights of the euro and the yen in the currency baskets of Indonesia, Korea, the Philippines, Singapore, and Thailand.

[24] Although the yen can be classified as freely floating, Japan has frequently intervened in the foreign exchange market to influence its dollar rate. See Fratzscher (2004).

[25] Such divergence analysis can help to identify idiosyncratic problems in a particular currency's market and help to address vulnerabilities that adversely affect the exchange rate. See Ogawa and Shimizu (2005).

Second, the ACU could be used as a region-wide "parallel currency" (Eichengreen, 2006) to circulate alongside national currencies. Because it would be more stable than any national currency in terms of aggregate regional production and trade, it would be interesting for private corporations and investors to use the ACU for invoicing and settling intraregional trade as well as for regional investment. The ACU could be also useful for developing new tradable financial market instruments and, more generally, for promoting the development of regional capital markets. Especially the development of a regional bond market has been given high priority by East Asian policymakers ever since the financial crisis. ACU-denominated bonds would be interesting for issuers as well as investors, because the currency risk of basket denominated bonds tends to be lower than that of local currency-denominated bonds (Ogawa and Shimizu, 2009). Moreover, Ogawa and Shimizu (2009) show that issuing currency-basket-denominated bonds would, in general, decrease the foreign borrowing costs for bond issuers in all East Asian countries. East Asian governments, as well as private corporations of any nationality investing in the region, would thus have an incentive to issue sovereign or corporate bonds denominated in ACU. On the buying side, ACU-denominated bonds would be attractive for institutional investors not only because of a lower currency risk than of single-currency-denominated securities, but also because a region-wide ACU bond market, if ever realized, would offer more liquidity and market depth than single national markets. Kawai (2009) points to other possible usage of an ACU. For instance, futures exchanges could offer ACU futures, which would provide hedging instruments for traders even in the absence of onshore derivatives markets for some highly regulated currencies. Finally, commercial banks could accept ACU deposits and make ACU loans, facilitating the financing of regional trade.

At an early stage of cooperation, the ACU would not need to fulfill any official function like the European Currency Unit did in the European Monetary System (EMS). In the beginning, neither the adoption of a currency basket regime nor the creation of the ACU would require concessions in national sovereignty or a binding commitment to monetary integration. In the longer term, however, as monetary authorities get acquainted with the management of currency baskets, and as markets increasingly rely on the ACU, countries could gradually increase integration efforts and develop the East Asian basket standard into a fully fledged regional exchange rate system. Gradually, cooperation could be increased and the composition of currency baskets could be harmonized. The ACU could then become the common reference point for exchange rate management of all countries of the region. Over time, when substantial credibility has been accumulated, currency bands could be introduced, developing a formal exchange rate system similar to the EMS, which should then also include intervention obligations in case of deviations from the parity grid. Only if a formal exchange rate system were to be created, would the ACU assume the function of an official unit of account for monetary and exchange rate policy coordination.

Parallel to increasing exchange rate cooperation, authorities would need to intensify monitoring and surveillance of financial markets, for example under the framework of ASEAN+3's Economic Policy and Review Dialogue. In this context the independent regional surveillance unit that is to be created in the process of the multilateralization of the Chiang Mai Initiative could play an important role. Exchange rate coordination would also need to be flanked by financing facilities, such as those under the extended Chiang Mai Initiative (see Volz, 2008, 2009).

The advantages of such a strategy are at hand. As shown before, currency baskets would help to stabilize NEERs and prevent negative effects of gyrations between major currencies, especially the dollar and the yen. No radical reorientation of exchange rate policies would be required, as most countries in the region have already allowed for more flexibility vis-à-vis the dollar. A gradual reduction of the dollar's weight in region-wide currency baskets would reduce the risk of a dollar crash. At the same time, the ACU could be introduced as a virtual parallel currency to be used for trade invoicing and settling and for developing financial products on a regional capital market. In the early stages, political commitment would be very limited, which would make cooperation easier to realize. Moreover, choosing currency baskets and the ACU to guide exchange rate policy circumvents the problem of selecting a regional currency to act as an anchor. Countries could gain experience with regional cooperation and develop trust before moving to more formal cooperation that would require sacrifices to a country's sovereignty. A gradual approach to monetary integration in East Asia would allow East Asian countries to get to know their partners more closely and develop a sense of community. If countries are still committed to regional monetary unification after having experienced what close monetary and exchange rate cooperation really means, they could eventually form an East Asian monetary union.

6. Conclusion

Given the economic interdependencies that have developed within East Asia over the past decades, this chapter recommends a cooperative approach to exchange rate stabilization within the region based on currency baskets. As financial linkages with the United States are still very important today, a quick dissolution of the still close ties with the U.S. dollar would not only be destabilizing for the region, it would also entail the risk of a severe dollar crisis. Instead, the chapter proposes a gradual approach in which East Asian monetary authorities steadily reduce their linkages with the dollar and at the same time increase weights of other currencies – including the yen and the euro – in their currency baskets. For constructing currency baskets, the chapter suggests a blend of "real" and "financial" exchange rates, which could help guide the "optimal" exchange rate policy. Even if all countries chose the "optimal" basket composition tailored to their own economic circumstances, the result would be a relatively homogenous exchange rate policy across the region. In time, East Asian monetary authorities could harmonize their basket compositions and also introduce a virtual basket unit, which could be then used for more formal exchange rate coordination, if this is politically desired.

Acknowledgments

Earlier versions of this chapter were presented at the 18th Conference of the American Committee for Asian Economic Studies (ACAES) on "Asian Economic Integration in a Global Context," August 29–31, 2008, at the University of Bologna, Rimini Campus; the Keio University/ADBI Workshop on "Exchange Rate Systems and Currency Markets in Asia" in Tokyo, March 24, 2009; and the WEAI Pacific Rim Conference in Kyoto, March 24–27, 2009. Comments and suggestions from Reid Click, Guonan Ma, Robert McCauley, Hiro Ito, Eiji Ogawa, Naoyuki Yoshino, Zhiwei Zhang, and other participants of these conferences, as well as comments by an anonymous referee are gratefully acknowledged. All remaining errors and shortcomings are my own.

Annex 1. Estimated basket weights of Thai baht, 1999–2008

	USD	Euro	Yen	Adj. R-squared
1999	0.8624***	0.0921	0.1199**	0.57
	(0.0884)	(0.0641)	(0.0480)	
2000	0.8972***	0.0340	0.0771	0.69
	(0.0724)	(0.0412)	(0.0514)	
2001	0.8195***	−0.0046	0.1130***	0.83
	(0.0416)	(0.0251)	(0.0307)	
2002	0.6120***	0.1907***	0.1250**	0.60
	(0.0636)	(0.0482)	(0.0536)	
2003	0.7799***	0.0340	0.1404***	0.83
	(0.0441)	(0.0281)	(0.0397)	
2004	0.7220***	0.0955***	0.1299***	0.89
	(0.0318)	(0.0199)	(0.0256)	
2005	0.6653***	0.1177***	0.1521***	0.84
	(0.0345)	(0.0257)	(0.0321)	
2006	0.6992***	0.1505***	0.1326**	0.58
	(0.0635)	(0.0519)	(0.0539)	
2007	0.8739***	−0.0618	0.0591	0.15

Annex 1. *(Continued)*

	(0.1699)	(0.1340)	(0.1053)	
2008	1.0045***	−0.0018	−0.0162	0.39
	(0.1565)	(0.1274)	(0.1319)	
1999–2008	0.7908***	0.0683***	0.1115***	0.58
	(0.0240)	(0.0169)	(0.0180)	

Note: The currency weights were estimated using the methodology introduced by Frankel and Wei (1994) with daily exchange rates. Estimates for 2008 were made with data ranging from January 1, 2008 to August 14, 2008.
Source: Own calculations with daily exchange rate data from Datastream (Reuters and Tenfore).

References

Bénassy-Quéré, A., Fontagné, L., Lahrèche-Révil, A. (2001), Exchange-rate strategies in the competition for attracting foreign direct investment. *Journal of the Japanese and International Economies* 15 (2), 178–198.

Calvo, G.A., Reinhart, C.M. (2002), Fear of floating. *Quarterly Journal of Economics* 117 (2), 379–408.

Dooley, M., Folkerts-Landau, D., Garber, P. (2003), An essay on the revived Bretton Woods System. NBER Working Paper 9971, National Bureau of Economic Research, Cambridge, MA.

Dooley, M., Folkerts-Landau, D., Garber, P. (2009a), Bretton Woods II still defines the international monetary system. *Pacific Economic Review* 14 (3), 297–311.

Dooley, M., Folkerts-Landau, D., Garber, P. (2009b), East Asia's role in the revived Bretton Woods System. In: Hamada, K., Reszat, B., Volz, U. (Eds.), *Toward East Asian Monetary and Financial Integration.* Edward Elgar, Cheltenham, pp. 141–158.

Eichengreen, B.J. (1994), *International Monetary Arrangements for the 21st Century*. Brooking Institution, Washington, DC.

Eichengreen, B.J. (2006), The parallel-currency approach to Asian monetary integration. *American Economic Review* 96(2) (AEA Papers and Proceedings), 432–436.

Eichengreen, B. J., Hausmann, R. (Eds.) (2005). *Other People's Money: Debt Denomination and Financial Instability in Emerging Market Economies*. University of Chicago Press, Chicago.

Fischer, S. (2001), Exchange rate regimes: is the bipolar view correct? *Journal of Economic Perspectives* 15 (2), 3–24.

Frankel, J.A. (1999), No single currency regime is right for all countries or at all times. NBER Working Paper 7338, National Bureau of Economic Research, Cambridge, MA.

Frankel, J.A., Schmukler, S.L., Serven, L. (2004), Global transmission of interest rates: monetary independence and currency regime. *Journal of International Money and Finance* 23 (5), 701–733.

Frankel, J.A., Wei, S.J. (1994), Yen bloc or dollar bloc? Exchange rate policies of the East Asian economies. In: Ito, T., Krueger, A. (Eds.), *Macroeconomic linkages: savings, exchange rates, and capital flows*, NBER East Asia Seminar on Economics, 3, University of Chicago Press, Chicago, pp. 295–329.

Fratzscher, M. (2002), The euro bloc, the dollar bloc and the yen bloc: how much monetary policy independence can exchange rate flexibility buy in an interdependent world?, Working Paper Series 154, European Central Bank, Frankfurt am Main.

Fratzscher, M. (2004), Exchange rate policy strategies and foreign exchange interventions in the group of three economies. In: Bergsten, C.F., Williamson, J. (Eds.), *Dollar Adjustment: How Far? Against What?*, Special Report 17, Institute for International Economics, Washington, DC, pp. 259–271.

Giavazzi, F., Pagano, M. (1988), The advantage of tying one's hands: EMS discipline and central bank credibility. *European Economic Review* 32 (5), 1055–1082.

Hamada, K. (1985), *The Political Economy of International Monetary Interdependence*. MIT Press, Cambridge, MA.

Ito, T. (Ed.) (2007). *A Basket Currency for Asia*. Routledge, London.

Kawai, M. (2009), The role of an Asian currency unit. In: Hamada, K., Reszat, B., Volz, U. (Eds.), *Towards East Asian Monetary and Financial Integration*. Edward Elgar, Cheltenham, pp. 304–322.

Lane, P.R., Milesi-Ferretti, G.M. (2001), The external wealth of nations: measures of foreign assets and liabilities for industrial and developing countries. *Journal of International Economics* 55 (2), 263–294.

Lane, P.R., Milesi-Ferretti, G.M. (2003), International financial integration. *IMF Staff Papers* 50 (Special Issue), 82–113.

Lane, P.R., Milesi-Ferretti, G.M. (2005), Financial globalisation and exchange rates. CEPR Discussion Paper No. 4745, London.

Lane, P.R., Shambaugh, J.C. (2007), Financial exchange rates and international currency exposures. NBER Working Paper 13433, National Bureau of Economic Research, Cambridge, MA.

Ma, G., McCauley, R.N. (2009), The evolving Renminbi regime and implications for Asian currency stability. Paper presented at the Keio University/ADBI Workshop on "Exchange Rate Systems and Currency Markets in Asia", Tokyo, March 24, 2009.

Ma, G., Remolona, E.M. (2009), Learning by doing in market reform: lessons from a regional bond fund. In: Hamada, K., Reszat, B., Volz, U. (Eds.), *Towards East Asian Monetary and Financial Integration*. Edward Elgar, Cheltenham, pp. 87–103.

McKinnon, R.I. (2001), After the crisis, the East Asian Dollar standard resurrected: an interpretation of high-frequency exchange rate pegging. In: Stiglitz, J.E., Yusuf, S. (Eds.), *Rethinking the East Asian Miracle*. Oxford University Press, Oxford, pp. 197–246.

McKinnon, R.I. (2005), *Exchange Rates Under the East Asian Dollar Standard. Living With Conflicted Virtue*. MIT Press, Cambridge, MA.

McKinnon, R.I., Schnabl, G. (2004), The East Asian Dollar standard, fear of floating, and original sin. *Review of Development Economics* 8 (3), 331–360.

McKinnon, R.I., Schnabl, G. (2009), Current account surpluses and conflicted virtue in East Asia: China and Japan under the dollar standard. In: Hamada, K., Reszat, B., Volz, U. (Eds.), *Towards East Asian Monetary and Financial Integration*. Edward Elgar, Cheltenham, pp. 159–191.

Mundell, R.A. (2003), Prospects for an Asian currency area. *Journal of Asian Economics* 14 (1), 1–10.

Ogawa, E., Ito, T. (2002), On the desirability of a regional basket currency arrangement. *Journal of the Japanese and International Economies* 16 (3), 317–334.

Ogawa, E., Shimizu, J. (2005), AMU deviation indicator for coordinated exchange rate policies in East Asia. RIETI Discussion Paper No. 05-E-017, Research Institute of Economy, Trade and Industry, Tokyo.

Ogawa, E., Shimizu, J. (2009), Currency denomination in Asian bond markets. In: Hamada, K., Reszat, B., Volz, U. (Eds.), *Towards East Asian Monetary and Financial Integration*. Edward Elgar, Cheltenham, pp. 104–137.

Pula, G., Peltonen, T. (2011), Has emerging Asia decoupled? An analysis of production and trade linkages using the Asian International Input-Output Table. In: Cheung, Y.-W., Kakkar, V., Ma, G. (Eds.), *The Evolving Role of Asia in Global Finance*. Bingley, UK: Emerald.

Reade, J.J., Volz, U. (2011), When you got nothing, you got nothing to lose. Monetary integration and monetary policy independence. In: Volz, U. (Ed.), *Regional Integration, Economic Development and Global Governance*. Edward Elgar, Cheltenham, pp. forthcoming.

Schnabl, G. (2009), Capital markets and exchange rate stabilization in East Asia – diversifying risk based on currency baskets. In: Hamada, K., Reszat, B., Volz, U. (Eds.), *Towards East Asian Monetary and Financial Integration*. Edward Elgar, Cheltenham, pp. 267–289.

Schou-Zibell, L. (2008), Regional cooperation and development of bond markets – the Asian experience. In: Volz, U. (Ed.), *Financial Innovation and Emerging Markets. Opportunities for Growth vs. Risks for Financial Stability*. InWEnt, Berlin, pp. 127–144.

Tille, C. (2003), *The impact of exchange rate movements on U.S. foreign debt, Current Issues in Economics and Finance 9-1*. Federal Reserve Bank of New York, New York.

Volz, U. (2006), On the feasibility of a regional exchange rate system for East Asia: lessons of the 1992–93 EMS crisis. *Journal of Asian Economics* 17 (6), 1107–1127.

Volz, U. (2008), Asian Monetary Fund, take two. *Far Eastern Economic Review*, Forum, June. Available at http://feer.com/economics/2008/june/an-asian-monetary-fund-second-try

Volz, U. (2009), A new era of financial cooperation. *Far Eastern Economic Review*, Forum, June. Available at http://www.feer.com/economics/2009/june53/A-New-Era-of-Financial-Cooperation

Volz, U. (2010), *Prospects for Monetary Cooperation and Integration in East Asia*. MIT Press, Cambridge, MA.

Williamson, J. (1982), A survey of the literature on the optimal peg. *Journal of Development Economics* 11 (1), 39–61.

Williamson, J. (2001), The case for a Basket, Band and Crawl (BBC) regime for East Asia. In: Gruen, D., Simon, J. (Eds.), *Future Directions for Monetary Policies in East Asia*. Reserve Bank of Australia, Sydney, pp. 97–111.

Williamson, J. (2009), East Asian currency baskets. In: Hamada, K., Reszat, B., Volz, U. (Eds.), *Towards East Asian Monetary and Financial Integration*. Edward Elgar, Cheltenham, pp. 290–303.

Yoshino, N., Kaji, S., Suzuki, A. (2004), The basket-peg, dollar-peg, and floating: a comparative analysis. *Journal of the Japanese and International Economies* 18 (29), 183–217.

CHAPTER 7

Stability of East Asian Currencies during the Global Financial Crisis

Junko Shimizu[a] and Eiji Ogawa[b]

[a]*School of Commerce, Senshu University, 2790031 Japan*
E-mail address: jshimizu@isc.senshu-u.ac.jp
[b]*Graduate School of Commerce and Management, Hitotsubashi University, 1868601 Japan*
E-mail address: ogawa.eiji@srv.cc.hit-u.ac.jp

Abstract

We investigate fluctuations in the nominal effective exchange rates (NEERs) of East Asian currencies and the Asian monetary unit (AMU), which is computed as a weighted average of East Asian currencies during the global financial crisis. We find that NEERs were more stable for countries that continued to follow a currency basket system during the global financial crisis.

Furthermore, we investigate the relationships among NEERs, AMU, and AMU deviation indicators, which indicate the extent of the deviation in the exchange rate of each East Asian currency from a benchmark rate given in terms of the AMU. By comparing NEERs with a combination of AMU and AMU deviation indicators, we find that there is a strong relationship between them, both before and after the global financial crisis. These results indicate that a coordinated exchange rate policy aimed at stabilizing the AMU deviation indicators will be effective in stabilizing the NEERs of East Asian currencies. In this respect, the AMU deviation indicators, which indicate intraregional exchange rates among East Asian currencies, play a crucial role.

Because NEER trade weights are widely similar among East Asian currencies, a policy aimed at stabilizing a home currency against its NEER may lead to a coordinated exchange rate policy without a common consensus among East Asian countries. In the future, however, coordinated monetary policies should be considered along with coordinated exchange rate policies.

Keywords: Asian monetary unit (AMU), AMU deviation indicator, *dė facto* US dollar peg system, currency basket system, nominal effective exchange rate (NEER), coordinated exchange rate policy, the Chiang Mai Initiative, trade weight, GDP measured at PPP, European currency unit

Frontiers of Economics and Globalization
Volume 9 ISSN: 1574-8715
DOI: 10.1108/S1574-8715(2011)0000009012

(ECU), implicit basket weights, currency regime, surveillance, European monetary system (EMS)

JEL classification: F31, F33, F36

1. Introduction

The global financial crisis that began in the United States during the summer of 2007 has significantly influenced the US domestic economy and Asian economies. It has also led to the possibility that production networks, which have been growing in East Asia, may undergo large-scale restructuring in the future. Considerable currency fluctuations not only against the US dollar but also against currencies of neighboring countries within the region bring unfavorable conditions for Asian economies. To determine the economic impact of exchange rate fluctuations on intraregional trade, it is essential to create a new currency system that will stabilize intraregional exchange rates within Asia while allowing them to fluctuate against the US dollar and euro.

In this chapter, we investigate the fluctuations in nominal exchange rates, nominal effective exchange rates (NEERs) of East Asian countries, and the Asian monetary unit (AMU), which is computed as a weighted average of Asian currencies, as proposed by Ogawa and Shimizu (2005), throughout the period of the most recent global financial crisis.[1] In particular, we analyze the differences among the exchange rate data of nominal exchange rates, NEERs of East Asian countries, and the AMU in order to determine an appropriate currency regime for stabilizing the NEER of each East Asian currency during the global financial crisis.

In addition, we investigate relationships among NEERs, AMU, and AMU deviation indicators for each East Asian country previously studied by Ogawa and Shimizu (2005). The AMU is computed as a weighted average of East Asian currencies, whereas the AMU deviation indicators indicate the extent of the deviation of East Asian currencies with respect to a benchmark rate set in terms of the AMU. The AMU and AMU deviation indicators are both considered surveillance measures under the Chiang Mai Initiative, and as such, they are coordinated exchange rate policies among East Asian countries. If fluctuations in the AMU deviation indicators for each East Asian currency are strongly related to their NEERs, monitoring and maintaining the indicators within a certain band is considered an effective exchange rate policy. Ogawa and Shimizu (2006) have previously investigated the relationship among NEERs, AMU, and AMU deviation indicators (AMUDI). In this chapter, we conduct the

---

[1] For details on the AMU and AMU deviation indicators, see the Appendix.

same analysis, but extend the sample period to include the global financial crisis to identify possible changes in the relationship among NEERs, the AMU, and the AMUDI.

The rest of this chapter is organized as follows. Section 2 presents an overview of previous studies aimed at identifying an appropriate currency regime for East Asian countries. Section 3 investigates the fluctuations in Asian currencies during the global financial crisis. Section 4 focuses on the fluctuations in the NEER of each East Asian currency to compare the relationships between the effective exchange rate weights assigned to the East Asian countries and their currency regimes. Section 5 investigates the relationship among the NEER, the AMU and the AMU deviation indicators for each East Asian currency. Section 6 discusses the manner in which the AMU deviation indicators should be used to promote the coordination of regional exchange rates. Finally, Section 7 summarizes our results and presents the conclusion.

2. What is an appropriate currency regime for East Asia?

Although the Asian currency crisis in 1997 provided an important lesson that *de facto* dollar peg may be dangerous for East Asian countries, the monetary authorities of East Asian countries were inclined to choose a *de facto* dollar peg system over a currency basket peg system. As highlighted in McKinnon (2000), Ogawa (2002), and Ogawa and Yoshimi (2008), the currencies of East Asian countries continue to be frequently linked to the US dollar, even following the Chinese currency regime reform in July 2005.[2] Using empirical evidence, Ogawa and Yoshimi (2008) indicated that the monetary authority of China continued to stabilize the Chinese yuan against the US dollar despite the adoption of a managed floating exchange rate system with reference to a currency basket. Simultaneously, it was found that the home currencies of a few East Asian countries were tied to a currency basket. A similar coordination failure in exchange rate policies among the monetary authorities of East Asian countries may increase the volatility and nonalignment of intraregional exchange rates among East Asian currencies.

Given an increasing dependency on intraregional trade within East Asian countries, the establishment of a currency system to minimize exchange rate risks in international trade and investments within the region is indispensable. A proposed approach in this regard is the creation of a common currency basket that would serve as a basis for East Asian currencies and enable the monetary authorities of East Asian countries to achieve a joint currency basket system. Ogawa and Shimizu (2005) proposed the Asian monetary unit (AMU), which is computed as the

[2] Ogawa and Ito (2000) regarded these movements as a type of coordination failure.

weighted average of 13 East Asian currencies (namely, ASEAN, China, Japan, and South Korea), and they developed the AMU deviation indicators, which serve as surveillance measures under the Chiang Mai Initiative.[3] The AMU deviation indicators are employed as benchmarks for enabling the monetary authorities of East Asian countries to maintain regional coordination in exchange rate policies, essentially ensuring that any East Asian currency does not deviate from the common currency basket or the AMU. This would enable East Asian countries to achieve stability in terms of intraregional exchange rates and float jointly against outside currencies, including the US dollar and euro.

A few East Asian countries, including Singapore, China, and Malaysia (the latter since July 2005), adopted a currency system in line with the BBC (Basket, Band, and Crawling) rule.[4] As an example proposal, Ogawa and Shimizu (2007) developed a stepwise approach to transitioning from an individual to a common currency basket system in East Asia. Ma and McCauley (2009) also discussed that intra-Asian exchange rate stability could build on similar national policies aimed at managing currencies against their own respective baskets.

In contrast, McKinnon (2005) proposed the so-called "East Asian dollar standard," which suggests that East Asian countries must coordinate their policies to maintain stable exchange rates against the US dollar. In addition, he highlighted the collective macroeconomic consequences on the governments of all East Asian countries that individually choose to peg their currencies against the US dollar. According to McKinnon, East Asian countries must coordinate their policies to maintain stability in their exchange rates against the US dollar. McKinnon and Schnabel (2009) also proposed that China must strictly maintain the nominal peg of the Chinese yuan to the US dollar for reasons of monetary and financial stability.

During normal, noncrisis periods, a majority of Asian currencies were strongly correlated with the US dollar; that is, they were stable vis-à-vis the US dollar. However, these currencies fluctuated vis-à-vis the euro and Japanese yen. Consequently, their effective exchange rates were unstable. The Bank of Thailand clearly explains on their website that they endeavor to ensure the value of the Thai baht under the condition of "maintaining national competitiveness, as measured through not just the US Dollar but the nominal effective exchange rate, which includes currencies of important trading partners for Thai economy."

Following the Lehman shock on September 15, 2008, a number of Asian currencies depreciated sharply vis-à-vis the US dollar, with the Japanese yen and Chinese yuan being notable exceptions. The monetary

---

[3] Such a unit has also been extensively discussed in East Asia, for example, in the ADB (Kuroda and Kawai, 2003).

[4] Please see Williamson (2000) for BBC rule.

authorities of East Asian countries have now recognized that exchange rate stability against the US dollar is not sufficient for sustaining the stability of their economy. At present, all monetary authorities should reassess whether it is more appropriate for the region to stabilize their exchange rates against the US dollar or a currency basket. Moreover, they must assess whether it is appropriate for the East Asian economy to adopt coordinated exchange rate policies.

3. Exchange rate fluctuations under the global financial crisis

First, we evaluated the most recent fluctuations in Asian currencies vis-à-vis the US dollar. Figure 1 indicates the index of Asian currencies vis-à-vis the US dollar (January 2008 = 100) from January 2008 to March 2009. Since September 2008, Asian currencies have been depreciating sharply against the US dollar on account of the sale of local currencies accompanying capital outflows associated with deleveraging by the US and European financial institutions. The only exception has been the Japanese yen, which has appreciated substantially against the US dollar. The Chinese yuan has remained relatively stable vis-à-vis the US dollar during this period due to its strong relationship with the US dollar. This is similar to the *de facto* dollar peg conducted by the monetary authority of China. In addition, the Singapore dollar and Malaysian ringgit did not significantly depreciate against the US dollar due to the existence of a currency basket system. Among all Asian currencies, the South Korean

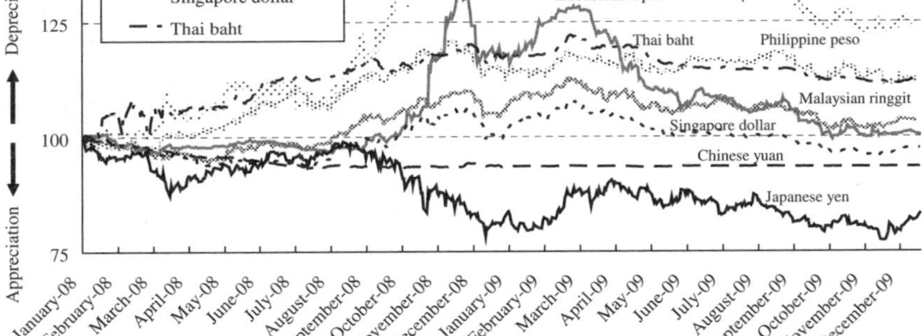

Fig. 1. Fluctuations in the exchange rates of Asian currencies against the US dollar. Source: Datastream.

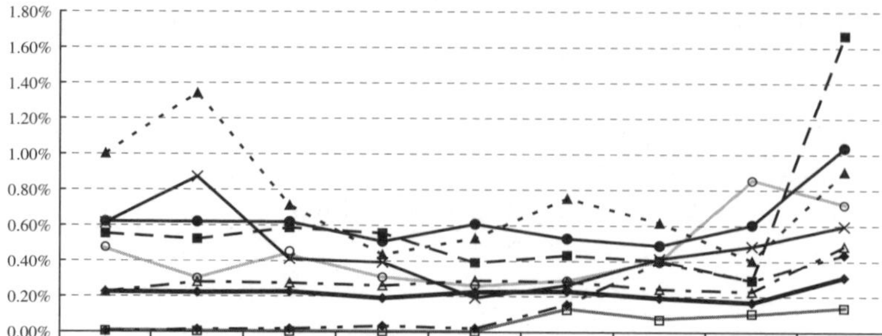

	2000	2001	2002	2003	2004	2005	2006	2007	2008
AMU	0.22%	0.22%	0.23%	0.19%	0.22%	0.23%	0.19%	0.17%	0.31%
China	0.00%	0.00%	0.00%	0.00%	0.00%	0.13%	0.07%	0.10%	0.14%
Indonesia	1.00%	1.34%	0.71%	0.44%	0.53%	0.75%	0.62%	0.40%	0.90%
South Korea	0.55%	0.52%	0.59%	0.56%	0.39%	0.43%	0.40%	0.29%	1.67%
Malaysia	0.00%	0.01%	0.02%	0.03%	0.02%	0.15%	0.39%	0.29%	0.44%
Philippines	0.61%	0.87%	0.41%	0.39%	0.19%	0.26%	0.41%	0.48%	0.60%
Singapore	0.22%	0.28%	0.27%	0.26%	0.29%	0.28%	0.24%	0.23%	0.48%
Thailand	0.48%	0.30%	0.45%	0.31%	0.26%	0.29%	0.39%	0.85%	0.72%
Japan	0.62%	0.62%	0.62%	0.51%	0.61%	0.53%	0.49%	0.60%	1.04%

Fig. 2. Foreign exchange fluctuations vis-à-vis the US dollar. Note: Standard deviation of daily exchange rates is in percentage.

won faced the most considerable depreciation against the US dollar. Other Asian currencies, particularly the Thai baht, have also depreciated following the subprime crisis and bankruptcy of Lehman Brothers.

Subsequently, we compared the fluctuations in the AMU, which is computed as a weighted average of East Asian currencies, and in each East Asian currency vis-à-vis the US dollar, euro, and Japanese yen. We calculated the standard deviation of daily nominal exchange rates by year. All exchange rates have been obtained from Datastream, whereas the AMU is available on the Research Institute of Economy, Trade and Industry (RIETI) website.[5]

Figure 2 indicates the fluctuations in nominal exchange rates vis-à-vis the US dollar. Essentially, there are considerable fluctuations in floating currencies (i.e., the Japanese yen, South Korean won, and Indonesian rupiah) and comparatively insignificant fluctuations in *de facto* US dollar-pegged currencies (i.e., the Chinese yuan) and currency basket pegged currencies (i.e., the Singapore dollar). The AMU acts as the second most stable East Asian currency. A majority of East Asian currencies, except the Chinese yuan, fluctuate more significantly than the AMU against the US dollar.

Figure 3 indicates the fluctuation in nominal exchange rates vis-à-vis the euro. Overall, fluctuations in Asian currencies are more significant vis-à-vis the euro than the US dollar. The AMU is the second least volatile; the

[5] Daily data on the AMU and AMU deviation indicators are freely available on the RIETI website (http://www.rieti.go.jp/users/amu/en/index.html).

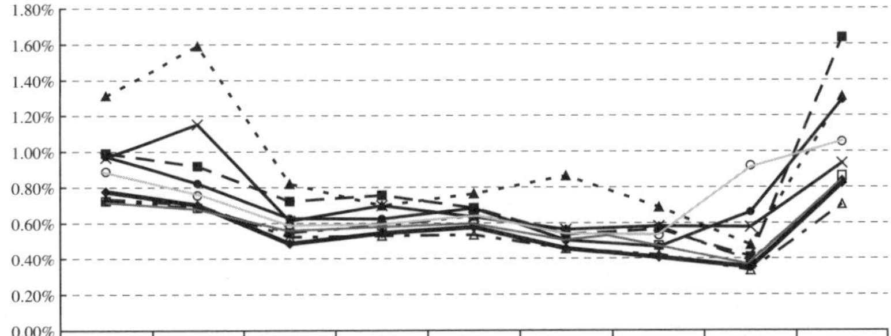

	2000	2001	2002	2003	2004	2005	2006	2007	2008
AMU	0.78%	0.70%	0.49%	0.54%	0.58%	0.46%	0.41%	0.35%	0.82%
China	0.72%	0.69%	0.55%	0.59%	0.64%	0.55%	0.47%	0.36%	0.86%
Indonesia	1.31%	1.59%	0.82%	0.70%	0.76%	0.86%	0.69%	0.48%	1.31%
South Korea	0.99%	0.92%	0.72%	0.76%	0.68%	0.54%	0.56%	0.41%	1.64%
Malaysia	0.72%	0.69%	0.55%	0.59%	0.64%	0.56%	0.58%	0.39%	0.83%
Philippines	0.97%	1.15%	0.61%	0.70%	0.63%	0.56%	0.58%	0.58%	0.93%
Singapore	0.74%	0.70%	0.52%	0.53%	0.53%	0.46%	0.42%	0.33%	0.70%
Thailand	0.89%	0.76%	0.59%	0.59%	0.60%	0.51%	0.53%	0.92%	1.05%
Japan	0.97%	0.82%	0.63%	0.62%	0.68%	0.50%	0.47%	0.66%	1.29%

Fig. 3. Foreign exchange fluctuations vis-à-vis the euro. Note: Standard deviation of daily exchange rates is in percentage.

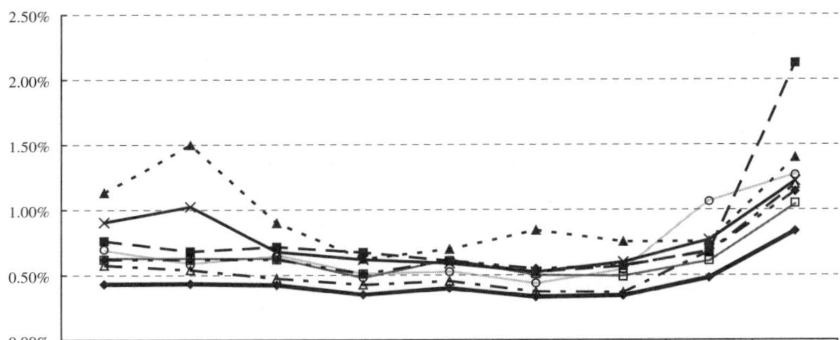

	2000	2001	2002	2003	2004	2005	2006	2007	2008
AMU	0.43%	0.43%	0.42%	0.35%	0.40%	0.33%	0.34%	0.48%	0.84%
China	0.62%	0.62%	0.62%	0.51%	0.61%	0.51%	0.49%	0.61%	1.05%
Indonesia	1.13%	1.50%	0.90%	0.62%	0.70%	0.84%	0.75%	0.76%	1.40%
South Korea	0.76%	0.68%	0.72%	0.67%	0.61%	0.52%	0.57%	0.68%	2.13%
Malaysia	0.62%	0.62%	0.62%	0.51%	0.61%	0.55%	0.57%	0.68%	1.14%
Philippines	0.91%	1.02%	0.68%	0.62%	0.59%	0.52%	0.60%	0.77%	1.22%
Singapore	0.58%	0.54%	0.47%	0.43%	0.45%	0.37%	0.37%	0.68%	1.19%
Thailand	0.70%	0.58%	0.65%	0.48%	0.52%	0.44%	0.54%	1.06%	1.27%

Fig. 4. Foreign exchange fluctuations vis-à-vis the Japanese yen. Note: Standard deviation of daily exchange rates is in percentage.

Singapore dollar was the least volatile. The Malaysian ringgit fluctuates less than other East Asian currencies. Figure 4 indicates the fluctuation in nominal exchange rates vis-à-vis the Japanese yen. In this case, the AMU is the most stable, while the Chinese yuan is the second most stable East Asian currency.

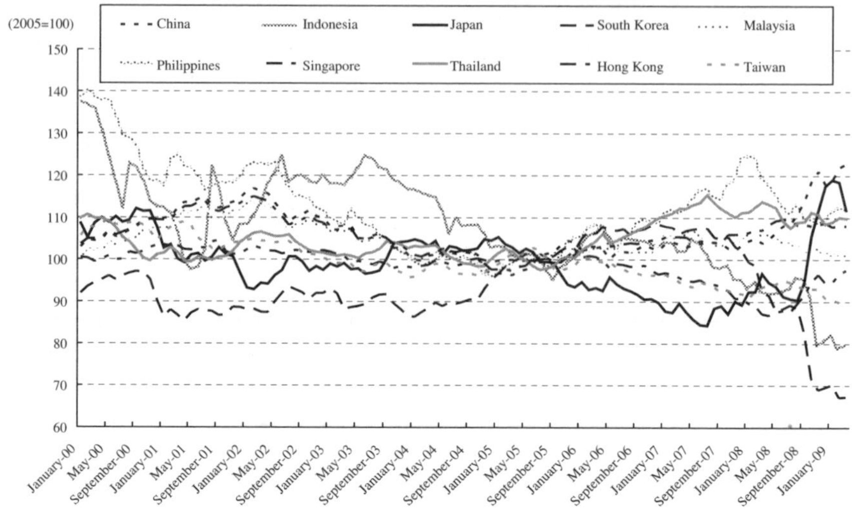

Fig. 5. The NEERs of East Asian currencies. Source: BIS.

Overall, we can summarize the abovementioned results in the following manner. The exchange rates of East Asian currencies vis-à-vis the three major currencies, that is, the euro, US dollar, and Japanese yen, became very volatile in 2008. However, there were comparatively less significant fluctuations in the exchange rates of currency basket pegged currencies (i.e., the Singapore dollar and Malaysian ringgit), especially vis-à-vis the euro and Japanese yen. At one point, the exchange rate was more stable for the AMU than for a majority of East Asian currencies.

4. The NEERs of East Asian currencies

In this section, we investigated fluctuations in the NEERs of East Asian currencies. The monthly data on NEERs were obtained from BIS (2005 = 100). Figure 5 indicates the fluctuations in the NEERs of East Asian currencies from January 2000 to March 2009. Figure 5 indicates that the NEER of the Chinese yuan fluctuated even prior to the Chinese currency regime reform in July 2005. NEERs began becoming volatile for a majority of the East Asian countries in mid-2007. Since September 2008, the NEERs of the Japanese yen and Chinese yuan have been sharply appreciating, whereas the NEER of the South Korean won has been dramatically depreciating.

What accounts for the volatility in the NEERs of a few East Asian currencies during the global financial crisis? To answer this question, we must first verify the effective exchange rate weights assigned to the currencies of trade-partner countries. Figure 6 indicates effective exchange rate weights assigned to East Asian currencies in 2005–2007 according to

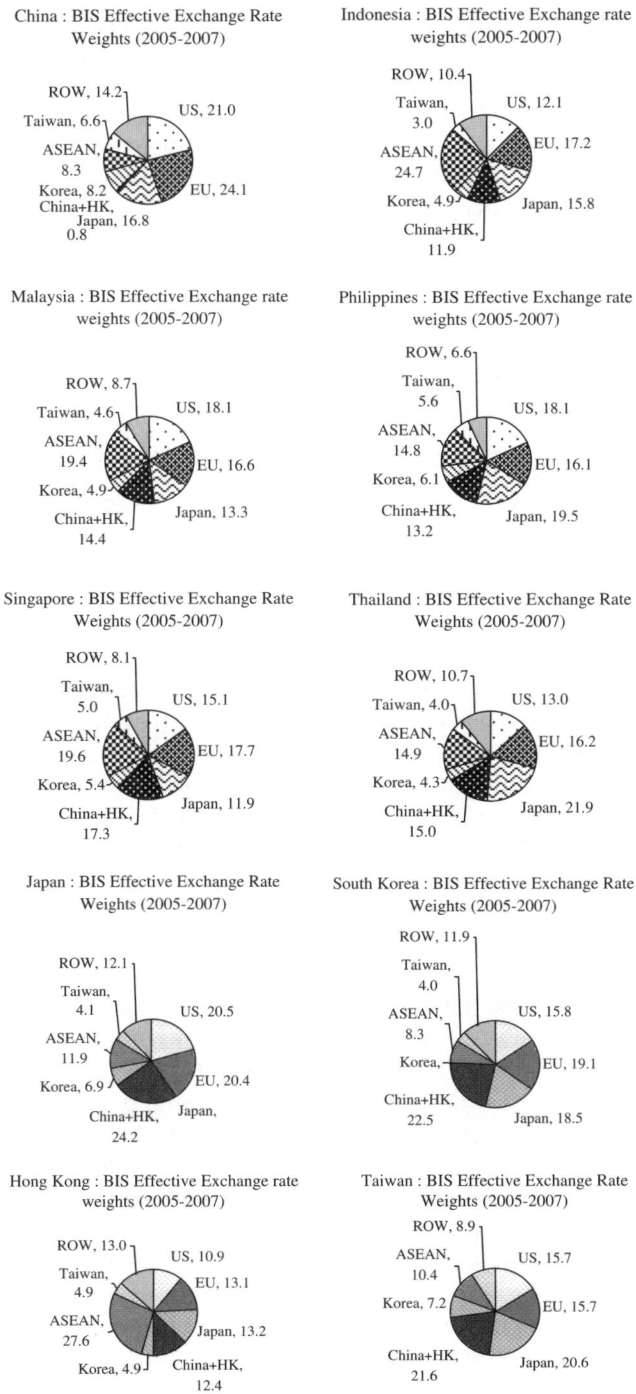

Fig. 6. BIS effective exchange rate weights (2005–2007). Source: BIS.

the BIS statistics.[6] As Ma and McCauley (2009) highlighted, we find that the pattern of assigning effective exchange rate weights to East Asian currencies are similar. Weights assigned to the US dollar range from 12.1% in Indonesia to 21.0% in China. Weights assigned to the euro range from 16.1% in Indonesia to 24.1% in China. Weights assigned to East Asian currencies (i.e., the Japanese yen, Chinese yuan, Hong Kong dollar, South Korean won, ASEAN currencies, and Taiwanese dollar) range from 47.1% in Japan to 68.63% in Taiwan. Among the East Asian currencies, the smallest weight is assigned to the Chinese yuan (40.7%), as it does not include a weight on itself. The US dollar does not carry the maximum weight consistently for all East Asian currencies. The maximum weight for the Chinese yuan is assigned to the euro. The maximum weight for the Japanese yen, South Korea won, and Taiwanese dollar is assigned to the Chinese yuan and thus the Hong Kong dollar. The maximum weight for the Thai baht, Philippine peso, and Hong Kong dollar is assigned to the Japanese yen. The maximum weight for the Singapore dollar, Malaysian ringgit, and Indonesian rupiah is assigned to the ASEAN currencies. These results indicate that significant weights are assigned to East Asian currencies. Consequently, this implies that the effective exchange rate for East Asian currencies may be stable if their intraregional bilateral exchange rates are stable.

We investigated the relationship between the effective exchange rate weights assigned to East Asian currencies and fluctuations in the NEER of each East Asian currency. For this, we plotted a scatter diagram indicating the volume of monthly fluctuations in NEERs on the vertical axis and the effective exchange rate weights assigned to East Asian currencies on the horizontal axis. The fluctuation in NEERs is calculated as a standard deviation from monthly NEER data. We divide the sample period into two subsample periods that comprise a normal period from January 2000 to December 2006 and a period of global financial crisis from January 2007 to March 2009.

Figure 7 indicates the results. During the normal period (Panel A, January 2000 to December 2006), we find no apparent relationship between the effective exchange rate weights assigned to the East Asian currencies and fluctuations in NEERs. During the global financial crisis period (Panel B, January 2007 to March 2009), the fluctuations in NEERs are less than 5% when the effective exchange rate weights assigned to East Asian currencies are approximately over 60%, except in the case of the Indonesian rupiah. In addition, the fluctuations in NEERs are just over 7% when the effective exchange rate weights on the East Asian currencies are below 55%. This implies that when the effective exchange rate weights assigned to East Asian currencies are considerable, NEERs become more

---

[6] BIS revises the effective exchange rate weights every two years.

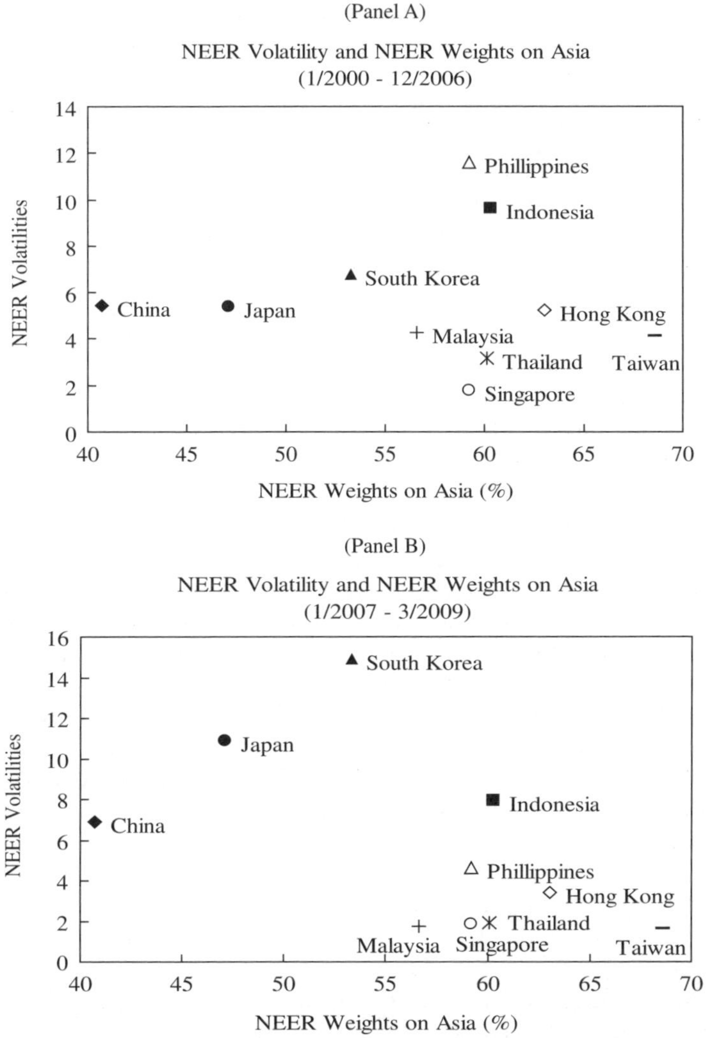

Fig. 7. NEER fluctuation weights assigned to East Asian currencies. NEER volatility and NEER weights on Asia from Panel A: 1/2000 to 12/2006; Panel B: 1/2007 to 3/2009.

stable. In other words, the NEERs of East Asian currencies that assign considerable weights to the US dollar and euro are relatively more stable as compared to other East Asian currencies.

Subsequently, we investigated the manner in which the currency regime affects fluctuations in NEERs. It is often believed that currency regimes vary across East Asian countries. We compare the fluctuations in NEERs during the normal and global financial crisis periods to investigate their relationships with East Asian currency regimes.

Table 1. Exchange rate policy in East Asian countries

	Exchange rate policy	Degree of fluctuation
Hong Kong	Currency board	Lowest
Taiwan	Managed float (reference to a currency basket)	↓
China	Managed float (reference to a currency basket)	↓
Malaysia	Managed float (reference to a currency basket)	↓
Singapore	Managed float (reference to a currency basket)	↓
Thailand	Managed float	↓
South Korea	Managed float	↓
Philippines	Free float	↓
Indonesia	Free float	↓
Japan	Free float	Highest

Source: IMF, Central Bank website.

Table 1 indicates the current exchange rate policy in East Asian countries. Only the monetary authority of Hong Kong adopted the hard peg system, also known as the "currency board." Five countries adopted a managed floating exchange rate system, whereas three countries adopted a free-floating exchange rate system. However, these classifications only indicate their *de jour* currency regime. To ascertain the *de facto* currency regime for these countries, we employed the estimation methodology proposed by Frankel and Wei (1994), which estimates the coefficients of the implicit basket weights for each East Asian currency on three anchor currencies, namely, the US dollar, euro, and Japanese yen.[7] The estimation equation is presented in the following manner.

$$\dot{e}_{i/\mathrm{Sfr}} = a_0 + a_1 \cdot \dot{e}_{\mathrm{USD/Sfr}} + a_2 \cdot \dot{e}_{\mathrm{Euro/Sf}r} + a_3 \cdot \dot{e}_{\mathrm{JPY/Sfr}} + \varepsilon$$

where $\dot{e}_{i/\mathrm{Sfr}}$ represents the degree of change in the daily currency exchange rate i in terms of the Swiss franc, which is a numeraire currency.[8] Therefore, $\dot{e}_{\mathrm{USD/Sfr}}, \dot{e}_{\mathrm{Euro/Sfr}}$ and $\dot{e}_{\mathrm{JPY/Sfr}}$ represent the degree of change in the daily exchange rates of the US dollar, euro, and Japanese yen in terms of the Swiss franc, respectively.

In the equation above, the coefficients a_1, a_2, and a_3 are interpreted as weights assigned to the three anchor currencies in an implicit basket peg system. If the coefficients a_1, a_2, and a_3 are significantly estimated and positive, then this implies that currency i pegs to a basket of the three major currencies. If only coefficient a_1 is significantly estimated, its value is approximately 1, and the other two coefficients are not significant, then this implies that currency i pegs to the US dollar. We analyze nine East

[7] Frankel and Wei (2007) confirmed that the *de facto* regime in China remained pegged to the dollar throughout 2005. However, they subsequently indicated that there was a modest but steady increase in flexibility.

[8] To analyze Asian currencies, the Swiss franc is usually used as a numeraire currency.

Asian currencies, of which five are ASEAN currencies. The four remaining currencies are the Chinese yuan, South Korean won, Hong Kong dollar, and New Taiwanese dollar. The sample period extends from January 2007 to May 2009. We employ the abovementioned estimation equation every six months during the sample period; as a result, five subsample periods were analyzed. All daily exchange rates were obtained from Datastream.

Table 2 indicates the results. We observed that despite China announcing the exchange rate reform in July 2005, the Chinese yuan continues to be pegged to the US dollar. The US dollar coefficient for the Chinese yuan remained at 98% throughout the sample period, except during the second subsample period (July 2007 to December 2007). In addition, the value of the adjusted R-squared for the Chinese yuan is considerable. These results indicate the existence of a strong relationship between the Chinese yuan and US dollar that persisted even during the global financial crisis. All other East Asian currencies, except for the Indonesian rupiah and South Korean won, are also closely associated with the US dollar. Their US dollar coefficients were above 80% during the global financial crisis. In contrast, the Singapore dollar was pegged to a currency basket with the US dollar and euro throughout the sample period. Apart from the Chinese yuan and the Hong Kong dollar, the other East Asian currencies were pegged to a currency basket with the US dollar and euro for the major part of the subsample periods. A few of the Japanese yen's coefficients are estimated to be significant; however, a majority of them are negative.

Based on the above results, we can evaluate the manner in which the *de facto* currency regime influences fluctuations in NEERs. Figure 8 indicates a scatter diagram that reflects the relationship between the *de facto* currency regime and fluctuations in NEER. The vertical axis indicates the extent of fluctuations in NEER (monthly), whereas the horizontal axis indicates the *de facto* currency regime moves from a hard peg (i.e., the Hong Kong dollar) toward a free-floating exchange rate system (i.e., the Japanese yen). Between the Hong Kong dollar and Japanese yen, the sequence of the remaining East Asian currencies is determined by the magnitude of their US dollar coefficients, which are estimated and reflected in the abovementioned results.

During the normal period (Panel A, January 2000 to December 2006), the Singapore dollar's NEER was most stable. The NEERs of the US dollar pegging countries, including the Hong Kong, China, and Taiwan, were less stable than that of Singapore. The NEERs of free-floating countries were relatively less stable than the NEERs of other countries. During the global financial crisis period (Panel B, January 2007 to March 2009), the NEERs of the Japanese yen, South Korean won (free-floating countries), and the Chinese yuan became increasingly volatile. It is remarkable that the NEER of the Singapore dollar remained stable throughout the two periods. Additionally, the NEERs of the Malaysian

Table 2. Estimated coefficients of the implicit basket weights for East Asian currencies

Country	China		Indonesia		Korea		Malaysia		Philippines		Singapore		Thailand		Hong Kong		Taiwan	
variable	Coef.	Std. dev.	Coef.	Std. dev.	Coef.	Std. dev.	Coef.	Std. dev.	Coef.	Std. dev.	Coef.	Std. dev.	Coef.	Std. dev.	Coef.	Std. dev.	Coef.	Std. dev.
January 2007 to June 2007																		
C	−0.0195***	(0.0075)	0.0192	(0.0364)	0.0015	(0.0192)	−0.0077	(0.0204)	−0.0380	(0.0333)	0.0040	(0.0133)	−0.1024	(0.0741)	0.0037	(0.0030)	0.0074	(0.0160)
USD	0.9857***	(0.0267)	0.7650***	(0.1292)	0.7725***	(0.0680)	0.8647***	(0.0724)	0.8316***	(0.1182)	0.7660***	(0.0472)	1.1783***	(0.2629)	0.9935***	(0.0107)	0.8935***	(0.0567)
EURO	−0.0305	(0.0485)	0.6350***	(0.2343)	0.3468***	(0.1233)	0.4590***	(0.1312)	0.3162	(0.2142)	0.3246***	(0.0855)	−0.5599	(0.4765)	−0.0202	(0.0194)	0.0902	(0.1028)
JPY	−0.0213	(0.0179)	−0.1031	(0.0865)	−0.0454	(0.0455)	−0.0124	(0.0485)	−0.0401	(0.0791)	0.0651***	(0.0316)	0.2233	(0.1760)	−0.0091	(0.0072)	0.0113	(0.0379)
Adj. R^2	0.9495		0.4258		0.6947		0.7322		0.4533		0.8381		0.2204		0.9918		0.7919	
July 2007 to December 2007																		
C	−0.0270**	(0.0104)	0.0423	(0.0328)	0.0223	(0.0284)	−0.0104	(0.0249)	−0.0788	(0.0506)	−0.0347	(0.0195)	−0.0449	(0.0763)	−0.0014	(0.0044)	−0.0069	(0.0129)
USD	0.9231***	(0.0276)	0.7789***	(0.0875)	0.8256***	(0.0756)	0.6483***	(0.0663)	0.8602***	(0.1348)	0.7723***	(0.0520)	0.8448***	(0.2035)	0.9933***	(0.0116)	0.9515***	(0.0345)
EURO	0.0412	(0.0469)	0.5280***	(0.1486)	0.5694***	(0.1285)	0.7523***	(0.1126)	0.4425*	(0.2290)	0.3629***	(0.0883)	0.0093	(0.3457)	0.0019	(0.0198)	0.0620	(0.0586)
JPY	−0.0013	(0.0165)	−0.0243	(0.0523)	0.0450	(0.0452)	0.0614	(0.0396)	−0.0138	(0.0805)	−0.1395***	(0.0310)	−0.2348*	(0.1216)	0.0001	(0.0070)	−0.0177	(0.0206)
Adj. R^2	0.9355		0.5984		0.7040		0.7223		0.4048		0.7772		0.1502		0.9893		0.9080	
January 2008 to June 2008																		
C	−0.0473***	(0.0107)	−0.0142	(0.0252)	0.0809	(0.0574)	−0.0106	(0.0471)	0.0524	(0.0651)	−0.0281	(0.0244)	0.0852	(0.0951)	0.0006	(0.0041)	0.0480	(0.0260)
USD	0.9835***	(0.0205)	0.9455***	(0.0480)	1.0752***	(0.1093)	0.8688***	(0.0897)	0.9911***	(0.1241)	0.7705***	(0.0465)	0.9683***	(0.1811)	0.9864***	(0.0078)	0.9614***	(0.0496)
EURO	−0.0408	(0.0348)	0.1145	(0.0816)	0.3174*	(0.1857)	0.1483	(0.1524)	0.0352	(0.2108)	0.2099***	(0.0789)	0.0103	(0.3077)	−0.0058	(0.0133)	0.0863***	(0.0842)
JPY	0.0166	(0.0180)	0.0357	(0.0422)	−0.1829*	(0.0960)	0.1571**	(0.0788)	0.2622**	(0.1090)	−0.0800*	(0.0408)	0.1919	(0.1591)	0.0102*	(0.0069)	−0.0410	(0.0436)
Adj. R^2	0.9760		0.8858		0.655		0.6835		0.5914		0.8476		0.3700		0.9965		0.8738	
July 2008 to December 2008																		
C	−0.0078	(0.0123)	0.1389	(0.1081)	0.0167	(0.1839)	0.0230	(0.0384)	0.0125	(0.0488)	−0.0026	(0.0414)	0.0167	(0.0260)	−0.0041	(0.0035)	0.0413	(0.0284)
USD	0.9879***	(0.0152)	1.1242***	(0.1338)	0.5987***	(0.2276)	0.8573***	(0.0475)	0.8068***	(0.0604)	0.7524***	(0.0512)	0.8718***	(0.0322)	0.9914***	(0.0044)	0.8632***	(0.0352)
EURO	0.0325	(0.0204)	0.0360	(0.1793)	1.2976***	(0.3050)	0.2116***	(0.0637)	0.4580***	(0.0809)	0.3496***	(0.0687)	0.1447***	(0.0431)	0.0014	(0.0058)	0.1859***	(0.0471)
JPY	−0.0129	(0.0105)	0.0834	(0.0920)	−0.2048	(0.1566)	−0.0203	(0.0327)	0.0253	(0.0415)	−0.0834**	(0.0352)	−0.0005	(0.0221)	0.0053*	(0.0030)	−0.0133	(0.0242)
Adj. R^2	0.9824		0.4866		0.2256		0.8244		0.7667		0.7614		0.9133		0.9986		0.8965	
January 2009 to May 2009																		
C	0.0007	(0.0034)	−0.0621	(0.0704)	0.0168	(0.1266)	0.0194	(0.0445)	0.0021	(0.0461)	0.0133	(0.0439)	−0.0110	(0.0242)	0.0001	(0.0014)	−0.0002	(0.0358)
USD	0.9831***	(0.0049)	0.8620***	(0.0999)	0.7491***	(0.1794)	0.8613***	(0.0631)	0.9788***	(0.0654)	0.8459***	(0.0622)	0.8294***	(0.0343)	0.9970***	(0.0020)	0.8619***	(0.0508)
EURO	0.0067	(0.0072)	0.0098	(0.1475)	0.4415*	(0.2650)	0.2767***	(0.0931)	0.1673*	(0.0966)	0.2152**	(0.0919)	0.1339***	(0.0506)	−0.0009	(0.0030)	0.1896**	(0.0750)
JPY	0.0011	(0.0040)	−0.0586	(0.0813)	−0.2806*	(0.1462)	−0.1377***	(0.0514)	−0.1119**	(0.0533)	−0.0542	(0.0507)	0.0145	(0.0279)	0.0021	(0.0017)	−0.0749*	(0.0413)
Adj. R^2	0.9987		0.5585		0.1980		0.7575		0.7905		0.7752		0.9235		0.9998		0.8375	

Significance level: *90%, **95%, ***99%.

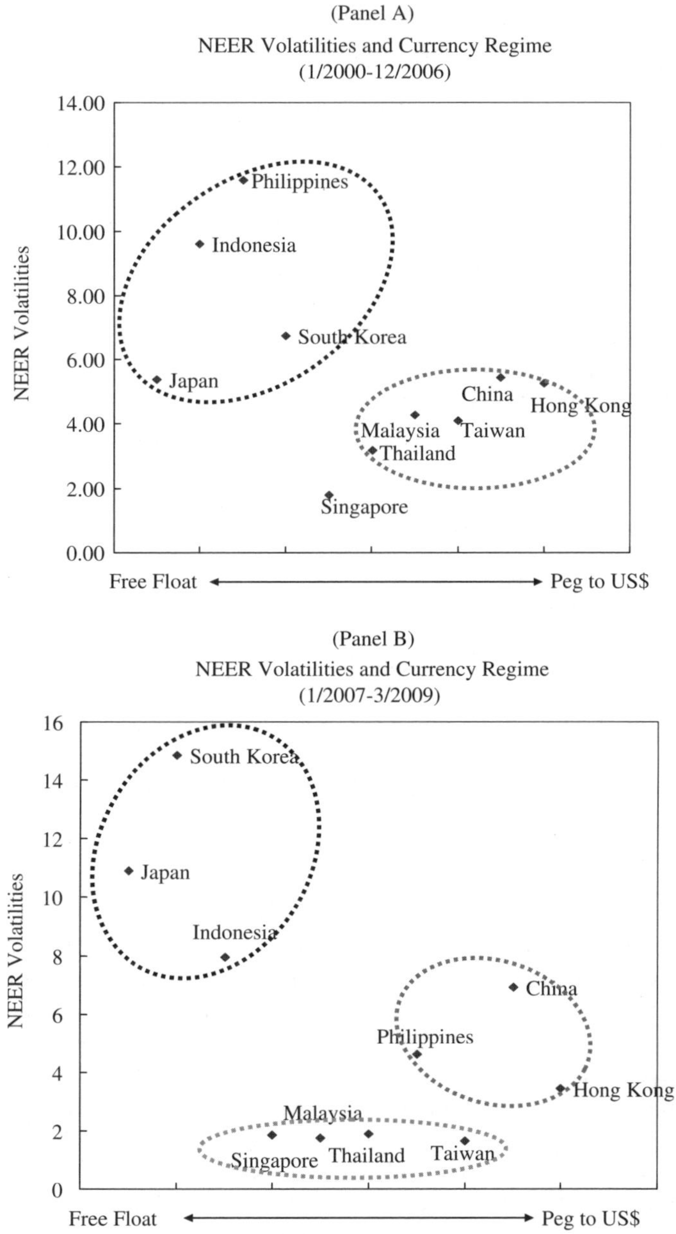

Fig. 8. ***NEER fluctuations and*** **de facto** ***currency regime. NEER volatilities and currency regime from Panel A: (1/2000 to 12/2006); Panel B: 1/2007 to 3/2009.***

ringgit, Thai baht, and New Taiwanese dollar became more stable. This implies that the currency basket system can provide stability to or further reduce the fluctuations in NEERs, even during the global financial crisis.

Taking into account the abovementioned results regarding the fluctuations in NEERs, we have established the following. The NEERs of East Asian countries that have assigned a considerable effective exchange rate weight to their own currency (i.e., Taiwan and Hong Kong) or have executed a currency basket system (i.e., Singapore, Malaysia, Thailand, and Taiwan) remained stable throughout the global financial crisis period. Those East Asian countries that assign a considerable effective exchange rates weight to the US dollar and euro, such as Japan, China, and South Korea, should adopt a currency-basket-type exchange rate policy to stabilize their NEERs.

5. The relationship among effective exchange rates, the AMU, and the AMU deviation indicators

Ogawa and Shimizu (2005) proposed the creation of an AMU, which is computed as a weighted average of East Asian currencies. In addition, they also calculated AMU deviation indicators, which indicate the extent of deviation of each East Asian currency vis-à-vis a benchmark rate set in terms of the AMU. Both the AMU and AMU deviation indicators are taken into account to support coordinated exchange rate policies in East Asia. Ogawa and Shimizu (2006) investigated the relationship among the NEERs of AMU composite currencies, the AMU, and the AMUDI. If the fluctuations in the AMU deviation indicators are strongly correlated with their NEERs, monitoring these indicators and maintaining them within a certain band is considered an effective exchange rate policy for the East Asian region. Ogawa and Shimizu (2006) collected data during the sample period from January 1999 to December 2004 and analyzed it to identify relationships between the AMU deviation indicators and the effective exchange rates for a majority of East Asian currencies.[9]

For this chapter, we conducted the same empirical analysis as Ogawa and Shimizu (2006), but extended the sample period to include the global financial crisis. We regressed the monthly percentage change in the NEERs, the AMU, and the AMU deviation indicators for each of the East Asian currencies to investigate the manner in which the fluctuation in the AMU and each AMU deviation indicator explain fluctuations in the NEER of each East Asian currency.[10] We estimate the regression equation

---

[9] In Ogawa and Shimizu (2006), the coefficients on the AMU are significant and positive for the Japanese yen and Chinese yuan. In addition, the coefficients on the AMU deviation indicator are positive and significant for eight East Asian currencies.

in the following manner.

$$\Delta(\log\ \mathrm{EER}_i) = \alpha_0 + \alpha_0 \cdot \Delta(\log\ \mathrm{AMU}) + \alpha_0 \cdot \Delta(\mathrm{AMUDI}_i).$$

We divided the entire sample period (January 2000 to March 2009) into two subsample periods, namely, the normal period (January 2000 to December 2006) and the global financial crisis period (January 2007 to March 2009).

Table 3 shows the analytical results. The coefficients on both the AMU and AMU deviation indicators are significant and positive. The value of the adjusted *R*-squared is also considerable during both subsample periods. Even throughout the global financial crisis period, the coefficients on the AMU and the AMU deviation indicators are significant and positive. The coefficients on AMU deviation indicators are more sizeable for China, Indonesia, Japan, and South Korea during the global financial crisis period over the normal period. These results imply that a coordinated exchange rate policy that involves monitoring the AMU and AMU deviation indicators is an effective approach to stabilizing the NEERs of East Asian currencies.

6. Coordinated exchange rate policies with the AMU and AMU deviation indicators

How do we encourage the adoption of coordinated exchange rate policies by employing the AMU and AMU deviation indicators?[11] Ogawa and Shimizu (2007) proposed the following stepwise approach toward regional monetary coordination.

- First step
  - Policy dialogue regarding exchange rates and exchange rate policies.
  - Surveillance using the AMU and AMU deviation indicators during Economic Review and Policy Dialogue (EPRD).
- Second step
  - Managed floating exchange rate system with reference to an individual currency basket.
  - Surveillance using the AMUDI.

[10] We conducted this regression analysis not according to the level but rather the percentage change, because the data on the NEERs, the AMU, and the AMU deviation indicators are not stationary according to level but rather are stationary in terms of the change in percentage (or in first differences for the AMU deviation indicator). We transpose the data on AMU deviation indicators into first differences, as they are quoted in terms of percentage change.

[11] In contrast, Eichengreen (2006) supported the G3 currency basket and believed that it was a more promising vehicle to provide improvements in moving toward monetary union (if that is the long-run objective), thus achieving more exchange rate stability within East Asia and integrating the financial markets of East Asian countries.

Table 3. Relationship among NEERs, the AMU, and the AMU deviation indicators

Variable	China		Indonesia		Japan		South Korea	
	Coef.	Std. error	Coef.	Std. error	Coef.	Std. error	Coef.	Std. error
(A) Sample period: January 2000 to December 2006 (83 observations)								
C	−0.0324	(0.0260)	−0.0014	(0.0542)	−0.0242	(0.0231)	−0.0153	(0.0289)
DLOG(AMU)	0.6405***	(0.0366)	0.4326***	(0.0633)	0.5803***	(0.0304)	0.4445***	(0.0372)
D(AMUDI)	1.4079***	(0.0338)	1.0342***	(0.0172)	1.1228***	(0.0201)	0.9843***	(0.0249)
Adj. R^2	0.9561		0.9788		0.9859		0.9725	

Variable	Malaysia		Philippines		Singapore		Thailand	
	Coef.	Std. error	Coef.	Std. error	Coef.	Std. error	Coef.	Std. error
C	−0.0094	(0.0183)	0.0234	(0.0320)	−0.0089	(0.0207)	−0.0165	(0.0320)
DLOG(AMU)	0.4783***	(0.0252)	0.3258***	(0.0367)	0.4171***	(0.0257)	0.3127***	(0.0392)
D(AMUDI)	1.1854***	(0.0237)	1.1390***	(0.0224)	0.9812***	(0.0337)	0.9367***	(0.0317)
Adj. R^2	0.9694		0.9694		0.9145		0.9151	

Variable	China		Indonesia		Japan		South Korea	
	Coef.	Std. error	Coef.	Std. error	Coef.	Std. error	Coef.	Std. error
(B) Sample period: January 2007 to March 2009 (27 observations)								
C	−0.0740	(0.1270)	0.0602	(0.1096)	0.0670	(0.1129)	0.0816	(0.0993)
DLOG(AMU)	1.1124***	(0.1710)	0.3362**	(0.1508)	0.5017***	(0.2169)	0.4192	(0.1347)
D(AMUDI)	1.5831***	(0.1357)	1.1621***	(0.0398)	1.2862***	(0.0643)	1.0979***	(0.0324)
Adj. R^2	0.8383		0.9722		0.9738		0.9813	

Variable	Malaysia		Philippines		Singapore		Thailand	
	Coef.	Std. error	Coef.	Std. error	Coef.	Std. error	Coef.	Std. error
C	0.0525	(0.0886)	0.0967	(0.0819)	0.1396*	(0.0766)	−0.0427	(0.1949)
DLOG(AMU)	0.4774***	(0.1239)	0.3451***	(0.1102)	0.3402***	(0.1209)	0.4911*	(0.2623)
D(AMUDI)	0.7914***	(0.0836)	1.0488***	(0.0469)	0.5515***	(0.0796)	0.2563***	(0.0769)
Adj. R^2	0.7723		0.9507		0.6431		0.3133	

Significance level: *90%, **95%, ***99%.

We have recognized that policy dialogue, especially regarding coordinated exchange rate policies among East Asian countries, is imperative for regional policy coordination. Under the current circumstances, however, taking even a first step in that direction is challenging because the governments of East Asian countries have limited policy consensus regarding coordinated exchange rate policies. However, is a consensus in policy required for policy coordination? As indicated in the previous section, a few East Asian countries have already adopted an individual currency basket system. In addition, we observe that the NEERs of these currencies continued to remain stable even during the period of global financial crisis. Ma and McCauley (2009) highlighted that coordination is not a prerequisite to reduce intra-Asian currency volatilities and that the

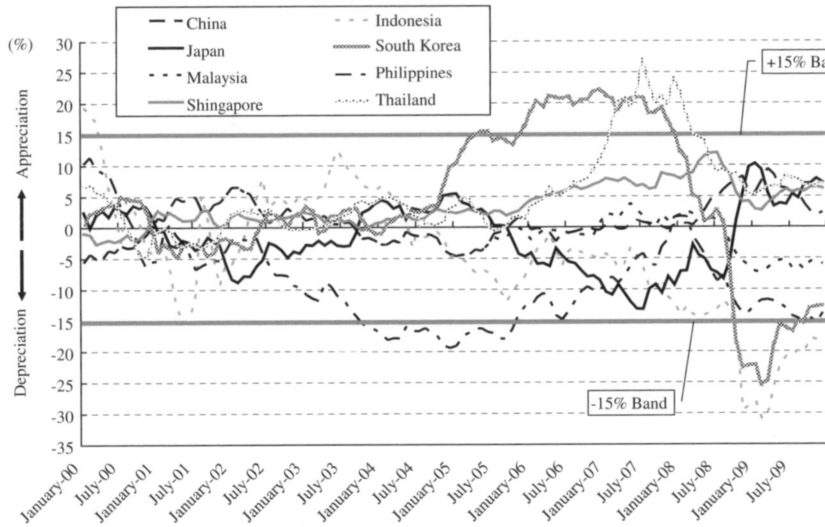

Fig. 9. AMU deviation indicators (monthly from January 2000 to December 2009). Source: RIETI.

first and second steps can be executed straightaway under the premise that each monetary authority adopts the policy to maintain stability in its own effective exchange rate.

For example, we can derive a coordinated exchange rate policy by employing the AMU deviation indicator. Figure 9 indicates the fluctuations in the AMU deviation indicators from January 2000 to March 2009. If we decide to utilize a fluctuation band of $\pm$ 15% for the AMU deviation indicators, which is equivalent to the currency band of the exchange rate mechanism (ERM) under the European monetary system (EMS) post-1992 and ERM II (except for the Denmark crone), all East Asian currencies except the Philippine peso and Lao kip would be placed within the $\pm$15% band for the period between 2000 and mid-2005. This implies that exchange rates of East Asian currencies can be managed within the band without any coordinated exchange rate policies. However, since 2006, the AMU deviation indicator for the South Korean won began appreciating beyond the upper limit of the fluctuation band of 15%, while the AMU deviation indicator for the Japanese yen depreciated and fell below zero. The AMU deviation indicators for the Thai baht and Singapore dollar also followed the South Korean won.

What instigated these currencies to deviate from the benchmark level? It was observed that trade between the Japanese yen and other appreciating currencies destabilized the AMUDI. This phenomenon suggests that coordinated monetary policies should also be considered along with coordinated exchange rate policies. Table 4 indicates the latest policy interest and three-month money market rate for East Asian

Table 4. Policy rate and three-month market rate (%)

	Policy rate	3-Month	Market rate	
China	2.25	1-Year deposit rate	1.207	SHIBOR
	5.31	1-Year lending rate		
Indonesia	7.25	Bank Indonesia rate	8.22	JIBOR
Japan	0.10	Target O/N call rate	0.567	TIBOR
South Korea	2.00	BOK base rate	2.41	KORIBOR
Malaysia	2.00	O/N policy rate	2.12	KLIBOR
Philippines	4.50	BSP O/N borrowing rate	3.688	PHIBOR
	6.50	BSP O/N lending rate		
Singapore		N/A	0.5	SIBOR
Thailand	1.25	1-Day repurchase rate	1.425	BKIBOR

Source: AsianBondOnlines (ADB). All data are as of May 2009.

countries. There are still vast differences between Japan and Indonesia, which have the lowest and highest policy interest and money market rates, respectively. However, the difference between the maximum and minimum three-month money market rates is diminishing due to the latest global financial crisis. Accordingly, this represents a suitable opportunity to discuss issues on coordinated monetary and exchange rate policies.[12]

7. *Conclusion*

In this chapter, we investigated the fluctuations in nominal exchange rates, the NEERs of East Asian currencies, and the AMU during the global financial crisis. We found that the exchange rates of the East Asian currencies vis-à-vis the three major currencies became increasingly volatile in 2008. However, there were relatively minor fluctuations in basket pegged currencies, especially vis-à-vis the euro and Japanese yen. Moreover, the AMU was generally more stable as compared to East Asian currencies. Regarding the fluctuation in NEERs, we found that the NEERs of a majority of East Asian currencies began fluctuating in 2007. Since September 2008, the NEERs of the Japanese yen and Chinese yuan appreciated considerably, while that of the South Korean won depreciated dramatically. The relationship between fluctuations in NEER and the effective exchange rate weights assigned to East Asian currencies suggested that as the share of weights assigned to the East Asian currencies increases,

[12] If we adopt coordinated exchange rate policies with a common currency basket, a coordinated intervention rule must also be discussed. For example, Kim (2009) proposed the establishment of common rules for exchange rate intervention by three countries, namely, Japan, China, and Korea.

NEERs become more stable. In addition, we found that a currency basket system could stabilize NEERs even during the global financial crisis.

Our analysis reveals the existence of a powerful relationship among the NEERs, the AMU, and the AMUDI. This relationship generally remained unchanged during the global financial crisis. Accordingly, the coordinated exchange rate policy to stabilize the AMU deviation indicators is also effective for stabilizing the NEERs of East Asian currencies. At present, an individual basket system is appropriate for East Asian countries. Because NEER weights are generally similar across East Asian currencies, a comparable policy for stabilizing a home currency against its NEER can result in a coordinated exchange rate policy, even in the absence of a common consensus among East Asian countries. In the future, however, coordinated monetary policies also should be considered along with coordinated exchange rate policies.

Turmoil in the US financial markets is still expected to have a significant impact on East Asian countries. Until recently, the direct impact of the global financial crisis on East Asia has been relatively insignificant; however, they have lately begun experiencing significant subprime mortgage fallout, with their domestic economies being increasingly affected by declining exports to the US and falling stock prices, among other factors. Sudden changes in capital flow caused by the global financial crisis have significantly influenced foreign exchange rates in East Asia. Under such circumstances, it is imperative to focus on foreign exchange rate fluctuations. In addition, due attention must be given to currency measurements in terms of effective exchange rates rather than solely focusing on their nominal exchange rate vis-à-vis the US dollar. In this respect, the AMU deviation indicators, which indicate intraregional exchange rates among East Asian currencies, play a crucial role.

Acknowledgments

This chapter is a revised version of a paper that was presented in the Fifth Asia-Pacific Economic Association Annual Conference at the University of California, Santa Cruz, on June 27–28, 2009. The authors are indebted to Shin-ichi Fukuda for his constructive observations. This research was partially supported by the Ministry of Education, Science, Sports and Culture, Grant-in-Aid for Scientific Research (C) 21530312, 2009.

Appendix. The AMU and AMU deviation indicators

A.1. Calculating the AMU

We calculated the AMU according to the approach employed for calculating the European currency unit (ECU) under the EMS before the introduction of the euro in 1999. Just as the ECU was defined as a basket of currencies of member countries of the European Union (EU), the AMU has been defined as a basket of currencies of the ASEAN 10 + 3 countries (namely, Brunei, Cambodia, Indonesia, Laos, Malaysia, Myanmar, the Philippines, Singapore, Thailand, Vietnam, Japan, China, and South Korea). The weight assigned to each currency in this basket is based on the share of GDP measured using purchasing power parity (PPP) and overall trade volumes (i.e., the sum of exports and imports) of each sample country. We calculated the share of GDP measured at PPP and trade volumes for each country using the average of the last three years to derive the currency shares of the AMU (the current version is based on the period from 2005 to 2007).

Because both the US and the EU countries are important trading partners for East Asia, the AMU is quoted in terms of a weighted average of the US dollar and the euro. The weighted average of the US dollar and the euro (US$–euro) is based on the trade volumes of East Asian countries with the United States and the EU. The weights assigned to the US dollar and the euro were 65% and 35%, respectively.

Subsequently, a benchmark period to calculate AMU deviation indicators was determined. The benchmark period was defined in the following manner. The total trade balance of member countries (i.e., intraregional trade balance), the total trade balance of the member countries (excluding Japan) with Japan, and the total trade balance of member countries with the rest of world must be approximately zero. Consequently, it was found that the trade balance in 2001 was the closest to zero. Assuming a one-year time lag before changes in exchange rates affect trade volumes, we chose 2000 and 2001 as the benchmark period. For the benchmark period, the exchange rate of the AMU in terms of the US$–euro was set at unity. We defined the exchange rate of each East Asian currency in terms of the AMU during the benchmark period as the benchmark exchange rate.

Overall, the AMU weights were calculated based on both the arithmetic share of trade volumes and GDP measured at PPP. The table below indicates the AMU basket weights and benchmark exchange rates.

	AMU basket weights of East Asian currencies				
	Trade volume* %	GDP measured at PPP** %	Arithmetic average shares % (a)	Benchmark exchange rate*** (b)	AMU weights (a)/(b)
Brunei	0.33	0.14	0.23	0.589114	0.0039
Cambodia	0.15	0.17	0.16	0.000270	5.8666
China	26.08	44.97	35.52	0.125109	2.8395
Indonesia	5.27	5.61	5.40	0.000113	477.8761
Japan	23.12	29.76	26.44	0.009065	29.1705

South Korea	13.01	8.12	10.56	0.000859	122.9905
Laos	0.11	0.08	0.10	0.000136	7.0288
Malaysia	7.51	2.40	4.95	0.272534	0.1818
Myanmar	0.33	0.30	0.31	0.159215	0.0198
Philippines	2.37	1.99	2.18	0.021903	0.9964
Singapore	12.80	1.50	7.15	0.589160	0.1213
Thailand	6.59	3.51	5.05	0.024543	2.0580
Vietnam	2.33	1.45	1.89	0.000072	262.4862

* The trade volume is calculated as the average of total export and import volumes in 2005, 2006, and 2007. The data has been obtained from DOTS (IMF).
** GDP measured at PPP is the average of GDP measured at PPP in 2005, 2006, and 2007. The data has been taken from the World Development Report, World Bank.
*** The benchmark exchange rate ($–euro/currency) is the average of the daily exchange rate in terms of US$–euro in 2000 and 2001.
Note: AMU shares and weights were revised in Oct. 2009. This was the 5th version.
Source: RIETI (http://www.rieti.go.jp/users/amu/en/index.html).

A.2. Calculating the AMU deviation indicators

The nominal exchange rate of each East Asian currency in terms of the AMU is used to determine its AMU deviation indicator, which signifies the deviation from the benchmark exchange rate vis-à-vis the AMU. It is represented by a formula in the following manner.

$$\text{AMU deviation indicator (\%)} = \frac{\text{Actual exchange rate of AMU/a currency} - \text{benchmark exchange rate of AMU/a currency}}{\text{Benchmarkexchangerateof AMU/a currency}} \times 100$$

When the AMU deviation indicator of currency A, for example, is positive, it implies that currency A's actual exchange rate vis-à-vis the AMU is higher than its benchmark exchange rate vis-à-vis the AMU. This represents an appreciation of currency A against the AMU. Similarly, when the AMU deviation indicator of currency A is negative, for example, it implies that currency A's actual exchange rate vis-à-vis the AMU is lower than its benchmark exchange rate vis-à-vis the AMU. This represents a depreciation of currency A against the AMU.

References

Eichengreen, B. (2006), The parallel-currency approach to Asian monetary integration. *American Economic Review* 96, 432–436.

Frankel, J.A., Wei, S.J. (1994), Yen bloc or dollar bloc? Exchange rate policies of the East Asian economies. In: Ito, T., Krueger, A.O. (Eds.), *Macroeconomic Linkage: Savings, Exchange Rates, and Capital Flows.* University of Chicago Press, Chicago, pp. 295–355.

Frankel, J.A., Wei, S.J. (2007). Assessing China's exchange rate regime. NBER Working Paper No. W13100.

Kim, I. (2009). The optimum currency basket approach to East. Asia's coordinated exchange rate intervention. Fukino Project Discussion Paper No. 014, Hitotsubashi University.

Kuroda, H., Kawai, M. (2003). Strengthening regional financial cooperation in East Asia. PRI Discussion Paper Series No. 03A-10.

Ma, G., McCauley, R. (2009). The evolving East Asian exchange rate system. Keio/ADBI/FSA workshop on "Asian exchange rates and currency markets", March 24.

McKinnon, R.I. (2000). After the crisis, the East Asian dollar standard resurrected: an interpretation of high-frequency exchange rate pegging. Economics Department, Stanford University. Available at http://wwwecon.standford.edu/faculty/workp/swp98010.pdf.

McKinnon, R.I. (2005), *Exchange Rates under the East Asian Dollar Standard: Living with Conflicted Virtue*. MIT press, MA.

McKinnon, R.I., Schnabel, G. (2009). China's financial conundrum and global imbalances. BIS Working Paper No. 277.

Ogawa, E. (2002), Should East Asian countries return to a dollar peg again?. In: Drysdale, P., Ishigaki, K. (Eds.), *East Asian Trade and Financial Integration: New Issues*. Asia Pacific Press, Australian National University, pp. 159–184.

Ogawa, E., Ito, T. (2000). On the desirability of a regional basket currency arrangement. NBER Working Paper No. 8002.

Ogawa, E., Shimizu, J. (2005). AMU deviation indicator for coordinated exchange rate policies in East Asia. RIETI Discussion Paper No.05-E-017.

Ogawa, E., Shimizu, J. (2006), AMU deviation indicators for coordinated exchange rate policies in East Asia and their relationships with effective exchange rates. *World Economy* 29 (12), 1691–1708.

Ogawa, E., Shimizu, J. (2007). Progress toward a common currency basket system in East Asia. RIETI Discussion Paper Series No. 06-E-038.

Ogawa, E., Yoshimi, T. (2008). Widening deviation among East Asian currencies. RIETI Discussion Paper Series No. 08-E-010.

Williamson, J. (2000), *Exchange rate regimes for East Asia: Reviving the intermediate option*. Institute for International Economics, Washington, DC.

CHAPTER 8

On Emerging Asian Equilibrium Exchange Rates

Antonia López-Villavicencio[a] and Valérie Mignon[b]

[a]*CEPN-CNRS, University of Paris 13, 93430 Villetaneuse, France*
E-mail address: lopezvillavicencio@univ-paris13.fr
[b]*EconomiX-CNRS, University of Paris Ouest, 92001 Nanterre Cedex, France; CEPII, Paris, France*
E-mail address: valerie.mignon@u-paris10.fr

Abstract
The aim of this chapter is to provide equilibrium exchange rates values for a large set of currencies and to study the adjustment process of observed exchange rates toward these levels by paying special attention to emerging Asian countries. Relying on panel smooth transition regression models, we show that real exchange rate dynamics in the long run are nonlinear for emerging Asian countries, and linear for the G7 currencies. Especially, there exists an asymmetric behavior of the real exchange rate when facing an over- or undervaluation, the adjustment speed being higher in the case of undervaluation in Asia. Although this result may be explained by the international pressure to limit undervaluation, the undervaluation may still persist over time, as has been observed since the beginning of 1990s.

Keywords: Equilibrium exchange rates, misalignments, panel smooth transition models, emerging Asia

JEL classifications: F31, C23

1. Introduction

The current context of global imbalances has led to a revival of interest in assessing equilibrium values for exchange rates. Indeed, since the mid-1990s – the beginning of a period characterized by the increasing contribution of emerging countries to global imbalances – the accelerating financial integration process has engendered a growing disconnection between exchange rate fluctuations and the real economic activity

Frontiers of Economics and Globalization
Volume 9 ISSN: 1574-8715
DOI: 10.1108/S1574-8715(2011)0000009013

(Béreau *et al.*, 2009). Moreover, fixed exchange rate regimes, and more specifically the Chinese exchange rate regime, have often been blamed for being one major building block of global imbalances (Bénassy-Quéré *et al.*, 2008). In particular, Chinese authorities have been frequently accused of maintaining the value of the yuan against major currencies at a very low level to foster China's spectacular growth, through the promotion of its exports. This export-led growth has generated surging Chinese current account surpluses, creating a major source of tension among trading partners who experienced important trade deficits with China (especially the United States and the European Union). The persistent misalignment of the yuan – and more generally of other emerging Asian currencies – may thus be a key factor influencing global imbalances.

Within this context of growing financial integration and global imbalances, it is crucial for monetary authorities to have a means to assess long-run values for the real exchange rates that would be consistent with the realization of a long-run stable macroeconomic equilibrium. To this end, various approaches have been proposed in the literature, among which are the fundamental equilibrium exchange rate (FEER) pioneered by Williamson (1983), the natural real exchange rate (NATREX) of Stein (1994), and the behavioral equilibrium exchange rate (BEER) introduced by Clark and MacDonald (1998).[1] In this chapter, we rely on the BEER methodology, which is based on the existence of a long-run, cointegrating relationship between the real exchange rate and a set of economic fundamentals, such as the net foreign asset position, the relative productivity, and the terms of trade. The estimation of this relationship provides the equilibrium value of the considered real exchange rate, and the speed of the adjustment of the observed exchange rate toward its equilibrium level may be obtained from the estimation of the corresponding vector error correction model (VECM).

According to the standard view, the deviations of the observed exchange rate from its equilibrium value are transitory and the adjustment process exhibits quick mean-reverting dynamics. This common wisdom may however be challenged by the observation of long-lasting misalignments, especially over the last two decades, notably concerning emerging Asian currencies. In this context, although the BEER can be thought of as a steady-state attractor for the actual rate, the adjustment process toward the equilibrium may however not be appropriately represented by linear equations (Dufrénot *et al.*, 2008). Indeed, the temporal dependence of misalignments implies that the adjustment is likely not to operate at a constant rate as assumed in linear models. Moreover, when disequilibrium

---

[1] It should be noted that various other concepts of equilibrium exchange rates (EER) exist, such as the capital enhanced EER, the intermediate-term model-based EER, the permanent EER, the atheoretical permanent EER, or the desired EER among others. For a survey, see Driver and Westaway (2004).

appears, prices – due to their imperfect flexibility – do not quickly and painlessly move to bring the actual real exchange rate to its equilibrium level. As a consequence, using an empirical framework based on nonlinear VECM is more appropriate than the standard linear error correction models to describe the adjustment of the observed real exchange rate to its equilibrium value.

In this chapter, we thus go further than the usual linear case by investigating the slow dynamics of the adjustment process of the observed real exchange rates to their equilibrium values within a nonlinear framework. More specifically, we retain a smooth transition model to describe the adjustment process, which can be thought as a reduced form of structural models of fundamental exchange rates accounting for nonlinearities produced by transaction costs (Dumas, 1992; Sercu *et al.*, 1995), heterogeneity of market participants (Taylor and Allen, 1992), presence of noise traders causing abrupt changes (De Long *et al.*, 1990), speculative attacks on currencies (Flood and Marion, 1999), existence of target zones (Krugman, 1991; Tronzano *et al.*, 2003), heterogeneity of central banks' interventions (Dominguez, 1998), and so on. Moreover, as highlighted by Béreau *et al.* (2010), smooth transition models help at modeling asymmetries in the adjustment process that may notably explain the unequal duration of undervaluations and overvaluations.

While various studies have investigated the nonlinear behavior of the adjustment process in a time series context,[2] very few contributions have been considered within a panel framework. We aim at filling this gap here by relying on a large panel of countries, including both industrialized and emerging economies. Considering such a panel seems to be a crucial point in deriving consistent equilibrium exchange rates by accounting for the rising share of developing countries – especially Asian – in global imbalances and, more generally, in the international monetary system.

On the whole, our aim in this chapter is to investigate the behavior of exchange rate misalignments by paying particular attention to the case of emerging Asian countries. To this end, the chapter is organized as follows. Section 2 presents the estimation of the currency misalignments. In Section 3, we address the question of the nonlinearity of the adjustment process of the observed real exchange rates toward their equilibrium value by estimating panel smooth transition models. Section 4 concludes.

---

[2] See Michael *et al.* (1997), Ma and Kanas (2000), Chen and Wu (2000), Taylor *et al.* (2001), Baum *et al.* (2001), Dufrénot and Mignon (2002), Dufrénot *et al.* (2006, 2008), López-Villavicencio (2008).

2. *Estimation of currency misalignments*

2.1. The BEER equation and data

We rely on the BEER approach introduced by Clark and MacDonald (1998) that consists in estimating a long-term relationship between the real effective exchange rate and its fundamentals. Based on previous studies (Bénassy-Quéré *et al.*, 2009; Béreau *et al.*, 2009, 2010), we consider the following determinants of the real effective exchange rate: the net foreign asset position, a measure of relative productivity, and terms of trade. More specifically, we estimate the following relationship:

$$q_{i,t} = \alpha_i + \beta_1 \text{nfa}_{i,t} + \beta_2 \text{prod}_{i,t} + \beta_3 \text{tot}_{i,t} + \varepsilon_{i,t}, \quad (1)$$

where $i = 1, \ldots, N$ denotes the country, and $t = 1, \ldots, T$ the time. $q_{i,t}$ is the real effective exchange rate (in logarithms),[3] $\text{nfa}_{i,t}$ denotes the net foreign asset position expressed as percentage of GDP, $\text{prod}_{i,t}$ stands for the logarithm of the relative productivity in the traded goods sector relative to the nontraded goods one, and $\text{tot}_{i,t}$ is the logarithm of terms of trade. Finally, $\varepsilon_{i,t}$ is an error term and α_i accounts for country-fixed effects.

We expect a positive link between the real effective exchange rate and all those potential determinants. Indeed, the real effective exchange rate is expected to appreciate if (i) the net foreign asset position increases, due to implied net interest receipts, (ii) productivity in the tradable sector increases relative to the rest of the world, according to the Balassa–Samuelson effect, and (iii) terms of trade follow an increasing trend, leading to an improvement of the trade balance.

More precisely, considering first the nfa variable, the real exchange rate is supposed to depend on capital flows, as well as imbalances between national savings and investment.[4] Indeed, there are several channels through which the stock of foreign assets can influence the real exchange rate. For instance, relying on a short-term horizon, portfolio-balances considerations suggest that a deficit in the current account creates an increase in the net foreign debt of a country, which has to be financed by international investors who demand a higher yield to adjust their portfolio. At given interest rates, this can only be achieved through a depreciation of the currency of the debtor country. In the long run, current deficits accumulate in net foreign debts, for which interests have to be paid. Facing these higher interest payments, the debtor country needs to strengthen its international price competitiveness. As a consequence, to increase the

---

[3] A rise (resp. decrease) in q denotes a currency appreciation (resp. depreciation).

[4] Lane and Milesi-Ferretti (2004), among others, explore the theoretical link between the real exchange rate and the net foreign assets, and provide evidence that the net foreign asset position is an important determinant of the real exchange rate for developing as well as developed countries.

attractiveness of its exports, the country needs to depreciate its currency (see Maeso-Fernandez *et al.*, 2004). We therefore expect an increase of the net foreign asset position of a country (i.e., a reduction of the foreign debt) to have a positive effect on the currency (i.e., an appreciation). Second, the impact of productivity differentials is expected to follow the well-known Balassa–Samuelson effect that depends on differences in the relative productivity of the tradable and nontradable sectors across countries. The productivity in the traded goods sector being higher than that in the tradable one, the real exchange rate is expected to appreciate for catching-up countries. Finally, the real exchange rate can also be affected by commodity price shocks through their impact on the terms of trade. Overall, a lasting deterioration of the terms of trade of a country should result in a depreciation of its real exchange rate.

To estimate Equation (1), we use annual data over the 1980–2007 period. To derive consistent equilibrium exchange rates, we rely on a large panel of countries including both developed and developing or emerging countries: Argentina, Australia, Brazil, Canada, Chile, China, Colombia, Costa Rica, Denmark, Egypt, Euro area, Hong Kong, India, Indonesia, Israel, Japan, Korea, Malaysia, Mexico, New Zealand, Norway, Peru, Philippines, Singapore, Sweden, Switzerland, Thailand, Turkey, United Kingdom, United States, Uruguay, and Venezuela.[5]

Turning to the variables that enter in the BEER equation, the real effective exchange rate for each country i is defined as the weighted average of real bilateral exchange rates against each j trade partner. Bilateral real exchange rates are expressed as the ratio of nominal rates to the corresponding consumer price indices (CPI); they are based in 2000. Nominal exchange rates and CPI data are taken from World Bank, World Development Indicators (WDI), except the EUR/USD exchange rate that was extracted from Datastream and China's real exchange rate that was calculated with GDP deflator (WDI). The weights correspond to the share of each partner in average values of imports and exports of goods and services over the 2000–2007 period and are extracted from the IMF, Direction of Trade Statistics.[6] Formally, we have

$$q_{i,t} = \sum_{j \neq i} w_{ij}\left(e_{i,t} - e_{j,t}\right) = \sum_{j \neq i} w_{ij} e_{ij,t}, \tag{2}$$

where $\sum_{j \neq i} w_{ij} = 1$, $e_{i,t}$ is the logarithm of the real bilateral exchange rate of currency i *vis-à-vis* the USD, $e_{ij,t}$ the logarithm of the real bilateral

[5] We included these high and middle income countries not only due to data availability (our estimations require balanced panels), but also because they account for most of the world trade.

[6] Note that intra-Eurozone flows have been excluded and trade weights have been normalized to sum to one across the partners included in the sample.

exchange rate of currency i against the j currency, and w_{ij} the trade weights.

Turning to the explanatory variables, the net foreign asset position is built using the Lane and Milesi-Ferretti online database from 1980 to 2004. The series have been completed from 2005 to 2007 using data on gross foreign assets and liabilities provided by IFS (International Financial Statistics, IMF) and WDI. Terms of trade are excerpted from WDI, except for the Euro zone and Chile (IFS). Concerning now the proxy for relative productivity, we use the relative labor productivity of tradables to nontradables, measured by output per worker.[7] The choice of this measure of the Balassa–Samuelson effect compared to other proxies – such as the ratio of the consumer price to the producer price index (PPI) for the home country relative to the same ratio for the country's major trading partners – may be especially relevant in the case of Asian countries. In particular, in China's case, elements of the CPI, such as utility prices, are still under government control, housing costs are imputed based on prices in rental markets that are not fully developed, and there is mismeasurement of price increases because adequate adjustments for improvements in quality – especially for durable goods – are not made.[8] Liberalization of price control in China has affected the CPI and the PPI by different amounts and at different times, with the resulting changes in the ratio of the two price series potentially being misinterpreted as changes in productivity (Dunaway *et al.*, 2009).

2.2. Estimation results

We start by applying panel unit root and cointegration tests. Regarding first the unit root case, various tests are considered. Levin and Lin (1992, 1993),[9] Breitung (2000), and Hadri (2000) tests are based on a common unit root process. The first two tests (Levin–Lin – LL – and Breitung) consider the unit root as the null hypothesis, while the Hadri's test uses a null of no unit root. The hypothesis that the autoregressive parameters are common across individuals is a rather restrictive assumption on the

[7] It is calculated on the basis of a dataset for output and employment for a six-sector classification (or three-sector when the six-sector data were not available). Data are taken from the following sources: the United Nations Statistics Division, International Labor Office Bureau of Statistics, Eurostat, World Bank, and Groningen Growth and Development Centre.

[8] Moreover, as noticed by Chinn (2000, 2005) and Cheung *et al.* (2005), another drawback of the relative price ratio is that it can be affected by factors unrelated to the Balassa–Samuelson effect, especially relative demand effects, tax changes, or the nominal exchange rate itself. See also Kakkar and Yan (2009) for a detailed study of the links between productivity and exchange rate movements in the case of Asian economies.

[9] See also Levin *et al.* (2002).

Table 1. Panel unit root tests

	q		nfa		prod		tot	
	Test	Prob	Test	Prob	Test	Prob	Test	Prob
LL	1.774	0.962	0.798	0.787	0.655	0.744	2.498	0.994
IPS	−1.386	0.083	0.239	0.594	0.553	0.709	4.159	1.000
MW	69.990	0.283	73.772	0.189	62.533	0.528	41.458	0.987
Breitung	−0.405	0.343	2.424	0.992	1.081	0.860	6.123	1.000
Hadri	7.798	0.000*	7.379	0.000*	8.236	0.000*	13.548	0.000*

Notes: * indicates the rejection of the null hypothesis at the 5% significance level. Lags selected according to the SIC criterion, with a maximum lag length of 2.

dynamics of the series under the alternative hypothesis. For this reason, we also consider two other tests. The IPS (Im *et al.*, 2003) test allows for heterogeneity in the value of the autoregressive coefficient under the alternative hypothesis. Thus, under the alternative hypothesis, some series may be characterized by a unit root, while some other series can be stationary. Like IPS, the Maddala and Wu's (1999) test (MW) is not based on the restrictive assumption that the autoregressive coefficient is the same across countries. This test is a nonparametric Fisher-type test that combines the p-values from individual unit root tests. The results are reported in Table 1. As can be seen, all the tests failed to reject the null hypothesis of unit root for the variables in levels. These results are corroborated by the Hadri's (2000) test, according to which the null hypothesis of stationarity is rejected for the (log) real exchange rate, the (log) productivity, the (log) terms of trade, and the net foreign assets to GDP ratio.

Turning now to the search for a cointegrating relationship between the real effective exchange rate and its three determinants, we apply panel cointegration tests. We consider here the seven tests proposed by Pedroni (1999, 2004). These tests are based on the null hypothesis of no cointegration. Some heterogeneity is introduced under the alternative hypothesis since there exists a cointegration relationship for each country, and this relationship is not necessarily the same for each country. Among the seven Pedroni's tests, four are based on the within dimension (panel cointegration tests) and three on the between dimension (group mean panel cointegration tests). Group mean panel cointegration statistics are more general in the sense that they allow for heterogeneous coefficients under the alternative hypothesis. Overall, if the null hypothesis of no cointegration is rejected, then it is possible to estimate the cointegration relationship. We also present the results of the Kao's (1999) cointegration test, which is an ADF-type test based on the residuals of the OLS panel estimation. The results of cointegration tests are displayed in Table 2.

Table 2. Panel cointegration tests

	Test statistic	*p*-value
Pedroni's tests		
Panel cointegration tests		
Panel v-statistic	1.516	0.064
Panel rho-statistic	−0.948	0.171
Panel PP-statistic	−3.210	0.000
Panel ADF-statistic	−5.153	0.000
Group mean panel cointegration tests		
Group rho-statistic	0.901	0.816
Group PP-statistic	−4.495	0.000
Group ADF-statistic	−6.424	0.000
Kao's test	−4.867	0.000

Note: Both tests are based on the null hypothesis of no cointegration.

With the exception of the rho-statistic in Pedroni's tests, the results point to cointegration between the four considered variables, since the null hypothesis of no cointegration is rejected at the 5% significance level.

Our results indicate that all our series are integrated of order 1 and cointegrated; thus, it is possible to proceed to the estimation of the long-run relationship (1). To this end, we rely on the pooled mean group (PMG) methodology proposed by Pesaran *et al.* (1999). This estimator combines two procedures that are commonly used in panels. The first one, known as the "mean group estimate," consists in estimating separate relationships for each country (or group) and averaging the group-specific coefficients. The second one is based on the traditional pooled estimators that allow only the intercepts to differ freely across countries, while all the other coefficients are constrained to be the same. The PMG estimator can be viewed as an intermediate estimator since it combines both pooling and averaging. Given that we are dealing with advanced and emerging economies, some degree of heterogeneity between countries would be recommended. In this sense, the advantage of the PMG estimation procedure over other techniques such as FM-OLS (fully modified OLS) and DOLS (dynamic OLS) is that, while slope homogeneity is imposed, short-run heterogeneity is allowed for each member of the panel. Given that we are estimating an equilibrium relationship, it is important to keep some degree of homogeneity in the long-run coefficients.[10] Indeed, the economic rationale behind a BEER equation states that, for all the countries involved, productivity gains, accumulation of foreign assets, and improvements in the terms of trade should appreciate the real exchange

[10] For a detailed study of the homogeneity hypothesis in the case of Asian countries, see Kakkar and Yan (2009).

Table 3. Estimation of the cointegrating relationship and Hausman test for homogeneity (PMG methodology)

	nfa	prod	tot
Coefficient	0.174	0.187	0.155
t-stat	3.969	3.267	4.722
Joint Hausman test: 2.22 (0.53)			

Notes: Under the slope homogeneity hypothesis, the Hausman's statistic is asymptotically distributed as a Chi-squared variate. The table reports the value of the test statistic and the corresponding *p*-value in parenthesis.

rate in the long run. Even though the impact of these variables can be different in magnitude among countries, we should expect at least positive and significant coefficients in the cointegration relationship. Yet, the slope homogeneity restriction imposed in the cointegration relationship can be tested using a Hausman test. This test is based on the result that an estimate of the long-run parameters in the model can be derived from an average of the country regressions, and this is consistent even under heterogeneity. However, if the parameters are in fact homogenous, the PMG estimates are more efficient. In other words, if the "poolability" assumption is invalid, then the PMG estimates are no longer consistent.

Results of both the estimation of the long-run coefficients and the Hausman test are given in Table 3. Regarding the estimation of the cointegrating relationship, all the coefficients have the expected positive sign. Indeed, the real effective exchange rate appreciates if net foreign assets rise, as well as the relative productivity and terms of trade. In addition, there seems to be some homogeneity across countries. Indeed, according to the Hausman test, the long-run parameters are homogeneous, implying that pooling leads to more efficient estimates than simple averaging of the coefficients. Note that this criterion for (slope) homogeneity does not imply that the parameters are exactly the same across countries, but rather that the pooled estimator provides an acceptable estimate of the mean of the parameters' distribution.

2.3. Exchange rate misalignments

Given the previous estimations, we can now proceed to the derivation of currency misalignments defined as:

$$m_{i,t} = q_{i,t} - \hat{q}_{i,t}, \tag{3}$$

where $\hat{q}_{i,t}$ is the equilibrium exchange rate given by the cointegrating relationship.

***Table 4.* Currency misalignments in 2007 (in percentage), based on the PMG estimates**

Undervalued currencies		Overvalued currencies		Currencies close to equilibrium	
Argentina	−54.79	Australia	21.92	Mexico	3.43
Brazil	−23.59	*Canada*	*11.29*	Peru	−1.66
Chile	−14.90	Colombia	13.43	**Philippines**	**−3.31**
China	**−20.90**	Denmark	6.96	Uruguay	1.40
Costa Rica	−9.38	*Eurozone*	*10.18*	*USA*	*−3.20*
Egypt	−52.06	**Korea**	**12.82**	Venezuela	−1.08
Hong Kong	**−27.61**	New Zealand	21.09		
Indonesia	**−14.91**	Turkey	30.70		
India	**−12.47**	*UK*	*14.37*		
Israel	−21.82				
Japan	*−19.85*				
Malaysia	**−34.70**				
Norway	−20.04				
Singapore	**−9.62**				
Sweden	−14.89				
Switzerland	−9.51				
Thailand	**−16.52**				

Notes: In bold: Emerging Asian countries. In italics: G7 countries. A positive (resp. negative) sign denotes an overvaluation (resp. undervaluation).

Table 4 reports the values of misalignments for 2007, the last point of our sample. With the exception of Japan whose currency is undervalued in 2007 and the USD which is slightly undervalued, but very close to its equilibrium value, all other G7 currencies are overvalued in 2007. Turning to the emerging Asian countries, all the currencies but the Korean won are undervalued. The amount of undervaluation is quite large, especially for Malaysia, Hong Kong, and China. The undervaluation of the yuan, around 20%, is in the range of the estimations generally found in the literature, as surveyed by Cline and Williamson (2007). Cheung *et al.* (2005, 2007, 2009), who have investigated in detail the behavior of the yuan,[11] report however some different results. More specifically, the authors evaluate the value of the yuan using three approaches – relative purchasing power parity (PPP), absolute PPP, and Balassa–Samuelson hypothesis – and show that the undervaluation of the Chinese currency widely varies according to the chosen procedure.

To account for this important finding and as a robustness check, we also estimate misalignments according to the PPP hypothesis. In this case, the equilibrium exchange rate is associated with an international version of the

[11] The article by Cheung *et al.* (2005) also provides a complete survey on the theoretical and empirical literature on the Renminbi misalignments.

law of one price and is obtained by regressing, on a country-by-country basis, the real exchange rate on a constant. We proceed to these estimations since PPP is a very widely used measure for misalignments, but it should be noticed that our unit root tests' results do not support the PPP hypothesis – real exchange rate series being nonstationary. Keeping this limitation in mind, our results (available upon request) show that while there exists some differences in terms of size of the misalignments, the global pattern obtained with the PPP-based measure is similar to that reported in Table 4: with a few exceptions, these are the same currencies that are over or undervalued.

Considering the whole period, 1980–2007, the misalignments of G7 currencies globally follow an increasing trend, as reported in Figure 1 for the British pound, the Japanese yen, the USD, and the euro. Consistent with common wisdom, the USD appears overvalued from 1983 to 1986. It is undervalued from 1988 to 1995, and overvalued again from 1997 to 2005. Since 2005, it is close to its equilibrium value, while being slightly undervalued at the end of the period. Turning to the euro, the misalignment is quite stable on the whole period even if the euro follows a clear appreciating trend since 2002 and is overvalued since 2003. The British pound tends to be overvalued since the end of the 1990s, and the Japanese yen, while being overvalued during a long period from the end of the 1980s to 2005, is now undervalued.

Considering emerging Asian currencies (Figures 2 and 3), for five of them their currencies' misalignments progressively move from overvaluation to undervaluation over the period: China, India, Indonesia, Malaysia, and Thailand. With the exception of the Thai bath whose undervaluation starts at the end of the 1990s, the other four currencies are undervalued since the beginning of the 1990s. Regarding more specifically the case of the Chinese currency, the yuan is undervalued since the liberalization of the economy; the undervaluation being reinforced at the beginning of the 2000s due to various factors – in addition to China's fixed exchange rate regime: (i) very low inflation rate (see Figure A1 in the appendix), (ii) depreciation of the USD, (iii) high current account surpluses that may be a sign of competitiveness advantage for Chinese exports (see Figure A2 in the appendix), and (iv) surging foreign exchange reserves, the latter having accelerated at the beginning of the 2000s due to recurrent Central bank's interventions in order to impede the yuan appreciation (see Figure A3 in the appendix). As noted by Coudert and Couharde (2005), in the absence of such interventions, the yuan would have appreciated, which can be viewed as a clear indication of undervaluation. Turning to Hong Kong, the Philippines, and Singapore, the pattern is less clear-cut. The misalignments exhibit a global decreasing trend on the whole period for the Philippines and Singapore, whose currencies have known important overvaluations most of the part of the 1990s and are undervalued since the end of the 1990s.

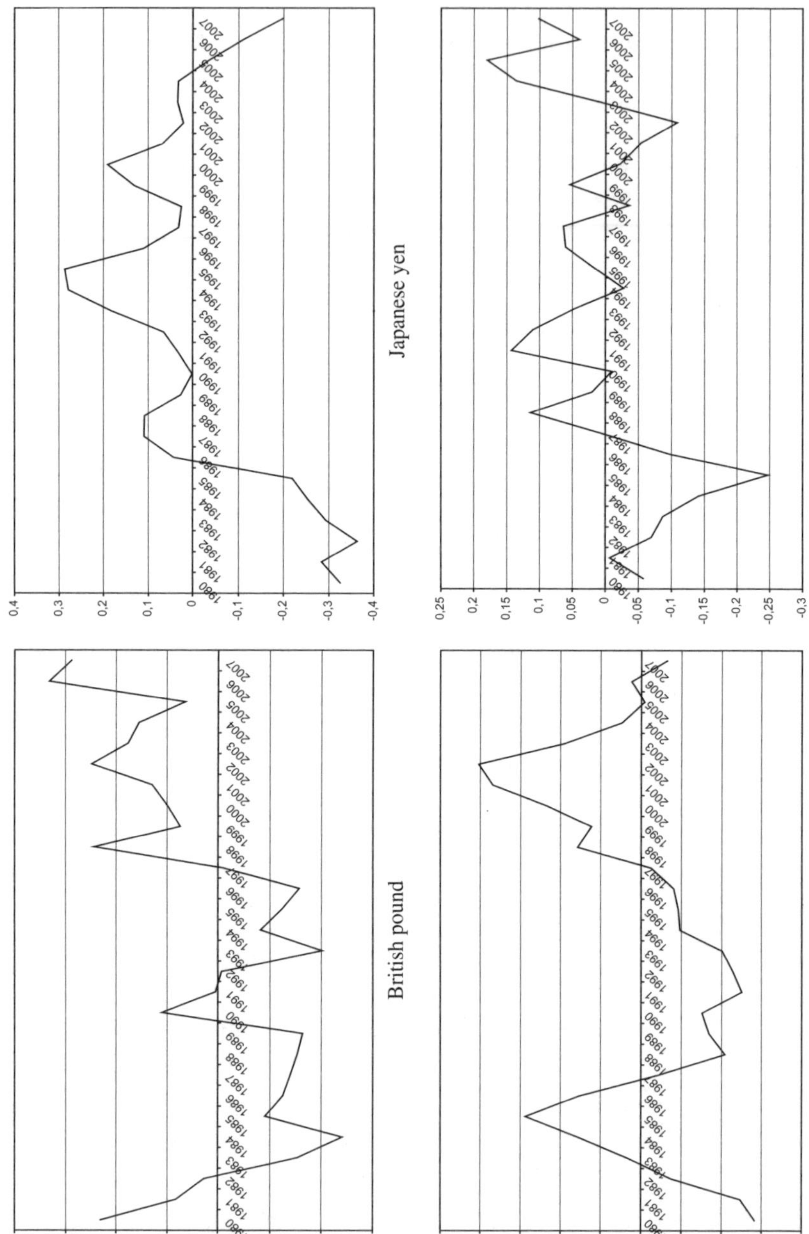

Fig. 1. ***Misalignments of some G7 currencies. Source: Authors' calculations.***

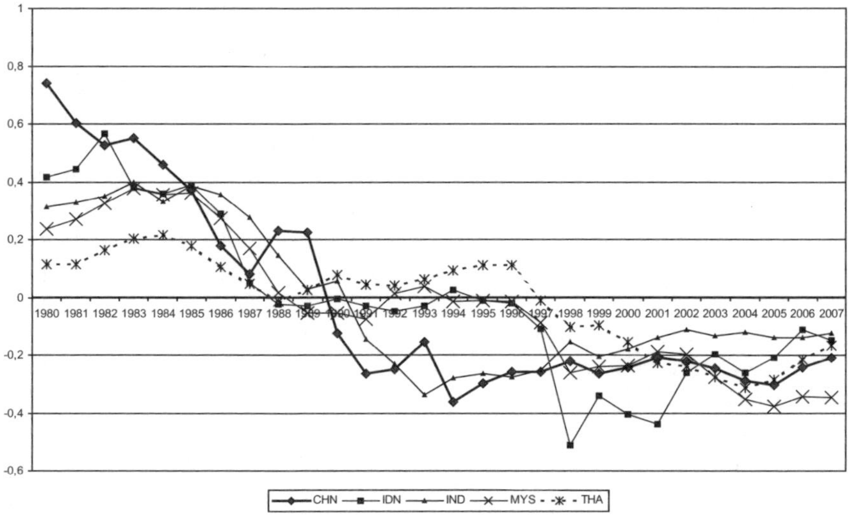

Fig. 2. Emerging Asia misalignments. Note: CHN: China, IDN: Indonesia, IND: India, MYS: Malaysia, THA: Thailand. Source: Authors' calculations.

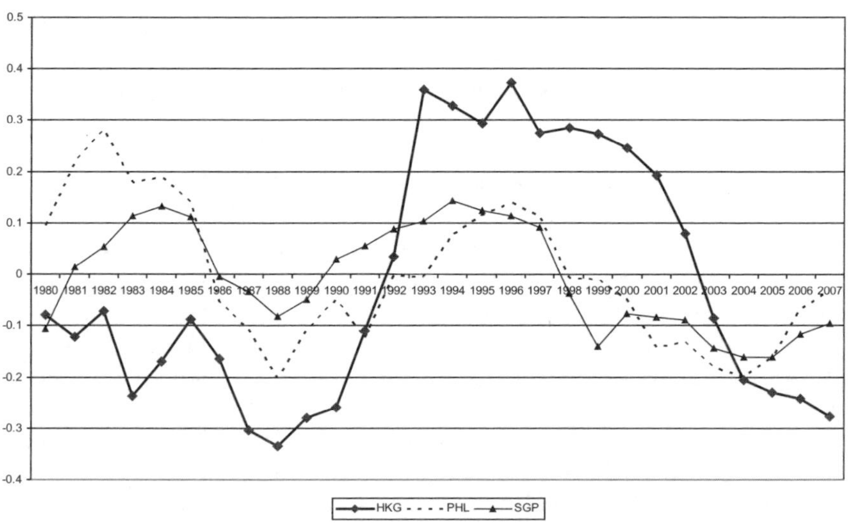

Fig. 3. Emerging Asia misalignments (continued). Note: HKG: Hong Kong, PHL: Philippines, SGP: Singapore. Source: Authors' calculations.

Figures 2 and 3 also display interesting facts regarding the Asian financial crisis of 1997–1998. Indeed, it is shown that the currencies for Thailand, Hong Kong, Philippines, and Singapore were overvalued prior to the crisis and undervalued after it. More precisely, most of these overvalued currencies reached a peak around 1996, and then displayed a decreasing trend toward equilibrium. However, as also noticed by Kakkar and Yan (2009), this downward adjustment was too important since the currencies have overshot the equilibrium during the adjustment process: they have depreciated below their equilibrium value, becoming undervalued. Kakkar and Yan (2009) explain this phenomenon by self-fulfilling expectations: due to the panic caused by movements on the financial markets, the speculators were expecting large further declines and behaved in a way that provoked such decreases. Currencies have thus depreciated more than the adjustment that was required according to the fundamentals. In this sense, long-lasting overvalued currencies may be viewed as an advanced indicator of financial crises and speculative attacks.

Not only are emerging Asia's real exchange rates, on average, highly undervalued in recent years, but they are also more volatile and unstable – particularly when compared with the evolution of the misalignment in most of the advanced economies (see Table A1 in the appendix).

On the whole, our estimations indicate that real exchange rates seem to exhibit more mean-reverting dynamics for G7 countries than for emerging Asian ones. Indeed, periods of over and undervaluations tend to alternate quite frequently for the currencies of industrialized countries. On the contrary, the dynamics for emerging Asian currencies' misalignments strongly differs: emerging Asian exchange rates are undervalued particularly since the 1990s, and spend a long time away from their equilibrium value, showing no clear mean-reverting dynamics.

3. Convergence to equilibrium: how long are the disequilibria?

Our aim in this section is to investigate the dynamics of the adjustment process of the exchange rate toward its equilibrium value. A standard way to proceed is to estimate vector error correction models that allow assessing the speed at which this adjustment takes place. However, as previously stated, these standard models may be too poor to account for the full dynamics of the adjustment process since they implicitly assume that (i) the adjustment speed toward equilibrium is both continuous and constant, regardless the extent of the real misalignment and (ii) any deviation from the equilibrium level is temporary since there exist forces ensuring quickly mean-reverting dynamics. This standard view may however be challenged by the results obtained in the previous section evidencing that some countries, especially Asian emerging ones, are characterized by long-lasting substantial misalignments. As an example, the yuan is found undervalued since 1990 and never recovers its equilibrium value until 2007, the last point of our sample. The fact that these exchange rates may spend long periods away from their equilibrium values may be explained by nonlinearities such as: transaction costs (Dumas, 1992, Sercu *et al.*, 1995), heterogeneity of market participants

(De Long *et al.*, 1990; Taylor and Allen, 1992), or existence of target zones (Krugman, 1991). All these factors may explain a nonlinear adjustment mechanism of the exchange rate toward its equilibrium level with time-dependent properties. This leads us to investigate in more detail the adjustment process within a nonlinear panel framework.

To this end, we consider panel smooth transition models, which allow us to investigate the slowness of the adjustment process by accounting for the potential aforementioned nonlinearities. They also offer a way to model possible asymmetries inherent to the adjustment process that may explain, for instance, the unequal duration of undervaluations and overvaluations.

3.1. Methodology[12]

Let $\{z_{i,t}, s_{i,t}, x_{i,t}; t = 1, ..., T; i = 1, ..., N\}$ be a balanced panel with $z_{i,t}$ denoting the dependent variable, $s_{i,t}$ the threshold variable, and $\boldsymbol{x}_{i,t}$ a vector of k exogenous variables. The panel smooth transition regression (PSTR) model introduced by González *et al.* (2005) can be written as follows:

$$z_{i,t} = \mu_i + \beta_0' x_{i,t} + \beta_1' x_{i,t} g(s_{i,t}; \gamma, c) + \upsilon_{i,t}, \tag{4}$$

where μ_i denotes the individual fixed effects, $g(s_{i,t}; \gamma, c)$ is the transition function, normalized and bounded between 0 and 1, γ the speed of transition from one regime to the other, and c the threshold parameter. The threshold variable $s_{i,t}$ may be an exogenous variable or a combination of the lagged endogenous one (see van Dijk *et al.*, 2002). In this model, the observations in the panel are divided into two regimes[13] depending on whether the threshold variable is lower or larger than the threshold c. The error term $\upsilon_{i,t}$ is independent and identically distributed.[14] The transition from one regime to another is smooth and gradual.

Following Granger and Teräsvirta (1993) and Teräsvirta (1994) in the time series context or González *et al.* (2005) in a panel framework, the following specification can be used for the transition function

$$g(s_{i,t}; \gamma, c) = \left[1 + \exp\left(-\gamma \prod_{j=1}^{m} (s_{i,t} - c_j)\right)\right]^{-1} \tag{5}$$

with $\gamma > 0$ and $c_1 \leq c_2 \leq \cdots \leq c_m$. When $m = 1$ and $\gamma \rightarrow \infty$, the PSTR model reduces to the panel threshold regression (PTR) model introduced by Hansen (1999), characterized by an abrupt change from one regime to

[12] This section is based on Béreau *et al.* (2009, 2010).

[13] Of course, it is possible to extend the PSTR model to more than two regimes.

[14] Since this is a strong assumption, we tested this hypothesis on the residuals for each of the nonlinear models presented. In all the cases, the residuals are found to be white noise processes.

the other. González *et al.* (2005) mention that from an empirical point of view, it is sufficient to consider only the cases of $m = 1$ (logistic) or $m = 2$ (exponential) to capture the nonlinearities due to regime switching. In the first case, the adjustment process is asymmetric and the two regimes are associated with small and large values of the transition variable (the misalignment) relative to the threshold. On the contrary, in the case of an exponential specification, the two regimes have similar structures – meaning that increases and reductions of the transition variable have similar dynamics – but the middle grounds are characterized by a different dynamics than that in the extremes.

Following the methodology used in the time series context, González *et al.* (2005) suggest a three-step strategy to apply PSTR models:

- Specification. The aim of this step is to test for homogeneity against the PSTR alternative. To this end, we rely on the LM-test statistic provided by González *et al.* (2005) that can be used to select (i) the appropriate transition variable as the one that minimizes the associated p-value and (ii) the appropriate order m in Equation (5) in a sequential manner.
- Estimation. Nonlinear least squares are used to obtain the parameter estimates, once the data have been demeaned.
- Evaluation and choice of the number of regimes. We apply misspecification tests in order to check the validity of the estimated PSTR model. We follow González *et al.* (2005) who propose to adapt the tests of parameter constancy over time and of no remaining nonlinearity introduced by Eitrheim and Teräsvirta (1996) in the time series context.

On the whole, putting together Equations (1) and (4), our complete model is given by:

$$\begin{aligned}\Delta q_{i,t} = \mu_i + (\theta m_{i,t-1} + \delta_1 \Delta \text{nfa}_{i,t} + \delta_2 \Delta \text{prod}_{i,t} + \delta_3 \Delta \text{tot}_{i,t}) + (\theta^* m_{i,t-1} \\ + \delta_1^* \Delta \text{nfa}_{i,t} + \delta_2^* \Delta \text{prod}_{i,t} + \delta_3^* \Delta \text{tot}_{i,t}) g(s_{i,t}; \gamma, c) + u_{i,t}, \quad (6)\end{aligned}$$

where $m_{i,t} = q_{i,t} - \hat{q}_{i,t}$, $\hat{q}_{i,t}$ being the BEER value, and $u_{i,t}$ is an error term.

3.2. Estimation results

We start by testing the null hypothesis of linearity in Equation (6) using the González *et al.* (2005) test with the misalignment series as the relevant transition variable. In other words, we test (i) if there exists a different reverting dynamics of the exchange rate toward its equilibrium value when facing positive and negative misalignments and (ii) if the transition from one regime to another depends on the size and the sign of the deviation of the real exchange rate to its equilibrium level. The results[15] conclude that

[15] Results are available upon request to the authors.

Table 5. PSTR model estimation, 1980–2007

	Regime 1					Regime 2				
	Speed of adjustment		Half-life	Range		Speed of adjustment		Half-life	Range	
	θ	t-stat		Lower (%)	Higher (%)	$\theta+\theta^*$	*t*-stat		Lower (%)	Higher (%)
Whole sample	−0.186	−5.80	4.3	−61.5	24.4	−0.238	−3.16	3.2	24.5	55.6
Emerging Asia	−0.233	−4.03	3.3	−51.5	−14.2	−0.013	−0.84	5.3	−14.3	56.7
G7					Linear					

Notes: This table reports the estimation of the error-correction terms in both the linear (θ) and the nonlinear ($\theta+\theta^*$) regimes (Equation (6)), together with their *t*-statistics. Half-life refers to the number of years for correcting 50% of the deviation from the equilibrium value. The range gives the minimum and the maximum values taken by the misalignment in each regime.

(i) the null of linearity is rejected at the 5% significance level and (ii) the logistic specification is preferred to the exponential one, evidencing that under and overvaluations are corrected differently. Indeed, given that the logistic function proved to be more appropriate than the exponential one, there is no support to the principle that it takes the same time to correct high undervaluations and high overvaluations, simply because the "costs" of correcting them might be different. Several reasons can explain this different correcting mechanism. For instance, to correct an undervaluation, the currency has to appreciate. This may happen through a Balassa–Samuelson effect, or similarly, through salaries increasing faster in the home country. We will go back to this idea latter on.

Table 5 reports the results of the estimation of the main parameters, i.e., the error correction coefficients in the two extreme regimes, θ and $\theta+\theta^*$, the threshold parameter c, and the half-lives of deviations from equilibrium. The estimated threshold is equal to 0.244. This means that the first regime, characterized by $g(\cdot)=0$, corresponds to undervaluations and overvaluations less than 24.4%. The second regime, corresponding to $g(\cdot)=1$, concerns overvaluations more than 24.4%. We found a negative and statistically significant error correction term in both regimes, implying that if the fundamentals in the last period dictate a lower real exchange rate than that observed, then it will depreciate in the current period. The estimated (average) error correction coefficients show that the adjustment is sizeable, slightly faster for higher overvaluations. In other words, whereas about 19% of the adjustment is corrected within a year in the case of undervaluations, 24% is corrected for high overvaluations, corresponding to half-lives of 4.3 and 3.2 years, respectively. As illustrated by Figure 4, there is a continuum of observations in each regime, with slightly more observations to the left of the threshold, indicating that most of the currencies were on average undervalued, with a high tendency to revert to equilibrium.

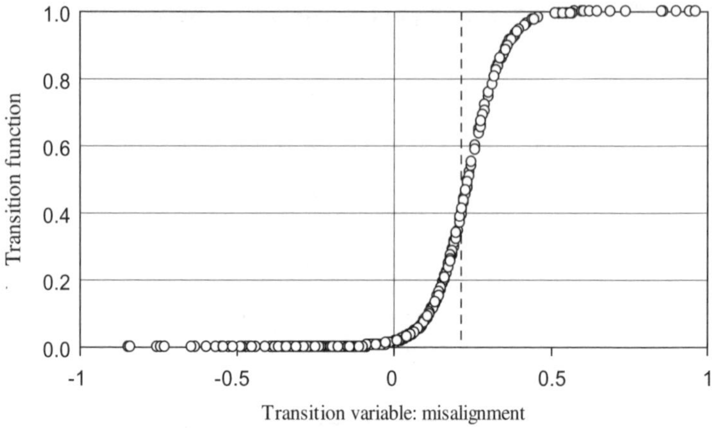

Fig. 4. Misalignment versus transition function, whole sample. Source: Authors' calculations.

Let us now turn to the panel constituted by emerging Asian countries. The results strongly differ from those obtained for the whole sample. Indeed, the estimated threshold is now equal to −0.142, corresponding to an undervaluation of 14.2%. The negative sign of the threshold parameter is consistent with the fact that Asian emerging currencies are undervalued on average (see Figures 2 and 3). The estimated error correction term θ is negative and significant in the first regime, corresponding to high undervaluations. On the contrary, the estimated coefficient is not significant in the second regime, taking a value close to zero ($\theta + \theta^* \cong -0.03$). This means that the adjustment process is clearly more effective in case of an undervaluation than when an overvaluation occurs, putting forward the asymmetric property of the real exchange rate adjustment toward equilibrium.[16] This asymmetric behavior may be explained by the fact that, while undervaluations can be viewed as a means for a country to enhance its growth through the promotion of its exports, the international pressure for limiting undervaluations is stronger than for overvaluations. This may explain why undervaluations tend to be corrected faster than overvaluations. One may also wonder whether this result comes from the nature of the exchange rate regime. Indeed, as recalled by Coudert *et al.* (2008) among others, a peg tends to hinder the adjustment of the real

[16] As a robustness check, we have estimated the PSTR model for Asian emerging countries on the two distinct subperiods characterizing the evolution of their real exchange rates: 1980–1989 (overvaluation period) and 1990–2007 (undervaluation period). Turning to the most recent period of undervaluation, our findings show that while undervaluations tend to be corrected (the error correction term being significantly negative), high overvaluations (more than 30%) are not corrected (the error correction term being positive). On the whole, these results tend to confirm that the adjustment process of the exchange rate toward its equilibrium value is more effective in case of undervaluations than for overvaluations.

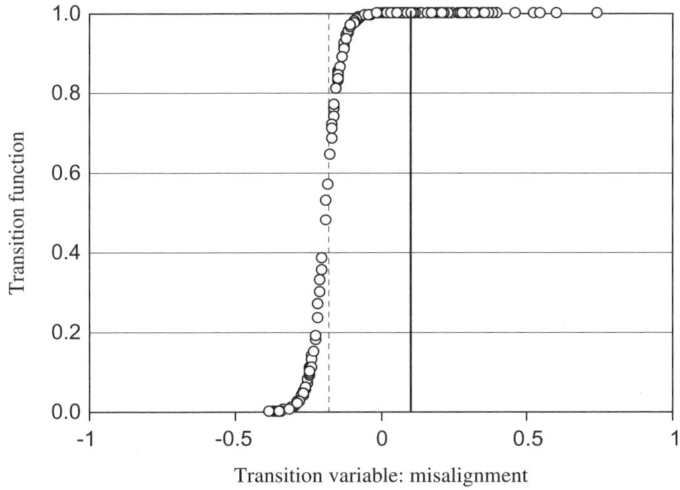

Fig. 5. Misalignment versus transition function, emerging Asia. Source: Authors' calculations.

exchange rate to its equilibrium value, as all the adjustment has to be made through prices, known to be rigid in the short run. This is especially true in the downward sense, making pegged currencies more prone to overvaluation. Hence, the nature of the exchange rate regime may be an explanation of the asymmetric adjustment process. To check this hypothesis, we investigate whether the misalignments obtained for 2007 (Table 4) are linked to the exchange rate regime, relying upon the IMF classification. As it can be seen from Table A2 in the appendix, there seems to be no systematic link between the nature of the exchange rate regime and the misalignments, confirming the results by Coudert *et al.* (2008).[17]

Note that, as for the calculation of the misalignments, we proceeded to robustness checks by estimating the PSTR model using the PPP-based measure of the real exchange rate misalignments. Our findings show that this asymmetric behavior is a robust phenomenon since the error correction term is negative and significant in the first regime ($\theta = -0.66$), while it is close to zero and nonsignificant in the second regime ($\theta + \theta^* \cong -0.05$).[18] Some potential explanations to this asymmetric adjustment of emerging Asian currencies are provided in Section 3.3.

As seen in Figure 5, even though most of the observations are to the left of the zero line (i.e., observations reflecting undervaluations), those that present an important mean reversion (i.e., with undervaluations higher than 18%) are less abundant. The results of the nonlinear estimation show

[17] As a robustness check, we did the same exercise using the Ilzetzki *et al.* (2008) classification, which leads to similar results.

[18] Complete results of the PSTR estimation are available upon request to the authors.

that mean reversion gets weaker the smaller the size of the undervaluation and for overvaluations in general. Most of the points to the right of the zero line in Figure 5 correspond to the overvaluations characterizing the beginning of the period under study (remember that most of the Asian currencies were overvalued between 1980 and 1990). As illustrated by Figure 2, the period of overvaluation lasted about 10 years, with a very slow descending trend toward, first, equilibrated real exchange rates and, then, to the period of undervaluation that has lasted since then.[19] In this second period, the average misalignment is considerably lower than in the first period, and reversion toward equilibrium seems to be more important.

Finally, results in Table 5 indicate that the case of G7 economies alone is strongly different from the rest of the panel. Indeed, the null hypothesis of linearity is not rejected when the misalignment is used as the threshold variable. As a consequence, in the most industrialized countries, reversion to equilibrium happens regardless of the size of the deviation from equilibrium.[20] This result is consistent with our previous findings relating to misalignments (see Section 2.3), in particular with the fact that periods of over and undervaluations tend to alternate quite frequently for the currencies of the most industrialized countries.

3.3. Explaining the asymmetric adjustment of emerging Asian currencies: the case of China

Two main facts emerge from our previous results. First, after a decade of high overvaluations, Asian real exchange rates have been, in general, undervalued since the beginning of the 1990s. Yet, this undervaluation is, on average, smaller in magnitude than the observed overvaluation during the 1980s. Second and related to the previous point, disequilibria in emerging Asia are corrected faster in case of undervaluations than in case of overvaluations. In other words, our results tend to indicate that real exchange rate appreciations are faster than depreciations.

Looking at the specific case of China, whereas the overvaluation reached levels higher than 50% at the beginning of the 1980s (almost 75% in 1980, during the exchange rate administered system), the undervaluation has not exceeded 40%. At the same time, there seems to be a tendency to reduce this undervaluation, which, in 2007, was approximately equal to 20% according to our presented BEER model. In other words,

[19] China, for instance, experienced an average overvaluation of 40% between 1980 and 1989 (with an overvaluation of almost 75% at the beginning of the period). Since 1990, the Chinese undervaluation has been 24.5% on average, reaching the highest value (36%) in 1994.

[20] This result confirms previous studies in a time series context; see López-Villavicencio (2008) among others.

whereas during the 1980s there was an important, lasting gap between the real effective exchange rate and the economic fundamentals with a corresponding significant overvaluation, since 1990 we observe a reduction of this deviation between the observed and the equilibrium exchange rates. Before attempting to explain this dynamics, it should be mentioned that the Chinese exchange rate regime was different during these two decades. Indeed, during the 1981–1994 period, it was characterized by a dual system composed by an official rate together with a foreign exchange market (swap market). In January 1994, this system was replaced by a unified exchange rate market, leading to a managed float regime.

There are several possible explanations for the behavior of the Chinese misalignment and, in particular, the asymmetric adjustment of the yuan when facing under or overvaluations. Certainly, given that the real effective exchange rate adjustment is, by definition, exerted through prices or nominal exchange rates, the flexibility of these factors would play a crucial role.

Regarding the flexibility of the nominal exchange rate, and as it was mentioned before, the argument according to which a stronger yuan would help reducing global imbalances in general, and the US trade deficit in particular, explains the increasingly international pressures to allow the Chinese currency to appreciate and therefore to limit the yuan undervaluation, especially during the 2005–2007 period. Even though the Chinese authorities have not strongly reacted to these urges, some changes can be seen in the reevaluation of their currency. In this respect, Frankel and Wei (2007) suggest that the increase in Chinese currency flexibility, small though it is, has been gradually accelerating, at a rate that would suggest the likelihood of some genuine flexibility. China allowed the yuan to rise by 21% against the dollar in the three years to July 2008, a fact that may be opposed to the long period of depreciation of the yuan between 1980 and the beginning of the 1990s.

Yet, in spite of these small nominal adjustments to increase the value of the Chinese currency, China keeps its exchange rate tightly fixed to the dollar. Therefore, the evolution of the USD exchange rate against other currencies, as well as the dynamics of the Chinese economic fundamentals – as the relative productivity and the terms of trade – which influence prices, should also be important to explain the reduction of the exchange rate misalignment and the fact that the real exchange rate seems to be closer to the fundamentals during recent years.

As it can be seen in Figure 6, after a long falling trend during the 1980s, relative productivity has been increasing *vis-à-vis* China's main trading partners since the beginning of the 1990s. In this respect, McKinnon and Schnabl (2006) suggest that, in order to preserve the exchange rate anchor and to balance international competitiveness, nominal wages have to rise in line with the rapid productivity growth and thereby much faster than in

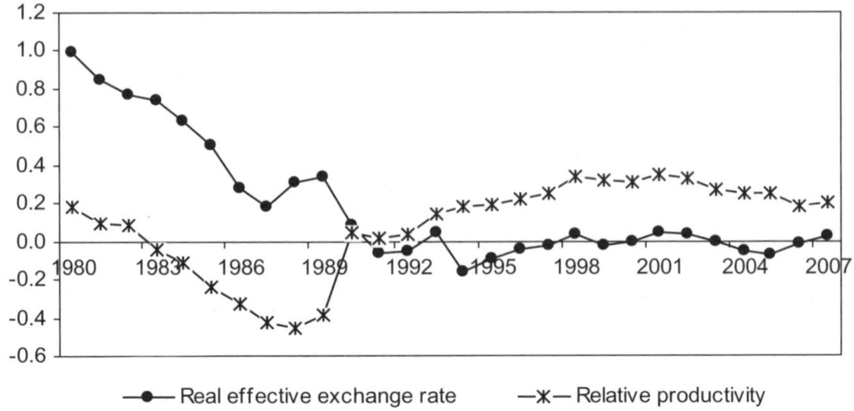

Fig. 6. Real effective exchange rate and relative productivity in China. Note: Real effective exchange rate and relative productivity are expressed in logarithms.

the rest of the world.[21] Indeed, balancing international competitiveness requires real wages in China to increase much faster than those in its trade partners to reflect China's much higher growth in labor productivity.[22] According to this proposition, given that the Chinese currency is, basically, fixed to the US dollar, wages (and prices) should adjust to preserve competitiveness. Therefore, as suggested by the Balassa–Samuelson hypothesis, this rapid economic growth and the increase in real wages should be accompanied by a real exchange rate appreciation. The increasing trend of wages in China is clearly illustrated in Figure 7, especially since the beginning of the 1990s.

In this context, even though our results do not allow us to draw any conclusion in that sense, we could conjecture that wages were characterized by more flexibility to increase since the 1990s and more rigidity to decrease during the 1980s. It is a widespread view that both wages and prices are "downward sticky," i.e., they take longer to go down than to increase. Indeed, it seems reasonable to think of wages and prices in China as flexible, despite its large size and Communist historical path: because

---

[21] For instance, from 1994 through 2004, money wages in manufacturing increased by 11.7% in China per year and by only 3.0% in the United States (see McKinnon and Schnabl, 2006). Much of this extraordinary growth in Chinese wages reflects the upgrading of skills and greater work experience of the manufacturing labor force.

[22] McKinnon and Schnabl (2006) suggest that, if the exchange rate is safely fixed (as it might be the case in China), wage growth can be highly responsive to varying rates of labor productivity growth so as to better balance international competitiveness. Based on the so-called "Scandinavian Model" of wage adjustment, they show that fixing the nominal exchange rate to a stable external monetary anchor facilitates faster adjustment (growth) in real wages than leaving the exchange rate "flexible" with the threat of appreciation.

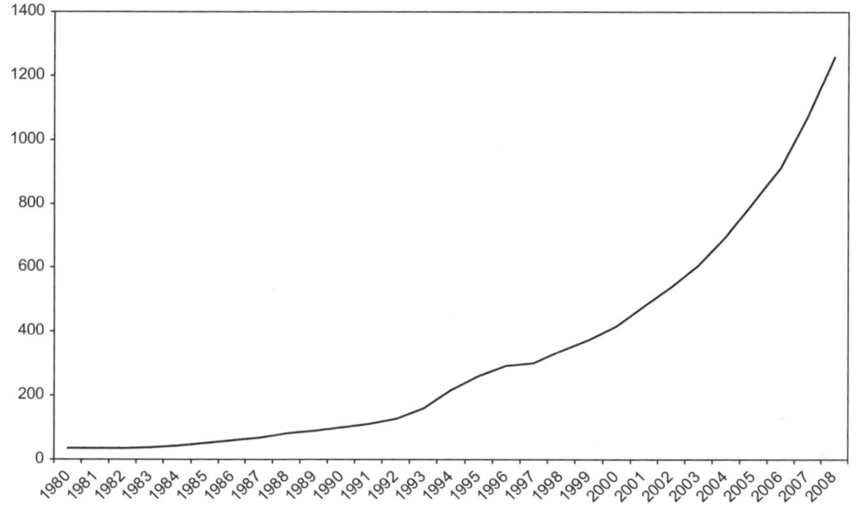

Fig. 7. Average wages in China (relative to the United States). Note: This figure reports the average wage in money terms per person for staff and workers in enterprises, institutions, and government agencies in China relative to the US (1990 = 100). Source: Datastream.

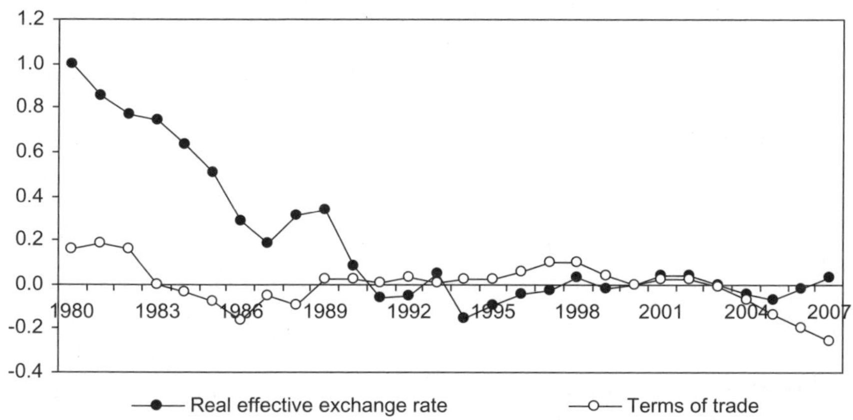

Fig. 8. Real effective exchange rate and terms of trade in China. Note: Real effective exchange rate and terms of trade are expressed in logarithms and are based in 2000.

the economy is so dynamic, wages are fluid, in the sense that they are growing rapidly in nominal terms – regardless of price inflation – because of productivity growth; so there is less reason to fear nominal stickiness (Frankel, 2006).

Regarding the terms of trade (Figure 8), after a decade of deterioration at the beginning of the period, since 1990, not only the real exchange rate

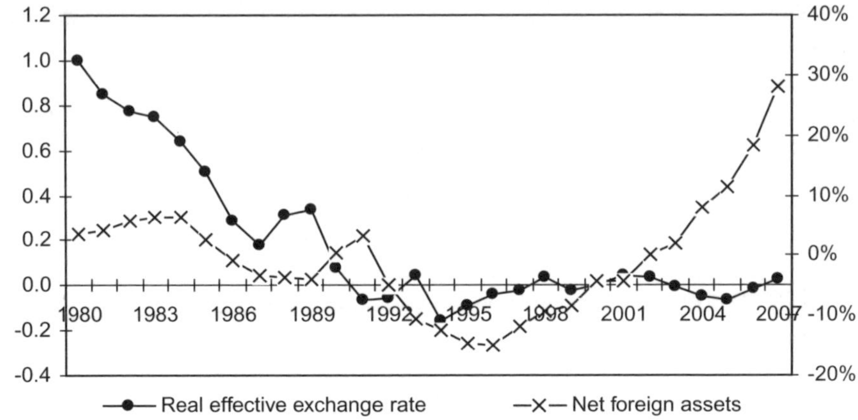

Fig. 9. Real effective exchange rate and net foreign asset position in China. Note: Real effective exchange rate is expressed in logarithms and the net foreign asset position is expressed as percentage of GDP.

has somehow stabilized, but also the terms of trade show a more stable path with small deviations of the exchange rate from the terms of trade.

Finally, turning to our third determinant, the nfa series exhibits a different pattern. Indeed, as reported in Figure 9, there is an important increasing gap between the net foreign asset position and the real effective exchange rate since the beginning of the 2000s, a fact that may explain the undervaluation of the Chinese currency in the recent period.

On the whole and to sum up, whereas it took longer to bring the real exchange rate close to its fundamentals, which explain the first period of overvaluation, since the 1990s, deviations of the exchange rate from its fundamentals are less pronounced, justifying the more rapid correction of undervaluations.

4. Conclusion

The aim of this chapter was to provide equilibrium exchange rate values and to study the adjustment process of observed exchange rates toward these levels by paying special attention to emerging Asian countries. Relying upon a wide sample of countries and on the BEER approach, we have shown that emerging Asian currencies are globally undervalued during the period under study, especially since the end of the 1990s. These undervaluations may be viewed as the result of competitive devaluations that drive the exchange rate to a level that encourages exports and reduces imports, stimulates domestic production and investment and, as a result, encourages economic growth.

Following a dynamic perspective, we have estimated panel smooth transition regressions in order to model the adjustment process of the real exchange rate toward its equilibrium BEER value. We have shown that real exchange rate dynamics in the long run are nonlinear for emerging Asian countries, and linear for the G7 currencies. More especially, there exists an asymmetric behavior of the real exchange rate when facing an over or undervaluation, the adjustment speed being more important in the case of undervaluations in Asia. This result is consistent with our findings that emerging Asian currencies have tended to be globally undervalued since the 1990s, but these undervaluations have been lower in size than the overvaluations observed at the beginning of the 1980s.

Acknowledgment

We would like to thank Agnès Bénassy-Quéré, Yin-Wong Cheung, and an anonymous referee for helpful comments and suggestions.

Appendix

Table A1. Currency misalignments, average (in percentage) and volatility, 2000–2007

Country	Misalignment	Volatility
Canada	*−3.71*	*0.12*
Eurozone	*3.54*	*0.10*
Japan	*0.01*	*0.12*
UK	*9.32*	*0.05*
USA	*7.48*	*0.09*
Average	*3.32*	*0.10*
China	**−24.56**	**0.33**
Hong Kong	**−6.52**	**0.23**
Indonesia	**−25.32**	**0.28**
India	**−13.56**	**0.24**
Korea	**−1.56**	**0.10**
Malaysia	**−28.56**	**0.24**
Philippines	**−12.09**	**0.13**
Singapore	**−11.63**	**0.10**
Thailand	**−23.40**	**0.16**
Average	**−16.35**	**0.20**

Notes: In bold: Emerging Asian countries. In italics: G7 countries.

Table A2. Exchange rate regimes and sign of the misalignments in 2007

Undervalued currencies		Overvalued currencies		Currencies close to equilibrium	
Argentina	(2)	Australia	(8)	Mexico	(8)
Brazil	(8)	*Canada*	*(8)*	Peru	(6)
Chile	(8)	Colombia	(6)	**Philippines**	**(8)**
China	(1)	Denmark	(10)	Uruguay	(6)
Costa Rica	(4)	*Eurozone*	*(8)*	*USA*	*(9)*
Egypt	(7)	**Korea**	**(8)**	Venezuela	(2)
Hong Kong	**(3)**	New Zealand	(8)		
Indonesia	**(6)**	Turkey	(8)		
India	**(7)**	*UK*	*(8)*		
Israel	(8)				
Japan	(9)				
Malaysia	**(7)**				
Norway	(8)				
Singapore	**(5)**				
Sweden	(8)				
Switzerland	(9)				
Thailand	**(6)**				

Notes: In bold: Emerging Asian countries. In italics: G7 countries. (1) Crawling peg, with the US dollar as exchange rate anchor.(2) Other conventional fixed peg arrangement, with the US dollar as exchange rate anchor. (3) Currency board arrangement, with the US dollar as exchange rate anchor. (4) Crawling band, with the US dollar as exchange rate anchor. (5) Managed floating with no predetermined path for the exchange rate, with a composite exchange rate anchor. (6) Managed floating with an inflation targeting framework. (7) Managed floating with other monetary policy framework. (8) Independently floating with inflation targeting framework. (9) Independently floating with other monetary policy framework. (10) Other conventional fixed peg arrangement, with the Euro as exchange rate anchor.
Source of the classification of exchange rate regimes: IMF (2008).

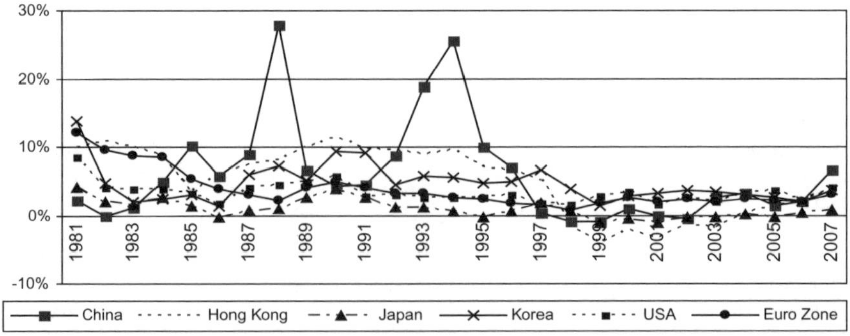

Fig. A1. Inflation, China, and main trade partners.

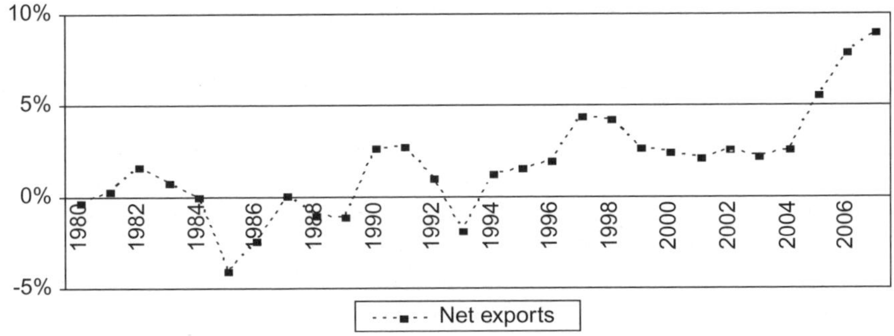

Fig. A2. Net exports (% GDP), China.

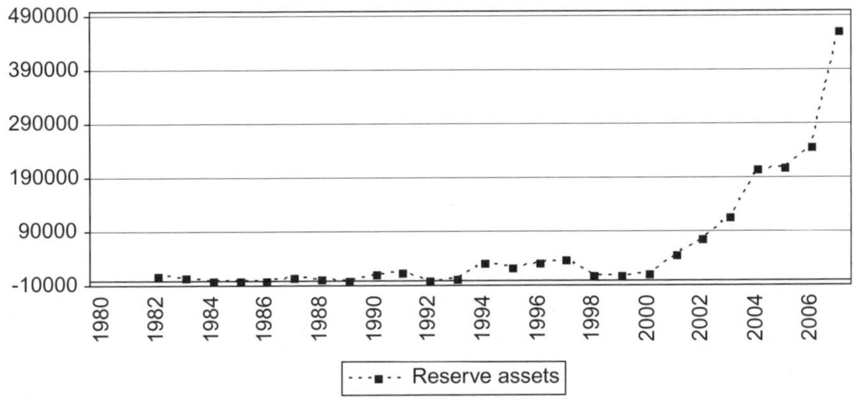

Fig. A3. Reserve assets (USD), China. Note: Sources for data used in Figures A1–A3: IFS, IMF.

References

Baum, C., Barkoulas, J., Caglayan, M. (2001), Nonlinear adjustment to purchasing power parity in the post-Bretton Woods era. *Journal of International Money and Finance* 20 (3), 379–399.

Bénassy-Quéré, A., Béreau, S., Mignon, V. (2009), Robust estimations of equilibrium exchange rates within the G20: a panel BEER approach. *Scottish Journal of Political Economy* 56 (5), 608–633.

Bénassy-Quéré, A., Lahrèche-Révil, A., Mignon, V. (2008), Is Asia responsible for exchange rate misalignments within the G20? *Pacific Economic Review* 13 (1), 46–61.

Béreau, S., López-Villavicencio, A., Mignon, V. (2009), Currency misalignments and growth: a new look using nonlinear panel data methods. Working Paper CEPII

Béreau, S., López-Villavicencio, A., Mignon, V. (2010), Nonlinear adjustment of the real exchange rate towards its equilibrium value: a panel smooth transition error correction modelling. *Economic Modelling* 27, 404–416.

Breitung, J. (2000), The local power of some unit root tests for panel data. In: Baltagi, B. (Ed.), *Advances in Econometrics, Vol. 15: Nonstationary Panels, Panel Cointegration, and Dynamic Panels*. JAI Press, Amsterdam, pp. 161–178.

Chen, S., Wu, J. (2000), A re-examination of purchasing power parity in Japan and Taiwan. *Journal of Macroeconomics* 22 (2), 271–284.

Cheung, Y-W., Chinn, M.D., Fujii, E. (2005), *Why the Renminbi might be overvalued (but probably isn't)?* University of California, Santa Cruz, USA.

Cheung, Y-W., Chinn, M.D., Fujii, E. (2007), The overvaluation of Renminbi undervaluation. *Journal of International Money and Finance* 26 (5), 762–785.

Cheung, Y-W., Chinn, M.D., Fujii, E. (2009), The illusion of precision and the role of the Renminbi in regional integration. In: Hamada, K., Reszat, B., Volz, U. (Eds.), *Towards Monetary and Financial Integration in East Asia*, Chapter 13. Edward Elgar Publishing, Cheltenham, pp. 325–356.

Chinn, M.D. (2000), The usual suspects: productivity and demand shocks and Asia-Pacific real exchange rate. *Review of International Economics* 8 (1), 20–43.

Chinn, M.D. (2005), A primer on real effective exchange rates: determinants, overvaluation, trade flows and competitive devaluation. NBER Working Paper No. 11521.

Clark, P.B., MacDonald, R. (1998), Exchange rates and economic fundamentals: a methodological comparison of BEERs and FEERs. IMF Working Paper No. 98/67.

Cline, W.R., Williamson, J. (2007), Estimates of the equilibrium exchange rates of the Renminbi: is there a consensus and, if not, why not? Paper presented at the Conference on China's Exchange Rate Policy, Peterson Institute for International Economics, Washington DC.

Coudert, V., Couharde, C. (2005), Real equilibrium exchange rate in China. Working Paper CEPII, 2005-01.

Coudert, C., Couharde, C., Mignon, V. (2008), Do terms of trade drive real exchange rates? Comparing oil and commodity currencies. Working Paper CEPII, 2008-32.

De Long, J.B., Shleifer, A., Summers, L.H., Waldmann, R.J. (1990), Noise trader risk in financial markets. *Journal of Political Economy* 98, 703–738.

Dominguez, K.M. (1998), Central bank intervention and exchange rate volatility. *Journal of International Money and Finance* 17 (1), 161–190.

Driver, R.L., Westaway, P.F. (2004), Concepts of equilibrium exchange rates. Bank of England Working Paper No. 248.

Dufrénot, G., Lardic, S., Mathieu, L., Mignon, V., Péguin-Feissolle, A. (2008), Explaining the European exchange rates deviations: long memory or non-linear adjustment? *Journal of International Financial Markets, Institutions and Money* 18 (3), 207–215.

Dufrénot, G., Mathieu, L., Mignon, V., Péguin-Feissolle, A. (2006), Persistent misalignments of the European exchange rates: some evidence from non-linear cointegration. *Applied Economics* 38 (2), 203–229.

Dufrénot, G., Mignon, V. (2002), *Recent Developments in Nonlinear Cointegration with Applications to Macroeconomics and Finance*. Kluwer Academic Publishers, Boston.

Dumas, B. (1992), Dynamic equilibrium and the real exchange rate in a spatially separated World. *Review of Financial Studies* 5 (2), 153–180.

Dunaway, S., Leigh, L., Li, X. (2009), How robust are estimates of equilibrium real exchange rates: the case of China. *Pacific Economic Review* 14 (3), 361–375.

Eitrheim, Ø., Teräsvirta, T. (1996), Testing the adequacy of smooth transition autoregressive models. *Journal of Econometrics* 74 (1), 59–75.

Flood, R., Marion, N. (1999), Perspectives on the recent currency crisis literature. *International Journal of Finance and Economics* 4 (1), 1–26.

Frankel, J. (2006), On the yuan. The choice between adjustment under a fixed exchange rate and a flexible exchange rate. *CESifo Economic Studies* 52 (2), 246–275.

Frankel, J., Wei, S. (2007), Assessing China's exchange rate regime. CEPR Discussion Paper No. DP6264.

González, A., Teräsvirta, T., van Dijk, D. (2005), Panel smooth transition regression models. Research Paper No. 165, Quantitative Finance Research Centre, University of Technology, Sydney.

Granger, C., Teräsvirta, T. (1993), *Modelling nonlinear economic relationships*. Oxford University Press, New York, USA.

Hadri, K. (2000), Testing for unit roots in heterogeneous panel data. *Econometrics Journal* 3, 148–161.

Hansen, B. (1999), Threshold effects in non-dynamic panels: estimation, testing, and inference. *Journal of Econometrics* 93 (2), 345–368.

Ilzetzki, E., Reinhart, C.M., Rogoff, K. (2008), The country chronologies and background material to exchange rate arrangements in the 21st century: which anchor will hold?. Available at http://terpconnect.umd.edu/˜creinhar/Papers/ERA-Country%20chronologies.pdf

Im, K.S., Pesaran, M.H., Shin, Y. (2003), Testing for unit roots in heterogeneous panels. *Journal of Econometrics* 115, 53–74.

IMF. (2008), De facto classification of exchange rate regimes and monetary policy frameworks. Available at http://imf.org/external/np/mfd/er/2008/eng/0408.htm

Kakkar, V., Yan, I. (2009), Real exchange rates and productivity: evidence from Asia. Manuscript, City University of Hong Kong.

Kao, C. (1999), Spurious regression and residual-based rest for cointegration in panel. *Journal of Econometrics* 90, 1–44.

Krugman, P. (1991), Target zones and exchange rate dynamics. *Quarterly Journal of Economics* 106, 231–254.

Lane, P.R., Milesi-Ferretti, G.M. (2004), The transfer problem revisited: net foreign assets and real exchange rates. *Review of Economics and Statistics* 86 (4), 841–857.

Levin, A., Lin, C.F. (1992), Unit root tests in panel data: asymptotic and finite sample properties. Discussion Paper No. 56, Department of Economics, University of California at San Diego.

Levin, A., Lin, C.F. (1993), Unit root tests in panel data: new results. Discussion Paper No. 92-93, Department of Economics, University of California at San Diego.

Levin, A., Lin, C.F., Chu, J. (2002), Unit root tests in panel data: asymptotic and finite sample properties. *Journal of Econometrics* 108, 1–24.

López Villavicencio, A. (2008), Nonlinearities or outliers in real exchange rates? *Economic Modelling* 25 (4), 714–730.

Ma, Y., Kanas, A. (2000), Testing for a nonlinear relationship among fundamentals and exchange rates in the ERM. *Journal of International Money and Finance* 19 (1), 135–152.

Maddala, G., Wu, S. (1999), A comparative study of unit root tests and a new simple test. *Oxford Bulletin of Economics and Statistics* 61, 631–652.

Maeso-Fernandez, F., Osbat, C., Schnatz, B. (2004), Towards the estimation of equilibrium exchange rates for CEE acceding countries: methodological issues and a panel cointegration perspective. ECB Working Paper No. 353.

McKinnon, R., Schnabl, G. (2006), China's exchange rate and international adjustment in wages, prices, and interest rates: Japan déjà vu? CESifo Working Paper No. 1720.

Michael, P., Nobay, A., Peel, D. (1997), Transactions costs and nonlinear adjustment in real exchange rates; an empirical investigation. *Journal of Political Economy* 105 (4), 862–879.

Pedroni, P. (1999), Critical values for cointegration tests in heterogeneous panels with multiple regressors. *Oxford Bulletin of Economics and Statistics*, S1, vol. 61, 653–670.

Pedroni, P. (2004), Panel cointegration. Asymptotic and finite sample properties of pooled time series tests with an application to the PPP hypothesis. *Econometric Theory* 20, 597–625.

Pesaran, M., Shin, Y., Smith, R.P. (1999), Pooled mean group estimation of dynamic heterogeneous panels. *Journal of the American Statistical Association* 94 (446), 621–634.

Sercu, P., Uppal, R., van Hulle, C. (1995), The exchange rate in the presence of transactions costs: implications for tests of purchasing power parity. *Journal of Finance* 50, 1309–1319.

Stein, J. (1994), The natural real exchange rate of the US dollar and determinants of capital flows. In: Williamson, J. (Ed.), *Estimating Equilibrium Exchange Rates*. Institute for International Economics, Washington, DC.

Taylor, M., Peel, D., Sarno, L. (2001), Nonlinear mean-reversion in real exchange rates: toward a solution to the purchasing power parity puzzles. *International Economic Review* 42 (4), 1015–1042.

Taylor, M.P., Allen, H. (1992), The use of technical analysis in the foreign exchange market. *Journal of International Money and Finance* 11, 304–314.

Teräsvirta, T. (1994), Specification, estimation, and evaluation of smooth transition autoregressive models. *Journal of the American Statistical Association* 89 (425), 208–218.

Tronzano, M., Psaradakis, Z., Sola, M. (2003), Target zones and economic fundamentals. *Economic Modelling* 20, 791–807.

van Dijk, D., Teräsvirta, T., Franses, P. (2002), Smooth transition autoregressive models: a survey of recent developments. *Econometric Reviews* 21 (1), 1–47.

Williamson, J. (1983), *The Exchange Rate System*. Institute for International Economics, Washington, DC, (MIT Press, Cambridge, MA, 1983).

PART III

Decoupling

CHAPTER 9

Global Contagion and the Decoupling Debate

Thomas D. Willett[a,b,c], Priscilla Liang[a,d] and Nan Zhang[a,c]

[a]*Claremont Institute for Economic Policy Studies, Claremont, CA 91711, USA*
E-mail address: Thomas.Willett@cgu.edu
[b]*Department of Economics, Claremont McKenna College, Claremont, CA 91711, USA*
E-mail address: priscilla.liang@csuci.edu
[c]*Department of Economics, School of Politics and Economics, Claremont Graduate University, Claremont, CA 91711, USA*
E-mail address: nzhangcgu@yahoo.com
[d]*Martin V. Smith School of Business & Economics, California State University, Channel Islands, Camarillo, CA 93012, USA*

Abstract

This chapter argues that there are a number of different versions of decoupling hypotheses and that rapid swings in their popularity are due largely to herding in popular mental models and shifts in short-run correlations. It is important to not put too much emphasis on such changes of correlations since these can vary substantially depending on the patterns of shocks. There are substantial differences in the effects of contagion during the current crisis on growth rates of both advanced and emerging economies, including Brazil, Russia, India, and China (the BRICs). Our estimates suggest that while countries like China and India have been able to maintain high growth rates, their short falls from trends have not been greatly smaller than for the United States itself. Thus, their decoupling has not been as great as many popular analyses have suggested.

Keywords: Contagion, financial crisis, decoupling

JEL Classifications: G15, F30, F42

1. Introduction

Fashion can change swiftly among commentators on the global economy. The media has a strong incentive to emphasize new area of stories to capture attention and there appears to be a quite elastic supply of experts to provide them. In the 1970s global interdependence was all the rage while in the middle of the first decade of this century decoupling theories gathered considerable attention to be followed again by recoupling

Frontiers of Economics and Globalization
Volume 9 ISSN: 1574-8715
DOI: 10.1108/S1574-8715(2011)0000009014

stories as the global financial crisis worsened, and contagion was felt across the globe.

Now as the crisis eases, advocates of decoupling stories are rising again. For example, in a 2010 book entitled *Fiscal Hangover: How to Profit from the New Global Economy*, the investment director for *Money Morning*, Keith Fitz-Gerald devotes a major part to advocacy of what he calls "The Great Decoupling." He argues that "The term decoupling … is widely misunderstood – and even more widely misapplied. Most people think of it solely in term of financial markets. However, what it really means is that the global economy will be disconnected…" (Fitz-Gerald, 2010). We strongly agree with Keith Fitz-Gerald that discussions of decoupling can at times be quite confusing because people have different concepts in mind. Unlike Fitz-Gerald, however, we believe that there are several different legitimate and useful concepts of decoupling and that the key to productive discussion and analysis is to closely identify the type or types of decoupling that are being discussed, not to spend time in debate about what a specific concept of decoupling should be. In this respect decoupling is much like contagion, where a number of useful concepts also coexist (Liang and Willett, 2008).

A major purpose of this chapter is to distinguish among several different concepts or uses of decoupling. A second major purpose is to illustrate the dangers of the popular practice of exaggerating the importance of recent correlations – whether of financial market performance or economic growth rates – as guides to the general relationships among these markets or economies. Changes in correlations may be products of changing structural relationships, market sentiment, or patterns of shocks and the last can be quite variable over time. In popular discussions changes in correlation that have been generated primarily by changes in patterns of shocks are often taken as evidence of new eras of structural relationships. We argue that neither the fall in stock market correlations that sparked much of the decoupling discussion nor the sharp increases in correlations from contagion as the financial crisis went global in 2008 should be taken as strong evidence about longer term relationships.

While the most highly publicized views on issues like contagion and decoupling are often highly over simplified, they raise important issues for investors, global businesses, and policy makers and have been the subject of considerable high quality research. In Section 2, we offer a brief history of the decoupling debates and document the rapid swings in the popularity of decoupling stories based on shifts in short-run correlations among financial markets and growth rates. In Section 3, we offer an interpretation of these rapid swings based on the concept of herding in popular mental models. In Section 4, we discuss more useful concepts of decoupling that go beyond simple correlations. In Section 5, we illustrate the substantial instability in the correlation among growth rates and stock markets over time. In Section 6, we turn to the argument that emerging market economies such as China and India have been able to largely insulate their economies, that is, decouple, from the Great Recession in the advanced economies. We show that while China and India were able to maintain growth rates that would be envied by any of the advanced economies, measures of their growth rates relative to estimated trends suggest that while they escaped the crisis with much less damage than did economies such as Mexico and Russia, their short falls from trend were not a great deal less than for the United States and on some measures were even a little greater. Section 7 offers concluding commends.

2. *A brief history of the decoupling debates*

In the 1970s global interdependence was highlighted by the breakdown of the Bretton Woods regime of adjustably pegged exchange rates, the oil shocks, and emergence of stagflation on a global scale. While citizens of most countries had long paid attention to the importance of the world economy, these developments came as a shock to many Americans who were used to being well insulated from most global economic developments. From ignoring global economies interactions, many switched to exaggerating its importance. By the 1980s, however, more balanced views were wide spread among leading researchers. Even for large economies like the United States, international economic interdependence was significant, both due to external shocks and the ways in which the external sector influenced the impacts of domestic policies. A prime example of the latter was the twin deficits analysis that argued that US budget deficits were a major cause of the strong dollar and US current account deficits in the 1980s. Discussions of the desirability of economic policy coordination received prominence and discussion of locomotive theories for global growth were popular.

Other than sources of commodity shocks, developing countries played little role in the discussions of macroeconomic policy coordination among the advanced economies. On the investment side, the 1980s are largely remembered as the decade of the Latin American debt crises. In Asia, there was early talk of decoupling from economic dependence on the advanced economies as "strong domestic demand and confident consumer became hallmarks of Asian countries." (Asian Economics Flash, 2007). However, the 1997–1998 Asian financial crises wiped this concept out of investors' minds. The buzzword reappeared after September 11, 2001 when the United States and Europe sank into recession, but emerging countries like India and China continued to grow at mid-to-high single digits. From 2002 to 2007, emerging nations sustained high growth. "The 'decoupling' thesis ... [became] a popular theme in Asian policy circles in the first decade of the new millennium... " (Athukorala and Kohpaiboon, 2009). In this context decoupling meant "the notion that the East Asian region had become a self-contained economic entity with potential for maintaining its own growth dynamism independent of the economics outlook for the traditional developed market economies" (Athukorala and Kohpaiboon, 2009).

Attention to the possibility of decoupling broadened as US growth began to slow in 2005 without noticeable effects on growth in other regions. This prospect was highlighted by the IMF in its World Economic Outlook (2007). Even after the slowing of US growth was followed by the early signs of the US subprime crises, many serious researchers as well as popular analysts emphasized decoupling – and with some justification. As Vanessa Rossi (2009) documents "Up to mid-2008, the emerging markets remained strong-'decoupling did work.'" In a 2007 report the IMF concluded "Overall, these factors suggest that most countries should be in a position to 'decouple' from the U.S. economy and sustain strong growth if the U.S. slowdown remains as moderate as expected"(IMF, 2007).

As will be documented in Section 5, over this period the decoupling of economic growth rates was accompanied by a decoupling of stock market behavior. Increasing liberalization of financial sectors, improvements in communication and computer technology, declines in transaction costs, and increased recognition of the benefits of diversification have all contributed to a substantial increase in international financial interdependence among advanced and emerging market economies. Indeed some even argued that the correlations among stock markets had increased so much that there was little benefit left to international diversification.

Big investment firms like Goldman Sachs and Morgan Stanley were the ones to popularize the notion of decoupling.[1] They believed "China, together with emerging Asia, stands a very good chance of outperforming and decoupling from the US economy in the coming few years." (Asian Economics Flash, 2007). In 2007, IMF data indicated that India and China accounted for a higher proportion of global growth than the United States (Esterhuizen, 2008). In the later part of 2007, as the crisis worsened in the United States, investors increasingly switched to emerging market assets. A $54 billion inflow to emerging market funds helped generate strong global stock performance outside the United States in 2007 (Prakash, 2008). These decoupling views were sharply dashed as 2008 progressed, however. In a careful study of the spread of the global crisis, Dooley and Hutchison (2009) pointed to May 2008 as the latest time that any plausible decoupling view could be held with respect to stock markets.

In fall 2008, after Lehman Brothers' collapse, the global financial system was strongly affected.[2] Emerging economies got caught in the fallout. Outflows from EM funds were $15 billion in January 2008 alone

---

[1] The main advocate was Jim O'Neill, chief economist of Goldman Sachs and the inventor of the BRIC acronym for the world's four biggest emerging markets of Brazil, Russia, India, and China in 2001.

[2] For more detailed analysis and references on the spread of the crisis see Rajan (2009) and Willett *et al.* (2010).

(Prakash, 2008). Some of the biggest stock markets drops were in emerging markets. Sell offs in China and India led the way. By mid-October 2008, the BRICs (Brazil, Russia, India, and China) index was down by 57 percent (Global Finance Magazine, 2008). Global funds fled the emerging markets and took refuge in US Treasury securities. By the beginning of 2008, Goldman Sachs raised the prospect of recoupling on the argument that "some parts of the rest of the world would now find it difficult to ignore the US slowdown" (O'Neil, 2008). Discussions of recoupling quickly replaced decoupling stories.

Not all analysts just followed the data. For example, Nouriel Roubini (2008), in a number of publications of his Global EconoMonitor, predicted that decoupling would not last. In early February of 2008 a Danske Bank Emerging Markets Brief was titled "From Decoupling to Recoupling" and a research paper by Barry Eichengreen and Yung Chul Park (2008) completed in May was titled "Asian and the Decoupling Myth." Still as far as the investment world was concerned Mohamed El-Erian (2009) judges that "The decoupling camp was firmly in control in the run-up to the 'sudden stop' experienced by the global economy in the last 3½ months of 2008 … market consensus increasingly viewed emerging economies as the growth locomotive for a world looking to reduce its dependence on highly-indebted U.S. consumers."

The victory of the recouplers was only temporary, however. Decoupling quickly returned in 2009 when Europe and the United States continued to show signs of contraction while China and India quickly rebounded. In its October 2009 WEO, the IMF said growing economies like "India and China will lead the expansion this year and will grow at rates of 5.4 and 8.5 percent, respectively." (Commodity Online, 2009). Decoupling was, once again, a hot topic. As El-Erian (2009) put it in August 2009, "With the ongoing normalization of the financial system, the decoupling camp is again in strong ascension today. It is buoyed by the developing pick-up in economic activities and the fact that equity valuations are now back above the pre-Lehman levels."

3. An interpretation of the swings in opinion

How should we interpret such rapid swings back and forth in opinion? For the investment community we believe that this is largely an example of the tendency to focus on popular models or stories to interpret events and sell investment strategies. An example is in the tendency for foreign exchange market participants and commentators to focus on one or two factors at a time, flitting from current account deficits to money growth to international indebtedness and back again. In dealing with a world of great complexity and uncertainty, recent developments in behavioral and neuroeconomics and finance suggest that it's quite understandable that investors grasp for simple mental models.[3] Such focus on problems of information and the cognitive limitation of the human brain suggest that it's quite understandable to have considerable herding in the adoption of popular models. Their views are also likely to be much more lightly held than deep-seated ideologies. With the frequency of surprise developments in the financial world, there are likely to be frequent shifts in focus. While confirmation bias dampens the frequency of switcher among investors the "latest thinking" will often show considerable flexibility.

In this light we can interpret the decoupling and recoupling theses as views on the short- or medium-term outlooks for correlations among countries' economic growth rates and financial market performance. And from this perspective it's perfectly reasonable to switch back and forth between decoupling and recoupling views based on the patterns of shocks that hit economies. On the other hand, taken as scientific hypotheses, such frequent switching is highly disturbing. This is likewise true for policy makers attempting to deal with the challenges of economic and financial interdependence.

Fortunately, however, international monetary analysis provides a framework within which we can make sense of a substantial portion of the otherwise bewildering array of comments made about decoupling – pros and cons. A beginning is to recognize that there are a number of different concepts of decoupling, not all of which go hand in hand. As was illustrated in the Section 2 some discussions focus on the behavior of stock markets, some on the real economy and some on both. While economic growth certainly has an influence on stock markets, the relationship is far from one to one. In general in recent decades we find higher correlations among stock markets than among economic growth rates across countries, indicating an increased degree of global capital mobility and financial integration. This is illustrated in Section 5.

4. Concepts of decoupling

Decoupling clearly implies a break in a relationship that was previously more coupled and closely linked. This definition lends itself naturally to discussions of changes in patterns of correlations and that is what commentators usually have in mind, especially in discussions of stock markets. Economists often offer more structural definitions, however. The definition of "decoupling … as growth in one area becoming less dependent on growth in another area" (Rossi, 2009) reflects this view. Discussions also frequently proceed in terms of the size of spillovers from one economy to another (IMF, 2007). Often the case for decoupling in the face of greater globalization is made in terms of greater regionalization.

[3] See, for example, Burnham (2005), Peterson (2007), and Zweig (2007).

This is especially common in Asia where intraregional trade has grown rapidly. Furthermore, while the discussions of such macroeconomic interdependence in the 1970s and 1980s focused heavily on the relationships among the advanced economies, with the spectacular growth of the BRICs and other emerging market economies in recent years, current discussions focus heavily on relationships with the emerging market countries as well.

A recent study by an IMF economist M. Ayhan Kose *et al.* (2008) describes the decoupling and recoupling debate as "largely about whether and how emerging markets will be affected by the U.S. business cycle." In a broader concept, decoupling means business cycles in emerging nations are more independent from business cycles in advanced nations like the United States. After they separated 106 countries into industrial and emerging economies, they found evidence of "business cycle convergence within each of these two groups of countries but divergence (or decoupling) between them."

These issues have been the subject of quite a number of recent empirical studies, especially for Asia and Europe, that don't directly address the decoupling debate but focus instead on economic interdependence more generally. The label under which most of this analysis goes is the degree of business cycle synchronization. Of course this can be measured in the same way as decoupling, just with a reversal of signs. A good deal of the literature has been motivated by the empirical implementation of optimum currency area criteria in the context of the pros and cons of regional monetary union or greater regional policy coordination.[4] The standard argument is that a greater degree of synchronization reduces the divergence in optimal monetary policies for the member of a prospective currency area and hence reduces the cost of giving up independent national monetary policies.

One common method of measurement is to divide the sources of a country's macroeconomic economic fluctuations into global, regional, and national factors. The difficulty with this approach, as with correlation analysis, is that it conflates the effects of direct interdependence or spillover effects with the nature of shocks. As a consequence changes in correlations are interpreted as indicating changes in the degree of interdependence or spillover when in fact they may largely reflect changes in the patterns of shocks. This point is emphasized in the paper by Kose *et al.* (2008). They find that for EMs group factors have become more important relative to global factors over the period 1985–2005 compared with 1960–1984. However, over this period estimates of the size of the spillover on EMs from fluctuations in the US economy have increased, not decreased.

---

[4] For discussion and references to this literature see Willett *et al.* (2009), and Willett *et al.* (2010a), and Willett *et al.* (2010b).

These seemingly conflicting results are easily explained. Global shocks were stronger in the earlier period. As the WEO comments "Export exposure to the United States has generally continued to increase, even for countries where the US share of total exports has declined" (IMF, 2007). The WEO goes on to stress that the magnitudes of these real linkages vary considerably across countries. They are especially strong for the United States' immediate neighbors, Canada and Mexico, and are generally stronger with the advanced than with the emerging and developing economies. Such econometric estimates of direct spillovers suggest that the old adage that when the United States sneezes the rest of the world catches a cold is greatly exaggerated except for Canada and Mexico. The IMF describes the spillovers from US fluctuations as "important" but "generally moderate in magnitude" (IMF, 2007).

Decoupling and recoupling (and changes in the degree of business cycle synchronization) are closely related to the size, nature, and source of shocks. Larger shocks get transmitted most strongly and faster. Similarly, we observe convergence, or recoupling, when shocks are generated from the intertwined and complex global financial system. In the beginning of the current credit crisis, neither the magnitude nor the natures of the shocks were initially fully recognized. So patterns diverged across countries. Initially it was viewed primarily as a shock to the United States and some European banks. As the crisis entered its more severe stages, however, the seizing up of the global financial system acted as a common shock across most countries, leading to a substantial increase in synchronization. The combination of the drying up of trade, finance, and the beginning of recessions in many countries then began to take its toll on international trade, in turn worsening the recessions in many countries.

The magnitudes of these spillovers will vary not only with patterns of trade and investment but also with the causes of fluctuations in the United States. Thus, it was not unreasonable that many analysts believed that the spillovers from what was initially viewed almost exclusively as a US domestic housing market problem would be relatively mild. Since housing has a relatively low import content and the effects on the aggregate US economy were expected to be moderate, it was quite plausible to expect little effect on growth in other countries. The growth effects abroad from the US recession in the early 1990s generated by the savings and loans crisis had been much weaker than from the US recession following the bursting of the tech bubble. Furthermore, historically the spillovers from US slowdowns in growth had been much weaker than from actual recessions.

As the magnitudes of the crisis slowly revealed itself, the outlook for emerging markets changed drastically. The banking systems in both the United States and Europe were much more heavily exposed to securities based on subprime mortgages than officials and analysts had been aware. As the sharp downturn in the housing market hit first the shadow banking system of conduits, hedge funds and special investment vehicles (SIVs), and then the parent banks themselves, even EMs with sound fundamentals were hit by a double whammy. First the freezing up of the credit system led to drastic reductions and in many cases actual reversals of financial flows from the advanced to the EM economies, even though the financial systems of the later had generally little direct exposure to the toxic assets. Then as the United States and Europe moved into recession, EM exports fell sharply. They were hit both by the drop in demand for imports in the recession countries and by a substantial drying up of trade credit. On top of this, EMs with weak fundamentals such as large current account deficits and high short-term foreign indebtedness were hit by speculative runs over and above the general increase in risk aversion and flight to quality in the financial sector.[5]

The strength of transmission channels can change decoupling quickly into recoupling and vice versa. India has a more open financial system than does China. So the credit crisis was transmitted more strongly to India through financial markets than to China. The large portfolio inflow to India in 2007 gave many a false impression of decoupling, but this was reversed to a huge outflow in 2008 as the crisis worsened. China, on the other hand, had built a much stronger trade relationship with the United States and rest of the advanced world than had India. Thus, China was hit harder through its export sector.

In terms of providing protection from economic fluctuations in the advanced economies much of the increases in intraregional trade in Asia gave misleading signals to those who did not analyze its composition carefully. Much of the increase had been in inputs to export platforms, especially in China. Thus, when the advanced economies demand for imports from China was hit, this was passed along as reductions in China's demand for imported inputs from the rest of Asia. As a result the extent of intraregional trade within Asia provided much less insulation from advanced country fluctuations than if there had been an equivalent expansion of trade in final products (Eichengreen and Park, 2008; Athukorala and Kohpaiboon, 2009).

A full analysis of decoupling (and synchronization) requires consideration not just of impact effects but also of countries' ability to respond to these shocks. This is an area where the decoupling camp has a stronger position. Many EMs have been developing greatly expanded domestic markets and strong international reserve positions. This combination has allowed many EMs to respond to the contagion from the advanced economies with strong macroeconomic stimulus. China has been the most prominent, but by no means the only example. As a result many EMs who took a hard hit have been able to begin their recoveries rather quickly. This is the major truth underlying the reemerging of the decoupling camp.

---

[5] See Willett *et al.* (2010).

One should be careful not to swing too far in this direction, however. There is a vast difference between the moderate decoupling view that many EMs will be able to resume substantial growth fairly quickly and the hope that the BRICs could be a new locomotive to drive the world economy. In some specific market segments such as particular commodities there may be some truth in the stronger argument, but not in the aggregate.

5. *Analysis of the instability of growth and financial market correlations*

Our theses that correlations are heavily influenced by the patterns of shocks and that since these can vary a great deal over time so will the correlations are strongly borne out by the calculations presented in Tables 1 and 2. In these we focus on correlations between the United States and three sets of countries, its closest neighbors, Canada and Mexico, advanced economies represented by Germany and Japan, and the BRICs. We consider growth correlations first. We present both simple correlations of annual growth rates against the United States over a series of five-year periods and the correlations of deviations from trend.[6] For the deviations from trend, we calculate them from the Hodrick—Prescott filter (HP filter). The HP filter is a data-smoothing technique that is commonly used to remove short-term fluctuations and reveal long-term trends. In contrast to the linear trend, HP filter produces a nonlinear presentation with a procedure of square error minimization. The HP filter is not without drawbacks, however. For example, the determinants of the variance of the trend or level of smoothness is arbitrary, and there is an end-point problem in which the calculation puts more weight on the observations in the end of the series (Marinheiro, 2004/2005). However, as Ravn and Uhlig (1997) have suggested, although the HP filter may be only optimal in special cases, "none of these shortcomings and undesirable properties are particularly compelling: the HP filter has withstood the test of the time and the fire of discussion remarkably well." With these considerations in mind, we adopted the HP filter for our calculations in this chapter.

5.1. Growth rate correlations

Our story line is strongly supported by both sets of calculations. The correlations are extremely variable over the different time periods (Table 1a and 1b). The differences between the simple correlations and the correlations of deviations from trend are usually quite small. They

[6] Two sets of GDP growth correlations against the US GDP growth in five-year intervals are calculated: the simple correlations and the correlations of deviations from trends after applying HP filter (Tables 1a and 1b).

Table 1. Correlations of GDP growth (vs. the United States)[a]

1a: Simple correlations of GDP growth in five-year intervals (1960–2008)

	1960–1964	1965–1969	1970–1974	1975–1979	1980–1984	1985–1989	1990–1994	1995–1999	2000–2004	2005–2008
Brazil		0.38	0.82	0.31	−0.05	−0.17	0.44	−0.72	0.78	−0.64
Canada	0.99	0.90	0.89	0.87	0.87	0.72	0.90	0.69	0.80	0.99
China					0.67	0.49	0.54	−0.88	0.24	0.55
Germany		0.18	0.56	0.84	0.88	0.39	−0.86	0.21	0.61	0.30
India	0.21	−0.98	−0.38	−0.23	0.00	−0.54	0.92	−0.52	0.06	0.98
Japan	−0.61	−0.53	0.51	0.87	0.49	0.87	−0.58	−0.49	0.97	0.90
Mexico	0.26	0.30	0.46	−0.05	−0.12	0.20	−0.18	0.86	0.96	0.82
Russia									0.90	0.43

1b: Correlations of the deviations from GDP growth trend (Hodrick–Prescott filter) in five-year intervals (1960–2008)

	1960–1964	1965–1969	1970–1974	1975–1979	1980–1984	1985–1989	1990–1994	1995–1999	2000–2004	2005–2008
Brazil		0.36	0.82	0.50	0.00	−0.27	0.41	−0.71	0.77	−0.22
Canada	0.99	0.90	0.86	0.89	0.90	0.70	0.89	0.63	0.79	0.98
China					0.62	0.38	0.54	−0.87	0.40	0.76
Germany		0.25	0.59	0.84	0.87	0.69	−0.85	0.64	0.50	0.45
India	0.25	−0.95	−0.40	−0.26	−0.02	−0.55	0.88	−0.60	0.15	0.99
Japan	−0.34	−0.48	0.54	0.85	0.45	0.89	−0.50	−0.39	0.96	0.95
Mexico	0.21	0.29	0.46	0.03	0.01	0.30	−0.25	0.83	0.91	0.83
Russia									0.55	0.82

[a] *Source:* GDP annul data are taken from the IFS and WEO October 2009.

Table 2. Simple correlations of equity returns (vs. the United States) in five-year intervals (1/1960–11/2009)[a]

	1/1960–12/1964	1/1965–12/1969	1/1970–12/1974	1/1975–12/1979	1/1980–12/1984	1/1985–12/1989	1/1990–12/1994	1/1995–12/1999	1/2000–12/2004	1/2005–11/2009
Brazil							−0.02	0.64	0.65	0.78
Canada	0.82	0.80	0.80	0.64	0.77	0.84	0.66	0.82	0.77	0.81
China								0.09	0.01	0.45
Germany	0.45	0.23	0.33	0.25	0.37	0.55	0.44	0.73	0.75	0.89
India					−0.07	−0.03	−0.02	0.15	0.28	0.77
Japan			0.32	0.41	0.42	0.55	0.43	0.43	0.47	0.72
Mexico								0.68	0.64	0.79
Russia									0.37	0.59

[a] *Source:* Equity returns are calculated from the major national equity prices from Bloomberg.

differ by less than 0.1 in 79 percent of the calculations. However, the differences can be big sometimes. For example, during 2005–2008, detrended correlations of three of the BRIC countries are significantly different from their simple correlations. The differences are 0.42 for Brazil–United States, 0.21 for China–United States, and 0.39 for Russia–United States. For other countries, the largest differences are 0.44 for Germany–United States during 1995–1999, and 0.27 for Japan–United States during 1960–1964.

We do find some expected regularities based on structural characteristics. The United States' closest trading partners, Canada and Mexico, display consistently high correlations with the United States over the entire sample period. The correlations between Canada and the United States vary only from 0.63 to 0.99, with 80 percent being 0.79 or above. Up to 1995 Mexico–United States correlations were quite variable, but since Mexico's economic liberalization and its joining NAFTA, the correlations have been consistently high, varying only between 0.82 and 0.96.

Due in considerable part to the major oil shocks the correlations of the industrial countries with the United States were especially high during the 1970s. While at the time there were many claims that we had entered a new era of global interdependence, by the late 1980s the correlations of Germany with the United States had fallen substantially and in the early 1990s they turned negative for both calculations. In the first decade of the new century they were positive again. Over our full sample the Germany–United States simple correlations varied from 0.88 in 1980–1984 to −0.86 in 1990–1994 (0.87 to −0.85 for detrended correlations). For Japan the simple correlations varied from 0.97 in 2000–2004 to −0.58 in 1990–1994 (0.96 to −0.50 for detrended correlations). The correlations of the United States and developing countries show high variability as well, often varying from large positive to large negative numbers. Using detrended data, the pairwise correlations for Mexico–United States vary from 0.91 to −0.25, for Brazil–United States 0.77 to −0.71, for China–United States 0.76 to −0.87 and for India–United States 0.99 to −0.95. (The Russian data does not go back far enough to make such comparisons.)

Table 1b, however, shows that compared with other countries in our sample, the BRICs generally had lower degrees of growth comovements with the United States. Evidence of low correlations can be found during 1980–1984 for Brazil and India, during 1985–1989 and 1995–1999 for Brazil, India, and China, and during 2000–2004 for India, China, and Russia. Nevertheless, the evidence is not strong enough to strongly support decoupling. During other time frames, the same sets of correlations are quite high. For example, China–United States growth correlations are 0.62 and 0.76 during 1980–1984 and 2005–2008, India–United States are 0.88 and 0.99 during 1990–1994 and 2005–2008, respectively, and Russia–United States are 0.82 during 2005–2008. Furthermore, simultaneous increases in correlations (other than Brazil) during

2005–2008 show the effect of increased globalization and interdependence rather than decoupling. With its seesaw-patterned correlations, Brazil's case shows volatility rather than decoupling.

Thus, our results caution that we should not place a good deal of weight on using correlations over short periods to either support or reject decoupling. The high variability in correlations over time suggests that the general increase in global economic interdependence reflected in growing international trade as a proportion of GDP and substantial increases in international capital mobility has been dominated by the variability in patterns of shocks.

5.2. Stock market correlations

Interestingly we find considerably less variability in correlations of equity returns. Negative correlations are less frequent and of smaller magnitudes (Table 2). Again Canada–United States correlations are the most stable, varying only between 0.64 and 0.82. Mexico's correlations are also rather stable for the three periods available, varying between 0.64 and 0.79. Germany–United States stock correlations show an upward trend, but Japan–United States correlations do not. From 1975 through 2004, the five-year correlations varied only between 0.4 and 0.55 for Japan, while Germany varied from 0.25 to 0.75 over the same period. The BRIC correlations generally start off low or negative and then rise substantially in the later periods. This is consistent with these economies becoming more integrated into the global financial system.

6. Did the BRICs insulate their economies successfully from the great recession?

Another relevant empirical issue is to look at how the BRICs and other EMs have weathered the financial crisis compared with the advanced economies. Of course, a full analysis of this question would require careful econometric estimations of the impacts of the interactions among countries. For example, the strong view of BRICs as locomotives sees their growth as helping to reduce the size of the recessions in the advanced economies. This version sees "the BRIC's vigorous consumption growth helping drag advanced economies out of recession" (Lex, 2009). As an initial investigation, however, we can compare how growth rates during the crisis in the BRICs and other EMs compared with those in the advanced economies.

A typical perception of the success of the BRICs is given by the Lex Column in the Financial Times. "The BRICs, excluding Russia, withstood the financial crisis better than the developed world: China and India maintained robust growth"(Lex, 2009). It is certainly true that China and

India maintained growth rates that the advanced economies would love to have, but this can give a misleading impression of the growth costs the crisis imposed on such economies.

More relevant is what happened to their growth rates compared with what they would have been without the crisis. This counterfactual is of course unobservable so we must rely on estimates and these may differ. Still it is an exercise worth pursuing. The simplest method is to compare growth rates during the crisis with those preceding it. Of course even this simple method raises a number of issues. What year or average of years of growth should we take as the benchmark for comparison? And how should we measure the crisis declines when they cut across various years? Furthermore, we don't know if the recent resumption of growth in most economies in 2009 will be continued. In a recent paper (Willett *et al.*, 2010), we used IMF estimates to compare growth rates for 2007 with 2009. The average differences across the advanced and emerging and developing economies as groups were quite similar, with declines of 6.1 and 6.6 percent, respectively, but with considerable variability within each group. For example, US growth fell less than 5 percent, from 2.1 to −2.7 percent, but Mexican growth fell by more than 10 percent, from 3.3 to −7.3 percent.

A likely better measure is to look at deviations from growth trend using a HP filter. Our analyses in some cases paint a quite different picture from the standard story (Table 3a and 3b). Depending on the time periods used for calculating the trends,[7] we estimated China's growth rate was 1.67–1.92 percent below its growth trend in 2009. This was much better than the growth reductions for many other countries. For example, we estimate Russia's economic growth was 8.57–10.16 percent less than its long-term trend, while estimated reduction for Mexico was 6.14–6.4 percent, Germany 4.25–4.39 percent, and Brazil 3.78–3.86 percent. By comparison, growth in the United States dropped only 2.53–2.61 percent. India and Canada's are in similar situations, decreased 2.2–2.53 percent and 2.28–2.56 percent, respectively. Since the growth rate for the United States in 2009 was among the least below the estimated normal growth, it suggests that the BRICs on average didn't weather the recent credit crisis much better than the United States did. In terms of these calculations, the BRICs were not as insulated from the crisis as some decoupling advocators have argued.

Using the HP filter may understate the effects of the crisis, however, since in its standard application the full time period is used and in our application this includes the crisis years at the end of the series. As noted previously, the mechanism of the HP filter's calculation produces the

---

[7] The deviations from trends here are based on the HP filter generated for the period of 1960–2009 and 2000–2009, respectively.

Table 3. Deviations of GDP growth from the trend[a]

3a: Deviations of GDP growth from the trend (Hodrick–Prescott filter for the whole period (1960–2009))[b]

	Brazil	Canada	China	Germany	India	Japan	Mexico	Russia	US
2006	0.67	1.08	1.58	2.76	2.16	1.70	3.52	2.12	1.08
2007	2.36	1.28	2.9	2.43	1.37	2.38	2.63	3.58	1.07
2008	1.82	−0.25	−1.21	1.37	−0.93	−0.08	1.27	2.28	−0.06
2009	−3.86	−2.56	−1.67	−4.39	−2.2	−4.23	−6.4	−10.16	−2.61

3b: Deviations of GDP growth from the trend (Hodrick–Prescott filter for 2000–2009)

	Brazil	Canada	China	Germany	India	Japan	Mexico	Russia	US
2006	0.59	1.32	1.38	2.77	2.06	1.68	3.74	2.73	1.23
2007	2.34	1.54	2.68	2.49	1.19	2.49	2.86	4.55	1.19
2008	1.86	0.01	−1.44	1.46	−1.19	0.15	1.51	3.57	0.03
2009	−3.78	−2.28	−1.92	−4.25	−2.53	−3.89	−6.14	−8.57	−2.53

3c: Deviations of GDP growth from the trend (linear trend for 1990–2006)

	Brazil	Canada	China	Germany	India	Japan	Mexico	Russia	US
2006	0.57	−1.10	1.81	3.08	1.59	1.08	1.88	NA	−0.64
2007	2.16	−1.59	3.20	2.67	0.61	1.40	0.29	NA	−1.21
2008	1.47	−3.87	−0.88	1.45	−1.93	−1.50	−1.89	NA	−2.96
2009	−4.41	−6.94	−1.33	−4.51	−3.46	−6.14	−10.43	NA	−6.14

3d: Deviations of GDP growth from the trend (linear trend for 2000–2006)

	Brazil	Canada	China	Germany	India	Japan	Mexico	Russia	US
2006	0.17	0.36	0.34	1.82	−0.21	0.02	1.47	0.86	−0.16
2007	1.67	0.20	1.19	1.11	−1.92	0.15	−0.32	1.81	−0.74
2008	0.87	−1.76	−3.43	−0.41	−5.20	−2.96	−2.69	−0.19	−2.49
2009	−5.11	−4.52	−4.42	−6.66	−7.47	−7.79	−11.42	−13.43	−5.67

[a]For the results in 2007–2009, deviations from the trend are calculated using the actual value from the Hodrick–Prescott filter trend and the forecasting value from the linear trend.
[b]The starting year of the whole period varies for different economies due to the data availability. For example, the GDP data for the United States, Canada, India, Japan, and Mexico start from 1960, for the other economies start later than 1960 (i.e., Brazil in 1964, China in 1979, Germany in 1961, and Russia in 1996).

"end-point bias," which means the last point of the series has an exaggerated impact on the trend at the end of the series (Bruchez, 2003).[8] Thus, the recession pulled down the calculated trend rates of growth. We, thus, also calculated linear trends based on data only through 2006 and

[8] The end-point problem can be adjusted by adding forecasting value to the end of the series, however, the forecast might also be biased due to factors such business cycle conditions (Bruchez, 2003). Discussions on the solution for the problem can be done in a future research.

compared 2009 growth rates with trend rate of growth.[9] On these measures the effects of the crisis on the United States appear much stronger, with the magnitude of subpar growth equaling 5.67 percent if the trend is started in 2000 and 6.14 percent if the trend is started in 1990 (Tables 3c and 3d). For China the growth gap is 4.42 percent if 2000 is used, but only 1.33 percent if 1990 is used. This reflects the acceleration of China's growth as more economic reforms took hold. The other two BRICs, Brazil and India, also appear to weather the crisis better than in the previous scenarios. Thus, one can argue from both sides as to which is more appropriate.

With the notable exception of the effect on China using the trend from 1990, the results are generally qualitatively similar to those from the HP filter with respect to the pattern of growth declines. Russia is still the hardest hit. Using the 1990 trend, we found Brazil and India performed somewhat better than the United States. The declines from their growth trends were −4.41 and −3.46 percent, respectively, compared with −6.14 percent for the United States. Using the 2000 trend, India appears harder hit. Its growth rate was 7.74 percent less than trend. Brazil and the United States were 5.11 and 5.67 percent less, respectively.

While we should not put too much weight on these specific calculations, they do strongly suggest that we should not be too quick to accept the conclusions that the BRICs, excluding Russia, have been able to largely insulate themselves from the Great Recession. It seems that some commentators have conflated the high trend growth rates of these countries with their degree of insulation from the global economy. This is clearly an important issue that deserves deeper structural analysis.

7. *Concluding remarks*

We have argued that there are a number of different versions of decoupling hypotheses and that it is important to keep these distinctions in mind if we are to avoid confusion. It is particularly important not to place too much emphasis on the latest patterns of correlations among economic growth rates and stock prices since these can vary substantially from one period to another depending on the patterns of shocks.

While we would not put much weight on the precise numbers of our calculations, they suggest that no relatively open economy was able to almost completely decouple from the effects of the global financial shock. But many were able to adopt policy responses that reduced the negative impact and most of these policy responses were not of the beggar-thy-neighbor variety. The failure of the shock to cumulate into anything like the Great Depression of the 1930s suggests that despite all of the miscues

[9] The deviations from trends here are based on the linear trend for the period of 1990–2006 and 2000–2006, respectively.

made by governments in fighting the crisis, we still have come a long way since the 1930s. Let us hope that this crisis in turn will help governments learn as much about sound financial regulation and supervision as was learned from the 1930s about macroeconomic policy making.

The United States was never a great locomotive of the global economy as was popularly imagined and neither will be the BRICs within the next few decades. But the United States has had and will continue to have an important (if possible somewhat declining) impact on the global economy and increasingly so will the BRICs. We have entered a world where no one country or group of countries is economically dominant. This is a world of complex economic interdependence that requires joint management by a sizeable group of countries if we are to achieve our collective economic potential.

In this regard, there is another aspect of economic interdependence that will return to prominence as we recover from the global financial crisis – the problem of global payments imbalances. To avoid global instability, it is important not only to restore growth, but to do so in ways that reduce global current account imbalances to safe proportions. The economics of this is well understood. Countries with large surpluses such as China and much of Asia need to rely more on the expansion of domestic demand and less on exports. Countries with large deficits, especially the United States, need to increase domestic savings (both public and private) while reducing domestic consumption. If this is to be done without generating another recession substantial expansion of exports will be required.

From the standpoint of standard economic models this is a simple problem with a simple solution. In practice there are substantial political problems because of the short-run costs of making such adjustments. The global costs of such adjustments will be much less if they are undertaken cooperatively across countries. This is a situation where there is much more commonality than divergence of economic interests from a longer term perspective.

The key obstacle is the status quo bias of short-run political pressures that can create substantial short-run conflicts of interest. There are also important technical economic issues concerning the most effective ways of going about the rebalancing of both surplus and deficit economies. In this policy sense economies will remain importantly coupled despite continued swings back and forth in the short-run correlations of their economic growth rates and stock market performances.

References

Asian Economics Flash (2007), China: decoupling – why do we believe this time would be different, economic research from the Gao Hua Portal, September 24. Available at http://portal.ghsl.cn

Athukorala, P.C., Kohpaiboon, A. (2009), East Asian exports in the global economic crisis: the decoupling fallacy and post-crisis policy challenges. The Australian National University Working Paper No. 2009/13.

Bruchez, P.A. (2003), A modification of the HP filter aiming at reducing the end-point bias. The Federal Finance Administration (FFA) of Switzerland Working Paper No. OT/2003/3.

Burnham, T. (2005), *Mean markets and lizard brains: how to profit from the new science of irrationality*. Wiley, Hoboken, NJ.

Commodity Online (2009), IMF says India, China to lead economic expansion, October 1. Available at http://www.commodityonline.com/news/IMF-says-India-China-to-lead-economic-expansion-21589-3-1.html

Dooley, M., Hutchison, M. (2009), Transmission of the U.S. subprime crisis to emerging markets: evidence on the decoupling-recoupling hypothesis. *Journal of International Money and Finance* 28 (8), 1331–1349.

Eichengreen, B., Park, Y.C. (2008), Asia and the decoupling myth. Policy Paper. Available at http://www.econ.berkeley.edu/˜eichengr/asia_decoup_myth.pdf

El-Erian, M. (2009), Insight: Decoupling versus recoupling. *Financial Times*, August 10, p. 18.

Esterhuizen, E. (2008), Commoditizing the 'Decoupling Theory', March 10th. Available at http://seekingalpha.com/article/67844-commoditizing-the-decoupling-theory

Fitz-Gerald, K. (2010), *Fiscal Hangover: How to Profit from the New Global Economy*. Wiley, Hoboken, NJ.

Global Finance Magazine (2008), Features: breaking up or breaking down?, December. Available at http://www.gfmag.com/archives/32-dec2008/382-features.html.

IMF (2007), Decoupling the train? Spillovers and cycles in the global economy. *World Economic Outlook: Spillovers and Cycles in the Global Economy*, International Monetary Fund.

Kose, M.A., Otrok, C., Prasad, E.S. (2008), Global business cycles: convergence or decoupling? IMF Working Paper No. 08/143.

Lex (2009). The rise of the BRICs. *Financial Times*, December 30, Lex Column, p.12.

Liang, P., Willett, T. (2008), Contagion. In: Reinert, K., Rajan, R., Class, A., Davis, L.S. (Eds.), *The Princeton Encyclopedia of the World Economy*, Vol. 1. Princeton University Press, Princeton, NJ, pp. 215–219.

Marinheiro, C.F. (2004/2005). Brief notes on the determination of the output gap. *Econometria Aplicada*. Available at https://woc.uc.pt/feuc/getFile.do?tipo = 6&id = 1703

O'Neil, J. (2008). Cloudy picture as concept of decoupling is put in context, July 31. Available at http://m.ftchinese.com/index.php/ft/story/001020927/en

Peterson, R.L. (2007), *Inside the investor's brain: the power of mind over money*. Wiley, Hoboken, NJ.

Prakash, A. (2008), Decoupling or recoupling? *Business Standard*, February 12. Available at http://www.business-standard.com/india/news/akash-prakash-decoupling-or-recoupling/313393/

Rajan, R.S. (2009), Financial crisis and private capital flows to emerging economies in Asia and elsewhere. Working Paper No. 09/06, United Nations UN-ESCAP.

Rossi, V. (2009), *Decoupling Debate will Return: Emergers Dominate in Long Run*. Chatham House, Briefing Note, IEP BN 08/01.

Roubini, N. (2008), 2008 US and global economic outlook and implications for financial markets, RGE Monitor, January.

Ravn, M., Uhlig, H. (1997), On adjusting the Hodrick Prescott Filter for the frequency of observations. CentER Discussion Paper. Available at http://arno.uvt.nl/show.cgi?fid = 3560

Willett, T., Auerbach, N. N., Kim, K. S., Kim, Y., Ouyang, A., Permpoorn, O., Sompornserm, T., Srisorn, L., Sula, O. (2009), The global crisis and Korea's international financial policies (special studies series: 5). Korea Economic Institute.

Willett, T., Liang, P., Zhang, N. (2010), The slow spread of the global crisis. *Journal of International Commerce, Economics and Policy* 1 (1), 33–58.

Willett, T., Permpoon, O., Srisorn, L. (2010a). Asian monetary cooperation: perspectives from the optimum currency area analysis. *Singapore Economic Review* 55 (1), 103–124.

Willett, T., Permpoon, O., Wihlborg, C. (2010b). Endogenous OCA analysis and the early Euro experience. *The World Economy* 33 (7), 851–872.

Zweig, J. (2007), *Your money and your brain: how the new science of neuroeconomics can help make you rich*. Simon and Schuster, New York.

CHAPTER 10

The Decoupling of Asia-Pacific?

James Yetman

Representative Office for Asia and the Pacific, Bank for International Settlements, 78th Floor, Two International Finance Centre, Central Hong Kong
E-mail address: james.yetman@bis.org

Abstract
Standard measures of business cycle comovement, based on correlation coefficients, are very sensitive to the phase of the business cycle, as well as to regional crises. Adjusting for these factors overturns the empirical result that Asia-Pacific economies are becoming decoupled from the United States over time. An alternative, intuitive, measure of business cycle comovement is proposed, based on the difference between output growth rates adjusted for its long-run average. The new measure suggests that Asia-Pacific economies are becoming more strongly coupled with the United States over time.

Keywords: Decoupling, correlation, comovement

JEL classifications: E32, F42

1. Introduction

International economic links between Asia-Pacific and the United States have strengthened over time due to growing trade and capital flows, both in absolute terms and as a percent of GDP. An existing theoretical literature (surveyed below) has argued that the effect of strengthening international links on comovement in real activity is ambiguous. An analogous empirical literature has examined low-frequency business cycle comovement dynamics, typically using Pearson correlation coefficients, and reported conflicting results, with some papers arguing that comovements are becoming stronger, while others argue for macroeconomic "decoupling."

In the context of the recent international financial crisis, this empirical evidence had been interpreted by some as suggesting that a recession in the United States would not have the same negative effects on Asia-Pacific economies as would have been expected in the past, due to decoupling. For

Frontiers of Economics and Globalization
Volume 9 ISSN: 1574-8715
DOI: 10.1108/S1574-8715(2011)0000009015

example, China and, to a lesser extent, India and Indonesia have become increasingly important drivers of global growth, and potential substitutes for a loss in demand for world output from the United States.

Here we demonstrate the fragility of arguments based on the standard, correlation-based, measure of business cycle comovement. Decomposing the correlation coefficient into its period-by-period components, we show that most of the variation in business cycle correlations is related to the phase of the business cycle. Correlations are high during recessions, but low during other periods. Further, the empirical conclusions related to decoupling are very sensitive to the end point of the sample. If we stop the sample in 2008, the empirical evidence points to decoupling. But there is little evidence of any change in the level of comovement over time if we include data for 2009.

We then construct an alternative measure of international links based on the difference in output growth rates adjusted for its long-run average. We argue that this alternative measure is more consistent with intuitive notions of business cycle comovement. For example, the new measure discriminates between the case where two countries are growing at their average rates and where only one country is growing at its average rate. Arguably the former case is consistent with high business cycle comovement, while the latter indicates a lack of comovement. In contrast, correlation-based measures treat both cases as consistent with complete decoupling.

Applying this new measure to our dataset, we find strong evidence against the decoupling of Asia-Pacific from the United States. With the exception of the Asian financial crisis period (1997–1998), deviations in growth rates from average levels have tended to move more closely in Asia-Pacific to those in the United States since 1990 than before.

We also examine the causes of business cycle comovement and find that economies whose banks are relatively integrated with the United States or experience higher growth rates in terms of GDP per capita tend to comove less strongly with the United States. Interestingly we find that standard measures of trade integration offer little explanatory power for the degree of business cycle comovement. Perhaps these results are not surprising, given the ambiguous implications of trade and financial integration for business cycle comovement discussed in the next section.

In the following section, we examine the existing theoretical and empirical literature on business cycle comovement. We then conduct our own empirical examination in Section 3, before concluding.

2. *Existing evidence*

An existing literature has outlined the possible effects of changing international links on business cycle comovement from a theoretical perspective. Akin and Kose (2008) highlight three effects. First, there are changes in the size distribution of economies, with the share of global GDP attributable to the United States declining while that attributable to China and India is growing, for example. Second, there are changes in the dynamics of trade and sectoral output due to the ongoing development of economies. Third, there are changes in financial linkages due to liberalization of capital accounts and increased links between emerging economies.[1] These changes in recent years have generally resulted in a strengthening of international links.

Theory would suggest that the effect of these strengthening links on the degree of comovement between economies may be ambiguous. On the one hand, sources of demand may become more strongly linked. With increased trade, for example, a slowdown in one economy may translate into a larger reduction in imports from trading partners. Similarly, increased consumption demand comovement may result from growing capital flows, due in increasing risk-sharing between economies, and contagion in the event of financial disruptions (Kose *et al.*, 2003b).

On the other hand, increased trade and capital flows may reduce the link between underlying demand and production so that stronger comovement in demand need not translate into stronger comovement in output. In particular, to the extent that economy-specific productivity and technology shocks drive business cycles, world demand for domestic output may become sufficiently elastic that output volatility increases, and becomes less correlated, across economies. Increased specialization in production may reduce output comovement still further (Kose *et al.*, 2003b).[2]

Given this potential ambiguity, the effect of increased international links on comovement in real activity is an empirical question. On this the existing literature provides mixed results, with some papers concluding that the degree of comovement is declining, as national economies increasingly "decouple" from each other, while others conclude that the degree of comovement is in fact increasing.

A common measure of the degree of business cycle comovement is the Pearson correlation coefficient between the cyclical components of GDP for countries i and j, constructed as follows:

$$\rho^{ij} = \frac{\sum_{t=1}^{T}(\Delta y_{it} - \Delta\bar{y}_i)(\Delta y_{jt} - \Delta\bar{y}_j)}{\sqrt{\sum_{t=1}^{T}(\Delta y_{jt} - \Delta\bar{y}_j)^2}\sqrt{\sum_{t=1}^{T}(\Delta y_{jt} - \Delta\bar{y}_j)^2}}, \tag{1}$$

where y_{it} = log real output for country i in period t and $\Delta\bar{y}_i$ is the arithmetic mean of the change in log real output over time. This

[1] See also Imbs (2004) for similar arguments.

[2] Furceri and Karras (2008) argue that increased intraindustry trade implies increased comovement, while increased interindustry trade will result in increased specialized and less comovement.

correlation may be constructed over many pairs of economies, either for the full sample or for subperiods. The resulting correlations are then typically used to study the causes of international economic links or the evolution of those links over time.

For example, Otto *et al.* (2001) use this approach to model cross-country variation in bilateral output growth correlations for 17 OECD countries. They find that cross-country correlations have declined in their sample between two subperiods, 1960–1979 and 1980–2000. Kose *et al.* (2004) consider correlations with "world" output based on 10-year subsamples and find that economies have generally become less highly correlated with world output over time, with the exception of industrial economies. Akin and Kose (2008) examine changes in correlations of average growth rates between three subperiods (1960–1972, 1973–1985, and 1986–2005) and find that links between developed economies and developing economies have weakened between the latter two subsamples.

Some papers seek to more formally model the source of these correlations. For example, Frankel and Rose (1998) consider 21 industrialized economies and find that business cycle correlations are increasing in bilateral trade.[3] Darvas *et al.* (2005) find that economies with similar government budgets (defined as deficits or surpluses as a percent of GDP) experience similar business cycle fluctuations. Imbs (2004, 2006) finds that trade, specialization patterns, degree of financial integration, similarities in sectoral patterns of production, convergence in macroeconomic policies, and the existence of currency unions are all important in explaining business cycle correlations. Calderón *et al.* (2007) examine 147 countries over 1960–1999 and argue that trade intensity increases business cycle correlation, but more so in industrial than developing economies. Clark and van Wincoop (2001) find that sharing a border increases business cycle synchronicity, Akin and Kose (2008) find that financial openness and global financial integration both increase correlations and Furceri and Karras (2008) find that the introduction of the common currency increased business cycle synchronization in Europe.[4,5]

Finally, there are a number of papers that study the degree of comovement using alternative methods that focus on shorter horizons. For example, Gregory *et al.* (1997), using dynamic factor analysis to identify a common component in output, consumption, and investment across the

[3] See also Gruben *et al.* (2002), Inklaar *et al.* (2008), and Abbott *et al.* (2008) who report similar results of the effect of trade on business cycle correlation. In contrast, Crosby (2003) finds that trade intensity does not explain synchronicity among Asia-Pacific economies.

[4] Other authors take alternative approaches, utilizing common factor analysis (e.g., Kose *et al.*, 2003a, 2008a, 2008b; Del Negro and Otrok, 2008) or error correction models (e.g., Hoffmaister *et al.*, 1998). Also see Baxter and Kouparitsas (2005) who use a band-pass filter that isolates fluctuations in GDP with periodicities between 2 and 8 years.

[5] Kumakura (2006) finds that the extent to which an economy specializes in electronics is an important determinant of business cycle correlation for Asia-Pacific economies.

G7 economies over 1970–1993, find large differences in the importance of the common factor between different business cycle episodes.

Others go further and explicitly link synchronicity with the phase of the business cycle. For example, Bordo and Helbling (2004), taking a long-term view, examine 121 years of annual data for 16 economies. While finding an increasing degree of business cycle synchronization across different exchange rate regimes, due to increased goods market and asset market integration, they also point out that the importance of global shocks appears to be particularly high when there is a worldwide downturn.[6] This corroborates Helbling and Bayoumi (2003), who obtain a similar result for the G7 countries during 1973–2001 using quarterly data and a dynamic factor model to isolate common cycles. They argue that this is due to the growing importance of global shocks, resulting from increased globalization. Similarly, Canova *et al.* (2007), in a multi-country Bayesian VAR model of G7 business cycles, find that business cycles are more synchronized during contractions than during expansions. But, in contrast to some of the earlier cited literature, they find no evidence of structural breaks in the degree of synchronization over time.

3. Empirical evidence

We focus our analysis on the comovement between the United States and the major economies of the Asia-Pacific (Australia, China, Hong Kong SAR, India, Indonesia, Japan, Korea, Malaysia, New Zealand, Philippines, Singapore, and Thailand). Our data source is the International Financial Statistics (IFS) published by the International Monetary Fund. We consider annual data for the 1971–2009 period. Our measure of output (Y_{it}) is real GDP, in local currency terms.[7]

3.1. Correlation coefficients

As a first step, we follow Otto *et al.* (2001), Kose *et al.* (2004), and Akin and Kose (2008) in computing the business cycle correlation between two subperiods: 1971–1989 and 1990–2008. The results are contained in columns (a) and (b) of Table 1. The correlation declines between the two subsamples for many of the individual economies, with the decline in the average correlation significant at the 10% level, consistent with decoupling.

---

[6] See also International Monetary Fund (2002, 2007).

[7] The series used are 99BVRZF ... and 99BVPZF .... For China, Indonesia, and the Philippines, we use mean forecasts from the November 2009 publication of Consensus Economics in place of actual data for 2009.

Table 1. GDP growth rate correlations: Asia-Pacific with United States

	(a) 1971–1989	(b) 1990–2008	(c) 1990–1996; 1999–2008[a]	(d) 1990–2009	(e) 1990–1996; 1999–2009[a]
Australia	0.47	0.73	0.70	0.72	0.69
China	0.49	0.12	0.22	0.17	0.26
Hong Kong SAR	0.50	0.04	0.38	0.31	0.63
Indonesia	0.29	−0.34	−0.22	−0.25	−0.04
India	−0.11	0.25	0.36	0.14	0.22
Japan	0.63	−0.14	0.00	0.35	0.49
Korea	0.49	−0.11	0.25	0.12	0.51
Malaysia	0.28	−0.06	0.30	0.23	0.60
New Zealand	0.34	0.33	0.45	0.51	0.60
Philippines	−0.15	0.12	0.28	0.24	0.39
Singapore	0.22	0.34	0.57	0.52	0.71
Thailand	0.39	−0.30	0.07	0.01	0.47
Mean	0.32	0.08	0.28	0.26	0.46
p-value[b]		0.07	0.70	0.51	0.10

Source: Author's calculations.
[a]Dropping the Asian Financial Crisis years (1997, 1998).
[b]*p*-value from a two-tailed test of no change in mean correlation with column (a).

One limitation of these results, however, is that they focus on low-frequency changes in the degree of comovement, which would provide an adequate description of changes in the degree of comovement only if it evolved smoothly and unidirectionally over time.[8] However, we will show that changes in business cycle comovement are dominated by variation over the business cycle, and that it is only during periods of recession or financial turmoil that there is significant evidence of any correlation in the growth of output across countries at all. In other periods, the degree of comovement is largely indistinguishable from random noise.

To illustrate this we decompose the Pearson correlation into its period-by-period contributions, as in Yetman (2011). First we construct a z-score of the growth rate of each economy in Asia-Pacific at each point in time:

$$x_{it} = \frac{(\Delta y_{it} - \Delta \bar{y}_i)}{\sqrt{(1/(T-1))\sum_{t=1}^{T}(\Delta y_{it} - \Delta \bar{y}_i)^2}}, \tag{2}$$

and the product of this measure with x_{jt}, constructed analogously for the United States, then yields a measure of the comovement between countries i and j that is year- and country pair-specific, as follows:

[8] This is true not just for papers that divide the sample into subperiods, but also for dynamic factor models that effectively preclude large changes in the "world" factor over short horizons.

$$\rho_t^{ij} = x_{it}x_{jt}. \tag{3}$$

Up to a degrees-of-freedom correction, the average of the comovement between economies i and j measured using Equation (3) will equal the Pearson correlation coefficient in Equation (1),[9] as in

$$\frac{1}{T}\sum_{t=1}^{T}\rho_t^{ij} = \frac{T-1}{T}\rho^{ij}. \tag{4}$$

We then regress ρ_t^{ij} on a series of time dummies, also including fixed effects for each country i. The use of fixed effects implies that we are allowing for differences in the amount of comovement between different economy pairs. These differences are not formally modeled, but may include the standard "gravity" variables (the distance between the two economies, and their average economic size), historical, cultural, and political drivers of business cycle comovement and the average level of exports and imports, for example.

The use of fixed effects means that our estimated coefficients are identified by changes in the degree of comovement over time. Suppose, for example, that the degree of comovement between national economies was steadily declining over time, due to long-run "decoupling." We would then expect to find positive coefficients on the time dummies corresponding to the early part of our sample and negative coefficients in the latter part. We would also expect the results to be consistent with those obtained using low-frequency methods, comparing correlation coefficients over subsamples, discussed earlier.

We illustrate our results by providing a plot of the time dummy estimates, together with 95% confidence intervals based on robust standard errors, in Figure 1. Additionally, we superimpose on the graphs vertical bars to coincide with years in which there were US recessions, as identified by the National Bureau of Economic Research.

The figure indicates that there is an almost one-to-one correlation between periods of significant business cycle comovement with the United States and periods when the United States was in recession. Additionally, while the confidence bands typically widen during recessions, the increases in comovement are still large enough to ensure that comovements are statistically significantly positive during recessions, but insignificantly different from zero at most other times.[10] The largest exception to this scenario is the Asian financial crisis, when Asian economies experienced a dramatic slowdown while the United States was enjoying above-average growth. Note also that 2009 stands out as an exceptional year, with a

---

[9] Note that, unlike the Pearson correlation, this measure of comovement may take on any real value. But the average of ρ_t^{ij} across the full sample for given i, j will lie between -1 and 1.

[10] Similar results are found for many different sets of countries *vis-à-vis* the United States.

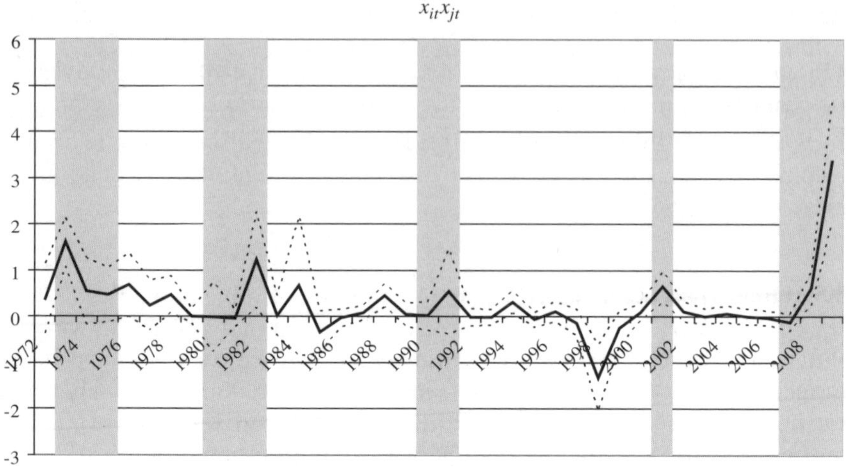

Fig. 1. Asia-Pacific business cycle phase comovement with the United States. Source: NBER Business Cycle Dating Committee and author's calculations.

much higher degree of business cycle comovement between Asia-Pacific and the United States than any other point in our sample.

3.2. Sensitivity to crises and recessions

These results suggest two possible sources whereby using correlation coefficients may result in misleading conclusions regarding the evolution of comovement over time. First, a regional crisis may dramatically decrease the measured level of business cycle comovement. Second, as Imbs (2004) suggests, the infrequency and irregularity of business cycles may bias the results. Indeed, the results suggest that the "Great Moderation" (Kim and Nelson, 1999; McConnell and Perez-Quiros, 2000), and the corresponding drop in the number and severity of recessions over 1990–2007, may result in the appearance of decoupling even if, conditional on the phase of the business cycle, there had been no underlying change in the degree of comovement.

We can illustrate the impact of each of these factors on the correlation coefficients. Regarding the effect of regional crises, column (c) of Table 1 repeats the correlation calculation from 1990 to 2008 from column (b), but excludes the Asian financial crisis years of 1997 and 1998. This increases the size of the correlation for all economies except Australia, and the average correlation is now almost identical to the earlier subsample. We also illustrate the effect of including 2009 data in column (d) of Table 1. The inclusion of 2009 data increases the degree of business cycle comovement for every economy except India, and dramatically reduces the difference in comovement between the two subsamples. Finally, in column (e), we demonstrate that dropping 1997 and 1998 data and including 2009 data is sufficient to completely overturn the decoupling hypotheses, and result in a substantially higher degree of business cycle comovement in the second subsample than in the first one. Also, in each of columns (c)–(e), there is no longer a statistically significant decline in the mean correlation between the two subperiods.

3.3. Other critiques of correlations

We now consider two further critiques of correlation coefficient-based measures of business cycle comovement discussed so far, first adjusting for heteroskedasticity and second the counter-intuitive treatment of data in the calculation of the correlation coefficient.

A possible critique of the analysis above is due to Forbes and Rigobon (2002). They argue that correlation coefficients may be biased due to heteroskedasticity, and suggest a correction for this bias. The source of the bias is that correlation coefficients are conditional on volatility, which tends to vary systematically with the level of correlation. They find that the bias is large enough that their correction overturns the well-known result that stock market comovement increases during crisis periods, for a number of different episodes. In principle this bias could also explain our results.

Suppose we are comparing the comovement between an Asia-Pacific economy and the United States across two subsamples, and obtain correlation coefficients ρ_1 and ρ_2, respectively. Following Forbes and Rigobon, we cannot simply compare the two but need to adjust one of them for the change in variability between the two time periods. In particular, we should compare ρ_1 with ρ_2^*, where

$$\rho_2^* = \frac{\rho_2}{\sqrt{1 + \delta[1 - (\rho_2)^2]}}, \tag{5}$$

and

$$\delta = \frac{V(\Delta y_{jt}^2)}{V(\Delta y_{jt}^1)} - 1 \tag{6}$$

is the relative increase in the variance of US growth between the two sample periods. While this correction is only strictly accurate when there are no omitted variables or endogeneity between markets, in our case it may provide an indication as to how sensitive the results are to changes in volatility.

The results, incorporating the Forbes and Rigobon correction, are given in Table 2. Columns (a)–(e) parallel Table 1 and indicate that, while the correction has quantitatively important effects in increasing correlations

Table 2. GDP growth rate correlations: Asia-Pacific with United States with Forbes–Rigobon (2002) correction[a]

	(a) 1971–1989	(b) 1990–2008	(c) 1990–1996; 1999–2008[b]	(d) 1990–2009	(e) 1990–1996; 1999–2009[b]	(f) No US recession	(g) US recession
Australia	0.47	0.88	0.87	0.82	0.80	0.12	0.65
China	0.49	0.20	0.38	0.23	0.35	0.23	−0.22
Hong Kong SAR	0.50	0.07	0.59	0.40	0.75	0.27	0.70
Indonesia	0.29	−0.54	−0.38	−0.33	−0.05	0.00	0.81
India	−0.11	0.42	0.58	0.19	0.30	−0.19	−0.03
Japan	0.63	−0.24	0.00	0.46	0.61	0.39	0.55
Korea	0.49	−0.19	0.42	0.17	0.64	0.13	0.51
Malaysia	0.28	−0.10	0.50	0.31	0.72	0.03	0.54
New Zealand	0.34	0.53	0.67	0.63	0.72	−0.16	0.72
Philippines	−0.15	0.21	0.46	0.32	0.50	−0.34	0.78
Singapore	0.22	0.53	0.78	0.64	0.81	0.11	0.45
Thailand	0.39	−0.48	0.12	0.01	0.60	−0.07	0.68
Mean	0.32	0.11	0.42	0.32	0.56	0.04	0.51
p-value[c]		0.20	0.49	1.00	0.02		0.00

Source: Author's calculations.
[a]The Forbes–Rigobon (2002) correction is applied to columns (b)–(e) with respect to column (a), and (g) with respect to column (f).
[b]Dropping the Asian Financial Crisis years (1997, 1998).
[c]*p*-value from a two-tailed test of no change in mean correlation between column (a) and columns (b)–(e); column (f) and column (g).

in the second subperiod, they do not change the overall interpretation that measured declines in GDP comovement between Asia-Pacific and the United States are largely driven by the Asian financial crisis and the absence of major recessions. The final two columns make this point even more clearly. Column (f) contains the correlation between Asia-Pacific economies and the United States for years when the United States is not in recession, while column (g) contains the correlation using only data from years when the United States was in recession. Even with the Forbes–Rigobon correction the mean correlation is 0.52 during recession years, compared with only 0.04 in other years, a difference that is highly statistically significant.

A second critique is that the correlation coefficient is counter-intuitive in its treatment of data. Consider, for example, the circumstances under which ρ_t^{ij} will take on a value of zero, suggesting that period t data is consistent with complete decoupling between economies i and j. There are three possible cases:

(1) $\Delta y_{it} = \Delta \bar{y}_i$; $\Delta y_{jt} \neq \Delta \bar{y}_j$;
(2) $\Delta y_{it} \neq \Delta \bar{y}_i$; $\Delta y_{jt} = \Delta \bar{y}_j$;
(3) $\Delta y_{it} = \Delta \bar{y}_i$; $\Delta y_{jt} = \Delta \bar{y}_j$.

While the contribution of observation t to the correlation coefficient is the same in each of these cases, they are very different from each other. Case (3), for example, looks a lot like strong comovement, since both economies are growing at average rates, while the other cases are more consistent with decoupling, since deviations from average growth in one economy occur simultaneously with average growth in the other economy.

Moreover, if $x_{it} = x_{jt}$ in period t, suggesting very strong comovement, this contributes no more to the correlation between economies i and j than in any period s where $x_{is} = (x_{it}x_{jt})/x_{js}$. That is, if the growth rate of one economy is slightly below average when the growth rate of the other economy is dramatically lower than average, then ρ_t^{ij} may take on a relatively large positive value, despite the fact that this may reasonably be viewed as consistent with decoupling.

3.4. An alternative measure of comovement

The point of the analysis so far is not intended to answer the question of whether Asia-Pacific has decoupled from the United States. Rather it is to illustrate the sensitivities of the standard approach used to answering this question.

An alternative measure that may remedy these critiques is to use the sum of deviations, rather than the product. Consider, for example, the following measure of business cycle comovement:

$$\xi_t^{ij} = -|x_{it} - x_{jt}|. \tag{7}$$

Now what matters for measuring business cycle comovement is the difference in the level of deviations in growth rates from average, normalized by the volatility of each country's growth rate. Note that the absolute difference is multiplied by negative one, so that an increase in value indicates stronger comovement, as with the correlation-based measures.

This measure is intuitively appealing. For example, the three cases discussed in Section 3.3 that each generate $\rho_t^{ij} = 0$, would be treated differently here. Case (3), where both economies are growing exactly at average levels, would be interpreted as consistent with strong comovement, rather than decoupling. And, for the other cases, ξ_t^{ij} would reflect the distance between the growth rate and average growth across the two economies.

We can illustrate the robustness of this alternative measure to the phase of the business cycle and regional crises by computing mean values over subsamples, as before:

$$\xi^{ij} = \frac{1}{T}\sum_{t=1}^{T} \xi_t^{ij}, \tag{8}$$

and repeating the analysis in Table 1. We do so in Table 3. While the results remain quantitatively sensitive to the Asian financial crisis and the inclusion of data for 2009, the evidence in all cases is inconsistent with Asia-Pacific decoupling from the United States. Instead there is strong evidence that business cycle comovement has strengthened in recent decades, especially if the Asian financial crisis dates are excluded or 2009 data are included.

We also regress ξ_t^{ij} on a series of time dummies, including fixed effects for each country pair, and plot the time dummies and 95% confidence bands in Figure 2. By this measure, Asia-Pacific economies tend to "decouple" in relative terms during US recessions, in sharp contrast with measures based on the correlation coefficient. This is because, while Asia-Pacific economies tend to experience slower-than-average growth in such times, the slowdown in the region is relatively smaller than that in the United States.

Also, while the Asian financial crisis has a significant quantitative effect on this measure of business cycle comovement, it does not reverse the long-run trend toward increased business cycle comovement between Asia-Pacific and the United States. Indeed, there is a statistically significant upward trend in ξ_t^{ij} over the full sample period (t-statistic 2.74), excluding the Asian financial crisis (t-statistic 4.28), excluding US recession periods (t-statistic 1.87), and excluding both (t-statistic 4.15).

The above analysis provides strong evidence for increased Asia-Pacific business cycle comovement with the United States over the past three

Table 3. Alternative measure of business cycle comovement: Asia-Pacific with United States

	(a) 1971–1989	(b) 1990–2008	(c) 1990–1996; 1999–2008[a]	(d) 1990–2009	(e) 1990–1996; 1999–2009[a]
Australia	−0.88	−0.41	−0.43	−0.47	−0.51
China	−0.76	−0.77	−0.69	−0.83	−0.76
Hong Kong SAR	−0.95	−0.75	−0.56	−0.67	−0.53
Indonesia	−1.04	−1.54	−0.85	−0.88	−0.70
India	−1.32	−0.68	−0.64	−1.12	−1.10
Japan	−0.81	−0.81	−0.67	−0.70	−0.59
Korea	−0.86	−0.93	−0.65	−0.73	−0.62
Malaysia	−1.10	−0.93	−0.67	−0.71	−0.55
New Zealand	−0.98	−0.59	−0.50	−0.61	−0.55
Philippines	−1.12	−0.63	−0.56	−0.69	−0.65
Singapore	−1.11	−0.87	−0.73	−0.71	−0.59
Thailand	−0.99	−1.31	−0.69	−0.86	−0.60
Mean	−0.99	−0.85	−0.64	−0.75	−0.65
p-value[b]		0.17	0.00	0.00	0.00

Source: Author's calculations.
[a]Dropping the Asian Financial Crisis years (1997, 1998).
[b]*p*-value from a two-tailed test of no change in mean correlation with column (a).

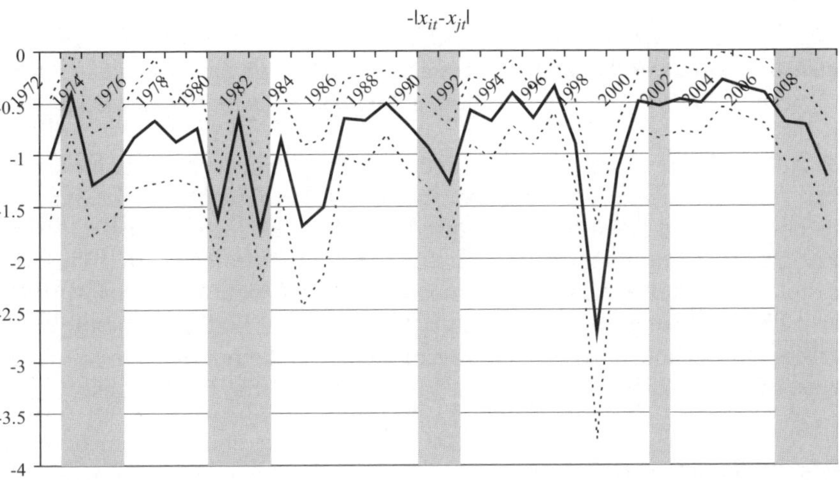

***Fig. 2.* Asia-Pacific business cycle phase comovement with the United States. Source: NBER Business Cycle Dating Committee and author's calculations.**

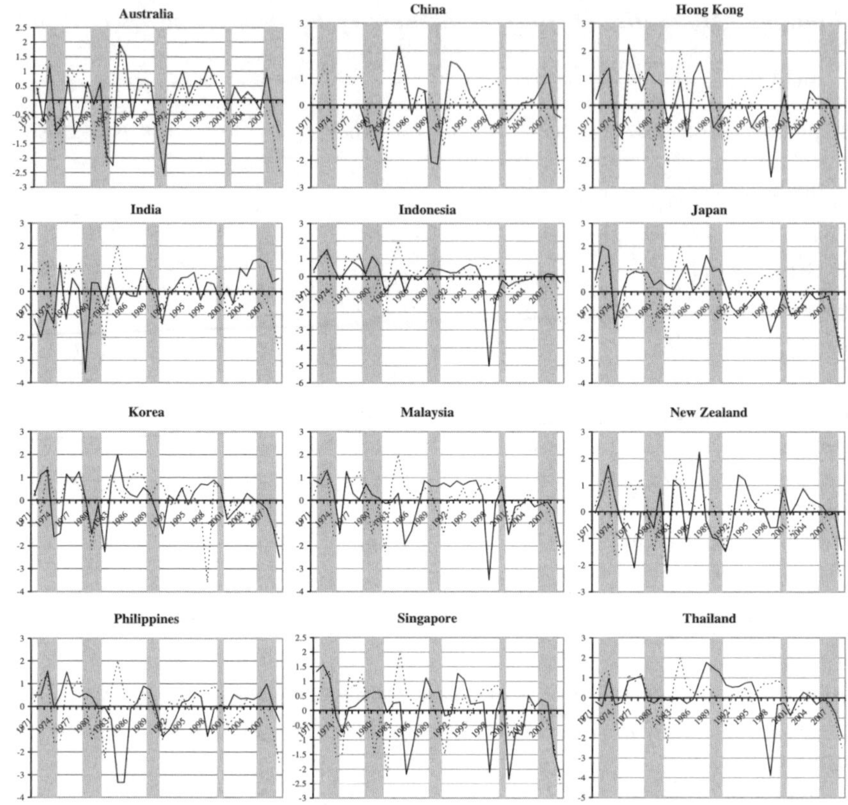

Fig. 3. Output deviations from average growth path. Dotted line in each figure indicates output deviation from average growth path for the United States. Source: NBER Business Cycle Dating Committee and author's calculations.

decades. However, the average increase in business cycle comovement masks a wide diversity of country experiences. Breaking down the data into its country-level constituents, Figure 3 plots x_{it} for each economy in Asia-Pacific (solid line) along with that for the United States (dotted line). We can now see that in fact all high income regional economies plus Malaysia and Thailand comoved very closely with the United States during the recent crisis. The decline in average comovement across the full panel in this recent episode is driven by China, India, Indonesia, and the Philippines.

3.5. Explaining comovement

Finally, we seek to identify the factors that influence the degree of business cycle comovement by regressing ξ_t^{ij} on banking sector integration, trade integration, population, and per capita income. The variables are defined as follows.

Population:

$$\ln(\mathrm{POP}^i_t) - \ln(\mathrm{POP}^j_t)$$

is the log difference between the population of country i and the United States in period t (*Source:* IFS).

Banking integration:

$$\mathrm{BInt}^{ij}_t = \ln\left(\frac{1}{4}\left[\frac{A^{ij}_t + L^{ij}_t + A^{ji}_t + L^{ji}_t}{\mathrm{GDP}^i_t/e^i_t}\right]\right),$$

where A^{ij}_t = stock of asset holdings of country i's banks in the United States, measured in USD million, taken from the BIS Locational Banking Statistics (similarly, L^{ij}_t is the stock of liabilities of country i's banks in the United States), GDP^i_t is nominal GDP of country i in year t (*Source:* IFS), and e^i_t is the average market value of country i's currency in year t defined as units of domestic currency per USD (*Source:* IFS).

Trade integration:

$$\mathrm{TInt}^{ij}_t = \ln\left(\frac{1}{4}\left[\frac{X^{ij}_t + M^{ij}_t + X^{ji}_t + M^{ji}_t}{\mathrm{GDP}^i_t/e^i_t}\right]\right),$$

where X^{ij}_t = exports from country i to the United States, measured in millions of USD, from the Direction of Trade statistics (similarly, M^{ij}_t is imports from the United States).

Real GDP per capita:

$$\mathrm{GDPPC}^i_t - \mathrm{GDPPC}^j_t = \ln\left(\frac{\mathrm{GDP}^i_t}{e^i_t\,\mathrm{CPI}^j_t\,\mathrm{POP}^i_t}\right) - \ln\left(\frac{\mathrm{GDP}^j_t}{\mathrm{CPI}^j_t\,\mathrm{POP}^j_t}\right)$$

is the difference in log GDP per capita between country i and the United States, where CPI^j_t is the level of CPI in the United States (*Source*: IFS).

US Recession:

US Recession is a dummy variable that takes on a value of 1 each year that the United States was in recession for at least part of that year, as defined by the National Bureau of Economic Research Business Cycle Dating Committee (*Source:* NBER).

The results are contained in Table 4 and show that, once country and time fixed effects are included (column (c)), greater banking integration is linked with less business cycle comovement between Asia-Pacific and the United States, while trade integration offers little explanatory power. Also more rapidly growing countries, as measured by GDP per capita, tend to be less correlated with the US business cycle. Interestingly, trade integration offers little explanatory power for the degree of business cycle comovement in any of our specifications. Perhaps these results are not surprising, given the ambiguous implications of both trade

Table 4. Dependent variable: $|x_{it}-x_{jt}|$[a]

	(a)	(b)	(c)
Population	−0.014	1.361	−0.175
	(0.701)	(0.106)	(0.781)
Banking integration	−0.048	−0.123	**−0.195**
	(0.475)	(0.187)	**(0.026)**
Trade integration	−0.001	0.051	−0.012
	(0.986)	(0.735)	(0.938)
Real GDP per capita	0.053	−0.260	**−0.454**
	(0.343)	(0.185)	**(0.014)**
US recession	**−0.187**	−0.153	
	(0.041)	(0.132)	
Country fixed effects	No	Yes	Yes
Year dummies	No	No	Yes
Observations	348	348	348
R^2 (within)		0.029	0.423
R^2 (between)		0.221	0.382
R^2 (overall)	0.017	0.002	0.138

Source: Author's calculations.
[a]*p*-values are in parentheses; significant coefficients at the 10% level are bold.

and financial integration for business cycle comovement discussed in Section 2.

4. Conclusion

Standard measures of business cycle comovement, based on correlation coefficients, are very sensitive to the phase of the business cycle, as well as regional crises. Adjusting for these factors overturns the empirical result that Asia-Pacific is decoupling from the United States.

An alternative, intuitive, measure of business cycle comovement, based on differences between output growth rates adjusted for their long-run averages, is relatively robust to these factors and suggests that Asia-Pacific economies are becoming more strongly coupled with the United States over time. Further empirical investigation suggests that increasing trade integration and banking integration cannot explain this evolution. In fact, trade integration plays little role in explaining business cycle comovement, and increasing banking integration between Asia-Pacific economies and the United States tends to result in weaker, rather than stronger, comovement. Investigating further the driving forces behind the stronger comovement between Asia-Pacific and the United States is left for future work.

Acknowledgments

The author would like to thank, without implication, seminar participants at the Bank of Canada and Bank of Thailand for comments on an early draft. Marek Raczko and Lillie Lam provided excellent research assistance. Any remaining errors are the author's sole responsibility. The opinions expressed herein are those of the author, and are not necessarily shared by the Bank for International Settlements.

References

Abbott, A., Easaw, J., Xing, T. (2008), Trade integration and business cycle convergence: is the relation robust across time and space? *Scandinavian Journal of Economics* 110 (2), 403–417.

Akin, C., Kose, M.A. (2008), Changing nature of north-south linkages: stylized facts and explanations. *Journal of Asian Economics* 19 (1), 1–28.

Baxter, M., Kouparitsas, M.A. (2005), Determinants of business cycle comovement: a robust analysis. *Journal of Monetary Economics* 52 (1), 113–157.

Bordo, M.D., Helbling, T.F. (2004), Have national business cycles become more synchronized? In: Siebert, H. (Ed.), *Macroeconomic Policies in the World Economy*. Springer-Verlag, Berlin, pp. 3–39.

Calderón, C., Chong, A., Stein, E. (2007), Trade intensity and business cycle synchronization: are developing countries any different? *Journal of International Economics* 71 (1), 2–21.

Canova, F., Ciccarelli, M., Ortega, E. (2007), Similarities and convergence in G-7 cycles. *Journal of Monetary Economics* 54 (3), 850–878.

Clark, T., van Wincoop, E. (2001), Borders and business cycles. *Journal of International Economics* 55 (1), 59–85.

Crosby, M. (2003), Business cycle correlations in Asia-Pacific. *Economics Letters* 80 (1), 35–44.

Darvas, Z., Rose, A.K., Szapáry, G. (2005), Fiscal divergence and business cycle synchronization: irresponsibility is idiosyncratic. National Bureau of Economic Research Working Paper No. 11580.

Del Negro, M., Otrok, C. (2008), Dynamic factor models with time-varying parameters: measuring changes in international business cycles. Federal Reserve Bank of New York Staff Report No. 326.

Forbes, K.J., Rigobon, R. (2002), No contagion, only interdependence: measuring stock market comovements. *Journal of Finance* 57 (5), 2223–2261.

Frankel, J.A., Rose, A.K. (1998), The endogeneity of the optimum currency area criteria. *Economic Journal* 108 (449), 1009–1025.

Furceri, D., Karras, G. (2008), Business-cycle synchronization in the EMU. *Applied Economics* 40 (12), 1491–1501.

Gregory, A.W., Head, A.C., Raynauld, J. (1997), Measuring world business cycles. *International Economic Review* 38 (3), 677–701.

Gruben, W.C., Koo, J., Millis, E. (2002), How much does international trade affect business cycle synchronization? Federal Reserve Bank of Dallas Working Paper No. 0203.

Helbling, T., Bayoumi, T. (2003), Are they all in the same boat? The 2000–2001 growth slowdown and the G-7 business cycle linkages. International Monetary Fund Working Paper No. 03/46.

Hoffmaister, A.W., Pradhan, M., Samiei, H. (1998), Have north-south growth linkages changed? *World Development* 26 (5), 791–808.

Imbs, J. (2004), Trade, finance, specialization, and synchronization. *Review of Economics and Statistics* 86 (3), 723–734.

Imbs, J. (2006), The real effects of financial integration. *Journal of International Economics* 68 (2), 296–324.

Inklaar, R., Jong-a-Pin, R., de Haan, J. (2008), Trade and business cycle synchronization in OECD countries-a re-examination. *European Economic Review* 52 (4), 646–666.

International Monetary Fund. (2002), *World Economic Outlook: April 2002: Recessions and Recoveries.* International Monetary Fund, Washington, DC, pp. 104–137.

International Monetary Fund. (2007), *World Economic Outlook: April 2007: Decoupling the Train? Spillovers and Cycles in the Global Economy.* International Monetary Fund, Washington, DC, pp. 121–160.

Kim, C.J., Nelson, C. (1999), Has the U.S. economy become more stable? A Bayesian approach based on a Markov-switching model of the business-cycle. *Review of Economics and Statistics* 81 (4), 608–616.

Kose, M.A., Otrok, C., Whiteman, C.H. (2003a), International business cycles: world, region and country-specific factors. *American Economic Review* 93 (4), 1216–1239.

Kose, M.A., Prasad, E.S., Terrones, M.E. (2003b), How does globalization affect the synchronization of business cycles? *American Economic Review* 93 (2), 57–62.

Kose, M.A., Prasad, E.S., Terrones, M.E. (2004), Volatility and comovement in a globalized world economy: an empirical exploration. In: Siebert, H. (Ed.), *Macroeconomic Policies in the World Economy.* Springer-Verlag, Berlin, pp. 89–122.

Kose, M.A., Otrok, C., Prasad, E. (2008a), Global business cycles: convergence or decoupling? International Monetary Fund Working Paper No. 08/143.

Kose, M.A., Otrok, C., Whiteman, C.H. (2008b), Understanding the evolution of world business cycles. *Journal of International Economics* 75 (1), 110–130.

Kumakura, M. (2006), Trade and business cycle co-movements in Asia-Pacific. *Journal of Asian Economics* 17 (4), 622–645.

McConnell, M., Perez-Quiros, G. (2000), Output fluctuations in the United States: what has changed since the early 1980s? *American Economic Review* 90 (5), 1464–1476.

Otto, G., Voss, G., Willard, L. (2001), Understanding OECD output correlations. Reserve Bank of Australia Discussion Paper No. 2001-05.

Yetman, J. (2011), Exporting recessions: international links and the business cycle. *Economics Letters* 110 (1), 12–14.

CHAPTER 11

Has Emerging Asia Decoupled? An Analysis of Production and Trade Linkages Using the Asian International Input–Output Table

Gabor Pula and Tuomas A. Peltonen

Senior Economist, European Central Bank, Kaiserstrasse 29, 60311 Frankfurt am Main, Germany
E-mail address: gabor.pula@ecb.europa.eu; tuomas.peltonen@ecb.europa.eu

Abstract

Due to the emergence of global production networks, trade statistics have became less accurate in describing the dependence of emerging Asia on external demand. This chapter analyses, using an update of the Asian International Input–Output (AIO) table, the interdependence of emerging Asian economies, the United States, the EU15, and Japan via trade and production linkages. According to the results, we do not find evidence of the decoupling of emerging Asia from the rest of the world. On the contrary, we find evidence on increasing trade integration, both globally and regionally. Nonetheless, our analysis indicates that emerging Asia's dependence on exports is only about one-third of its GDP, that is, well below the 50% exposure suggested by trade data. This finding can be explained by the high import content of exports in these economies, which is a result of the increasing segmentation of production across the region.

Keywords: Emerging Asia, Asian International Input–Output table, real linkages, decoupling, resilience

JEL classifications: F14, C67, E23

1. Introduction

Since 1998, emerging Asia's[1] exports has more than doubled in value, an increase well above the growth rate of overall world demand. As a result,

[1] In general, emerging Asia is defined in the chapter as consisting of China, Hong Kong S.A.R., Indonesia, Korea, Malaysia, the Philippines, Singapore, Taiwan (R.O.C.), and Thailand. However, in the trade analysis using UN COMTRADE data (Chapter 2), Taiwan (R.O.C.) is not included due to missing data. In contrast, in the analyses with the Asian International Input–Output (AIO) tables, emerging Asia does not include Hong Kong due to the fact that this economy is not included in the production matrix of the AIO table.

Frontiers of Economics and Globalization
Volume 9 ISSN: 1574-8715
DOI: 10.1108/S1574-8715(2011)0000009016

the share of emerging Asia's exports in total world exports increased from 17% in 1998 to 22% in 2007. Moreover, by accounting for 14% of the world's GDP[2] and contributing nearly half of world's GDP growth,[3] emerging Asia has become a key to world's economic growth and dynamics.

The slowdown of the US economy since the second half of 2007 and the continued strength of growth in emerging Asia have set off the so-called "decoupling" debate on whether emerging Asia has decoupled from the global business cycle. In general, decoupling can be defined as "*the emergence of a business cycle dynamic that is relatively independent of global demand trends and that is driven mainly by autonomous changes in internal demand*" (ADB, 2007). We use this definition of decoupling in the analysis of this chapter.

In the early stages of the recent financial crisis, the shocks hitting the global economy seemed to be primarily US based, emanating from the collapse of the US housing bubble. Since early 2008, however, a broader set of shocks has appeared, including a global banking and liquidity crisis with negative implications on financing costs, risk premia, and availability of credit; various commodity price shocks; and emergence of housing-related problems in several non-US economies. Thus, the relevant question today is more to what extent emerging Asia has decoupled not only from the United States, but from extraregional demand in general. For this reason, our analysis focuses on the extra versus intraregional determinants of economic growth in emerging Asia.

The main arguments behind the decoupling theory are threefold. First, according to the trade statistics, trade linkages of emerging Asia with the G3 economies,[4] and in particular with the United States, are less important today than in the past. Indeed, the steady slowdown of exports to the United States since 2006 has been compensated by dynamically expanding export markets to other emerging economies. Second, prolonged productivity and income growth, as well as rising purchasing power are increasing emerging Asia's own final demand. A major reason why emerging Asia's business cycle may have decoupled is China's emergence with a domestic market of 1.3 billion consumers. In view of the supporters of the decoupling theory, China is an engine of growth in emerging Asia, that is, it increasingly demands for goods produced in other economies of the region. Finally, unlike in the earlier episodes of a global slowdown, emerging Asian economies are now better able to weather adverse external conditions by active economic policies. This is because most economies now have current account surpluses, large

[2] Measure in USD 2007 values.

[3] Based on the IMF *World Economic Outlook* April 2008 projections for 2008 using PPP weights.

[4] By the G3 economies, we mean the United States, the euro area (EU15), and Japan.

foreign reserves, and many even budget surpluses, leaving room for a fiscal stimulus.

The chapter aims at analyzing the dependence of emerging Asia through trade linkages on the demand both from the region itself and on the advanced economies, especially the United States, the EU15, and Japan. There are three main questions that we intend to answer.

1. To what extent value added in emerging Asia is determined by domestic versus external demand? Has the dependence on external factors decreased over time? (In the latter question, "yes" supports the decoupling view).
2. How important is intraregional trade in emerging Asia? Has the increasing purchasing power in China and other emerging Asian economies provided an expanding market for products from the region, helping to isolate emerging Asia from global business cycle fluctuations? ("yes" for the latter supports the decoupling view).
3. To what extent value added in emerging Asia depends on demand from the United States, Japan and the euro area, and the rest of the world? Has the relative importance of these regions changed?

Due to the emergence of global production networks, it is less accurate to analyze economic dependences between economies by using only trade data. The main shortcoming of trade data lies with its inability to capture the source of value added, that is, to quantify the contribution of each economy to the total value added in the production chain. This can be overcome by using the Asian International Input–Output (AIO) table to analyze the real linkages between economies and sectors. The AIO tables provide detailed information on trade and production linkages among nine economies in the Asia-Pacific region: China, Indonesia, Malaysia, the Philippines, Singapore, South Korea, Taiwan (R.O.C.), Thailand, and Japan as well as the United States. The geographical breakdown for trade also includes Hong Kong S.A.R., the EU, and rest of the world.[5]

One should note, however, there are some limitations to this approach. The analysis with the AIO table can only capture the "direct" trade effects, that is, neither any "second-round" effects of an export slowdown on domestic demand via, for example, lower employment, wages, or investment, nor any financial or policy-related channels can be taken into account. Thus, the actual impacts of negative external demand shock may be underestimated by the numbers provided in the chapter. The chapter also lacks a sector-level analysis. Although the 1995 and 2000 AIO tables provide information on sectors, the update of the AIO table at the sectoral

[5] The fact that Hong Kong is not included in the production matrix of the AIO table implies that the production linkages with Hong Kong cannot be taken into account, but only trade linkages. However, given that Hong Kong is more prominent trade center than a production center, we do not consider it as a major limitation to the analysis.

level is currently not possible due to severe data limitations. However, an extensive literature of sectoral studies is available (see, e.g., Dieter (2007), Gangnes and Van Assche (2008), Nag *et al.* (2007), and Luthje (2004)), which can be used to supplement the findings of this chapter.

Compared to the study closest to our work, Mori and Sasaki (2007), this chapter contains at least three improvements. First, as regards the updating procedure of the AIO table, the chapter takes into account the compositional shift in the imports from final to intermediate goods, and also applies an adjustment for Hong Kong's entrepot trade. Second, it gives a picture of production linkages in the region using the Leontieff coefficients of the AIO table. Finally, it presents a broad set of descriptive results on income dependency, with specific attention paid to the reliance of emerging Asia's GDP on European markets.

The chapter has some interesting contributions to the decoupling debate. We find no evidence of decoupling of the emerging Asian region from the rest of the world. On the contrary, we find evidence on increasing trade integration, both globally and regionally. Our results indicate that emerging Asia's GDP is increasingly driven by exports, in line with the stronger economic integration of the world economy. Intraregional markets, despite gaining substantial importance in the recent years, still account for only 7% of value added in the region. Nevertheless, the chapter finds that domestic demand, with a share of around two-thirds of the final demand, is still key to the economic growth in the region. Consequently, the share of external demand of around one-third is, therefore, significantly lower than the 50% exposure suggested by aggregate trade data.

The chapter is organized as follows. Section 2 briefly discusses the related literature. Section 3 introduces some stylized facts based on trade statistics and describes the limitations of these data. Section 4 presents the methodology used to update the AIO table, and Section 5 the main analysis. Finally, Section 6 concludes. The updating procedure and the derivation of measures used in the analysis are presented in the appendices.

2. *Brief review of the literature*

The existing empirical evidence on the decoupling of emerging Asia is ambiguous. In support of the decoupling view, several recent studies suggest that global (common) factors play a relatively less important role in driving business cycles in emerging Asia than in other regions of the world (see, e.g., IMF (2007) and Dees and Vansteenkiste (2007)). Moreover, the importance of common factors seems to have declined since the mid-1980s. In parallel, the studies indicate an increasing role of regional factors, in line with ongoing trade and financial integration in emerging Asia (see ADB, 2008).

In contrast, several studies indicate an increasing synchronization of business cycles of advanced and emerging Asian economies. According to calculation of IMF (2007a) and ADB (2008), import demand from the United States, the euro area, and Japan is assumed to be now more important for the region than ever before. Indeed, estimations suggest that the comovements between (nonoil) import demand from the aforementioned G3 economies and economic growth of emerging Asia became stronger in the last decade compared to earlier periods.[6]

Moreover, evidence based on existing trade data does not support the view that intraregional demand for final goods is increasing, and that China is emerging as an engine of growth for the region. Although intraregional exports are increasing fast, it is mostly due to trade in intermediate goods. In fact, there is no indication that exports of final goods from emerging Asia to China, or to other economies of the region would have risen strongly (ADB 2008).

One should note, however, that decoupling does not mean that a slowdown of the growth in the United States or the global economy would not have an impact on growth in emerging Asian economies. It means that the GDP growth in these economies will slow by much less than in previous recession episodes. Combining elasticities from panel estimates[7] and actual trade data, IMF (2007a) calculates that the impact of a 1% slowdown in the US GDP growth has a −0.15 percentage point (pp) impact on growth in emerging Asia. The finding that a 1% slowdown in the euro area would have an impact closely similar in size implies that a broader slowdown within the G3 group can have an economically significant effect on emerging Asia's growth. However, these elasticities, given that they do not allow for spillovers between economies, are assumed to be underestimated. Indeed, VAR estimates that allow for intercountry dependencies estimate the impact of a 1% slowdown in the US GDP growth at around −0.4 pp (IMF, 2007a; ADB, 2008). Moreover, Dees and Vansteenkiste (2007) using a global VAR model estimate the impact in the range of −0.16 to −0.30 pp.[8] Macromodel simulations that also take into account changes in relative prices and allow for a depreciation of the US dollar indicate impacts in the range of −0.5 to −1.5 pps (IMF, 2007a; ADB, 2008). Finally, when simulations take into account factors, such as cross-country interlinkages in business and consumer confidences, integration of financial markets, and

---

[6] According to the IMF estimates, the rise in the openness of emerging Asia from 4.8% in 1981–1985 to 7.1% in 2001–2005 (measured as merchandize exports to GDP) resulted in an increase of elasticity of growth to US growth by 0.2 pp.

[7] The sample contains 130 economies and data from 1970 to 2005. For more details see IMF (2007a, p. 132).

[8] Including "echo effects" via trade links between third economies, the authors estimate an impact in the range of 0.2–0.4 pp.

synchronization of policy decisions, the elasticities may easily exceed those cited above.

In a study methodologically close to our chapter, Mori and Sasaki (2007) use the updated version of the AIO table to quantify interdependencies in the Asia-Pacific region. According to their results, interdependencies between the Asia-Pacific economies in terms of global production networks deepened further in 2000–2005, while China became the main production center in the region. The authors also find that the East Asian economies, rather being more autonomous, became more exposed to economic developments outside of the region.

Finally, Inomata and Uchida (2009) use the AIO table for several interesting questions related to the global financial crisis, for instance, on the shock transmission mechanisms, the impact on employment, vertical specialization, and Asian production network.

3. Emerging Asia's external dependence based on trade data

This section briefly summarizes the stylized facts on emerging Asia's external dependence based on trade statistics. The trade data we use is from UN COMTRADE, and it only contains data on traded goods for 1998–2006.

First, we start the analysis with aggregated exports data. The main findings are the following (see Table 1):

- Exports (in goods) contributed 45% of GDP in 2006, which indicates a strong exposure of the region to external demand. Moreover, the exports to GDP ratio increased significantly from 34% in 1998 to 45% in 2006, giving no support to the decoupling theory. Using the more complete National Accounts statistics, which include trade in both goods and services, and serve as a benchmark for the final findings of the chapter, exports of emerging Asia accounted for 53% of GDP in 2006. As for comparison, in 2006, the exports-to-GDP ratio in the United States was 11%, in the EU15 16%, and in Japan 16%.
- Intraregional demand determines 17% of GDP. The role of intraregional market has increased, mainly driven by a robust expansion of the Chinese market. The contribution of exports to China in the total value added increased from 6% to 12% in 1998–2006.
- As regards extraregional demand, exports to the G3 economies accounts for 19% of GDP, slightly up from 16% in 1998. The US markets are the most important (8%), followed by the EU15 (7%), and Japan (4%). Demand from the rest of the world determined 10% of total value added in 2006.

Aggregated (total) exports data indicate that emerging Asian economies are relatively open, are increasingly integrated in global trade networks, and

Table 1. Exports by type of goods and by destination

	In million USD						In percentage of GDP					
	Total		Final		Intermediate		Total		Final		Intermediate	
	1998	2006	1998	2006	1998	2006	1998	2006	1998	2006	1998	2006
Exports to G3 countries	363.0	905.1	143.0	289.2	220.0	615.9	16.2	18.7	6.4	6.0	9.8	12.7
within that to United States	164.5	378.6	70.8	138.8	93.7	239.8	7.3	7.8	3.2	2.9	4.2	4.9
to the EU	114.7	327.1	39.5	96.3	75.2	230.9	5.1	6.7	1.8	2.0	3.4	4.8
to Japan	83.9	199.4	32.8	54.2	51.0	145.2	3.7	4.1	1.5	1.1	2.3	3.0
Intraregional exports	245.4	800.9	45.7	84.5	199.7	716.4	11.0	16.5	2.0	1.7	8.9	14.8
within that exports to China*	78.3	271.9	9.4	13.0	68.9	258.8	6.2	12.1	0.8	0.6	5.5	11.5
RoW	160.6	492.2	47.1	121.2	113.6	370.9	7.2	10.2	2.1	2.5	5.1	7.7
Exports of goods, total	**769.1**	**2,198.2**	**235.8**	**495.0**	**533.2**	**1,703.2**	**34.4**	**45.3**	**10.5**	**10.2**	**23.8**	**35.1**
Memo item												
Exports of goods and services	*958.9*	*2,588.3*				*42.8*	*53.4*					

Note: The numbers refer to exports of goods. * GDP ratio is based on non-China emerging Asia GDP.
Source: UN COMTRADE database.

are increasingly dependent on external markets. In a word, aggregated trade data reject the decoupling theory. Nevertheless, when a more detailed dataset is used and the analysis includes exports by types of goods, the picture becomes more ambiguous.

Intermediate goods exports accounted for 77% of total exports in 2006. Moreover, exports of intermediate goods have expanded more dynamically than exports of final goods, and have been the main contributor to increasing openness of emerging Asia in most country relations. However, one may argue that trade of intermediate goods, being a result of production segmentation and prone to double counting, should be excluded from the analysis. When calculating final demand dependence, it is the exports of final goods that matter.

According to final goods exports, openness of emerging Asia is low and has not increased over the last decade (10.2% in 2006 vs. 10.5% in 1998). Extraregional demand contributed to GDP by 8.5% in 2006, similarly to 1998. However, the importance of US and Japanese markets have declined, while the importance of EU and rest of the world has increased. *Unlike data on total exports, final goods trade statistics do not justify the high and increasing exposure of emerging Asia to external demand.*

Which data should we trust? Assuming that production networks aim at supplying export markets, and thus intermediate goods should partly be included in the analysis, we believe the actual exposure of emerging Asia should lie somewhere between the numbers suggested by total and final goods export data. However, trade statistics itself do not provide enough information to tell the exact exposure.

With the emergence of global production networks, trade data has become less accurate in describing the interdependencies of the economies in emerging Asia. There are two main shortcomings of trade data. First, trade statistics are unable to capture the source of value added (i.e., to quantify the contribution of each economy to the total value added) in the production chain. Thus, trade statistics provide inaccurate information about the dependence of each economy in the production chain on external demand. Second, because trade data are gross statistics, they are prone to double counting. The more the production is segmented across economies, the higher the total volume of trade will be, and thus, the more trade data overestimate the openness of emerging Asia as a region. Let us illustrate these problems with a numerical example.

Assume that the production chain contains three economies: Malaysia supplies China with intermediate inputs; China uses these inputs for both producing final goods to its domestic market and to exports to EU markets. In order to calculate the impact of changes in demand from the EU on the value added of Malaysia and China, one needs to know the share of inputs from Malaysia in the value of final goods produced by China to its domestic and export markets. This information, however, is not provided by the trade data.

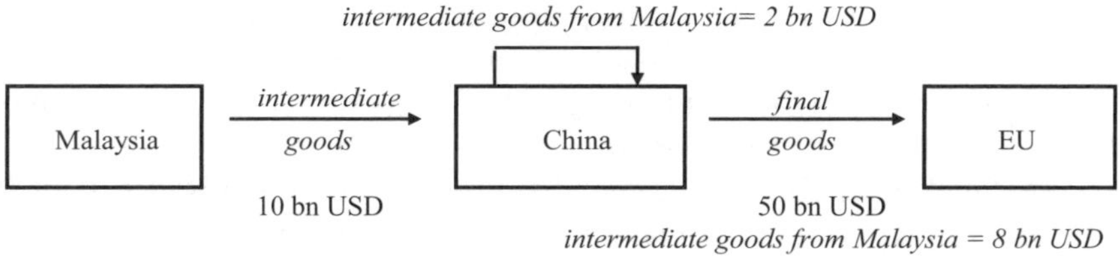

Fig. 1.* *Sources of value added in the production chain – an illustrative example.

Assume that the value of inputs exported from Malaysia to China is USD 10 bn, and the value of final goods exports from China to the EU15 is USD 50 bn[9] (see Figure 1). Assuming that USD 2 bn of inputs from Malaysia ends up in products that are consumed in China, the products exported to the EU15 will contain USD 8 bn value added from Malaysia and USD 42 bn value added from China. Consequently, fall in the demand of EU15 by 50 bn US dollars would have an 8 bn impact on Malaysia and a 42 bn impact on China. Aggregate trade data (similar to trade data on final goods), however, would indicate a 50 bn USD impact on China and no impact on Malaysia.

The above example can also be used to illustrate the problem of double counting. Malaysian inputs that end up in Chinese exports to the EU are counted twice: once when they are exported from Malaysia to China and once when they are exported from China to the EU. As a result, while the actual value added that is exported from the region is USD 50 bn, trade data would indicate a USD 60 bn of total exports of the region as a whole.

A possible way to compass these problems is to use input–output tables. These tables are built on a broad set of disaggregated statistics and take into account not only trade flows, but also information on flows of inputs within the production process. In the following analysis, we will use the AIO tables to describe the dependence of emerging Asian economies on intra- and extraregional demand.

4. Methodology

This section describes the structure of the AIO, the updating methodology, as well as the sensitivity analysis applied.

The AIO tables are compiled by the Institute of Developing Economies Japan External Trade Organization (IDE-JETRO), and can be used to analyze the structures of industry and trade linkages, as well as intertemporal changes in the interdependencies of the economies in the Asia-Pacific region.

[9] The illustrative numbers closely track actual export values in 2006, by both types of goods and economy relations.

The AIO tables provide detailed information on trade and production linkages among nine economies in the Asia-Pacific region: China, Indonesia, Malaysia, the Philippines, Singapore, South Korea, Taiwan (R.O.C.), Thailand, and Japan as well as the United States. The geographical breakdown for trade also includes Hong Kong S.A.R., the EU, and the rest of the world. The AIO tables contain the input–output tables of these economies linked together using detailed trade matrices. Accordingly, the AIO tables have both an economy and a sectoral dimension, which makes it possible to describe interlinkages between various sectors of different economies.[10]

To date, the AIO tables have been compiled for the years 1985, 1990, 1995, and 2000. Given the rapid changes in production and trade structures, however, these data look inadequate to describe the current situation. For this reason, we update the AIO table at the economy level for 2006, and use it to analyze the research questions of the chapter. The updating procedure is described in detail in Appendix A.

To test the validity of the updating procedure, we did the following two sensitivity analyses. First, we examined the residuals from the GDP identity. Input–output tables are closed systems, meaning that they are constructed so that total demand equals total supply. Given that we use import data to update the trade linkages in the input–output table, any discrepancy between import data reported by the importer and export data reported by the exporter (after the items of freight, insurance, and import duties are controlled for) would cause a discrepancy between supply and demand in the updated table. For example, trade balances from the Chinese statistical sources do not necessarily match the trade balances reported by its trading partners.[11] Moreover, any assumption we use in the updating, such as the assumptions on services trade, on the share of freight, insurance, and import duties in total imports, may all result in discrepancies.

Nevertheless, with the exceptions of Singapore and Taiwan (R.O.C.), the residuals calculated from the GDP identity are below 5% of the GDP. In the case of Singapore, the high residual may be explained by Singapore's relatively significant re-export trade that we could not correct for given data limitations. The discrepancies in the case of Taiwan (R.O.C.) may have to do with the fact that the COMTRADE database does not contain data for Taiwan (R.O.C.), and thus we had to make some assumptions on Taiwanese trade.[12] For transparency purposes, we report

[10] For more technical details on the AIO tables, see AIO table 2000, Volume 1. Explanatory Notes, JETRO, March 2006.

[11] US Department of the Treasury (2007), Report to Congress on International Economic and Exchange Rate Policies, Appendix II China's Trade Data, June 2007.

[12] Although we tried alternative estimates for Taiwanese trade assuming similarities in the trade structure of Taiwan (R.O.C.) and China and other NIE3 economies, we could not lower the residuals.

a residual line when presenting the contribution ratios of final demand to value added. This residual line stands for a part of value added, which remains unexplained.

A second way of checking the sensitivity of the updating procedure is to update the 1995 AIO table to year 2000 values, derive the main indicators used in our analysis, and compare the results from this updated table with the "official" 2000 AIO table by IDE-JETRO. To do this, we calculate two measures: the Leontieff coefficients and the so-called "Contribution ratios of final demand to value added." The Leontieff coefficients from the updated 1995 AIO table indicate less significant changes in the production network between 1995 and 2000, and a stronger concentration of suppliers of inputs than the "official" 2000 AIO. The results from the impact of final demand on value-added analysis are not significantly different from the findings of the "official" 2000 AIO table, the main difference being that the updated 1995 AIO table overestimates the dependence on domestic demand by 2 pps and underestimates the dependence on the rest of the world by the same extent.[13]

5. *Analysis using the AIO tables*

We use the updated 2006 AIO table in two different analyses. First, we calculate the "backward linkages" of production, which helps us to describe the interlinkages of the emerging Asian economies in the production process. Second, as the main contribution of our chapter, the reliance of each economy's value added on domestic demand, intraregional and extraregional demand is computed. Comparing results from the 1995, 2000, and the updated 2006 AIO tables, we also report the evolution of major trends in emerging Asia's production and trade dynamics.

5.1. "Backward linkages" of production

The backward linkages of production are measured by the Leontieff coefficients of the 2006 AIO table. The Leontieff coefficients of the AIO table are calculated as follows:

$$\text{Let } \alpha^{ij} = \frac{A^{ij}}{X^j}, \tag{1}$$

where $i =$ (Indonesia, Malaysia, ..., USA) is the supplier economy, $j =$ (Indonesia, Malaysia, ..., USA) is the demand economy, A^{ij} is input from supplier economy i used in the demand economy j's production, and X^j is total production of demand economy j. Then the AIO table can be

[13] For more details, see Appendix D.

written in a matrix form as:

$$\begin{bmatrix} \alpha^{II} & \alpha^{IM} & . & \alpha^{IU} \\ \alpha^{MI} & \alpha^{MM} & . & \alpha^{MU} \\ . & . & . & . \\ \alpha^{UI} & \alpha^{UM} & . & \alpha^{UUI} \end{bmatrix} x \begin{bmatrix} X^{I} \\ X^{M} \\ . \\ X^{U} \end{bmatrix} + \begin{bmatrix} F^{II} \\ F^{MI} \\ . \\ F^{UI} \end{bmatrix} + \begin{bmatrix} F^{IM} \\ F^{MM} \\ . \\ F^{UM} \end{bmatrix} + \ldots + \begin{bmatrix} Q^{I} \\ Q^{M} \\ . \\ Q^{U} \end{bmatrix} = \begin{bmatrix} X^{I} \\ X^{M} \\ . \\ X^{U} \end{bmatrix}, \tag{2}$$

where $\boldsymbol{F}^{ij}$ is vector of final demand (sum of consumption and investment), $\boldsymbol{Q}^{j}$ are export vectors to Hong Kong, the EU, and the rest of the world. For details see Appendix D.

The matrix notation can be written in short as

$$\mathbf{AX} + \mathbf{Y} = \mathbf{X}. \tag{3}$$

To answer the question how much production is needed to meet 1 unit of demand, the system of equations should be solved to X:

$$\mathbf{X} = (\mathbf{I} - \mathbf{A})^{-1}\mathbf{Y} = \mathbf{BY}, \tag{4}$$

where B is called the Leontieff coefficient matrix.

The B^{ij} element of the matrix indicates the number of units of production needed in economy i (the supply economy) to produce 1 unit of value added in economy j (the demand economy). The Leontieff coefficient matrix helps us to analyze production linkages across the economies in the region via trade of intermediate inputs.

The results of the analysis of backward linkages of production are summarized in Figure 2, which illustrates the Leontieff coefficients of the 1995, 2000, and updated 2006 AIO tables. The vertical axis of the figure shows the supplier economies, and the horizontal axis represents the demand economies. For example, in the bottom-left corner, one can read the number of units of production needed in the United States to produce 1 unit of value added in Indonesia, or alternatively, the share of imports from the United States in Indonesian value added. The number of units is represented by the different colors in the figure. According to Figure 2, in order to produce 1 unit of value added in Indonesia in 2006, approximately 0.03 units of production were needed in the United States. To put it differently, the import content of the Indonesian production from the United States was approximately 3%.

There are two main facts that stand out as results of the analysis. First, the dominance of horizontal formations in Figure 2 indicates *that suppliers are highly concentrated in emerging Asia*, that is, there are only a few economies that provide the bulk of inputs for production in the region. According to Figure 2, the main suppliers of inputs in the region are Japan, the United States, and most recently also China. As regards economies of demand, Malaysia, Singapore, and Taiwan (R.O.C.) are the economies where imported inputs account for the highest share of value

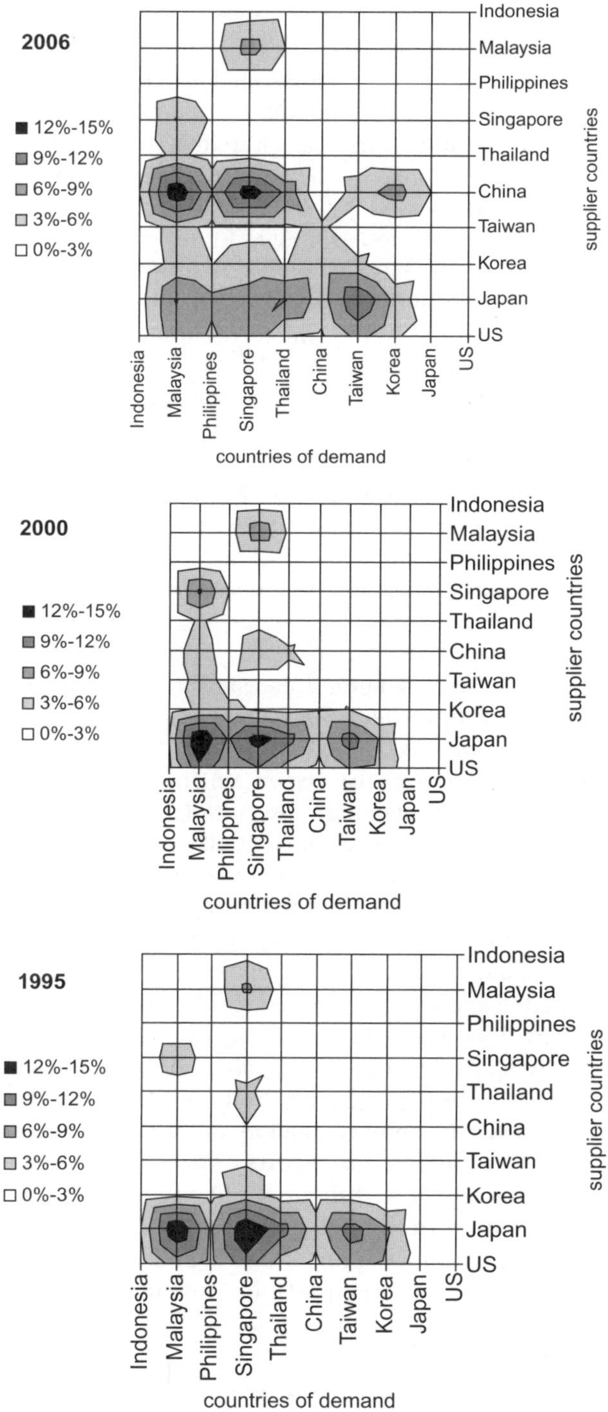

Fig. 2. Backward linkages of production (Leontieff coefficients). Note: The figure depicts the Leontieff coefficients of the AIO matrices. Sources: AIO tables 1995, 2000, and authors' calculations.

added, while in the larger, less open economies such as Korea and China the import content of value added is lower.

Second, *the role of major supplier is changing*. In 1995, emerging Asia used inputs mostly from Japan and the United States in its production process. (The EU is not in the production matrix of the AIO table, that is, it is not included in this exercise.) The pattern of production segmentation in the region was determined by the offshoring activities from these economies. By 2000, Japan and the United States still being dominant, the NIE3s and China seem to have emerged as suppliers of input material. A major change occurred by 2006, when for most economies in the region, China became a more important source of inputs than Japan and the United States.

This trend can be explained by the increasing delocalization of manufacturing production from advanced economies. For example, Toyota has created a global operating platform in recent years that operates without major Japanese inputs (Dieter, 2007). Nevertheless, the phenomenon does not come down to auto industry exclusively, but is also present in other sectors, as documented by a wide range of literature (see, e.g., Dieter (2007), Gaulier *et al.* (2005), Gangnes and Van Assche (2008), and Luthje (2004)).

Figure 2 shows no evidence of clear specialization on final-stage assembling in any of the economies. Final-stage assembling would show up as a vertical formation in the figure, indicating that several suppliers provide inputs for the assembler economy. Although the supply of inputs is increasingly diversified across the region due to intensifying production segmentation, no clear vertical pattern has emerged. This finding is striking in the case of China in particular, an economy that has become the major export platform in the region supposedly via specializing in final-stage assembling.

However, when interpreting the results one has to keep in mind that Figure 2 hides a significant heterogeneity in the data. Production linkages can differ by firms and sectors. Haddad (2007) describes various production networks within the machinery sector. In the road vehicles industry, all economies in East Asia including China export a significant share of parts to Japan, and China also exports a large share of parts to the EU and the United States. The electrical machinery sector, on the other hand, provides examples of final-stage assembling. In electronics, inputs come from Japan and the NIEs, and assembling and exports of final goods is done by several East Asian economies (China, Indonesia, Malaysia, and the Philippines) independently. In the electrical appliances and the computer industry, East Asian economies export a high share of parts to China for final assembling, and China exports the final products to the EU and the United States.[14]

[14] According to the 2000 AIO table, China's role as final assembler also prevails in the textile industry.

Due to data limitations, however, we are unable to update the 2000 AIO table at the sectoral level, and thus our analysis cannot take into account the data heterogeneity across sectors.

5.2. Contribution ratios of final demand to value added

In the previous exercise we described production linkages via flows of intermediate inputs. Leontieff coefficients measured the production needed in the supply economies in order to produce 1 unit of value added in the demand economy. Now, we extend the analysis further. First, we not only take into account inputs needed for production, but also direct imports needed to meet final demand (consumption, investments, and exports) in the demand economy. Thus, rather than focusing on intermediate goods only, we also include flows of final goods in the analysis. Moreover, rather than gross production, the analysis focuses on value added implied in the supply economy.

These changes make it possible, in the first step, to calculate the impact of final demand from demand economies on the value added of supply economies. In the next step, we can split up the value added of the supply economies by final demand components: by domestic demand and by final demand from other economies, that is, exports to different destinations.[15] By doing so we are able to measure the dependence of the supply economies' value added on domestic, intraregional, and extraregional demand.

The calculations are made in two steps.

The impact of final demand on value added (*IFv*). The impact of final demand (from demand economy *j*) on the value added of supply economies is calculated according to the following formula:

$$IFv^j = \widehat{v} \times B \times f^j, \tag{5}$$

where v is a diagonal matrix consisting the elements of $v^j = V^j/X^j$ (the ratio of V value added to total production X in the demand economy), B is the Leontieff coefficient matrix, f^j is a column vector of final demand in the demand economy j.[16]

[15] Intuitively the split up of the value added is based on the supply–demand identity: the value added in the supply economy is either consumed domestically, or exported to other economies.

[16] For interpretation purposes, let's assume the case of a 1-unit increase in final demand of Indonesia (f^I). The impact of Indonesian final demand on production of economies in the matrix ($\mathbf{IFv}^I$) is the following:

$$\mathbf{IFv}^I = \begin{array}{c} v^I B^{II} f^{II} + v^I B^{IM} f^{MI} + ... + v^I B^{IU} f^{UI} \\ v^M B^{MI} f^{II} + v^M B^{MM} f^{MI} + ... + v^M B^{MM} f^{UI} \\ ... \\ v^U B^{UI} f^{II} + v^U B^{UM} f^{MI} + ... + v^U B^{UU} f^{UI} \end{array}$$

Table 2. ***The impact of final demand on value added, emerging Asia (%)***

	1995	2000*	2000	2006
Domestic demand	72.3	70.3	68.9	64.3
Intraregional trade	5.3	5.8	5.8	6.8
G3	11.4	13.8	16.1	15.7
within that EU	2.1	2.4	4.7	5.8
Japan	3.9	4.1	4.1	3.2
United States	5.3	7.3	7.3	6.6
RoW	11.2	10.1	10.1	14.2
Residual				−1.3

Table 3. ***The impact of final demand on value added, China (%)***

	1995	2000*	2000	2006
Domestic demand	79.7	79.3	79.4	69.7
Intraregional trade	2.0	1.8	1.8	2.4
G3	10.7	12.5	13.9	16.6
within that EU	2.1	2.3	3.8	6.4
Japan	4.1	3.6	3.6	3.0
United States	4.5	6.6	6.6	7.1
RoW	8.0	6.5	6.5	13.2
Residual				−2.4

Contribution ratios of final demand to value added. The contribution ratio (CR) of final demand from demand economy j to the value added of supply economy i is given by the formula:

$$\mathrm{CR}_i^j = \frac{IFv_i^j}{\sum_j IFv_i^j}, \tag{6}$$

where IFv_i^j stands for the ith row of matrix IFv^j, representing the impact of final demand from economy i on the value added of supply economy j.

The main findings of the analysis of the contribution ratios are summarized in Tables 2–4.

Tables 2–4 present the contribution ratios of four major final demand aggregates: domestic demand, intraregional demand (the sum of exports to emerging Asian economies), the G3 demand (exports to United States,

where the first row of the matrix indicates the impact of a 1-unit increase in Indonesian final demand on Indonesian value added, the second row the impact on Malaysian value added, etc. Interpreting the elements in the first row (from left to right), the Indonesian value added is stimulated by Indonesian domestic demand to the extent that Indonesian domestic demand consumes products from domestic supply ($B^{II}f^{II}$), plus the production of Indonesian inputs needed to produce the final goods imported from Malaysia ($B^{IM}f^{MI}$), from the Philippines ($B^{IP}f^{PI}$), etc.

Table 4. The impact of final demand on value added, NIE3, and ASEAN4 (%)

	1995	2000*	2000	2006
Domestic demand	68.4	63.0	60.3	57.9
Intraregional trade	7.0	9.0	9.0	11.9
within China	2.1	3.8	3.8	7.2
G3	11.7	14.9	17.8	14.6
within that EU	2.1	2.5	5.4	5.1
Japan	3.9	4.5	4.5	3.5
United States	5.8	8.0	8.0	6.0
RoW	12.9	13.1	13.1	15.3
Residual				0.0

Note: 2000* refers to EU3 under the EU line, and is directly comparable with 1995 results. Emerging Asia consists of China, the NIE3 (Korea, Singapore, and Taiwan (R.O.C.)), and the ASEAN4 (Indonesia, Malaysia, the Philippines, and Thailand). Adjusted for Hong Kong's trade, the original (not re-exported) imports of Hong Kong is taken as intraregional demand. The residual indicates the nonstatistical discrepancy in the GDP identity of the updated 2006 AIO table (for details see Section 4).
Sources: AIO tables 1995, 2000, and authors' calculations.

EU15, and Japan), and exports to the rest of the world. The contribution ratios are presented separately for the following supply economies: emerging Asia (Table 2), China (Table 3), and non-China emerging Asia (Table 4).

The tables contain two columns for 2000, which refer to different economy composition of the EU. The column marked with asterisks refers to EU3 (Germany, France, and the United Kingdom) data, and is thus comparable with 1995 numbers in the first column, while the other column with no asterisks refers to EU15 and is comparable with 2006 data in the last column.

The following results stand out from the analysis of emerging Asia as a whole (Table 2). Approximately two-thirds of the value added of emerging Asian economies is determined by domestic demand, while the share of external demand is around one-third.[17] More precisely, external factors accounted for 36.7% of the value added in 2006, implying *a significantly lower dependency of emerging Asia on exports than suggested by total trade data* (53%[18]). In addition, 6.8% of emerging Asia's value added was due to

[17] The share of domestic demand of total value added in emerging Asia is significantly lower than in the advanced economies. Based on the AIO, the share of domestic demand of value added in 2006 was 91% in the United States, and in Japan 86%. Given that EU15 is not included in the production matrix of the AIO, comparable statistics is not available. See Table Appendix E for more details.
[18] Calculated as exports per GDP after aggregating National Accounts data at the economy level from the CEIC database.

intraregional demand, lowering the reliance of value added on extra-regional markets to below 30%. In 2006, the G3 economies accounted for slightly more than half of the extraregional demand (15.7% of the value added) with the United States (6.6% of the value added) being the most important market, followed by the EU15 (5.8%) and Japan (3.2%).

The changes in the impact of the final demand components give some interesting insights. Since 1995, there is a trend increase in export dependence, indicating no sign of "decoupling," but more an increasing integration of emerging Asian economies to global trade. Dependence on intraregional trade has also increased, in line with the strengthening of economic integration in emerging Asia. Despite its rising importance however, intraregional trade has not compensated for the falling share of domestic demand in value added. Consequently, *the exposure of emerging Asia to extraregional markets has increased.*

There have been differing trends in the sources of extraregional demand in 1995–2006. The share of US demand increased between 1995 and 2000 from 5.3% to 7.3%, with a relatively stable share of the EU3 and Japan (close to 2% and 4%, respectively). After 2000, however, both the US and Japanese shares started to decline, in parallel with a significant increase in the share of EU15 from 4.7% to 5.8%. As a result, the *dependence of emerging Asia's value added on demand from the G3 economies declined slightly between 2000 and 2006*. However, the higher exposure of emerging Asia to extraregional markets after 2000 was due to *stronger trade linkages with the rest of the world*, with its share in emerging Asia's value added increasing from 10.1% to 14.2% between 2000 and 2006.[19]

China, partly due to its size, is still less dependent on external markets than other economies in the region (Table 3). However, between 2000 and 2006, the share of external demand in the value added of China increased substantially from 20% to 30%.

The comparison of China with the NIE3 and ASEAN4 economies by the sources of demand reveal an interesting pattern of division of labor within the region. Since 2000, China "outcrowded" the NIE3 and ASEAN4 economies from the G3 trade, and albeit its lower degree of openness, China had a higher exposure to the G3 markets in 2006 than the non-China block (16.6% vs. 14.6%, respectively). This finding is in line with the previous remark on the emergence of China as a major export platform in the region. As regards their exposure to demand from the rest of the world, China, the NIE3, and ASEAN4 economies were all more dependent on these markets in 2006 than in 2000. However, the

---

[19] The reasons behind China's opening up to the rest of the world are still to be investigated. One possible explanation being that China increased its manufacturing trade surplus against the rest of the world in order to compensate its growing trade deficit in oil and raw materials in this relation.

increase in China's dependence was substantially stronger than that of the non-China block.

Finally, Table 4 also provides some information on the importance of China as a source of final demand within the region. *The dependency of the NIE3 and ASEAN4 economies' value added on Chinese markets was relatively low, at 7.2% in 2006*. The main channel of this impact, as shown by the import content analysis before, is via imported inputs to local production rather than direct imports of final goods. Albeit still at low level, *the exposure to demand from China increased substantially in recent years and almost doubled since 2000*. Moreover, by 2006 China became a more important market for the NIE3 and ASEAN4 economies than the United States. More detailed economy-by-economy results are shown in Appendix E.

6. Conclusions

The chapter contributed to the "decoupling debate," – that is, whether the business cycle dynamics in emerging Asia have recently become less sensitive to the global demand trends – using a novel method based on an update of the AIO table. In particular, the study analyzed the dependence of emerging Asia's value added through trade and production linkages on intraregional demand, and on demand from the advanced economies; especially the United States, the EU15, and Japan. The updated 2006 AIO table was used in two ways. First, we calculated the "backward linkages" of production, which allowed us to describe the interlinkages of the emerging Asian economies in the production process. Second, as the main contribution of our chapter, the dependency of each economy's value added on domestic demand, and intraregional and extraregional demand was computed.

The main findings of the chapter are the following. First, only about one-third of the value added in emerging Asian economies is determined by external demand, significantly lower than the 50% exposure suggested by the aggregate trade data, while domestic demand contributes around two-thirds to the value added. Second, the dependence of emerging Asia's value added on export markets has steadily risen since 1995, a phenomenon in line with increasing global trade integration, and a clear evidence against the decoupling view. Third, although intraregional and Chinese markets have both gained importance, they still account for only around 7% of the final demand. This share is also below the one suggested by trade data.

As it is evident from these results, the chapter finds no support for the decoupling view. At the same time, however, it finds that if the bias in trade data due to the segmentation of production is accounted for, the exposure of emerging Asia is significantly lower than suggested by trade statistics. In other words, on the one hand we find no evidence of decoupling, but on the other hand we calculate that emerging Asia is less "coupled" with the rest of the world than trade data suggests.

When interpreting the results, one should note the caveat that the analysis of the real linkages with the AIO table can only capture the direct trade effects, that is, neither any "second-round" effects of an export slowdown on domestic demand via lower employment, wages, or investment, nor any financial market or policy-related channels are accounted for.

Acknowledgments

The views presented in this chapter are those of the authors and do not necessarily reflect those of the European Central Bank (ECB).

We would like to thank Ettore Dorrucci, Marcel Fratzscher, Frank Moss, Daniel Santabarbara, Roland Straub, Christian Thimann, Robert Anderton, as well as the conference participants at the 16th Central Banking Seminar, Seoul, October 21–24, 2008.

Appendix A. The updating procedure

The scheme of the updating procedure is shown in Figure A1. The updating procedure and the data sources used are similar to Mori and Sasaki (2007), with two main improvements. First, the trade data used for the update differs by type of goods, and thus takes into account the shift in the composition of trade from final to intermediate goods. Second, the data are adjusted for Hong Kong's entrepot trade.[20]

The starting point of the updating procedure is the 2000 AIO table. In general, the 2006 value of a specific cell in the AIO table is calculated by multiplying the 2000 value of the cell by its nominal growth rate in 2000–2006. The steps of the procedure and the estimation of the 2006/2000 growth rates are as follows:

Intermediate demand block (A)

- Value added (V^j_{t+1}). The value added growth rates for each economy are taken from National Account statistics (data source: CEIC database).

[20] In 2006, 95% of the Hong Kong's exports were re-exported. These re-exports are overwhelmingly originated from China and aimed at overseas markets. As Hong Kong is considered as part of the emerging Asian region, then if not corrected for, the Hong Kong re-exports may result in an overestimation of the intraregional and underestimation of extraregional demand. Given that Hong Kong is not included in the production matrix of the AIO table, the adjustment has to be made as an additional exercise.

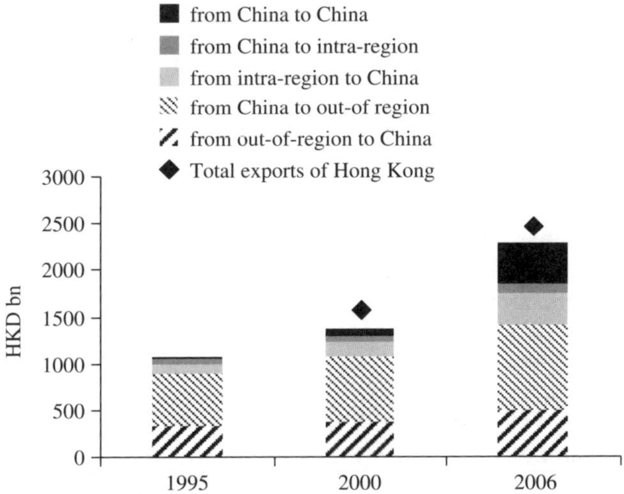

Fig. A1. Schematic chart of the updating procedure.

- Total output (X^j_{t+1}). With the exception of the United States, direct information on total economy's output is not available. Thus, total (gross) output is estimated by applying the output/value added ratio in the manufacturing sector to the total economy's value added. Data on manufacturing value added is from national accounts sources; output data are from industrial statistics (data source: CEIC).
- Imported inputs (A^{ij}_{t+1}). The calculation of growth rates of imported inputs draws on two data sources. First, in order to keep consistency, we use the growth rate of imports from the National Accounts statistics. The advantage of using this statistics is that it includes trade of goods and services, while the disadvantage is that it does not provide information by the direction of trade. To get an estimate for changes in the direction of trade, we combined National Accounts import growth with the information from the COMTRADE. The COMTRADE database provides information on imports not only by direction, but also by type of good, that is, it helps us to take into account the increasing share of intermediate inputs in total imports. (The classification of imports by type of goods I described in Appendix C.) However, the COMTRADE only includes data on goods trade; thus we have to assume that changes in imports by direction and by type of goods are similar for goods and services.[21]

The formula used to estimate the imported input growth rate is the following:

$$\left(\frac{\text{int}M^{*ij}_{t+1}}{\text{int}M^{*ij}_{t}}\right) = \left(\frac{M^{\text{NA}}_{t+1}}{M^{\text{NA}}_{t}}\right) \times \frac{(\text{int}M^{\text{COM}ij}_{t+1}/\text{int}M^{\text{COM}ij}_{t})}{(M^{\text{COM}}_{t+1}/M^{\text{COM}}_{t})}, \tag{A.1}$$

where the superscripts NA and COM stand for National Accounts and COMTRADE, respectively, and int$M$ indicates imports of intermediate goods and M is for total imports.[22]

- Freight and insurance and import duties (BA^{j}_{t+1}, DA^{j}_{t+1}). The growth rates of items' freights and insurance and import duties are chosen to be the same as the import growth rate from the National Accounts. This implies the assumption of unchanged share of these items in total imports from 2000 to 2006.
- Domestic input of production (A^{jj}_{t+1}). The domestic input content of production is calculated as a residual of the column, that is, total inputs minus total imported inputs ($= X^{j}_{t+1} - V^{j}_{t+1} - BA^{j}_{t+1} - DA^{j}_{t+1} - \sum A^{ij}_{t+1}$).

The update of the *final demand block (F)* follows the same pattern. The final demand of each economy is calculated by updating the components of consumption and investments separately.

- Total consumption and investments (C^{j}_{t+1}, I^{j}_{t+1}). The growth rates of consumption and investments are taken from the National Accounts statistics. Consumption is defined as the sum of private and government consumption, while investments equal gross capital formation (gross fixed capital formation plus inventories).
- Imported final goods (cF^{ij}_{t+1}) and imported capital goods (iF^{ij}_{t+1}). The growth rates are calculated according to the formula given for the imported inputs above, with the difference that the COMTRADE data on final and capital goods are used instead of the data on intermediate goods.

$$\left(\frac{cM^{*ij}_{t+1}}{cM^{*ij}_{t}}\right) = \left(\frac{M^{\text{NA}}_{t+1}}{M^{\text{NA}}_{t}}\right) * \frac{(cM^{\text{COM}ij}_{t+1}/cM^{\text{COM}ij}_{t})}{(M^{\text{COM}}_{t+1}/M^{\text{COM}}_{t})}, \tag{A.2}$$

$$\left(\frac{\text{cap}M^{*ij}_{t+1}}{\text{cap}M^{*ij}_{t}}\right) = \left(\frac{M^{\text{NA}}_{t+1}}{M^{\text{NA}}_{t}}\right) * \frac{(\text{cap}M^{COMij}_{t+1}/\text{cap}M^{\text{COM}ij}_{t})}{(M^{\text{COM}}_{t+1}/M^{\text{COM}}_{t})}, \tag{A.3}$$

---

[21] COMTRADE data are not available for Taiwan. Import growth rate for Taiwan is taken from the National Accounts statistics, that is, it lacks heterogeneity by economies of origin and types of goods.

[22] Note that if the growth rate of total goods imports from COMTRADE (M^{COM}) would equal the growth rate of total goods and services imports from National Accounts (M^{NA}), then the growth rate would be simply the growth rate of intermediate goods imports.

where the superscripts NA and COM stands for National Accounts and the COMTRADE, respectively, and cM and cap$M$ indicates imports of consumption and capital goods and M total imports.

- Freight and insurance, and import duties (cBF^{j}_{t+1}, iBF^{j}_{t+1}, cDF^{j}_{t+1}, iDF^{j}_{t+1}). Similar to the intermediate demand block.
- Domestically produced final and capital goods (cF^{jj}_{t+1}, iF^{jj}_{t+1}). Residual similar to the intermediate demand block.

Export block (L)

- Exports to Hong Kong, EU15, and RoW (L^{iH}_{t+1}, L^{iO}_{t+1}, L^{iW}_{t+1}). Growth rates are calculated in a similar manner as before, that is, as a combination of the National Accounts' export growth rates and the COMTRADE export growth rates by economy of destination (HK, EU15, RoW).

$$\left(\frac{EX^{*ij}_{t+1}}{EX^{*ij}_{t}}\right) = \left(\frac{EX^{\mathrm{NA}}_{t+1}}{EX^{\mathrm{NA}}_{t}}\right)\left(\frac{EX^{\mathrm{COM}ij}_{t+1}/EX^{\mathrm{COM}ij}_{t}}{EX^{\mathrm{COM}}_{t+1}/EX^{\mathrm{COM}}_{t}}\right) \tag{A.4}$$

- Statistical discrepancy (Q^{i}_{t+1}). To calculate the discrepancy, the data for 2006 data are taken from the National Accounts.

Adjusting for Hong Kong's entrepot trade

According to Hong Kong trade statistics, re-exports accounted for 95% of the economy's exports in 2006. Re-exports consists of goods that pass through Hong Kong without having undergone "a manufacturing process which has changed permanently the shape and nature, form or utility of the product."[23] Hong Kong's re-exports are overwhelmingly related to trade between China and the overseas markets. In total re-exports of Hong Kong, the share of China's exports to out-of-region markets was 39% in 2006, while the share of imports of China from out-of-region markets was 22% (Figure A2). Thus, if not corrected for, the Hong Kong re-exports may result in an overestimation of the intraregional and underestimation of extraregional demand.

The Hong Kong trade statistics provides information on re-exports by economy of origin, destination, and also by type of goods and destination. Based on this information, we used the following formulas to adjust the imports of intermediate, consumer, and capital goods, respectively, for the Hong Kong entrepot trade.

$$A^{ij}_{\mathrm{HK}} = A^{ij} + \eta^{j}_{\mathrm{int}} * \gamma^{ij} * LH^{i} \tag{A.5}$$

[23] US Department of the Treasury (2007) Report to Congress on International Economic and Exchange Rate Policies, Appendix II Chain's Trade Data, June 2007.

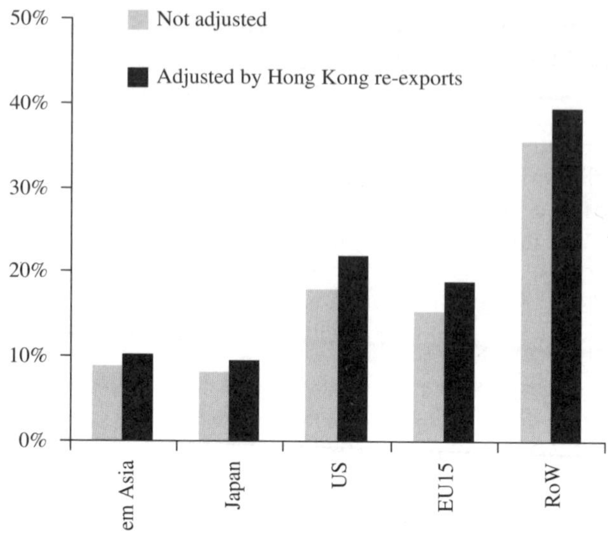

Fig. A2. The value of China-related trade in the total exports of Hong Kong. Source: CEIC.

$$cF^{ij}_{\text{HK}} = cF^{ij} + \eta^{j}_{\text{cons}} * \gamma^{ij} * LH^{i} \tag{A.6}$$

$$iF^{ij}_{\text{HK}} = iF^{ij} + \eta^{j}_{\text{cap}} * \gamma^{ij} * LH^{i} \tag{A.7}$$

where LH^i is exports from (origin) economy i to Hong Kong, $\gamma^{ij} = \text{RX}^{*ij}/M^{*i}$ is the share of re-exports (RX) from (origin) economy i to (destination) economy j in total imports of Hong Kong from (origin) economy i, and $\eta^{j}_{g} = \text{RX}^{*j}_{g}/\text{RX}^{*j}$ is the share of intermediate, capital, and consumption goods ($g = \{\text{int, cons, cap}\}$ type of good) in re-exports to (destination) economy j.[24]

As a result of the adjustment, the new trade weights of China indicate a significantly higher share for the United States, the EU15, and rest of the world markets, while intraregional markets and Japan gain relatively less in importance (Figure A3). In fact, the share of the United States in China's total exports rises from 18% to 22% in 2006, the share of EU15 from 15% to 19%, and the rest of the world from 36% to 39%, an almost 4 pp increase on average. The adjustment's impact on the shares of emerging Asia and Japan are lower, that is, a 1.4 pp on average.

[24] Given that data on re-exports by type of goods is only available in relation to destination economies, we apply the assumption that the distributions across the types of goods are similar regardless of the economy of origin of re-exports.

	code	Intermediate Demand (A): Indonesia (AI)	Malaysia (AM)	Philippines (AP)	Singapore (AS)	Thailand (AT)	China (AC)	Taiwan (AN)	Korea (AK)	Japan (AJ)	U.S.A. (AU)	Final Demand (F): Indonesia (FI) C I	Malaysia (FM)	Philippines (FP)	Singapore (FS)	Thailand (FT)	China (FC)	Taiwan (FN)	Korea (FK)	Japan (FJ)	U.S.A. (FU)	Export (L): Export to Hong Kong (LH)	Export to EU (LO)	Export to R.O.W. (LW)	Statistical Discrepancy (QX)	Total Outputs (XX)
Indonesia	(AI)	A^{II}										cF^{II} iF^{II}										L^{IH}			Q^{I}	X^{I}
Malaysia	(AM)	A^{MI}	$A^{ij}_{t+1}=X^{j}_{t+1}-V^{j}_{t+1}-DA^{j}_{t+1}-BA^{j}_{t+1}-\sum A^{ij}_{t+1}$									cF^{MI} iF^{MI}	$cF^{ij}_{t+1}=C^{j}_{t+1}-cDA^{j}_{t+1}-cBA^{j}_{t+1}-\sum cF^{ij}_{t+1}$									L^{MH}			Q^{M}	X^{M}
Philippines	(AP)	A^{PI}										cF^{PI} iF^{PI}	$iF^{ij}_{t+1}=I^{j}_{t+1}-iDA^{j}_{t+1}-iBA^{j}_{t+1}-\sum iF^{ij}_{t+1}$									L^{PH}			Q^{P}	X^{P}
Singapore	(AS)	A^{SI}										cF^{SI} iF^{SI}										L^{SH}			Q^{S}	X^{S}
Thailand	(AT)	A^{TI}										cF^{TI} iF^{TI}										L^{TH}			Q^{T}	X^{T}
China	(AC)	A^{CI}										cF^{CI} iF^{CI}										L^{CH}			Q^{C}	X^{C}
Taiwan	(AN)	A^{NI}	} $A^{ij}_{t+1} = A^{ij}_{t} * (intM*^{ij}_{t+1} / intM*^{ij}_{t})$									cF^{NI} iF^{NI}	} $cF^{ij}_{t+1} = cF^{ij}_{t} * (cM*^{ij}_{t+1} / cM*^{ij}_{t})$									L^{NH}			Q^{N}	X^{N}
Korea	(AK)	A^{KI}										cF^{KI} iF^{KI}	$iF^{ij}_{t+1} = iF^{ij}_{t} * (capM*^{ij}_{t+1} / capM*^{ij}_{t})$									L^{KH}			Q^{K}	X^{K}
Japan	(AJ)	A^{JI}										cF^{JI} iF^{JI}										L^{JH}			Q^{J}	X^{J}
U.S.A.	(AU)	A^{UI}										cF^{UI} iF^{UI}										L^{UH}			Q^{U}	X^{U}
Freight and Insurance	(BF)	BA^{I}	$BA^{j}_{t+1} = BA^{j}_{t} * (intM*^{j}_{t+1} / intM*^{j}_{t})$									cBF^{I} iBF^{I}	$cBF^{j}_{t+1} = cBF^{j}_{t} * (consM*^{j}_{t+1} / consM*^{j}_{t})$													
Import from Hong Kon(	(CH)	A^{HI}										cF^{HI} iF^{HI}	$cF^{ij}_{t+1} = cF^{ij}_{t} * (consM*^{ij}_{t+1} / consM*^{ij}_{t})$									$L^{ij}_{t+1} = L^{ij}_{t} * (EX*^{ij}_{t+1} / EX*^{ij}_{t})$				
Import from EU	(CO)	A^{OI}	} $A^{ij}_{t+1} = A^{ij}_{t} * (intM*^{ij}_{t+1} / intM*^{ij}_{t})$									cF^{OI} iF^{OI}	} $iF^{ij}_{t+1} = iF^{ij}_{t} * (capM*^{ij}_{t+1} / capM*^{ij}_{t})$									$Q^{ij}_{t+1} = Q^{ij}_{t} * (Q*^{ij}_{t+1} / Q*^{ij}_{t})$				
Import from the R.O.W	(CW)	A^{WI}										cF^{WI} iF^{WI}														
Duties and Import Commodity Taxes	(DT)	DA^{I}	$DA^{j}_{t+1} = DAjt * (intM*^{j}_{t+1} / intM*^{j}_{t})$									cDF^{I} iDF^{I}	} $cDF^{j}_{t+1} = cDF^{j}_{t} * (consM*^{j}_{t+1} / consM*^{j}_{t})$ $iDF^{j}_{t+1} = iDF^{j}_{t} * (capM*^{j}_{t+1} / capM*^{j}_{t})$													
Value Added	(VV)	V^{I}	$V^{j}_{t+1} = V^{j}_{t} * (V*^{j}_{t+1} / V*^{j}_{t})$									C^{I} I^{I}	$C^{j}_{t+1} = C^{j}_{t} * (C*^{j}_{t+1} / C*^{j}_{t})$, $I^{j}_{t+1} = I^{j}_{t} * (I*^{j}_{t+1} / I*^{j}_{t})$													
Total Inputs	(XX)	X^{I}	$X^{j}_{t+1} = X^{j}_{t} * (X*^{j}_{t+1} / X*^{j}_{t})$																							

$X*^{j}_{t}$ = Gross production of country j (National Accounts data) or industrial gross output
$V*^{j}_{t}$ = GDP of country j (National Accounts)
$C*^{ij}_{t}$ = total consumption of country j (National Accounts)
$I*^{ij}_{t}$ = capital accumulation of country j (National Accounts)
$EX*^{ij}_{t}$ = exports of country j to country i (COMTRADE)

$intM*^{j}_{t}$ = intermediate goods imports of country j (COMTRADE)
$intM*^{ij}_{t}$ = intermediate goods imports of country j from country i (COMTRADE)
$consM*^{j}_{t}$ = consumption goods imports of country j (COMTRADE)
$consM*^{ij}_{t}$ = consumption goods imports of country j from country i (COMTRADE)
$capM*^{j}_{t}$ = capital goods imports of country j (COMTRADE)
$capM*^{ij}_{t}$ = capital goods imports of country j from country i (COMTRADE)

Fig. A3. China's adjusted and nonadjusted export weights. Source: AIO updated.

Appendix B. Classification of goods by broad economic categories (BEC)

1. Capital goods
Sum of categories:
41 Capital goods (except transport equipment)
521 Transport equipment, industrial

2. Intermediate goods
Sum of categories:
111 Food and beverages, primary, mainly for industry
121 Food and beverages, processed, mainly for industry
21 Industrial supplies not elsewhere specified, primary
22 Industrial supplies not elsewhere specified, processed
31 Fuels and lubricants, primary
322 Fuels and lubricants, processed (other than motor spirit)
42 Parts and accessories of capital goods (except transport equipment)
53 Parts and accessories of transport equipment

3. Consumption goods
Sum of categories:
112 Food and beverages, primary, mainly for household consumption
122 Food and beverages, processed, mainly for household consumption
522 Transport equipment, nonindustrial
61 Consumer goods not elsewhere specified, durable
62 Consumer goods not elsewhere specified, semidurable
63 Consumer goods not elsewhere specified, nondurable

4. Other goods
Sum of categories:
21 Motor spirit
51 Passenger motor cars
7 Goods not elsewhere specified

Note: When the breakdown of goods to capital, intermediate, and consumption goods is used in the chapter, the three first categories are used. However, in the cases where total trade is used, then the data also includes the fourth category of other goods.

Appendix C. Sensitivity analysis – results from the updated 1995 AIO table

As a sensitivity check of the updating procedure, we also updated the 1995 AIO table to year 2000 and compared the results from this updated table with that from the "official" 2000 AIO table.

The updating procedure was similar to the one used in the chapter: we took the 1995 AIO table as a starting point and updated each cell according to the steps described in Appendix A. Data limitations were somewhat more severe than in the original exercise. First, as no

COMTRADE import data was reported by the Philippines for 1995, we used the export data reported by partner economies adjusted for the freight and insurance and import duties component. Second, Indonesian producer prices were proxied by the average producer price inflation in Malaysia, the Philippines, and Thailand. Similar to the original exercise we lack COMTRADE trade data for Taiwan, applying the output/value added ratio in the manufacturing sector to the total economy's value added and assume changes in imports by direction and by type are similar for goods and services.

To test the sensitivity of our findings to the updating procedure, we calculated the Leontieff coefficients and the impacts of final demand on value added from the updated 1995 table and compared the results with the ones from the "official" 2000 AIO table.

The Leontieff coefficients from the updated 1995 AIO table indicate less significant changes in the production network between 1995 and 2000, and a stronger concentration of suppliers of inputs than the "official" 2000 AIO (Figures C1 and C2).

However, the results from the impact of final demand on value added analysis with the updated 1995 AIO table are not significantly different from the findings of the "official" 2000 AIO table, the main difference being that the updated 1995 AIO table overestimates the dependence on domestic demand by 2 pps and underestimates the dependence on the rest of the world by the same amount.

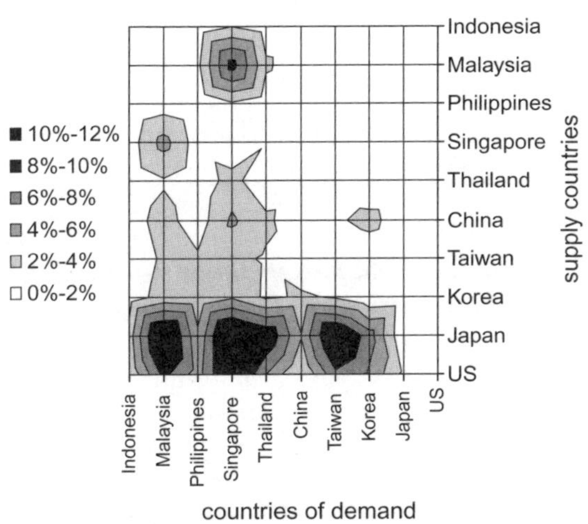

Fig. C1. Leontieff coefficients from the updated 1995 AIO table.

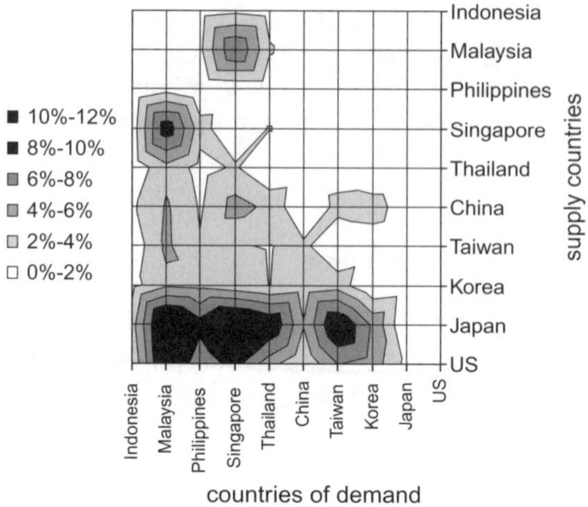

Fig. C2. Leontieff coefficients from the "official" 2000 AIO table.

Table C1. The impact of final demand on value added, not adjusted for Hong Kong trade (%)

	Updated 1995 AIO table	Official 2000 AIO table	Difference in pps
Domestic demand	70	68	2
Intraregional trade	8	7	0
G3	13	13	0
within that EU3	2	2	0
Japan	4	4	0
United States	7	7	0
RoW	10	12	−2
Residual	0	−1	1

Appendix D. The derivation and interpretation of the main indicators used in the analysis of backward linkages (Leontieff coefficients)

$$\text{Let } \alpha^{ij} = \frac{A^{ij}}{X^{j}}, \tag{D.1}$$

where index $i = (I, M, \ldots, U)$ depicts the supplier economy and $j = (I, M, \ldots, U)$ is the economy of demand. X is total production and A is intermediate inputs from the supplier economy used in the production of the economy of demand.

Then the AIO table can be written as

$$\begin{aligned}
\alpha^{II}X^{I} + \alpha^{IM}X^{M} + \ldots + \alpha^{IU}X^{U} + F^{II} + F^{IM} + \ldots + Q^{I} &= X^{I}\\
\alpha^{MI}X^{I} + \alpha^{MM}X^{M} + \ldots + \alpha^{MU}X^{U} + F^{MI} + F^{MM} + \ldots + Q^{M} &= X^{M}\\
&\ldots\\
\alpha^{UI}X^{I} + \alpha^{UM}X^{M} + \ldots + \alpha^{UU}X^{U} + F^{UI} + F^{UM} + \ldots + Q^{U} &= X^{U}
\end{aligned} \tag{D.2}$$

or in a matrix form

$$\begin{bmatrix} \alpha^{II} & \alpha^{IM} & . & \alpha^{IU} \\ \alpha^{MI} & \alpha^{MM} & . & \alpha^{MU} \\ . & . & . & . \\ \alpha^{UI} & \alpha^{UM} & . & \alpha^{UUI} \end{bmatrix} x \begin{bmatrix} X^{I} \\ X^{M} \\ . \\ X^{U} \end{bmatrix} + \begin{bmatrix} F^{II} \\ F^{MI} \\ . \\ F^{UI} \end{bmatrix} + \begin{bmatrix} F^{IM} \\ F^{MM} \\ . \\ F^{UM} \end{bmatrix} + \ldots + \begin{bmatrix} Q^{I} \\ Q^{M} \\ . \\ Q^{U} \end{bmatrix} = \begin{bmatrix} X^{I} \\ X^{M} \\ . \\ X^{U} \end{bmatrix}. \tag{D.3}$$

In short

$$\mathbf{AX} + \mathbf{Y} = \mathbf{X}. \tag{D.4}$$

To answer the question how much production is needed to meet 1 unit of demand, the system of equation should be solved to **X**:

$$\mathbf{X} = (\mathbf{I} - \mathbf{A})^{-1}\mathbf{Y} = \mathbf{BY}, \tag{D.5}$$

where **B** is called the Leontieff coefficient matrix.

The B^{ij} element of the matrix indicates the number of unit of production needed in economy i to produce 1 unit of value added in economy j.

The impact of final demand on value added

The formula used is

$$IFv^{j} = \widehat{\upsilon} \times B \times f^{j}, \tag{D.6}$$

where B is the Leontieff coefficient, f^{j} is final demand of economy j, and v is a diagonal matrix constructed from the elements of $v^{j} = V^{j}/X^{j}$, and f^{j} is the demand vector of economy j.

For interpretation purposes let's assume the case of a 1 unit increase in final demand of Indonesia (f^{I}). The impact of Indonesian final demand on production of economies in the matrix $\mathbf{IF}^{\mathbf{I}}$ is the following:

$$\mathrm{IF}^{I} = \begin{matrix} B^{II}f^{II} + B^{IM}f^{MI} + \ldots + B^{IU}f^{UI} \\ B^{MI}f^{II} + B^{MM}f^{MI} + \ldots + B^{MM}f^{UI} \\ \ldots \\ B^{UI}f^{II} + B^{UM}f^{MI} + \ldots + B^{UU}f^{UI} \end{matrix}, \tag{D.7}$$

where the first row of the matrix indicates the impact on Indonesian production, the second row the impact on the Malaysian production, etc.

Interpreting the elements of the formula in the first row, the Indonesian production is stimulated by Indonesian domestic demand to the extent that Indonesian domestic demand consumes products from domestic supply ($B^{II}f^{II}$), plus the production of Indonesian inputs needed to produce the final goods imported from Malaysia ($B^{IM}f^{MI}$), the Philippines ($B^{IP}f^{PI}$), etc.

Multiplying the $\mathbf{IF}^i$ matrix with the v diagonal matrix, the formula gives the level of induced value added rather than that of the induced production.

Appendix E. detailed results from the impact of final demand on value-added exercise

Year 2006 with adjustment for Hong Kong entrepot trade

	Demand countries												
	Indonesia	Malaysia	Philippines	Singapore	Thailand	China	Taiwan	Korea	Japan	United States	HK	EU15	RoW
Source countries													
Indonesia	**74%**	1%	0%	0%	1%	2%	1%	1%	4%	3%	0%	3%	9%
Malaysia	1%	**31%**	1%	2%	2%	9%	2%	2%	5%	12%	1%	9%	20%
The Philippines	0%	1%	**55%**	0%	1%	8%	1%	1%	4%	6%	1%	6%	7%
Singapore	1%	2%	1%	**26%**	1%	6%	1%	2%	2%	8%	4%	8%	32%
Thailand	1%	1%	0%	1%	**54%**	5%	1%	1%	5%	7%	1%	5%	21%
China	0%	0%	0%	0%	0%	**70%**	0%	1%	3%	7%	0%	6%	13%
Taiwan	0%	1%	0%	0%	1%	16%	**49%**	1%	5%	12%	1%	8%	17%
Korea	0%	0%	0%	0%	0%	6%	1%	**65%**	2%	4%	1%	4%	14%
Japan	0%	0%	0%	0%	0%	2%	1%	1%	**84%**	3%	0%	2%	5%
United States	0%	0%	0%	0%	0%	0%	0%	0%	0%	**91%**	0%	1%	6%

Note: The percentages indicate the ratio of demand from each economy to the total value added in the source economies. The rows should sum up to 100%, the difference being the sum of the residual and the statistical discrepancy (not included in the table). Bold refers to the ratio of domestic demand in the total value added of the economy. Bold refers to the ratio of domestic demand in the total value added of the economy.

References

Asian Development Bank (ADB). (2007), Uncoupling Asia: myth and reality. *Asian Development Outlook 2007*. Available at www.adb.org

Asian Development Bank (ADB). (2008), *Emerging Asian regionalism – A partnership for shared prosperity*. Available at http://aric.adb.org/emergingasianregionalism/

Dees, S., Vansteenkiste, I. (2007), The transmission of US cyclical developments to the rest of the world. ECB Working Paper No. 798, August. Available at www.ecb.int

Dieter, H. (2007), Transnational production networks in the automobile industry. Notre Europe Studies and Research No. 58. Available at www.notre-europe.eu/uploads/tx_publication/Etud58.pdf

Gangnes, B., Van Assche, A. (2008), China and the future of Asian electronics trade. CIRANO, Scientific Series, Montreal. Available at www.cirano.qc.ca/pdf/publication/2008s-05.pdf

Gaulier, G., Lemoine, F., Unal-Kesenci, D. (2005), China's integration in East Asia: production sharing, FDI and high-tech trade. CEPII Working Paper No. 2005-09. Available at www.cepii.fr

Haddad, M. (2007), Trade integration in East Asia: the role of China and production networks. World Bank Policy Research Working Paper No. 4160, March. Available at Available at www.worldbank.org

Inomata, S., Uchida, Y. (2009), Asia beyond the crisis. visions from international input–output analyses. Institute of Developing Economies IDE-JETRO Spot Survey 31. Available at http://www.ide.go.jp/English/

International Monetary Fund (IMF). (2007), Decoupling the train? Chapter 4 in the *World Economy Outlook 2007*, April. Available at www.imf.org

Mori, T., Sasaki, H. (2007), Interdependence of production and income in Asia-Pacific economies: an international input–output approach. Bank of Japan Working Paper Series No.07-E-26, November. Available at www.boj.or.jp/en/

Nag, B., Banerjee, S., Chatterjee, R. (2007), Changing features of the automobile industry in Asia. Asia-pacific Research and Training Network on Trade Working paper Series No. 37, July. Available at http://ideas.repec.org/p/esc/wpaper/3707.html

Luthje, B. (2004), Global production networks and the industrial upgrading in China: the case of electronics contract manufacturing. East-West Center Working Papers Economics Series No. 74. Available at http://ideas.repec.org/p/ewc/wpaper/wp74.html

US Department of the Treasury. (2007), Report to Congress on international economic and exchange rate policies. Appendix II Chain's Trade Data, June. Available at www.ustreas.gov/

CHAPTER 12

The Australia–Asia Business Cycle Evolution

Shawn Chen-Yu Leu[a] and Jeffrey Sheen[b]

[a]*School of Economics and Finance, La Trobe University, Melbourne, VIC. 3086, Australia*
E-mail address: C.Leu@latrobe.edu.au
[b]*Department of Economics, Macquarie University, Sydney, NSW 2109, Australia*
E-mail address: jsheen@efs.mq.edu.au

Abstract
We consider whether there has been a gradual decoupling of the Australian business cycle from its trading partners in Europe and North America and a closer convergence toward its trading partners in Asia. We set up a dynamic latent factor model to estimate common dynamic components or factors for the real GDP growth rate of 19 countries. From variance decomposition over the 1991–2009 sample, we find that a global factor contributed the most in explaining Australian output growth variations, followed by a European factor, an Asian factor, and finally a North American factor. However, the correlation between Australian output growth movements and the Asian business cycle factor evolved from negative and small to positive and large after 2002. The European and North American factors were negatively correlated with Australian output growth for most of the sample period before turning positive in the global financial crisis of 2007–2008. This evidence supports the hypothesis that the Australian economy has decoupled to some extent from Europe, was not much coupled with North America except insofar as the United States drove the global factor, and has increasingly become positively coupled with Asia.

Keywords: International business cycle, decoupling, dynamic latent factor model, Kalman filter, dynamic correlation, variance decomposition

JEL classifications: E32, E37, O47

1. Introduction

In this chapter, we examine the evolving business cycle linkages between Australia and key regional groupings. We test to see whether Australia's links with Asian economies have become more intense in recent years, relative to Europe and North America. Using dynamic factor analysis,

Frontiers of Economics and Globalization
Volume 9 ISSN: 1574-8715
DOI: 10.1108/S1574-8715(2011)0000009017

we find evidence to support this hypothesis, thus going a long way to understanding why Australia's performance was relatively robust in the recent global financial crisis and the ensuing global recession.

The financial turmoil that began in 2007 and peaked in September 2008 in the United States led to perhaps the most severe global financial and real crisis since the Great Depression. This financial malfunction spread quickly to the real global economy by impacting on the costs and confidence of consumers and firms, thus, severely reducing the level of economic activity. Aggregate demand, global industrial production and trade volumes fell rapidly, unemployment rose almost everywhere, and as a result, most countries experienced one of the worst recessions in the postwar era. Against this difficult backdrop, the Australian economy was remarkably resilient. Among the main developed economies in the world, Australia is the only country that did not register negative year-end output growth during this global downturn. In addition, it did not record a drop in export volume during that period, and its terms of trade began to increase early in the piece. Unemployment did rise, but only to reach its long-run average. There are several factors that contributed to this remarkably robust performance. First, the large and timely monetary and fiscal stimulus measures of the central bank and the federal government were important in supporting aggregate demand. However, most other countries also responded with quite similar stimulus packages. Second, the banking sector in Australia was in a healthier state compared to some other advanced economies, with minimal exposure to the subprime debt problems originating in the United States. Even so, there were a number of other developed countries with a similar low financial exposure, whose economies performed much worse. Third, the Australian dollar depreciated in trade-weighted terms by 15% in the six months after September 2008, which helped to support exports. Nevertheless, a number of countries also experienced depreciation over that period, but performed worse. Fourth, increasing trade links over the decade with Asian economies, in particular China and India, which rebounded quickly in the crisis, provided an important driver for the relatively robust growth that Australia continued to enjoy through the crisis. It is this last point that might be the one that distinguished Australia's response to the crisis, and it is the one that we test in this chapter.

Few doubt that Australia has benefited from the resource boom arising from its Asian trading partners. Lowe (2009), the assistant governor of the Reserve Bank of Australia, was optimistic that this shift of economic weight to Asia not only had positive effects for the Australian economy in the short run but would also be sustained in the medium run. We therefore ask the following question: "For the last twenty years, has there been a degree of decoupling of the Australian business cycle from its trading partners in Europe and North America, and a greater coupling with its trading partners in Asia?"

We proceed to answer this question by drawing from the literature that examines the key characteristics of international business cycles. Using pairwise correlations, Backus *et al.* (1995) and Baxter (1995) found that the business cycles in major industrialized countries are similar. In Mendoza (1995) and Kose (2002), the business cycles of emerging market economies were found to share many similar features to those of the advanced countries. Gregory *et al.* (1997) employed the Kalman filter and dynamic factor analysis to identify common macroeconomic fluctuations across G7 countries. Using a VAR factor model, Clark and Shin (2000) studied the importance of common and country-specific shocks in accounting for variation in industrial production in European countries. Lumsdaine and Prasad (2003) developed a weighted aggregation procedure to examine the correlations between the industrial output fluctuations of 17 OECD countries. They found evidence for a world business cycle and a European business cycle. While most of these studies focus on smaller groups of countries, Kose *et al.* (2003) used a sample of 60 countries to estimate a world factor that could represent the common business cycle factor for all countries, a set of regional factors that could be common to countries within their regions, and country-specific factors that could capture fluctuations of individual countries. Kose *et al.* (2008) categorized a sample of 106 countries into developed countries, emerging markets and other developing economies for the estimation of global, region-specific and country-specific factors. This large literature, although spanning a variety of techniques, datasets and sample periods, has provided strong evidence of cross-country links for macroeconomic fluctuations in the context of international business cycles.

However, an interesting related question has resurfaced recently[1], which asks whether the emerging market economies of Asia have decoupled from the business cycles of the advanced economies. In recent years the impressive growth performance of emerging market economies, especially China and India, seems to have been only mildly affected by growth slowdowns in industrial countries. This has led to suggestions that the international channels of business cycle transmission might have weakened, with some even conjecturing that these emerging markets have "decoupled" from industrial economies, in the sense that their business cycle dynamics are no longer tightly linked to industrial country business cycles.

The decoupling hypothesis challenges the alternative view that increasing globalization through intercountry trade and financial linkages increases output comovement by widening the channels for external shocks to spill across countries. However, economic theory is ambiguous about the impact of greater international linkages on cross-country output

---

[1] See for example, "The Decoupling Debate", *The Economist*, March 6, 2008.

comovements. Stronger financial linkages may increase cross-country comovements via the correlated wealth effects of external shocks. However, they may also reduce these output comovements by encouraging specialization in production consistent with countries' comparative advantage arising from international capital diversification. Greater trade linkages generate both demand- and supply-side spillovers across countries, which can result in more highly correlated output fluctuations. On the other hand, if stronger trade linkages facilitate greater specialization of production across countries, and if sector-specific shocks are dominant, then the degree of output comovement could fall (see Baxter and Kouparitsas, 2005). Thus, the degree of business cycle coupling across countries may be different in the short term (due to wealth effects and activity spillovers) than in the longer term (insofar as forces for specialization take root).

With Australia's exports now more closely aligned with its Asian trading partners, the question arises whether its business cycle is now driven more (positively) by an Asian economic factor, than by other regional or global factors. To answer this question, we set up a dynamic latent factor model to estimate common dynamic components for the real GDP growth rate of 19 countries. Australia is viewed as the home country and the remaining 18 countries are divided into three regions: Asia, Europe, and North America. Apart from Australia, real GDP growth of each country is decomposed into two factors: (1) a global factor, which picks up fluctuations that are common to all countries, and (2) a region-specific factor, which captures fluctuations that are common to countries within each of the three regions. Since the objective of the study is to investigate the evolution of Australian business cycles and its correlation with that of the rest of the world, Australia is classified as a "member" for all three regions and, hence, the decomposition of its output growth involves the global factor and the three regional factors.

To estimate the dynamic latent factor model, we use maximum likelihood with quarterly data over the period 1991Q1 to 2009Q1, and extract the latent (or unobservable) factors with the Kalman filter. We obtain the following main findings. First, the fluctuations of the global factor are found to be highly persistent. The movements track the major economic events of the past two decades quite closely and possibly represent the influences of coordinated policy responses across countries. In contrast, the fluctuations of the region-specific factors exhibit lower persistence and their higher-frequency cyclicality may be capturing real exchange rate variations between the regions, or uncoordinated policy responses across countries. Second, our estimated regional factors suggest that the negative impact of the global recession from 2008 was transmitted to the three regions at different speeds. The growth rates of most Asian economies were among the earliest to fall below zero and registered the largest decrease. The negative impact on North America started in late

2008 delivering three quarters of (small) negative growth. The European region seemed to weather the storm by producing positive (but low) growth throughout 2008 before turning negative in 2009. Third, we perform variance decompositions to determine the relative contributions of the latent factors to Australian output growth variations. The global factor is found to be the most important external driver, explaining 11% of the variations. Of the regional factors, the European one ranks first with a contribution of 5.7%, the Asian factor picks up 2.3%, while the North American factor contributes 1.1%. Fourth, the correlation between the Australian and Asian business cycles changed from negative to positive after 2002, and then increased significantly after the 2007–2008 global financial crisis. The European and North American factors were negatively correlated with the Australian cycle for most of the sample period, turning positive only at the onset of the global financial crisis in 2007–2008. When the effects of the global crisis finally subside, these results suggest that Australia will return to a negative relation with the European and North American factors, but remain positively connected to Asia. This provides support for the hypothesis that the Australian economy has decoupled to some degree from the idiosyncratic component of European and North American business cycles, and enhanced its coupling with Asia.

The chapter is organized as follows. Section 2 describes the data and lays out the dynamic latent factor model. In Section 3, we present the empirical results that include the parameter estimates, variance decomposition of Australian output growth, the estimated latent factors, and the dynamic correlations between Australian output growth and the latent factors. We close this section with a brief discussion of robustness checks on model specification. Section 4 concludes.

2. *Data and methodology*

2.1. Data

The primary data is real GDP for the 19 countries in the sample, which we extracted from three different sources – Datastream, the IFS, and the OECD databases (see Data Appendix for more information). The sample period is quarterly and covers 1990Q1 to 2009Q1. Given our focus on Australia and its cyclical output linkages with its trading partners, we chose 18 countries that were among its top 27 export trading partners[2] during the sample period. With Australia as the home country, the 18 foreign countries are divided up into three international regions: nine

[2] We excluded countries in this set for which there were data availability problems and which were unlikely to be contributing drivers of the Australian economy (e.g., Papua New Guinea and the Philippines).

countries in the Asian region that includes China, Hong Kong, India, Indonesia, Japan, Korea, New Zealand, Singapore, and Taiwan; seven countries in the European region that includes Belgium, France, Germany, Italy, Netherlands, Spain, and the United Kingdom; and the North American region comprising Canada and the United States. The global economy is proxied by the "aggregate" of all the countries in the sample. We compute year-end output growth rates from the real GDP data and remove the mean for each country for the empirical analysis so that we can focus on business cycle correlations over the 19-year sample.

2.2. A dynamic factor model

For the set of output growth rates, we construct a dynamic factor model that allows for the identification of one global factor and three regional factors as drivers of cyclical output fluctuations, and accounts for their dynamic persistence. We cast the model into a state-space representation and estimate the parameters by maximum likelihood, using the Kalman filter to extract the global and regional latent factors. Modeling common fluctuations of a set of macroeconomic variables using a dynamic factor model approach has become popular recently. One reason is that this approach can characterize the degree and source of synchronization in various dimensions without having to make strong identifying assumptions to disentangle the different types of common shocks. The factor structure is motivated by general equilibrium models as shown in Altug (1989). The factors are interpreted as capturing the effects of many types of common shocks, including technology shocks and monetary policy shocks, rather than just representing specific types of shocks.

In the international business cycle literature, the estimated factors can capture common fluctuations across the entire dataset (which represents the "world") and across subsets of the data (which represents a particular grouping of countries). Examples of studies that have applied this technique, for example, are Stock and Watson (1989), Monfort *et al.* (2003), and Kose *et al.* (2003, 2008). Another common approach in the literature to measuring the level of comovement is to calculate a set of bivariate correlations for all variables in the dataset[3], for example, Backus *et al.* (1995), Baxter (1995), and more recently Doyle and Faust (2002). There are two advantages of using the dynamic factor model rather than the bivariate correlation approach. First, the analysis of simple correlation cannot allow for the separation of idiosyncratic components from the

[3] Two other measures are: (1) the concordance statistic by Harding and Pagan (2002), which measures the synchronization of turning points; and (2) the measurement of coherences, which is the equivalent of correlations in the frequency domain Unlike static correlations, the latter can allow for lead–lag relationships between variables.

common source of joint comovements. Second, static correlation analysis cannot capture dynamic persistence in the data as well as common fluctuations.

In our implementation, the real GDP growth rate for each country, denoted by $y_{i,t}$ and indexed by $i = 1, \ldots, 19$, is assumed to evolve according to an AR(1) process. There is an unobservable global factor (f_t) that is common to all 19 countries in the sample. For the regional groupings, the three unobservable factors are the Asian factor (n_A), the European factor (n_E) and the North American factor (n_{NA}), which are indexed by $j = A$, E and NA. Hence, each observable output growth series is decomposed as

$$y_{i,t} = \alpha_i y_{i,t-1} + \beta_i f_t + \gamma_i^j n_{j,t} + \varepsilon_{i,t}, \tag{1}$$

where the parameters β and γ are the factor loadings that capture the sensitivity of individual output growth rates to the latent factors. The estimated factor loadings quantify the extent to which output growth moves with the global factor and the regional factors, respectively. The idiosyncratic shocks are assumed to be normally distributed and serially uncorrelated, $\varepsilon_{i,t}$ is distributed NID$(0, \sigma^2_{\varepsilon_i})$, and are uncorrelated with each other, $E(\varepsilon_{i,t}\varepsilon_{k,t-s}) = 0$ for $i \neq k$ with $s \geq 0$.

Since the focus is on the business cycle synchronicity between Australia as the home country and the rest of the world, we allow the global factor and all three regional factors to enter into the Australian output growth equation:

Australia

$$y_{1,t} = \alpha_1 y_{1,t-1} + \beta_1 f_t + \gamma_1^A n_{A,t} + \gamma_1^E n_{E,t} + \gamma_1^{NA} n_{NA,t} + \varepsilon_{1,t}.$$

As a result, we can compute the dynamic correlations between Australian output growth and the estimated latent factors. The correlation statistics can shed light on the degree and evolution of synchronization between the Australian business cycle and the global and regional factor cycles. It is worth noting, for example, that the U.S. economy's business cycle will impact on Australia's cycle via both the global factor and the idiosyncratic North American factor.

For the remaining countries in the sample that are classified into one of the three regions, the global factor and only the assigned regional factor enter into their output growth equations:

Asian region, $i = 2, \ldots, 10$

$$y_{i,t} = \alpha_i y_{i,t-1} + \beta_i f_t + \gamma_i^A n_{A,t} + \varepsilon_{i,t},$$

European region, $i = 11, \ldots, 17$

$$y_{i,t} = \alpha_i y_{i,t-1} + \beta_i f_t + \gamma_i^E n_{E,t} + \varepsilon_{i,t},$$

North American region, $i = 18, 19$

$$y_{i,t} = \alpha_i y_{i,t-1} + \beta_i f_t + \gamma_i^{NA} n_{NA,t} + \varepsilon_{i,t}.$$

The evolution of the global factor and the regional factors is governed by the following first-order autoregressive process:

$$f_t = \phi_{f,1} f_{t-1} + \eta_{f,t} \tag{2}$$

$$n_{j,t} = \phi_{j,1} n_{j,t-1} + \eta_{j,t}, \tag{3}$$

where η's are assumed to be normally distributed and serially uncorrelated, $\eta_{f,t}$ is distributed NID$(0, \sigma^2_{\eta_f})$ and $\eta_{j,t}$ is distributed NID$(0, \sigma^2_{\eta_j})$, and the factor innovations are uncorrelated with each other. In addition, there is orthogonality between the idiosyncratic shocks and the factor innovations, $E(\eta_{f,t}\varepsilon_{i,t-s}) = E(\eta_{j,t}\varepsilon_{i,t-s}) = 0$ for all i, j, and s. Thus, all comovement is driven by the latent factors, which in turn have autoregressive representations. The lag orders for Equation (1) through Equation (3) can in principle be different to each other, however, for simplicity and parsimony, these are restricted to be AR(1). At the end of Section 3, we will discuss the results of some robustness checks carried out on model specification.

To identify the scales of the factors and factor loadings we follow Sargent and Sims (1977) and Stock and Watson (1989) by assuming that the variances of factor innovations are constant. The constant is chosen based on the scale of the data so that the innovation variance is equal to the average innovation variance of a set of univariate autoregressions for each time series. In other words, we calibrate $\sigma^2_{\eta_f}$ to equal the average innovation variance of the global set. For the regional innovation variances, $\sigma^2_{\eta_A}$, $\sigma^2_{\eta_E}$, and $\sigma^2_{\eta_{NA}}$, these are calibrated to equal the average innovation variance of their respective regional groups. Note that in casting the model into state-space representation for the estimation of the parameters and latent factors, Equation (1) can be viewed as the measurement equation and Equations (2)–(3) make up the transition equations (see the Technical Appendix for the matrix representation).

3. *Empirical results*

We now present the estimation results of our global model, Equations (1)–(3). Since this chapter focuses on the evolving linkages of the Australian business cycle with the rest of the world, our discussion will concentrate on the implications of the model estimates for Australia.

3.1. Parameter estimates

The parameter estimates of the model are given in Table 1. The estimates for the lagged dependent variables are all highly significant (at 1%),

Table 1. Parameter estimates of the dynamic factor model Equations (1)–(3)

	α_i	β_i	σ_{ε_i}		γ_i
Australia	0.58***	0.20***	0.67***	*Australia*	
				Asia factor	0.06**
China	0.36***	0.29	2.71***	EU factor	−0.27***
Hong Kong	0.80***	0.78***	1.38***	NA factor	−0.20
India	0.68***	0.52***	2.23***		
Indonesia	0.90***	0.60***	3.65***	*Asian region*	
Japan	0.75***	0.39***	0.94***	China	0.81***
Korea	0.68***	0.66***	1.94***	Hong Kong	0.51***
New Zealand	0.61***	0.41***	1.19***	India	0.14*
Singapore	0.67***	1.01***	1.90***	Indonesia	0.38***
Taiwan	0.68***	0.84***	1.22***	Japan	0.31***
				Korea	0.52***
Belgium	0.60***	0.52***	0.78***	New Zealand	0.01
France	0.79***	0.32***	0.48***	Singapore	0.59***
Germany	0.42***	0.44***	1.02***	Taiwan	0.48***
Italy	0.80***	0.42***	0.74***		
Netherlands	0.79***	0.40***	0.55***	*EU region*	
Spain	0.80***	0.30***	0.71***	Belgium	0.34***
United Kingdom	0.78***	0.31***	0.37***	France	0.18***
				Germany	1.18***
Canada	0.70***	0.29***	0.00	Italy	0.30***
United States	0.66***	0.30***	0.52***	Netherlands	0.28***
				Spain	0.22***
ϕ_f	0.72***	σ_f	1.21	United Kingdom	−0.03
ϕ_A	0.40***	σ_A	1.78		
ϕ_E	0.53***	σ_E	0.66	*NA region*	
ϕ_{NA}	0.34***	σ_{NA}	0.40	Canada	−1.25***
Log-likelihood	−2090			United States	−0.25*

Note: * designates significance at 10%, ** at 5%, and *** at 1%.

thus supporting the AR(1) specification. Apart from China, the impact coefficients for the global factor are positive and significant at 1% indicating a positive comovement between individual output growth rates and global economic fluctuations. The global factor also exhibits a high and significant degree of autocorrelation, as indicated by the autoregressive parameter $\phi_f = 0.72$ that suggests a high persistence of global business cycle fluctuations, which then impact on individual output growth rates.

Looking at the impact coefficients for the regional factors, most are significant except for the Asian factor loading for New Zealand, the European factor loading for the United Kingdom, and the North American factor loading for Australia. Concentrating on the two significant regional factor loadings for Australia leads us to suggest that Australian business cycles comove positively with the Asian regional cycles but in the opposite direction to the European regional cycles. The regional factors also exhibit positive autocorrelation, however, these are lower than that of the global factor (which are $\phi_A = 0.41$, $\phi_E = 0.53$, and $\phi_{NA} = 0.35$). This result indicates that most of the persistent, or low-frequency, comovement across economies is generated by the global factor. The higher-frequency fluctuations would seem to be better captured by the regional factors.

3.2. Variance decomposition

We decompose the variance of Australian output growth into the relative contributions that are due to each of the four latent factors and the idiosyncratic shock. Given the factors are orthogonal to each other by construction, the variance of the Australian output growth rate can be written as

$$\begin{aligned}\text{var}(y_{1,t}) = {} & \frac{(\beta_1)^2}{1-(\alpha_1)^2}\text{var}(f_t) + \frac{(\gamma_1^A)^2}{1-(\alpha_1)^2}\text{var}(n_{A,t}) + \frac{(\gamma_1^E)^2}{1-(\alpha_1)^2}\text{var}(n_{E,t}) \\ & + \frac{(\gamma_1^{\text{NA}})^2}{1-(\alpha_1)^2}\text{var}(n_{NA,t}) + \frac{1}{1-(\alpha_1)^2}\text{var}(\varepsilon_{1,t}). \qquad (4)\end{aligned}$$

Hence, the shares of volatility due to each component are

$$\begin{array}{ll}\text{Global factor:} & (((\beta_1)^2/1-(\alpha_1)^2)\text{var}(f_t))/\text{var}(y_{1,t}) \\ \text{Asian factor:} & (((\gamma_1^A)^2/1-(\alpha_1)^2)\text{var}(n_{A,t}))/\text{var}(y_{1,t}) \\ \text{European factor:} & (((\gamma_1^E)^2/1-(\alpha_1)^2)\text{var}(n_{E,t}))/\text{var}(y_{1,t}) \\ \text{North American factor:} & (((\gamma_1^{NA})^2/1-(\alpha_1)^2)\text{var}(n_{NA,t}))/\text{var}(y_{1,t}) \\ \text{Idiosyncratic Australian shock:} & ((1/1-(\alpha_1)^2)\text{var}(\varepsilon_{1,t}))/\text{var}(y_{1,t}).\end{array} \qquad (5)$$

Table 2 reports the relative contributions of the global and regional factors to variations in the Australian output growth rate over the whole sample period (since 1991). The global factor plays a major role and accounts for 11% of the output growth variation. From the regional factors, the European factor is the most dominant, accounting for 5.7%, while the Asian factor explains 2.3% and the North American factor contributes just 1.1% of the output growth variation. Over the whole

Table 2. Variance decomposition of Australian output growth

Global factor	0.11
Asian factor	0.02
European factor	0.06
North American factor	0.01
Idiosyncratic Australian shock	0.80

sample then, we cannot conclude that the Asian region has played a significant role in Australian output growth variance. Nevertheless, it may have begun to play an increasingly important role, something we will try to establish later.

3.3. Estimated factor roles

Figure 1 presents the estimated global factor and the three regional factors with Australian output growth. The fluctuations of the global factor reflect the major world economic events of the past two decades and perhaps the coordinated policy responses to them: the global recession in the early 1990s due to tight anti-inflationary policies of major industrialized countries and the uncertainty created by the first Gulf war; the 1997–1998 Asian financial crisis that was followed by a quick recovery; the global slowdown associated with the first dot-com bubble in 2000 and then the terrorist attack in the United States in 2001; the beginning of the second Iraq war in 2004 that had a short impact with a subsequent economic turnaround; and the spectacular collapse of the world output growth associated with the global financial crisis that began in late 2007 and peaked in September 2008. According to the estimates, the global factor growth rate was −0.1% in December 2007, but fell to a dismal −8.3% in March 2009.

The region-specific factors are orthogonal to the global factor by construction and any common shocks affecting all countries will show up in the global factor, hence, the region-specific factors capture the remaining, more high-frequency, comovements among countries within each group. They may be capturing real exchange rate variations between the regions, or uncoordinated policy responses across countries. One interesting feature is that the Asian factor exhibits the most volatility with a standard deviation of 1.95, followed by 1.19 for Europe, and 0.41 for North America, while the global factor has a measure of 1.84. The fluctuations in the region-specific factors highlight some important cyclical episodes specific to each region. While the 1990–1991 recession had a relatively mild effect on the Asian region, it was particularly hard hit by the Asian financial crisis that started in 1997 with the growth rate sinking to −5.7% in March 1998. Since most of the countries in the Asian region rely heavily on exports to drive their economic growth, the global collapse of industrial production and trade after the 2007–2008 global financial crisis negatively affected the region with its factor growth rate falling rapidly to −2.9% in December 2008. This was followed by a rebound (although still with negative growth, −0.8%) in March 2009. The European regional factor started off with a 7.2% growth rate in June 1991, but this was followed by three extended periods of negative growth from 1992 to 2005. During the global financial crisis, according to the estimated

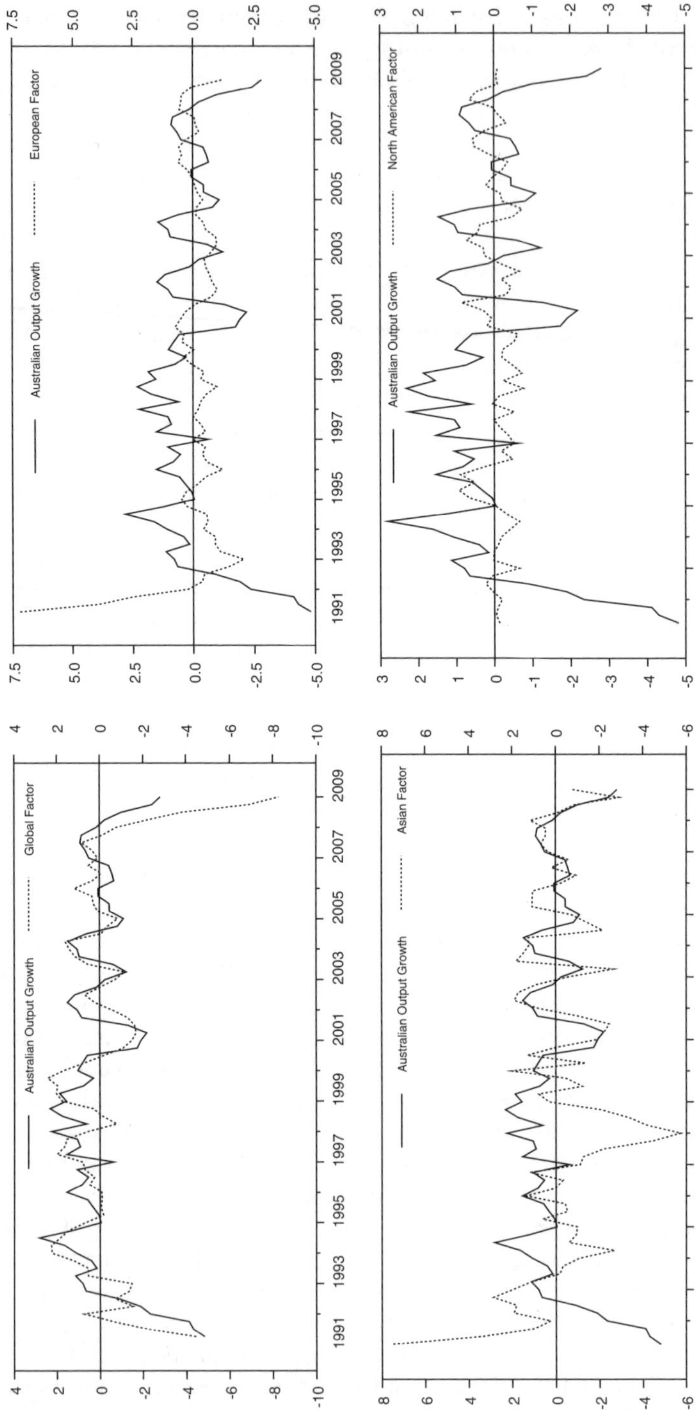

Fig. 1. Australian output growth and dynamic latent factors.

factor, the European region managed to maintain positive but low growth rates throughout 2008. However, the regional economy could not sustain the performance and the growth rate dipped into the negative territory with −1.2% at the end of the sample. The cyclical fluctuations exhibited by the North American factor broadly mirror most of the main economic events that we discussed for the global factor. Comparing the effect of the global financial crisis on the three regions, the negative impact hit the Asian region the quickest and its growth rate suffered the deepest loss given that most of the countries are small open economies. The North American region experienced three quarters of (small) negative growth starting in September 2008. The spillover of the cyclical downturn affected the European region with a delay after displaying some economic resilience (although weak) throughout 2008.

It is well known that Australian output growth over a number of decades appears remarkably similar to that of the United States. Given this fact, an interesting puzzle is why the North American factor had an insignificant effect on Australia. The resolution of this apparent puzzle is that the marginal effect of the global factor on Australia was large, positive, and significant, and this global factor was heavily influenced by the largest economy in the world, the United States.[4] The global factor is likely to be picking up intercountry transmission channels beyond trade links. In particular, international financial integration is likely to go a long way in understanding its global characteristic.

3.4. Dynamic correlations

Figures 2–5 plot the dynamic correlations with a four-year rolling window between Australian output growth and the four latent factors – the global, Asian, European, and North American growth rates. These results will help to answer whether there has been some decoupling of the Australian business cycles from the European and North American business cycles and an increasing convergence toward the Asian business cycles. Figure 2 shows that the degree of synchronization was high between the Australian business cycle and the global factor – the average dynamic correlation for the sample is 0.54. However, there was a marked fall in the correlation that turned negative in 1999 to reach a low of −0.08. Since 2001 the correlation hovered around 0.67 but with substantial and increasing variability. At the start of the global financial crisis in late 2007, the correlation decreased. However, by the peak of the crisis in the second half of 2008, the

[4] Indeed the (static) correlation between the global factor and U.S. output growth is 0.8 and the global factor loading on the U.S. output growth is highly significant and large, $\beta_{\text{U.S.}} = 0.3$. Both of these facts support the hypothesis that the United States represents an important source of global economic fluctuations.

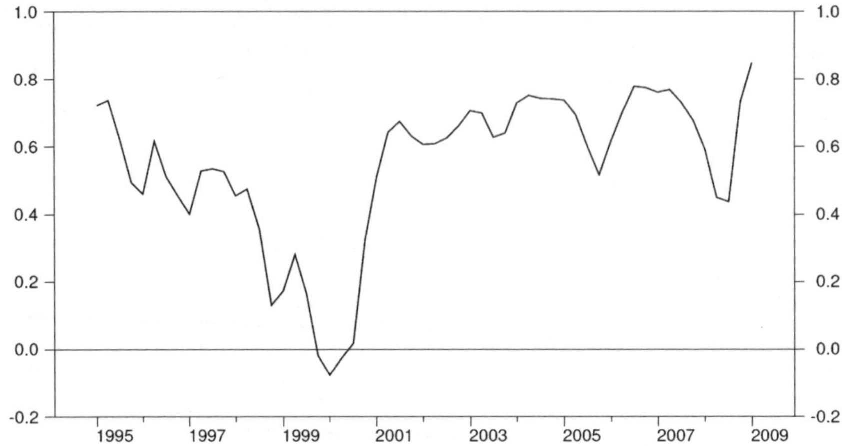

Fig. 2. Dynamic correlation between Australian output growth and global factor output growth.

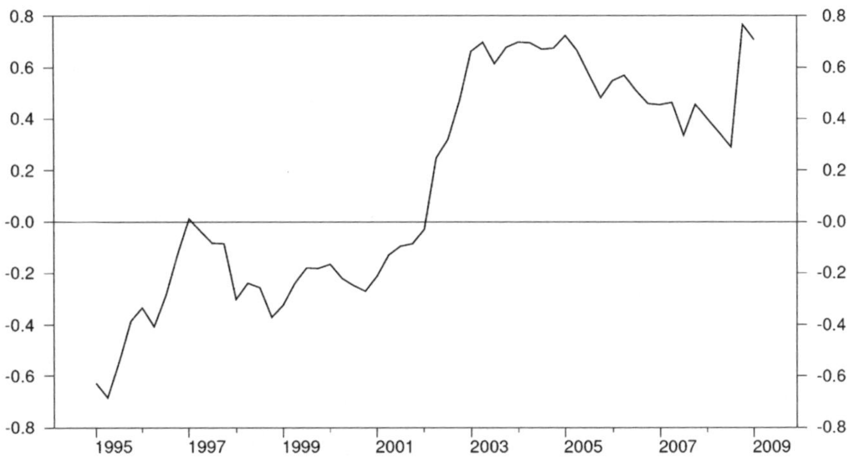

Fig. 3. Dynamic correlation between Australian output growth and Asian factor output growth.

correlation had risen rapidly, reaching a high of 0.85 in March 2009. At the height of the crisis, the global business cycle factor was an important driver in dragging down the Australian output growth, which supports the variance decomposition result that the global factor was the most important external driver in explaining the variations of Australian output growth.

An interesting pattern emerges from the dynamic correlation between Australian output growth and Asian factor growth rates as shown in Figure 3. The correlation statistic suggests that there were two distinct phases of business cycle linkage. Before June 2002, the Australian business

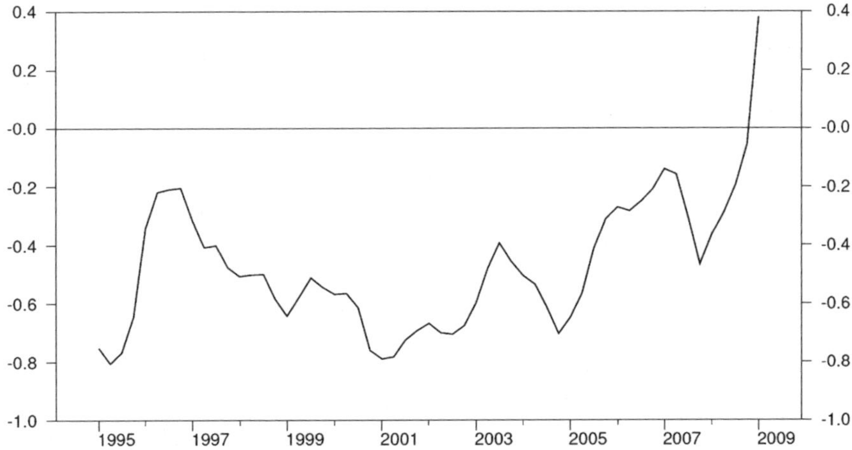

Fig. 4. Dynamic correlation between Australian output growth and European factor output growth.

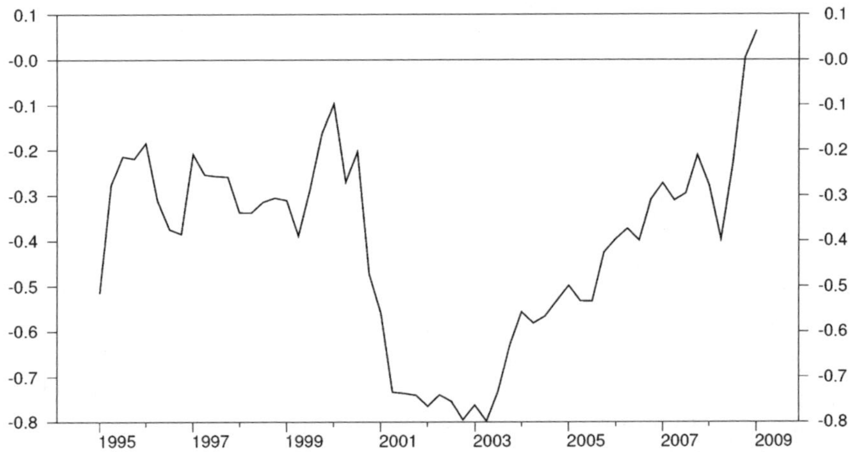

Fig. 5. Dynamic correlation between Australian output growth and North American factor output growth.

cycle moved in the opposite (or counter-cyclical) direction to that of the Asian factor. The correlation turned positive briefly around the 1997–1998 Asian financial crisis, suggesting that Australia was not immune from this regional shock. However, Australia reoriented its trading relationships by boosting links with its Asian neighbors, and so we observe that the correlation became positive after June 2002 reaching a local peak of 0.72 in March 2005 before falling to 0.29 in September 2008. However, in the last two quarters of the sample, the correlation jumped up again, reflecting the additional importance of Asia for Australia in the latest global economic downturn. In fact, this meant that Australia actually benefited from the relatively quick recovery of Asia in 2009, so that its experience of the crisis was the most benign among rich industrialized countries.

Figures 4 and 5 show that Australian output growth movements have been negatively correlated with the European and North American factors throughout much of the sample period, except in the latest financial crisis. In both cases, the degree of synchronization increased with the onset of the global financial crisis, and turned positive at the end of the sample, reflecting the additional impact of the crisis on Australia in weighing down the growth rates of countries in these two regions. Although the correlations in March 2009 for Europe (0.38) and North America (0.06) took the highest values for the whole sample period, these were still lower than that for the Asian region (0.71) at the end date. While the level of synchronicity between Australia and North America fluctuated over time below zero, the correlation measure fell dramatically in 2001 and reached its lowest point in June 2003 at −0.80. This decrease in synchronicity evidences the fact that Australia was not as badly affected by the 2001 slowdown as Canada and the United States. Inspecting the output growth rates we observe that they fell dramatically from 5.1% in 2000 to 1.8% in 2001 for Canada and from 3.6% to 0.8% for the United States, while the Australian economy performed relatively well, with the growth rate falling from 3.4% to a mere 2.1%.

3.5. Some robustness checks

To check the robustness of the results, we estimated a dynamic factor model with an AR(2) specification in both the output growth and latent factor equations.[5] Most of the second-order lagged autoregressive parameters for the output growth equations are not statistically significant. Figure 6 compares the estimated latent factors of the AR(1) and AR(2) models. The two series for each factor are very similar and the turning points match quite closely. However, the AR(2) model offers a more exaggerated amplitude for some end points and turning points of the latent factors. Inspecting the dynamic correlations shown in Figure 7, the basic story does not change between the two models, except in the correlation between Australia and North America where we do not observe the same decrease in the 2000–2001 slowdown.

To what extent are our results driven by the specification that the Asian region is dependent on the global and only the Asian regional

[5] We restrict our attention to AR(2) but acknowledge that in principle higher order autoregressive specifications might also be considered. However, this increases dramatically the number of parameters to be estimated and we could not achieve numerical convergence during estimation. Further, it is unlikely that such high-order models will be consistent with the univariate time-series process for GDP growth.

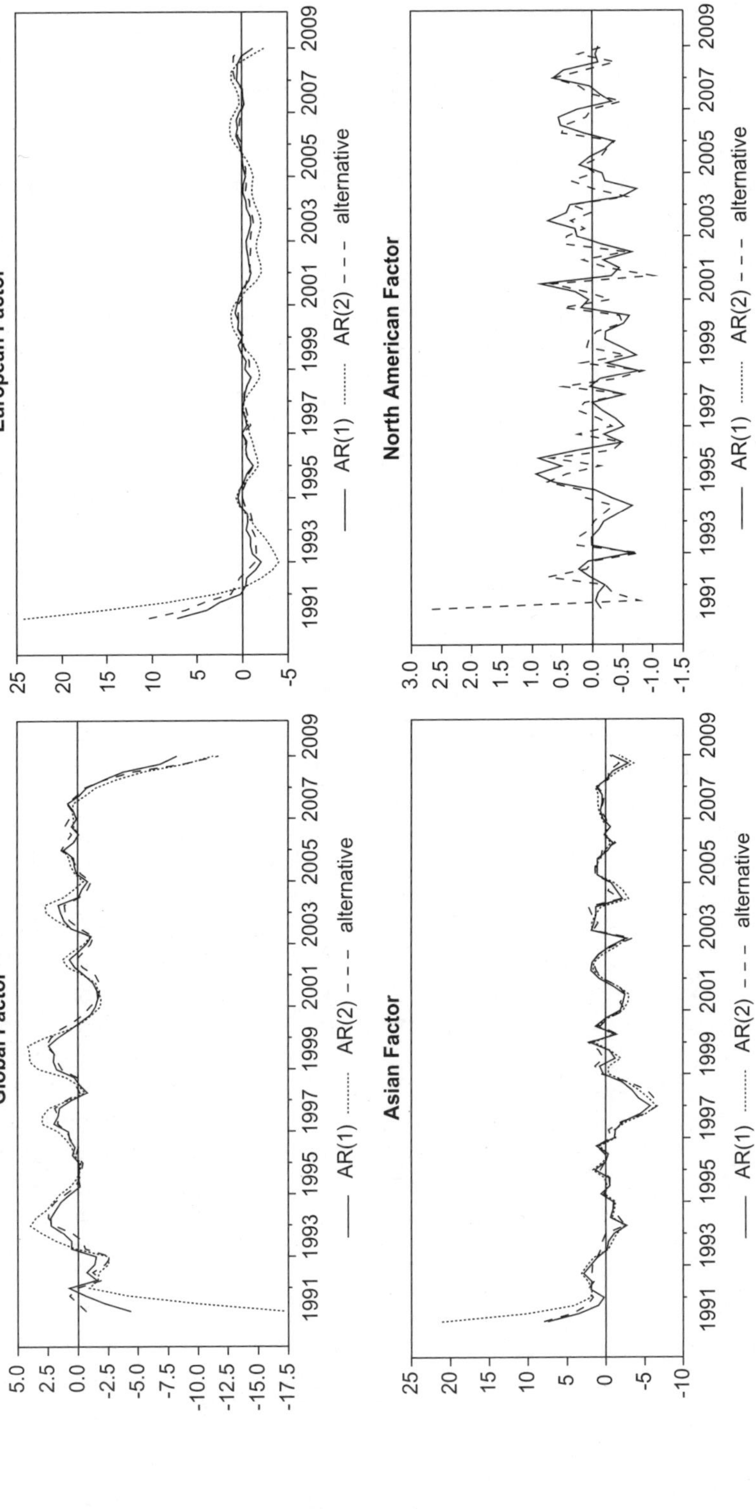

Fig. 6. Comparison of estimated latent factors between the AR(1), AR(2) and alternative models.

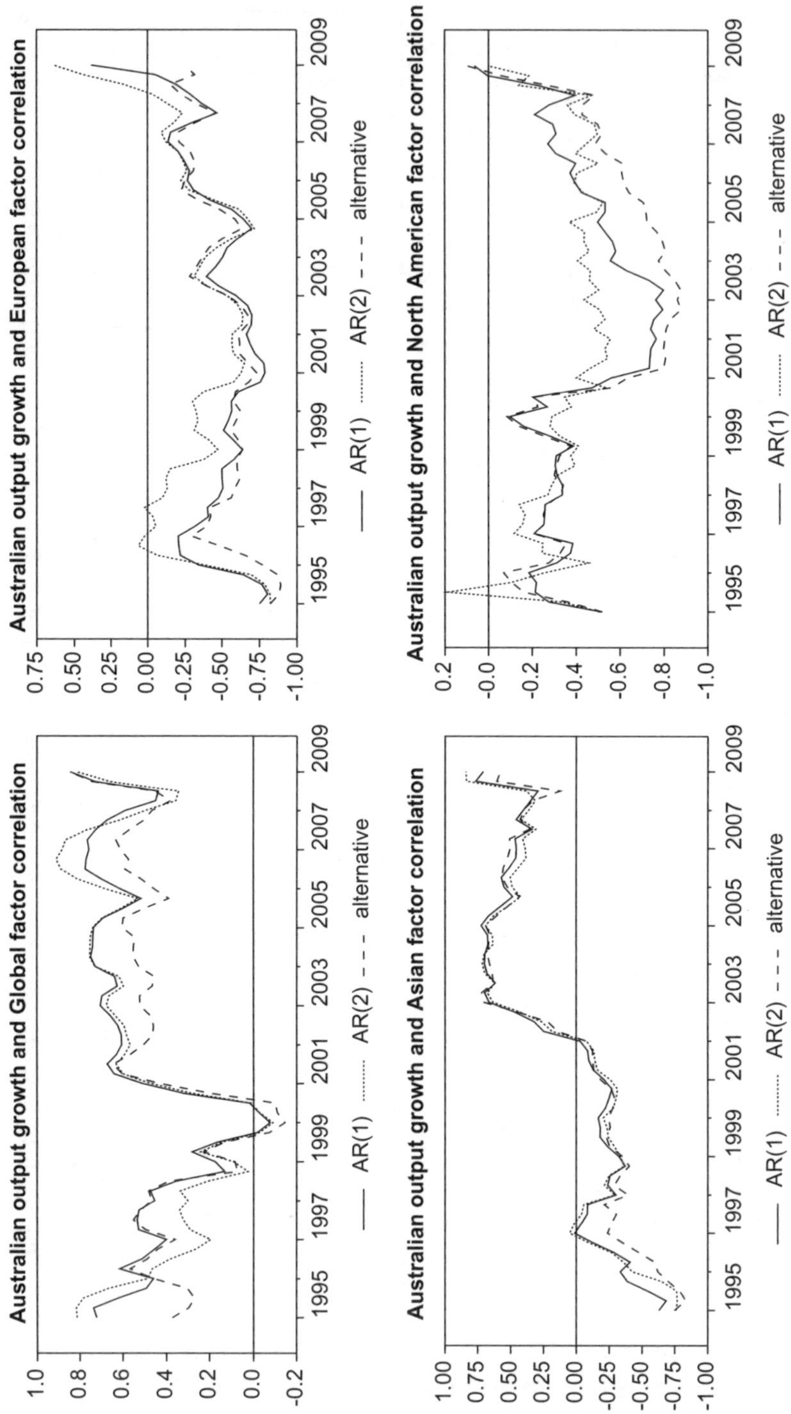

Fig. 7. ***Comparison of dynamic correlations between the AR(1), AR(2) and alternative models.***

factor? Given many countries in the region are small open economies that rely heavily on the global export markets, it is plausible to modify our assumption that the Asian region is influenced also by European and North American factors. The estimated results of the latent factors and dynamic correlations from this "alternative" model are included in Figures 6 and 7. In general, the result from the alternative model is not different qualitatively from our AR(1) model. Adding the European and North American factors to the Asian region does not change our conclusions in regard to the Australia–Asia business cycle evolution, which is the focus of this chapter.

4. Conclusions

In the aftermath of the global financial crisis of 2007–2008, it appears that emerging market countries recovered from the crisis sooner and faster than advanced economies in general. It has even been suggested that these emerging market countries are the "new engines of global growth." This suggests that business cycles in emerging market economies have become less dependent on those of advanced economies. Among the developed economies in the world, Australia performed remarkably well in response to the global financial crisis of 2007–2008. One contributing factor is the increasing trade links Australia has developed with Asian economies, in particular China and India, which has kept up its level and value of its exports and hence helped output growth.

We posed the question about whether there has been a gradual decoupling of the Australian business cycle from its trading partners in Europe and North America, and a closer convergence toward its trading partners in Asia. We set up a dynamic latent factor model to estimate common dynamic components or factors for the real GDP growth rate of 19 countries. We performed variance decomposition over the whole sample to examine the sources of Australian output growth variations and found that the global factor contributed the most to explaining the variations, followed by the idiosyncratic European factor, then the Asian factor and finally the North American factor in a distant last place. However, we found that the correlation between Australian output growth movements and Asian business cycle factor evolved from being small and negative to positive and large after 2002. The idiosyncratic business cycle factors for Europe and North America were negatively correlated with Australian output growth for most of the sample period before turning positive owing to the intense effects of the global financial crisis of 2007–2008. This evidence supports the hypothesis that the Australian economy has decoupled to some extent from Europe, was not much coupled with North America except insofar as the United States drove the global factor, and has increasingly and positively coupled with Asia.

Acknowledgments

We wish to thank the editor Yin-Wong Cheung and an anonymous referee for their helpful comments and suggestions. A substantial amount of work was carried out while Shawn Leu visited the Department of Economics at Macquarie University, Shawn would like to gratefully acknowledge their support and hospitality.

Appendix

Data Appendix

The table below displays the source of the real GDP series for the 19 countries in the sample and the regional classification of countries, except for Australia that is set up as the home country.

Australia	OECD				
Asia		*Europe*		*North America*	
China	Datastream	Belgium	IFS	Canada	OECD
Hong Kong	Datastream	France	IFS	United States	OECD
India	Datastream	Germany	IFS		
Indonesia	Datastream	Italy	IFS		
Japan	IFS	Netherlands	OECD		
Korea	IFS	Spain	OECD		
New Zealand	Datastream	United Kingdom	OECD		
Singapore	Datastream				
Taiwan	Datastream				

Technical Appendix

The state-space representation consists of a measurement equation:

$$\boldsymbol{w}_t = \boldsymbol{z}_t + F\boldsymbol{\xi}_t + \boldsymbol{v}_t$$

and a transition equation:

$$\boldsymbol{\xi}_t = G\boldsymbol{\xi}_{t-1} + \boldsymbol{\upsilon}_t,$$

where $\boldsymbol{w}_t$ is the vector of observable variables (output growth rates), $\boldsymbol{\xi}_t$ is the vector of latent variables (the unobservable global and regional factors), and $\boldsymbol{z}_t$ is a vector of exogenous or predetermined variables (lagged output growth). $\boldsymbol{v}_t$ and $\boldsymbol{\upsilon}_t$ are white noise innovation vectors that are assumed to be uncorrelated at all lags, $E(\boldsymbol{v}_t\boldsymbol{\upsilon}_\tau) = 0$ for all t and τ.

Transforming Equation (1) into the measurement equation yields:

$$\left[\begin{array}{c} y_{1,t} \\ \hline y_{2,t} \\ \vdots \\ y_{10,t} \\ \hline y_{11,t} \\ \vdots \\ y_{17,t} \\ \hline y_{18,t} \\ y_{19,t} \end{array}\right] = \left[\begin{array}{c} \alpha_1 y_{1,t-1} \\ \hline \alpha_2 y_{2,t-1} \\ \vdots \\ \alpha_{10} y_{10,t-1} \\ \hline \alpha_{11} y_{11,t-1} \\ \vdots \\ \alpha_{17} y_{17,t-1} \\ \hline \alpha_{18} y_{18,t-1} \\ \alpha_{19} y_{19,t-1} \end{array}\right] + \left[\begin{array}{cccc} \beta_1 & \gamma_1^A & \gamma_1^E & \gamma_1^{NA} \\ \hline \beta_2 & \gamma_2^A & 0 & 0 \\ \vdots & \vdots & \vdots & \vdots \\ \beta_{10} & \gamma_{10}^A & 0 & 0 \\ \hline \beta_{11} & 0 & \gamma_{11}^E & 0 \\ \vdots & \vdots & \vdots & \vdots \\ \beta_{17} & 0 & \gamma_{17}^E & 0 \\ \hline \beta_{18} & 0 & 0 & \gamma_{18}^{NA} \\ \beta_{19} & 0 & 0 & \gamma_{19}^{NA} \end{array}\right] \begin{bmatrix} f_t \\ n_{A,t} \\ n_{E,t} \\ n_{NA,t} \end{bmatrix} + \left[\begin{array}{c} \varepsilon_{1,t} \\ \hline \varepsilon_{2,t} \\ \vdots \\ \varepsilon_{10,t} \\ \hline \varepsilon_{11,t} \\ \vdots \\ \varepsilon_{17,t} \\ \hline \varepsilon_{18,t} \\ \varepsilon_{19,t} \end{array}\right] \tag{A.1}$$

where the top partition corresponds to Australia as the home country, and the other partitions correspond to the Asian, European, and North American countries, respectively.

Combining Equations (2) and (3) gives the transition equation:

$$\begin{bmatrix} f_t \\ n_{A,t} \\ n_{E,t} \\ n_{NA,t} \end{bmatrix} = \begin{bmatrix} \phi_{f,1} & 0 & 0 & 0 \\ 0 & \phi_{A,1} & 0 & 0 \\ 0 & 0 & \phi_{E,1} & 0 \\ 0 & 0 & 0 & \phi_{NA,1} \end{bmatrix} \begin{bmatrix} f_{t-1} \\ n_{A,t-1} \\ n_{E,t-1} \\ n_{NA,t-1} \end{bmatrix} + \begin{bmatrix} \eta_{f,t} \\ \eta_{A,t} \\ \eta_{E,t} \\ \eta_{NA,t} \end{bmatrix}. \tag{A.2}$$

The covariance matrix for $\boldsymbol{v}_t$ is

$$\begin{bmatrix} \sigma_{\varepsilon_1}^2 & 0 & 0 & 0 \\ 0 & \sigma_{\varepsilon_2}^2 & 0 & 0 \\ \vdots & \vdots & \ddots & \vdots \\ 0 & 0 & 0 & \sigma_{\varepsilon_{19}}^2 \end{bmatrix} \tag{A.3}$$

and the covariance matrix for $\boldsymbol{\upsilon}_t$ is

$$\begin{bmatrix} \sigma_{\eta_f}^2 & 0 & 0 & 0 \\ 0 & \sigma_{\eta_A}^2 & 0 & 0 \\ 0 & 0 & \sigma_{\eta_E}^2 & 0 \\ 0 & 0 & 0 & \sigma_{\eta_{NA}}^2 \end{bmatrix} \tag{A.4}$$

References

Altug, S. (1989), Time-to-build and aggregate fluctuations: some new evidence. *International Economic Review* 30 (4), 889–920.

Backus, D., Kehoe, P., Kydland, F. (1995), International business cycles: theory and evidence. In: Cooley, T. (Ed.), *Frontiers of Business Cycle Research*. Princeton University Press, Princeton, NJ, pp. 331–357.

Baxter, M. (1995), International trade and business cycles. In: Grossman, G., Rogoff, K. (Eds.), *Handbook of International Economics*, vol. 3. North-Holland, Amsterdam, pp. 1801–1864.

Baxter, M., Kouparitsas, M. (2005), Determinants of business cycle co-movement: a robust analysis. *Journal of Monetary Economics* 52 (1), 113–157.

Clark, T., Shin, K. (2000), The sources of fluctuations within and across countries. In: Hess, G., van Wincoop, E. (Eds.), *International Macroeconomics*. Cambridge University Press, Boston, MA, pp. 189–220.

Doyle, B., Faust, J. (2002), An investigation of co-movements among the growth rates of the G7 countries. *Federal Reserve Bulletin* October, 427–437.

Gregory, A., Head, A., Raynauld, J. (1997), Measuring world business cycles. *International Economic Review* 38 (3), 677–702.

Harding, D., Pagan, A. (2002), Dissecting the cycle: a methodological investigation. *Journal of Monetary Economics* 49 (2), 365–381.

Kose, M. (2002), Explaining business cycles in small open economies: how much do world prices matter? *Journal of International Economics* 56 (2), 299–327.

Kose, M., Otrok, C., Whiteman, C. (2003), International business cycles: world, region, and country-specific factors. *American Economic Review* 93 (4), 1216–1239.

Kose, M., Otrok, C., Prasad, E. (2008). Global business cycles: convergence or decoupling?. NBER Working Paper No. 14292.

Lowe, P. (2009). The growth of Asia and some implications for Australia, Talk to Citi Australia Inaugural Australian Investment Conference, Sydney – 19 October 2009. Available at http://www.rba.gov.au/speeches/2009/sp-ag-191009.html

Lumsdaine, R., Prasad, E. (2003), Identifying the common component in international economic fluctuations. *Economic Journal* 113 (484), 101–127.

Mendoza, E. (1995), The terms of trade, the real exchange rate, and economic fluctuations. *International Economic Review* 36 (1), 101–137.

Monfort, A., Renne, J.-P., Ruffer, R., Vitale, G. (2003). Is economic activity in the G7 synchronized? Common shocks versus spillover effects. CEPR Discussion Paper No. 4119.

Sargent, T., Sims, C. (1977), Business cycle modeling without pretending to have too much a priori economic theory. In: Sims, C. (Ed.), *New Methods in Business Cycle Research*. Federal Reserve Bank of Minneapolis, Minneapolis, MN, pp. 45–108.

Stock, J., Watson, M. (1989), New indexes of coincident and leading economic indicators. In: Blanchard, O., Fischer, S. (Eds.), *NBER Macroeconomics Annual*. MIT Press, Cambridge, MA, pp. 351–394.

PART IV

Domestic Finance and Capital Flows

CHAPTER 13

What are the Sources of Financing for Chinese Firms?

Galina Hale[a] and Cheryl Long[b]

[a]*Research Department, Federal Reserve Bank of San Francisco, Economic Research, 101 Markeet St., San Francisco, CA 94105, USA*
E-mail address: galina.b.hale@sf.frb.org
[b]*Department of Economics, Colgate University, Economics, 13 Oak Dr., Hamilton, NY 13346, USA*
E-mail address: cxlong@colgate.edu

Abstract
In this chapter we study internal and external, formal and informal, financing sources of Chinese firms during the period 1997–2006, by analyzing balance sheet data from the *Chinese Industrial Surveys of Medium-sized and Large Firms* for 2000–2006 and survey data from the *Large-Scale Survey of Private Enterprises in China* conducted in 1997, 2000, 2002, 2004, and 2006.
The following stylized facts emerge from our analysis: (1) State-owned firms continue to enjoy more generous external finances than other types of Chinese firms. (2) Chinese private firms have resorted to various ways of overcoming financial constraints, including reliance on the increasingly more mature informal financial markets, cost savings through lower inventory and other working capital requirements, and greater reliance on retained earnings. (3) Substantial variations exist in financial access among private firms, with small private firms facing more financial constraints whereas more established firms having financial access more equal to their SOE counterparts. (4) Although not as accessible as for SOEs, the Chinese formal financial sector does provide Chinese private firms with substantial financial resources, especially for their short-term needs during daily operations. (5) The most pressing financial constraint facing Chinese private firms is their limited ability to secure long-term funds to invest for growth, and resolving this issue should be one of the top goals of financial reforms in China.

Keywords: Formal and informal financing, financial constraints, China, firm ownership

JEL classifications: O16, O17

Frontiers of Economics and Globalization
Volume 9 ISSN: 1574-8715
DOI: 10.1108/S1574-8715(2011)0000009018

1. Introduction

One big puzzle in China's rapid economic growth over the past three decades relates to the financial sector. On the one hand, the Chinese economy has continuously achieved one of the fastest growth rates in the world since the late 1970s, with a large part of the growth driven by the rapid development of the private sector, which outpaced the growth rate of the state sector. On the other hand, a vast majority of researchers believe that the formal financial sector in China lacks efficiency, especially when it comes to financing private firms. In this section, we review the relevant literature, appraise China's financial reforms, and discuss potential theories and corresponding evidence that help reconcile the apparent paradox.

The importance of finances for economic development has long been advocated and empirically tested in the economic literature. As early as 1911, Schumpeter linked the importance of financial services to firms' capacity to engage in technological innovation and thus a country's economic development. Based on a country-level analysis, King and Levine (1993) provide evidence that multiple indicators of financial development are not only positively correlated with the present levels of multiple economic indicators but also with their future values. Using industry-level data for a large number of countries, Rajan and Zingales (1998) show that industries with higher external finance requirements tend to grow faster in countries with more developed capital markets. In the Chinese context, Cull and Xu (2005) provide evidence that firms with better access to bank loans are more likely to reinvest.

Lardy (2004) provides an overview of the historical background of Chinese economic reforms and argues that reforms in the product and labor markets have been much faster than those in the financial market. While the Chinese economy is very close to completing the transition from planned to market-oriented product and labor markets, interest rates are still subject to government intervention to a large degree. The work by Cull and Xu provides further evidence that there have been reversals in the reforms of the banking sector (by far the most important component of the Chinese financial sector) in the 1990s. In particular, Cull and Xu (2000, 2003) show that in the late 1980s banks proved to be more efficient in allocating funds to more productive and more profitable firms than bureaucrats in charge of direct government transfers; but by the mid-1990s, the correlation between loans and productivity (or profitability) had disappeared or weakened as banks increasingly assumed bailout responsibility. In contrast, however, Demetriades *et al.* (2008) provide evidence that bank loans are positively correlated with firm productivity in China using data from a later time period.

Other studies provide evidence that private firms, which are the most productive and profitable firms in China, have been discriminated against in the financial market. Using matched bank-firm data from two coastal provinces in China, Brandt and Li (2003) provide direct evidence that in 1994 and 1997 private firms were discriminated against by township branches of the Agricultural Bank of China (one of the "Big Four" in China[1]) and the local Rural Credit Cooperatives, compared to township enterprises, in two main ways: Private firms were less likely to obtain a loan, and were required more loan collateral. In addition, Ferri and Liu (2009) use a representative sample of Chinese firms to show that the cost of financing is significantly lower for SOEs than for nonstate firms.

Using survey data that cover all regions in China between 2002 and 2004, Dollar and Wei (2007) show that on average Chinese domestic private firms have significantly higher returns to capital than SOEs, implying excess funds going to the SOEs, that is, an inefficient allocation of financial resources. Using the generalized method of moments (GMM) to estimate the investment Euler equation models (based on a balanced panel of medium to large firms for 2000–2004), Liu and Siu (2006) similarly show that the implied cost of capital derived from their estimated structural parameters is substantially higher for private and foreign-invested firms than for SOEs in China. Boyreau-Debray and Wei (2005) take a different perspective and show that in the 1990s the Chinese financial system was associated with low efficiency of allocating funds across regions (low capital mobility across regions) and low efficiency in providing consumption risk sharing for households. More generally, Hsieh and Klenow (2009) estimate that the Chinese manufacturing sector could improve its total factor productivity by 30–50% through more efficient capital allocation.

The existence of these problems and the continued failure to resolve them are discussed in Dobson and Kashyap (2006), where the authors make the astute observation that China's gradualist approach to reforms largely accounts for its continued struggle in reforming the financial sector. A related way of viewing the continued difficulty in reforming the financial sector in China is that it has shouldered much of the reform costs in China since the beginning of the reform era. In doing so, many of the obstacles encountered in reforming the fiscal system, the exporting sector, and the SOEs have been overcome by shifting the costs away from the targeted sectors to the banking sector.

Thus, it may only be natural that during the first two decades of China's reforms the financial sector was the least reformed in the economic realm.

---

[1] The largest four banks in China, often referred to as the "Big Four," are the Industrial and Commerce Bank of China (ICBC), the Bank of China (BOC), the Construction Bank of China (CBC), and the Agricultural Bank of China (ABC). Increasingly, the Bank of Communications (BoCom) has been included in the group known as the "Big Five." The shares of these banks are all largely owned by the state, with small percentages of shares owned by foreign shareholders.

For example, when SOEs were required to become independent accounting units subject to hard budget constraints in the 1980s, they first had to be weaned away from direct government budgetary funds. The banks, which had just begun to transition from their old role of government accountants/cashiers to their new status as modern financial institutions, were ordered to offer loans at government-set rates to replace the direct government transfer, often without regard to efficiency standards. Other examples include preferential bank loans offered to SOEs in the 1990s to help discharge former employees when they went through "restructuring" (which often was a thinly veiled privatization) and other mandates in later years to make preferential loans to firms and organizations that help solve various social issues (such as employment opportunities for people with disabilities, etc.).

Since the mid-1990s, the government has gone through multiple rounds of reforms to help transform the old financial institutions into authentic commercial banks. By the end of 2006, in preparation for China's commitment to open its domestic financial market under the World Trade Organization (WTO) rules, most of China's "Big Five" had obtained foreign partners as shareholders and were listed on foreign stock exchanges, although the government still maintained controlling stakes in these banks.[2] These reforms, however, have not truly improved the efficiency of the major state banks (Dobson and Kashyap, 2006).

A puzzle related to this discussion then is the following: In spite of the numerous inefficiencies in the financial sector and the apparent discrimination against private firms, the Chinese economy has maintained one of the fastest growth rates throughout human history. In particular, private firms have proven to be the most energetic and productive sector in the economy, with their share in total national industrial output quickly rising from less than 1% in 1978 to 23% in 2006.[3]

To explain the apparent paradox, Allen *et al.* (2005, 2008) argue that the informal financial sector must have somehow compensated for the inefficiency of the formal financial market in China such that the private sector has been able to develop rapidly. Following this argument, one big task for researchers would be to investigate what informal mechanisms exist and how they work to alleviate the financial obstacles faced by Chinese private firms.

Studies of various authors on the development of informal mechanisms to overcome financial constraints or facilitate firm finances in China can be categorized into this line of research, and several mechanisms have been suggested in these investigations. First of all, internal finances are an important source for firm finances in China, whether they are private firms

---

[2] The only exception is the Agricultural Bank of China (ABC).
[3] Authors' calculation using the *Statistical Yearbook of China* for various years.

or SOEs (Lardy, 1998, 2004; Allen *et al.*, 2005). Lardy (2004) points out that in 2002, close to 50% of investment was funded by firms' own retained earnings in China. In addition, Allen *et al.* (2005) discuss the important role of funds from family, relatives, and friends in both the start-up stage and the continued growth period of private firms.

Other potential channels for funding private firms are foreign direct investment (FDI) into Chinese private firms and trade credit, especially from the state-owned sector to the private sector (Ge and Qiu, 2007; Cull *et al.*, 2009). Based on case studies, Huang (2004) argues that private firms have faced the highest degree of financial constraints in China throughout the reform era, which explains to a large degree the rapid inflow of FDI into China, as FDI serves to ease the financial constraints faced by Chinese private firms. Hèricourt and Poncet (2008) use data from a World Bank survey of Chinese firms to provide supporting evidence of Huang's argument. Poncet *et al.* (2008) further confirm this finding using the annual industrial survey data. Regarding the channel of trade credit, we will discuss it in more detail in Section 4.2, where we provide evidence refuting its importance.

Finally, rather than studying the supply of funds, at least one paper addresses the issue of private firm finances from the demand side. Using firm-level data from China's two recent censuses (Industry Census 1995 and Economic Census 2004) and a new measure of industry proximity based on the Hausmann–Klinger product proximity matrix (Hausmann and Klinger, 2006), Long and Zhang (2010) show that Chinese firms have become more interconnected during this period, which helps ease firms' credit constraints through two mechanisms: (1) Finer division of labor among interconnected firms lowers the capital barriers to entry and thus reduces the fixed investment required and (2) closer proximity makes the provision of trade credit among firms easier. The authors thus argue that institutional innovations such as those in production organizations could help alleviate firms' financial constraints. In line with these authors' emphasis on the demand side of finances, we will discuss two additional mechanisms that Chinese private firms rely on to help overcome financial constraints.

Following the literature, we pursue two main tasks in the chapter. First, we investigate whether in 2006, the last full year before the outbreak of the liquidity crisis and the global recession, private firms still had more restricted access to formal external finance than SOEs, despite all the reforms. Second, once we establish that private firms still find it hard to access formal external finance, we study sources that private firms rely on to substitute for external finance, including ones studied in the literature (informal lending, trade credit, and internal funds), as well as additional mechanisms that we have newly uncovered.

The rest of the chapter is organized as follows. Section 2 describes our data. Section 3 compares different firms in their access to finance, while Section 4 explores how Chinese private firms obtain finances. Section 5 concludes.

2. Data

Our data come from two main sources. First, we use balance sheet and ownership information from the *Chinese Industrial Surveys of Medium-sized and Large Firms for 2000–2006*, which includes all state-owned firms and firms of other ownership types that are in excess of a certain scale. This dataset is commonly referred to as the National Bureau of Statistics (NBS) industrial census, and it is an unbalanced panel with a total of 496,738 firms for 2000–2006.[4] For short, we will refer to this dataset as the "census" data. We use two versions of these data – the cross-section of firms in the last year of our sample (297,665 firms) and a balanced panel that includes only firms that were in our data in each of the years from 2000 to 2006 (48,382 firms, 338,674 observations).

Second, we use survey data from the *Large-Scale Survey of Private Enterprises in China* jointly conducted by the All China Federation of Industrial and Commerce (ACFIC) and the United Front of the Chinese Communist Party in 1997, 2000, 2002, 2004, and 2006, often with help from the Bureau of Industry and Commerce (the government agency in charge of firm registration). This survey is a repeated cross-section in which firms are not matched across years. A total of 18,527 firms are surveyed over these years, and only private firms are included. For short, we will refer to this dataset as the "survey" data.

The census data cover firms of all ownership types, including those with foreign shares. We classify firms by ownership types in two ways – by their registration type, and by the type of investor holding the majority share of the paid-up capital. While the first measure may be outdated, because the firm's registration information may not change as soon as its capital structure changes, it may be the registered ownership type, rather than the *de facto* ownership structure that determines the access to finance. We will refer to the two classifications as the *de jure* ownership (by registration) and the *de facto* ownership (by actual shares).

Table 1 shows, using the 2006 cross-section, that in most cases there is a good match between the two classifications. Note that one exception is the set of firms with the majority share held by a "legal person," which is mostly registered as private firm but could also be in other *de jure* ownership categories. In what follows, we will analyze results using both classifications, but for brevity we will only report results based on *de facto* classification.

While the census data mainly include medium-sized and large firms, there are many small firms in the data set as well, both because all SOE firms are included in these data sets and due to time lags in excluding firms

[4] While the raw data include 622,424 firms, after we drop observations with missing values for year, location, industry code, and observations with key variables missing or erroneously reported, we are left with 496,738 firms in the unbalanced panel data set.

Table 1. Firm distribution by* de facto *and* de jure *ownership type in 2006 census cross-section

De facto ownership	*De jure* ownership						Total
	State	Private	Collective	FRN	HMT	Other	
State	**12,309**	37	46	325	262	2,807	15,786
Private	104	**111,610**	862	2,054	1,600	27,843	144,073
Collective	100	378	**10,556**	354	344	4,324	16,056
FRN	2	112	3	**21,976**	251	173	22,517
HMT	3	102	9	380	**21,220**	155	21,869
Legal person	2,754	35,962	2,736	5,898	5,081	**23,590**	76,021
Other[a]	55	136	48	304	237	563	1,343
Total	15,327	148,337	14,260	31,291	28,995	59,455	297,665

Note: The numbers represent number of firms for each pair of *de jure* and *de facto* ownership types. Boldface numbers indicate number of firms that are categorized in the same way by either approach.
FRN, ownership by firms outside greater China area; HMT, ownership by firms from Hong Kong, Macao, and Taiwan.
[a]No group holds more than 50% shares.

that have fallen below the size threshold. For the purposes of our analysis, we classify all firms into four groups: small firms with assets less than 40 million renminbi (RMB), medium firms with assets between 40 million and 400 million RMB, large firms with assets between 400 million and 4 billion RMB, and giant firms with assets exceeding 4 billion RMB. The top panel of Table 2 gives the distribution of firms in 2006 from the NBS census data by these size categories and their *de facto* ownership types, for both our 2006 cross-section and for those firms that were in the data set continuously since 2000. The panel shows that small firms are predominantly private, while giant and large firms are mostly state owned, and that the balanced panel data set includes disproportionately fewer small and private firms. Panel B of Table 2 shows the size distribution of firms in the private firm survey data for both the pooled sample of 2000–2006 and for the 2006 survey. We can see that the private firm surveys almost exclusively cover small firms and as a result include many small private firms that are excluded from the census data. This distinction between the census data and the survey data is crucial, as it points to the importance of the latter in studying private firms, which are predominantly small firms.

3. Do state-owned firms have easier access to external financing?

As discussed previously, an important indicator of how efficiently the financial system operates in China is whether banks treat firms of different

Table 2. Size distribution (by assets) of firms by ownership type and sample (number of firms in each cell)

Panel A: NBS census data

2006 full cross-section

De facto ownership	Size distribution by assets				Total
	Small	Medium	Large	Giant	
State	8,383	5,681	1,467	255	15,786
Private	121,638	21,045	1,347	34	144,064
Collective	12,463	3,333	250	10	16,056
FRN	12,188	8,716	1,523	90	22,517
HMT	14,100	7,052	691	24	21,867
Legal person	55,124	17,877	2,706	310	76,017
Other	597	487	223	36	1,343
Total	224,493	64,191	8,207	759	297,650

Balanced panel sample as of 2006

De facto ownership	Size as				Total
	Small	Medium	Large	Giant	
State	3,396	2,708	690	127	6,921
Private	7,076	3,920	386	15	11,397
Collective	2,353	1,082	81	5	3,521
FRN	1,307	1,985	519	33	3,844
HMT	1,879	1,665	214	11	3,769
Legal person	4,363	3,678	793	116	8,950
Other	114	175	105	21	415
Total	20,488	15,213	2,788	328	38,817

Panel B: Size distribution of firms from private firm survey data

Pooled private firm sample for 2000, 2002, 2004, and 2006

	Small	Medium	Large	Giant	Total
Survey data	8,977	733	38	1	9,749

Private firm sample for 2006

	Small	Medium	Large	Giant	Total
Survey data	2,253	242	10	0	2,505

Note: We adopt the same size categories as used by the national statistical Bureau of China since 2003, where small firms are those with assets less than 40 million RMBs, medium firms are those with assets between 40 million and 400 million RMB, large firms are those with assets between 400 million and 4 billion RMB, and giant firms are those with assets exceeding 4 billion RMB.
FRN, ownership by firms outside greater China area; HMT, ownership by firms from Hong Kong, Macao, and Taiwan.

ownership types the same when extending loans. Thus, we first study whether and how SOEs differ in their access to formal loans as compared to private firms.

Using the sample of all firms in the last year of our census data, 2006, we first show that state-owned firms still have easier access to external financing: They tend to have higher leverage (debt/total assets) and a higher share of financial expense in total expense,[5] while they pay half as much interest per unit (or RMB) of their external financing as private firms (see Table 3).[6] Repeating the same analysis for the balanced panel of the firms, we see that leverage was more or less unchanged during our sample period for SOEs, holding the sample constant. Moreover, for older and larger private firms that were in our sample since 2000, leverage is a bit higher than for SOEs and has declined. If we include new firms, however, in our 2006 sample, the average leverage of the private firms is substantially lower than in the balanced sample, suggesting that new entrants have more restricted access to financing than older private firms and SOEs. The leverage of smaller private firms, the ones included in our survey data, is less than half of that for private firms in the census, indicating that access to finance is particularly limited for young small private firms.

One possibility is, therefore, that differences in access to finance are not due to ownership *per se*, but rather reflect the fact that private firms are on average younger and smaller and therefore lack credit history and reputation. We address this difficulty in interpretation in two ways: by estimating the effects of ownership controlling for size, liquidity, and profitability in a regression analysis that follows next, and by focusing on the survey data that covers mostly small firms in the next section. The focus on the survey data is important because the NBS census data focus more on large and medium-sized firms and the balanced firm panel especially includes large firms disproportionately.

Looking at the share of financial expense in total expense, we find that even in the balanced panel the share is substantially lower for private firms than for the SOEs. The share is even lower when we include all firms in our 2006 cross-section, implying less access to external finances by private firms. At the same time, interest expense as a ratio to total debt is almost twice as high for private firms as it is for SOEs, in both the cross-section

[5] In Table 3, financial costs include interest payments, money exchange losses, and other financial charges (e.g., fees for bank drafts, wire transfers, etc.).

[6] Note that the per unit cost for external financing computed here is different from average interest rate for two reasons: (1) A firm's total debt may include liabilities that do not bear interest such as various accounts payable and (2) even if the firm's total debt comprises only interest-bearing bank loans, the year-end total debt may not correspond to the amount of bank loans that incurred the interest payment in that year. However, this ratio still gives a proxy for the average cost of obtaining finances faced by firms of different types.

Table 3. Mean leverage, financial, and interest expense ratios

Mean leverage (total debt/total assets):

Year	Ownership						
	State	Private	Collective	FRN	HMT	Legal person	Other
Census full 2006 cross-section							
2006	0.560	0.554	0.539	0.470	0.476	0.529	0.527
Balanced panel (census)							
2000	0.567	0.622	0.597	0.473	0.496	0.572	0.571
2001	0.561	0.614	0.587	0.454	0.481	0.567	0.554
2002	0.561	0.610	0.581	0.450	0.476	0.567	0.545
2003	0.559	0.610	0.577	0.451	0.475	0.564	0.550
2004	0.566	0.609	0.568	0.468	0.465	0.574	0.530
2005	0.568	0.597	0.562	0.453	0.470	0.562	0.528
2006	0.565	0.590	0.560	0.446	0.470	0.556	0.540

Survey data (private firms only)

Year	Leverage (total debt/total assets)
2000	0.171
2002	0.177
2004	0.184
2006	0.217

Mean financial expense/total expense

Year	Ownership						
	State	Private	Collective	FRN	HMT	Legal person	Other
Census full 2006 cross-section							
2006	0.046	0.015	0.018	0.015	0.012	0.020	0.026
Balanced panel (census)							
2000	0.063	0.028	0.032	0.030	0.019	0.040	0.045
2001	0.062	0.027	0.030	0.028	0.017	0.038	0.041
2002	0.059	0.024	0.029	0.024	0.014	0.037	0.041
2003	0.057	0.023	0.026	0.022	0.014	0.032	0.034
2004	0.055	0.023	0.022	0.018	0.013	0.032	0.034
2005	0.050	0.022	0.023	0.016	0.013	0.030	0.029
2006	0.050	0.022	0.020	0.016	0.015	0.027	0.030

Mean interest expense/total debt

Year	Ownership						
	State	Private	Collective	FRN	HMT	Legal person	Other
Census full 2006 cross-section							
2006	0.016	0.031	0.025	0.015	0.012	0.029	0.027

Table 3. (*Continued*)

Mean interest expense/total debt							
Year	Ownership						
	State	Private	Collective	FRN	HMT	Legal person	Other
Balanced panel (census)							
2000	0.022	0.033	0.036	0.023	0.017	0.032	0.032
2001	0.021	0.032	0.033	0.020	0.016	0.030	0.032
2002	0.020	0.030	0.032	0.017	0.015	0.031	0.027
2003	0.019	0.029	0.030	0.015	0.014	0.029	0.025
2004	0.017	0.029	0.026	0.014	0.013	0.027	0.023
2005	0.017	0.030	0.027	0.015	0.014	0.027	0.023
2006	0.016	0.031	0.025	0.016	0.013	0.026	0.026

Note: Financial expenses include interest payments, money exchange losses, and other financial charges.

FRN, ownership by firms outside greater China area; HMT, ownership by firms from Hong Kong, Macao, and Taiwan.

and the balanced panel. This indicates that when private firms do have access to external finance, they pay more for it than SOEs. In addition, we see that total financial expenses and interest expenses have declined on average for SOEs during our sample period, but they remained unchanged for private firms, suggesting more differential treatment between SOEs and private firms in more recent years.

Rather than prejudice against private firms in the formal financial sector, one potential reason for state-owned firms' easier access to finances could be their better creditworthiness. To study this possibility, we test whether the apparent SOE advantage in accessing external credit shown in Table 3 persists when we control for size and measures of creditworthiness, namely profitability and liquidity. Table 4 reports the results of the regression analysis based on the 2006 cross-section. We do see that all three measures of firm size matters, as well as ownership type. In the case of leverage, once we control for log of assets, the coefficient on the SOE indicator falls by about half, indicating that half of the difference in leverage between private firms and SOEs in the 2006 census cross-section is due to the fact that state-owned firms tend to be larger. The reduction in the SOE effect on financial cost ratio is not only small but also non-negligible. Nevertheless, we still find that state-owned firms have significantly higher leverage, a larger ratio of financial to total expenses, and a lower share of interest payment in financial expenses, even after controlling for size, profitability, and liquidity measures. These findings confirm that even as recently as 2006, state-owned firms had easier access to formal external financing than other firms.

Table 4. OLS regressions in the 2006 NBS census cross-section

	Dependent variable is leverage				
I(State owned)	0.027***	0.015***	0.027***	0.024***	0.015***
	(0.0023)	(0.0023)	(0.0023)	(0.0023)	(0.0023)
Log(assets)		0.013***			0.011***
		(0.00034)			(0.00034)
Pretax ROE			−0.000017		−0.000020
			(0.000040)		(0.000039)
Liquidity				−0.0000040***	−0.0000041***
				(0.00000062)	(0.00000062)
Constant	0.53***	0.40***	0.53***	0.54***	0.44***
	(0.00050)	(0.0034)	(0.00050)	(0.00049)	(0.0034)
Observations	286,993	286,993	286,894	279,662	279,628
Adjusted R^2	0.00047	0.0058	0.00049	0.00054	0.0040
	Dependent variable is financial expenses/total expenses				
I(State owned)	0.029***	0.024***	0.029***	0.029***	0.024***
	(0.00042)	(0.00042)	(0.00042)	(0.00043)	(0.00042)
Log(assets)		0.0062***			0.0062***
		(0.000062)			(0.000063)
Pretax ROE			0.0000032		0.0000015
			(0.0000072)		(0.0000071)

Liquidity				−0.000000079	−0.00000015
				(0.00000014)	(0.00000013)
Constant	0.017***	−0.043***	0.017***	0.017***	−0.044***
	(0.000091)	(0.00061)	(0.000091)	(0.000093)	(0.00062)
Observations	265,672	265,670	265,630	258,509	258,472
Adjusted R^2	0.018	0.052	0.018	0.018	0.053
Dependent variable is interest expense/total debt					
I(State owned)	−0.11***	−0.11***	−0.11***	−0.12***	−0.11***
	(0.0024)	(0.0024)	(0.0024)	(0.0024)	(0.0024)
Log(assets)		−0.0099***			−0.012***
		(0.00038)			(0.00038)
Pretax ROE			0.000015		0.000017
			(0.000045)		(0.000044)
Liquidity				−0.0000020***	−0.0000018***
				(0.00000070)	(0.00000070)
Constant	0.29***	0.39***	0.29***	0.30***	0.41***
	(0.00055)	(0.0037)	(0.00055)	(0.00056)	(0.0038)
Observations	293,435	293,435	293,391	287,813	287,774
Adjusted R^2	0.0077	0.0100	0.0077	0.0082	0.011

Note: Pretax ROE is the ratio of pretax net profit to equity. Liquidity is the ratio of liquid assets to total assets. Standard errors are in parentheses.
***Significance at 1% level; **Significance at 5% level; *Significance at 10% level.

Table 5. ***Equity composition of private firms in the survey data (percent of total capital)***

Survey year	State	Private	Collective	Foreign
1995	0.608	94.226	0.656	1.985
1997	1.414	97.811	1.533	1.886
2000	0.792	97.877	2.121	4.671
2002	0.670	99.199	1.578	1.271
2004	0.442	97.078	0.412	0.679
2006	0.436	97.120	0.356	0.615
Overall	0.568	96.644	0.722	1.268

4. How do private firms finance themselves?

Our findings suggest that as late as 2006, SOEs still enjoyed better access to external finances. The natural question then is: How do Chinese private firms finance their fast growth? As discussed above, the NBS data set has very little information on small private firms. Thus, we will need to rely on the private entrepreneur survey data to explore this issue. We first look at survey responses by private-firm owners on how they overcome financial constraints, and then use both the NBS census data and the private firm survey data to evaluate the various mechanisms for private firm financing.

4.1. Survey responses

4.1.1. Initial finances

Firms included in the survey data are exclusively private firms, as shown in Table 5, which presents the average composition of equity for firms included in the survey. The predominant majority of firm shares (96.6% on average) are owned by the private owner of the firm, other private individuals, or other private firms, whereas foreign capital and investment from collective firms and SOEs play insignificant roles in financing private firms. Table 6 shows that such ownership structure has remained largely unchanged since the founding of these firms and since the late 1970s when the economic reforms began in China.

How did private owners fund the firms' initial investment? Information provided in Table 7 suggests that the vast majority of firm owners relied on their own savings from previous work (80% of the respondents), a large percentage (42%) received financial help from other individuals (including relatives and friends), 30% obtained loans from banks and other formal

Table 6. Equity composition of private firms by founding year (percent of total capital)

Founding year	State	Private	Collective	Foreign	Number of firms
1975	0.000	100.000	0.000	0.000	3
1976	0.000	100.000	0.000	0.000	4
1977	0.000	100.000	0.000	0.000	2
1978	0.000	85.600	7.500	0.000	25
1979	0.000	98.892	0.568	0.506	37
1980	0.094	90.698	1.765	0.000	53
1981	0.638	96.739	1.170	0.000	47
1982	0.494	98.875	0.063	0.000	81
1983	0.889	93.948	0.809	0.667	135
1984	0.617	92.985	1.317	2.316	201
1985	0.687	94.668	1.541	1.235	252
1986	0.369	95.099	1.447	2.039	244
1987	0.657	96.224	1.069	0.424	216
1988	0.534	93.508	1.680	1.727	357
1989	0.583	94.628	1.621	1.146	350
1990	0.639	96.965	0.791	0.891	349
1991	1.690	95.356	1.191	1.754	343
1992	0.564	95.648	0.550	2.125	557
1993	1.014	95.969	0.284	1.923	808
1994	0.374	96.339	0.808	0.851	710
1995	0.225	97.564	0.740	1.122	490
1996	0.817	97.860	1.220	1.325	534
1997	1.061	97.407	1.238	0.908	490
1998	0.596	97.155	0.825	0.945	668
1999	0.591	97.696	0.631	1.025	552
2000	1.012	97.380	0.798	0.388	670
2001	0.536	96.786	1.164	0.634	615
2002	0.546	97.435	0.460	0.486	548
2003	0.498	97.877	0.601	0.050	498
2004	0.472	97.757	0.558	1.000	265
2005	0.094	97.956	0.338	0.807	160
Overall	0.670	96.481	0.895	1.069	10,277

financial institutions, and a very small number (less than 5%) used inheritance in starting the firm.[7]

4.1.2. Ongoing finances

The percentage of firms that received initial help from banks and other formal financial institutions is surprisingly high (30%, from Table 7). A similarly surprising finding comes from Table 8, which summarizes the sources of ongoing finances for private firms: A large percentage of private

[7] Numbers add up to more than 100% because each respondent could indicate multiple funding sources.

Table 7. Sources of initial financing of private firms by founding year (share of responses)

Founding year	Own saving	Individuals	Banks	Inheritance
1975	0.333	1.000	0.333	0.333
1976	0.875	0.500	0.625	0.125
1977	1.000	0.500	0.500	0.000
1978	0.839	0.677	0.355	0.129
1979	0.804	0.588	0.490	0.255
1980	0.830	0.625	0.318	0.102
1981	0.770	0.608	0.446	0.054
1982	0.858	0.575	0.381	0.071
1983	0.775	0.647	0.353	0.098
1984	0.762	0.635	0.414	0.101
1985	0.758	0.570	0.427	0.089
1986	0.825	0.565	0.370	0.096
1987	0.748	0.576	0.415	0.089
1988	0.732	0.569	0.379	0.108
1989	0.759	0.561	0.337	0.096
1990	0.797	0.534	0.309	0.044
1991	0.790	0.575	0.327	0.081
1992	0.801	0.495	0.293	0.074
1993	0.792	0.533	0.316	0.053
1994	0.822	0.484	0.316	0.040
1995	0.834	0.318	0.244	0.019
1996	0.781	0.330	0.249	0.008
1997	0.802	0.327	0.260	0.021
1998	0.779	0.335	0.304	0.018
1999	0.806	0.291	0.238	0.018
2000	0.805	0.305	0.258	0.021
2001	0.785	0.312	0.268	0.024
2002	0.842	0.308	0.239	0.006
2003	0.828	0.265	0.250	0.015
2004	0.866	0.303	0.222	0.006
2005	0.868	0.231	0.278	0.019
Overall	0.798	0.425	0.301	0.046

Note: Shares may add up to more than 1 because respondents could name more than one source.

firms continue to secure loans from banks and other formal financial institutions during their ongoing operations (41%). In comparison, only 25% of firms in our sample have obtained loans from informal channels. In terms of loan amounts, slightly more than half of an average private firm's total debt is in the form of loans from banks or other formal financial institutions, with the rest almost equally accounted for by informal finances and trade credit (measured as a ratio of accounts payable to total debt). In particular, the ratio between the average amount of bank loans and that of informal finances (excluding trade credit) is

Table 8. Sources of ongoing financing

Survey year	Share of firms using bank loans	Share of firms using informal loans	Bank loans as a share of assets	Informal loans as a share of assets	Accounts payable as a share of debt	Share of firms reporting financing difficulty
1995						0.703
2000	0.381	0.275	0.657	0.343		0.730
2002	0.432	0.278	0.675	0.325	0.256	
2004	0.390	0.233	0.682	0.318	0.242	
2006	0.435	0.230	0.733	0.267	0.207	
Overall	0.411	0.253	0.688	0.312	0.235	

Note: Assets do not include accounts receivable.

slightly above two, implying that bank loans play a much more important role in firm finances than informal finances. Furthermore, the percentage of firms using informal loans has shown steady decrease (from 27% in 2000 to 23% in 2006), probably implying a smaller need for informal finances over time.

4.1.3. Financing costs of private firms

An additional angle to study the financial access of Chinese private firms is through their financing costs. For two of the survey years, we have detailed information on the interest rates paid by private firms to obtain various kinds of loans, as well as the maturity of these loans. Of the private firms in our sample, 43% were able to obtain bank loans at the government-stipulated interest rate (of 5.84%) in 2000, 9% obtained bank loans at higher interest rates (8.85%), while 29% got informal loans at rates similar to those of bank loans with adjusted rates (8.17%). On average, the loans obtained are short-term loans, with the average maturity of bank loans at 9½ months, whereas the term of informal loans is slightly longer at a little over 11 months.

One somewhat surprising finding is how similar interest rates charged by banks are to those charged for informal loans. This suggests that the formal financial sector and the informal financial sector in China may be better integrated than we thought. The usual concern with firms' reliance on the informal financial sector is its lack of efficiency in allocating funds, yet our evidence suggests that this concern may be exaggerated.

4.1.4. Are private firms financially constrained?

Despite the surprisingly high proportion of private firms with access to formal finances, the concern with private firms' financial constraints remains. Compared to firms of other ownership types (and even private firms of larger size), private firms in the survey data have substantially lower leverage (see Table 3).[8] This suggests that Chinese private firms, especially younger and smaller ones, have much less access to external finance than firms of other ownership types, especially SOEs, and therefore are more likely to face financial constraints.

In fact, informal finances and trade credit are crucial to private firms, and their importance can be demonstrated by comparing total debt and the total amount of funds needed. In the private firm surveys, firms report two types of funds needed: daily working capital and funds for expansion. The survey data suggest that the daily working capital requirement is easily fulfiled by bank loans (as the ratio of bank loan amount to working capital amount is substantially greater than 1), although neither informal loans nor trade credit alone can fully cover it, amounting to 76% and 93% of daily working capital, respectively. But when expansion funds are included, even the sum of bank loans and informal loans is not sufficient to meet firms' financial needs – without informal loans, bank credit amounts to only 74% of the expansion funds, and bank credit together with informal loans amounts to 89%. In fact, only with the addition of accounts payable can the total debt cover the total funds needed.

Therefore, both informal loans and trade credit are essential for the healthy growth of private firms, although they are relatively small in magnitude. In other words, private firms would be financially constrained without the informal financial mechanisms such as informal loans and trade credit. This pattern is confirmed by the responses from firms to questions on whether they face difficulty in obtaining finances, which were asked in 1995 and 2000. In both years, over 70% of firms gave affirmative answers to the above questions (see the last column of Table 8).

One caveat of the above discussion is that it ignores the compatibility in the maturity of debt and capital required. Because both formal and informal loans are mostly short term, as are accounts payable, it may not be feasible after all to provide expansion funds with the formal and informal credit discussed earlier. In addition, note that the calculation does not include the actual investment made in the current year. Instead, the main source for such longer-term investment is most likely firms' own retained earnings, which we will discuss later.

To summarize, the responses from private firm owners demonstrate that the initial funds for Chinese private firms come mainly from informal channels (personal savings and support from family and friends), while ongoing finances have relied more on formal finances such as bank loans, albeit limited to short-term ones. Private firms do face financial constraints, especially for financing growth, but they have become more

---

[8] Trade credit is included as part of total liability.

able to overcome the constraints over time. We now turn to the analysis of the specific mechanisms for private firm financing in China.

4.2. Financing Mechanisms for Chinese Private Firms

4.2.1. Informal finances

As we have seen from the earlier discussion, informal finances, especially informal loans, play an important role in private firms' everyday operations, amounting to over a quarter of their daily financial needs. A brief overview of the informal financial market in China seems helpful here.

By one account, the total amount of informal funds flowing around in the Chinese economy was between 0.7 and 0.8 trillion RMB in 2003, which is about one-fifth the total amount of the stimulus package China put together to combat the current financial crisis (PBOC and JICA, 2005). Circulation of funds of this magnitude may involve more than just small circles of family, relatives, and friends. In fact, several forms of informal financial institutions have emerged in some Chinese regions since the early 1980s, a phenomenon that at one time alarmed the Chinese government. In the city of Wenzhou, for example, groups of individuals formed organizations such as Qianzhuang, Yinbei, and Juhui, which pool funds together and lend to members to fund potentially profitable investment projects. Because they lack the formal recognition of the government and thus cannot rely on any legal protection from the courts or the government, these groups start by drawing their members largely from relatives, friends, and local acquaintances. Although this may have constrained the size of the groups and the scale of total funds, the reputation effects seem to have functioned well in enforcing the implicit financial contracts among members. The largely successful operations of these organizations have gradually eased the concern of the Chinese government, which has now established Wenzhou as one of the sites for monitoring rates for informal loans. But caution is called for when interpreting the above patterns, as Wenzhou is arguably a special region of China, which is long known for its extraordinary entrepreneurship; thus, it may not be representative of the whole country.

In response to the spontaneous emergence of various informal financing arrangements and their popularity among business owners, the Chinese government legitimized informal loans in 1991, allowing interest rates to be as high as four times the bank loan rates. It also explicitly recognized the validity of loan contracts signed between two willing parties, even when neither party is a formal financial institution. The change in the government's attitude toward informal loans may have resulted from the important finding that the interest rates of informal loans are not as high as believed by many. In addition, these rates have been declining over time and have been largely moving together with interest rates charged by formal institutions (Que 2009).

Table 9. Tax rates and profitability

Survey data					
Survey year	Tax/profit	Tax+fees/profit	Profit/sales	Profit/assets	Profit/equity
1993	0.071	0.086			
1995	0.074	0.107	0.150		0.223
1997	0.064	0.092	0.122		0.343
2000	0.059	0.086	0.096	0.193	0.245
2002	0.059	0.081	0.080	0.156	0.212
2004	0.066	0.102	0.047	0.194	0.257
2006	0.063	0.094	0.077	0.146	0.241
Overall	0.064	0.091	0.087	0.170	0.247

Census data: 2006 cross-section			
Ownership	Tax/sales	Net profit/assets	Net profit/equity
State	0.077	0.001	0.044
Private	0.050	0.093	0.064
Collective	0.065	0.097	0.048
FRN	0.033	0.064	0.000
HMT	0.034	0.047	0.037
Legal person	0.052	0.090	0.109
Others	0.053	0.060	0.109

Note: Total tax is computed as the sum of corporate income tax, value-added tax, and operation tax.
FRN, ownership by firms outside greater China area; HMT, ownership by firms from Hong Kong, Macao, and Taiwan.

4.2.2. *Internal finances*

We next study the role of internal finances in funding private firms' daily operations and expansion needs. As Lardy (2004) points out, in 2002 close to 50% of firm investment was funded by firms' own retained earnings in China. Profit is the ultimate source for internal finances for all firms; thus we start by looking at profit data in Table 9, which also provides information on tax rates to partially explain profit rates. The average ratio of after-tax profit to sales for private firms in our survey sample is 9%, while the tax rate (tax amount as a percentage of sales) is slightly over 6%, or 9% when levies are included in the calculation. These tax rates correspond to those computed using the census data, which also include firms of other ownership types.[9] We can see that among firms of various ownership types, the tax rate of SOEs is the highest, followed by that of

[9] Total tax rate is computed by dividing the sum of income tax, value-added tax, and business tax by sales.

Table 10. Uses of after-tax profit (share of total)

Survey year	Investment	Dividend	Special assessment	Donation	Public relations	Other
1995	0.416	0.093	0.094	0.127	0.190	0.155
1997	0.587	0.192	0.069	0.066	0.142	0.106
2000	0.743	0.187	0.060	0.083	0.167	0.087
2002	0.308	0.145	0.091	0.109	0.208	0.031
2004	0.404	0.239	0.098	0.099	0.203	0.083
2006	0.465	0.173	0.065	0.075	0.155	0.032
Overall	0.536	0.166	0.080	0.095	0.179	0.093

corporations, then by that of collective firms, and then private firms. Foreign-invested firms enjoy the lowest tax rates.

Even though profit rates and returns are substantially lower in the census data than in the survey data,[10] we find that state-owned firms have much lower profit and return measures. Given lower tax rates and higher profit rates, private firms have access to more retained earnings, which can potentially be used as financial sources for investment and further expansion. Indeed, as we can see from Table 10, firms in our survey sample allocate the majority (54%) of their retained earnings to investment, 17% to dividend payments, and the rest to special assessments, donations, public relations, and others.

4.2.3. Trade credit

Using a small sample of private firms and SOEs for 1994–1999, Ge and Qiu (2007) provide evidence that private firms use trade credit as a net source of credit (i.e., incur higher accounts payable than accounts receivable), while SOEs on average are a net supplier of trade credit. Using a large panel data set of Chinese industrial firms (1999–2003), Cull *et al.* (2009) similarly find that SOEs tend to carry more accounts receivable than private firms. However, they argue that these findings are more likely explained by the fact that SOEs extended credit to their failing partners that were in arrears. Furthermore, the magnitudes of their estimates suggest that redistribution of bank loans through trade credit cannot be an important explanation for how private firms obtain funds.

In this section, we evaluate the role of trade credit in financing firms of different ownership types using our census data. Specifically, we focus on accounts payable and accounts receivable as one type of informal external financing. Table 11 provides the related information using the full sample cross-section in 2006. The first two columns give the total amount of accounts payable and that of accounts receivable for firms by ownership

[10] This is most likely due to the different coverage of private firms in the two samples, with large ones in the census and small ones in the survey.

Table 11. Accounts payable (AP) and accounts receivable (AR)

De facto ownership	Sum AP (mil. RMB)	Sum AR (mil. RMB)	Mean					
			AP/ assets	AR/ assets	AP/ sales	AR/ sales	AP/ debt	AR/ debt
NBS 2006 cross-section								
State	501.5	328.9	0.107	0.106	0.146	0.161	0.176	0.166
Private	584.2	684.5	0.145	0.191	0.100	0.131	0.262	0.296
Collective	105.9	135.8	0.150	0.206	0.120	0.165	0.265	0.290
FRN	794.0	741.0	0.196	0.193	0.159	0.166	0.413	0.335
HMT	398.5	356.0	0.210	0.203	0.170	0.173	0.432	0.329
Legal person	1036.6	833.2	0.145	0.168	0.114	0.134	0.272	0.274
Other	66.6	65.2	0.131	0.165	0.131	0.172	0.250	0.283
Survey (2006)			0.071	0.207	0.075	0.158	0.203	0.824

FRN, ownership by firms outside greater China area; HMT, ownership by firms from Hong Kong, Macao, and Taiwan.

type, which shows that private firms collectively are a net creditor, while all other firms (with the only exception of collective firms) are net debtors.[11] The most probable explanation for this is that private firms tend to operate in more competitive sectors.

As accounts payable and accounts receivable are routine by-products of a firm's daily sales, the most common way of measuring their levels and usage is to compute their ratios to sales. Based on these measures, private firms tend to be offered a lower level of accounts payable, again consistent with their being in more competitive sectors. The lower accounts receivable to sales ratio, on the other hand, is a response of private firms to manage funds more efficiently due to constraints in accessing external financial resources.

In contrast, ratios of accounts payable to debt and accounts receivable to assets are higher in private firms than in SOEs. This is due to the much easier access to finances enjoyed by SOEs and their consequent high levels of assets and liabilities. In other words, the higher share of accounts payable in total debt suggests that private firms have to rely more on trade credit to finance their operating expenses because other forms of credit are not available. The lower share of accounts receivable in total assets for the state-owned firms suggests that they tend to engage less in informal financing. The pattern is the same in our balanced sample and has not

[11] One thing to note is that firms of the legal-person type also include private firms, so the specific numbers in Table 11 column 1 need to be adjusted. Yet the same patterns remain after the adjustment, with only private firms and collective firms carrying more accounts receivable than accounts payable as a group. Similar results are also obtained when the *de jure* ownership classifications are used.

changed much since 2003, when these variables were first reported in the census data.[12]

Put together, the empirical evidence provided in Table 11 falls more in line with the findings in Cull *et al.* (2009) in challenging the importance of trade credit as a funding source for private firms. As shown in Table 11, when the amount of trade credit is compared to their asset or debt level, it is clear that accounts payable and accounts receivable are much less important for SOEs than for private firms. Yet when compared to private firms, SOEs have higher accounts receivable and accounts payable as percentages of sales, implying that they have greater access to trade credit. In other words, the SOEs have greater access to all kinds of credit including trade credit. Furthermore, the implication of the SOEs' greater access to trade credit for private firms is negative, in contrast to what is argued in Ge and Qiu (2007). As shown in Table 11, the SOE sector as a whole carries more accounts payable than accounts receivable, while the opposite holds for the private sector. As a result, trade credit is unlikely to be a main channel through which SOEs provide informal financing to other types of firms, in particular to private firms.

4.2.4. Inventory

All the mechanisms discussed above focus on the supply side of the story, i.e., how private firms increase financial access to solve their financial needs. The demand side, however, may also be important in resolving private firms' financial constraints. As Long and Zhang (2010) point out, certain organizational arrangements such as clustering may lead to a lower level of financial need for private firms, thus alleviating their financial hardship.

Here we point to another potential mechanism that works along the demand dimension. Table 12 shows that private firms have much lower inventory to sales ratios than their SOE counterparts: 14% as opposed to 31%. As these firms are all industrial firms exceeding a certain size, such large differences in inventory to sales ratios most likely indicate much more efficient inventory management and thus less need for working capital in private firms compared to SOEs. In fact, the inventory to sales ratio in private firms is even lower than that in foreign-invested firms. If we assume that foreign-invested firms are both unconstrained financially and efficient at managing their inventory, this implies that private firms may in fact be reducing their inventory below the optimal level. Yet, a comparison with firms in Japan and Korea suggests that the inventory level in Chinese private firms is still within the norm.

The same logic may also explain the lower ratios of accounts payable and accounts receivable to sales in private firms than in SOEs discussed

---

[12] We do not present the balanced panel results in the interest of space.

Table 12. Average inventory/sales ratios by ownership in 2006 census cross-section

Ownership	Inventory/sales
State	0.306
Private	0.138
Collective	0.171
FRN	0.195
HMT	0.222
Legal person	0.172
Others	0.221

FRN, ownership by firms outside greater China area; HMT, ownership by firms from Hong Kong, Macao, and Taiwan.

earlier. Much like with inventory management, easy access to cheap external finance by SOEs reduces their incentives to manage their accounts payable and accounts receivable efficiently. Private firms that face borrowing constraints, on the other hand, are more likely to actively manage their trade credit to maintain their cash flow.

5. *Conclusion*

The findings we have presented suggest the following patterns. First, in 2006, before the onset of the global recession, SOEs still had better access to external finances as compared to private firms in China. This is shown in higher leverage rates, higher financial costs, and lower interest payments. Moreover, evidence based on the census data (Table 3) suggests that there may have been more differential treatment between SOEs and private firms in more recent years. Second, to counter their limited access to external finances, Chinese private firms have resorted to a variety of mechanisms. Using both the NBS census data and the private entrepreneur survey data, we show that these mechanisms include a greater reliance on retained earnings (facilitated by lower tax rates and higher profit rates), the flexible yet reasonably efficient use of informal finances, and very efficient management of working capital (by reducing the required levels of inventory and accounts receivable). In contrast, we present evidence that trade credit from state-owned firms to the private sector cannot be a plausible mechanism to resolve financial constraints for Chinese private firms, since the funds appear to be flowing in reverse. Third, there is a great amount of variation in private firms' access to external finances: While small private firms have difficulty obtaining external finances, larger private firms are able to achieve high leverage rates by paying higher financial costs. We estimate that about half of the observed differential access to finances between SOEs and private firms can be explained by the size of the firm, which is often a good indicator of reputation and creditworthiness.

One finding is somewhat surprising to us: Although not as accessible as for SOEs, the formal financial sector in China does provide Chinese private firms with substantial financial resources, especially for their short-term needs during daily operations. In addition, there is some evidence that the access of small private firms to formal bank loans has improved moderately in the past decade. Based on the survey data, Table 3 shows that the leverage (debt/asset ratio) has increased from 0.17 to 0.22 from 2000 to 2006, while Table 9 shows that during the same period the percentage of firms with access to bank loans has increased from 38% to 43%, and simultaneously the proportion of firms using informal loans has dropped from 27% to 23%.

As discussed previously, private firms included in the NBS balanced panel tend to be well-established large private firms, and thus they are not representative of all private firms. So it is possible that the patterns summarized above are completely consistent with one another, and there indeed has been improvement in the financial access of small private firms, the most constrained sector, in the past few years. Such a development would definitely be a welcome one. A more robust conclusion, however, will await further investigation.

Finally, as we have shown, both the ingenuity and resilience of Chinese private firms and the gradual improvements in the financial sector, formal or informal, have helped provide funds for private firms' daily operations. Yet the main source for long-term investment remains firms' own internal funds. As a result, the most pressing financial constraint facing Chinese private firms in our minds is their limited ability to secure long-term funds to invest for growth, and resolving this issue should be one of the top goals of financial reforms in China.

Acknowledgments

The views expressed in this chapter are those of the authors and do not necessarily represent the views of the Federal Reserve Bank of San Francisco or the Federal Reserve System. Part of this work was conducted while Hale was visiting the Hong Kong Institute of Monetary Research, for whose hospitality she is most grateful. We thank Hirotaka Miura for excellent research assistance.

References

Allen, F., Qian, J., Qian, M. (2005), Law, finance, and economic growth in China. *Journal of Financial Economics* 77 (July), 57–116.

Allen, F., Qian, J., Qian, M. (2008), China's financial system: past, present, and future. In: Brandt, L., Rawski, T. (Eds.), *China's Great Economic Transformation*. Cambridge University Press, UK.

Boyreau-Debray, G., Wei, S.-J. (2005), Pitfalls of a state-dominated financial system: the case of China. NBER Working Paper No. W1121, March.

Brandt, L., Li, H. (2003), Bank discrimination in transition economies: ideology, information or incentives?. *Journal of Comparative Economics* 31, 1–31.

Cull, R., Xu, L.C. (2000), Bureaucrats, state banks, and the efficiency of credit allocation: the experience of Chinese state-owned enterprises. *Journal of Comparative Economics* 28 (March), 1–31.

Cull, R., Xu, L.C. (2003), Who gets credit? The behavior of bureaucrats and state banks in allocating credit to Chinese state-owned enterprises. *Journal of Development Economics* 71 (2), 533–559.

Cull, R., Xu, C. (2005), Institutions, ownership, and finance: the determinants of reinvestments of profit among Chinese firms. *Journal of Financial Economics* 77, 117–146.

Cull, R., Xu, L.C., Zhu, T. (2009), Formal finance and trade credit during China's transition. *Journal of Financial Intermediation* 18, 173–192.

Demetriades, P.O., Du, J., Girma, S., Xu, C. (2008), Does the Chinese banking system promote the growth of firms? Working Paper No. 08/6, University of Leicester, UK.

Dobson, W., Kashyap, A. (2006), The contradiction in China's gradualist banking reforms. *Brookings Papers on Economic Activity*, Fall, 103-48.

Dollar, D., Wei, S. (2007), Das (wasted) Kapital: firm ownership and investment efficiency in China. NBER Working Paper No. 13103.

Ferri, G., Liu, L.G. (2009), Honor thy creditors beforan thy shareholders: are the Profits of Chinese state-owned enterprises real? HKIMR Working Paper No.16/2009.

Ge, Y., Qiu, J. (2007), Financial development, bank discrimination and trade credit. *Journal of Banking and Finance* 31 (2), 513–530.

Hausmann, R., Klinger, B. (2006), Structural transformation and patterns of comparative advantage. Center for International Development Working Paper No. 128, Harvard University, Cambridge, MA.

Hèricourt, J., Poncet, S. (2009), FDI and credit constraints: firm level evidence from China. *Economic Systems*, 33(1), 1–21.

Hsieh, C.-T., Klenow, P. J. (2009), Misallocation and manufacturing TFP in China and India. *Quarterly Journal of Economics* 124 (4), 1403–1448.

Huang, Y. (2004), *Selling China*. Cambridge University Press, UK.

King, R., Levine, R. (1993), Finance and growth: Schumpeter might be right. *Quarterly Journal of Economics* 108, 717–738.

Lardy, N. (1998), *China's Unfinished Economic Revolution*. The Brookings Institution, Washington, DC.

Lardy, N.R. (2004), State-owned banks in China. In: Caprio, G., et al. (Eds), *The Future Of State-Owned Financial Institutions*. Brookings Institution Press, Washington, DC.

Liu, Q., Siu, A. (2006), Institutions, financial development, and corporate investment: evidence from an implied return on capital in China. Available at SSRN: http://ssrn.com/abstract = 965631

Long, C., Zhang, X. (2010), Industrial clusters and firm financing in China with Xiaobo Zhang. The International Food Policy Research Institute Discussion Papers (IFPRI DP).

PBOC and JICA (Research Bureau of People's Bank of China, and Japan International Cooperation Agency). (2005), *Investigation Report on Chinese Small and Medium Firm Financial System*. Zhongxin Publishing, Beijing.

Poncet, S., Steingress, W., Vandenbussche, H. (2008), Financial constraints in China: firm-level evidence. LICOS Discussion Paper No. 226/2008.

Que, Z. (2009), Financial support systems for small and medium-sized firms: theory, evidence, and public policy. Shenzhen Stock Exchange Research Institute Research Report No. 0173.

Rajan, R.G., Zingales, L. (1998), Financial dependence and growth. *American Economic Review* 88 (3), 559–586.

CHAPTER 14

Foreign Direct Investment in China: Performance, Characteristics, and Prospects

Chunlai Chen

Policy and Governance Program, Crawford School of Economics and Government, ANU College of Asia & the Pacific, The Australian National University, Canberra, ACT 0200, Australia
E-mail address: chunlai.chen@anu.edu.au

Abstract
Large foreign direct investment (FDI) inflow is one of the most important features of China's economic reform and opening up to the outside world. Over the past 30 years, China has attracted over US$940 billion FDI inflows, making it the largest FDI recipient among the all developing countries. This chapter argues that FDI inflows into China have mostly come from developing economies, concentrated in China's east and southeast coastal regions, and biased toward the manufacturing sector. The large FDI inflows have greatly contributed to China's economic development. FDI has been playing an increasingly important role in China's economy in terms of capital formation, employment creation, export promotion, and integrating with the world economy. The global financial and economic crisis has had negative impact on FDI inflows into China. However, as compared to the large decline in FDI globally, FDI inflows into China have been resilient. China will continue to be one of the most attractive destinations for FDI in the future.

Keywords: Foreign direct investment, composition of sources, regional and sectoral distribution, contributions, prospects, China

JEL classifications: F14, F21, F23

1. Introduction

Foreign direct investment (FDI) is one of the most dramatic features of China's economic reform and opening up to the outside world. Since 1979 China has gradually liberalized its FDI regime, and an institutional framework has been developed to regulate and facilitate such investments. The liberalization of the FDI regime and the improved investment

Frontiers of Economics and Globalization
Volume 9 ISSN: 1574-8715
DOI: 10.1108/S1574-8715(2011)0000009019

environment have greatly increased the confidence of foreign investors in China. Foreign firms have been attracted by its huge domestic market and pool of relatively well-educated, low-cost labor, which have made China one of the most attractive destinations for FDI in the world.

During the last three decades, China has attracted a huge amount of FDI inflows. By the end of 2009, China had attracted a total of over US$940 billion FDI inflows cumulatively,[1] making it the largest FDI recipient among the developing countries in the world. The large FDI inflows have made great contributions to China's economic development, in terms of promoting capital formation, employment creation, export promotion, technology transfer, and integration with the world economy.

This chapter aims to present an overview of FDI in China. It is structured as follows. Section 2 reviews the trends of FDI inflows into China. Section 3 analyzes the characteristics of FDI inflows into China in terms of the composition of FDI sources, and the regional and sectoral distribution of FDI inflows. Section 4 examines the contribution of FDI to China's economy. Section 5 discusses the prospects of FDI inflows into China. Section 6 summarizes the main findings.

2. *The growth of FDI inflows into China*

During the past three decades, FDI inflows into China can be broadly divided into three phases (see Figure 1): the experimental phase from 1982 to 1991, the boom phase from 1992 to 2001, and the post-WTO phase from 2002 to 2009.

During the experimental phase, FDI inflows into China were at a very low level but grew steadily, and were mainly concentrated in the Chinese southeast coastal areas, particularly in the four special economic zones (SEZs).[2]

In the second phase, FDI inflows into China rose rapidly during 1992–1996, but slowed down after 1997 and even declined in 1999 and 2000, before a moderate recovery in 2001. The slowdown during 1997–2000 was mainly caused by the Asian financial crisis.

After the entry into the WTO, FDI inflows into China rose rapidly, from US$47 billion in 2001 to US$92 billion in 2008. However, because of the 2007–2009 global financial crisis, FDI inflows into China declined to US$90.03 billion in 2009.

---

[1] Excluding FDI inflows into the financial sector. China first published FDI inflows into the financial sector in 2005. During the period 2005–2008, FDI inflows into the financial sector were US$46.52 billion. In this chapter, the data for FDI inflows into China do not include FDI inflows into the financial sector unless otherwise specified.

[2] The four special economic zones are Shenzhen, Zhuhai, Shantou in Guangdong Province, and Xiamen in Fujian Province.

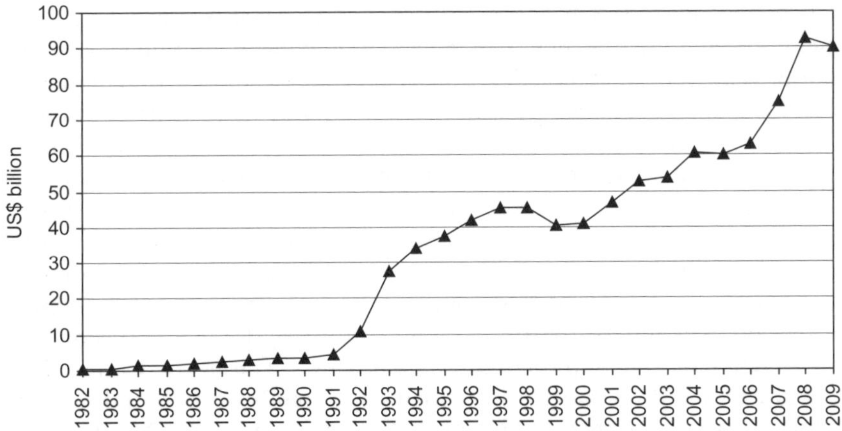

***Fig. 1.* FDI inflows into China (US$ billion and at current prices). Source: National Bureau of Statistics of China (NBS) (various issues-a); Invest in China. Note: The data do not include FDI inflows into the financial sector.**

There has long been an issue of "round-tripping" of FDI in the case of China. Because the funds originate in the host economy itself, round-tripping inflates actual FDI inflows. According to the UNCTAD (2007), a significant share of FDI inflows into China is round-tripping, mainly via Hong Kong and more recently and increasingly via some tax heaven islands – Virgin Islands, Cayman Islands, and Samoan Islands. Official estimates by the Chinese government are not available. One estimate made by Dr. Guonan Ma suggested that round-tripping inward FDI accounted for 25 percent of China's FDI inflows in 1992[3] and the same figure was also estimated by Harrold and Lall (1993). However, Xiao (2004) estimated that the round-tripping FDI accounted for 40 percent of China's total FDI inflows during 1994–2001.[4]

Round-tripping typically involves three steps: (1) the accumulation of new capital in China, (2) the capital flight out of China, and (3) the round-tripping FDI back to China. Because of the fast economic growth and high saving, China has accumulated a large amount of new capital. However, a large part of the new capital has found its way abroad through misinvoicing in international trade, smuggling, and other channels of capital flight since the people who are creating the new capital have strong incentives to diversify domestic risks and to seek better protection of property rights (Xiao, 2004). Some of this capital has stayed abroad

---

[3] In the conference of "China Update 2007" held in The Australian National University in 2007, Dr. Guonan Ma informed the author that he estimated in 1993 that the round-tripping FDI accounted for 25 percent of China's total FDI inflows in 1992.

[4] For a detailed study on "round-tripping" FDI in China, please see Xiao (2004).

waiting for opportunities to return back to China. On average, the round-tripping FDI – the returning Chinese capital, is about 20–30 percent of the capital flight (Xiao, 2004). The accumulated capital flight then forms the base for sustained round-tripping FDI back home when the opportunities to make profits and create new capital at home continue to exist.

Round-tripping is driven by a number of incentives. In the case of China, preferential treatments offered to FDI and property rights protection are the two main incentives for round-tripping FDI. First, since the beginning of economic reform, the Chinese government has used tax incentives, tariff concessions, and various preferential treatments intensively and selectively to attract FDI flowing into the designed areas and industries. These preferential treatments offered to FDI are the primary incentives for domestic firms to do round-tripping FDI. Second, China's property rights protection enforcement is weak. Many private enterprises operate in the environment of very restrictive regulations with loose property rights protection. So, the private sector has strong incentives to move their profits out of China and then move them back in the form of FDI when they see profit opportunities exist as the Chinese governments tend to give better protection of property rights to foreign investors. In addition, China's foreign exchange control regime, and better financial services overseas also play some roles in FDI round-tripping.

After China's accession to the WTO, China has strengthened property rights protection, and gradually introduced national treatment to FDI firms, providing better protection of property rights and offering more market access for FDI firms. However, with the implementation of the national treatment, a lot of preferential treatments offered to FDI firms have also been reduced and eventually eliminated. In March 2007 China passed the new corporate income tax law, unifying the corporate income tax rates for foreign and domestic enterprises, at 25 percent. The unification of the corporate income tax rate, the elimination of preferential treatments to FDI firms, and improved property rights protection will reduce the incentives for FDI round-tripping.

China has been very successful in attracting FDI inflows, particularly after its WTO accession. However, China's success in attracting FDI inflows has caused increasing concerns that China has crowded out FDI inflows into other countries, particularly into other Asian developing countries.

2.1. Has China attracted excessive FDI inflows from the world?

To answer this question, the author (Chen, 2010a) has developed a multiregression empirical model[5] to establish a norm of FDI inflows

[5] The empirical model is a multiregression model with panel data. The data set contains 50 developing countries for a period of 17 years from 1992 to 2008.

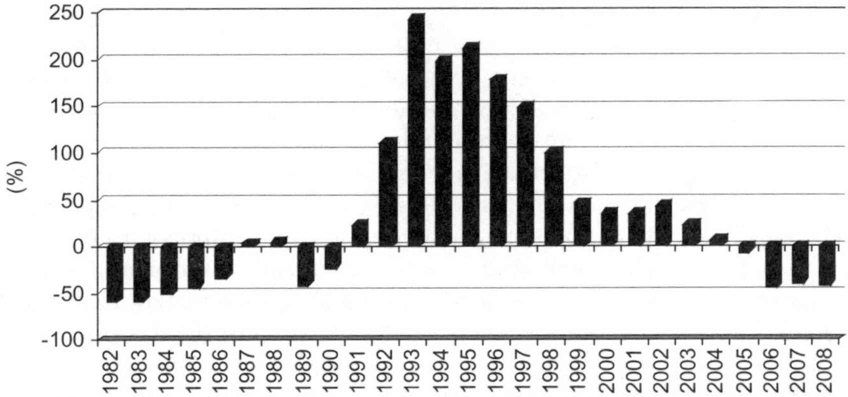

Fig. 2. China's annual relative performance in attracting FDI inflows, 1982–2008. Source: Chen (2010a). Note: The relative performance index is defined as the ratio of the difference between actual and the predicted FDI inflows over the predicted FDI inflow. A positive (negative) figure indicates that actual FDI inflow is more (less) than the model's prediction. FDI inflows cover inflows into the financial sector.

from all source countries into a developing host country for the period 1992–2008. According to the model, after controlling the aggregate supply-side effect of world FDI outflows, FDI inflows from all source countries into developing host countries are a function of a developing host country's market size, economic growth, per capita income level, efficiency wages, and creditworthiness. Using the model's prediction and the actual FDI inflows, the author examines the relative performance of China in attracting FDI inflows during 1982 and 2008. The study found that between 1982 and 2008 China attracted 5.88 percent or US$38.77 billion (at the 1990 constant US dollar price) more FDI inflows (including FDI inflows into the financial sector) than its potential. Therefore, though China is the largest FDI recipient among the developing countries, after controlling for its huge market size, fast economic growth, low labor cost, relatively well-educated human resources, and other economic and geographical characteristics, China's relative performance in attracting FDI inflows is only marginally above its potential.

From a dynamic point of view, as shown in Figure 2, China's relative performance in attracting FDI inflows fluctuated during the 1980s and 1990s. China attracted less FDI inflows than its potential during 1982–1986 but more between 1987 and 1988. However, from 1989 to 1990 China received less FDI inflows than it might have received.[6] Starting from

[6] China's poor performance in attracting FDI inflows during 1989–1990 was largely due to foreign countries' reaction to the Tiananmen Square Incident.

1992, FDI inflows into China surged at an unprecedented pace, mainly owing to a series of market-opening policies in the early 1990s. As a result, China received more FDI inflows than its potential from 1992 to 2000, but the relative performance fell during 1997–2000, mainly because of the Asian financial crisis. After China's accession into the WTO, China's relative performance was stable around its potential during 2001–2005, which is attributed to a series of domestic factors in China, including macroeconomic stability, steady economic growth, improved investment environment, accelerated trade and investment liberalization, social stability, and the integration with the global economy. However, since 2006 China's relative performance has been declining, especially in 2008, mainly due to the current global financial crisis.

The above analysis reveals that China's relative performance in attracting FDI inflows was only at a level moderately above its potential. Therefore, despite the fact that China is the largest FDI recipient among the developing countries and has attracted a large amount of FDI inflows in absolute dollars, China has received only its fair share of global FDI inflows, or at most marginally more than its potential.

2.2. Has China crowded out FDI inflows into other countries?

China's success in attracting FDI inflows has raised increasing concerns that China has crowded out FDI inflows into other countries, particularly into other Asian developing countries? A growing China can add to other countries' FDI inflows by creating more opportunities for production-networking and raising the need for raw materials and resources. At the same time, the extremely low Chinese labor costs may lure multinationals away from other Asian sites when the foreign corporations consider alternative locations for low-cost export platforms. Theoretically, competition in any resource flow may obviously occur when the resource in question is available in limited amounts. However, this "zero-sum" hypothesis is difficult to justify in the case of FDI. For example, as FDI inflows accounted for only 14.8 percent of the world gross fixed capital formation in 2007 (UNCTAD, 2008), additional FDI resources can be easily diverted from domestic resources and other international capital flows should investment opportunities arise.

As China attracts more FDI inflows, there have been more empirical studies focusing on the effects of FDI into China on FDI into other countries.

Chantasasawat *et al.* (2004) use data for eight Asian economies (Hong Kong, Taiwan, Republic of Korea, Singapore, Malaysia, Philippines, Indonesia, and Thailand) in addition to China over the period 1985–2001 and estimate equations for China's FDI inflows and other Asian countries' FDI inflows by two-stage least squares. They find that the level of China's

FDI is positively related to the levels of these economies' inward FDI, and the "China Effect" is generally not the most important determinant of the inward FDI of these economies. Policy and institutional factors such as openness, corporate tax rates, and the level of corruption tend to be more important. Zhou and Lall (2005) and Wang *et al.* (2007) estimate panel models to investigate the effect of FDI into China on FDI into Asian economies and find that, on average, FDI into China has raised rather than diverted FDI into neighboring countries.

Mercereau (2005) developed an empirical model to investigate the impact of China's emergence on FDI flows to Asia, using data from 14 Asian economies from 1984 to 2002. In contrast to the above studies, he does not find positive relationship between China's FDI inflows and FDI inflows to other Asian economies, however, he does not find much evidence that China's success in attracting FDI has been at the expense of other countries in the region either. China does not seem to have diverted FDI flows from countries in the region, with the exception of Singapore and Myanmar. Low-wage economies, which compete with China for low-wage investment, do not appear to have been particularly affected by China's emergence. Low levels of education or scientific developments are not associated with increased crowding out by China either.

Eichengreen and Tong (2005) employ a gravity model to show that the emergence of China as a leading FDI destination has encouraged FDI flows to other Asian countries via supply-chain production linkages. However, they also find evidence suggesting that FDI inflows into China have substituted FDI inflows into European countries. They explain this diversion effect by the negative effect of distance on supply-chain production linkages. In contrast, Resmini and Siedschlag (2008) estimate an augmented gravity model to analyze the effects of FDI into China originating in OECD countries on FDI into European Union (EU) and other countries over the period 1990–2004. Their results suggest that on average, *ceteris paribus*, over the analyzed period, FDI inflows into China have been complementary to FDI inflows into other host countries and into the EU as well. However, this complementary relationship is not constant across countries, being less strong in Europe than outside Europe. Also these complementarities follow a decreasing trend over the analyzed period of time.

Cravino *et al.* (2007) examine the effect of foreign capital stock in China on the Latin American and Caribbean (LAC) countries and find no evidence for a FDI diversion from OECD countries, in particular from the United States into China at the expense of the LAC countries. While the growth of capital stocks in China originating from the OECD especially from the United States was faster than in LAC countries over the period 1990–1997, this relative growth has slowed down since 1997.

Using data for 12 Asian developing economies over the period of 1992 and 2008, Chen (2010b) investigate the impact of FDI inflows into China on FDI inflows into other Asian developing economies and find that FDI inflows into China have statistically significant positive impact on FDI inflows into other Asian developing economies. This complementary relationship between Chinese and Asian FDI inflows may be linked to the increased resource demand by a rapidly growing Chinese economy and the production-networking activities among the Asian economies.

The above empirical studies suggest that there is not much evidence that China's success in attracting FDI inflows has crowded out FDI inflows into other countries. On the contrary, there is a strong evidence that FDI inflows into China have been complementary to FDI inflows into other host countries, especially to Asian and China's neighboring economies.

3. Characteristics of FDI inflows into China

FDI inflows into China come overwhelmingly from developing economies, are highly concentrated in the Chinese east and southeast coastal regions, and are biased toward the manufacturing sector.

3.1. Developing economies are the dominant source of FDI into China

In terms of the composition of FDI sources, FDI in China is characterized by overwhelming dominance of developing economies, particularly the Asian newly industrializing economies (NIEs). During the period of 1992 and 2008, developing economies accounted for 77.5 percent of the total accumulated FDI inflows into China,[7] while developed economies only 22.5 percent of the total. As shown in Figure 3, among the developing economies, Hong Kong is the largest single investor (41 percent), followed by Virgin Islands (10 percent), Taiwan (6 percent), South Korea (5 percent), Singapore (4.5 percent), and ASEAN-4 (1.6 percent). Among developed economies, Japan (7.5 percent) and the United States (7 percent) are the largest investors, while the EU-15 as a group accounted for 7 percent of the accumulated FDI inflows.

Figure 4 presents the annual FDI inflows into China by developing and developed economies during the period of 1992–2008. Two interesting observations emerge. First, FDI inflows into China slowed down and declined during 1997–2000, entirely because of the decline of FDI inflows from developing economies in the Asian financial crisis. During the same period, FDI inflows into China from developed economies were relatively stable.

---

[7] This figure includes round-tripping FDI. However, even after deducting the estimated 40 percent of round-tripping FDI, the developing economies still accounted for 67 percent and Hong Kong still accounted for 26 percent of the total accumulated FDI inflows into China.

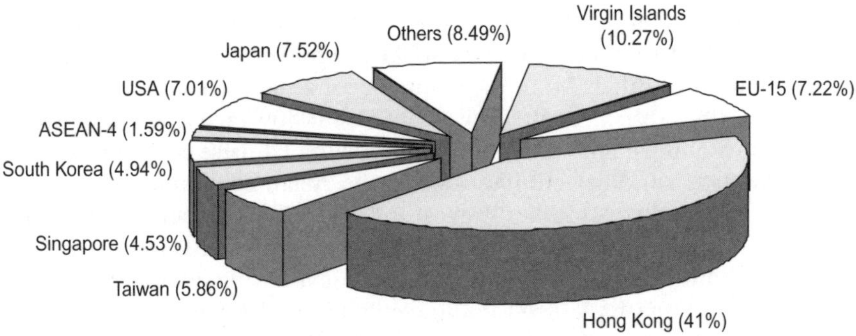

Fig. 3. Shares of accumulated FDI by sources economies in China (1992–2008). Source: Calculated from National Bureau of Statistics of China (NBS) (various issues-a); Invest in China. Note: The calculation is based at 2000 constant US dollar prices.

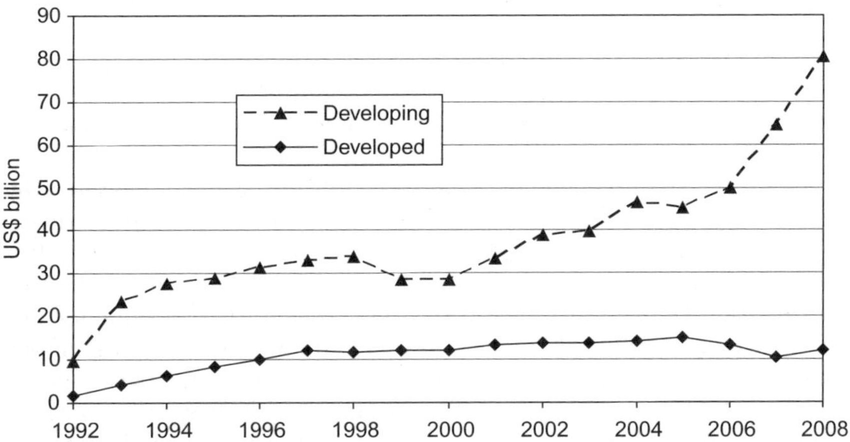

Fig. 4. FDI inflows into China by developing and developed economies (US$ billion and at current prices). Source: National Bureau of Statistics of China (NBS) (various issues-a); Invest in China.

Second, after China's accession into the WTO, FDI inflows into China increased rapidly, almost entirely coming from developing economies. FDI inflows from developing economies increased from US$33.5 billion in 2001 to US$80.3 billion in 2008. However, FDI inflows from developed economies only increased marginally during 2002–2005 and even declined during 2006–2008. As a result, the relative importance of FDI in China for developed economies has declined since 2002.

Why has China been so successful in attracting FDI inflows from developing economies, especially from Hong Kong and Taiwan, but not much in attracting FDI inflows from developed economies, especially from the European countries, even though they are the major investors for world FDI?

The domination of developing economies in FDI in China could be attributed to their economic development level and the nature and characteristics of their firms. Firms in developing economies have moderate technological and innovative capabilities, are at the mid-level of economic development and more concentrated in labor-intensive production technology, standardized manufacture products and better export market networks. With relatively abundant in labor resources, China is a very attractive location for the developing economies' investors to explore overseas investment opportunities, particularly for export-oriented FDI.[8] In addition, Hong Kong, Taiwan, and to a lesser extent Singapore, South Korea, and the ASEAN-4 (Thailand, the Philippines, Malaysia, and Indonesia) have high proximity with China. The extensive Chinese business networks and close geographical distance greatly reduce the costs of doing business in China for these investors and have facilitated the companies of these economies to venture in China. Therefore, China will likely remain an important host country for FDI from the developing economies in the future.

There are many reasons for the low level of FDI flows into China from the developed countries. Apart from the relatively large economic and technological development gaps and the low proximities, several other factors may be important in hindering FDI flows into China from the developed countries. First, the firms of developed countries usually possess more advanced technology and production techniques. Since the legal framework for protecting intellectual property rights in China is weak, the firms from the developed countries are more reluctant to invest in China. Second, the services sector in developed countries is advanced and has recorded the highest growth rates in global FDI flows over the last three decades. Most of China's service industries were closed to FDI before its 2001 accession to the WTO. Third, the large multinational enterprises (MNEs) are the main carriers of FDI from developed countries and cross-border mergers and acquisitions (M&As) are the increasingly important means by which they carry out FDI. However, cross-border M&As transactions by foreign investors in China have only been allowed at an experimental fashion in recent years. All these have negative impacts on the investment decision of the developed countries' investors. Not surprisingly, the magnitude of investment from developed countries in China is low compared with their total investments in the world.

---

[8] Export-oriented FDI refers to FDI that mainly aims to export from host country to other markets.

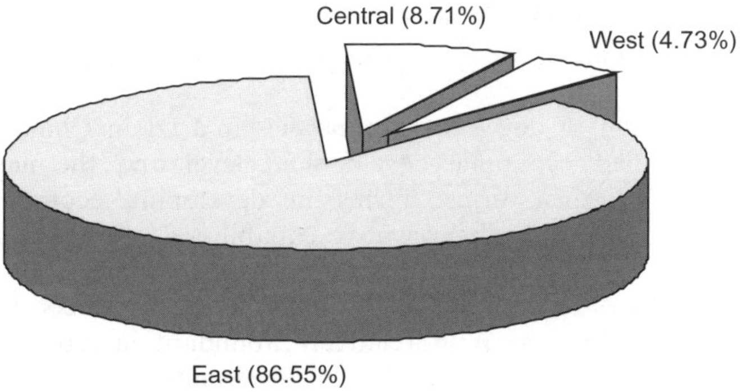

Fig. 5. Shares of accumulated FDI in China by regions (1983–2008). Source: Calculated from National Bureau of Statistics of China (NBS) (various issues-a); Ministry of Commerce of China (MOFCOM) (various issues). Note: The calculation is based at 2000 constant US dollar prices.

Obviously, the current composition of FDI sources in China needs to be diversified if China wants to benefit more from FDI. The diversification of FDI sources not only is necessary for China to attract more quantity of FDI, but also is very important for it to attract high quality FDI. In general, enterprises from developed countries with high technological and innovative capabilities have advantages in high technology, product differentiation, managerial and entrepreneurial skills, and knowledge-based intangible assets. Because of these advantages, FDI from developed countries is more interested in the Chinese market. The general implication is that host countries with larger market size, faster economic growth, and higher income will attract more market-oriented FDI.[9] China's huge domestic market, fast growth, and rising income are very attractive to market-oriented FDI from developed countries. Therefore, China has a great potential to attract FDI from developed countries. However, to realize its potential, China should fulfill its commitments to the WTO in trade and investment liberalization, particularly in strengthening the intellectual property rights protection, opening more services sector to FDI, and relax restrictions in cross-border M&As.

3.2. Unbalanced regional distribution of FDI inflows

The regional distribution of FDI inflows into China has been very uneven. FDI inflows into China were highly concentrated in the eastern region. Though there have been small fluctuations, the gap between the east and the central and western regions in receiving FDI has been increasing, especially since the early 1990s. As shown in Figure 5, by the end of 2008,

[9] Market-oriented FDI refers to FDI that mainly targets the host country's domestic market.

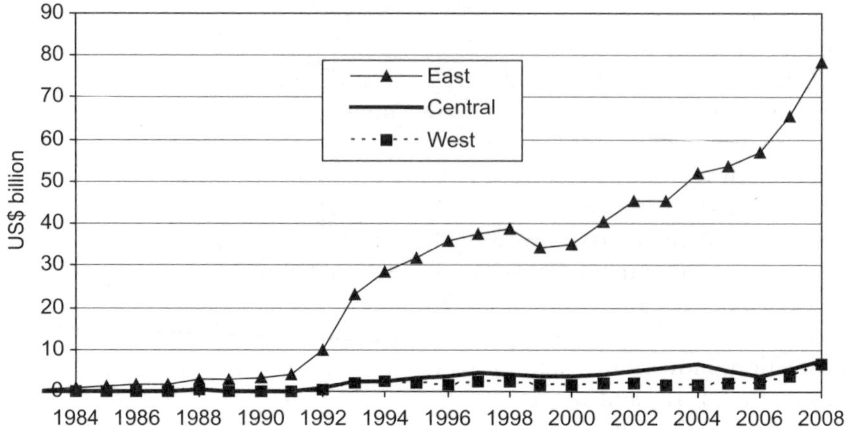

Fig. 6. FDI inflows into China by regions (at current prices). Source: National Bureau of Statistics of China (NBS) (various issues-a); Ministry of Commerce of China (MOFCOM) (various issues).

the eastern region[10] attracted 86.6 percent of the total FDI inflows while the central region[11] and the western region[12] received only 8.7 percent and 4.7 percent of the total.

As Figure 6 shows, after the 2001 entry into the WTO, FDI inflows continue to concentrate in the eastern region. FDI inflows into the eastern region increased from US$40.3 billion in 2001 to US$78.3 billion in 2008. In contrast, during the same period, FDI inflows into both the central region and the western region increased only slightly by 2008.

What are the reasons for this uneven regional distribution of FDI inflows into China? Empirical studies reveal that the uneven regional distribution of FDI inflows within China is primarily caused by the regional differences in location determinants (Chen, 2003). However, can this uneven regional distribution of FDI inflows within China be improved in the near future? Chen (2003) calculates the FDI inward attractiveness index for China's provinces and regions,[13] and reveals large differences across China's provinces and regions in the attractiveness index. The attractiveness of the eastern region to FDI is its more open and developed economy, closer connections with outside world, better infrastructure,

---

[10] The eastern region includes Beijing, Tianjin, Hebei, Liaoning, Shanghai, Jiangsu, Zhejiang, Shandong, Fujian, Guangdong, and Hainan.

[11] The central region includes Shanxi, Jilin, Heilongjiang, Henan, Hubei, Hunan, Anhui, and Jiangxi.

[12] The western region includes Inner Mongolia, Guangxi, Chongqing, Sichuan, Yunnan, Guizhou, Tibet, Shaanxi, Gansu, Qinghai, Ningxia, and Xinjiang.

[13] The inward FDI attractiveness index is the average of the scores on 15 variables (including 3 dummy variables) for each province or region. The value of the index ranges from 0 to 1. The higher the value of the index, the more attractive a province or a region is to inward FDI.

higher level in scientific research and technical innovation, and higher quality of labor forces.

Compared with the eastern region, although there has been some improvement in the investment environment for FDI, the central and the western regions are still less attractive and lag 10–15 years behind that of the eastern region. Therefore, the poor performance of the central region and particularly the western region in attracting FDI inflows is mainly attributed to their poor investment environments. To reduce the gap of economic development between the eastern region and the central and western regions, the Chinese government launched the "West Development Strategy" in 1998, which emphasizes on infrastructure, environment protection, industrial structural readjustment, sciences and education, and economic reform and openness.

Undoubtedly, the west development strategy has provided great opportunities for foreign investors. However, because the investment environment is largely based on structural factors that tend to change slowly over time, it is unrealistic to expect that the central and the western regions will attract large FDI inflows in the near future. Therefore, the eastern region will continue to attract most of the FDI inflows into China, and the uneven regional distribution of FDI inflows into China will persist.

3.3. Sectoral distribution of FDI inflows

As of the end of 2008, the sectoral distribution of FDI in China was characterized by a high concentration in the manufacturing sector. As shown in Figure 7, the manufacturing sector attracted 62.7 percent, the services sector attracted 34.7 percent, while the primary sector attracted only 2.5 percent of the total cumulative FDI inflows into China during 1997 and 2008.[14]

The sectoral structure of FDI in China is different to that of the world in which services sector accounted for more than 60 percent of the total world FDI. However, the sectoral structure of FDI in China has been gradually changing from heavily concentrating in the manufacturing sector toward more in the services sector. As Figure 8 shows, since China's accession into the WTO in 2001, although the manufacturing sector continued to receive large amount of FDI inflows, the growth rate of FDI inflows into the manufacturing sector has slowed down since 2004. In contrast, FDI inflows into the services sector have risen rapidly since 2005. By 2008, the share of FDI inflows into the services sector increased to 44 percent, while the share of FDI inflows into the manufacturing sector declined to 54 percent. FDI inflows into the primary sector have been relatively stable.

---

[14] Data for actual FDI inflows by sectors are not available before 1997.

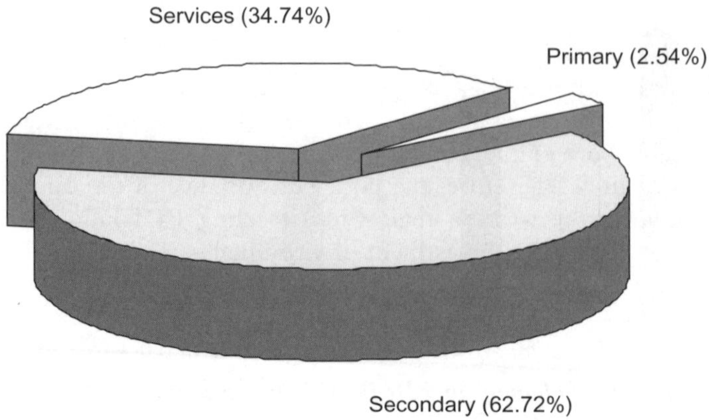

Fig. 7. Sectoral distribution of accumulated FDI inflows in China (1997–2008). Source: Calculated from National Bureau of Statistics of China (NBS) (various issues-a); Invest in China. Note: The calculation is based at 2000 constant US dollar prices.

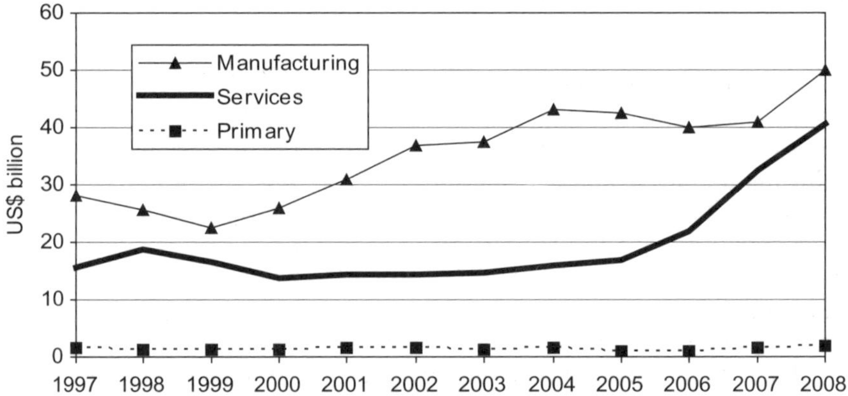

Fig. 8. FDI inflows into China by sectors (US$ billion and at current prices). Source: National Bureau of Statistics of China (NBS) (various issues-a); Invest in China.

In the last three decades, FDI inflows into China's manufacturing sector have gradually shifted from being heavily concentrated in labor-intensive industries, which is mainly export-oriented FDI, toward more investments in capital-intensive industries and technology-intensive industries, which are mainly domestic market-oriented FDI. As shown in Figure 9, between 1995 and 2006, the share of labor-intensive industries declined from 47 to 30 percent while the share of capital-intensive and technology-intensive industries increased from 25 and 27 percent to 31 and 38 percent,

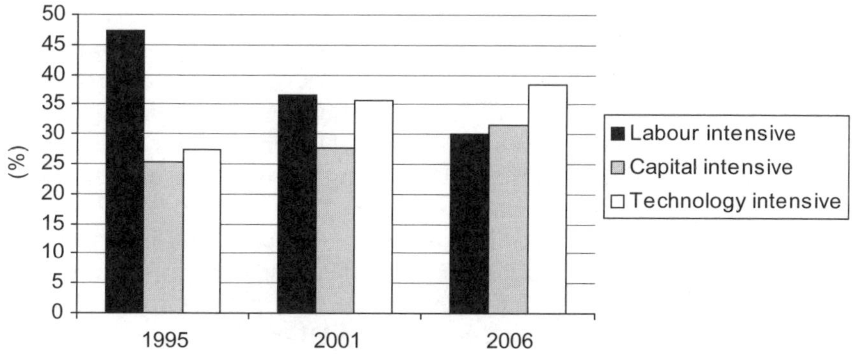

Fig. 9. Structural changes of FDI firms in manufacturing (by total assets). Source: Calculated from National Bureau of Statistics of China (various issues-a).

respectively, in the industrial composition of FDI firms in the manufacturing sector.

The changing industrial structure of FDI firms from the high concentration in labor-intensive industries toward more investments in capital-intensive and technology-intensive industries is clearly an indication that FDI inflows have been increasingly targeting China's huge domestic market. As China maintains high economic growth and increases per capita income, its domestic market demand provides good opportunities for market-oriented FDI. Therefore, market-oriented manufacturing FDI inflows into China will continue in the future.

China's labor-intensive industries are still quite competitive, with abundant and well-educated human resources and low labor costs, making it one of the most attractive locations for export-oriented FDI. Therefore, despite the declining share, FDI will continue to flow into China's labor-intensive industries, particularly for export-oriented FDI.

China made substantial WTO commitments to open its services sector to international trade and FDI. However, China takes a step-by-step approach to implement its commitments. In most services industries, especially in telecommunications, banking and insurance, wholesale and retail, storage and transportation, China will fulfill its commitments in 3–5 years after its WTO accession. As a result, FDI inflows into the services sector have been increasing slowly during 2002–2005, but started to increase sharply since 2006, reaching US$40.7 billion in 2008. With further and full implementation of its WTO commitments, China will attract more FDI into its services sector.

FDI inflows into China's primary sector have been low but relatively stable around 2.5 percent. This has been more because of institution and policy factors than economic factors. China's agricultural land tenure system and the traditional small-scale family-based agricultural production pattern have limited the inflows of agricultural FDI with large scale of production and advanced technology. Therefore, China would not attract large amount of FDI inflows into its agricultural sector without changing its land tenure system and reforming the traditional small-scale family-based farming pattern. China's FDI policies for the mining industries are relatively restricted. According to its "Industrial Guideline for Foreign Direct Investment (amended 2007)," except the industries of coal (excluding special coal), petroleum, natural gas, iron ore, and manganese, most mining industries are either restricted or prohibited to FDI. Therefore, unless China liberalizes its FDI policies for the mining industries, there would not be a big rise in FDI into its mining industries.

4. Contributions of FDI to China's economy

In the FDI literature, FDI is believed to have played some major roles in the development process of a host country economy, via capital formation, the creation of employment opportunity, promotion of international trade, transfer of technology, and the introduction of competition to the domestic economy. Over the past three decades, China has attracted huge amounts of FDI inflows and FDI firms have generated some important impacts on China's economy.

4.1. Capital formation

How important FDI inflows have been in China's domestic capital formation? To answer this question we analyze the ratio of FDI inflows in China's domestic gross fixed capital formation and the share of FDI in China's total investment in fixed assets[15] for the period 1994–2006.[16]

FDI has provided an important external finance to China's economic development. As shown in Figure 10, FDI inflows reached 17.3 percent of China's domestic gross fixed capital formation in 1994. However, since then the ratio of FDI inflows in China's domestic gross fixed capital formation has declined, falling to 6.4 percent in 2006. The main reason for the declining trend of the ratio of FDI inflows to China's domestic gross fixed capital formation is the much higher growth rate of China's domestic

[15] Gross fixed capital formation refers to the value of acquisitions less those disposals of fixed assets during a given period. Gross capital formation equals gross fixed capital formation plus changes in inventories. Total investment in fixed assets refers to the volume of activities in construction and purchases of fixed assets and related fees, expressed in monetary terms during the reference period of the whole country.

[16] China unified its dual exchange rate system in 1994. As a result, the exchange rate of RMB to US dollar depreciated sharply from 5.76 RMB per US dollar in 1993 to 8.62 RMB per US dollar in 1994. For consistency, data before 1994 were excluded in the analysis.

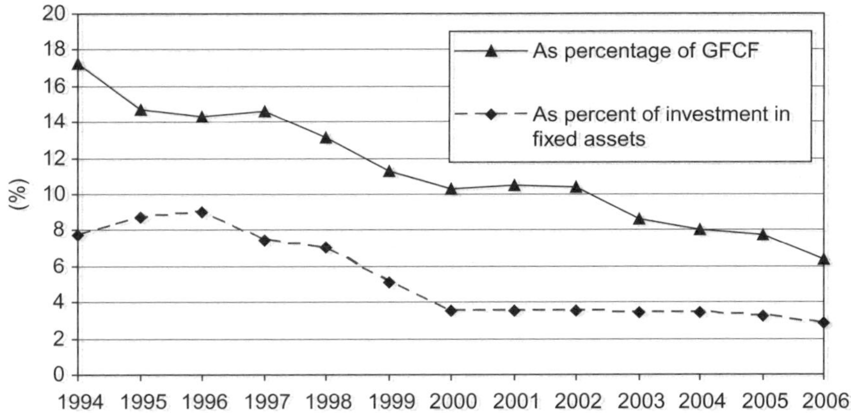

Fig. 10. FDI inflows as a percentage of gross fixed capital formation and shares of FDI in total investment in fixed assets in China (1994–2006). Source: Calculated from National Bureau of Statistics of China (NBS) (various issues-a). Note: GFCF = gross fixed capital formation.

gross fixed capital formation relative to that of FDI inflows into China. During 1994–2006, the annual growth rate of China's domestic gross fixed capital formation was 14.7 percent, while that of FDI inflows into China was 6.6 percent.

The above figure may also overestimate the real contribution of FDI to China's domestic gross fixed capital formation. In fact, total FDI inflows into China have not all been used in investment in fixed assets. There is evidence that investment in fixed assets made by FDI firms accounted for only a portion of the total FDI inflows into China each year. FDI firms' investment in fixed assets accounted for around 80 percent of the total FDI inflows into China in the late 1990s, and the figure for earlier years was much lower. The remainder (around 20 percent) of FDI inflows may have been used by FDI firms as working capital and for inventory investment (Chen, 2002).

To evaluate the contribution of FDI to China's domestic capital formation, we use the share of FDI in China's total investment in fixed assets. As shown in Figure 10, the share reached the highest level of 9 percent in 1996. Since then it fell to around 3.5 percent or less after 2000.

The above analysis suggests that FDI made important contribution to China's domestic capital formation during the 1990s. However, since 2000, the role of FDI in China's domestic capital formation has been declining. Nevertheless, for a large and fast growing economy like China – the third largest economy in the world with average annual GDP growth around 10 percent for the last three decades – FDI has provided an important supplementary source of finance to its domestic capital formation.

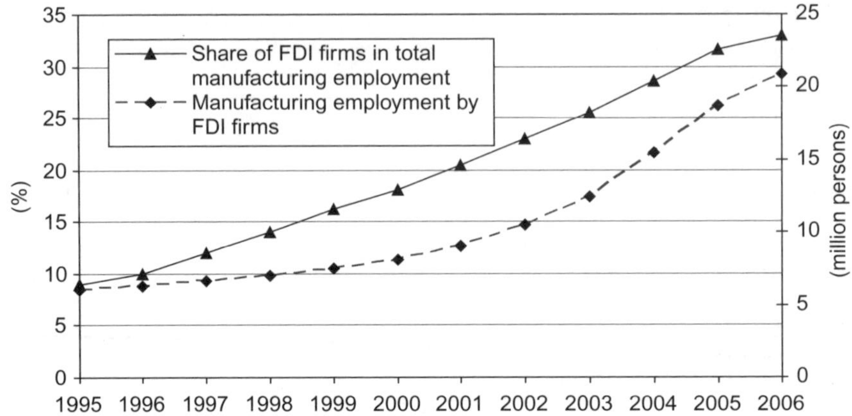

Fig. 11. FDI firms' manufacturing employment in China (1995–2006). Source: Data for 1995, 1999–2001, 2003, and 2005–2006 are calculated from National Bureau of Statistics of China (NBS) (various issues-a). Data for the other years are estimated by author.

4.2. Employment opportunities

In the developing countries, where capital is relatively scarce but labor is abundant, one of the most prominent contributions of FDI to the local economy is the creation of employment opportunities. In general, FDI has direct and indirect employment effects in a host country. The direct employment refers to the total number of people employed within the FDI firms. The indirect employment effects refer to the employment opportunities indirectly generated by FDI firms' activities in the host country. The indirect employment effects are difficult to measure, but country case studies conducted by the International Labour Organization (ILO) show that the indirect employment effects associated with inward direct investment may be as, if not more, important than the direct effects (Dunning, 1993).

Because of the difficulties in measuring the indirect employment effects of FDI, we confine our analysis within the scope of the direct employment effect of FDI in China's manufacturing sector. Figure 11 shows FDI firms' employment in the manufacturing sector during 1995–2006 and indicates that FDI firms' manufacturing employment increased significantly after 2001. While they employed 6.05 million workers or 8.9 percent of China's manufacturing employment in 1995, the figures have increased to 20.9 million workers or 33 percent in 2006. In other words, by the end of 2006, FDI firms employed one-third of China's manufacturing labor force.

Table 1. FDI firms' international trade performance (1980–2008)

Year	Value of FDI firms' trade (billion $US)			FDI firms as % of China's total		
	Total trade	Exports	Imports	Total trade	Exports	Imports
1980	0.04	0.01	0.03	0.11	0.05	0.17
1985	2.36	0.29	2.06	3.39	1.09	4.89
1990	20.12	7.81	12.31	17.43	12.58	23.07
1995	109.82	46.88	62.94	39.10	31.51	47.66
2000	236.71	119.44	117.27	49.91	47.93	52.10
2001	259.10	133.24	125.86	50.84	50.07	51.68
2002	330.24	169.99	160.25	53.20	52.21	54.29
2003	472.17	240.31	231.86	55.48	54.84	56.17
2004	663.18	338.61	324.57	57.44	57.07	57.83
2005	831.64	444.18	387.46	58.49	58.30	58.71
2006	1036.27	536.78	472.49	58.87	58.19	59.70
2007	1254.928	695.52	559.408	57.73	57.10	58.53
2008	1410.576	790.62	619.956	55.07	55.34	54.71

Sources: National Bureau of Statistics of China (NBS) (various issues-a); National Bureau of Statistics of China (NBS) (various issues-b); and Invest in China.

4.3. Export promotion

There is considerable evidence that FDI contributes to the growth of host countries' international trade. The most direct way to measure the impact of FDI on China's international trade growth is to examine the international trade performance of FDI firms. Table 1 presents the international trade performance of FDI firms from 1980 to 2008. FDI firms' trade rose from US$0.04 billion in 1980 to US$236 billion in 2000 and to US$1,410 billion in 2008. As a result, the importance of FDI firms in China's international trade has increased from only 0.1 percent in 1980 to 49.9 percent in 2000 and further to 58.8 percent in 2006, before falling slightly to 55 percent in 2008. One reason for this is that China's policy in relation to FDI has been deliberately biased toward export-oriented FDI. As a result, FDI firms have rapidly become a major exporter (Table 1).

FDI firms have played even more important role in China's manufacturing export. According to the annual enterprise census conducted by the National Bureau of Statistics (NBS) of China, during 2000–2003, on average, FDI firms' export propensity (export to sales ratio) was 42 percent, while that of domestic firms was only 10 percent. Among the 29 manufacturing industries, in 10 industries FDI firms' export propensity exceeded 50 percent, including cultural, educational, and sports goods (82 percent), leather and fur products (73 percent), furniture (71 percent), other manufacturing (71 percent), and instruments and meters (70 percent).

In 18 industries, FDI firms have dominated the industries' exports. For example, the share of FDI firms' exports in the industry's total exports was 92 percent in electronics and telecom equipment, 90 percent in instruments and meters, 87 percent in printing, 78 percent in plastic products, 76 percent in furniture, 75 percent in paper and paper products, and 72 percent in cultural, educational, and sports goods. Overall, FDI firms accounted for 67 percent of China's total manufacturing exports.

5. Prospects for FDI inflows into China

The global financial crisis started in 2008 has severely affected the world economy as well as world FDI flows. According to the "World Investment Report 2009," global FDI inflows declined by almost 30 percent, from US$1.7 trillion in 2008 to below US$1.2 trillion in 2009. China is not immune from this crisis. FDI inflows into China have also been affected by the crisis.

FDI inflows into China's financial sector dropped sharply. In the first half of 2009, FDI inflows into the financial sector were only US$1.5 billion, declining 48.3 percent than the same period in 2008 (MOFCOM, 2009). This sharp decline was mainly attributed to two factors. First, the financial crisis has severely weakened the ability of foreign financial institutions, especially those of developed countries, to undertake strategic investment in China's financial sector. Second, some foreign strategic investors sold stakes in Chinese banks in order to improve their own balance sheets. For example, in January, United Bank of Switzerland (UBS) sold its entire 3.378 billion shares in Bank of China (BOC) for US$800 million; Bank of America (BOA) cut its 19.13 percent stake in China Construction Bank (CCB) to 16.72 percent by selling 5.62 billion shares for US$2.8 billion (ETCN, 14 January 2009). Also in January, Royal Bank of Scotland (RBS) sold its entire stake in BOC for US$2.43 billion. In April, American Express Co. and German insurer Allianz sold half of their shares in Industrial and Commercial Bank of China (ICBC) for US$318 million and US$1.6 billion, respectively (*The Sydney Morning Herald*, 28 April 2009). In May, BOA again sold 5.7 percent of its stake in CCB for US$7.3 billion (The Wall Street Journal, 2009). In June, Goldman Sachs Group Inc. sold 20 percent of its shares in ICBC for US$2 billion (Caijing, 2009). The above transactions amounted to around US$18 billion of divestments by foreign strategic investors in Chinese banks in 2009.

FDI inflows into China's nonfinancial sectors dropped from US$92.4 billion in 2008 to US$90 billion in 2009. FDI inflows from the developed countries declined by more than 6 percent, while FDI inflows from the developing countries declined by 2 percent.

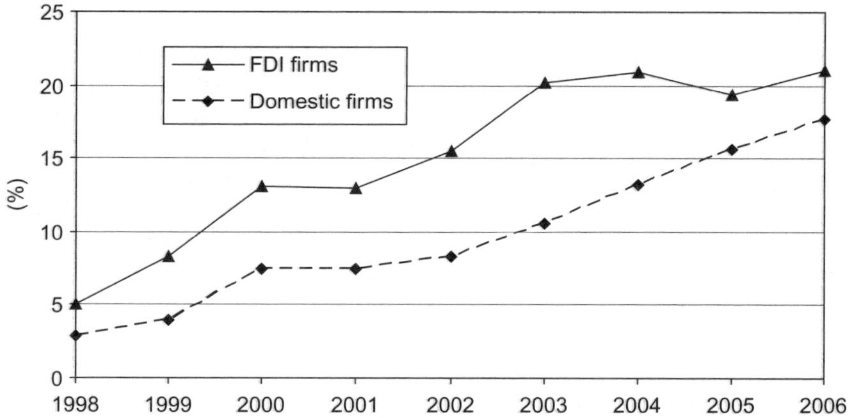

***Fig. 12.* Ratio of profits to net value of fixed assets of domestic firms and FDI firms in manufacturing sector in China (1998–2006). Source: Calculated from National Bureau of Statistics of China (NBS) (various issues-a).**

Undoubtedly, the global financial crisis has had negative impact on FDI inflows into China. However, as compared with the sharp decline of world FDI inflows, its negative impact on FDI inflows into China has been moderate. There are a number of reasons why FDI inflows into China have been resilient and why MNEs remain committed to investing in China.

First, China's overall investment environment remains attractive, with relatively efficient public services, good infrastructure, abundant and well-educated human resources, low labor costs, macroeconomic and political stability. This makes China one of the most attractive locations for FDI.

Second, China, as the largest developing and fast growing economy, has remained attractive to FDI, particularly to the market-seeking FDI. FDI firms in China are very profitable. As shown in Figure 12, the profit rate (measured by profits to the net value of fixed assets) of FDI firms is not only higher than that of domestic firms but has been increasing over time and reached over 20 percent since 2003. China maintained relatively high economic growth rate in 2008, 2009, and into the first quarter of 2010 (China Daily, 2010). A survey by the United States–China Business Council in March 2009 revealed that 88 percent of foreign businesses in China are profitable, 81 percent have a higher profit margin in China than elsewhere, and 89 percent select China as their first-time investment location (Xinhuanet, 2009). Therefore, China is very attractive to FDI and provides huge market opportunities for MNEs.

Third, China's abundant and relatively well-educated labor force with low labor costs is attractive to labor-intensive and export-oriented FDI projects. Despite the global economic recession, China's labor-intensive products are still very competitive in the world markets. On the one hand, with good quality and low prices, China's labor-intensive products are preferred by consumers. On the other, China's labor-intensive products mainly are daily consumer goods with low elasticity of demand. Therefore, the negative impact of the economic recession on demand for China's labor-intensive products is relatively small. In 2009, although China's total exports declined by 16 percent, exports of major labor-intensive products declined by a smaller margin. For example, exports of clothing, shoes, furniture, toys, suitcase and bags, declined by 11, 5.7, 6, 10, and 9.2 percent, respectively. In the first quarter of 2010 China's exports increased 28.7 percent over the same period last year (MOFCOM, April 15, 2010). This is a good sign of recovery of China's exports and is also a positive signal to export-oriented FDI to increase investment in China.

Fourth, in face of the global financial crisis, the Chinese government announced in November 2008 a renminbi (RMB) 4 trillion yuan (about US$600 billion) economic stimulus package in public investment plan to boost economic growth for three years. It may help keep the annual GDP growth rate of China at 8–9 percent for the period. By enhancing growth prospects and increasing investor confidence, the plan may help maintain FDI inflows into China.

Fifth, China has implemented a series of favorable FDI and trade policies to promote FDI inflows. China decentralized FDI approval rights in March 2009, allowing provincial authorities approve FDI project under US$100 million. China has increased the tax rebate rates for exports six times for some export products since 2008. As a result, the comprehensive tax rebate rates reached 12.4 percent.[17] These policy changes are necessary to cope with the global financial crisis and will help attract FDI inflows.

On April 13, 2010, the Chinese State Council released new regulations on foreign investment (State Council, 2010). According to the new regulations, China will improve good business conditions, welcome foreign investment in high-tech industries, services sectors, energy-saving, and environmental protection, but FDI into pollution- and energy-intensive projects or industries running at overcapacity are strictly prohibited. China will continue to support Chinese A-share listed companies in further introducing strategic investors from home and abroad, and standardize foreign companies' investment in domestic securities and M&A transactions. Qualified foreign-funded companies are allowed to go public, issue corporate bonds, or medium-term bills in China. Multinationals are encouraged to set up regional headquarters, R&D centers, procurement hubs, financial management, and other functional offices in China.

[17] The full tax-rebate rate for export is 17 percent.

Importing items for scientific and technological development by qualified foreign-funded R&D centers will be exempt from tariffs, importing value-added tax, and goods and services tax by the end of 2010. And foreign-funded enterprises are also encouraged to increase their investment in China's central and western regions, particularly in environment friendly and labor-intensive companies (People's Daily Online, April 14, 2010). The new regulations are expected not only to increase FDI inflows into China but also to improve the industrial and sectoral structure, regional distribution, and the quality of FDI inflows.

However, one policy factor that may create some uncertainties on FDI inflows is China's foreign exchange rate policy. Since the beginning of 2010, the developed countries led by the United States have renewed the pressure on China to reform its foreign exchange rate policy and to appreciate the RMB, as it is assumed to be 40 percent undervalued by C. Fred Bergsten, head of the Peterson Institute for International Economics (Cleveland.com, 2010). Paul Krugman claimed that China's policy to keep its currency undervalued has become a significant drag on global economic recovery (*The New York Times*, 2010). But the Chinese government rejected the claim and resisted the pressure to revalue its currency.

However, what would be the possible impacts of RMB appreciation on FDI inflows into China? First, as the value of RMB increases, so does the value of Chinese assets in terms of foreign currency. As a result, it will be more expensive for foreign investors to invest in China, thus having a negative impact on FDI inflows into China. Second, as the RMB appreciates, Chinese-made products become more expensive, which will reduce the competitiveness of Chinese products in international markets. As a result, the profit margin of export firms will be reduced, thus having a negative impact on export-oriented FDI inflows into China. Third, there might be a capital flight out of China soon after the sharp appreciation of the RMB. Some foreign investors might sell their assets (especially in the real estate sector) and repatriate their profits abroad so as to make windfalls from the sharp change in the exchange rate. Undoubtedly, in the short term, a sharp appreciation of the RMB will have a negative impact on FDI inflows into China.

As China's economy grows faster and larger, China will play a more important role in the global economy. So, it is an inevitable trend that the RMB will appreciate. However, the question is how fast and how much the RMB will appreciate. During a visit in April 2010 by the Chinese President Hu Jintao to Washington, DC, the United States and China seem to have reached an agreement with regard to the exchange rate between their two currencies. The agreement is that the United States government will stop yelling about it, and China will do whatever it can to reform its exchange rate regime, including a modest rise in the RMB some time in the near future (China.org.cn, April 16, 2010).

6. Conclusion

This chapter analyzes the growth trend of FDI inflows into China, evaluates China's performance in attracting FDI inflows, analyzes the composition of FDI sources, the regional and sectoral distribution of FDI in China, assesses the contributions of FDI to China's economy, and examines the prospects of FDI inflows amid the global financial crisis.

China has been successful in attracting FDI inflows, particularly after its 2001 WTO accession. This success could be attributed to several factors. They include China's increasingly liberalized FDI regime, much improved investment environment both in infrastructure and in legal framework, a potentially huge and fast growing domestic market, rising per capita income, relatively well-educated and low-cost labor forces, and extensive connections with overseas Chinese business communities.

However, China's success in attracting FDI inflows has not been at the expense of other countries. First, although China has been the largest FDI recipient among developing countries and has attracted over US$940 billion FDI inflows in the last three decades, based on its location variables, it only received its fair share of global FDI flows. Second, there is not much evidence that China's success in attracting FDI inflows has crowded out FDI flows into other countries. On the contrary, there is strong evidence that FDI inflows into China have been complementary to FDI flows into other countries, especially to Asian and China's neighboring economies.

FDI inflows into China have been overwhelmingly sourced from developing economies, particularly from the Asian NIEs and the ASEAN-4. The domination of developing economies as sources of FDI inflows into China could attribute to their similar economic development level, the nature and characteristics of their firms, and the high proximity with China. China will likely remain an important host country for the investments from the developing economies for a long period in the future. However, the current composition of FDI sources in China needs to be diversified if China wants to benefit more from FDI. China's huge and growing domestic market, fast economic growth, and rising per capita income are attractive to developed countries' investors, particularly to market-oriented FDI. Therefore, China has a great potential to attract FDI from developed countries. However, to realize its potential, China should fulfill its WTO commitments in trade and investment liberalization, particularly in the areas of strengthening the intellectual property rights protection, opening more sectors especially the services sector to FDI, and relax restrictions in cross-border M&As.

The regional distribution of FDI inflows inside China has been uneven, as FDI inflows into China have been mostly concentrated in the eastern region. This uneven regional distribution is primarily attributed to the regional differences in location determinants. The attractiveness of the east region to FDI is its relatively more open and developed economy, closer connections with outside world, better infrastructure, higher level in scientific research and technical innovation, and higher quality of labor forces. Although there has been some improvement, the central and the western regions are still less attractive to FDI in terms of location factors. Therefore, the eastern region will continue to attract most of the FDI inflows into China, and the uneven regional distribution of FDI inflows into China will persist.

The sectoral distribution of FDI in China was characterized by the concentration of FDI in the manufacturing sector. China's huge pool of relatively well-educated and low-cost labor is attractive to manufacturing FDI, which made China the processing and assembling "factories" of the world. FDI will likely continue to flow into China's manufacturing sector. FDI inflows into the services sector started to increase since 2006, mainly due to China's fulfilment of its WTO commitments to open its services sector. With further implementation of its WTO commitments, China will attract more FDI inflows into the services sector.

Large and growing FDI has greatly contributed to the Chinese economy in terms of capital formation, employment creation, and export promotion. The global financial crisis has had negative impact on FDI inflows into China, especially into the financial sector. However, as compared to the decline of world FDI inflows, the negative impact of the crisis on FDI inflows into China has been moderate. There are a number of reasons why FDI inflows into China have been resilient. China's sound and competitive overall investment environment, a large and fast growing domestic market, abundant and relatively well-educated labor resources, macroeconomic and political stability, government's strong policy response to counter the crisis and to further liberalization in trade and investment, all have made China one of the most attractive locations for FDI. Therefore, China will remain one of the most attractive destinations for FDI globally.

References

Caijing. (2009), Goldman Sachs Selling 0.9% Stake in ICBC for US$2 Billion, June 2. Available at http://english.caijing.com.cn/2009-06-02/110174882.html, accessed on April 19, 2010.

Chantasasawat, B., Fung, K., Iizaka, H., Siu, A. (2004), Foreign Direct Investment in China and East Asia. Available at http://www.hiebs.hku.hk/working_paper_updates/pdf/wp1135.pdf, accessed on April 19, 2010.

Chen, C. (2002), Foreign direct investment: prospects and policies. In: Charles A. P. (Ed.), *China in the World Economy: The Domestic Policy Challenges*. OECD, Paris, pp. 321–358.

Chen, C. (2003), Location determinants and provincial distribution of FDI. In: Garnaut, R., Song, L. (Eds.), *China: New Engine of World Growth*. Asia Pacific Press, The Australian National University, Canberra, pp. 189–216.

Chen, C. (2010a), Has China attracted excessive FDI inflows? Paper prepared for the 22nd ACESA Annual Conference, 'China: Economic Prosperity and Business Opportunities in the New Decade', to be held at the Graduate School of Management, La Trobe University, Melbourne, Australia, July 15–17, 2010.

Chen, C. (2010b), Asia foreign direct investment and the 'China effect'. In: Garnaut, R., Golley, J., Song, L. (Eds.), *China: The Next 20 years of Reform and Development*. ANU E Press, The Australian National University, Canberra, pp. 221–239.

China Daily. (2010), China's GDP Grows 11.9% in Q1, CPI up 2.2%, April 15. Available at http://www.chinadaily.com.cn/china/2010-04/15/content_9734449.htm, accessed on April 19, 2010.

China.org.cn. (2010), US, China "Agree" on RMB, Iran, April 16. Available at http://www.china.org.cn/opinion/2010-04/16/content_19832000.htm, accessed on April 19, 2010.

Cravino, J., Lederman, D., Olarreaga, M. (2007), Foreign Direct Investment in Latin America during the Emergence of China and India: Stylized Facts. World Bank, Policy Research Working Paper No. 4360. Available at http://ideas.repec.org/p/wbk/wbrwps/4360.html, accessed on April 19, 2010.

Dunning, J. (1993), *Multinational Enterprises and the Global Economy*. Addison-Wesley, Wokingham, England.

Eichengreen, B., Tong, H. (2005), Is China's FDI Coming at the Expense of Other Countries? NBER Working Paper No. 11335. Available at http://www.nber.org/papers/w11335, accessed on April 19, 2010.

ETCN. (2009), Share Sales "Don't Shake Relations" Between Chinese, Foreign Banks, January 14. Available at http://www.e-to-china.com/financial_crisis/analysis_comments/Authoritative_interpretation/2009/0114/15669.html, accessed on April 19, 2010.

Harrold, P., Lall, R. (1993), China Reform and Development in 1992–93. World Bank Discussion Paper No. 215, The World Bank, Washington, DC.

Mercereau, B. (2005), FDI Flows to Asia: Did the Dragon Crowd Out the Tigers?, September, IMF Working Paper No. WP/05/189. Available at http://ssrn.com/abstract = 888058, accessed on April 19, 2010.

Invest in China, *FDI Statistics*. Available at http://www.fdi.gov.cn/pub/FDI_EN/Statistics/FDIStatistics/default.htm

Ministry of Commerce of China (MOFCOM) (various issues), *China Foreign Investment Report*, MOFCOM, Beijing.

Ministry of Commence of China (MOFCOM). (2009), Regular News Conference of Ministry of Commence, July 30. Available at http://

www.mofcom.gov.cn/aarticle/ae/ah/200907/20090706431078.html, accessed on April 19, 2010.

Ministry of Commence of China (MOFCOM). (2010), Regular News Conference of Ministry of Commence, April 15. Available at http://www.mofcom.gov.cn/aarticle/ae/ai/201004/20100406869841.html, accessed on April 20, 2010.

National Bureau of Statistics of China (NBS). (various issues-a), *China Statistical Yearbook*, China Statistics Press, Beijing.

National Bureau of Statistics of China (NBS). (various issues-b), *China Foreign Economic Statistical Yearbook*, China Statistics Press, Beijing.

People's Daily Online. (2010), China Unveils New Rules for Foreign Investment, April 14. Available at http://english.peopledaily.com.cn/90001/90778/90861/6949654.html, accessed on April 19, 2010.

Resmini, L., Siedschlag, I. (2008), Is FDI into China Crowding out the FDI into the European Union? Available at http://www.etsg.org/ETSG2008/Papers/Siedschlag.pdf, accessed on April 19, 2010.

State Council. (2010), State Council's Regulations on Further Improvement on the Work of Utilising Foreign Direct Investment, April 13. Available at http://www.gov.cn/zwgk/2010-04/13/content_1579732.htm, accessed on April 19, 2010.

The New York Times. (2010), Taking on China, March 14, 2010. Available at http://www.nytimes.com/2010/03/15/opinion/15krugman.html, accessed on April 19, 2010.

The Sydney Morning Herald. (2009), Allianz, AmEx Sell Half of Stakes in China's ICBC, April 28, 2009. Available at http://news.smh.com.au/breaking-news-world/allianz-amex-sell-half-of-stakes-in-chinas-icbc-20090429-am6m.html, accessed on April 19, 2010.

The Wall Street Journal. (2009), BofA Gets $7.3 Billion in CCB Sale, May 13, 2009. Available at http://online.wsj.com/article/SB124210827820109929.html, accessed on April 19, 2010.

United Nations Conference on Trade and Development (UNCTAD). (2007), *Rising FDI into China: The Facts Behind the Numbers*. UNCTAD Investment Brief, Number 2. Available at http://www.unctad.org/en/docs/iteiiamisc20075_en.pdf, accessed on April 19, 2010.

United Nations Conference on Trade and Development (UNCTAD). (2008), World Investment Report, Transnational Corporations and the Infrastructure Challenge, United Nations Publication, New York.

Wang, C., Wei, Y., Liu, X. (2007), Does China rival its neighbouring economies for inward FDI. *Transnational Corporation* 16 (3), 35–60.

Xinhuanet. (2009), China's FDI Decline Slows in March, April 14, 2009. Available at http://news.xinhuanet.com/english/2009-04/14/content_11181782.htm, accessed on April 19, 2010.

Xiao, G. (2004), People's Republic of China's Round-tripping FDI: Scale, Causes and Implications. ADB Institute Discussion Paper No. 7. Available at http://www.adbi.org/files/2004.06.dp7.foreign.direct.

investment.people.rep.china.implications.pdf, accessed on April 15, 2010.

Cleveland.com (2010), Pressure Growing on China to Revalue Currency, March 24. Available at http://www.cleveland.com/business/index.ssf/2010/03/pressure_growing_on_china_to_r.html, accessed on December 23, 2010.

Zhou, Y., Lall, S. (2005), The impact of China's surge on FDI in South-East Asia: panel data analysis for 1986–2001. *Transnational Corporation* 14 (1), 41–65.

CHAPTER 15

Deviations from Covered Interest Parity: The Case of China

Yin-Wong Cheung[a] and XingWang Qian[b]

[a]*Department of Economics E2, University of California, Santa Cruz, CA 95064, USA; Department of Economics and Finance, City University of Hong Kong, and School of Economics, Shandong University, China*
E-mail address: cheung@ucsc.edu
[b]*Department of Economics and Finance, SUNY Buffalo State, Buffalo, NY 14222, USA*
E-mail address: qianx@buffalostate.edu

Abstract
We study the empirical determinants of the Chinese renminbi (RMB) covered interest differential. The canonical macroeconomic variables including capital flight and the factors that affect country risk, and a few China-specific regulatory and institutional factors are considered. It is found that the effects of these canonical macroeconomic variables on the RMB covered interest differential are largely consistent with those reported in the literature. Further, the covered interest differential was affected by China's general capital control policy and its exchange rate reform program, but not its political risk index. The effects of these explanatory variables on the covered interest differential appear to work mainly via the forward premium rather than the interest rate differential component. The results are largely the same across the onshore and offshore RMB forward rates that cover different sample periods.

Keywords: Covered interest differential, forward premium, expected depreciation, macrodeterminants

JEL classifications: F3, F32, G15

1. Introduction

China's official stance on exchange rate policy is to provide a stable exchange rate environment that is deemed to be a crucial factor for promoting trade and investment and, hence, economic growth. In recent years, China has been frequently criticized for pegging the value of its currency – renminbi (RMB) – at an artificially low level. The Mundell–Fleming trilemma framework

Frontiers of Economics and Globalization
Volume 9 ISSN: 1574-8715
DOI: 10.1108/S1574-8715(2011)0000009020

suggests that a country may only choose two of the three macroeconomic policy goals: free capital flows, independent monetary policy, and stable foreign exchange rate. With a revealed preference for exchange rate stability, China imposes capital controls and retains monetary policy independence.[1] How effectively China could restrict free capital flows is critical for its exchange rate and macroeconomic stabilization policies.

China, in recent years, has seen its economy getting more and more integrated with the world economy. While the pace of trade integration is phenomenal, it is hard to ignore the growing financial integration between China and the world economy. For instance, the gross cross-border capital flow per gross domestic product (GDP) increased from about 1% in 1982 to more than 12% in 2007. Despite the relatively fast integration process, China is arguably far from being perfectly integrated with the world economy. Further, the trade and financial integration processes do not come along smoothly and without any costs.

Conceivably, the progressing integration process could make it increasingly difficult for China to maintain tight capital controls. Anecdotal evidence suggests that, since 2003, China has experienced large swings in both inward and outward capital flight. For instance, Cheung and Qian (2010) document that, for some periods, illicit capital outflows and inflows could be larger than the official foreign direct investment or the change in external debts. These large capital movements, in the absence of an efficient capital market, could inflict huge economic costs on China's economy.

Indeed, in the last few years, China has issued quite a few policy directives targeting capital flight and hot money. In general, China's policy is shifting from being more restrictive on capital outflows toward gradually balanced controls on both capital inflows and outflows.[2] Before establishing an efficient capital market, China's ability to maintain an effective capital control policy has significant implications for its ability to manage the economy and for the development of future policies of liberalizing capital management.

In the current exercise we study the RMB covered interest differential that is closely related to capital control effectiveness. In the absence of impediments to capital movement, covered interest parity suggests that assets of similar risk characteristics in different countries should commend the same rate of return. Capital controls that prohibit free capital flow between countries could drive a substantial wedge between returns across countries and lead to covered interest differentials. Perfectly effective capital control policies could sustain persistent covered interest

---

[1] See, for example, Cheung *et al.* (2008) for China's monetary policy independence.
[2] See, for example, Hung (2008) and Prasad and Wei (2007) for a detailed description of China's capital control policy.

differentials and partially effective policies could only maintain temporary deviations.

In the literature, the covered interest differential is shown to be determined by existing and future capital control policies and macroeconomic factors that could affect country risk and, hence returns; see Aliber, (1973), Dooley and Isard (1980), Ito (1983), and Melvin and Schlagenhauf (1985). In the case of China, Cheung *et al.* (2003), for example, use *ex post* uncovered interest differentials to examine China's degree of integration with other economies. Ma and McCauley (2008) use the covered interest differential directly to study the effectiveness of China's capital control policy. They suggest that China's capital control is binding but not perfect; that is, there is capital flight but it is not large enough to equalize onshore and offshore yields on the Chinese RMB.

In the next section, we briefly discuss the empirical determinants of covered interest differentials considered in our empirical exercise. Some of these determinants are drawn from the literature and some are specific to China.

One data issue for our empirical exercise is the choice of forward rates for constructing the RMB covered interest differential. In our exercise, we use both the nondeliverable and onshore forward rates. One advantage of nondeliverable forward rates is that these rates are determined outside China and are not subject to Chinese jurisdiction. Thus, they could be interpreted as a proxy for the market expected future RMB exchange rate. The onshore forward rates are prices local Chinese firms could use to hedge their exchange rate risk and have only been available recently.

Another data issue is the choice of capital flight measure, which is an important factor for assessing the effectiveness of capital controls. In this exercise, we adopt the Chow and Lin method to construct the monthly version of the World Bank measure of capital flight. These data issues are discussed in Section 3.

The estimation results are discussed in Section 4 and some concluding remarks are offered in Section 5.

2. *Determinants of cover interest differential*

Covered interest differential exists in the presence of capital controls and country risk (Aliber, 1973; Dooley and Isard, 1980; Frankel and Engel, 1984). By restricting capital movement in and/or out of a country, capital control policies could create a gap between returns of domestic and foreign investments. A perfect control policy offers authorities a tight grip on, say, domestic interest rates. The folklore, however, is that capital controls are never perfect – people always find some ways to circumvent regulations. Thus, capital controls impede but do not eliminate capital flows between countries.

To what extent does a given capital control policy affect capital movement? The policy's potency depends on, among other things, how it is being implemented and the country's economic structure. The same capital control policy could yield different outcomes in different countries. Thus, the use of *de jure* capital control classifications may not accurately represent the effect of capital controls on observed covered interest differentials.[3]

In the subsequent sections, we use capital flight as a proxy for *de facto* capital control effort. Capital flight, the illicit capital movement that circumvents control measures, indicates the effectiveness of capital controls. We take a low level of capital flight as a result of serious capital controls. A high level of capital flight suggests a porous control environment. It is postulated that capital flight has a negative effect on the country's currency covered interest differential.

Besides capital controls, covered interest differentials are affected by macroeconomic factors that contribute to country risk. Because country risk is not directly observable, we follow the literature and consider three components of country risk.[4] Specifically, the three components are: (a) solvency, (b) liquidity, and (c) economic stability. Intuitively, the country risk increases if a country has a deteriorating solvency position, worsening liquidity condition, or destabilizing economic climate. The effect of these three components on a country's covered interest differential follows from the axiom that investors demand a higher yield margin to assume a higher level of risk. Thus, factors that increase country risk have a positive impact on covered interest differentials.

The macroeconomic factors used to capture a country's solvency position (and their effect on covered interest differentials given in parentheses) are the real GDP growth rate (−), total external debt (+), and government budget deficits (+). The liquidity condition is assessed by the international reserves to GDP ratio (−). The economic stability factors are the inflation rate (+), inflation volatility (+), exchange rate change (+/−), and exchange rate volatility (+).[5]

In studying the RMB covered interest differential, we include three China-specific regulatory and institutional factors. The first factor is a dummy variable that represents China's capital control policy. It captures the shift of China's policy bias from tightening to loosening and from primarily controlling outflow to controlling both inflow and outflow.

---

[3] See, for example, Magud and Reinhart (2007) for issues related to *de jure* capital control measures.

[4] See for example, Edwards (1984, 1986), Favero *et al.* (1997), Eichengreen and Mody (1998), Kamin and von Kleist (1999), Kaminsky and Schmukler (2001), Merrick (2001), Mauro *et al.* (2002), Rigobon (2002), and Baek *et al.* (2005).

[5] Some studies used the probability of debt default or eurocurrency spreads as proxies for country risk. However, both proxies could be problematic (Melvin and Schlagenhauf, 1985).

We expect a narrow covered interest differential in the presence of a loose capital control policy.

The second factor is a dummy variable for the foreign exchange reform that took place in July 2005. The long awaited foreign exchange reform is conducted in the typical Chinese style of gradualism – a 2.1% one-off RMB revaluation in July 2005 followed by gradual appreciation.[6] The policy change reduces the probability of a one-off sharp appreciation risk. Thus, the policy is likely to reduce covered interest differential.

The third factor is related to China's political risk. It is expected that a higher RMB covered interest differential follows a higher level of political risk. We use the political risk index variable from ICRG, which is constructed from 12 elements including bureaucracy quality, corruption, and law and order.

3. *The basic empirical specification and data*

Following the discussion in the previous section, the basic covered interest differential regression specification is given by

$$Y_t = \alpha + \sum_{i}^{p} \beta_i Y_{t-i} + \theta' \boldsymbol{X_t} + \psi' Z_t + \varepsilon_t, \tag{1}$$

where Y_t is the RMB covered interest differential at time t, $\boldsymbol{X_t}$ is a vector that includes the canonical explanatory variables including capital flight and other macroeconomic factors mentioned in the previous section, Z_t contains the three China-specific explanatory variables, and ε_t is the error term.

Monthly data from January 1999 to June 2008 are considered. The starting point of the sample period is determined by data availability.

Data on one-month RMB interbank offer rates (Chibor), one-month US dollar London interbank offer rates (Libor), spot RMB exchange rates per US dollar, and one-month nondeliverable forward rates of RMB per US dollar are used to construct the RMB covered interest differential variable.[7] A large value of Y_t implies a high covered return on RMB. In addition to nondeliverable forward rates, we consider onshore forward rates – see Section 4.3. The lags of Y_t are included to describe dynamics not captured by macroeconomic variables and China-specific factors.

The capital flight variable – a measure of *de facto* capital control intensity – is derived from the World Bank residual method, which is a common approach to assess the amount of capital flight. In essence, the

---

[6] The gradual appreciation came to a halt in the second half of 2008 in the midst of the global financial crisis.

[7] See, for example, Ma *et al.* (2004) for a discussion of the RMB nondeliverable forward market.

method assesses the magnitude of capital flight by comparing capital inflows and outflows reported in the balance of payments statistics.[8] The use of balance of payments statistics yields only quarterly capital flight data. The monthly quarterly data are interpolated from quarterly data using the Chow and Lin (1971) method. The data construction procedure is described in appendix.[9] The monthly Chinese GDP data used are also obtained using the same procedure from quarterly data.

These variables and others used in the empirical analysis are defined in the appendix.

4. Empirical results

We examine the stationary property of each variable considered in our regression analysis using the Elliott *et al.* (1996) ADF-GLS unit root test, which assumes the highest test power among unit root tests. The finite sample critical values from Cheung and Lai (1995) are used to assess statistical significance. For brevity, the unit root test results are not reported but are available upon request. It is found that the covered interest differential variable, capital flight, and most other macroeconomic variables considered are stationary variables. For variables that are determined to be I(1) nonstationary, they enter the regression in their first differences.

Since capital flight may be endogenous with respect to covered interest differentials, we estimate Equation (1) using the instrumental variable method. Specifically, the instrument for capital flight is trade openness. The choice of trade openness is motivated by the link between capital flight and misinvoicing of exports and imports. Indeed, it is widely perceived that trade misinvoicing via under- and overinvoicing imports and exports is a common strategy to evade capital controls and to move money in and out of China, and thus, is an important conduit for capital flight. A higher level of openness offers a better chance to manipulate the reported trade prices and the related capital flight.[10]

4.1. Basic estimation results

The results of estimating Equation (1) are reported in the first column of Table 1. With a few exceptions, we only present variables with a significant

---

[8] See, for example, Claessens and Naude (1993) and Kar and Cartwright-Smith (2008) for a detailed description of various capital flight measures and their limitations.

[9] Essentially, information from monthly data on comparable and related variables is used to obtain the monthly capital flight and GDP data from the corresponding quarterly data. Wilcox (1983), for example, reports that the Chow and Lin method can successfully recover the essential dynamic characteristics of a data series, including autocorrelation structure and turning points.

[10] Qualitatively similar results were obtained when the lagged KF was used as the instrument.

Table 1. Determinants of China's covered interest differentials (offshore forward rates)

CID		RDIFF		PREM	
CID(−1)	0.774***	RDIFF(−1)	0.955***	PREM(−1)	0.528**
	(0.13)		(0.09)		(0.24)
CID(−2)	−0.467***	KF	−0.113	PREM(−2)	−0.484*
	(0.15)		(0.45)		(0.25)
CID(−3)	0.156	*d*FISC	2.461*	KF	−1.757
	(0.10)		(1.38)		(2.21)
KF	−0.757			RGDPG	−0.080**
	(0.86)				(0.04)
RGDPG	−0.083**			*d*NEER	−0.034***
	(0.04)				(0.01)
*d*NEER	−0.046***			EV	8.197***
	(0.01)				(2.78)
EV	9.090***			InflV	0.068
	(3.00)				(0.05)
InflV	0.063***				
	(0.02)				
CONTROL	−0.063*				
	(0.03)				
REFORM	−0.202***				
	(0.08)				
Trend	0.122**		0.004		0.200*
	(0.06)		(0.02)		(0.10)
Constant	−0.439**		−0.009		−0.644**
	(0.18)		(0.05)		(0.28)
Adj. R-square	0.86		0.86		0.81
Obs.	111		113		112
Q-stat(12)	1.81		10.01		17.76
Q-stat(24)	7.11		15.60		28.03

Note: The table reports the results of the IV regression with *d*OPEN (trade openness) as the instrument for KF. Robust standard errors are given in the parentheses. ***, **, and * denote significance at the 1%, 5%, and 10% levels, respectively. Q-stat(12) and Q-stat(24) are the Box–Ljung Q-statistics calculated from the first 12 and 24 estimated residual autocorrelations. None of the Q-statistics is significant.

coefficient estimate in the table for brevity.[11] The lag structure of the lagged dependent variable covered interest differential (CID) is determined by the Bayesian information criterion and the properties of the estimated residuals. The marginally significant Y_{t-3} is included to ensure that there is no serial correlation among the estimated residuals. The covered interest differential variable displays rather complex dynamics that is not explained by the selected macroeconomic variables and China-specific factors. The coefficient estimates suggest that there is considerable amount

[11] The complete result is available upon request.

of one-period persistence that is mostly reversed in the subsequent period. In passing, it is noted that the use of quarterly data would not reveal this kind of dynamics and, thus, could lead to distorted results.

The RMB covered interest differential is negatively affected by capital flight (KF). A higher level of capital flight that is indicative of less restrictive capital control efforts reduces the RMB covered interest return. The result is in line with the findings of Dooley and Isard (1980), Ito (1983), and Melvin and Schlagenhauf (1985). Nevertheless, it is not statistically significant.

Not all the macroeconomic factors used as proxies for country risk are statistically significant. For instance, the liquidity factor represented by the international reserves to GDP ratio is not significant and, thus, not reported in the table. The significant macroeconomic factors, however, mostly have a sign that is consistent with theoretical predictions. For instance, the real GDP growth (RGDPG) has a negative coefficient estimate – high economic growth lowers RMB covered interest differentials. The finding is in accordance with the notion that high economic growth alleviates the level of country risk and, hence, reduces the level of covered interest differential.

*Three of the four economic stability proxy variables are significant. High exchange rate volatility (EV) and high inflation volatility (InflV) – the symptoms of economic instability – have the expected positive impact on RMB covered interest differentials. Again, a high covered return is required to assume a high level of country risk. The nominal effective exchange rate (NEER) is an index measuring the general strength of RMB. A positive value of the change in NEER (*d*NEER) means RMB appreciates against a basket of foreign currencies. Given the conservative Chinese exchange rate policy, we expect a high NEER reduces the possibility of a jump in its value in the near future and, thus, does not add to the required covered return. Thus, the negative estimate of *d*NEER suggests that an appreciation of RMB softens the pressure (or the expectations) of further RMB appreciation and, hence, a negative coefficient estimate.

While China's political risk does not affect RMB covered interest differentials, the other two China-specific factors show up significantly in the regression. Specifically, the policy control dummy variable (CONTROL) and the foreign exchange reform variable (REFORM) have a negative coefficient. During the sample period, China is loosening its grip on capital control and the CONTROL variable is decreasing. In the content of China, a weaker capital control environment makes it more difficult to deter hot money inflow and to resist the pressure to appreciate RMB. If it is the case, then a looser control leads to an expected RMB appreciated, a lower RMB forward discount, and a higher covered return, *ceteris paribus*.

The estimated negative effect of the reform variable REFORM is in line with the conventional wisdom. With a one-time appreciation in July 2005 and the subsequent managed appreciation process, the possibility of another large jump in the future value of RMB is subsided. Thus, covered interest differentials in the postreform period are lower than those in the prereform period, *ceteris paribus*.

Overall, specification (1) explains the RMB covered interest differential variable quite well with the sample adjusted R-square statistic of 86% and estimated residuals pass the Box–Ljung test.

4.2. Components of covered interest differential

The covered interest differential variable considered in the previous section is the sum of two components: interest rate differential and forward premium. Although China's onshore money market is undergoing a liberalization process and transiting from a mostly government directed to a more market-force-driven market, the RMB interest rate is *de facto* a government-dictated rate. Further, the domestic money market is not open to all investors – especially foreign investors.[12]

The nondeliverable forward rates used to construct the forward premium, however, are determined outside China and, in principle, are not subject to the Chinese jurisdiction. These rates are the result of the interplay between market forces and could be interpreted as a market proxy for the expected future Chinese RMB exchange rate. For instance, during 2003–2005, the speculation of RMB revaluation drove up its nondeliverable forward rate and induced an average of about US$55 billion hot money inflow per year.[13]

Given their different determination mechanisms, the interest rate differential and the forward premium components could react differently to the determinants of covered interest differential. Some explanatory variables may affect the RMB covered interest differential via the forward premium channel and some via the interest rate differential. To capture this idea, we decomposed the covered interest differential into its interest rate differential (RDIFF) and forward premium (PREM) component; that is, CID = RDIFF+PREM. Then, we regressed each one of these two components on the explanatory variables included in Equation (1). The results are reported in the second and third columns of Table 1.

The interest differential variable (RDIFF) displays a high level of persistence with an AR(1) coefficient estimate of 0.955. The capital flight (KF) variable is negative but not significant. The first-differenced fiscal deficit variable (*d*FISC) that is related to solvency is the only significant macroeconomic factor. It is significant at the 10% level with a

---

[12] See, for example, Nagai and Wang (2007) and Xie (2002).

[13] Authors' calculation based on the notion of hot money = errors and omissions+portfolio investment inflows (Prasad and Wei, 2007).

negative sign, indicating a high government deficit widens the interest rate differential.

The forward premium (PERM) yields estimation results that are comparable to those for the covered interest differential regression presented under the first column. The capital flight variable again has a negative coefficient and is insignificant. It is of interest to compare the capital flight estimates across these three regressions despite their insignificance. While all these estimates are negative, the one for PERM is much larger than the RDIFF one. If these estimates are significant, then we would say that the capital flight effect on covered interest differentials works mainly through the forward premium, instead of the interest rate differential, channel.

The macroeconomic factors, real GDP growth (RGDPG), nominal effective exchange rate (*d*NEER), exchange rate volatility (EV), and inflation volatility (InflV) have the same signs as those under the first column. All four variables with the exception of InflV are statistically significant. The inflation volatility variable is reported because its inclusion raises the adjusted R-square estimate from 73% to 81%.[14]

Comparing the results in these three columns, we observed that the two components of covered interest differential respond differently to the determinants. The dissimilar response patterns could be attributed to their different determination mechanisms noted in the beginning of this section. The interest rate differential component is quite persistent and responds only to a few economic factors. The forward premium component, on the other hand, behaves quite similarly to the covered interest differential. Interestingly, none of the China-specific factors show up significantly in both the interest rate differential and forward premium equations.

4.3. Onshore forward data

In Sections 4.1 and 4.2, the forward premium and the resulting covered interest differential variable is based on nondeliverable forward rates that are determined outside China. Since the exchange rate reform in July 2005, the Chinese central bank, People's Bank of China, has encouraged the trading of RMB forwards in China. State banks, nonbank financial institutions, foreign banks and financial institutions, and even nonfinancial enterprises are allowed to register and participate in the onshore RMB forward market. Forward contracts of RMB vis-à-vis five major foreign currencies – the US dollar, euro, Japanese yen, Hong Kong dollar, and British pound – are currently offered in the onshore forward market. Compared with the offshore nondeliverable RMB forward market, the

---

[14] In fact, if the openness instrumental variable is not used, the InflV variable is positively significant.

onshore market is a relatively shallow market in which transactions are mostly hedge demands from corporations. It is under close government supervision and regulations. Apparently, the pricing in this market is influenced by interest rate parity (Peng *et al.*, 2007).

Despite the fact that onshore RMB forward data are available only for a relatively short time period, we would like to investigate if the results reported in Table 1 are robust to the choice of forward data. Further, it is of interest to know if the onshore and offshore variables have different responses to the selected macroeconomic factors. To this end, we re-estimated Equation (1) using the RMB covered interest differential constructed from the onshore RMB forward rate as the dependent variable. For comparison purposes, we also repeated the regressions for the two components of the alternative covered interest differential variable. The sample size of these regressions is from October 2005 to June 2008. The results are presented in Table 2. It is noted that the

Table 2. Determinants of China's covered interest differentials (onshore forward rates)

OSCID		OSRDIFF		OSPREM	
OSCID(−1)	0.750***	RDIFF(−1)	0.542***	OSPREM(−1)	0.464***
	(0.07)		(0.18)		(0.07)
OSCID(−2)	−0.630***	KF	−0.277	OSPREM(−2)	−0.605***
	(0.09)		(0.40)		(0.14)
OSCID(−3)	0.482***			KF	−1.755**
	(0.08)				(0.72)
KF	−0.924*			*D*NEER	−0.031**
	(0.52)				(0.01)
*d*NEER	−0.050***			EV	18.148***
	(0.01)				(4.41)
EV	15.734***			InflV	0.137***
	(2.79)				(0.04)
InflV	0.127***				
	(0.03)				
Trend	−1.028***		0.579**		−1.105***
	(0.30)		(0.25)		(0.38)
Constant	4.439***		−2.708**		4.989***
	(1.36)		(1.15)		(1.68)
Adj. R-square	0.88		0.81		0.64
Obs.	30		32		31
Q-stat(12)	7.65		11.64		11.34
Q-stat(24)	16.29		28.62		24.15

Note: The table reports the results of the IV regression with *d*OPEN (trade openness) as the instrument for KF. Robust standard errors are given in the parentheses. ***, **, and * denote significance at the 1%, 5%, and 10% levels, respectively. Q-stat(12) and Q-stat(24) are the Box–Ljung Q-statistics calculated from the first 12 and 24 estimated residual autocorrelations. None of the Q-statistics is significant.

two China-specific factors, namely CONTROL and REFORM, are not included because these two dummy variables show no variation in the shortened sample. The political risk factor, again, is not significant. Thus, these three China-specific variables are not listed in Table 2.

Besides the absence of the China-specific factors and the real GDP growth variable, the estimates from the regression based on the RMB covered interest differential constructed from the onshore forward rate (OSCID) are quite comparable to the corresponding ones in Table 1. The dynamic structure of the OSCID resembles that of CID in Table 1. In both cases, three lagged dependent variables are required to remove serial correlation in estimated residuals. The coefficient estimates of the included variables are qualitatively the same as those in Table 1 – they have the same signs. However, the coefficient estimates of the OSCID regression are larger in magnitude than the corresponding ones for CID.

For instance, the capital flight variable (KF) has a more negative and, more importantly, statistically coefficient estimate. That is, the capital flight is significant for the covered interest differential based on onshore forward rates though it is not significant for the differential derived from offshore forward rates. Further, the nominal effective exchange rate (*d*NEER), exchange volatility (EV), and inflation volatility (InflV) variables that capture economic stability have a larger impact on OSCID than on CID. Compared with CID, OSCID is more responsive to the significant macroeconomic determinants.

The second column in Table 2 is labeled OSRDIFF for "consistency." It presents the results on the interest rate differential regression based on the sample in which the offshore RMB forward rate data are available. The only significant variable is the lagged interest rate differential. The capital flight variable is not significant as it is in Table 1 – we reported it for comparison purposes. The *d*FISC variable is not significant with the reduced sample size.

The "OSPREM" regression that has forward premiums based on the onshore RMB forward rates as the dependent variable shares some similarities with the OSCID regression. The macroeconomic variables – capital flight, nominal effective exchange rate, exchange volatility, and inflation volatility – that affect OSCID are also statistically significant. In fact, the coefficient estimates in the OSPREM equation are usually larger (in magnitude) than the corresponding ones in the OSCID equation. That is, the forward premium is likely to be the conduit through which these macroeconomic factors affecting (affect) the covered interest differential.

In sum, when we take the substantial reduction in sample size into consideration, the estimates in Tables 1 and 2 are qualitatively similar. The identified empirical determinants appear robust to the alternative choices of forward data.

5. *Concluding remarks*

With the growing importance of China in the global market, a plethora of studies on China emerge. These studies cover, for example, its phenomenal economic growth trajectory, its ability to attract foreign direct investment and its deployment of outward direct investment, its exchange rate policy, the international reserves it amassed in the new millennium, and its real and financial integration with the world economy.[15] There are, however, only a few studies on China's capital control policy. In this exercise, we study the determinants of the RMB covered interest differential, which is a proxy for the effectiveness of capital controls.

Our empirical exercise considers the canonical macroeconomic variables including capital flight and the factors that affect country risk, and a few China-specific regulatory and institutional factors. It is found that the effects of these canonical macroeconomic variables on the RMB covered interest differential are largely consistent with those reported in the literature. The results, again, are largely the same across the two different choices of RMB forward rates (onshore and offshore rates) that cover different sample periods. In that sense, the China case is not much different from the other cases. Further, there is evidence that the RMB covered interest differential was affected by China's general capital control policy and its exchange rate reform program but not China's political risk index.

Since its economic reform policy started in the late 1970s, China has embarked on the process of integrating with the global economy. At the same time, the Chinese economy is undergoing a swift transition from a planned economy to a market economy. In the process, China has gradually loosened its grip on both the trade and finance areas. Policies are instituted to direct the path of economic development and, from time to time, are formulated to accommodate economic reality. Capital control policies are of no exception. They offer the authorities an extra degree of freedom in contemplating macroeconomic policies for the so-called "unorthodox" China-style economic experiment.

The Chinese authorities have repeatedly proclaimed their ultimate policy goal is to lift capital controls and let market forces play the role in, say, determining the RMB exchange rate.[16] Understandably, China would like to be in charge of the transition process to a less controlled

---

[15] See, for example, Blanchard and Giavazz (2006), Cheung *et al.* (2007), Cheung and Qian (2009), Eichengreen and Tong (2007), Feenstra and Wei (2009), Hale and Long (forthcoming), Jeanne (2007), and Lane and Schmukler (2007).

[16] The Chinese President Hu Jintao repeated the similar message in, say, the recently held second summit of Brazil, Russia, India and China; see http://www.fmprc.gov.cn/chn/gxh/tyb/zyxw/t682096.htm

policy environment and be sure the process is controllable and does not jeopardize the stability of the Chinese economy. One issue China has to face is the ability of its relatively underdeveloped financial sector to handle and absorb shocks – both real and financial – to the economy.

Compared with, say, the US financial system, the Chinese financial sector is quite underdeveloped and is commonly perceived to have only limited capacity to handle volatility and shocks that are commonly observed in the modern financial world. Thus, before China has developed a well-functioning and efficient financial sector, the authorities are likely to leverage on capital control measures to manage capital movements and foreign exchange transactions. At the same time, the effectiveness of these control measures could have implications for China's progress in liberalizing its financial market and conducting monetary policy, when it is in the process of building a robust financial system that could sustain real and financial shocks.

Our exercise suggests that the RMB covered return differential is affected by both the canonical macroeconomic determinants and some China-specific factors. Thus, we have the usual prescription of a stable economic environment that is essential for China to manage capital flows and, hence, its macroeconomy, especially before its financial sector has both the depth and breadth to handle the considerable shocks to the economy.

Acknowledgments

Cheung gratefully acknowledges the financial support of faculty research funds of the University of California, Santa Cruz. Qian acknowledges the financial support from the dean of the School of Natural and Social Science at Buffalo State.

Appendix

A.1. Data: definition and sources

The appendix lists the definitions of the variables used in the study and their sources.

KF The stock of China's capital flight in trillion US dollars. The US dollar LIBORs are used to compound capital flight data, and the compounded series is adjusted by the US inflation rates. The World Bank residual method is used to construct the capital flight data. The required balance of payments data are obtained from the State Administration of Foreign Exchange (SAFE) of China.

CID	The covered interest differential. It is given by $(r-r^*)/(1+r^*) -(F-S)/S$, where r is the Chinese interbank offer rate (CHIBOR), r^* is the US\$ LIBOR, F is the RMB nondeliverable forward rate, and S is the spot exchange rate (yuan/\$).
OSCID	The covered interest differential when China's onshore forward rate is used.
RGDPG	China's real GDP growth rate calculated from seasonal adjusted data from CEIC.
FISC	China's government deficit scaled by GDP (Data source: CEIC).
NEER	The RMB nominal effective exchange rate (Data source: IFS).
InflV	China's inflation volatility, calculated from the conditional variance in a GARCH(1,1) model.
EV	The RMB exchange rate volatility, calculated as the standard deviation daily RMB exchange rate (Data source: CEIC).
REFORM	A dummy variable for China's July 2005 exchange rate policy reform, I($t>$ = July 2005).
CONTROL	A dummy variable to capture the timing of China's capital control policy changes. It is assigned a value of +1 for the observations before September 2001, when China tightened capital outflow; a value 0 for the observations between September 2001 and October 2002, when it is deemed as a transition period; and a value −1 for the observations after October 2002, when Chinese authorities start to encourage or promote capital outflow.
RDIFF	Interest rate differential, expressed as $(r-r^*)/(1+r^*)$. The data is calculated by subtracting the US\$ LIBOR from CHIBOR.
PREM	The RMB nondeliverable forward premium given by, $(\mathrm{NDF}_{t+k} - e_t)/e_t$, where NDF_t and e_t are, respectively, nondeliverable forward and spot rates expressed as the price of RMB. The 90-day and 30-day forwards are used in, respectively, quarterly and monthly data regressions.
OSPREM	The RMB onshare forward premium.
OPEN	China's trade openness, calculated from $(X+M)$/GDP.
Trend	A time trend variable.

A.2. Constructing the monthly capital flight and GDP data

Following Cheung and Qian (2010), we use the Chow and Lin (1971) method that is built upon Chang and Liu (1951) to extract the information to construct monthly capital flight and GDP data. For example, to construct the monthly GDP series, the Chow and Lin method uses information on variables that are closely related to GDP and, at the same time, available on the monthly frequency. Usually, these monthly variables are components of GDP. Wilcox (1983), for example, reports that the Chow and Lin method can successfully recover the essential dynamic characteristics of a data series, including autocorrelation structure and turning points.

The residual-method-based capital flight is given by

$$\text{Capital flight} = \Delta\text{ExD} + \text{NFDI} - \text{CAD} - \Delta\text{IR}.$$

where ΔExD is the change in external debts, NFDI is the net foreign direct investment, CAD is the current account deficit, and ΔIR is the change in international reserves. Monthly data on international reserves are available. Thus, we have to construct the monthly data on CAD, NFDI, and ΔExD. In our exercise, data on China's trade balance are used to derive the monthly current account balance. The net foreign direct investment series is derived using data on inward foreign direct investment. The monthly external debt series is derived from the regression framework given in Eaton and Gersovitz (1981) with a dummy variable capturing China's Qualified Foreign Institutional Investor program that was instituted in 2002 and allows designated foreign entities to participate in the local Chinese stock markets.

For the GDP data, only data on the aggregate consumption component are not available at the monthly frequency. Thus, we derived monthly consumption data using information on monthly retail sales on consumer goods, and the consumption of transportation and telecommunication services (Chang and Liu, 1951).

References

Aliber, R.Z. (1973), The interest rate parity theorem: a reinterpretation. *Journal of Political Economy* 81 (6), 1451–1459.

Baek, I.-M., Bandopadhyaya, A., Du, C. (2005), Determinants of market-assessed sovereign risk: economic fundamentals or market risk appetite?. *Journal of International Money and Finance* 24 (4), 533–548.

Blanchard, O., Giavazz, F. (2006), Rebalancing growth in China: a three-handed approach. *China & World Economy* 14, 1–20.

Chang, C.G., Liu, T.C. (1951), Monthly estimates of certain national product components, 1946–1949. *The Review of Economics and Statistics* 33, 219–227.

Cheung, Y.-W., Lai, K.S. (1995), Lag order and critical values of a modified Dickey–Fuller test. *Oxford Bulletin of Economics and Statistics* 57, 411–419.

Cheung, Y.-W., Qian, X. (2009), Empirics of China's outward direct investment. *Pacific Economic Review* 14, 312–341.

Cheung, Y.-W., Qian, X. (2010), Capital Flight: China's Experience. *Review of Development Economics* 14, 227–247.

Cheung, Y.-W., Chinn, M.D., Fujii, E. (2003), China, Hong Kong, and Taiwan: a quantitative assessment of real and financial integration. *China Economic Review* 14, 281–303.

Cheung, Y.-W., Chinn, M.D., Fujii, E. (2007), *The Economic Integration of Greater China: Real and Financial Linkages and the Prospects for Currency Union*. Hong Kong University Press, Hong Kong.

Cheung, Y.-W., Tam, D., Yiu, M.S. (2008), Does the Chinese interest rate follow the US interest rate? *International Journal of Finance and Economics* 13, 53–67.

Chow, G.C., Lin, A-L. (1971), Best linear unbiased interpolation, distribution, and extrapolation of time series by related series. *The Review of Economics and Statistics* 53, 372–375.

Claessens, S., Naude, D. (1993), Recent estimates of capital flight. Policy Research Working Paper Series No. 1186, The World Bank, Washington, DC.

Dooley, M.P., Isard, P. (1980), Capital controls, political risk, and deviations from interest-rate parity. *The Journal of Political Economy* 88 (2), 370–384.

Eaton, J., Gersovitz, M. (1981), Debt with potential repudiation: theoretical and empirical analysis. *The Review of Economic Studies* 48, 289–309.

Edwards, S. (1984), LDC foreign borrowing and default risk: an empirical investigation, 1976–80. *American Economic Review* 74 (4), 726–734.

Edwards, S. (1986), The pricing of bonds and bank loans in international markets. *European Economic Review* 30, 565–589.

Eichengreen, B., Mody, A. (1998), What explains changing spreads on emerging-market debt: fundamentals or market sentiment? NBER Working Paper No. W6408.

Eichengreen, B., Tong, H. (2007), Is China's FDI coming at the expense of other countries? *Journal of the Japanese and International Economies* 21, 153–172.

Elliott, G., Rothenberg, T.J., Stock, J.H. (1996), Efficient tests for an autoregressive unit root. *Econometrica* 64, 813–836.

Favero, C., Giavazzi, F., Spaventa, L. (1997), High-yields: The spread on German interest rates. *Economic Journal* 107 (443), 956–985.

Feenstra, R., Wei, S-J. (2009). Introduction to China's growing role in World Trade. NBER Working Paper No. 14716.

Frankel, J., Engel, C.M. (1984), Do asset-demand functions optimize over the mean and variance of real returns? a six-currency test. *Journal of International Economics* 17 (3–4), 309–323.

Hale, G., Long, C. (forthcoming). Are there productivity spillovers from foreign direct investment in China? *Pacific Economic Review*.

Hung, J.H. (2008), China's approach to capital flows since 1978: a brief overview. In: Cheung, Y.-W., Wong, K.-Y. (Eds.), *China and Asia: Economic and Financial Interactions*. Routledge, New York, pp. 44–63.

Ito, T. (1983), Capital controls and covered interest parity. NBER Working Paper No. 1187.

Jeanne, O. (2007), International reserves in emerging market countries: too much of a good thing? In: Brainard, W.C., Perry, G.L. (Eds.),

Brookings Papers on Economic Activity 1. Brookings Institution Press, Washington, DC, pp. 1–55.

Kamin, S., von Kleist, K. (1999). The evolution and determinants of emerging market credit spreads in the 1990s. International Finance Discussion Paper No. 1999-653, Federal Reserve Board.

Kaminsky, G., Schmukler, S. (2001). Emerging markets instability: do sovereign ratings affect country risk and stock returns? World Bank Policy Research Working Paper No. 2678.

Kar, D., Cartwright-Smith, D. (2008). Illicit financial flows from developing countries: 2002–2006. Global Financial Integrity, Washington, DC.

Lane, P.R., Schmukler, S.L. (2007). The international financial integration of China and India. Policy Research Working Paper Series No. 4132, The World Bank.

Ma, G., Ho, C., McCauley, R.N. (2004). The markets for non-deliverable forwards in Asian currencies. *BIS Quarterly Review* June, 81–94.

Ma, G., McCauley, R.N. (2008), The efficacy of China's capital controls – evidence from price and flow data. *Pacific Economic Review* 13, 104–123.

Magud, N., Reinhart, C. (2007), Capital controls: an evaluation. In: Edwards, S. (Ed.), *Capital Controls and Capital Flows in Emerging Economies: Policies, Practices, and Consequences*. University of Chicago Press, Chicago, pp. 64–74.

Mauro, P., Sussman, N., Yafeh, Y. (2002), Emerging market spreads: then versus now. *Quarterly Journal of Economics* 117 (2), 695–733.

Melvin, M., Schlagenhauf, D.E. (1985), A country risk index: econometric formulation and an application to Mexico. *Economic Inquiry* 23 (4), 601–619.

Merrick, J. (2001), Crisis dynamics of implied default recovery ratios: evidence from Russia and Argentina. *Journal of Banking and Finance* 25 (10), 1921–1939.

Nagai, S., Wang, H. (2007), Money market operations in China: monetary policy or FX policy? Working Paper, Bank of Japan.

Peng, W., Shu, C., Yip, R. (2007), Renminbi derivatives: recent development and issues. *China & World Economy* 15 (5), 1–17.

Prasad, E., Wei, S-J. (2007), China's approach to capital inflows: patterns and possible explanations. In: Edwards, S. (Ed.), *Capital Controls and Capital Flows in Emerging Economies: Policies, Practices and Consequences*. University of Chicago Press, Chicago, pp. 421–480.

Rigobon, R. (2002), The curse of non-investment grade countries. *Journal of Development Economics* 69 (2), 423–449.

Wilcox, J.A. (1983), Disaggregating data using related series. *Journal of Business and Economic Statistics* 1, 187–191.

Xie, D. (2002), Analysis of the development of China's money market. *China & the World Economy* 10, 29–37.

CHAPTER 16

Hong Kong's Future as a Securities Market

Peter T. Treadway

Historical Analytics LLC, New York, USA
E-mail address: pttreadway@hotmail.com
CTRISKS, Hong Kong
E-mail address: pttreadway@hotmail.com

Abstract
This chapter explores Hong Kong's future as a major public securities market. It concludes that Hong Kong has the potential to become one of the world's major – if not the number one – public securities market in the coming decades. However, there are four major factors that will affect how much this potential is realized: (1) How Hong Kong's market is treated by the Central Government in Beijing *vis-a-vis* its competitors in Shanghai and Shenzhen. If Hong Kong is allowed full access to the Chinese saver/investor and Chinese firms are allowed the choice of listing in Hong Kong, then Hong Kong will outcompete its Shanghai and Shenzhen rivals regardless of whether Shanghai and Shenzhen are opened for listings by foreign companies and to foreign investors. Hong Kong will thrive in an environment of no capital constraints on the renminbi. Conversely, a retention of the renminbi capital controls combined with free access of foreign firms to list on Shanghai or Shenzhen and/or restrictions on Chinese firms listing in Hong Kong would be very harmful to Hong Kong. (2) How skillful and aggressive Hong Kong and the Hong Kong Exchanges and Clearing Ltd. are in making Hong Kong into a global competitor as a securities market. Hong Kong's principal competitors on a global basis are New York and London and the new electronic exchanges that have sprung up in Western countries. (3) The full force of new technologies is not inhibited in Hong Kong to protect a monopoly position of the Hong Kong Exchanges and Clearing Ltd. (4) Hong Kong maintains its stable relationship with the US dollar, no capital controls are introduced in Hong Kong, and that Beijing continues to respect Hong Kong's information freedom as specified in the Basic Law.

Keywords: Alternative Trading Systems (ATS), dark pools, path dependence, renminbi, H Share companies, Red Chip companies, Initial Public Offerings (IPOs), securities market, Hong Kong peg, Basic Law,

Frontiers of Economics and Globalization
Volume 9 ISSN: 1574-8715
DOI: 10.1108/S1574-8715(2011)0000009021

Qualified Domestic Institutional Investor Program (QDII), convertible, capital account, through train, technology

JEL classification: G15

This chapter will explore the most likely future for Hong Kong as a public securities market. Along with its banking sector, a key feature of any financial center is its public securities market including securities-related derivatives. Note that as used in this chapter the term "public securities market" implies a broader scope than Hong Kong's major stock and derivatives exchanges, of which the holding company Hong Kong Exchanges and Clearing Ltd. (HKEx) is the sole owner. For example, as developed in the United States and the United Kingdom, one would expect that various off-exchange electronic Alternative Trading Systems (ATS) such as virtual exchanges, electronic communications networks (ECNs), and nonexchange dark pools would become important in Hong Kong. Since 2000, HKEx has been a profit making, publicly traded entity, and could become a major competitor of off-exchange ATS as well as sell-side brokerage firms that are now its customers.

That said, Hong Kong's securities market is at a very important juncture in its history. Hong Kong has come a long way from just over a decade ago when it was more or less a protected colonial exchange serving its local equity market. Depending on events, some of which are and some of which are not under its control, Hong Kong has the potential to become perhaps the world's most important equity market venue. Unfortunately, under equally plausible but less optimistic assumptions, Hong Kong could also find itself relegated to a less important (though still significant) regional public securities market. This chapter will lean toward a more optimistic conclusion with the caveat that at this point nothing is assured.

1. Brief overview of Hong Kong market

The major exchanges operating in Hong Kong at this moment are the Stock Exchange of Hong Kong Ltd. and the Hong Kong Futures Exchange Ltd. Both, along with the Hong Kong Securities Clearing Co. Ltd., are owned by HKEx. HKEx is shareholder owned and trades on the Hong Kong Stock Exchange under the code 0388. It has been very profitable with a recent ROE (return on equity) of approximately 65%.

The Hong Kong Stock Exchange consists of the Main Board and the Growth Enterprises Market (GEM) for newer, riskier companies. The latter advertizes itself as "A 'Buyers Beware' Market for Informed Investors."[1]

---

[1] Hong Kong Exchanges and Clearing Ltd. Available at http://www.hkex.com.hk

There are several classifications of note used by the HKEx regarding Chinese equities in Hong Kong:

H Share Companies – Enterprises that are incorporated in the Mainland, which are either controlled by Mainland Government entities or individuals.
Red Chip Companies – Enterprises that are incorporated outside of the Mainland and are controlled by Mainland Government entities.
Non-H Share Mainland Private Enterprises – Non-H Share Mainland Private Enterprises are companies that are incorporated outside of the Mainland and are controlled by Mainland individuals.

The government of Hong Kong owns 5.88% of HKEx. This government ownership position has been criticized as a conflict of interest, insofar as a government agency, the Securities and Futures Commission (SFC) has primary responsibility for the regulation of Hong Kong's stock and derivatives exchanges. Regulation takes place at two levels in Hong Kong with the HKEx and the stock exchange and futures exchange engaged in self-regulation.

The year 2009 for the HKEx was a banner year and 2010 is looking good as well. In 2009, the HKEx was the number one exchange in the world for Initial Public Offerings (IPOs) with a total of US$24.1 billion raised (see Table 1). H shares played a prominent role in Hong Kong's IPOs (see Table 2). Mainland enterprises accounted for 58% of HKEx market capitalization and 72% of average daily equity turnover. Worldwide, the total value of HKEx listings ranked seventh globally (see Table 3). One hundred and twenty-one overseas companies are listed on HKEx's securities market, with 41 based in Taiwan. Many have operations in or business connections with the Mainland.

Table 1. IPO equity funds raised (January–November 2009)

Rank	Exchange	IPO Equity funds raised (US$ million)
1	Hong Kong	24,112.10
2	Shanghai	13,996.80
3	NYSE Euronext (US)	13,747.60
4	BM&F BOVESPA (Brazil)	12,193.00
5	NASDAQ OMX	7,920.60
6	Shenzhen	6,391.40
7	Australia	4,782.00
8	Bursa Malaysia	3,528.80
9	National Stock Exchange of India	3,128.40
10	Warsaw SE	2,411.00

Source: Hong Kong Exchanges and Clearing Ltd.

Table 2. Ten largest IPO funds raised by newly Hong Kong listed companies in 2009

Rank	Company name	IPO funds raised HK$ billion
1	China Minsheng Banking Corp. Ltd. – H Shares (1988)	31.23
2	China Pacific Insurance (Group) Co. Ltd. – H Shares (2601)	24.12
3	China Longyuan Power Group Corporation Ltd. – H Shares (916)	20.11
4	Sands China Ltd. (1928)	19.41
5	Metallurgical Corporation of China Ltd. – H Shares (1618)	18.23
6	Wynn Macau Ltd. (1128)	14.49
7	Glorious Property Holdings Ltd. (845)	10.54
8	Sinopharm Group Co. Ltd. – H Shares (1099)	10.04
9	China Zhongwang Holdings Ltd. (1333)	9.84
10	Longfor Properties Co. Ltd. (960)	8.13

Table 3. Market value of shares of domestic-listed companies (main and parallel markets) (as at the end of November)

Exchange	Rank	November 2009	Rank	December 2008
		Market value US$ million		Market value US$ million
NYSE Euronext (US)	1	11,582,517.40	1	9,208,934.10
Tokyo	2	3,288,766.80	2	3,115,803.50
Nasdaq OMX	3	3,052,581.30	3	2,248,976.50
NYSE Euronext (Europe)	4	2,808,354.60	4	2,101,745.90
London	5	2,719,373.00	5	1,868,153.00
Shanghai	6	2,616,812.80	6	1,425,354.00
Hong Kong	7	2,259,942.70	7	1,328,768.50
TSX Group	8	1,611,638.20	9	1,033,448.50
BME Spanish Exchanges	9	1,391,417.60	10	948,352.30
BM&F BOVESPA (Brazil)	10	1,298,058.20	15	591,965.50

Source: Hong Kong Exchanges and Clearing Ltd.

2. Forecasting the role of Hong Kong's public equity market

Anyone forecasting Hong Kong's equity role must take into account a number of important and not always predictable factors. These are:

1. Political realities
2. Future of the Hong Kong peg
3. Future the renminbi and Hong Kong's role as a major securities market for China
4. Impact of technology on Hong Kong as a securities market

5. Future of Hong Kong as a global and regional securities market
6. The impact of globalization on Hong Kong's public equity markets

3. Political realities always shape the structure and scope of public equity markets

Political realities in the sense this phrase is being used here mean anything from national boundaries to regulations requiring or encouraging local investors to only own domestic stocks to inconvertibility of neighboring country currencies. In other words, all restrictions and preferences emanating from the government sector.

Countries have traditionally viewed their domestic stock markets as national assets to be protected. Countries generally do not restrict their companies from raising capital on foreign markets (although there are certainly exceptions to this, e.g., India) and thus tapping additional foreign savings. But generally the politically preferred route is for domestic saving to be channeled into domestic companies via domestic securities exchanges and for domestic companies' shares to be traded on those exchanges.

Two examples of this phenomenon can be cited. The first is Canada and the xxxxxx United States. It is said that 90% of Canadians live within 20 miles of the US border. Many Canadian stocks do trade on American exchanges. But the bulk do not and are traded on the Toronto or Vancouver Stock exchanges. Were there no political boundary between the two countries, the likelihood is that most Canadian stocks would migrate to American exchanges. The American exchanges would be the primary source of IPO capital for Canada, and Canadian savings would be routed to Canadian companies via public securities markets that ignored the US/Canadian border. Certainly this would not pose a great technological challenge even with the currency difference.

A second example is Singapore. Singapore withdrew from the Federation of Malaysia in 1965. While the split did not take place immediately, ultimately the stock exchange of the two countries that had been unified since colonial times had to be divided. At the time of Singapore's withdrawal from Malaysia, the Stock Exchange of Malaysia became known as the Stock Exchange of Malaysia and Singapore. Trading rooms existed in Singapore and Kuala Lumpur which were linked by telephone. In 1973, currency interchangeability between Malaysia and Singapore ceased, and the Stock Exchange of Malaysia and Singapore was divided into the Kuala Lumpur Stock Exchange Berhad and the Stock Exchange of Singapore. Politics – rooted in well-known historical, nationalistic, and demographic factors – ultimately trumped technology and economics.[2]

[2] Bursa Malaysia. Available at http://www.klse.com.my/website/bm/about_us/the_organisation/history.html

It is not far-fetched to assume that if there were no political obstacles and had Singapore remained in the Federation of Malaysia, given the technological forces (to be discussed) pushing toward stock market consolidation, Singapore would have emerged as the equity hub for all of Malaysia. Moreover, economic logic might dictate that the Singapore exchange would also come to dominate trading and listing activity for Indonesia and Brunei as well. Political constraints make such an outcome implausible.

3.1. So what does this mean for Hong Kong?

Let's start with China. How will the central government in Beijing view the Hong Kong's securities market versus so-called "domestic" markets in Shanghai and Shenzhen? The official "mantra" is that Hong Kong including its securities market will remain as China's external international financial center and that the Shanghai and Shenzhen exchanges will serve China's internal market. This makes some sense in the intermediate run provided the renminbi remains blocked on capital account and access to the Shanghai and Shenzhen markets essentially remains closed to foreign listings and foreign investors. The opening of an international board in Shanghai however, where non-Chinese firms could list and raise capital, would be a significant negative for Hong Kong especially if foreign investors would have easy access to the Shanghai international board and access to Hong Kong remained essentially blocked for Mainland investors. This situation would of course be worsened were Mainland Chinese companies be prohibited or discouraged from listing in Hong Kong. We would term this "an asymmetric capital control opening" with a definite bias against Hong Kong.

There are two "prizes" at stake here: (1) the Chinese saver/investor and (2) the international saver/investor. Other things equal, the securities market that can access both wins. Even without central government forcing Mainland firms to list on Shanghai or Shenzhen exchanges, both Chinese and non-Chinese firms, if they could, would choose to list where they can access both foreign and Chinese saver/investors.

We will assert two important principles that certainly hold for derivative contracts but also with some qualifications for equities. First, trading of the same financial instrument or security in the same time zone will move to one market. Investors and issuers will go where the liquidity is greatest. In the absence of regulatory or currency barriers, one market will dominate the trading of an identical financial instrument or security.

Second, comparing Hong Kong with the so-called Mainland exchanges, Hong Kong is far ahead in terms of regulatory fairness and transparency, freedom of information, and all the "human software" that goes with a securities market including a substantial supply of human financial and legal capital. Hong Kong also has resolutely maintained its tolerance of short sales, a factor that most financial analysts would regard as extremely important. Moreover, Hong Kong as a securities venue benefits from what economists call path dependence, i.e., once an economic activity develops in a particular region it tends to stay and develop there as the costs of moving elsewhere are high. Were the exchange controls on the renminbi to be dropped today and Chinese savers allowed to invest in Hong Kong securities as they can do now in Shanghai and Shenzhen, it is very likely that both international and Chinese investors would prefer to trade on the Hong Kong market. Chinese issuers would prefer to list on the Hong Kong market. I have no doubt that Hong Kong could host listings and trading in securities denominated in HK dollars or a fully convertible renminbi.

The overall superiority of Hong Kong versus Shanghai securities markets has, in effect, been publicly conceded by Shanghai officials. At the 2010 Asian Financial Forum held in Hong Kong, Shanghai deputy mayor Tu Guanshou said "Shanghai cannot prosper without Hong Kong's mentoring."[3] Similar sentiments were echoed at the conference by the president of the Shanghai Stock Exchange, Zhang Yujun. "Hong Kong has always been our model and benchmark," Mr. Zhang remarked.

But Hong Kong's technological, legal, and human capital advantages will not be enough to compete should Beijing institute a form of asymmetric capital control loosening biased against Hong Kong. Foreign investors and listing companies will not want to be confined to less liquid markets designated for foreigners only.

3.2. Hong Kong as a Chinese financial center – is Hong Kong part of China or not?

Of course, the legal and political answer is that Hong Kong on July 1, 1997 was returned to Chinese sovereignty, an event now referred to as the "Handover." Hong Kong is now classified as a Special Administrative Region (SAR) of the Peoples Republic of China. Legally and politically, Hong Kong is part of China. Hong Kong is governed under what is called the Basic Law. The Basic Law was drafted in accordance with the Sino-British Joint Declaration on the question of Hong Kong (the Joint Declaration), signed between the Chinese and British governments on December 19, 1984. The Basic Law allows Hong Kong to retain its British derived common law legal system, respect for property rights, and rights of freedom of information and expression at least until 2047 – all hugely important factors in the functioning of an efficient and fair securities market.

---

[3] Yan (2010).

But this invites two questions. The first is whether the Central Government in Beijing will observe the terms of the Basic Law. Thus far since the Handover, the Beijing's record on this is excellent and there is every reason to be optimistic that the Central Government will continue to respect the Basic Law.

The second political question is less predictable, however. Briefly put, what role does Beijing envision for Hong Kong's securities market? In other words, does Beijing really consider Hong Kong to be functionally part of China or is Hong Kong viewed as sort of a Cantonese-speaking liberal rich cousin, not always to be fully trusted in China's still command and control capital allocation process? Political decisions from Beijing could trump those legal, economic, and technological assets that currently give Hong Kong an advantage over Shanghai and Shenzhen.

Such an asymmetric policy by Beijing would imply the waste of the assets already built up over the century that the Hong Kong stock market has been functioning. Overall, the Chinese government's approach to economic policy and Hong Kong has been consistently pragmatic and shows an awareness of the value of Hong Kong's assets to China. It is probably reasonable to expect a Central Government bias toward Shanghai and Shenzhen but not one carried to extremes. It is also reasonable to expect that Shanghai officials will behind the scenes lobby for an expansion of the Shanghai Exchange's international role and the limitation of HKEx as a listing venue for Chinese companies. It is up to Hong Kong to capitalize and build on its many advantages, lobby Beijing, and overcome these biases.

4. The future of the Hong Kong peg

A major advantage that Hong Kong has today is that its currency, the Hong Kong dollar, is freely convertible into all currencies without restrictions and that the value of the Hong Kong dollar is pegged via a quasi currency board system to the US dollar. Since 1983 the Hong Kong dollar has been pegged at HK$7.80 to US$1.00. The Hong Kong dollar actually is allowed to move in a band from HK$7.85 (the weak side) to HK$7.75 (the strong side). Issuers and investors have had complete confidence that Hong Kong's currency is freely convertible and set at a fixed exchange rate against the world's major reserve currency, the US dollar. Prior to 1983 from 1974 to 1983 the Hong Kong dollar was allowed to float. Technically, there is nothing sacrosanct about the Hong Kong dollar/US dollar peg.

Any forecast of Hong Kong's role as a financial center must make some assumption about its continued monetary stability. Unfortunately, this could be impacted by events beyond Hong Kong's control. In the last year, a significant body of observers forecasts the demise of the US dollar as the world's leading reserve currency. As the result of dollar weakness, for most of 2009, the US dollar traded on the strong side of the HK currency band and there were consequently been significant inflows of US dollars into Hong Kong which under the currency board system had significantly increased Hong Kong's monetary base. As this goes to press, the US dollar is under some pressure again. Some observers have therefore recommended that Hong Kong therefore drop its peg against the US dollar.

The focus of this chapter is not on Hong Kong's monetary policy. But monetary matters do play an important role in Hong Kong's functions as a financial center. It is quite evident that Hong Kong has limited, and not altogether great, choices as far as its dollar peg goes. One alternative would be for Hong Kong to repeg to the renminbi. Perhaps one day that will happen. However, at this time this is not technically feasible because the renminbi is not convertible on capital account and is not regarded as a reserve currency. Moreover, China's return to the global financial system is of relatively short duration. Investors may require a longer "track record" before the renminbi could join the dollar and the euro as a major reserve currency. Alternative suggestions of Hong Kong pegging against a basket of currencies also have several drawbacks. From the viewpoint of a securities market, investors would suddenly have to worry about exchange risk and possible political manipulation of the Hong Kong dollar.

Suffice it to say that the best possible outcome for the foreseeable future for Hong Kong as a securities market and financial center is that the US dollar retains its global dominance and that the Hong Kong dollar peg remains in place and no restrictions are placed on the Hong Kong dollar's convertibility. An IPO and listing in Hong Kong really are equivalent to doing an IPO and trading in US dollars. Funding in US dollars no doubt is an attraction for Hong Kong, both for Chinese and non-Chinese companies.

5. *Future of the renminbi and Hong Kong's role as a major securities market for China*

Partly underlying the notion that Hong Kong should be China's international financial market is a rather simple economic model. The model suggests that developing countries will be labor intensive and capital short, run a current account deficit, and need to import capital. Developed countries on the other hand would be capital intensive, run a current account surplus, and export capital. The United States and the United Kingdom were good examples of this in the nineteenth century. The capital-intensive United Kingdom exported capital. The developing United States imported foreign capital to augment its domestic savings. So in theory Hong Kong could serve as the financial venue for foreign portfolio capital to enter China and augment Chinese savings.

Chart 1. AH premium chart. Source: Bloomberg.

Except that this model has been turned on its head so far in the twenty-first century. It is developing China that has been running a current account surplus. The developed supposedly capital-intensive United States has been importing capital from China and running a current account deficit.

Either something is very wrong with this model or something is very wrong with the international monetary system. It is curious that China can be a capital surplus and labor surplus country at the same time. The fact that the A shares in Shanghai have frequently sold at premiums to otherwise identical H share equivalents in Hong Kong (see Chart 1) is consistent with the view of China as a capital surplus country.

The fact that A–H share differences persist is the result of capital controls on the renminbi which prevent the law of one price from operating and arbitrage equating the prices of otherwise identical A and H shares. Of course, the capital controls are not airtight. One legal exception is the Qualified Domestic Institutional Investor Program (QDII) that has authorized approved Chinese mutual funds to invest in "foreign" markets including Hong Kong. And no doubt, there is plenty of "suitcase" capital that makes its way one way or another over the border to Hong Kong. But legally, outside of QDII, Chinese nationals and institutional investors cannot open stock trading accounts in Hong Kong and the A–H differences persist.

5.1. What would be the effect of making the renmimbi convertible on capital account?

It is a conclusion of this chapter that a total synchronous removal of capital controls on the renminbi in a reasonably near future would be highly advantageous to Hong Kong as a securities market. As mentioned, Hong Kong's superior regulatory and legal environment, established international linkages, technological strengths, cluster of money managers, and extensive human capital in terms of research, personnel etc., give Hong Kong an edge over Shanghai and Shenzhen. If Chinese savers, both retail and institutional, had complete freedom to open accounts and trade securities in Hong Kong, they would likely do so. If Chinese companies had complete freedom to choose which exchange to list on, they would go where the most liquidity and the highest price was. Hong Kong if it had unrestricted access to international *and* Chinese saver/investors would be the market of the most liquidity. Hong Kong no doubt could offer renminbi as well as HK dollar denominated securities. Not only would the A–H share differences disappear, but trading would migrate to Hong Kong and the A share market would see trading disappear in all securities that were also listed in Hong Kong. Actually, in this circumstance dual listings would disappear with trading migrating to Hong Kong.

Looked at in this way, from the viewpoint of Hong Kong as a securities market, the capital controls on the renminbi can be viewed as a protectionist measure. Shanghai and Shenzhen are being protected from competition from Hong Kong for Chinese saver/investors, at least until that day when from a regulatory, legal, technological, and human capital perspective, they can compete with Hong Kong. This is a type of "infant industry" protection so often encountered in so many countries. Hong Kong in this economic context is not 100% part of China.

The abandonment by Beijing of the so-called "through train" mechanism has to be seen as a disappointment for the Hong Kong securities market. Although the details were never released, the through train would have allowed Mainland saver/investors through a specially designed mechanism to invest directly in Hong Kong securities.

Note we are *not* predicting that Hong Kong would become the only major securities market in China were the renminbi capital controls to be eliminated tomorrow. In the United States, for example, market forces have determined that there are more than one major securities exchanges, including the legacy exchanges, i.e., the New York Stock Exchange (now part of NYSEEuronext), the NASDAQ (now part of NasdaqOMX), and a host of electronic exchanges including BATS and Direct Edge.

5.2. What happens if the renmimbi is not made convertible in the near future?

Realistically, if the pronouncements of Chinese leaders are to be believed, this is the most likely intermediate term scenario. Assuming there is no asymmetric favoring of Shanghai and Shenzhen as discussed above, the case for Hong Kong as China's international financial and securities center is a real one. Chinese and non-Chinese companies will find it attractive to list in Hong Kong. Cross listings with Shanghai and Shenzhen exchanges, and ETFs tracking Chinese markets make a great deal of sense in this type of environment. But the Mainland exchanges continued near-exclusive access to the vast savings of China remains an advantage that may be worth more than all of Hong Kong's technological, legal, freedom of information, and "human software" strengths.

6. *Impact of technology on Hong Kong as a securities market*

Besides political factors, the second important determinant of the structure of securities markets is technology and the power of technology to drive economics. Securities markets have come a long way since traders began buying and selling stocks in London coffee houses at the end of the seventeenth century. For example, at the end of the nineteenth century, there were over 250 exchanges in the United States and over 30 in the United Kingdom. Local exchanges were needed for specific markets and specific products. In the early part of the nineteenth century, information had to be delivered by foot or horseback, so that every urban center needed its own market. Settlement and clearing required close physical proximity. Distance dictated that there be a multitude of local exchanges.

Gradually, technology overcame distance and promoted the consolidation of exchanges. The telegraph (first introduced in 1837), the subsea intercontinental cable (1866), the ticker tape (1867), and the telephone (1870s) all ultimately forced the consolidation of the various regional exchanges. Information had become available over distance. The survivors in the process gained increased liquidity and reinforced their position. This is the network effect and path dependence at work.[4]

In the absence of political constraints and increasingly despite political constraints, technology is now driving the consolidation of securities and improving the efficiency of securities markets on a global basis. Information now flows instantly on a global basis. Today the new technologies are the computer and the internet. Computer processing power and bandwidth have become cheap, abundant, and ubiquitous and allowed for phenomenal increases in trading volume at ever-reduced cost. Cheap, abundant, and ubiquitous computer processing power and bandwidth are driving the continued national and now cross-border consolidation of securities markets, the globalization of securities markets, the replacement of floor trading with electronic trading (pits to bits), and

[4] A considerable part of the technological and historical issues discussed in this section comes from "Electronic Exchanges, The Global Transformation from Pits to Bits" (Gorham and Nidhi, 2009).

the conversion of mutually owned securities exchanges owned by their members to publicly traded stockholder-owned companies.

The structure of the global securities markets is rapidly being changed by technology, and even for many experienced participants the latest technologies are an imperfectly understood subject. High frequency trading, algorithmic trading, direct market access, dark pools, ECNs, multilateral trading facilities (MCNs), co-location, flash trading – all these are new words for phenomena that have come to dominate modern securities markets and have been made possible by cheap, abundant, and ubiquitous computer processing power and bandwidth.

The world securities markets are rapidly becoming seamlessly integrated. Even retail investors in the United States can trade Hong Kong stocks online and in real time through their US brokers. In the words of BATS CEO Bill O'Brien spoken in a Forbes interview, orders "can be executed in less than a second from anywhere on the planet."[5]

It is not the purpose of this chapter to evaluate the new technologies or comment on the regulatory issues they raise. But the history of securities markets, and indeed the entire history of the advance of civilization, suggests that technology and the more efficient flow of information are something that ultimately cannot be resisted. For the potential of computer power and bandwidth to be realized, full freedom must be granted to the new market technologies and information must be allowed to flow unimpeded.

Here Hong Kong may have an advantage *vis-a-vis* its Mainland competitors. Anyone who has recently visited China has experienced the phenomenon of landing in a spacious ultramodern new airport, being whisked to a gleaming new hotel and then finding when he (or she) plugs in his computer that many international and Hong Kong internet sites are inaccessible. Google's recent problems in China are another manifestation of the contradiction between China's enthusiasm for new information technologies and its unwillingness to allow them full freedom.

Hong Kong operates in an environment of complete freedom of information and competitive markets. Shanghai and Shenzhen do not. For example, will Beijing be comfortable with dark pools, ECNs and MTFs, and competing electronic ATS structures?

Hong Kong's major challenge is to protect all its investors and at the same time to keep its market technologically competitive and allow the new technologies to be implemented and information to flow. Globally, HKEx has the reputation for improving but still lagging technologically behind New York and London. The interests of HKEx and the Hong Kong securities market as a whole may not always be identical.

---

[5] Intelligent Investing with Steve Forbes. Available at http://www.forbes.com/2009/11/25/obrien-stock-exchange-intelligent-investing-video.html

Along with his counterparts in other countries, HKEx Chairman Ronald Arculli has warned against the potential of fragmentation of markets implied by some of the new electronic off-exchange alternatives.[6] Certainly, the May 6, 2010 so-called flash crash in the US markets, whereby structural problems rooted in the new securities trading technologies caused significant price anomalies, needs to be studied. However, it is in Hong Kong's overall interest that the promotion of an HKEx monopoly may not be its best competitive weapon in enhancing its position as a competitive global player in the securities markets. Hong Kong must remain completely open to all new technology that drives down the cost of trading, reduces latency, and is competitive in the quantitative high speed trading world of today.[7]

Flash trading is the "practice of some financial exchanges whereby certain customers are allowed to see incoming orders to buy or sell."[8] It is a controversial issue in the United States where it is legal. At the moment, HKEx's systems do not allow flash orders.[9]

Dark pools are off-exchange orders that cannot be seen by all market participants. In relation to dark pools and off-exchange electronic markets, HKEx's position is that it has always been open to competition from overseas markets and OTC markets as long as the regulatory playing field is level. HKEx maintains that to solidify its competitive position, it provides a central, transparent order book based on a strict price and time priority and makes available comprehensive market data on a nondiscriminatory basis. There are off-exchange trades by Exchange Participants and their affiliated ATS licensed by the SFC, but these trades are required to be reported to the Exchange. The HKEx's objective is that the investing public and the regulatory authorities can access all trade records based on the Exchange's transparent data feed.

In a November 2009 speech, SFC CEO Martin Wheatley disclosed that "off-exchange transactions reported to the exchange account for only about 3% of total market turnover on most trading days." According to Wheatley, this figure included transactions conducted on the dark pools operated by brokers. However, on days when there is an index rebalancing exercise, Wheatley said the SFC estimated that "average off-exchange

---

[6] Boey (2009).

[7] The global drive to reduce latency, the time it takes to process an order, is particularly important. For example, as a result of HKEx's latest technical revamp of its Third Generation Automatic Order Matching and Execution System, which is also known as AMS/3.5, the order processing capacity of AMS/3 has been doubled to 3,000 orders per second and the average end-to-end system response time halved to 0.15 seconds. An important step forward, HKEx now expects to migrate to AMS/3.8 over the next 12–18 months. Next generation AMS/4 is approximately two years in the future. A new data center is under construction in Tseung Kwan O in Hong Kong's New Territories.

[8] Wikipedia. Available at http://en.wikipedia.org/wiki/Flash_trading

[9] This statement was made to the author in an e-mail from HKEx.

transactions could exceed 10% of total market turnover but we (the SFC) have seen it go up to as high as 24% of total market turnover." Wheatley concluded that thus far relative to Western markets the importance of dark pools in Hong Kong was rather small. He also stated that the monopoly position of most exchanges in Asia inhibited the growth of dark pools.[10]

Wheatley went on to argue that dark pools and traditional exchanges could coexist:

> *Nonetheless, it is possible to make out a case for dark pools to operate in jurisdictions which consider their domestic exchanges to be national interests. The argument is founded on the fact that dark pools are really not exchanges. They are two very different creatures. We are basically going back to the basics of marketing theory i.e. product differentiation. Dark pools can offer something exchanges cannot, e.g. a wide range of order types including algorithmic trading tools. Thus, it is arguable that dark pools are not competing with the exchanges, they are in fact offering a different type of service or servicing a different segment of the market. I always believe that the pie is big enough for everyone to have a slice; the question is how big is the slice you get. In fact, dark pools and exchanges have complementary roles and together they may actually increase the size of the pie.*

There are a number of areas where Hong Kong might improve its competitive advantage. For example, HKEx does not facilitate collocation at this time. One might guess that this will have to change. Also on a global basis, Hong Kong's current trading hours of 10:00 a.m. to 12:30 p.m. and 2:30 p.m. to 4:00 p.m. with a break from 12.30 p.m. to 2.30 p.m. seems like a historical anachronism compared with New York and London that do not have such a break. Hong Kong also imposes a stamp tax on each stock transaction. This can be regarded as a barrier to high frequency trading. Finally, the new HKEx CEO Charles Li has mentioned that Hong Kong's three clearing facilities are an inefficiency that will have to be addressed.

It has been reported that the Singapore Stock Exchange will team up with Chi-X Global to introduce the first Asian exchange-backed dark pool. Apparently it is contemplated that Hong Kong stocks will be traded. It will be interesting to see whether this venture can solve problems of clearance and settlement. Nevertheless, if successful it represents a competitive threat to Hong Kong that cannot be ignored.

Finally, the recent push by CEO Li to extend HKEx's trading hours would seem to be a positive step.

---

[10] Securities and Futures Commission. Available at http://www.sfc.hk/

7. *Future of Hong Kong as a global and regional securities market*

In addition to Hong Kong registered companies, Hong Kong today competes for listing for both Chinese H share companies and non-Chinese foreign companies. Recent efforts by the HKEx to attract non-Chinese listings of global companies make a great deal of sense.

For global companies, the competition for listings and trading is global. Choice of an exchange can be based on valuation and liquidity reasons as well as for a variety of business reasons.

For listings, Hong Kong competes with a number of exchanges around the world including:

1. New York Stock Exchange
2. NASDAQ
3. London Stock Exchange Main Board
4. London Stock Exchange AIM
5. Singapore Stock Exchange
6. In addition as part of "Greater China," the Taipei Stock Exchange should probably be considered as a potential competitor.

Hong Kong's main foreign competitor for Chinese listings is New York, and to a much lesser extent London and Singapore. In New York, a substantial portion is level 2 or level 3 ADRs and cross listed with Hong Kong although the majority (many very small) are directly listed, either the product of a US IPO or a reverse merger.[11] There is an added cost to cross listing but the advantage is that a company's stock is then traded in two time zones with presumably a substantial addition to the investor base.

Trading is another matter. Competition for the legacy exchanges exists in the United States and Europe from electronic ATS and exchanges. As discussed, it is coming to Hong Kong. Despite all the worries about

[11] There are three different types of ADR issues:

- *Level 1* – This is the most basic type of ADR where foreign companies either don't qualify or don't wish to have their ADR listed on an exchange. Level 1 ADRs are found on the over-the-counter market and are an easy and inexpensive way to gauge interest for its securities in North America. Level 1 ADRs also have the loosest requirements from the Securities and Exchange Commission (SEC).
- *Level 2* – This type of ADR is listed on an exchange or quoted on Nasdaq. Level 2 ADRs have slightly more requirements from the SEC, but they also get higher visibility trading volume.
- *Level 3* – The most prestigious of the three, this is when an issuer floats a public offering of ADRs on a US exchange. Level 3 ADRs are able to raise capital and gain substantial visibility in the US financial markets.

Source: INVESTOPEDIA. Available at http://www.investopedia.com/

fragmentation and issues of fairness implied by such phenomena as flash trading, it is my view that ATS enhance liquidity.

7.1. Chinese companies

There are a number of possible factors that might lead a Chinese company to choose a Hong Kong or an alternative foreign listing such as New York, even though valuations are often higher in Shanghai and Shenzhen for Chinese issuers.

1. Company is privately controlled. Most Chinese companies that have listed abroad have been genuine private companies as opposed to companies with state ownership. For reasons of their own portfolio management etc., these owners may be selling some of their own shares and would prefer that these funds stay abroad.
2. Denial of access to the Shanghai and Shenzhen markets. In the past 10 years, preferential access to doing an IPO listing in Shanghai and Shenzhen has been given to state controlled enterprises (SOEs). Also for certain periods due to problems in the markets the Mainland markets were closed to all IPOs.
3. Preference for HK/US dollar rather than remminbi financing.
4. Knowledge factor. Certain markets are regarded as having a "knowledge advantage" in terms of research and investor understanding of certain industries. Thus Hong Kong has done IPOs for a number of property, banking, and low-tech China companies. New York on the other hand is regarded as having a knowledge advantage in technology. A number of private Chinese technology companies have done IPOs in New York, and the analytical community there is deep and sophisticated.
5. Regulatory treatment. Hong Kong's regulatory advantages have been discussed. Here New York is now perceived to be at disadvantage. The passage of the Sarbanes Oxley (SOX) legislation in 2002 may have lessened New York's attractiveness in this regard. The SOX is very demanding as to disclosure and personal obligations of issuing company executives and is thought by many to have become a barrier to listing in New York. This is a controversial subject with researchers differing as to their opinion.
6. Desire to establish or reinforce a presence or brand in the US. Chinese companies with significant business in the United States may believe that a US listing will improve their visibility in the United States.

7.2. Non-Chinese companies

Similarly there are a number of reasons why non-Chinese companies might decide to list in Hong Kong.

1. Competitive valuations and liquidity compared with New York or London.
2. Desire to establish or reinforce a presence or brand in China and Hong Kong.
3. Regulatory. Desire to avoid the SOX requirements in the United States.
4. Knowledge factor. For companies with substantial business in China, a Hong Kong listing may offer a more understanding and sophisticated analytical community.
5. Establish a 24-hour continuous high liquidity trading cycle. Global corporations may find it advantageous to have their securities traded in liquid markets on a more or less 24-hour basis. Hong Kong becomes the Asia/China link in the trading day.

8. A note on language

In terms of documentation and other functions, HKEx has operated in recent years increasingly on a bilingual Chinese and English basis. However the word "Chinese" brings some problems. The Chinese used on the Mainland is spoken Mandarin and written simplified Chinese characters. However, historically Hong Kong has been a Cantonese-speaking city and has used traditional Chinese characters. HKEx, if it wants to attract both international and Chinese savers/investors as well as Chinese and global issuers, must become fully trilingual.

9. Conclusion

Contrary to the pessimism expressed from time to time in the press, it is the conclusion of this chapter that Hong Kong can increase its importance as a securities market and can enhance its position as a preeminent market both globally and for China. Three major factors have determined the development of securities markets, viz. technology, political (broadly defined), and path dependence. Hong Kong to succeed must remain open to the huge changes that computer technology and unlimited global communications bandwidth have brought. At the same time, it must receive equal treatment from the (Mainland) Government of China *vis-a-vis* the so-called Mainland Exchanges in Shanghai and Shenzhen. Regarding path dependence this is simple: Hong Kong's current technological, legal, information freedom, and linguistic advantages carry their own momentum and will be difficult to overcome for competitors. A free-floating renminbi devoid of capital controls coupled with a Hong Kong dollar pegged to a stable US dollar would be the best case scenario for the Hong Kong securities market.

References

Boey, D. (2009), Dark Pools Pose Risks to the Markets, Hong Kong's Arculli Says, Bloomberg. Available at http://www.bloomberg.com/apps/news?pid = newsarchive&sid = aBFcQ8EMJV.4

Bursa Malaysia. Available at http://www.klse.com.my/website/bm/about_us/the_organisation/history.html

Gorham, M., Nidhi, S. (2009), *Electronic Exchanges, The Global Transformation from Pits to Bits*. Elsevier Inc., Burlington.

Hong Kong Exchanges and Clearing Ltd. Available at http://www.hkex.com.hk

Intelligent Investing with Steve Forbes. Available at http://www.forbes.com/2009/11/25/obrien-stock-exchange-intelligent-investing-video.html

Yan, S. (2010), Money Matters, South China Morning Post, p. B8.

ABOUT THE AUTHORS

Bertrand Candelon is a professor in International Monetary Economics. He received a PhD from Universite Catholique de Louvain. After a postdoctoral fellowship at the Humboldt Universität zu Berlin, he joined University Maastricht, School of Business and Economics in 2001. He has written extensive works in the area of international finance, in particular on contagion and on the analysis of financial market co-movements. He is one of the founders of the Methods in International Finance Network.

Chunlai Chen is a senior lecturer in the Crawford School of Economics and Government, the Australian National University. He received B.S. from Beijing Forestry University, China, MPA from Kennedy School of Government of Harvard University, USA, and Ph.D. in economics from Adelaide University, Australia. His research interest includes foreign direct investment, international trade, agricultural economics and Chinese economy. He teaches macroeconomics, microeconomics, services and investment policy, and the Global Trading System in Crawford School of Economics and Government. He is also a visiting professor at the Centre for Chinese Agricultural Policy of the Chinese Academy of Sciences, a visiting senior research fellow of International Food and Agricultural Economic Research Centre of Nanjing Agricultural University, China.

Yin-Wong Cheung obtained his bachelor's and master's degrees from the University of Hong Kong and the University of Essex, respectively. After graduating from the University of Pennsylvania in 1990, Cheung joined the University of California in Santa Cruz. Currently, Cheung is a professor in the Economics Department at the University of California, Santa Cruz. Concurrently, Cheung is member of the Council of Advisers, HKIMR/HKMA, a research fellow of the CESifo in Germany, a founding and board member of the Methods in International Finance Network in Europe, an adjunct professor of the City University of Hong Kong, and a chair professor of the Shandong University.

Tsz-Kin Chung is a research analyst in the Market Research Division of the Research Department, Hong Kong Monetary Authority. He obtained his B.Sc. and M.Phil. in physics from The Chinese University of Hong Kong. His research interest is in derivative pricing and stochastic modeling.

Chadwick C. Curtis is currently a graduate student in economics at the University of Notre Dame. His main research interests center around the major changes in the Chinese economy over the past 30 years. In particular, he studies the causes and consequences of the rise in household saving and the changing nature of the business cycle during China's economic reforms. He is drawn to China because of its rapid growth and increasing importance in the world economy - the possibility of this being 'the China Century' is very real.

Hans Genberg is assistant director at the Independent Evaluation Office of the International Monetary Fund since August 2010. Before joining the IMF he was an adviser at the Hong Kong office of the Bank for International Settlements for one year after having been the executive director of research at the Hong Kong Monetary Authority and Director of the Hong Kong Institute for Monetary Research since February 2005. Before joining the HKMA he was professor of international economics at the Graduate Institute of International Studies in Geneva, Switzerland. Mr. Genberg holds a Ph.D. degree in economics from the University of Chicago. His publications include *Asset Prices and Central Bank Policy* and *Official Reserves and Currency Management in Asia: Myth, Reality and the Future*.

Galina Borisova Hale is a senior economist at the Federal Reserve Bank of San Francisco, where she worked since 2006. Prior to joining the Federal Reserve she was an assistant professor in the economics department of Yale University. She also taught as a visiting faculty in economic department at both Stanford and UC Berkeley (economics department) and Haas School of Business. Galina received her bachelor's and master's degrees in economics from, respectively, the Moscow State University and the New Economic School in Russia. She briefly worked as a consultant for the Russian Ministry of Finance. She received her Ph.D. in economics in 2002 from UC Berkeley, under the supervision of Barry Eichengreen. She has published her work in a number of professional journals.

Cho-Hoi Hui is the head of Market Research Division of the Research Department, Hong Kong Monetary Authority (HKMA). His responsibilities include analyzing financial market developments and surveillance. He was a senior manager in the Banking Policy Department, where he is responsible for policy developments. Prior to joining the HKMA, he was a derivative analyst at Citibank. His research papers have appeared in a number of journals, including the *Journal of International Money and Finance*, *Journal of Money, Credit and Banking*, and *Journal of Fixed Income*. He is the coeditor (with Hans Genberg) of a book entitled *The Banking Sector in Hong Kong*. He holds a B.S. in physics from the University of Wisconsin-Madison and a Ph.D. in applied physics from Cornell University.

Shawn Chen-Yu Leu is a lecturer of economics at La Trobe University in Melbourne. He received his Ph.D. in economics at the University of Sydney in 2006. He has held visiting positions at the International Monetary Fund and Macquarie University. His research areas are open economy macroeconomics, monetary economics, and international finance with a substantial interest in Australia. His recent work examined monetary policy transmission mechanism in a New Keynesian structural VAR model; the level of managed floating by constructing index measures of the exchange market pressure and intervention activities; asymmetric monetary policy with a nonlinear Taylor rule; and natural rate measures of output, unemployment, and the real interest rate from a state-space model.

Priscilla Liang (Ph.D., Claremont Graduate University) is an assistant professor at California State University, Channel Islands. Her research interests focus on behavioral finance and development of emerging financial markets. Her recent publications include *The Slow Spread of the Global Crisis* (2010, coauthor), *Leveraging and Deleveraging, Financial* (2010), *Systemic Financial Crises* (2010), *The RMB Debate and International Influences on China's Money and Financial Markets* (2009, coauthor), *Contagion* (2008, coauthor), *Testing Four Strong Behavioral Hypotheses about the Effects of Asian and Russian Crises on Asian Financial Markets* (2008, coauthor), "*Explaining the Risk/Return Mismatch of the MSCI China Index: A Systematic Risk Analysis* (2007), *A Critical Analysis of Behavioral International Finance* (2007), *The Impact of Strategic Announcements on Corporate Value* (2006), and *Global and Regional Systematic Risks and International Assets Allocation in Asia* (2006).

Cheryl Long is an associate professor at Department of Economics, Colgate University. She was a Glenn Campbell and Rita Ricardo-Campbell National Fellow with the Hoover Institution, Stanford University in 2005–2006, and has been on the faculty of the Ronald Coase Institute Workshop on Institutional Analysis since 2009. Cheryl's research interests include transition economics and law and economics, with a focus on issues related to China's economic transformation. Her work appeared in a number of professional journals. After getting a B.S. degree in business and engineering from Xi'an Jiaotong University and an M.A. degree in economics from University of International Business and Economics (both in China), Cheryl received her Ph.D. in economics from Washington University in St. Louis in 2001.

Antonia López-Villavicencio is an associate professor at the University of Paris 13 (France). She got her Ph.D. in economics from the universities of Autónoma de Barcelona (Spain) and Paris Ouest (France). Her research focuses on areas of international finance and econometrics. She has written many articles, paying special attention to the presence of nonlinearities in economic relationships going from models of exchange rate dynamics to complementarities in the labor market. She is a member of the CEPN-CNRS research Lab at the University of Paris 13.

Guonan Ma is a senior economist at the Representative Office for Asia and the Pacific of the Bank for International Settlements (BIS). Before joining the BIS in 2001, he worked as a chief North Asia economist for 10 years at various investment banks, including Merrill Lynch, Salomon Smith Barney and Bankers Trust. Prior to his investment bank career, he was a lecturer of economics and research fellow at the Australian National University for four years following the completion of his Ph.D. in economics at the University of Pittsburgh (1990). Dr. Ma was born in China where he obtained his undergraduate degree at Beijing University (1982). Guonan Ma has many publications on the Asian and Chinese economies and financial markets over the years.

Nelson C. Mark is the DeCrane professor of international economics at the University of Notre Dame and Research Associate at the National Bureau of Economic Research. He received his Ph.D. from the University of Chicago in 1983 and has written extensively on international finance and open economy macroeconomic issues. He is the author of the graduate textbook *International Macroeconomics and Finance*. His current research interest is on understanding external imbalances with a particular focus on saving behavior of Chinese households.

Robert N. McCauley is the senior advisor in the Monetary and Economic Department of the Bank for International Settlements (BIS). Before October 2008, he served as the BIS Chief Representative for Asia and the Pacific in Hong Kong. Prior to joining the BIS, he worked for 13 years for the Federal Reserve Bank of New York, leaving as head of the International Finance Department in research. He taught international finance and the multinational firm at the University of Chicago's Graduate School of Business in 1992.

Norbert Metiu is a Ph.D. candidate in economics at Maastricht University, which he joined in 2008. He received a master's degree in economics from Corvinus University of Budapest. His fields of research include Time Series Econometrics, International Finance, and Monetary Economics.

Valérie Mignon holds a Ph.D. in economics, Valérie Mignon is professor at the University of Paris Ouest (France). She is a specialist of time series analysis, applied to finance and macroeconomics. She is responsible of the research group on "International Macroeconomics and Financial Econometrics" of EconomiX, the CNRS research center in economics at the University of Paris Ouest. She is also the scientific advisor to the CEPII, the French leading research institute in international economics, and coeditor of the academic journal *Economie Internationale/International Economics*. Her main research interests are in international macroeconomics and finance (exchange rates, oil prices, stock markets, economic growth, etc.), and in econometrics. She is the author of many books and articles, including textbooks in econometrics and macroeconomics.

Eiji Ogawa has been affiliated with Graduate School of Commerce and Management, Hitotsubashi University, since 1988. He received Ph.D. in commerce at Hitotsubashi University in 1999. His major field includes international currency and international monetary coordination. He is a faculty fellow of the Research Institute of Economy, Trade and Industry. He wrote many articles in the field. "Regional Monetary Coordination in East Asia," in *Exchange Rate, Monetary and Financial Issues and Policies in Asia*. "External adjustments and coordinated exchange rate policy in Asia" (with Kentaro Iwatsubo), *Journal of Asian Economics*.

Tuomas A. Peltonen holds a Ph.D. degree in economics from the European University Institute (EUI) Florence, as well as M.A. and B.Sc. degrees in economics from the University of Turku. He is currently working as a senior economist in the International Policy Analysis Division of the European Central Bank (ECB), where he has been since April 2006. His current assignments include analysis and development of tools for global financial stability surveillance and assessment. His prior assignments have included analysis and coordination of macroeconomic forecasting of emerging market economies. In January 2004–April 2006, he worked as an operations expert in the Front Office Division of the ECB and as a dealer at the Bank of Finland in May 1998–August 2000.

Gabor Pula holds an M.A. and B.Sc. degrees in economics from the Budapest University of Economics (BUES), Hungary. He is currently working as a senior economist in the International Policy Analysis Division of the European Central Bank (ECB), where he has been since November 2007. His current assignments include analysis of emerging market economies, in particular China. His recent research activity has focused on trade integration in Asia and technology upgrading in trade. Between 2005 and 2007, he worked as an economist in the Euro Area Macroeconomic Analysis Division of the ECB mainly focusing on issues related to globalization. In the 1998—2005, period he was an economist in the Ministry of Finance and the National Bank of Hungary.

Xingwang Qian is an assistant professor at the Economics and Finance Department of the State University of New York, Buffalo State College. He obtained his Bachelor Degree from the Nankai University of China and Masters and Ph.D. Degree from the University of California, Santa Cruz.

Jeffrey Sheen is a professor and the head of Department at Macquarie University in Sydney. He is the editor of the Economic Record, and the secretary of the Economic Society of Australia until 2010. His research areas are macroeconomics, macroeconometrics, international finance, labor economics and trade. He has published widely in journals, such as the *Journal of Monetary Economics*, *Economic Journal*, *Oxford Economic Papers*, *Journal of International Money and Finance*, *Journal of Banking* *and Finance*, and *Economic Record.* He is the coauthor with Olivier Blanchard of the best-selling Australasian intermediate macroeconomics textbook.

Junko Shimizu has been affiliated with School of Commerce, Senshu University, since 2008. She has also joined at the Research Institute of Economy, Trade and Industry as a researcher of the project on "The Optimal Exchange Rate Regime for East Asia" since 2005. She also worked as a research member of ASEAN+3 Research Group in 2007–2008, 2009—2010, and uptill now. She obtained her Ph.D. in commerce from Hitotsubashi University in 2004. Her latest paper is "Why Has the Yen Failed to Become a Dominant Invoice Currency in Asia? A Firm-Level Analysis of Japanese Exporters' Invoicing Behaviour."

Peter T. Treadway is an independent consultant and money manager. He is currently the principal of Historical Analytics LLC. Historical Analytics is consulting/investment management firm dedicated to global portfolio management. Its investment approach is based on his combined top-down and bottom-up Wall Street experience as economist, strategist, and securities analyst. A regular letter entitled *The Dismal Optimist* is produced for clients and interested readers. In addition Peter has served as adjunct professor at City University in Hong Kong in the Department of Economics and Finance. He also serves in a part-time capacity as chief economist, CTRISKS, a Hong Kong company that assists Asian financial institutions with their risk management problems. From 1965 to 2000 Peter had a distinguished career on Wall Street and with major American financial institutions. For example, from 1978 to 1981, he served as chief economist at Fannie Mae. From 1985 to 1998 he served as institutional equity analyst and managing director at Smith Barney following savings and loans and government sponsored entities (GSEs). While at Smith Barney he also served for a time as Latin American strategist and Latin American telecoms analyst. He was ranked as "all star" analyst 11 times by Institutional Investor Magazine. Peter holds a Ph.D. in economics from the University of North Carolina at Chapel Hill, an MBA from New York University, and a B.A. in English from Fordham University in New York.

Ulrich Volz is a senior economist at the German Development Institute in Bonn. He also teaches graduate courses in International Finance and International Monetary Relations at the Free University of Berlin. His research interests focus on international finance, monetary and financial cooperation and integration, financial market development, and development and transition economics. Together with Koichi Hamada and Beate Reszat, Ulrich is the editor of *Towards Monetary and Financial Integration in East Asia*, published in May 2009 by Edward Elgar Publishing. He is the author of *Prospects for Monetary Cooperation and Integration in East Asia*, published by the MIT Press in June 2010.

Thomas D. Willett (Ph.D., University of Virginia) serves as the director of the Claremont Institute for Economic Studies and is Horton Professor of Economics at Claremont Graduate University and Claremont McKenna College. He has previously served on the faculties at Cornell and Harvard University and as a senior economist at the Council of Economic Advisors and Deputy Assistant Secretary and Director of International Research at the US Treasury. He has written widely in areas such as exchange rate policy, inflation, international capital flows and currency and financial crises, the political economy of domestic and international economic policies and international organization, reform of the international finance architecture, regional integration, and the implications of conflicting mental models.

Alfred Wong is senior manager at the Hong Kong Monetary Authority. He works in the Research Department, having served over the past decade in the Monetary Management, External and Banking Development Departments, and seconded twice to the International Monetary Fund. Prior to joining the Hong Kong Monetary Authority, he was an economist at the HKSAR Government Land Fund Secretariat, Wardley Investment Services, and Reserve Bank of New Zealand. Due to different nature of the work of the organizations, his research work covers on a wide range of microeconomic and macroeconomic issues and appears in a number of journals including the New Zealand Economic Papers and European Economic Review. He received his economics training at the University of Western Australia.

James Yetman is senior economist at the Representative Office for Asia and the Pacific, Bank for International Settlements. His primary responsibility is to conduct research on macroeconomic issues of relevance to central banks in the region. Prior to taking up his current appointment James taught macroeconomics for seven years at the University of Hong Kong (2001–2008) and worked in the Research Department of the Bank of Canada (1998–2001). James obtained a bachelor's degree in economics from the University of Canterbury, New Zealand, followed by a master's degree from the University of British Columbia and a Ph.D. from Queen's University at Kingston, Canada. He has published extensively in academic journals including the *Journal of Business and Economic Statistics*, *Journal of Money, Credit and Banking*, and *Journal of International Money and Finance*.

Yushi Yoshida is a rofessor of economics at Kyushu Sangyo University. His research interests lie in the area of international finance, including exchange rate pass-through, foreign exchange intervention, and international financial transmission. He has also written on empirical international trade, including intraindustry trade, and extensive margin of exports. His recently published articles appear in the *IMF Staff Papers*,

International Review of Economics and Finance, *Atlantic Economic Journal* and *Asia Pacific Business Review*.

Nan Zhang is currently a Ph.D. student in economics at Claremont Graduate University. She has a B.A. degree in international business from University of International Business and Economics (UIBE) in Beijing, China, an MBA and an M.S. degree in economics from California State Polytechnic University, Pomona. Her research focuses on international monetary finance such as global and regional financial crises, international monetary union, and optimal currency areas. She is also interested in Asian economics, behavioral finance, environmental economics, and is continuously developing her professional knowledge both in depth and broadness through her Ph.D. study. She has coauthored in several publications in the current financial crisis and the endogenous OCA analysis in the Euro zone.

SUBJECT INDEX